Contributions to Economics

The series *Contributions to Economics* provides an outlet for innovative research in all areas of economics. Books published in the series are primarily monographs and multiple author works that present new research results on a clearly defined topic, but contributed volumes and conference proceedings are also considered. All books are published in print and ebook and disseminated and promoted globally. The series and the volumes published in it are indexed by Scopus and ISI (selected volumes).

More information about this series at https://www.springer.com/bookseries/1262

Nezameddin Faghih • Amir Forouharfar
Editors

Socioeconomic Dynamics of the COVID-19 Crisis

Global, Regional, and Local Perspectives

 Springer

Editors
Nezameddin Faghih ⓘD
Cambridge, MA, USA

Amir Forouharfar ⓘD
Shiraz, Iran

ISSN 1431-1933   ISSN 2197-7178   (electronic)
Contributions to Economics
ISBN 978-3-030-89998-1   ISBN 978-3-030-89996-7   (eBook)
https://doi.org/10.1007/978-3-030-89996-7

This Springer imprint is published by the registered company Springer Nature Switzerland AG
The registered company address is: Gewerbestrasse 11, 6330 Cham, Switzerland

*This book is dedicated to the loving
memory of Banu Bibi Taj Bahrololoum
Faghih (1900–1985), a cherished
philanthropist, a devoted mother, and
a great narrator and raconteur of the
1918 influenza pandemic in Estahban
(Fars, Iran), the land of figs and saffron.*

Acknowledgements

The editors would like to express their sincere gratitude to Lorraine Klimowich for her great efforts in the publication process of this book, and to all chapter authors as without their generous contributions, this volume would not have been possible. They would also like to wholeheartedly thank those who have devoted their time, effort, support, and generosity throughout the chapter review processes: Enokela Ebiega Abel, Samuel O. Adams, Memunat T. Ajadi, Angela Ajodo-Adebanjoko, Gabriel T. Akwen, Mohammad Hossein Alamatsaz, Peter Asare-Nuamah, Shayegheh Ashourizadeh, Pedro Baena-Luna, Samaneh Bahrololoum, Andrea Bellucci, Ebrahim Bonyadi, Alireza Bostani, Paul Bukuluki, Diala Kabbara, Mario Coccia, Jamshid Damooei, Mozhgan Danesh, Ender Demir, Hamid Reza Dowlatabadi, Ondřej Dvouletý, Vasilii Erokhin, Negar Razieh Esmaeilpour, Gerald E. Ezirim, Benson O. Igboin, Aristotle I. Jacobs, Qianying Jin, Mohammad Hossein Kaveh, Kristiaan Kerstense, Mohammadreza Khalesi, Mohsen Labbafi-mazraeh-shahi, Arvind Mahindru, Adrino Mazenda, Dipti Mehta, Okoro P. Mmahi, Hadijah Mwenyango, Musiwaro Ndakaripa, Tereza Němečková, Luke Nowlan, Hadijah Mwenyango, Jude Ogbodo, Najeem O. Oladosu, Maliheh Omidvar, Toyosi O. S. Owolabi, Feyisayo Oyolola, Shahamak Rezaei, Ali Hussein Samadi, Leyla Sarfaraz, Lida Sarreshtehdari, Mohammad Sayadi, Mahshid Sazegar, Babayo Sule, Jackson J. Tan, Oyinkan Tasie, Catherine C. Umenze, Mansoureh Vahabzadeh, Xiaocan L. Wang, Klaus Weyerstrass, and Haochang Yang.

Contents

List of Figures

List of Tables

Contributors

Angela Ajodo-Adebanjoko Department of Political Science, Federal University Lafia, Lafia, Nasarawa State, Nigeria

K. A. Al-Mustapha Department of Mathematics, Baze University, Abuja, Nigeria

Peter Asare-Nuamah University of Environment and Sustainable Development, Somanya, Ghana

H. S. Asthana Department of Psychology, Banaras Hindu University, Varanasi, India

Adel Azar Faculty of Management and Economics, Tarbiat Modares University, Tehran, Iran

Mahdi Azizi Systems Management, Faculty of Management and Economics, Tarbiat Modares University, Tehran, Iran

Xiang Chen Department of Geography, University of Connecticut, Storrs, CT, USA

Amrita Choudhary Department of Psychology, Banaras Hindu University, Varanasi, India

Mario Coccia CNR – National Research Council of Italy, Moncalieri, TO, Italy

Emmanuel Gbenga Dada Faculty of Science, Department of Mathematical Sciences, University of Maiduguri, Maiduguri, Borno State, Nigeria

Jamshid Damooei Center for Economics of Social Issues (CESI), School of Management, California Lutheran University, Thousand Oaks, CA, USA

Mozhgan Danesh Faculty of Entrepreneurship, University of Tehran, Tehran, Iran

Kürşat Demiryürek Faculty of Agriculture, Ondokuz Mayis University, Samsun, Turkey

Christopher Dick-Sagoe University of Botswana, Gaborone, Botswana

Nezameddin Faghih UNESCO Chair Professor Emeritus, Cambridge, MA, USA

Anisur Faroque LUT University School of Business and Management, Lappeenranta, Finland

Oluwadamilola Tosin Fasina Faculty of Social Sciences, Department of Economics, Federal University Oye, Oye, Ekiti State, Nigeria

Amir Forouharfar Independent Scholar, Shiraz, Iran

Merve Yanar Gürce Department of Business Administration, School of Business, American International University, Al Jahra, Kuwait

Pegah Hosseini-Nezhad Semmelweis Medical University (SOTE), Budapest, Hungary

Sara Hosseini-Nezhad Faculty of Education and Psychology, Doctoral School of Psychology, Eötvös Loránd University (ELTE), Budapest, Hungary

Asabe Ibrahim Department of Mathematics and Computer Science, Federal University Kashere, Gombe, Nigeria

Benson Ohihon Igboin Department of Religion and African Culture, Adekunle Ajasin University, Akungba-Akoko, Ondo State, Nigeria

Academic Associate of the Research Institute of Theology and Religion, University of South Africa, Pretoria, South Africa

Asef Karimi Faculty of Management and Accounting, College of Farabi, University of Tehran, Tehran, Iran

Hiroko Kawamorita Faculty of Economics and Administrative Sciences, Ondokuz Mayis University, Samsun, Turkey

Kingsley Obeng Kessie Kwame Nkrumah University of Science and Technology, Kumasi, Ghana

David A. Kirby Global Education Career Centre, London, UK

Joao Nuno Lopes Department of Management and Economics, Miguel Torga Institute of Higher Education, Coimbra, Portugal

Department of Management and Economics, University of Beira Interior and NECE – Research Unit in Business Sciences, Covilhã, Portugal

Lan Anh Nguyen Luu Faculty of Education and Psychology, Eötvös Loránd University (ELTE), Budapest, Hungary

David Mandiyanike Department of Political and Administrative Studies, University of Botswana, Gaborone, Botswana

Tyanai Masiya School of Public Management and Administration, University of Pretoria, Hatfield, Pretoria, UK

Adrino Mazenda School of Public Management and Administration, University of Pretoria, Hatfield, Pretoria, UK

Navid Mohammadi University of Tehran, Tehran, Iran

Thobeka Ncanywa Department of Economics, University of Limpopo, Mankweng, South Africa

Philip Ifeakachukwu Nwosa Faculty of Social Sciences, Department of Economics, Federal University Oye, Oye, Ekiti State, Nigeria

Justina Adwoa Onumah CSIR – Science and Technology Policy Research Institute, Accra, Ghana

Sakine Owjimehr Department of Economics, School of Economics, Management and Social Sciences, Shiraz University, Shiraz, Iran

David O. Oyewola Department of Mathematics and Computer Science, Federal University Kashere, Gombe, Nigeria

Richard L. Parcia Graduate School, University of Santo Tomas, Manila, Philippines

Mangena Phetole Faculty of Science and Agriculture, Department of Biodiversity, School of Molecular and Life Sciences, University of Limpopo, Sovenga, Republic of South Africa

Kunibert Raffer Department of Economics (Emeritus), University of Vienna, Vienna, Austria

Ombeswa Ralarala Department of Economics, University of Limpopo, Mankweng, South Africa

Jay Kumar Ranjan Department of Psychology, Banaras Hindu University, Varanasi, India

Saba Safdar University of Guelph, Guelph, ON, Canada

Shaghayegh Sakhteh University of Tehran, Tehran, Iran

Aidin Salamzadeh Faculty of Management, University of Tehran, Tehran, Iran

Ali Hussein Samadi Department of Economics, School of Economics, Management and Social Sciences, Shiraz University, Shiraz, Iran

Payal Sharma Department of Psychology, Banaras Hindu University, Varanasi, India

Jackson J. Tan Entrepreneurship Department, College of Commerce and Business Administration, University of Santo Tomas, Manila, Philippines
Ivory Research Interface Data Analysis Services, Pasig City, Philippines

Lasse Torkkeli Turku School of Economics, University of Turku, Turku, Finland

Mansoureh Vahabzadeh Faculty of Entrepreneurship, University of Tehran, Tehran, Iran

Hannes Velt LUT University School of Business and Management, Lappeenranta, Finland

Yiru Wang Department of Marketing and Management, School of Business, State University of New York at Oswego, Oswego, NY, USA

Tite Xu Department of Management, Jilin University, Changchun, China

Chapter 1
An Introduction to Socioeconomic Dynamics of the COVID-19 Crisis: Global, Regional, and Local Perspectives

Nezameddin Faghih ⓘ **and Amir Forouharfar** ⓘ

I am reminded of the story of the people of (the Great) Saba (City): how their zephyr (Saba) was turned into pestilence by the words of the foolish;
The life-increasing wind becomes unhealthy and pestilential: a fire turns to ashes and dust;
The orchard which resembled Paradise becomes the abode of disease: its leaves yellow and dropping in decay;
When the people of Saba carried beyond bounds, saying: "In our opinion, pestilence is better than the zephyr";
A wrath and a mercy like the zephyr and the plague: the former is the iron-attracting and the latter the straw attracting amber;
Their fundamental was bad: those inhabitants of Saba ….
Rumi (1207–1273): The story of the people of Saba (zephyr) and their folly.

Pandemics are a side effect of globalization. The trend of pandemics reveals, as human communication, trade, and travel developed more – besides new discoveries, pharmaceutical advancements, and innovative remedies and cures – it paved the way toward more technological spreading of contagious diseases. For instance, between 165 and 180 AD – during the Plague of Antoninus – when smallpox finally reached Rome via the trade routes, many Roman citizens were infected and consequently killed. Three centuries later, in the sixth century, the Plague of Justinian broke out in the Byzantine Empire and hit the Mediterranean, Europe, and the Middle East. Once the Plague of Justinian came back forcefully, it hit Europe as the Black Death in the fourteenth century at a time when a new global trade route facilitated the speedy transition of flea-infested furs from Central Asia, which was already plague-ridden (IOM, 2006). The countries and regions located on the trade and traveling crossroads were usually the first victims of globalization of infectious

N. Faghih (✉) · A. Forouharfar
UNESCO Chair Professor Emeritus, Cambridge, MA, USA

Independent Scholar, Shiraz, Iran

© The Author(s), under exclusive license to Springer Nature Switzerland AG 2022
N. Faghih, A. Forouharfar (eds.), *Socioeconomic Dynamics of the COVID-19 Crisis*,
Contributions to Economics, https://doi.org/10.1007/978-3-030-89996-7_1

diseases. For example, Persia, a mountainous several-thousand-year-old country which is encapsulated by the Caspian Sea in the North and the Persian Gulf and Gulf of Oman in the South and a major land and maritime trade and traveling route connecting the West and the East, has shown multiple plague epidemics in its history. Additionally, one of the political features of globalization which was the antagonistic and hostile feelings between the rival empires that most often culminated in long-lasting wars was the other reason for the transmission of contagious diseases. Large armies, when residing or besieging a place for a long time, due to poor sanitation, malnutrition and dense population, were usually conflicted with contagious diseases. A familiar instance is in 544 AD when the Sassanid Persian Empire army and the army of the Roman Empire were at war. The plague overran both armies (Smith, 1996). The pandemics were advancing as waves and contaminating the cities and populated areas on their way through ripple effects. In 627 AD, the capital of the Persian Sassanid Empire, Ctesiphon, was hit by the plague pandemics and killed nearly 100,000 citizens (Hashemi Shahraki et al., 2016, citing Zarrinkoub, 2006). Sometimes, the infected corpses – in a modern sense – were used as biologic weapons against the hostile forces in order to push the besieged city or castle dwellers to succumb. The transmission of Black Death to medieval Europe was speeded up from one such incidence when in 1347 AD the army of *Kipchak khan Janibeg* besieged Kaffa (now Feodosiya), a trading port southeast of Crimea. He catapulted decaying corpse died of plague to the besieged port to infect the inhabitants. Later the ships departing Kaffa transferred the plague westward to other Mediterranean ports. The catastrophic wave in 1347 AD affected Sicily and in 1348 AD ravaged North Africa, and then mainland Italy, Spain, and subsequently France. From Calais – a port in northern France – a ship transferred the plague in the same year to the Melcombe Regis, part of Weymouth port in Dorset, South West England. In 1349 AD, it afflicted Austria, as well as Hungary, Switzerland, Germany, and the Low Countries, and in 1350, it rushed through Scotland, as well as Scandinavia, and the Baltic countries (Encyclopaedia Britannica, 2020). In the history of global pandemics and regional epidemics, usually port cities were the forerunners. For instance, in the colonial African cities, the plague epidemics were closely correlated to the enhanced travel and trade via the sea routes once the steamship developed (Echenberg, 2002). However, if the maritime trade routes in the medieval and subsequent periods had a major role in spreading the pandemics, in our age, air travelling and fast-moving merchandise handling and transportation trade routes play one of the leading roles, which overwhelmingly contributed to the speed, distance, and complication of COVID-19 virus. Nevertheless, in a big picture, it is not only limited to the trade routes. Globalization has begot a gigantic *connectedness* mostly among all the global villagers of our era. Thus, "in the context of infectious diseases, there is nowhere in the world from which we are remote and no one from whom we are disconnected" (IOM, 1992, p. v). Now in order to slower the COVID-19 transmission besides mass vaccination programs and travel and border restriction policies, the governments are trying to break this connectedness at least for a limited time and in limited domains. Hence, the states are tended toward national protectionism and state *separateness*.

It is true that the pandemic worsened the condition in the developed countries, but the case was much more catastrophic in the underdeveloped and developing countries. Still there are some countries which could not succeed in vaccinating their public after more than 1 year and a half from the global recognition of this disease, and the public vaccination percentage in some other countries is under 5%. COVID-19 brought out, magnified, and proved the prevailing mismanagement rampant in these states. It was a mere fiasco for their public health administration.

On the other hand, different regions had different priorities which cast light on how incidents could raise complicated reactions and interpretations. For example, once we requested a reviewer for a chapter review, he mentioned, "Developing countries challenges are still immense. For instance, the water levels of Lake Victoria have reached a record level of 13.42 meters above sea level! This is apart from the pandemic...." Human sphere is cognitively separated from the biosphere. Although ecologically we belong to the same sphere as the other animates, our cognition makes us different creatures at least from our points of view. We see the world and the surroundings based on our perceived priorities and how close we feel a danger. Hunger, poverty, starvation, political conflicts and civil wars, forced immigrations, massacres, etc. are still preoccupied in the minds of millions of people, and once some states are fighting back COVID-19, many must strive for life to an extent that COVID-19 is not their number one priority. Now Ethiopia, a war-ravaged state, is struggling for food and famine is widespread. A war that displaced 1.7 m, killed thousands, pushed 1.8 m near to the starvation brink, and made more than 400,000 people live in a famine-like condition is still ongoing (Financial Times, 2021). In Afghanistan, the homeland of Jalāl ad-Dīn Mohammad Balkhī (Rumi) – once a region in Persia – the thirteenth-century Persian poet who was preaching tolerance, love, and understanding, is under the crushing retrospective ambitions of the extremist Taliban that currently controls a third of the Afghanistan districts (The Guardian, 2021). In a larger perspective, fighting COVID-19 needs considering global ecosystem embracing political, economic, social, technological, cultural, environmental, and psychological aspects with a systems thinking approach. In a recent joint report issued by the UNCTAD (United Nations Conference on Trade and Development) and UNWTO (UN World Tourism Organization), it is accentuated that, in respect to the global economy, the pandemic impact on tourism could lead to a more than $4 trillion loss (UN News, 2021). Moreover, the pandemic has curbed, made imbalances, and delayed the global endeavors for reaching the 2030 Agenda for Sustainable Development. The pandemic affected the socioeconomic gains achieved hard by promoting sustainable development goals before the COVID-19 global spread especially in weak economies in small island developing states (SIDS), landlocked developing countries (LLDCs), and least developed countries (LDCs) (UNCTAD, 2021a). However, according to UNCTAD's Business-to-Consumer (B2C) E-commerce Index 2020, e-commerce expanded in 2020 due to the pandemic lockdowns with Europe, which has the best-prepared infrastructure for e-commerce (UNCTAD, 2021b). Nevertheless, children were among the biggest victims of this pandemic all over the world and in every country, especially in the poorest countries (UNSDG, 2020). At least the national lockdown measures threatened the well-being of many – consisting the children – in developed countries. The global closure of the schools has had no historical precedent affecting more than 1.5 billion youth and children (UNSDG, 2020, p. 7). These incidents were coincided with widespread repercussion of *infodemic* as "too much information including false or misleading information in digital and physical environments during a disease outbreak" (WHO, 2021). Too much misinformation as well as disinformation were fabricated and transmitted via online social media and word of mouth in a magnitude that induced the *UN Pause Campaign* in order to reduce the misleading spread of unverified information. A recent MIT (Massachusetts Institute of Technology) study has proved the positive impact of the campaign especially among those who were familiar with the initiative. They were considerably less likely to share fake headlines (UN, 2021). The campaign tried to promote responsible sharing as a counterbalance against global infodemic (see Pledge to Pause, 2021).

The policy briefs, which were issued by the UN DESA (Department of Economic and Social Affairs, 2021) during the pandemic, show some of the major concerns on the socioeconomic dimensions derived from the COVID-19 pandemic. These concerns embrace a large arena from fiscal stimulus plans for addressing the social crisis (Policy Brief 58); turmoil in financial markets (Policy Brief 59); commodity-dependent economies affected by the pandemic in the developed countries (Policy Brief 60); digital government (Policy Brief 61); inducing better cooperation among scientific organizations (Policy Brief 62); inequality (Policy Brief 65); protecting youth in the responses to COVID-19 (Policy Brief 67); elders (Policy Brief 68); gender and disability concerns (Policy Brief 69); indigenous peoples (Policy Brief 70); consequences of the pandemic on the manufacturing exports from LDCs (Policy Brief 71); debt crisis (Policy Brief 72); social development, sports, well-being, and physical activity (Policy Brief 73); national institution accountability, participation, and the need for their transparency in the fight against COVID-19 (Policy Brief 74); the state-people governance relationships (Policy Brief 75); challenges of landlocked developing countries (Policy Brief 76); financial markets and investors (Policy Brief 77); achieving the sustainable development goals (SDGs) (Policy Brief 78); public servants and service (Policy Brief 79); forests (Policy Brief 80); social protection systems (Policy Brief 82); global public goods for health (Policy Brief 83); policymaking scenarios for achieving SDGs (Policy Brief 84); lessons for overcoming the pandemic (Policy Brief 85); poverty (Policy Brief 86); integrated national financing frameworks (Policy Brief 87); COVID-19 sustainable recovery and forest management (Policy Brief 88); big data and open data for fighting COVID-19 – data governance – (Policy Brief 89); economic security and its necessary politics (Policy Briefs 90 and 91); social inclusion via digital technologies (Policy Brief 92); post-COVID-19 social policies for Africa (Policy Brief 93); jobs' crisis (Policy Brief 94); economic insecurity and those who are at risk (Policy Brief 95); statistical and data community (Policy Brief 96); SDGs and private investment and finance (Policy Brief 97); blended finance (Policy Brief 100); food security (Policy Brief 102); partnership for achieving global goals after COVID-19 (Policy Brief 103); agriculture (Policy Brief 105); poverty and inequality in villages and rural regions (Policy Brief 106); to last but not the least trust in public institutions (Policy Brief 108). Some socioeconomic aspects of the above-mentioned concerns were also skillfully responded out of the global, regional, and local lenses by the chapter contributors of this volume.

The book is divided into six parts and contains 22 chapters (including this "Introduction"), as follows:

Chapter 1 is the introduction to the book. It introduces the book and discusses how this edited volume on the socioeconomic dynamics of the COVID-19 crisis embraces a wide spectrum of topics, such as reallocation of economic resources, financial markets, government policy response to COVID-19, stock market return, social relief packages, spread of the disease in polluted cities, public health strategies and biopolitics, healthcare, donation efficiencies, global hegemony, psychological perspectives, mental health outcomes, cultural challenges, and organization and management research in the post-COVID-19 era, as well as entrepreneurial universities, entrepreneurial frugality, and the international entrepreneurship future. Through each chapter, the authors, who are experts in this area of study, have tried to unfold an emerging aspect in the COVID-19 crisis which could benefit not only the academic readers but also the institutional, economic, social, and developmental policymakers as well as the health practitioners on the ground. Subsequently, the book proceeds with six consecutive parts containing 21 chapters.

Part I investigates the impacts of the COVID-19 crisis on entrepreneurship and management studies, in Chaps. 2, 3, 4, 5 and 6.

Chapter 2 considers entrepreneurial frugality in crisis, as an interpretative phenomenological approach. This chapter develops a more in-depth consideration of entrepreneurial frugality in the crisis regarding the continuing effect of the COVID-19 pandemic in entrepreneurship by applying an interpretative phenomenological approach. The interpretive phenomenology analysis is a qualitative method that examines entrepreneurs' lived experiences. A qualitative method is used to provide situated insights, rich details, and in-depth descriptions. Moreover, it offers in-depth processual and contextualized knowledge. The purpose of the current study is to analyze why and how the COVID-19 outbreak affected the entrepreneurial frugality in Iran. It demonstrated that entrepreneurs are frugal in such situation, and in the crisis, they shift their expense pattern. The main reason for them being frugal is themselves and self-constraint. Also, qualitative research revealed that human resources and the network are the two main levers of entrepreneurs in crisis. The study also showed that entrepreneurs could survive and grow their business by focusing and replanning for human resources, marketing, market development, and equipment. Fundamental theoretical contribution is the first methodology chosen for the research that provides new insight into entrepreneurial frugality. The second method is to reduce the gap between theoretical approaches to entrepreneurial frugality and the practical field. The last contribution highlights the importance of human and social support for entrepreneurs in times of crisis.

Chapter 3 studies the future of international entrepreneurship in the post-COVID-19 era. The COVID-19 pandemic has had a major impact on international entrepreneurship. The purpose of this study is to assess the future of international entrepreneurship as a field of research and to propose the main consequences for scholars and practitioners post-COVID-19. We examine the three main macro-level global phenomena (digitalization, ecosystems, and institutional support) that are impacting the consequences and repercussions of international entrepreneurship during and post-COVID-19. Specifically, we present arguments for the rise of born-digitals as the predominant form of internationalizing enterprises as well as for the importance of the local entrepreneurial ecosystem and export support for sustaining international entrepreneurship post-COVID-19 and beyond. Based on the analysis, we provide recommendations for researchers on international entrepreneurship for potential future research avenues. The study also includes recommendations for policy and practice on public support of digital international entrepreneurship, small- and medium-sized enterprise export promotion, and ecosystem support.

Chapter 4 considers the impact of the COVID-19 pandemic on the development of entrepreneurial universities, by studying the higher education institutions in Turkey. This chapter focuses on the impact of the COVID-19 pandemic on the development of entrepreneurial universities and the provision of entrepreneurship education in Turkey. It does so via a 10.67 response rate questionnaire survey of all 206 universities in Turkey, conducted online in August 2020. The results revealed that those Turkish HEIs that responded (i) have a good understanding of what entrepreneurial universities are and are in the transformation process, (ii) are involved in entrepreneurial activities to deal with the COVID-19 crisis, (iii) have or expect to have financial challenges as a result of the pandemic and believe that entrepreneurship is one of the key factors to survive in the market, and (iv) are fully supporting online education as a result of COVID-19 crises, though much needs to be done to improve the current performance. Thus, the study addresses a critical gap in the body of understanding on the impact of the pandemic and suggests that it might be creating the conditions that will encourage Turkish universities to become more entrepreneurial. This has relevance for policymakers, university managers, entrepreneurship academics, and industry.

Chapter 5 investigates the opportunities and threats facing early-stage digital startups during the COVID-19 pandemic. The pandemic has significantly influenced entrepreneurship and new venture creation to this point. Besides, it has caused consumer lifestyle modifications as well as alterations in business products and services, leading to paradigm shifts in the market. In this respect, startups have been also coping with numerous challenges and prospects in this period, and COVID-19 has even resulted in the rise and fall of many companies. This condition has been far more for early-stage startups, particularly the ones in their infancy life cycle. On the other hand, thanks to the changes in people's lifestyles, digital and online businesses have gained much popularity. For this purpose, the present study aimed to identify and analyze opportunities and threats encountering early-stage digital startups during the COVID-19 pandemic. Accordingly, in-depth interviews were conducted with a total number of 30 members working in 13 startup teams, and their data were finally examined using thematic analysis. Ultimately, 13 opportunities and 19 threats within 4 categories of "market and marketing," "startup team," "operational and management issues," and "financial and economic activities" were introduced.

Chapter 6 studies the developments and changes in organization and management research in the post-COVID-19 era, through a Foundationalist approach. Today, management, like all other areas of human life, has been severely affected by the COVID-19 crisis. The challenges that the crisis have created for various areas of management have had many consequences and, in many cases, have led to the loss and bankruptcy of many businesses. Hence, management theorists and practitioners need to address each of these challenges and issues in detail. Therefore, the year of the COVID-19 crisis has created a critical and epoch-making year for management knowledge. Accordingly, a big picture of changes caused by the COVID-19 crisis in the organization and management studies is essential and vital. Thus, the chapter has pursued this important goal in three parts. In the first part, we examine theoretical foundations of organization and management that have changed due to the COVID-19 crisis. The second part deals with organizational areas affected by the crisis. In the last section, we will review the recommendations made by management theorists in the face of the crisis. Finally, in the conclusion section, using the results of the studies conducted in these three sections, we focus on research currents in the organization and management studies faced with the crisis. In this section, two research currents were identified: the revolutionary current and the developmental current. Each of these currents can totally transform the future of management theory and practice. Then, the effects of the COVID-19 crisis on collapse and creation of businesses were examined.

Part II is devoted to shock economy and financial dynamics, in Chaps. 7, 8, 9, 10 and 11.

Chapter 7 explores lessons from the COVID-19 pandemic and its impact on the reallocation of resources, through a cross-country comparison in search of a global perspective. Pandemics and infectious diseases have brought fundamental changes throughout history by exposing the problems of societies. We know that climate change alters human relationships with other species on Earth and the process enhances the risk of pandemics. This chapter takes a cross-country comparison to look into the existing economic and social problems faced during the COVID-19 pandemic across the nations. It brings attention to an important fact that some of the most essential elements of a balanced and humanly conceivable life on Earth are not based on demand, but rather on meeting the needs of the individuals, groups, and communities. While the need is obvious, there is no clear mechanism for resolving the problem of production of Global Public Goods. Trust in governments is an essential asset for the success of nations in dealing with calamities and disasters. Helping people to stay in lockdown can only be successful when people are given the choice by setting in place economic measures which can support people out of jobs through relevant fiscal policies. Pandemics may inflict severe damage to globalization, free trade, multilateralism, and cooperative international development. This chapter reveals that problems witnessed during this crisis are systemic and caused by the dysfunctional neoliberal corporate capitalism. It is hard to imagine the way forward with any degree of certainty, but we should come to agree that without a systemic change, we will threaten our own existence and the pressure for change will become even more compelling.

Chapter 8 discusses the effects of the COVID-19 crisis on financial markets. The present Corona crisis has damaged the global economy more gravely than any crisis before. This contribution discusses its effects on the financial sector and on debtors globally. Fighting this crisis needs enormous sums of money, resulting in highly increased debts, often on top of already high debt burdens. Unfortunately, the COVID-19 crisis seems to be used to reinforce neoliberalism, as were debt crises in the past. Anti-Keynesian Maastricht criteria are temporarily suspended but not abolished. Back into force after the crisis, they will be used to destroy the welfare state. The IMF, e.g., is becoming more powerful due to the present emergency lending. Higher debts will allow more neoliberal pressure for austerity, causing more poverty and more inequality, as well as weakening democracy.

Interest rates are bound to be kept low not to create problems for borrowing Northern governments and the EU – with grave impacts on market-financed pension schemes and savers. Poor people in the South will suffer under increased debt pressure. While consequences are dire for people, especially the poor, and for democracy, there are also winners. International Financial Institutions are able to increase their importance, leverage, and incomes. The EU is likely to be happy to have another "reason" to destroy democracy further, rolling back national legislations' rights, especially regarding the budget. The financial consequences of the COVID-19 crisis thus go very much beyond financial markets only.

Chapter 9 forecasts monetary policy rates in the COVID-19 era for South Africa. It is of great importance to find accurate forecasts of monetary policy rates for economies to make better decisions for future performance of the overall economy and trading issues. For a proper decision-making process, regulatory authorities need to consider forecasting as one of the most important elements. This chapter aims to determine which forecast monetary policy rates such as bank lending, exchange, and inflation rates could be considered during the COVID-19 pandemic in South Africa. The chapter adopted univariate and multivariate modeling as a way to accomplish as many accurate forecasts as possible. Findings from the forecast modeling link the chosen monetary policy rates with ways that the economy can come back to normal through the transmission mechanism of monetary policy. Inflation rate portrayed the best forecast indicating that South Africa needs to maintain the adopted inflation rate between 3% and 6%. The bank rate as an instrument used by policymakers to influence the whole economy including inflation indicated best forecasts for the future movements of the economy in the post-COVID-19 era. As South Africa has an open economy trading globally, the foreign exchange rate showed that paying attention to it can give good forecasts for the future performance of the economy. It is thus recommended that South African policymakers closely monitor these monetary policy rates as their changes determine some major economic consequences during the pandemic.

Chapter 10 considers the effectiveness of the COVID-19 crisis economic and social relief package as a poverty alleviation strategy in South Africa. In South Africa, the COVID-19 pandemic has subjected the population to abject poverty. In response to the challenges posed by the pandemic, the South African government disbursed R500 billion (US\$ 2 879 935 450) Economic and Social Relief Package

(ESRP), to help fight the negative effects of COVID-19 pandemic on the economy and cushion vulnerable societies from extreme poverty for 6 months (May to October 2020). Of interest to this chapter is the delivery of targeted assistance to households and individuals to relieve poverty and social distress. A qualitative research approach was adopted. Data was gathered from authoritative secondary sources while a thematic approach was utilized to analyze the data. A major finding of this chapter is that the ESRP intervention was necessary to cushion households against income-induced food insecurity by providing a social grant, food parcel, and unemployment benefits, including paid holidays. However, the intervention was affected by numerous issues including administrative bottlenecks, inadequacy given that the average South African household size is much bigger, and irregular costing of food parcels as well as travel and contact restrictions. It is recommended that the government adopts a multisectoral response to ensure an increase in cash and non-cash resources to poor households and children.

Chapter 11 examines oil price, foreign reserves, and exchange rate nexus during the COVID-19 pandemic. This chapter analyzes the nexus among oil price, foreign reserve, and exchange rate in pre-COVID-19 era and during the COVID-19 pandemic. It employs descriptive, VAR (Vector Auto-Regression) and SVAR (Structural Vector Auto-Regression) estimation techniques. This chapter observes that oil price, foreign reserves, and exchange rate had undergone major changes during the COVID-19 pandemic compared to the pre-COVID-19 period. The VAR causality estimate showed the absence of causality among the variables in the pre-COVID-19 era, while during the COVID-19 period, the study observes unidirectional causality from oil price to foreign reserves and exchange rate, and a one-way causal influence from foreign reserves to exchange rate. The impulse response function from the SVAR estimate showed that a sudden decline in oil price affected foreign reserves and exchange rate more during the COVID-19 period than in the pre-COVID-19 period. Thus, this chapter concludes that the COVID-19 pandemic had significant adverse impact on oil price, foreign reserves, and exchange rate in Nigeria. The chapter recommends that the palliative measures of the ₦50 billion CBN COVID-19 intervention program should be judiciously executed to lessen the consequences of the pandemic on households and business firms.

Part III considers the politics and sociology of the COVID-19 crisis in Chaps. 12 and 13.

Chapter 12 discusses the COVID-19 crisis and China's quest for global hegemony. The COVID-19, a new strain of the coronavirus, is currently the public health emergency rocking the globe. From its discovery in Wuhan, China, in December 2019 to its declaration by the World Health Organization (WHO) in January 2020, COVID-19 has assumed the center stage of all national and international discourses in recent times. This is because of the negative impact of the disease on all aspects of human life: social, cultural, economic, and political. While its discovery has been traced to Wuhan, the origin of the disease remains unclear and unknown as there are mixed messages or accusations and counter-accusations from China and the United States. While China claims that the virus originated naturally from the Huanan seafood market in Wuhan, the United States and a host of other countries are skeptical, believing it to be man-made and originating from a laboratory in Wuhan. China's claims have been disputed because there are no bat markets in Wuhan amidst allegations that China has banned all forms of investigation into the origin of the virus. This latter allegation has raised the question of the possibility of China having released the virus as a biological weapon aimed at weakening other economies, particularly that of the United States and achieving its imperial ambition of becoming a global hegemon. This chapter investigated the role of China in the spread of the coronavirus disease and the rationale behind this. The research was conducted using secondary sources obtained from news organizations and the internet, among others. While there are still ongoing investigations to find out if China deployed the coronavirus as a bioweapon in its quest for global hegemony, the country's reluctance to share critical information or to provide timely and sufficiently detailed information about the potential public health emergencies of the virus with the WHO is an internationally wrongful act and a breach of international obligations which states could challenge at the International Court of Justice.

Chapter 13 examines the COVID-19 and the cultural challenges of the rights of contemporary African ancestors. The emergence of the COVID-19 has disrupted almost every aspect of human life globally. The first reaction of various governments was to place restriction on human movement, which raised questions about the right of free movement. While scientists and sociologists have mostly focused on human health and economic and political situations of nations in panic, little or no attention has been paid to the cultural rights of the dead, particularly from the African perspective that believes in the hereafter of the dead as ancestors or as legends. This chapter thus intervenes in this gap by critically analyzing the rights of the African ancestors, particularly those that transcended in the fight against the pandemic. Phenomenological methods are used to elicit data, which are subjected to cosmotheandric theory. It argues that since proper burial is a prerequisite for attaining the status of ancestorhood and it can be conducted via e-burial processes, it would then be reasonable to adopt it at this moment of the pandemic in order to keep the living safe from the novel coronavirus and accord the dead their rights.

Part IV studies the psychology of the COVID-19 crisis in Chaps. 14 and 15.

Chapter 14 explores the psychological perspectives on the COVID-19. A considerable quantity of research supports the findings that the COVID-19 pandemic has significantly influenced individuals' psychological well-being and behaviors. This chapter aims to provide an overview of some of the current studies examining psychological responses of various groups across cultures in relation to the COVID-19 pandemic employing the behavioral immune system (BIS) framework and terror management theory (TMT) as a theoretical lens. Online databases are used to conduct a literature review of some of the studies carried out during the global pandemic between 2019 and 2021. It is shown that the pandemic has had an overall detrimental effect on everyone to some extent, with a disproportionate impact on more vulnerable populations. In fact, people continue to cope with the death anxiety from the perspective of the TMT and are driven to avoid pathogens from the BIS viewpoint in the face of the COVID-19 pandemic; however, given the disproportionate impact of the pandemic on vulnerable groups, the chapter recommends that societies prioritize equity-oriented public health measures to ensure the population's future well-being.

Chapter 15 incorporates the outcomes of the COVID-19 with recent other pandemic outbreaks on healthcare workers through a systematic review and meta-analysis. The community transmission of the coronavirus disease-2019 (COVID-19) has created a sense of panic and anxiety around the world. There is rich pandemic-based evidence that shows the effect of disease outbreaks on the mental health of healthcare workers. However, inconsistencies and discrepancies have been observed among the findings of most of the reported studies. Therefore, this meta-analysis was conducted to identify the mental health issues faced by the doctors, nurses, and other paramedical staffs as a result of any health emergency. Firstly, databases of several web sources, namely, EBSCOhost, PubMed, and Google Scholar, were explored for searching the articles that dealt with the psychological distress faced by healthcare professionals during any pandemic. Thereafter, retrieved articles were systematically selected using specific inclusion and exclusion criteria. The quality of the included studies was assessed through guidelines of the Strengthening the Reporting of Observational Studies in Epidemiology (STROBE). Meta-analysis was computed using R software (3.5.3) with "metafor" package. The present meta-analysis includes 49 epidemiological studies consisting of 59,552 healthcare workers across the globe. The results of the analyses indicated that 7% of the healthcare workers reported anxiety issues (95% CI: 0.42–1.01), 5% reported stress (95% CI: 0.29–0.69) and depressive symptoms (95% CI: 0.40–0.52), 8% reported sleep problems (95% CI: 0.53–1.07), and 6% reported post-traumatic stress symptoms (95% CI: 0.41–0.70) during the COVID-19 pandemic. Prevalence of sleep problems among healthcare workers was the highest during the current pandemic, as compared to previous ones. Hence it would be reasonable to conclude that medical healthcare workers involved in controlling any infectious disease outbreak are under increased psychological burden and, hence, are at a high risk of developing and experiencing mental health problems.

Part V investigates the COVID-19 crisis, public health management, and biopolitics, in Chap. 16, 17, 18, 19 and 20.

Chapter 16 studies the spread of the novel coronavirus disease-2019 in polluted cities and explores lessons learned from environmental and demographic factors for prevention of pandemic diseases. This chapter analyzes coronavirus disease-2019 (COVID-19) cases alongside environmental and demographic data in a case study in Italy, the first European country to experience a rapid increase in confirmed cases and deaths. Sample is based on Italian province capitals considering data of air pollution given by total days exceeding the limits set for PM_{10} (particulate matter 10 micrometers or less in diameter) or, for ozone, diffusion of the COVID-19 measured with daily infected individuals, meteorological information based on average temperature in °C and wind speed, and finally a proxy of interpersonal contacts given by population density of cities under study. This chapter finds that geo-environmental and demographic factors may have accelerated the spread of the COVID-19 in polluted cities, leading to a higher number of infected individuals and deaths in society. In particular, results reveal that cities with little wind and frequently high levels of air pollution had higher numbers of COVID-19-related infected individuals and deaths. This chapter suggests policy implications for polluted cities to constrain future epidemics of viral agents similar to severe acute respiratory syndrome coronavirus 2 (SARS-CoV-2) that is the strain of novel coronavirus that causes COVID-19.

Chapter 17 presents high-performing machine learning algorithms for predicting the spread of COVID-19. COVID-19 is a strain of coronavirus that first broke out in Wuhan, China, in December 2019 and has since become a global pandemic. In this chapter, we apply four machine learning techniques which are logistic regression (LR), support vector machine (SVM), recurrent neural network (RNN), and long short-term memory (LSTM) in predicting transmission of the coronavirus (COVID-19). Data were collected from patients who have contacted the coronavirus disease from January 22, 2020, to March 14, 2020, obtained from Kaggle database. The data consisted of the confirmed, death, and recovered cases of all the countries infected with coronavirus (COVID-19). The performance of each machine learning techniques was compared using mean absolute error (MAE), root mean square error (RMSE), and mean absolute scaled error (MASE). The results indicate that logistic regression (LR) is effective in predicting accurately different continents such as Africa, Asia, Australia/Oceania, Europe, North America, Cruise ship, and South America with 0.4590, 57005.25, 0.6829, 44.35, 2.2764, 4.7508, and 0.5401, respectively. This is an indication that it is a promising technique in predicting the spread of the coronavirus. The study reveals that there are upward trends of the COVID-19 in Africa, Europe, Australia/Oceania, North America, and South America, while trends of transmission of pandemic diseases have been stable in Asia and Diamond Cruise ship. As COVID-19 cases continue to rise in Africa, Europe, Australia/Oceania, North America, and South America, there are urgent needs to curtail transmission of this disease.

Chapter 18 explores the perceptions and coping strategies to COVID-19 in a rural Ghanaian community. While rural communities are vulnerable and at risk to the coronavirus, there is, however, scarcity of information on how such communities perceive and respond to the pandemic. This chapter adopted a qualitative descriptive phenomenology to investigate the perceptions and coping strategies to the coronavirus pandemic in a rural Ghanaian community. Both purposive and snowball sampling techniques were employed to select 40 participants for interviews, in addition to overt observation. Findings show that participants have knowledge of the coronavirus, which they reported to spread through inter-human transmission. Symptoms such as difficulty in breathing, dyspnea, fever, sore throat, and dry cough were perceived to be associated with the coronavirus. The pandemic has disrupted sociocultural norms and activities such as funerals and burials in the community. Results further show that wearing nose masks, regular washing of hands, and applying sanitizer have been adopted as precautionary measures in the community. In addition, traditional measures, such as bathing nyanya leaves (*Momordica foetida*), sniffing local snuff, and drinking solution from the bark and leaves of neem trees (*Azadirachta indica*) as well as drinking local alcohol, sobolo (*Hibiscus sabdariffa*), and a mixture of ginger, garlic, and lemon solution, have been adopted. This chapter recommends intensification of coronavirus education especially in rural communities.

Chapter 19 explores the government policy response to COVID-19 and stock market return, by studying the case of Iran. This chapter uses four indices showing government intervention in facing COVID-19, including stringency index, government response index, containment and health index, and economic support index. The stock market return of Iran from February 22, 2020, to June 12, 2021, is the dependent variable. Using a threshold regression, the chapter shows that government intervention indices have different effects on the stock market return in the country under study, so that when the growth rate of confirmed cases of the COVID-19 is less than 0.06%, government intervention cannot affect the stock market return. However, in a situation with a higher growth rate of confirmed cases of the COVID-19, stringency index, government response index, and containment and health index reduce the return, but the economic support index increases return. In summary, first, the impact of government intervention on the stock market in this study depends on the growth rate of confirmed cases. Second, the government faces a trade-off between citizens' health and stock market return during the high incidence rate of the COVID-19.

Chapter 20 investigates the request and donation efficiencies in a crisis by data envelopment analyses of a Philippine web-based emergency response system. On March 16, 2020, the island of Luzon was placed under lockdown to curtail the spread of the COVID-19 in the Philippines. Soon thereafter, a web-based emergency response platform was developed to counteract effects from the outbreak. As a free service to strengthen a debilitated national hospital supply chain, the platform connected community organizations (as hospitals) with donors (individuals). From concepts and techniques that addressed Information Flows in Healthcare Logistics and Supply Chain Management, several input-oriented Data Envelopment Analyses were conducted to find the efficiencies for each of the 75 hospitals serviced by websites in terms of donors, individual items requested, total quantity of items requested, number of requested individual items that received a pledged, and average days a request pended to fulfillment. Results from the DEA technique found that hospitals on the platform made requests that exceeded optimal quantities of inputs from donors. Further, hospital requests aggregated at the city level stood unanswered an average of 14.39 days for inefficiently served cities. Findings from the analyses produce three recommendations to improve the web-based emergency response system service efficiency. The first recommendation is to reallocate donors over more hospitals, such that a few hospitals do not receive a majority of donations. A second recommendation is to reduce the number of individually requested items. The third recommendation is to reduce the quantities of items requested in order to bring service efficiency to optimality.

Part VI examines the COVID-19 crisis, food, and agriculture in Chaps. 21 and 22.

Chapter 21 investigates how COVID-19 reshaped food procurement around the globe and the effective operation and redesign of the food retail industry in China, Portugal, Turkey, and the United States. During the COVID-19 pandemic, consumers' food procurement activities underwent considerable transformations due to restrictive policies on social distancing. These behavioral changes induced a new industrial landscape within the food retail sector, with franchise stores gaining more consumers and more intensive competition occurring across online food retail plat-forms. This study employs cross-sectional survey data from China, Portugal, Turkey, and the United States to examine the major changes in consumer food procurement behaviors during the pandemic worldwide, as compared to behaviors before the pandemic. Based on the findings, we provide operable implications necessary for food retailers to sustain their businesses in a post-pandemic context.

Chapter 22 considers the potential impact of the COVID-19 pandemic on agri-culture and legumes and their economic value chain. It argues that the pandemic outbreak of the novel coronavirus (COVID-19) represents a serious global public health emergency crisis and has potential impacts on the society, agriculture, and the economy. Dry grains and oil legumes are among some of the major agricultural commodities that are projected to be severely affected by this outbreak. Therefore, this chapter focuses on the critical value chain activities involved in the food legume production, cross-border trade, and impact of these events on the socioeconomic uplifting of populations during the COVID-19 quarantines and other restrictions. The chapter analyzes already emerging trends on downstream distribution and demand that is currently influenced by unavailable labor force and loss of income by individual in poorer communities as a result of COVID-19 restrictions. Finally, the review examines how the pandemic exacerbate some of the already existing challenges such as the slow pace of crop productivity, impact on crop improvement, and other climate-change-related production constraints.

It is unfortunate that, during the review process of this volume, some of the authors who submitted chapters as well as some of the reviewers or their family members had expired. This pandemic, as one of the most strange, catastrophic, and unprecedented incidents – at least in modern human existence – which could not be compared with any other incidents in scale, degree of impact, repercussions, and magnitude, has had an intense effect on human life with unpredictable consequences in the future. It is hoped that this book presenting socioeconomic dynamics of the COVID-19 crisis in the global, regional, and local perspectives is appealing to a wide spectrum of global audience and academics and can provide a useful reference work in the socioeconomic research on the COVID-19. Academics, researchers, and scholars, from wide domain of disciplines and through experienced approaches, have contributed chapters and addressed the most recent issues on the COVID-19 crisis. Thus, it is also hoped that the book can provide creative discussions and align well with scholarly and intellectual interests in perceiving the present trends and main research streams on the COVID-19 crisis and add to the insight for better responses to the future changing and emerging consequences and repercussions.

It should also be noted that facts, information, opinions, views, findings, conclu-sions, comments, positions, and strategies expressed by the contributors and chapter authors are theirs alone and do not necessarily reflect the views, opinions, positions, or strategies of the editors of this contributed volume and do not constitute endorse-ment or approval by the editors. The authors and contributors are responsible for their citing of sources and the accuracy of their references and bibliographies. The editors of this book cannot be held responsible for any errors or for any conse-quences arising from the use of the information contained in the chapters or any lacks or possible violations of third parties' rights. Although every effort is made by the editors to see that no inaccurate or misleading data, opinion, or statements appear in this contributed volume, the data, their use and interpretations, and opinions appearing in the chapters are the sole responsibility of the authors and contributors concerned. The editors accept no liability whatsoever for the consequences of any such inaccurate or misleading data, information, opinion, or statements.

References

Echenberg, M. (2002). *Black death, white medicine: Bubonic plague and the politics of public health in colonial Senegal, 1914–1945*. Heinemann.

Encyclopaedia Britannica. (2020). *Black Death*. https://www.britannica.com/event/Black-Death

Financial Times. (2021, July 5). Fighting and food shortages fray hopes for Ethiopia's ceasefire. https://www.ft.com/content/17e3b3a4-94e1-4537-8316-b18298f85116

Hashemi Shahraki, A., Carniel, E., & Mostafavi, E. (2016). Plague in Iran: Its history and current status. *Epidemiology and Health, 38*, e2016033. https://doi.org/10.4178/epih.e2016033

IOM, Institute of Medicine. (1992). *Emerging infections: Microbial threats to health in the United States*. National Academy Press.

IOM, Institute of Medicine. (2006). *The impact of globalization on infectious disease emergence and control: Exploring the consequences and opportunities, workshop summary* (S. Knobler, A. Mahmoud, S. Lemon, & L. Pray, Eds.). The National Academies Press. https://doi.org/10.17226/11588

Pledge to Pause. (2021). https://pledgetopause.org/

Rumi. (1207–1273). *The Mathnawí of Jalaladdín Rumi* (p. 163) (R. A. Nicholson, Translation and commentary, Volume III, 1926). Messrs Luzac & Co. Ltd.

Smith, C. A. (1996). Plague in the ancient world: A study from Thucydides to Justinian. *Student Historical Journal, 28*, 1–19.

The Guardian. (2021, July 4). Hundreds of Afghan security forces flee as districts fall to Taliban. https://www.theguardian.com/world/2021/jul/04/hundreds-of-afghan-security-forces-flee-as-districts-fall-to-taliban

UN DESA, Department of Economic and Social Affairs. (2021). *Policy briefs documents*. https://www.un.org/en/desa/covid-19

UN News. (2021, June 29). COVID-19 impact on tourism could deal $4 trillion blow to global economy: UN report. https://news.un.org/en/story/2021/06/1095052

UN, United Nations. (2021). *COVID-19 response*. https://www.un.org/en/coronavirus and https://www.un.org/sites/un2.un.org/files/press_release_campaign_final_1_july.pdf

UNCTAD, United Nations Conference on Trade and Development. (2021a, July 2). *How countries are faring on global goals amid COVID-19*. https://unctad.org/news/how-countries-are-faring-global-goals-amid-covid-19

UNCTAD, United Nations Conference on Trade and Development. (2021b, February 17). *Switzerland climbs to top of global e-commerce index*. https://unctad.org/news/switzerland-climbs-top-global-e-commerce-index

UNSDG, UN Sustainable Development Group. (2020). *Policy brief: The impact of COVID-19 on children*. https://unsdg.un.org/sites/default/files/2020-04/160420_Covid_Children_Policy_Brief.pdf

WHO, World Health Organization. (2021). *Infodemic*. https://www.who.int/health-topics/infodemic#tab=tab_1

Zarrinkoub, A. (2006). *History of the Iranian people* (pp. 110–128). Amir Kabir Publications.

Part I
Impacts on Entrepreneurship and Management Studies

Chapter 2
Entrepreneurial Frugality in Crisis: An Interpretative Phenomenological Approach

Nezameddin Faghih (iD)**, Mansoureh Vahabzadeh, and Mozgan Danesh**

2.1 Introduction

The world is facing widespread societal upheaval. Due to the COVID-19 pandemic, most economic sectors' activities have been affected, and in some countries, even these activities have stopped (Purbasari et al., 2021). With the imposition of "lockdown," people are forced to stay home, not travel, and cut off social connections in fear of transmitting the Coronavirus (Deb et al., 2020). The International Monetary Fund (IMF) predicts that the Coronavirus will significantly impact the economy unmatched by any other economic downturn in world history. The IMF estimates the global damage caused to the economy by the COVID-19 crisis at 3% of average GDP in the world in April 2020, and this amount of damage is increasing due to the continuous lockdown epoch (IMF, 2020).

The COVID-19 pandemic's velocity and intensity have been so great that only a small number of countries have been able to continue their activities as before. Nevertheless, because of insufficient resources in most countries, the COVID-19 crisis has required unique and innovative responses (Harris et al., 2020). One of these innovative ways is frugality. Frugality has been a concern over time, and economic crises have reduced consumption while accumulating wealth (Michaelis, 2017a, b, c). Frugality is a concept and mindset that can be used at any time, but in today's severe economic conditions created by the COVID-19 pandemic, it can help entrepreneurs (Giones et al., 2020). Frugality is an individual characteristic related to entrepreneurs and goes back to their general preference for preserving current

N. Faghih
Cambridge, MA, USA

M. Vahabzadeh · M. Danesh (✉)
Faculty of Entrepreneurship, University of Tehran, Tehran, Iran
e-mail: Mozhgan.Danesh@ut.ac.ir

N. Faghih, A. Forouharfar (eds.), *Socioeconomic Dynamics of the COVID-19 Crisis*, Contributions to Economics, https://doi.org/10.1007/978-3-030-89996-7_2

19

resources and acquiring new ones, taking into account economic logic (Lastovicka et al., 1999).

The quality of the entrepreneur's frugality reveals the entrepreneur's resourcefulness behavior (Bradley, 2015). It helps entrepreneurs in times of economic crisis (Williams & Shepherd, 2016), so having a desire for frugality may improve the effects of the COVID-19 pandemic on businesses. From the perspective of researchers, frugality is an essential element for achievement in entrepreneurship. There has been some research on entrepreneurial frugality (Giones et al., 2020; Michaelis et al., 2020; Michaelis, 2017a, b, c). However, less research has been done to recognize why and how entrepreneurs engage in resourceful behaviors that are not dependent on situational limitation and are self-imposed. So the purpose of this chapter is to examine entrepreneurial frugality in times of the COVID-19 crisis.

The current study begins with a discussion of frugality, its origins, and necessity. The critical point in this section is to mention that frugality is fundamentally different from self-control. The following section of the chapter considers the topic of entrepreneurial frugality. This section refers to the resourceful behaviors of entrepreneurs. For enriching the literature, an attempt is made to link the underlying logic of the existing insights into considering the frugality arising from environmental constraints with the frugality emerging from entrepreneurs' self-imposed constraints. The last part of the theoretical framework is dedicated to the COVID-19 pandemic. The current crisis has posed a significant challenge for businesses, and entrepreneurial frugality is an effective way for businesses to survive. Since the purpose of this chapter is to examine why and how Iranian entrepreneurs show entrepreneurial frugality in their activities, exploring this concern requires a profound understanding of the entrepreneurs' lived experiences in crisis (Thompson et al., 1989). This chapter is based on interpretive phenomenology. Qualitative methods' strength is due to the profound insight, comprehensive details, and ample descriptions it indicates (Jack & Anderson, 2002). The present chapter articulates what areas entrepreneurs have frugality and "how" and "why" (Whetten, 1989) they are frugal. To know each entrepreneur, a profile of them has been prepared. Regarding time, the period for this research is the COVID-19 pandemic era, and regarding location, it returns to the point where entrepreneurs start their businesses. In this regard, the sample of the present study includes seven Iranian entrepreneurs. Startups and junior entrepreneurs under the age of three years are selected. Sampling is purposive and snowball (Marshall, 1996). The data collection tool is a loosely structured interview (Thompson et al., 1989). Then, after analyzing the data, a set of analytical findings is presented in three sections.

In the first part, the findings indicate that Iranian entrepreneurs have a common understanding of the concept of entrepreneurial frugality and consider it as economic spending. In fact, in the face of the COVID-19 crisis and the resulting constraints, Iranian entrepreneurs have tried to change the way resources are used to lead to frugality. The second section's findings acknowledge that regardless of the COVID-19 crisis, self-constraint is the principal cause of frugality. Due to their characteristics, childhood instruction, family, etc., Iranian entrepreneurs show entrepreneurial frugality. Finally, the third part of the findings demonstrates Iranian entrepreneurs considered human resources and networking as essential levers to survive and achieve their goals in this period. They have also changed the expense pattern in COVID-19 crises. For instance, they decrease domestic and offline marketing expenses to better focus on necessary costs. According to the results, Iranian entrepreneurs have made significant changes in four areas of human resources, marketing, market development, and equipment to survive their businesses during the COVID-19 crisis.

Finally, this chapter identifies three fundamental theoretical contributions. The first contribution is that given the type of methodology chosen for the study, this chapter provides new insight into entrepreneurial frugality. Examining entrepreneurs' lived experience and looking closely at their activities in the crisis can provide a comprehensive understanding and attitude towards entrepreneurial frugality, guiding other business owners to deal with the crisis. The second contribution is to reduce the gap between theoretical approaches to entrepreneurial frugality and the practical field. The last contribution highlights the importance of human and social support for entrepreneurs in times of crisis.

2.2 Literature Review

2.2.1 Frugality

Frugality was initially developed as a theory in consumer behavior and was created to understand how consumers make decisions about resources (Lastovicka et al., 1999). Although the word frugality is well known, it is often a misapprehended concept. As far as it is thought, frugal people have opposed consumption (Witkowski, 2010). A person who opposes consumption thinks that a frugal person does not use resources. However, the truth is that a frugal person consumes resources economically. Frugality is a unique feature achieved through experiences in one's life (Aldrich & Yang, 2012). Always frugality throughout history has been accompanied by necessity and survival in hostile and impoverished environments. In this regard, and according to previous research, we find that the concept of frugality has evolved with time and is derived from the concept of Weber's asceticism (Adair-Toteff, 2010; Swedberg, 2009). Generally, Weber's opinion was that asceticism, frugality, and thrift are influential factors in entrepreneurial prosperity (Weber, 1930).

It is essential to mention that frugality is not self-control. Their distinction is in why self-constraints are imposed. In fact, in frugality, the importance and priority of the person are saving resources and maximizing the use of resources, which does not pay attention to the situation (Michaelis et al., 2020). Self-control is a behavior which helps individual to choose valued goals instead of a short-time attractive alternatives (Duckworth et al., 2019). Finally, to achieve a favorable goal, self-control determines a mindset with more certainty in the process of self-activation of one's behavior (Vohs & Faber, 2007). In comparison, frugality encourages resourceful behaviors that have not been planned to achieve a desirable goal. This difference between frugality and self-control has fundamental effects on entrepreneurial resource utilization behaviors.

2.2.2 *Entrepreneurial Frugality*

So far, little research has provided a common definition of entrepreneurial frugality. According to Lastovicka et al. (1999) and Witkowski (2010), entrepreneurial frugality is "A tendency to (a) conserve resources (financial, material, …) and (b) an economical rational in acquiring products (i.e., both goods and services) concerning one's venture."

One of the most critical issues of entrepreneurship is investigating entrepreneurial actions in ambiguous conditions (Bylund & McCaffrey, 2017). In this regard, according to the research that Kuckertz et al. (2020) have done on the suffering of entrepreneurs from the effects of the COVID-19 pandemic in Germany, it has been determined that in times of crisis, entrepreneurs need flexibility in their actions on the one hand and readiness to identify new opportunities on the other. Entrepreneurial frugality is an option for flexibility and response from entrepreneurs in times of crisis. Frugal entrepreneurs are people who, first, sell all the capital that does not affect the growth of their business income; second, they maintain and organize the assets and resources that will immediately increase their income by focusing on frugal choices; and, finally, they try to decrease short-term debt and financial costs (Giones et al., 2020). Frugal entrepreneurs are more proficient than other entrepreneurs at using inefficient resources in new opportunities and successfully achieving long-term goals. As a result, frugality is associated with crucial entrepreneurial achievements, such as maintenance and business progress (Michaelis, 2017a, b, c). Despite the existence of different theories regarding the use of resources, there are three fundamental theories in this area, which are a) effectuation, b) resource-based view, and c) bricolage.

An effectuation approach describes how entrepreneurs set ultimate goals based on the available resources and how entrepreneurs alter goals based on resource restrictions (Sarasvathy, 2001). In this approach, because the goals are planned according to preexisting resources, frugality is meaningless, and the effectuation approach is not an appropriate approach to explain frugality.

The resource-based view (RBV) is an approach to achieving competitive advantage and states that resources are the most important reason for good company performance (Wernerfelt, 1984). Although it seems that the RBV can explain the frugality in entrepreneurship, this approach has been developed in terms of entrepreneurial cognition and does not explain how entrepreneurs make decisions about resources (Alvarez & Busenitz, 2001).

The bricolage approach is based on the principle that goals are achieved by combining available and scarce resources with limited resources (Baker & Nelson, 2005). However, there are resource constraints in the bricolage approach that this restriction does not necessarily exist in frugality. An entrepreneur may be frugal in situations where resources are not limited, so the bricolage approach is incapable of describing frugality behavior.

In general, these three theoretical approaches in the entrepreneurship literature state how entrepreneurs use resources to form new ventures. The literature considers the environment an influential factor in resourceful behavior. Besides, although resource constraints can be the cause of resourceful behavior (Baker & Nelson, 2005; Bradley et al., 2011), it is unable to answer why entrepreneurs engage in resourceful behavior in conditions without resource constraints. So, none of these theories can explain why entrepreneurs make frugal decisions.

According to the socio-cognitive theory, human behavior is widely stimulated and regulated through continuous actions of self-influence. As Bandura (1991, 248) has pointed out, "self-regulatory systems lie at the very heart of causal process... and provides the very basis for purposeful action" and thus "being purposive, is regulated by forethought." The three fundamental axioms of the self-regulatory mechanism are a) the self-monitoring of one's behavior, b) the judgment of one's behavior, and c) the self-reactive influences (Bandura, 1991).

Self-regulation theory (SRT) has been used in various fields. For example, SRT has been used in the field of customer behavior to describe impetuous purchasing behaviors (Baumeister, 2002) or to express the effect of goal setting on self-regulation in organizational behavior (Latham & Locke, 1991) and lately in the entrepreneurial circle to explain the decision-making process of entrepreneurs (Bryant, 2007). Time assumption is implicit in the self-regulation theory. Because persons act on their current wants and needs, on the one hand, and plan to achieve the desired long-term states, on the other hand, SRT is the contradiction between short-term and long-term preferences. Thus the SRT states that a behavior change is apparent from the self-reflective inconsistency between a present and a desirable future state (Hall & Fong, 2007). Under these conditions, entrepreneurs control and save resources based on personal standards of desirable behavior.

2.2.3   An Overview of the COVID-19 Pandemic and Its Impact

In December 2019, a virus appeared in Wuhan, China, infecting people in the area with a disease called the Corona (Mora Cortez & Johnston, 2020). Researchers have done much research to determine the origin of the virus. However, there is not much certainty about how the virus is transmitted from animals to humans. Following the COVID-19 outbreak and the infection of many people, and increased mortality, Wuhan, China, was locked down by the Chinese government, and an order was issued banning the movement of people except in urgent cases. Coronavirus is one of the cases that can be considered as a Black Swan. Because the Black Swan events are unexpected, unknown unknown, and have very severe consequences, facing these swans is a feature of modern societies (Kuckertz et al., 2020).

The crisis has also had severe economic effects. Despite economic policies to reduce the effects of the virus by governments, many of the economic effects are still unclear, and many businesses are severely damaged. This crisis raises concerns about the recession in the global economy (Ratten, 2020). Sectors of the global economy that have been dependent on close relationships with individuals have been more affected by these constraints than others. Like tourism, hospitality industries and many related businesses are at risk due to travel bans. The effects of this crisis have been such that it has closed different countries' borders and stopped international travel. Some industries are also facing supply chain problems, as most workers are forced to stay at home, and industry connections are disrupted (Kraus et al., 2020). However, some IT businesses and online businesses have grown under COVID-19 pandemic.

Entrepreneurs, like other economic actors, have been affected by the crisis. Entrepreneurship studies in the face of crisis and uncertainty have received more attention from an economic perspective and less from a behavioral perspective (Devece et al., 2016). A crisis inadvertently creates a sense of urgency to respond to the situation. In the current context of uncertainty, entrepreneurs need to be quick to identify opportunities and risks. On the one hand, entrepreneurs are agents of opportunity in society, and on the other hand, they may be pressured in uncertain situations, which can lead changes in their expected results (Williams et al., 2017). Entrepreneurs can overcome the crisis with innovation in their actions and can even gain a competitive advantage in global markets with their creative solutions. One of the most innovative ways for entrepreneurs to respond to crises is frugality. Frugality means that entrepreneurs achieve maximum efficiency at the lowest cost by using resources correctly and intelligently and generating creative ideas (Radjou & Prabhu, 2015).

In general, a review of previous research on frugality reveals the lack of substantial and rich evidence to support the importance of frugality in entrepreneurship. Table 2.1 summarizes the mainstream literature discussions.

2.3   Methodology

To answer the research question, we must choose an appropriate approach consistent with the research question and purpose (Davidsson, 2004). Entrepreneurs' cognitive issues and their activities have always been of interest to entrepreneurial researchers (Berglund, 2015). Researchers have either sought to study entrepreneurs' cognitive issues (Busenitz & Barney, 1997; Mitchell et al., 2002) or sought to investigate their activities (Berglund, 2015; Fletcher, 2006). This study aims to study why and how entrepreneurial frugality has been affected during the COVID-19 outbreak in Iran. This study examines entrepreneurs' lived experiences (Lindseth & Norberg, 2004) during the COVID-19. A qualitative method is used because it can provide situated insights, rich details, and in-depth descriptions (Jack & Anderson, 2002). Besides, it offers in-depth processual and contextualized knowledge (Hjorth

Table 2.1 Key contributions to recognizing frugality in business firms (source: authors' own table)

Article	Author	Type of research	Summary of key contribution(s)	Research gaps/areas for development
Revising entrepreneurial action in response to exogenous shocks:Considering the COVID-19 pandemic	Giones et al. (2020)	Conceptual	Identifying how entrepreneurs respond to the COVID-19 crisis using three fields of frugality behavior, entrepreneurial social support, and business planning. Providing an appropriate framework for risk-taking entrepreneurs' actions by integrating these three fields with crisis response steps, including crisis action, post-crisis action, and pre-crisis action. Providing insights to entrepreneurs and preparing them in the face of crisis	Paying attention to the more advanced social skills of entrepreneurs and examining them psychologically. Exploring new emotional and financial ways to support entrepreneurs and their business survival
The frugal entrepreneur: a self-regulatory perspective of resourceful entrepreneurial behavior	Michaelis et al. (2020)	Empirical	The importance of self-regulation theory and its application in SMEs success in terms of being frugal in time and resources. Providing a comprehensive understanding of entrepreneurs' resource constraints and frugality and further emphasis on long-term goals using social cognitive approach. Determining how resources are prioritized by frugal entrepreneurs and their long-term consequences for their business. Developing the concept and multidimensional measure of frugality	Clearly stating how people and their environment interact concerning resource-based decisions. The focus of future research is on determining the individual and environmental factors of thoughtful behaviors

(continued)

Table 2.1 (continued)

Article	Author	Type of research	Summary of key contribution(s)	Research gaps/areas for development
Leveraging frugal innovation in micro and small enterprises at the base of the pyramid in Brazil: an analysis through the lens of dynamic capabilities	Borchardt et al. (2020)	Empirical	Understanding how to innovate in a resource-constrained environment and selecting frugal innovation ways based on the target market. Using the input–process–output (I-P-O) framework to analyze the frugal innovation (frugal inputs, frugal processes, and frugal outputs) applied by micro and small enterprises (MSEs) at the base of the pyramid (BOP) concerning market orientation. Identify the factors affecting frugal innovation in the context of MSEs at the BOP using the dynamic capabilities approach. Providing structural factors that prevent and succeed in using frugal innovation in the company in MSEs at the BOP	Focusing on analyzing frugal innovation structures and their relationship to dynamic capabilities due to the target market. Considering environmental issues. Determining and identifying solutions for regional development and reducing inequalities and improving the MSEs at the BOP's situation
Frugal innovation in developed markets – adaption of a criteria-based evaluation model	Winkler et al. (2020)	Conceptual	Developing a criteria-based model for frugal innovation and the use of "second-degree frugal innovation" in developed countries. Dependence on the success or failure of frugal innovation and its definition on the type of market. Contributing to a better understanding of frugal products and services in developed markets. Suggest tools and guidelines on how to achieve the desired output of the model	A comprehensive and general definition of frugal innovation. Need to collect and analyze more data and readjust the model. Extend existing criteria by integrating with user-related elements

Table 2.1 (continued)

Article	Author	Type of research	Summary of key contribution(s)	Research gaps/areas for development
How entrepreneurship ecosystem influences the development of frugal innovation and informal entrepreneurship	Igwe et al. (2020)	Empirical	Responding to the gap in the importance of entrepreneurial ecosystem and institutional environment on frugal innovation and informal entrepreneurship development. Presenting a model of determinants of frugal innovation and informal entrepreneurship ecosystem	Need to focus on developing policies to support informal entrepreneurs using the "entrepreneurship as practice" perspective. Conducting more studies in different areas of Africa because of increasing entrepreneurship and internationalization of companies to enrich the field of frugal innovation and entrepreneurship
Opportunities of frugality in the post-Corona era	Herstatt and Tiwari (2020)	Conceptual	Demonstrating the role of the Corona crisis in individuals' choices (economic and social). Conceptualizing the impact of these choices resulting from the Corona crisis on innovation management. Emphasis on frugal innovation in managing the Corona crisis's consequences and clarifying these implications for companies and policymakers using a normative-conceptual approach	The need to develop a more comprehensive and multifaceted view of the various aspects of affordability. Further, exploring frugality to address post-Corona crisis issues and consider frugality as a global trend. Paying attention to the overlap of frugal innovation and the principles of circular economics

(continued)

Table 2.1 (continued)

Article	Author	Type of research	Summary of key contribution(s)	Research gaps/areas for development
Business models for frugal innovation in emerging markets: the case of the medical device and laboratory equipment industry	Winterhalter et al. (2017)	Empirical	Providing insights into the value proposition of business models in frugal innovation. Demonstrate increased efficiency in the medical sector through frugal business models. Creating new markets through frugal innovation by launching new programs. The importance of the necessity to adjust the components of the business model. Companies achieve new customer segments through appropriate value creation mechanisms and use research and development strategies for frugal innovation	Conducting longitudinal studies focusing on the dynamics of frugal business models and their change and evolution in specific circumstances. Investigating the multifaceted value proposition in emerging markets. The role of frugal business models in advanced markets
Frugal innovations and actor-network theory: a case of bamboo shoots processing in Manipur, India	Devi and Kumar (2018)	Empirical	Understanding the complex process of frugal innovation in the informal sector using actor-network theory. Identify the importance of diverse actors' negotiating role in creating frugal innovation and the desire to develop and maintain their network. Increasing the understanding of frugal innovation processes by considering the presence of non-human actors alongside human actors using actor-network theory	Emphasis on networking is an important factor in the success of frugal innovation Incorporating social realities into the process of frugal innovation to create deep understanding and knowledge in this area. utilizing other approaches and theories to enrich the field of frugal innovation

(continued)

Table 2.1 (continued)

Article	Author	Type of research	Summary of key contribution(s)	Research gaps/areas for development
The role of internal and external sources of knowledge on frugal innovation: moderating role of innovation capabilities	AlMulhim (2021)	Empirical	Recognizing the vital role of internal and external knowledge resources on frugal innovation. The importance of innovative capabilities on moderate the relationship between knowledge resources and frugal innovation	Investigating the information validity as a moderator of the relationship between knowledge resources and frugal innovation. Explaining the effect of knowledge resources from the view of emerging markets and SMEs
Linking transformational leadership and frugal innovation: the mediating role of tacit and explicit knowledge sharing	Lei et al. (2021)	Empirical	Helping to understand the managers of companies in developing countries about increasing their companies' frugal innovation competencies through leadership performance and knowledge resources. Connecting transformational leadership to frugal innovation through knowledge sharing	The necessity to consider knowledge management processes as a mediator between leadership styles and frugal innovation

et al., 2008). Interpretive phenomenology is used to deeply study the phenomenon of entrepreneurial frugality among Iranian entrepreneurs in the COVID-19 outbreak. This approach goes beyond description and does not preclude the use of a conceptual framework or theoretical orientation (Lopez & Willis, 2004). In addition to the frugality causes, the research explores how entrepreneurs are frugal and create strong descriptive themes (Starks & Trinidad, 2007). The research is based on the principles of Jonathan Smith's interpretive phenomenological analysis (Smith et al., 1999), as shown in Table 2.2.

2.3.1 Sampling and Data Collection

Sampling in interpretive phenomenological analysis is purposive (Greening et al., 1996). Through purposive sampling, snowball sampling has also been used (Hartley, 1994). Convenience and accessibility are the reasons for purposive sampling (Patton, 1990). The sample consists of seven entrepreneurs who are geographically

Table 2.2 Levels of interpretive phenomenology analysis

Levels of analysis	Description of analysis
Collecting data	It is better to use loosely structured interviews.
Interviews	Interviews can be transcript later, or notes can be taken at the interview.
Reading and re-reading	This effectively engages the analyst in the participants' statements. Besides, by focusing the analyst on the texts, she/he becomes aware of her/his and the participants' assumptions. So the analyst will analyze rigorously.
Exploring meaningful statements	Analysts attempt to select and specify meaningful statements, sentences, and phrases by reading the transcript several times.
Searching for themes	The analyst tries to link meaningful statements, sentences, and phrases and introduce themes below themes.
Writing up	This stage involves the formal writing of the participants' experiences. An analyst is obliged to share the real participants' experiences. Also, related theories are mentioned in the results.

Authors' table adopted from Smith et al. (1999)

Table 2.3 Participants' profile. (Source: authors' own table)

Bakhtiari S. is the founder of Avayar. Her startup is providing audio tour guides for those who visit tourist attractions. It explains that tourist attraction is a story to the visitor in multiple languages. Then the visitor can select a personal tour guide.

Ghowsi A. is the cofounder of Boks. His startup is an innovative advertising agency. Based on methods such as gamification or digital advertising, they design interactive advertising. They have promoted the conversion rate of the audience to the customer.

Khademi Moghaddam M. is the cofounder of Speed. His startup is an intra-city postal system. As a service, his startup serves online businesses and businesses which have group delivery.

Moridi M. is the cofounder of Moneyar. Her startup activity is about financial technology. There is a mobile financial application in which people could have financial communications with their phone contacts, in addition to chatting with them. Firms can also utilize these services in the same way.

Shabestanipour A. A. is the founder of Rozane. His startup focuses on data and artificial intelligence to help businesses. It allows companies to make better decisions by informing them about their costs, sales, forecasting demand, and various market conditions.

Soleimani M. is the cofounder of SalamCinema. His startup is an online reference that addresses any concerns about cinema professionals and enthusiasts. They provide data about professionals to promote their films. On the other hand, they provide data for enthusiasts for better decision-making about movies.

Soleymanian A. is the cofounder of LifeandMe. His startup is about e-health and personalized medicine. By investigating the individuals' genetic data, they provide them personalized health recommendations.

located in the capital of Iran, Tehran. Table 2.3 exhibits the profiles of the participants, which provide a brief description of their businesses. This research is based on small samples and, in addition to contextualization, allows a theoretical approach to be developed (Chapman & Smith, 2002). In IPA, six to eight participants are suitable (Smith & Eatough, 2006). For the sample to be homogeneous, the businesses of all the selected entrepreneurs are based on providing service. The establishment time frame of the selected enterprises was within three years (Davidsson, 2004).

2.3.2 Data Analysis

The robustness of qualitative methods in entrepreneurship requires that all data collected from participants be represented precisely (Leitch et al., 2010). IPA is a method that has a comprehensive and specific guideline. This method is not descriptive and allows the scholar to have individual flexibility (Smith & Eatough, 2006). Simultaneously, this method has well-defined procedures that would enable data to be strictly monitored and analyzed (Smith, 2004). The distinct levels in IPA can be observed in Table 2.2.

Using qualitative methods and small samples prevents research's generalizability (Bhattacherjee, 2012), but this study aims to present local and contextualized knowledge in detail (Steyaert, 1997). It does not mean that IPA cannot make a theoretical contribution. Berglund (2007) emphasizes that such research can help to create new theoretical concepts and improve existing theories. Such research can also lessen the gap between theoretical concepts and real-life events (Berglund, 2007). The theory building is entirely evolutionary, and theories are developed and built by examining a question in diverse contexts (Lincoln & Guba, 1985).

The results of data analysis are discussed in the findings section and under three subheadings: the meaning of entrepreneurial frugality, the determinants affecting entrepreneurial frugality, and the actions of entrepreneurial frugality in the COVID-19 crisis.

2.4 Findings

The following data analysis section seeks to examine several critical issues in detail. First, the meaning of entrepreneurial frugality in crisis is reviewed from the perspective of the seven entrepreneurs. Second, the factors affecting frugality are examined from the entrepreneurs' point of view. Michaelis et al. (2020) also suggest that future entrepreneurship studies should focus on factors of frugal behaviors. Finally, it looks at how entrepreneurial frugality was implemented during the COVID-19 era. As Giones et al. (2020) argue, new emotional and financial ways must be found to support entrepreneurs in crisis and survive their businesses. There are diverse points in this section that provide entrepreneurs the proper perspective to better manage everything in a crisis where people face uncertainty, and it is more difficult for them to make decisions (Shrivastava, 1993).

2.4.1 What Was Entrepreneurial Frugality in the COVID-19 Outbreak Crisis from the Entrepreneurs' Perspective?

As the entrepreneurs' responses were studied, all seven entrepreneurs' descriptions were almost similar for entrepreneurial frugality. Each entrepreneur came up with frugality with their own expressions and examples. Ghowsi, the Boks cofounder, mentioned, "The entrepreneur has hypotheses in her/his mind for value creation; she/he has to make the inevitable expenses to reject or confirm these hypotheses to reach the result as soon as possible. Otherwise, she/he will lose the time and opportunity." He also said, "If entrepreneurs identify their goals and where they want to go, they can recognize what expenses are extra and what expenses are required, and they will spend properly." Moridi, the Moneyar cofounder, expressed, "If you know you have chosen the right goal, you have to try to find the best way to reach the goal, and you have to pay to achieve it." Overall, these seven entrepreneurs believed that entrepreneurial frugality does not involve consuming less but rather spending rationally and optimally (Michaelis, 2017a, b, c). Entrepreneurs believed that they had experienced fast development to survive in the COVID-19 crisis (Ratten, 2020). Otherwise, they would have failed (Sheth, 2007, 2020). To achieve this development favorably, they have not decreased expenses, and their costs have also increased in some sectors. It is based on the claim that entrepreneurs are frugal and bootstrap in hostile and uncertain environments (Michaelis, 2017a, b, c). They have increased their expenses in two parts. Some of them have hired new human resources or changed the payment system. Others have provided the equipment they need to reduce their long-term costs and overcome constraints and have even been forced to use the financial facility. Soleimani, the SalamCinema cofounder, articulated, "We did not fire up the workforce, we also hired staff during this period so that we could develop one of our products as soon as possible, which is profitable for the days when people are at home." Soleymanian, the LifeandMe cofounder, expressed, "Not only did our employee numbers not decrease, but we recruited some people. We tried to work as hard as possible to prepare the test results concerning the Coronavirus. So clients can adjust their diet based on their genetics toward Coronavirus." Shabestanipour, the Rozane founder, pointed out, "To reduce the server cost and even generate revenue from it, we decided to have a server, and we paid for it in such circumstances." He also stressed, "In the Covid-19 pandemic, we raised staff salaries to speed up the development process. We also changed the payment system to output-driven to achieve the results faster." Soleymanian articulated, "Because the borders were closed during the Covid-19 crisis, we immediately purchased the equipment we needed with the financial facilities so that we would be needless out of borders."

All of the statements represent that entrepreneurs have been remarkably resilient in the COVID-19 era. They can respond to existing circumstances and required changes and have been able to survive and flourish in uncertainty (Maritz et al., 2020). They believe that it is not only environmental factors that cause an entrepreneur to be frugal and use resources rationally but other factors are also involved. Accordingly, the COVID-19 crisis did not reduce resource consumption but merely changed the form of resource consumption. We will develop this further below.

2.4.2 Why Were Entrepreneurs Frugal in the COVID-19 Outbreak Crisis from the Entrepreneurs' Perspective?

To understand the antecedents of entrepreneurial frugality, we investigated them from entrepreneurs' point of view. For entrepreneurs, factors such as childhood instruction, life experiences, living conditions, personal characteristics, and inherent resource constraints affected entrepreneurial frugality. Bakhtiari, the Avayar founder, mentioned, "My father was always sensitive about resources, especially time, and tried to train me." Ghowsi expressed, "The entrepreneur's experience in building something from scratch allows her/him to determine which expenses are extra and which are essential. Ultimately, the entrepreneur spends in the best way and does not waste." Soleimani mentioned, "It is right that being frugal is an individual characteristic, but people who live in less fertile and productive areas are more cautious about spending and using resources." Shabestanipour believed that "Frugality is due to individual characteristics, but also, resources are inherently limited, and this causes us to be concerned in consuming them in life."

All seven entrepreneurs believed that one of their frugality reasons was the inherent limitation of resources, but they acknowledge that the main reason for their entrepreneurial frugality is self-constraint (Michaelis, 2017a, b, c). According to the socio-cognitive theory, human behavior is widely stimulated and regulated through continuous actions of self-influence. As Bandura (1991) has pointed out, "Self-regulatory systems lie at the very heart of causal process… and provides the very basis for purposeful action."

Khademi Moghaddam, the Speed cofounder, mentioned, "It is right that there are inherent constraints on resources, but my main reason for frugality is myself." Moridi declared, "An entrepreneur must be mature enough to know how to use the resources, regardless of external constraints." Soleimani articulated, "If I were the richest person in the world, then I would optimally use the resources."

Considering these seven entrepreneurs and the logic for their frugality, it seems that the reason for their frugality was not the COVID-19 pandemic. They have just changed their cost model during the outbreak, which we will expand in the following. Entrepreneurs have tried to look at the COVID-19 situation as a point for finding new opportunities so that they can survive and ultimately succeed (Devece et al., 2016).

2.4.3 How Have Entrepreneurs Been Frugal in the COVID-19 Outbreak Crisis from Entrepreneurs' Perspective?

The current section is supposed to provide an entrepreneurial frugality approach in crisis from the entrepreneurs' perspective and explore their lived experiences (Lindseth & Norberg, 2004). This section tries to explain entrepreneurs' statements without shortcomings so that their solutions can be used operationally and concretely in times of crisis. Besides, with this approach, we can have pre-crisis predictions and constant preparedness (Bishop, 2019; Doern et al., 2019; Kuckertz et al., 2020; Williams & Vorley, 2015). This study aims to go beyond theory to examine what had happened in practice and lessen the gap between theory and practice (Berglund, 2007).

To understand what changes entrepreneurs initiated in resource consumption during the COVID-19 pandemic, they were asked, "What areas were you frugal during the Covid-19 crisis?" They gave several examples. The interesting information was that human resources and the network played the most critical role in their statements. The following is a brief description of human resources and the network. Entrepreneurial frugality behaviors were then categorized according to their words.

As it is clear, human resources play a vital role in business development and achieving goals in a crisis (Mirzapour et al., 2019; Sparrow et al., 2013; Wang et al., 2009). Ghowsi mentioned, "Our team structure was such that we considered new targets. They were so talented that we decided to add revenue lines." He also said, "Our employees were so purposeful that they worked under pressure and during day and night to launch new products." Soleimani expressed, "Our team is so friendly that when a problem appears in this situation, even if it is not related to them, they help to solve it as soon as possible." Soleymanian said, "Spreading the Coronavirus, employees announced that they did not want wage and the survival of the business was important to them." These are just some statements about the condition of human resources and the help they provided to entrepreneurs during the COVID-19 crisis so that they could carry out their planned development as soon as possible. In the following, the entrepreneurs' statements regarding the network's impact on their activities in the COVID-19 crisis is going to be elaborated.

Moynihan (2008) argues that network supports businesses in times of crisis. By learning from their network, businesses try to make the most in the crisis (Saunders et al., 2014). They also try to avoid failure and overcome the crisis by combining their internal resources with external resources provided by the network (Baker & Nelson, 2005). In this regard, Shabestanipour states,

> It is such a situation that everyone knows it will be a definite failure if they do not help each other. My network helps me to develop the market immediately. Before Coronavirus, I was focusing on digital businesses. By its initiation, I decided to move on to traditional businesses because they had to sell their products online; otherwise, they would have failed. The network allows me to know more traditional businesses.

He also mentioned, "I needed talented human resources for rapid development, and my acquaintances helped me find them as quickly as possible." Moridi expressed, "I was constantly talking to other friends and acquaintances who have a business, and we shared and learned the most reliable technique we could use for any problem. For example, when the staff was teleworking, it was difficult to check their output, and we were constantly transferring information to find the best way to evaluate them." Soleimani said, "We held a virtual festival during the Covid-19 pandemic to identify talents who are not present in the capital and are rarely seen. The sponsor of the festival awards was a familiar businessman." Bakhtiari states, "We met some of our needs by interacting with friends who had businesses. For example, I provided content for a business and received psychological counseling for staff in return." Khademi Moghaddam said, "Whenever I needed a place or hardware, I immediately turned to my friends in other businesses, and they were as responsive as possible." These are just a few examples of the network position and contribution to entrepreneurial business development during the COVID-19 pandemic. In the following, frugal behaviors of entrepreneurs are developed in a categorized mode.

For elucidating entrepreneurs' frugal behaviors during the COVID-19 pandemic, we tried to raise issues based on categories and entrepreneurs' statements. As mentioned before, for entrepreneurs, frugality did not mean consuming less, but consuming optimally and rationally (Michaelis, 2017a, b, c). Therefore, according to entrepreneurs' statements, the costs could have decreased, not changed, or increased based on the matter. They have changed consumption and cost structure in human resource, marketing, market development, and equipment, each of which is developed in detail and according to their statements below.

There is much effort for human resources that is gradually being developed here. Recruiting an expert person who has a network has accelerated the development process. Bakhtiari expressed, "I had to fire out a number of my human resources, but instead I recruited someone who was an expert and had a great network." Some entrepreneurs have developed online games according to their tasks to improve the productivity of their team. Some have allotted shares to employees (Brandes et al., 2003) or changed their payment systems (Pak et al., 2019). Shabestanipour states, "We have developed an online game so that people can do their work without constant control and be attractive to them. They can also communicate with each other utilizing this game on weekends." Bakhtiari expressed, "I have never done this before, and I had to give shares to key employees to work with more motivation. Now I realize how effective it can be." Soleymanian said, "We have been developing faster, and our payment system was changed to project-oriented and output-oriented. It has led to the maximum productivity of individuals." Shabestanipour expressed, "As I said, with the start of the Covid-19 pandemic, we approached the traditional market and designed the website for those who were not in the digital environment and started advertising for them. Our staff did all this, and we tried to use staff abilities and their idle time. We had constant planning for this." One of the most interesting ideas that human resources have done is collective purchases. Soleimani said, "Employees collectively provide the food they need to reduce their expenses." Recruiting human resources from outside the capital has lessened expenses. Soleymanian pointed out, "Some human resources returned to their cities due to the difficult conditions of the capital during the Covid-19 pandemic. Besides, due to the need for development, we recruited some human resources from other cities. Now I have a center with happier human resources. They are teleworking, and each of them works for a lower salary." These are some of the entrepreneurs' statements about their frugal behaviors. The following is an explanation of the marketing and entrepreneurial frugality behaviors.

Significant changes have also been made in marketing. The first change that most entrepreneurs emphasize is online advertising instead of offline advertising, which has reduced advertising expenses (Herhausen et al., 2020). Due to the online sessions of presenting products and services, the costs of advertising materials and transportation have been reduced. Advertising on social media is another solution that entrepreneurs have chosen instead of costly platforms. Ghowsi pointed out, "With Covid-19 initiation, offline advertising was ineffective, so we focused on online advertising." Bakhtiari said, "Before Covid-19, I used to prepare advertising materials for meetings in a very luxurious way, and I would definitely print them, but now I am content with online advertising." Moridi expressed, "Online meetings have helped us to manage our team better and reduce expenses. The situation is so great that we will continue to do so after the Covid-19." Shabestanipour expressed, "We have decreased the expense of advertising and customer acquisition, and instead of advertising on high-priced platforms, we are advertising on social media." Some entrepreneurs interact with other businesses to reduce their advertising payments (Zahra, 2021). Bakhtiari said, "Instead of doing the advertising myself and tolerating costs, I use the marketing staff of another company and produce content for them instead." While entrepreneurs have tried to reduce their advertising costs, some have to do foreign marketing to expand their market (Zahra, 2021). Ghowsi pointed out, "We thought, we can serve an Iranian customer in digital space, why not serve a foreign customer." Some businesses offer philanthropic services to help people from one side (Popkova et al., 2021) and show goodwill to customers on the other side. Soleimani expressed, "We have considered the option that customers can pay the price at the round price if they like. Then that overpayment will be given to the charity." Moridi pointed out, "We have given paying links to traditional businesses so they could exchange easily. Besides, we give paying links to charities." After reviewing the marketing issues in the COVID-19 pandemic, the following is a description of the market development in this period.

Nearly all entrepreneurs believed that they would fail (Sheth, 2007, 2020) if they did not develop their market according to the conditions. So they have developed their market in some way (Zahra, 2021). They entered foreign markets, traditional markets, and domestic online markets. Ghowsi pointed out, "We thought, we can serve an Iranian customer in digital space, why not serve a foreign customer." Shabestanipour expressed, "As I said, with the start of the Covid-19 pandemic, we approached the traditional market and designed a website for those who were not in the digital environment." Moridi pointed out, "In the Covid-19 outbreak, we have given traditional businesses the paying link and QR Code to make their exchanges more comfortable." Soleimani articulated, "We held a virtual festival during the Covid-19 pandemic to identify talents who were not present in the capital and were rarely seen." He also mentioned, "We focused on one of our products, which was entertaining and proper for the days which people were at home, and we developed it to make an extensive profit from it." These are some of the entrepreneurs' statements about frugal behaviors concerning market development. The following is an expansion of the equipment and frugal behaviors of entrepreneurs.

Almost all entrepreneurs believed that with the start of the COVID-19 pandemic and remoting staff, space, and equipment expenses were reduced, except for the costs of fundamental assets and health items. Some entrepreneurs have asked employees to work in shifts, and some have used coworking spaces. The remoted employees have used their equipment such as laptops. All of this is due to protection against the Coronavirus as well as being frugal. Shabestanipour said, "The expense of workspace has been reduced because we have only provided space for fifty percent of the staff. The employees attend work in shifts to reduce the risk of infection." He also mentioned, "We wanted the employees to be in the office and use the firm's equipment, but with Covid-19 pandemic initiation, the employees had to telework and use their laptops, so our costs were reduced." Soleymanian said, "With the remoted employees, the expense of staff commuting and some incidental costs has decreased." He also mentioned, "We use co-working space to lessen our costs." Bakhtiari pointed out, "After staff adjustment, I rented part of my office to cover other expenses." As mentioned, the cost of health items and fundamental assets has increased during the pandemic. Concerning the cost increase of health items, Khademi Moghaddam expressed, "We have disinfected the packages to protect the customers." Shabestanipour said, "Instead of tea, coffee, etc., we provide health items for the staff." Regarding the increase of fundamental assets expense, Shabestanipour pointed out, "To reduce the server cost and even generate revenue from it, we decided to have a server, and we paid for it in such circumstances." In this regard, Soleymanian articulated, "Because the borders were closed during the Covid-19 crisis, we immediately purchased the equipment we needed with the financial facilities so that we would be needless out of borders." These statements were part of what entrepreneurs explain about the use of space and equipment during the pandemic, concerning entrepreneurial frugality.

As mentioned, this section was supposed to provide an entrepreneurial frugality approach in crisis from the entrepreneurs' perspective and investigate their lived experiences (Lindseth & Norberg, 2004).

2.5   Discussion

We would like to conclude this chapter by quoting Michaelis (2017a, b, c: 1), who has proposed that: "frugality has been used throughout history as a way for countries to bounce back from economic hardships following war and periods of economic decline." There is no reason to presume that the COVID-19 crisis is an exception to that rule. This study represents that in response to the question that "what" is (Whetten, 1989) (There must be four essential elements to developing a theory. "What" deals with what factors, variables, constructs, and concepts must exist to explain the phenomenon. "How" addresses how these factors relate to each other. "Why" deals with the psychological, economic, and social reasons that led to choosing the prementioned factors. "When," "where," and "who" are the conditions that limit the generalizability of a theory.) entrepreneurial frugality in crisis, entrepreneurial frugality does not involve consuming less but instead spending rationally and optimally (Michaelis, 2017a, b, c). For the development of "why" (Whetten, 1989) entrepreneurs are frugal, from entrepreneurs' perspective, self-constraint (Michaelis, 2017a, b, c) is the fundamental reason, despite several reasons such as childhood instruction and life experiences, living conditions, personal characteristics, and inherent resource constraints were stated. Entrepreneurs do not need to be controlled by external factors to be frugal. They want to be frugal because they want to achieve their idealistic goals (Lastovicka et al., 1999). Regarding the "how" (Whetten, 1989) entrepreneurs are frugal in crisis, human resources (Mirzapour et al., 2019; Sparrow et al., 2013; Wang et al., 2009) and network (Baker & Nelson, 2005; Moynihan, 2008; Saunders et al., 2014) are two of the most crucial factors influencing the passing of the COVID-19 crisis. It highlights the importance of human and social support for entrepreneurs in times of crisis. To be frugal, entrepreneurs developed notable immediate changes in expense patterns, especially in the four divisions of human resources, marketing, market development, and equipment, to prevent their definitive failure (Ratten, 2020; Sheth, 2007, 2020).

The current research aimed to provide an entrepreneurial frugality approach in crisis from the entrepreneurs' perspective and explore their lived experiences (Lindseth & Norberg, 2004). This study explained entrepreneurs' statements so that their solutions can be used operationally and concretely in times of crisis. Besides, with this approach, we can have pre-crisis predictions and constant preparedness (Bishop, 2019; Doern et al., 2019; Kuckertz et al., 2020; N. Williams & Vorley, 2015). This study aimed to go beyond theory to examine what had happened in practice and lessen the gap between theory and practice (Berglund, 2007).

To examine "why" and "how" (Whetten, 1989) entrepreneurial frugality exists and "what" it is, we had to confine to the Iranian context. Entrepreneurial activities relate to the institutional environment, economic conditions, and government quality (Thai & Turkina, 2014). Still, with the relentless search for foreign entrepreneurs, it has not been possible to interview them and increase the research's generalizability (Bhattacherjee, 2012). Also, phenomenological studies comprise two interpretations. First, the participant interprets the subject and their world, and second, the researcher tries to interpret the world perceived by the participant (Smith et al., 1999). It may cause a trivial deviation in the result.

One of the critical concerns for entrepreneurs is coming up with a world full of uncertainty (Magnani & Zucchella, 2018). We can have pre-crisis predictions and constant preparedness (Bishop, 2019; Doern et al., 2019; Kuckertz et al., 2020; N. Williams & Vorley, 2015). By applying entrepreneurs' statements, it is possible to achieve the required preparation in the considered areas. For example, entrepreneurs can pay special attention to human resources issues and networking concerning the crisis to not get into trouble in the crisis. Future studies can examine these two areas in more depth to focus on pre-crisis preparedness and how entrepreneurs can equip for the crisis. Besides, longitudinal studies increase the validity of the research (Rindfleisch et al., 2008). This research is cross-sectional. The value of qualitative longitudinal studies in social studies is significant because the analyses based on measurement alone do not obtain a comprehensive understanding (Higgins et al., 2015; McLeod & Thomson, 2009). In longitudinal studies, it is possible to investigate the entrepreneurs' statements at the beginning of the crisis and recognize their activities in detail during the crisis. It is even possible to look deeply at businesses that failed during the crisis and explore how they use their resources to prevent future failures (Lattacher & Wdowiak, 2020).

2.6 Conclusion

The study illustrated that entrepreneurs had just shifted their expense pattern in the crisis. The foremost reason for this change, i.e., being frugal, was themselves and self-constraint. Human resources and network were two fundamental levers of entrepreneurs through the crisis. The research also exhibited that entrepreneurs could survive and grow their businesses by replanning for human resources, marketing, market development, and equipment. The current study has multiple contributions from the theoretical approach to the practical field. The first is the chosen methodology that gives valuable insight into the topic. The second is the gap reduction between the theoretical approach and practical field in entrepreneurial frugality. The last contribution highlights the importance of human and social support for entrepreneurs in crises that could put down future concerns.

In conclusion, frugality is one of the latest and complex topics worth studying meticulously due to the future unprecedented crises and limited resources. Entrepreneurs who have been successful during the pandemic and have even achieved significant growth are the right people to study more comprehensively, turn their tacit knowledge into explicit, and share it with other entrepreneurs. It is also possible to attain helpful knowledge about entrepreneurial frugality by studying failed entrepreneurs and their activities during the pandemic.

References

Adair-Toteff, C. (2010). Max Weber's notion of asceticism. *Journal of Classical Sociology, 10*(2), 109–122. https://doi.org/10.1177/1468795X10370071

Aldrich, H. E., & Yang, T. (2012). Lost in translation: Cultural codes are not blueprints. *Strategic Entrepreneurship Journal, 6*(1), 1–17. https://doi.org/10.1002/sej.1125

AlMulhim, A. F. (2021). The role of internal and external sources of knowledge on frugal innovation: Moderating role of innovation capabilities. *International Journal of Innovation Science.* https://doi.org/10.1108/ijis-09-2020-0130

Alvarez, S. A., & Busenitz, L. W. (2001). The entrepreneurship of resource-based theory. *Journal of Management, 27*(6), 755–775. https://doi.org/10.1177/014920630102700609

Baker, T., & Nelson, R. E. (2005). Creating something from nothing: Resource construction through entrepreneurial bricolage. *Administrative Science Quarterly, 50*(3), 329–366.

Bandura, A. (1991). Social cognitive theory of self-regulation. *Organizational Behavior and Human Decision Processes, 50*(2), 248–287. https://doi.org/10.1016/0749-5978(91)90022-L

Baumeister, R. F. (2002). Yielding to Temptation: Self-Control Failure, Impulsive Purchasing, and Consumer Behavior. *Journal of Consumer Research, 28*(4), 670–676. https://doi.org/10.1086/338209

Berglund, H. (2007). Researching entrepreneurship as lived experience. In H. Neergaard & J. P. Ulhøi (Eds.), *Handbook of qualitative research methods in entrepreneurship* (pp. 75–96). Edward Elgar. https://doi.org/10.4337/9781847204387.00011

Berglund, H. (2015). Between cognition and discourse: phenomenology and the study of entrepreneurship. *International Journal of Entrepreneurial Behavior & Research, 21*(3), 472–488.

Bhattacherjee, A. (2012). Social science research: Principles, methods, and practices. In *Book 3*. http://scholarcommons.usf.edu/cgi/viewcontent.cgi?article=1002&context=oa_textbooks

Bishop, P. (2019). Knowledge diversity and entrepreneurship following an economic crisis: an empirical study of regional resilience in Great Britain. *Entrepreneurship and Regional Development, 31*(5–6), 496–515. https://doi.org/10.1080/08985626.2018.1541595

Borchardt, M., Pereira, G., Ferreira, A. R., Soares, M., Sousa, J., & Battaglia, D. (2020). Leveraging frugal innovation in micro- and small enterprises at the base of the pyramid in Brazil: An analysis through the lens of dynamic capabilities. *Journal of Entrepreneurship in Emerging Economies*. https://doi.org/10.1108/JEEE-02-2020-0031

Bradley, S. W. (2015). Entrepreneurial Resourcefulness. In *Wiley encyclopedia of management* (pp. 1–3). https://doi.org/10.1002/9781118785317.weom030031.

Bradley, S. W., Wiklund, J., & Shepherd, D. A. (2011). Swinging a double-edged sword: The effect of slack on entrepreneurial management and growth. *Journal of Business Venturing, 26*(5), 537–554. https://doi.org/10.1016/j.jbusvent.2010.03.002

Brandes, P., Dharwadkar, R., & Lemesis, G. V. (2003). Effective employee stock option design: Reconciling stakeholder, strategic, and motivational factors. *Academy of Management Perspectives, 17*(1), 77–93. https://doi.org/10.5465/AME.2003.9474813

Bryant, P. (2007). Self-regulation and decision heuristics in entrepreneurial opportunity evaluation and exploitation. *Management Decision*. https://doi.org/10.1108/00251740710746006

Busenitz, L. W., & Barney, J. B. (1997). Differences between entrepreneurs and managers in large organizations: Biases and heuristics in strategic decision-making. *Journal of Business Venturing, 12*(1), 9–30. https://doi.org/10.1016/S0883-9026(96)00003-1

Bylund, P. L., & McCaffrey, M. (2017). A theory of entrepreneurship and institutional uncertainty. *Journal of Business Venturing, 32*(2), 461–475. https://doi.org/10.1016/j.jbusvent.2017.05.006

Chapman, E., & Smith, J. A. (2002). Interpretative phenomenological analysis and the new genetics. *Journal of Health Psychology, 7*(2), 125–130. https://doi.org/10.1177/1359105302007002397

Davidsson, P. (2004). *Researching entrepreneurship*. Springer. https://doi.org/10.1108/ijebr.2005.16011faa.001

Deb, P., Furceri, D., Ostry, J., & Tawk, N. (2020). The effect of containment measures on the COVID-19 pandemic. *IMF Working Papers*. https://doi.org/10.5089/9781513550268.001

Devece, C., Peris-Ortiz, M., & Rueda-Armengot, C. (2016). Entrepreneurship during economic crisis: Success factors and paths to failure. *Journal of Business Research, 69*(11), 5366–5370. https://doi.org/10.1016/j.jbusres.2016.04.139

Devi, W. P., & Kumar, H. (2018). Frugal innovations and actor-network theory: A case of bamboo shoots processing in Manipur, India. *European Journal of Development Research, 30*(1), 66–83. https://doi.org/10.1057/s41287-017-0116-1

Doern, R., Williams, N., & Vorley, T. (2019). Special issue on entrepreneurship and crises: business as usual? An introduction and review of the literature. *Entrepreneurship and Regional Development, 31*(5–6), 400–412. https://doi.org/10.1080/08985626.2018.1541590

Duckworth, A. L., Taxer, J. L., Eskreis-Winkler, L., Galla, B. M., & Gross, J. J. (2019). Self-control and academic achievement. *Annual Review of Psychology, 70*, 373–399. https://doi.org/10.1146/annurev-psych-010418-103230

Fletcher, D. E. (2006). Entrepreneurial processes and the social construction of opportunity. *Entrepreneurship and Regional Development, 18*(5), 421–440. https://doi.org/10.1080/08985620600861105

Giones, F., Brem, A., Pollack, J. M., Michaelis, T. L., Klyver, K., & Brinckmann, J. (2020). Revising entrepreneurial action in response to exogenous shocks: Considering the COVID-19 pandemic. *Journal of Business Venturing Insights, 14*, e00186. https://doi.org/10.1016/j.jbvi.2020.e00186

Greening, D. W., Barringer, B. R., & Macy, G. (1996). A qualitative study of managerial challenges facing small business geographic expansion. *Journal of Business Venturing, 11*(4), 233–256. https://doi.org/10.1016/0883-9026(95)00108-5

Hall, P. A., & Fong, G. T. (2007). Temporal self-regulation theory: A model for individual health behavior. *Health Psychology Review*. https://doi.org/10.1080/17437190701492437

Harris, M., Bhatti, Y., Buckley, J., & Sharma, D. (2020). Fast and frugal innovations in response to the COVID-19 pandemic. *Nature Medicine, 26*(6), 814–817. https://doi.org/10.1038/s41591-020-0889-1

Hartley, J. F. (1994). Case studies in organisational research. In: Cassell, C., Symon, G. (Eds.), *Qualitative methods in organisational research*. Sage. http://publications.lib.chalmers.se/records/fulltext/245180/245180.pdf%0A, https://hdl.handle.net/20.500.12380/245180%0A, https://doi.org/10.1016/j.jsames.2011.03.003%0A, https://doi.org/10.1016/j.gr.2017.08.001%0A, https://doi.org/10.1016/j.precamres.2014.12.0

Herhausen, D., Miočević, D., Morgan, R. E., & Kleijnen, M. H. (2020). The digital marketing capabilities gap. *Industrial Marketing Management, 90*(March), 276–290. https://doi.org/10.1016/j.indmarman.2020.07.022

Herstatt, C., & Tiwari, R. (2020). Opportunities of frugality in the post-corona era. *International Journal of Technology Management, 83*(1-3), 15–33. https://doi.org/10.1504/IJTM.2020.109276

Higgins, D., Trehan, K., McGowan, P., Galloway, L., Kapasi, I., & Whittam, G. (2015). How not to do it!! A salutary lesson on longitudinal and qualitative research approaches for entrepreneurship researchers. *International Journal of Entrepreneurial Behavior & Research, 21*(3), 489–500. https://doi.org/10.1108/IJEBR-12-2013-0224

Hjorth, D., Jones, C., & Gartner, W. B. (2008). Introduction for "Recreating/Recontextualising Entrepreneurship". *Scandinavian Journal of Management, 24*(2), 81–84. https://doi.org/10.1016/j.scaman.2008.03.003

Igwe, P. A., Odunukan, K., Rahman, M., Rugara, D. G., & Ochinanwata, C. (2020). How entrepreneurship ecosystem influences the development of frugal innovation and informal entrepreneurship. *Thunderbird International Business Review, 62*(5), 475–488. https://doi.org/10.1002/tie.22157

IMF. (2020). The great lockdown. In *World economic outlook*. International Monetary Fund.

Jack, S. L., & Anderson, A. R. (2002). The effects of embeddedness on the entrepreneurial process. *Journal of Business Venturing, 17*(5), 467–487. https://doi.org/10.1016/S0883-9026(01)00076-3

Kraus, S., Clauss, T., Breier, M., Gast, J., Zardini, A., & Tiberius, V. (2020). The economics of COVID-19: Initial empirical evidence on how family firms in five European countries cope with the corona crisis. *International Journal of Entrepreneurial Behaviour and Research*. https://doi.org/10.1108/IJEBR-04-2020-0214

Kuckertz, A., Brändle, L., Gaudig, A., Hinderer, S., Reyes, C. A. M., Prochotta, A., Steinbrink, K. M., & Berger, E. S. (2020). Startups in times of crisis – A rapid response to the COVID-19 pandemic. *Journal of Business Venturing Insights, 13*(e00169). https://doi.org/10.1016/j.jbvi.2020.e00169

Lastovicka, J. L., Bettencourt, L. A., Hughner, R. S., & Kuntze, R. J. (1999). Lifestyle of the tight and frugal: Theory and measurement. *Journal of Consumer Research, 26*(1), 85–98. https://doi.org/10.1086/209552

Latham, G. P., & Locke, E. A. (1991). Self-regulation through goal setting. *Organizational Behavior and Human Decision Processes, 50*(2), 212–247. https://doi.org/10.1016/0749-5978(91)90021-K

Lattacher, W., & Wdowiak, M. A. (2020). Entrepreneurial learning from failure. A systematic review. *International Journal of Entrepreneurial Behaviour and Research, 26*(5), 1093–1131. https://doi.org/10.1108/IJEBR-02-2019-0085

Lei, H., Gui, L., & Le, P. B. (2021). Linking transformational leadership and frugal innovation: the mediating role of tacit and explicit knowledge sharing. *Journal of Knowledge Management.* https://doi.org/10.1108/JKM-04-2020-0247

Leitch, C. M., Hill, F. M., & Harrison, R. T. (2010). The philosophy and practice of interpretivist research in entrepreneurship: Quality, validation, and trust. *Organizational Research Methods, 13*(1), 67–84. https://doi.org/10.1177/1094428109339839

Lincoln, Y. S., & Guba, E. G. (1985). *Naturalistic inquiry.* Sage.

Lindseth, A., & Norberg, A. (2004). A phenomenological hermeneutical method for researching lived experience. *Scandinavian Journal of Caring Sciences, 18*(2), 145–153.

Lopez, K. A., & Willis, D. G. (2004). Descriptive versus interpretive phenomenology: Their contributions to nursing knowledge. *Qualitative Health Research, 14*(5), 726–735. https://doi.org/10.1177/1049732304263638

Magnani, G., & Zucchella, A. (2018). Uncertainty in Entrepreneurship and Management Studies: A Systematic Literature Review. *International Journal of Business and Management, 13*(3), 98. https://doi.org/10.5539/ijbm.v13n3p98

Maritz, A., Perenyi, A., de Waal, G., & Buck, C. (2020). Entrepreneurship as the unsung hero during the current COVID-19 economic crisis: Australian perspectives. *Sustainability (Switzerland), 12*(11), 4612. https://doi.org/10.3390/su12114612

Marshall, M. N. (1996). Sampling for qualitative research. *Family Practice, 13*(6), 522–526. https://doi.org/10.1093/fampra/13.6.522

McLeod, J., & Thomson, R. (2009). Researching social change: Qualitative approaches. Sage https://doi.org/10.4135/9780857029010

Michaelis, T. (2017a). Entrepreneurial frugality: A new measure. *Academy of Management Proceedings, 1,* 16970. https://doi.org/10.5465/ambpp.2017.16970abstract

Michaelis, T. L. (2017b). *Entrepreneurial frugality: Validation of a new construct.* North Carolina State University.

Michaelis, T. L. (2017c). Entrepreneurial frugality: Validation of a new construct. In *Dissertation abstracts international section A: Humanities and social sciences.* University Microfilms.

Michaelis, T. L., Carr, J. C., Scheaf, D. J., & Pollack, J. M. (2020). The frugal entrepreneur: A self-regulatory perspective of resourceful entrepreneurial behavior. *Journal of Business Venturing, 35*(4), 105969. https://doi.org/10.1016/j.jbusvent.2019.105969

Mirzapour, M., Toutian, S. S., Mehrara, A., & Khorrampour, S. (2019). The strategic role of human resource management in crisis management considering the mediating role of organizational culture. *International Journal of Human Capital in Urban Management, 4*(1), 43–50. https://doi.org/10.22034/IJHCUM.2019.01.05

Mitchell, R. K., Busenitz, L., Lant, T., McDougall, P. P., Morse, E. A., & Smith, J. B. (2002). Toward a theory of entrepreneurial cognition: Rethinking the people side of entrepreneurship research. *Entrepreneurship Theory and Practice, 27*(2), 93–104.

Mora Cortez, R., & Johnston, W. J. (2020). The Coronavirus crisis in B2B settings: Crisis uniqueness and managerial implications based on social exchange theory. *Industrial Marketing Management, 88,* 125–135. https://doi.org/10.1016/j.indmarman.2020.05.004

Moynihan, D. P. (2008). Learning under uncertainty: Networks in crisis management. *Public Administration Review, 68*(2), 350–365.

Pak, K., Kooij, D. T., De Lange, A. H., & Van Veldhoven, M. J. (2019). Human resource management and the ability, motivation and opportunity to continue working: A review of quantitative studies. *Human Resource Management Review, 29*(3), 336–352. https://doi.org/10.1016/j.hrmr.2018.07.002

Patton, M. Q. (1990). *Qualitative evaluation and research methods.* Sage. http://publications.lib.chalmers.se/records/fulltext/245180/245180.pdf%0A, https://hdl.handle.net/20.500.12380/245180%0A, https://doi.org/10.1016/j.jsames.2011.03.003%0A, https://doi.org/10.1016/j.gr.2017.08.001%0A, https://doi.org/10.1016/j.precamres.2014.12.0

Popkova, E., DeLo, P., & Sergi, B. S. (2021). Corporate social responsibility amid social distancing during the COVID-19 crisis: BRICS vs. OECD countries. *Research in International Business and Finance, 55,* 101315. https://doi.org/10.1016/j.ribaf.2020.101315

Purbasari, R., Muttaqin, Z., & Silvya Sari, D. (2021). Digital entrepreneurship in pandemic Covid 19 Era: The digital entrepreneurial ecosystem framework. In *Review of integrative business and economics research*. GMP Press & Printing Co.

Radjou, N., & Prabhu, J. (2015). Frugal Innovation – How to do more with less. In *Learning and leading with technology*, Hachette India.

Ratten, V. (2020). Coronavirus and international business: An entrepreneurial ecosystem perspective. *Thunderbird International Business Review, 62*(5), 629–634. https://doi.org/10.1002/tie.22161

Rindfleisch, A., Malter, A. J., Ganesan, S., & Moorman, C. (2008). Cross-sectional versus longitudinal survey research: Concepts, findings, and guidelines. *Journal of Marketing Research, 45*(3), 261–279. https://doi.org/10.1509/jmkr.45.3.261

Sarasvathy, S. D. (2001). Causation and effectuation: Toward a theoretical shift from economic inevitability to entrepreneurial contingency. *Academy of Management Review, 26*(2), 243–263. https://doi.org/10.5465/AMR.2001.4378020

Saunders, M. N. K., Gray, D. E., & Goregaokar, H. (2014). SME innovation and learning: The role of networks and crisis events. *European Journal of Training and Development, 38*(1–2), 136–149. https://doi.org/10.1108/EJTD-07-2013-0073

Sheth, J. N. (2007). *Self-destructive habits of good companies and how to break them*. Wharton School Publishing.

Sheth, J. N. (2020). Business of business is more than business: Managing during the Covid crisis. *Industrial Marketing Management, 88*(May), 261–264. https://doi.org/10.1016/j.indmarman.2020.05.028

Shrivastava, P. (1993). Crisis theory/practice: Towards a sustainable future. *Organization & Environment, 7*(1), 23–42. https://doi.org/10.1177/108602669300700103

Smith, J. A. (2004). Reflecting on the development of interpretative phenomenological analysis and its contribution to qualitative research in psychology. *Qualitative Research in Psychology, 1*(1), 39–54. https://doi.org/10.1191/1478088704qp004oa

Smith, J. A., & Eatough, V. (2006). Interpretative phenomenological analysis. In G. M. Breakwell, S. Hammond, C. Fife-Schan, & J. A. Smith (Eds.), *Research methods in psychology*. Sage.

Smith, J. A., Jarman, M., & Osborn, M. (1999). Doing interpretative phenomenological analysis. In *Qualitative health psychology: Theories and methods* (pp. 218–240). Sage. https://doi.org/10.4135/9781848607927.n11

Sparrow, P., Farndale, E., & Scullion, H. (2013). An empirical study of the role of the corporate HR function in global talent management in professional and financial service firms in the global financial crisis. *International Journal of Human Resource Management, 24*(9), 1777–1798. https://doi.org/10.1080/09585192.2013.777541

Starks, H., & Trinidad, S. B. (2007). Choose your method: A comparison of phenomenology, discourse analysis, and grounded theory. *Qualitative Health Research, 17*(10), 1372–1380. https://doi.org/10.1177/1049732307307031

Steyaert, C. (1997). A qualitative methodology for process studies of entrepreneurship. *International Studies of Management & Organization, 27*(3), 13–33. https://doi.org/10.1080/00208825.1997.11656711

Swedberg, R. (2009). The protestant ethic and the spirit of capitalism: The Talcott Parsons translation interpretations. In *Norton critical editions in the history of ideas*. Norton.

Thai, M. T. T., & Turkina, E. (2014). Macro-level determinants of formal entrepreneurship versus informal entrepreneurship. *Journal of Business Venturing, 29*(4), 490–510. https://doi.org/10.1016/j.jbusvent.2013.07.005

Thompson, C. J., Locander, W. B., & Pollio, H. R. (1989). Putting consumer experience back into consumer research: The philosophy and method of existential-phenomenology. *Journal of Consumer Research, 16*(2), 133–146. https://doi.org/10.1086/209203

Vohs, K. D., & Faber, R. J. (2007). Spent resources: Self-regulatory resource availability affects impulse buying. *Journal of Consumer Research, 33*(4), 537–547. https://doi.org/10.1086/510228

Wang, J., Hutchins, H. M., & Garavan, T. N. (2009). Exploring the strategic role of human resource development in organizational crisis management. *Human Resource Development Review, 8*(1), 22–53. https://doi.org/10.1177/1534484308330018

Weber, M. (1930). Asceticism and the spirit of capitalism. In *The protestant ethic and spirit of capitalism*. Charles River Editors.

Wernerfelt, B. (1984). A resource-based view of the firm. *Strategic Management Journal*. https://doi.org/10.1002/smj.4250050207

Whetten, D. A. (1989). What constitutes a theoretical contribution? *Academy of Management Review, 14*(4), 490–495.

Williams, T. A., & Shepherd, D. A. (2016). Victim entrepreneurs doing well by doing good: Venture creation and well-being in the aftermath of a resource shock. *Journal of Business Venturing, 31*(4), 365–387. https://doi.org/10.1016/j.jbusvent.2016.04.002

Williams, N., & Vorley, T. (2015). The impact of institutional change on entrepreneurship in a crisis-hit economy: the case of Greece. *Entrepreneurship and Regional Development, 27*(1–2), 28–49. https://doi.org/10.1080/08985626.2014.995723

Williams, T. A., Gruber, D. A., Sutcliffe, K. M., Shepherd, D. A., & Zhao, E. Y. (2017). Organizational response to adversity: Fusing crisis management and resilience research streams. *Academy of Management Annals, 11*(2), 733–769. https://doi.org/10.5465/annals.2015.0134

Winkler, T., Ulz, A., Knöbl, W., & Lercher, H. (2020). Frugal innovation in developed markets – Adaption of a criteria-based evaluation model. *Journal of Innovation and Knowledge, 5*(4), 251–259. https://doi.org/10.1016/j.jik.2019.11.004

Winterhalter, S., Zeschky, M. B., Neumann, L., & Gassmann, O. (2017). Business models for frugal innovation in emerging markets: The case of the medical device and laboratory equipment industry. *Technovation, 66*, 3–13. https://doi.org/10.1016/j.technovation.2017.07.002

Witkowski, T. H. (2010). A brief history of frugality discourses in the united states. *Consumption Markets and Culture, 13*(3), 235–258. https://doi.org/10.1080/10253861003786975

Zahra, S. A. (2021). International entrepreneurship in the post Covid world. *Journal of World Business, 56*(1), 101143. https://doi.org/10.1016/j.jwb.2020.101143

Chapter 3
The Future of International Entrepreneurship Post-COVID-19

Lasse Torkkeli, Anisur Faroque, and Hannes Velt

3.1 Introduction

The COVID-19 pandemic has, since its global onset in 2020, had a major impact on entrepreneurs and businesses worldwide. Global foreign direct investment (FDI) in 2020 fell by 42%, with the trends for FDI expected to remain weak in 2021 (UNCTAD, 2021). The pandemic also heavily impacts research on both international business (Caligiuri et al., 2020) and international entrepreneurship (Zahra, 2020), disrupting global value chains (Kano & Oh, 2020) and calling into question a host of recurring decisions on internationalization and international operations (see Verbeke & Yuan, 2021).

In a recessionary period, such as the pandemic is exerting on markets across the world, the importance of high-growth enterprises as drivers of economic development is even more important than normal (Greene & Rosiello, 2020). High-growth enterprises in the international domain have been conceptualized as "born globals" (Rennie, 1993; Knight et al., 2004), which are small, rapidly internationalizing firms, often from knowledge-intensive industries (Madsen & Servais, 2017), ventures whose purpose is to exploit a global niche from the inception of the company (Tanev, 2012). Such rapidly internationalizing enterprises have also been termed international new ventures (McDougall et al., 1994) among a host of other terms (see Rialp et al., 2005; Romanello & Chiarvesio, 2019). The study of such firms crucial for the present economic recovery is conducted within the international

L. Torkkeli (✉)
Turku School of Economics, University of Turku, Turku, Finland
e-mail: lasse.torkkeli@utu.fi

A. Faroque · H. Velt
LUT University School of Business and Management, Lappeenranta, Finland
e-mail: anisur.faroque@lut.fi; hannes.velt@lut.fi

© The Author(s), under exclusive license to Springer Nature Switzerland AG 2022   45
N. Faghih, A. Forouharfar (eds.), *Socioeconomic Dynamics of the COVID-19 Crisis*,
Contributions to Economics, https://doi.org/10.1007/978-3-030-89996-7_3

entrepreneurship domain of research (Jones et al., 2011). Therefore, when assessing the COVID-19 aftermath from business and management perspectives, considering how the pandemic impacts international entrepreneurship, and how international entrepreneurship can and should be supported from policy and practice perspectives, is essential.

The purpose of this chapter is to assess the future of international entrepreneurship as a field of research (cf. Servantie et al., 2016; Zucchella, 2021) and a phenomenon and to propose the main consequences for scholars and practitioners post-COVID-19. In this chapter, we posit that three macro-level global phenomena impact entrepreneurship today: digitalization, ecosystems, and institutional support are strengthening and will have a major impact on the consequences and repercussions of international entrepreneurship post-COVID-19. Specifically, we propose that (1) born digital enterprises will perform better globally post-COVID-19 than other types of internationalizing enterprises, (2) the entrepreneurial ecosystem is critical for sustaining international entrepreneurship resilience post-COVID-19, and (3) countries that provide more export support for small- and medium-sized enterprises (SMEs) post-COVID-19 will see an increase on their global share of international entrepreneurship. The chapter concludes with suggestions for ways forward for international entrepreneurship as a field of research as well as for policymakers and entrepreneurs looking to not only cope with the COVID-19 pandemic but also to leverage it in decision-making to ensure continued success for international entrepreneurs post-pandemic.

The chapter continues as follows. The next section will discuss the origins and state of international entrepreneurship as a field of study. We then build on this in section three by discussing the growing role of digitalization in the field, marking the emergence and evolution of digital international entrepreneurship as a stream of research. This is followed by outlining the role of the ecosystemic view in taking the field forward post-COVID-19, after which we outline how export assistance by nations and governments is expected to impact the trajectories of entrepreneurial internationalization post-pandemic. The chapter concludes by discussing the future of international entrepreneurship post-COVID-19 in light of these developments, while also describing the main resulting managerial and policy implications.

3.2   International Entrepreneurship as a Field

International entrepreneurship as a field of study arose during the 1990s at the intersection of international business and entrepreneurship research. Traditional models of internationalization (Johanson and Wiedersheim-Paul, 1975; Bilkey & Tesar, 1977; Johanson & Vahlne, 1977; Cavusgil, 1980; Reid, 1981; Czinkota, 1982) were increasingly questioned and critiqued partly due to the fact that scholars (McDougall, 1989; Oviatt & McDougall, 1995) noted that global developments such as the rise of the internet and the progress of globalization were increasingly giving rise to new types of enterprises whose international expansion did not match the process and patterns that the earlier models of internationalization in international business literature would predict.

Instead, the new types of ventures were characterized by rapid and intensive internationalization across culturally and geographically distant markets, as well as the closer ones. Oviatt and McDougall (1994, p. 49) define such firms as international new ventures, "a business organization that, from inception, seeks to derive significant competitive advantages from the use of resources and the sale of outputs in multiple countries." New types of rapidly internationalizing (often) small enterprises have subsequently been conceptualized in the international entrepreneurship domain as born globals (Rennie, 1993; Knight et al., 2004), global start-ups (Oviatt & McDougall, 1995), and micromultinationals (Dimitratos et al., 2003). The growth and relevance of international entrepreneurship research owes much to the study of such novel phenomena that were found to challenge the existing models and theories on internationalization (Zucchella, 2021).

As international entrepreneurship research initially developed around the (mostly) empirical research of the early internationalizing firms, and while it has been criticized as theoretically fragmented (Keupp & Gassmann, 2009), later studies have established that international entrepreneurship has reached a mature stage (Hånell et al., 2013) and developed into a proper field of research (Servantie et al., 2016; Zucchella, 2021) with a domain ontology encompassing entrepreneurial internationalization, international comparisons of entrepreneurship, and comparative entrepreneurial internationalization (Jones et al., 2011). International entrepreneurship has been defined along two lines of argument. First, international entrepreneurship is defined as the combination of innovative, proactive, and risk-seeking behavior that crosses national borders and is intended to create value in organizations (McDougall & Oviatt, 2000). This definition aligns the field with the concept of international entrepreneurial orientation (Kuivalainen et al., 2007; Covin & Miller, 2014). A second, later definition of international entrepreneurship is "the discovery, enactment, evaluation, and exploitation of opportunities—across national borders—to create future goods and services" (Oviatt & McDougall, 2005, p. 540), or as the "identification and exploitation of opportunities for international exchange" (Ellis, 2011, p. 99). This second definition in turn aligns the domain with the concept of international opportunity recognition (Zahra et al., 2005; Mainela et al., 2014).

The COVID-19 pandemic is having a major impact on international entrepreneurship in general, and on born globals and international new ventures in particular. As Zahra (2020) has noted, it is expected that the post-COVID world will provide an international environment where agile and resilient international new ventures should be able to leverage their entrepreneurial orientation to find new international opportunities. Post-disaster environments in general are uncertain and volatile by nature, which further emphasizes the advantage of being able to develop capabilities and resources for new opportunity recognition (Battisti & Deakins, 2017). Rapidly internationalizing small firms such as born globals are characterized by their unique capabilities (Weerawardena et al., 2007; Cavusgil & Knight, 2015) and tend to reside in high-tech industry sectors (e.g., Cannone & Ughetto, 2014) such as software and other information and communication technology sectors that are more digitalized by nature compared to more traditional manufacturing industries. They comprise what we place under the umbrella term of digital international entrepreneurship.

3.3 Digital International Entrepreneurship

Digitalization is commonly defined as "the process of converting something to digital form" (Merriam-Webster, 2021). The intersection of digital technologies and entrepreneurship gives rise to digital entrepreneurship, which considers how the distinct characteristics of digital technologies shape entrepreneurial pursuits (Nambisan, 2017). The international entrepreneurship field of research has, since its foundation, shed light on how more or less digitally enabled, often small and young enterprises, internationalize. Bell and Loane (2010) have termed such firms "new-wave" global firms, SMEs that make use of web 2.0 tools and technologies to develop the capabilities necessary for rapid internationalization.

Other studies (e.g., Wentrup, 2016) have shed light on how enterprises balance an online and offline presence during their internationalization and on the intricacies of internationalization in platform firms (e.g., internationalization of ibusiness firms) (Brouthers et al., 2016). In sum, the phenomenon of digitalization has permeated the international entrepreneurship literature for the majority of its existence; however, unlike its parent field of research, the domain of *digital* international entrepreneurship has also tended to lack in coherent unifying frameworks and in robust theoretical foundations.

That is, until recently, several recent studies (Vadana et al., 2019, 2020; Monaghan et al., 2020) have shed light on the internationalization of *born digitals.* Monaghan et al. (2020) discuss internationalization of digitally intensive firms by contrasting them with earlier models of internationalization such as the revised U-model (Johanson & Vahlne, 2009). In this analysis, the main distinguishing factors of born digitals are twofold: they are firms that leverage digital infrastructure to enter foreign markets, and they rely on digital infrastructure to accrue the capabilities necessary for creating and selling their offerings online through a digital business model that is accessible to international markets (Monaghan et al., 2020).

The conceptualization by Vadana et al. (2019, 2020) takes a partly distinct view of the internationalization of born digitals, defining them as a product or services company in which the value chain activities are digitalized in full at the inception of the company or soon after. This distinction allows for assessing the extent of digitalization and internationalization by explaining how and why firms that digitalize different parts of their value chain activities can strategize and perform in their international expansion, and it also allows for incorporating the research on born digitals with that of global value chains (Gereffi et al., 2005; Cattaneo et al., 2010).

In sum, the conceptualizations of born digitals by both Monaghan et al. (2020) and Vadana et al. (2019, 2020) suggest that, thanks to their extent of digitalization, born digitals are able to start international business activities either from their inception or soon after their inception.

We posit that born digital firms are in a position to benefit after the pandemic has passed. For one thing, digital enterprises are in a position to effectively respond to disruptions in global supply chains (e.g., Qermane & Mancha, 2020). SMEs in general tend to be agile, and it has been suggested (Papadopoulos et al., 2020) that SMEs can develop capabilities for sensing, seizing, and transforming activities that would enable them to deal with COVID-19. International digital competence allows digital companies to pursue international expansion via increasing online presence (Cahen & Borini, 2020) and is therefore an important capability.

A similar tendency is seen in exporting firms as they can prioritize investments in digitalization instead of further export diversification during the pandemic, thus overcoming crises through increased digitalization, in addition to simply diversifying their exports (Jaklič & Burger, 2020). We therefore consider it likely that highly digitalized enterprises will, on average, be among the "winners" of post-pandemic global trade and international entrepreneurship, and we posit the following:

- Proposition 1: Born digital enterprises will perform better globally post-COVID-19 pandemic than other types of internationalizing enterprises.

3.4 Entrepreneurial Ecosystem Support in International Entrepreneurship

An entrepreneurial ecosystem is "a set of interconnected entrepreneurial actors, entrepreneurial organisations, institutions and entrepreneurial processes which formally and informally coalesce to connect, mediate and govern the performance within the local entrepreneurial environment" (Mason & Brown, 2014, p. 4). Another, more recent definition of entrepreneurial ecosystem is "a regional community of hierarchically independent, yet interdependent heterogeneous participants who facilitate the start-up and scale-up of entrepreneurial new ventures who compete with innovative business models" (Thomas & Autio, 2020). This latter definition further highlights the geographical and high-growth entrepreneurship supporting the nature of the ecosystem.

The entrepreneurial ecosystem is a complex adaptive system (Phillips & Ritala, 2019) with a number of elements and sub-elements to be considered (Cavallo et al., 2019). Structurally, the entrepreneurial ecosystem has been conceptualized as consisting of the three interconnected dimensions of structural, cognitive, and relational (Theodoraki et al., 2018). Theodoraki and Catanzaro (2021) found that the sub-ecosystems of business creation and internationalization support each other.

Research on entrepreneurial ecosystems has been called under-theorized and in need of more development (Acs et al., 2017). Studies (Velt et al., 2018, 2020) have highlighted the role of regional and transnational entrepreneurial ecosystems in the development of born globals. Recently, Theodoraki and Catanzaro put forth the argument for incorporating international entrepreneurship and entrepreneurial ecosystem literature; they propose that one of the primary objectives of entrepreneurial ecosystems should be facilitating the internationalization of firms (Theodoraki & Catanzaro, 2021).

We posit that the role of entrepreneurial ecosystems will be particularly important in the post-COVID-19 global business environment and that this is due to the crucial role that entrepreneurial ecosystems have in supporting otherwise viable born globals and born digitals through the initial shock of the pandemic. Entrepreneurial ecosystems have a critical role in making sure SMEs can survive the COVID-19 pandemic. As Kuckertz et al. (2020) recently argued, the pandemic will require policy measures to support start-ups with both short-term cash flow and long-term measures aimed at strengthening the entrepreneurial ecosystems in their home countries. Born globals are in general small firms characterized by their resource constraints (Sasi & Arenius, 2012) and their rapid development (Nummela et al., 2016). They also make use of unique sets of knowledge and resources to speed up their internationalization (Fan & Phan, 2007; Gassmann & Keupp, 2007). Those resources are acquired from local contexts, which means that the role of the local regional entrepreneurial ecosystem for born globals is critical (Velt et al., 2018). Born globals often require endowments to support their internationalization in the best of times, and thus they are the type of entrepreneurship that have also required and will require entrepreneurial ecosystem support through and post-COVID-19.

The importance of the entrepreneurial ecosystem to entrepreneurial internationalization extends from born globals to internationalizing SMEs in general: the latter face a variety of barriers to international growth (Hutchinson et al., 2009; Hessels & Parker, 2013; Kahiya, 2013), barriers that the entrepreneurial ecosystem can help mitigate (Theodoraki & Catanzaro, 2021). More specifically, many of the typical barriers for successful entrepreneurial internationalization—outsidership to networks (Schweizer, 2013), lack of financial resources (Freeman et al., 2006), lack of international entrepreneurial culture (cf. Dimitratos & Plakoyiannaki, 2003), and lack of knowledge (Fernhaber et al., 2009)—correspond to the specific elements of the entrepreneurial ecosystem, as outlined by Stam and van de Ven (2019). Therefore, we posit that regional entrepreneurial ecosystems will have an important role in sustaining international entrepreneurial behavior and international entrepreneurship in general:

- Proposition 2: The entrepreneurial ecosystem is critical for sustaining international entrepreneurship resilience post-COVID-19.

3.5 Export Support in International Entrepreneurship

Given that international entrepreneurship contributes more to the local economy than local entrepreneurship (González-Pernía & Peña-Legazkue, 2015), governments in most countries offer pro-international entrepreneurship policy incentives to assist existing and aspiring entrepreneurs to cross borders (Minniti, 2008). In a broader sense, governments offer two types of export assistance: financial and marketing. Financial assistance includes direct and indirect financial incentives such as easily accessible and affordable export loans, duty-free provisions for export/import, tax breaks or lower taxes, export credit guarantees, and cash incentives. Marketing assistance consists mostly of information (Diamantopoulos et al., 1993), though there may be some other forms of such assistance, such as aiding connections with potential exporters, product development, and product promotion. Additionally, general economic diplomacy as a soft public intervention also caters to the export promotion based on international relations through foreign trade missions and embassies.

Research on the relationship between export assistance and export performance has largely focused on traditional exporting firms, without paying attention to the needs of born global or digital firms (Faroque & Takahashi, 2012, 2015). Furthermore, only a few studies have investigated how government support has helped firms to weather crises, especially recessions. Van Biesebroeck et al. (2016), based on firm-level data for Belgium and Peru, found that after the global recession of 2009, firms that availed of government assistance programs did better during the crisis in terms of survival and continuation of exports to countries hit by recession.

We posit that in the post-COVID-19 era, governments all around the world, regardless of whether they are in developed or developing countries, will realize the importance of such assistance more than ever. Since 1920, the world has witnessed more than 15 recessions, each of which lasted just over a year. However, considering the unique nature of the recession caused by the COVID-19 pandemic and the overwhelming impact of it, it is considerably difficult to predict specific consequences and the time period of the recession.

The pandemic has contributed to geo-economic instability, a lack of trust between nations, and an escalating fragmentation of economic space. A reduction in economic activity has caused a reduction in exports and imports of all countries, which has ultimately altered the international maps of supply/demand (Malysheva & Ratner, 2020). Lin and Zhang (2020) found that the impact of COVID-19 on smaller firms is more severe than on larger firms. SMEs are more vulnerable to the pandemic and hence are in need of government intervention and incentives for exporting; at the same time, they have the potential to contribute more to the economy than large firms. Therefore, if SMEs receive sufficient and appropriate export assistance, they will guarantee economic recovery by confirming their global share of international entrepreneurship. Hence, we propose the following:

- Proposition 3: Countries that provide more export support for SMEs post-COVID-19 will see an increase in their global share of international entrepreneurship.

3.6   Discussion and Conclusion

This chapter sought to discuss the field of international entrepreneurship in light of the consequences and repercussions of the COVID-19 pandemic. In doing so, we identified three major forces impacting the future of international entrepreneurship: those related to digitalization, entrepreneurial ecosystems, and export promotion. The three propositions put forth in this chapter and pertaining to these forces help outline high-potential post-COVID-19 research trajectories in the international entrepreneurship research field.

The COVID-19 pandemic has resulted in global disruptions in logistics, global value chains, and entrepreneurship. Consequently, international business, entrepreneurship, and scholars from other business and management fields have rushed to describe how the restrictions and environmental volatilities introduced by the pandemic will impact their fields.[1] In a piece pertaining to the international entrepreneurship field, Zahra (2020) provides a relatively pessimistic view on how the effects of the pandemic would be expected to impact international new ventures, thanks to the disrupted networks, ecosystems, and platforms. However, this study does not consider in detail how some companies with digitally enabled value chains (such as born digitals) can not only survive but thrive in an environment characterized by the remote work and lack of face-to-face services that the COVID-19 pandemic has introduced. Born digital business models and business model innovation (Clauss et al., 2019; Westerlund, 2020) will be crucial for international entrepreneurs post-COVID-19. Digital platform firms also continue to provide interesting research questions related to internationalization and innovation (Rasmussen & Petersen, 2017).

Similarly, we have seen many governments around the world react to the crushing impact of the pandemic on global value and supply chains and on international business in general, by looking to make maximal use of country- and region-specific institutional support mechanisms, often through national export promotion organizations and through more or less well-functioning regional entrepreneurial ecosystems. Consequently, our view on the future of international entrepreneurship post-COVID-19 is much more positive. In essence, this study suggests that international entrepreneurship during and after the immediate COVID-19 crisis will undergo a process of Schumpeterian creative destruction, the winners of which will be the enterprises that are born digital, regions that are endowed with

---

[1] Our cursory search of the related literature for the present study yielded over 130 journal articles on the topic published in business and management journals from 2020 to February 2021.

well-functioning entrepreneurial ecosystems, and nations that have effective and efficient export support organizations that help internationalizing enterprises through the initial shock phases of the pandemic.

In continuing the exploration of the presented propositions empirically, research on international entrepreneurship will be able to combine research most critical to consequences and repercussions of COVID-19 with the theoretically most important areas of further development for the field. The former is supported by our arguments for the propositions outlined in the present study; the latter were recently highlighted by Zucchella (2021), who outlined digitalization and "novel networked opportunities endeavors like platforms," as high-potential future research opportunities for anyone looking to explain contemporary entrepreneurial internationalization. From a theoretical perspective, the entrepreneurial ecosystem literature can serve as a basis for shedding light on the dynamics of international entrepreneurship post-COVID-19. As discussed, the international entrepreneurship literature has been criticized as lacking in unifying theoretical foundations, and this criticism of a "scattered" literature is valid for research on born globals as well (e.g., Baier-Fuentes et al., 2019). Moreover, since barriers that born globals and other types of internationalizing enterprises face in their efforts to do so are linked to specific entrepreneurial ecosystem elements within the ecosystemic framework (Stam & van de Ven, 2019; Velt et al., 2020), we conclude that employing an entrepreneurial ecosystem framework within the international entrepreneurship field of research would help advance research in this field by presenting a coherent theoretical framework that looks to be more relevant than ever in a post-COVID-19 world.

The study also provides practical implications and guidelines for international entrepreneurs and public policymakers looking to come out on the other side of the COVID-19 pandemic more resilient than before. For one thing, there is clearly a need to transfer from general entrepreneurship support policy toward SME export promotion and ecosystem-level policy in particular (cf. Autio & Levie, 2017). Since so many elements of the entrepreneurial ecosystem are linked to successful international entrepreneurship originating from a given country, governments and local municipal decision-makers should focus on strengthening the weaknesses of their regional entrepreneurial ecosystems, instead of trying to pinpoint specific SMEs considered "most in need" for support during the COVID-19 pandemic. Focusing merely on the latter risks misattributing support based on subjective assessments of the extent of the predicament a given enterprise faces instead of ensuring a level and well-functioning playing field on which growth- and internationalization-seeking small firms are able to "weather the storm" of the COVID-19 pandemic and retain their competitive international advantage and globally scalable business models (cf. Hennart, 2014).

The present study makes similar suggestions for policymakers in charge of organizing and distributing financial and other types of resource support for entrepreneurs and their enterprises in that we recommend such assistance to be organized under export assistance for SMEs specifically. To date, in most countries, we have mainly witnessed support for entrepreneurs based on the extent of the immediate effects that the COVID-19 pandemic is having on the industry sector and the type of services it provides (e.g., in the tourism and hospitality sectors, such as hotels and restaurants). However, this short-term support should be complemented by a more long-term view of which exporting small firms are in most need for assistance to cope with the challenges that the pandemic has exerted on global value and supply chains and to conduct international business in general. Based on our analysis, we consider it very likely that those countries prioritizing export support presently will reap the benefits in the post-COVID-19 world through more competitive international entrepreneurship originating from within the country. Such policies are expected to be particularly important for developed, small, open economies, in which the small domestic market size tends to coincide with highly technology-intensive industries and a digital entrepreneurship scene with a substantial share of local start-ups with globally scalable business models. Nordic countries in particular fit this description closely. The main implications for theory and practice are summarized below in Table 3.1.

Every study naturally also comes with limitations, some of which provide potentially fruitful avenues for future research. We acknowledge that, due to the focus of this chapter on the macro- and ecosystemic levels, future studies should look to establish a similar propositional view at the microfoundational level. For instance, entrepreneurial resilience has previously been established as a significant differentiator between failure and success in entrepreneurship in general (Bullough et al., 2014; Korber & McNaughton, 2018). As the definition of resilience, the "ability to go on with life, or to continue living a purposeful life after hardship or adversity" (Tedeschi & Calhoun, 2004), seems even more necessary during a pandemic, we suggest that research looking to establish determinants of entrepreneurial success in the aftermath of COVID-19 explore the role of resilience in international entrepreneurship as it is linked to long-term survival and success post-COVID-19. The role of entrepreneurship in building resilient economies post-COVID-19 will be essential (Korsgaard et al., 2020), and the microfoundational view can allow for ambidextrous use of exploitation and exploration capabilities (e.g., Faroque et al., 2021). Thus, this microfoundational aspect of international entrepreneurship is likely to remain a potential topic for important research beyond the immediate effects of the pandemic on societies and entrepreneurs.

We also note that, when it comes to international entrepreneurship, the meso-level, most often taking the firm as the unit of analysis, provides interesting potential for future research seeking to map the consequences and repercussions of the COVID-19 pandemic. For instance, it is an established fact that internationalizing small enterprises are forced to make trade-offs between international expansion and capability development during the best of times (e.g., Fernhaber & McDougall-Covin, 2014; Torkkeli et al., 2015). How an extended external shock such as the COVID-19 pandemic impacts the choices available and the trade-off decisions necessary for internationalizing small firms is to date an unexplored issue. Moreover, capabilities of many firms are embedded in network relationships and can change in line with changes in network structure (Hånell et al., 2013). The COVID-19 pandemic has already exerted major changes in global supply chains (Ivanov, 2020; Miroudot, 2020), and thus network structures of international entrepreneurs are

Table 3.1 Implications for theory and practice (authors' own table)

Proposition	Arising research questions	Managerial implications	Policy implications
Born digital enterprises will perform better globally post-COVID-19 than other types of internationalizing enterprises	How do international digital entrepreneurs operate post-COVID-19? How does international digital competence facilitate post-COVID-19 internationalization? How does increasing digitalization of their value chains enable small businesses to widen the intensity of their foreign operations from exporting to include other types of foreign operation modes?	Internationalizing enterprises need to digitalize parts of their value chains for resiliency Some of the changes brought on by the pandemic, such as increased remote work and digitalized entertainment, may remain; business models must be innovated to account for them	Provide SMEs the resources and training necessary for them to develop digital competence Prioritize support for those growth enterprises exhibiting born digital tendencies (digitalized value chains)
The entrepreneurial ecosystem is critical for sustaining international entrepreneurship resilience post-COVID-19	How can COVID-19-related export barriers be mitigated by the entrepreneurial ecosystem? How has COVID-19 reconfigured the free movement of endowments (financial, knowledge, human capital) needed for internationalization? How do local entrepreneurial ecosystems facilitate networks essential for internationalization?	Entrepreneurs need to focus on efficiency and self-sufficiency when acquiring resources Entrepreneurs need to increase global presence even more to tackle issues related to internationalization Entrepreneurs should familiarize themselves with the particular strengths and weaknesses of their local regional ecosystems and prioritize exports to contexts where the host entrepreneurial ecosystem is welcoming to exporting foreign firms	Transfer from general entrepreneurship support policy toward the SME export promotion and ecosystem-level policy needed Focus on strengthening the weaknesses of regional entrepreneurial ecosystems Transfer from general entrepreneurship support policy to SME export promotion and ecosystem-level policy

(continued)

Table 3.1 (continued)

Proposition	Arising research questions	Managerial implications	Policy implications
Countries that provide more export support for SMEs post-COVID-19 will see an increase on their global share of international entrepreneurship	To which type of internationalizing enterprises is export support the most beneficial for successful rebounding post-pandemic? How do countries compete nationally with export support post-pandemic? In what form should developed and emerging economies primarily provide post-COVID-19 export support to SMEs?	Entrepreneurs and small business managers need to educate themselves on the export support systems within their home countries, particularly the types of support specific to the COVID-19 pandemic Using the available export support to increase the scope of exports to a wider range of host countries can help mitigate risks arising from COVID-19 restrictions in specific areas in the world	Governments should organize their assistance for small business management and entrepreneurship primarily under export assistance for SMEs Countries with small open economies are in the position to economically benefit the most from prioritizing export support over other types of support for entrepreneurs

likely to be on the receiving end of such changes in network structures and, by extension, their capabilities. Therefore, what capabilities are most useful in international entrepreneurship post-COVID-19 remains an enticing area of future research.

To conclude, we highlight the role of international entrepreneurship in general as an important phenomenon helping global trade and business move forward from the pandemic. Though the COVID-19 crisis is proving to be an ongoing, serious threat to humankind, long-term global challenges such as climate change and environmental pollution are not going away during or after the pandemic but remain to be solved. In that process, sustainable international entrepreneurship (Torkkeli et al., 2017; Morozova ct al., 2019) rcmains kcy, and through continucd support of internationalizing SMEs promoting such change (for instance, renewable energy SMEs) (cf. Asemokha et al., 2019), these macroeconomic developments will mean that the future of international entrepreneurship post-COVID-19 remains bright.

References

Acs, Z. J., Stam, E., Audretsch, D. B., et al. (2017). The lineages of the entrepreneurial ecosystem approach. *Small Business Economics, 49*(1), 1–10.

Asemokha, A., Ahi, A., Torkkeli, L., et al. (2019). *Renewable energy market SMEs: Antecedents of internationalization*. Critical Perspectives on International Business. https://doi.org/10.1108/cpoib-05-2018-0043

Autio, E., & Levie, J. (2017). Management of entrepreneurial ecosystems. In *The Wiley handbook of entrepreneurship* (Vol. 43, pp. 423–444). Wiley-Blackwell.

Baier-Fuentes, H., Hormiga, E., Miravitlles, P., et al. (2019). International entrepreneurship: A critical review of the research field. *European Journal of International Management, 13*(3), 381–412.

Battisti, M., & Deakins, D. (2017). The relationship between dynamic capabilities, the firm's resource base and performance in a post-disaster environment. *International Small Business Journal, 35*(1), 78–98.

Bell, J., & Loane, S. (2010). 'New-wave' global firms: Web 2.0 and SME internationalisation. *Journal of Marketing Management, 26*(3–4), 213–229.

Bilkey, W. J., & Tesar, G. (1977). The export behavior of smaller Wisconsin manufacturing firms. *Journal of International Business Studies, 9*(Spring/Summer), 93–98.

Brouthers, K. D., Geisser, K. D., & Rothlauf, F. (2016). Explaining the internationalization of ibusiness firms. *Journal of International Business Studies, 47*(5), 513–534.

Bullough, A., Renko, M., & Myatt, T. (2014). Danger zone: The importance of resilience and self-efficacy for entrepreneurial intentions. *Entrepreneurship Theory & Practice, 38*(3), 473–499.

Cahen, F., & Borini, F. M. (2020). International digital competence. *Journal of International Management, 26*(1), 100691.

Caligiuri, P., De Cieri, H., Minbaeva, D., et al. (2020). International HRM insights for navigating the COVID-19 pandemic: Implications for future re-search and practice. *Journal of International Business Studies, 51*, 697–713.

Cannone, G., & Ughetto, E. (2014). Born globals: A cross-country survey on high-tech start-ups. *International Business Review, 23*(1), 272–283.

Cattaneo, O., Gereffi, G., & Staritz, C. (Eds.). (2010). *Global value chains in a postcrisis world: A development perspective.* The World Bank.

Cavallo, A., Ghezzi, A., & Balocco, R. (2019). Entrepreneurial ecosystem research: Present debates and future directions. *International Entrepreneurship and Management Journal, 15*(4), 1291–1321.

Cavusgil, T. S. (1980). On the internationalization process of firms. *European Research, 8*(November), 273–281.

Cavusgil, S. T., & Knight, G. (2015). The born global firm: An entrepreneurial and capabilities perspective on early and rapid internationalization. *Journal of International Business Studies, 46*(1), 3–16.

Clauss, T., Abebe, M., Tangpong, C., et al. (2019). Strategic agility, business model innovation, and firm performance: An empirical investigation. *IEEE Transactions on Engineering Management, 68*(3), 767–784.

Covin, J. G., & Miller, D. (2014). International entrepreneurial orientation: Conceptual considerations, research themes, measurement issues, and future research directions. *Entrepreneurship Theory and Practice, 38*(1), 11–44.

Czinkota, M. R. (1982). *Export development strategies: US promotion policies.* Praeger Publishers.

Diamantopoulos, A., Schlegelmilch, B. B., & Katy Tse, K. Y. (1993). Understanding the role of export marketing assistance: Empirical evidence and research needs. *European Journal of Marketing, 27*(4), 5–18.

Dimitratos, P., & Plakoyiannaki, E. (2003). Theoretical foundations of an international entrepreneurial culture. *Journal of International Entrepreneurship, 1*(2), 187–215.

Dimitratos, P., Johnson, J., Slow, J., et al. (2003). Micromultinationals: New types of firms for the global competitive landscape. *European Management Journal, 21*(2), 164–174.

Ellis, B. (2011). Social ties and international entrepreneurship: Opportunities and constraints affecting firm internationalization. *Journal of International Business Studies, 42*, 99–127.

Fan, T., & Phan, P. (2007). International new ventures: Revisiting the influences behind the "born-global" firm. *Journal of International Business Studies, 38*(7), 1113–1131.

Faroque, A. R., & Takahashi, Y. (2012). Export assistance: The way back and forward. In *Export assistance: The way back and forward.* Springer.

Faroque, A. R., & Takahashi, Y. (2015). Export marketing assistance and early internationalizing firm performance: Does export commitment matter? *Asia Pacific Journal of Marketing and Logistics, 27*(3), 421–443.

Faroque, A. R., Morrish, S. C., Kuivalainen, O., et al. (2021). Microfoundations of network explo-ration and exploitation capabilities in international opportunity recognition. *International Business Review, 30*(1), 101767.

Fernhaber, S. A., Mcdougall-Covin, P. P., & Shepherd, D. A. (2009). International entrepreneur-ship: leveraging internal and external knowledge sources. *Strategic Entrepreneurship Journal, 3*(4), 297–320.

Fernhaber, S. A., & McDougall-Covin, P. P. (2014). Is more always better? Risk trade-offs among internationalizing new ventures. *European Business Review, 26*(5), 406–420.

Freeman, S., Edwards, R., & Schroder, B. (2006). How smaller born-global firms use networks and alliances to overcome constraints to rapid internationalization. *Journal of International Marketing, 14*(3), 33–63.

Gassmann, O., & Keupp, M. M. (2007). The competitive advantage of early and rapidly interna-tionalising SMEs in the biotechnology industry: A knowledge-based view. *Journal of World Business, 42*(3), 350–366.

Gereffi, G., Humphrey, J., & Sturgeon, T. (2005). The governance of global value chains. *Review of International Political Economy, 12*(1), 78–104.

González-Pernía, J. L., & Peña-Legazkue, I. (2015). Export-oriented entrepreneurship and regional economic growth. *Small Business Economics, 45*(3), 505–522.

Greene, F. J., & Rosiello, A. (2020). A commentary on the impacts of 'Great Lockdown' and its aftermath on scaling firms: What are the implications for entrepreneurial research? *International Small Business Journal, 38*(7), 583–592.

Hånell, S. M., Nordman, E. R., Tolstoy, D., et al. (2013). International entrepreneurship research during the last decade: A review. *Journal for International Business and Entrepreneurship Development, 7*(2), 116–138.

Hennart, J. F. (2014). The accidental internationalists: A theory of born globals. *Entrepreneurship Theory and Practice, 38*(1), 117–135.

Hessels, J., & Parker, S. C. (2013). Constraints, internationalization and growth: A cross-country analysis of European SMEs. *Journal of World Business, 48*(1), 137–148.

Hutchinson, K., Fleck, E., & Lloyd-Reason, L. (2009). An investigation into the initial barriers to internationalization: Evidence from small UK retailers. *Journal of Small Business and Enterprise Development, 16*(4), 544–568.

Ivanov, D. (2020). Predicting the impacts of epidemic outbreaks on global supply chains: A simulation-based analysis on the coronavirus outbreak (COVID-19/SARS-CoV-2) case. *Transportation Research Part E: Logistics and Transportation Review, 136*, 101922.

Jaklič, A., & Burger, A. (2020). Complex internationalisation strategies during crises: The case of Slovenian exporters during the great recession and COVID-19 pandemic 1. *Teorija in Praksa, 57*(4), 1018–1041.

Johanson, J., & Vahlne, J.-E. (1977). The internationalization process of the firm: A model of knowledge development and increasing foreign market commitments. *Journal of International Business Studies, 8*(1), 23–32.

Johanson, J., & Vahlne, J.-E. (2009). The Uppsala internationalization process model revisited: From liability of foreignness to liability of outsidership. *Journal of International Business Studies, 40*(9), 1411–1431.

Johanson, J., & Wiedersheim-Paul, F. (1975). The internationalization of the firm: Four Swedish cases. *Journal of Management Studies, 12*(3), 305–323.

Jones, M. V., Coviello, N., & Tang, Y. K. (2011). International entrepreneurship research (1989–2009): A domain ontology and thematic analysis. *Journal of Business Venturing, 26*(6), 632–659.

Kahiya, E. T. (2013). Export barriers and path to internationalization: A comparison of conven-tional enterprises and international new ventures. *Journal of International Entrepreneurship, 11*(1), 3–29.

Kano, L., & Oh, C. H. (2020). Global value chains in the post-COVID world: Governance for reli-ability. *Journal of Management Studies, 57*(8), 1773–1777.

Keupp, M. M., & Gassmann, O. (2009). The past and the future of international entrepreneurship: A review and suggestions for developing the field. *Journal of Management, 35*(3), 600–633.

Knight, G., Cavusgil, S. T., & Innovation, O. C. (2004). The born-global firm. *Journal of International Business Studies, 35*(2), 124–141.

Korber, S., & McNaughton, R. B. (2018). Resilience and entrepreneurship: A systematic literature review. *International Journal of Entrepreneurial Behavior and Research, 24*(7), 1129–1154.

Korsgaard, S., Hunt, R. A., Townsend, D. M., et al. (2020). COVID-19 and the importance of space in entrepreneurship research and policy. *International Small Business Journal, 38*(8), 697–710.

Kuckertz, A., Brändle, L., Gaudig, A., et al. (2020). Startups in times of crisis—A rapid response to the COVID-19 pandemic. *Journal of Business Venturing Insights, 13*, e00169.

Kuivalainen, O., Sundqvist, S., & Servais, P. (2007). Firms' degree of born-globalness, international entrepreneurial orientation and export performance. *Journal of World Business, 42*(3), 253–267.

Lin, B. X., & Zhang, Y. Y. (2020). Impact of the COVID-19 pandemic on agricultural exports. *Journal of Integrative Agriculture, 19*(12), 2937–2945.

Madsen, T. K., & Servais, P. (2017). *The internationalization of born globals: An evolutionary process?* Routledge.

Mainela, T., Puhakka, V., & Servais, P. (2014). The concept of international opportunity in international entrepreneurship: A review and a research agenda. *International Journal of Management Reviews, 16*(1), 105–129.

Malysheva, E. V., & Ratner, A. V. (2020). Small and medium-sized business export support in terms of global economy changed by coronavirus. *International Trade and Trade Policy, 6*(3), 79–96.

Mason, C., & Brown, R. (2014). *Entrepreneurial ecosystems and growth oriented entrepreneurship*. Background paper prepared for the workshop organized by the OECD LEED Program and the Dutch Ministry of Economic Affairs on Entrepreneurial Eco-systems and Growth Oriented Entrepreneurship. The Hague, Netherlands.

McDougall, P. P. (1989). International versus domestic entrepreneurship: New venture strategic behavior and industry structure. *Journal of Business Venturing, 4*(6), 387–400.

McDougall, P. P., & Oviatt, B. M. (2000). International entrepreneurship: The intersection of two research paths. *Academy of Management Journal, 43*(5), 902–906.

McDougall, P. P., Shane, S., & Oviatt, B. M. (1994). Explaining the formation of international new ventures: The limits of theories from international business research. *Journal of Business Venturing, 9*(6), 469–487.

Merriam-Webster. (2021). *Digitalization*. https://www.merriam-webster.com/dictionary/digitalization. Accessed 28 Feb 2021.

Minniti, M. (2008). The role of government policy on entrepreneurial activity: Productive, unproductive, or destructive? *Entrepreneurship Theory and Practice, 35*(5), 779–790.

Miroudot, S. (2020). Reshaping the policy debate on the implications of COVID-19 for global supply chains. *Journal of International Business Policy, 3*(4), 430–442.

Monaghan, S., Tippmann, E., & Coviello, N. (2020). Born digitals: Thoughts on their internationalization and a research agenda. *Journal of International Business Studies, 51*(1), 11–22.

Morozova, I. A., Popkova, E. G., & Litvinova, T. N. (2019). Sustainable development of global entrepreneurship: Infrastructure and perspectives. *International Entrepreneurship and Management Journal, 15*(2), 589–597.

Nambisan, S. (2017). Digital entrepreneurship: Toward a digital technology perspective of entrepreneurship. *Entrepreneurship Theory and Practice, 41*(6), 1029–1055.

Nummela, N., Saarenketo, S., & Loane, S. (2016). The dynamics of failure in international new ventures: A case study of Finnish and Irish software companies. *International Small Business Journal, 34*(1), 51–69.

Oviatt, B. M., & McDougall, P. P. (1994). Toward a Theory of International New ventures. *Journal of International Business Studies, 25*(1), 45–64.

Oviatt, B. M., & McDougall, P. P. (1995). Global start-ups: Entrepreneurs on a worldwide stage. *Academy of Management Perspectives, 9*(2), 30–43.

Oviatt, B. M., & McDougall, P. P. (2005). Defining international entrepreneurship and modeling the speed of internationalization. *Entrepreneurship Theory and Practice, 29*(5), 537–554.

Papadopoulos, T., Baltas, K. N., & Balta, M. E. (2020). The use of digital technologies by small and medium enterprises during COVID-19: Implications for theory and practice. *International Journal of Information Management, 55*, 102192.

Phillips, M. A., & Ritala, P. (2019). A complex adaptive systems agenda for ecosystem research methodology. *Technological Forecasting and Social Change, 148*, 119739.

Qermane, K., & Mancha, R. (2020). WHOOP, Inc.: Digital entrepreneurship during the Covid-19 pandemic. *Entrepreneurship Education and Pedagogy, 4*(3), 500–514.

Rasmussen, E. S., & Petersen, N. H. (2017). Platforms for innovation and internationalization. *Technology Innovation Management Review, 7*(5), 23–31.

Reid, S. T. (1981). The decision-maker and export entre and expansion. *Journal of International Business Studies, 12*(Fall), 101–112.

Rennie, M. W. (1993). Born global. *The McKinsey Quarterly, 4*, 45–53.

Rialp, A., Rialp, J., & Knight, G. A. (2005). The phenomenon of early internationalizing firms: What do we know after a decade (1993–2003) of scientific inquiry? *International Business Review, 14*(2), 147–166.

Romanello, R., & Chiarvesio, M. (2019). Early internationalizing firms: 2004–2018. *Journal of International Entrepreneurship, 17*(2), 172–219.

Sasi, V., & Arenius, P. (2012). Strategies for circumventing born global firms' resource scarcity dilemma. In *New technology-based firms in the new millennium*. Emerald Group Publishing Limited.

Schweizer, R. (2013). SMEs and networks: Overcoming the liability of outsidership. *Journal of International Entrepreneurship, 11*(1), 80–103.

Servantie, V., Cabrol, M., Guieu, G., et al. (2016). Is international entrepreneurship a field? A bibliometric analysis of the literature (1989–2015). *Journal of International Entrepreneurship, 14*(2), 168–212.

Stam, E., & van de Ven, A. (2019). Entrepreneurial ecosystem elements. *Small Business Economics, 56*, 1–24.

Tanev, S. (2012). Global from the start: The characteristics of born-global firms in the technology sector. *Technology Innovation Management Review, 2*(3), 5–8.

Tedeschi, R. G., & Calhoun, L. G. (2004). Posttraumatic growth: Conceptual foundations and empirical evidence. *Psychological Inquiry, 15*(1), 1–18.

Theodoraki, C., & Catanzaro, A. (2021). Widening the borders of entrepreneurial ecosystem through the international lens. *Journal of Technology Transfer,* 1–24. https://doi.org/10.1007/s10961-021-09852-7

Theodoraki, C., Messeghem, K., & Rice, M. P. (2018). A social capital approach to the development of sustainable entrepreneurial ecosystems: An explorative study. *Small Business Economics, 51*(1), 153–170.

Thomas, L. D., & Autio, E. (2020). Innovation ecosystems in management: An organizing typology. In *Oxford research encyclopedia of business and management*. Oxford University Press.

Torkkeli, L., Saarenketo, S., & Nummela, N. (2015). The development of network competence in an internationalized SME. In *Handbook on international alliance and network research*. Edward Elgar Publishing.

Torkkeli, L., Saarenketo, S., Salojärvi, H., et al. (2017). Sustainability and corporate social responsibility in internationally operating SMEs: Implications for performance. In *Value creation in international business*. Palgrave Macmillan.

UNCTAD. (2021). *Global investment trend monitor*, no. 38. https://unctad.org/system/files/official-document/diaeiainf2021d1_en.pdf. Accessed 10 May 2021.

Vadana, I. I., Torkkeli, L., Kuivalainen, O., et al. (2019). The internationalization of born-digital companies. In *The changing strategies of international business*. Palgrave Macmillan.

Vadana, I. I., Torkkeli, L., Kuivalainen, O., & Saarenketo, S. (2020). Digitalization of companies in international entrepreneurship and marketing. *International Marketing Review, 37*(3),
471–492.

Van Biesebroeck, J., Konings, J., & Volpe Martincus, C. (2016). Did export promotion help firms
weather the crisis? *Economic Policy, 31*(88), 653–702.

Velt, H., Torkkeli, L., & Saarenketo, S. (2018). Uncovering new value frontiers: The role of
the entrepreneurial ecosystem in nurturing born globals. *International Journal of Export
Marketing, 2*(4), 316–342.

Velt, H., Torkkeli, L., & Saarenketo, S. (2020). Transnational entrepreneurial ecosystems: The
perspectives of Finnish and Estonian born-global start-ups. In *Research handbook on start-up
incubation ecosystems*. Edward Elgar Publishing.

Verbeke, A., & Yuan, W. (2021). A few implications of the COVID-19 pandemic for international
business strategy research. *Journal of Management Studies, 58*(2), 597–601.

Weerawardena, J., Mort, G. S., Liesch, P. W., et al. (2007). Conceptualizing accelerated internationalization in the born global firm: A dynamic capabilities perspective. *Journal of World
Business, 42*(3), 294–306.

Wentrup, R. (2016). The online-offline balance: Internationalization for Swedish online service
providers. *Journal of International Entrepreneurship, 14*(4), 562–594.

Westerlund, M. (2020). Digitalization, internationalization and scaling of online SMEs. *Technology
Innovation Management Review, 10*(4), 48–57.

Zahra, S. A. (2020). International entrepreneurship in the post Covid world. *Journal of World
Business, 56*, 101143.

Zahra, S. A., Korri, J. S., & Yu, J. (2005). Cognition and international entrepreneurship: Implications
for research on international opportunity recognition and exploitation. *International Business
Review, 14*(2), 129–146.

Zucchella, A. (2021). International entrepreneurship and the internationalization phenomenon:
Taking stock, looking ahead. *International Business Review, 30*, 101800.

Chapter 4
The Impact of the COVID-19 Pandemic on the Development of Entrepreneurial Universities: A Study of Higher Education Institutions in Turkey

Hiroko Kawamorita, Aidin Salamzadeh, David A. Kirby, and Kürşat Demiryürek

4.1 Introduction

In recent years, universities have been required, increasingly, to behave more entrepreneurially. In part, this has been to reduce their dependence on government funding and, in part, to them contributing to economic and social development through the exploitation of the intellectual property stemming from their research. However, there is a third important reason that is often overlooked. If universities are to create entrepreneurial or enterprising graduates, as they are also required to do, they will not be able to do so effectively unless they are entrepreneurial.

So, there are good reasons for this development, but all too frequently, it is resisted, not least because it is not fully understood. Traditionally, universities have never had to be entrepreneurial, and many in academia are concerned that it will "drive out their other more fundamental university qualities, such as intellectual integrity and commitment to learning and understanding" (Williams, 2002, p. 19).

H. Kawamorita (✉)
Faculty of Economics and Administrative Sciences, Ondokuz Mayis University,
Samsun, Turkey
e-mail: hiroko.kawamorita@omu.edu.tr

A. Salamzadeh
Faculty of Management, University of Tehran, Tehran, Iran
e-mail: salamzadeh@ut.ac.ir

D. A. Kirby
Global Education Career Centre, London, UK

K. Demiryürek
Faculty of Agriculture, Ondokuz Mayis University, Samsun, Turkey
e-mail: kursatd@omu.edu.tr

© The Author(s), under exclusive license to Springer Nature Switzerland AG 2022
N. Faghih, A. Forouharfar (eds.), *Socioeconomic Dynamics of the COVID-19 Crisis*,
Contributions to Economics, https://doi.org/10.1007/978-3-030-89996-7_4

Accordingly, except for international student recruitment, there has not been widespread adoption of the concept, despite various measures introduced to expedite its take-up.

As Kirby (2020b) has suggested, the COVID-19 pandemic could cause universities to become more entrepreneurial and expedite the process of change. However, at least in the short term, there is likely to be a reduction in student numbers and tuition fee income, and despite support from government funds, several universities are likely to face a shortfall in their revenues. Doubtless, some institutions will have to trim their budgets, and some may be required to close or merge, but many will probably look to diversify their income streams by being more entrepreneurial. Already this has begun to happen, with the UK university sector, for example, carrying out vital research into finding a vaccine; providing much-needed equipment, facilities, and extra staff to frontline National Health Services; and exploring ways to help the people's health and well-being (Universities UK, 2020).

The same is happening elsewhere, and in Egypt, a country not known for its entrepreneurial universities (Kirby & Ibrahim, 2016), Mowafy (2020) has demonstrated how: "with the current COVID-19 pandemic, several Egyptian universities have responded in an entrepreneurial manner". However, while such actions may be entrepreneurial, whether commercial or social, it does not mean that "universities themselves have suddenly been transformed into Entrepreneurial institutions".

Therefore, this chapter aims to explore in Turkey the likely impact of COVID-19 on the country's universities with respect to their understanding of the concept and the progress they are making in terms of becoming more entrepreneurial and developing more enterprising graduates.

4.2   Literature Review

Over the years, there has developed an extensive body of literature on both entrepreneurship education and the development of the entrepreneurial university. More specifically, the research has focused on the definitions and impact of both and how entrepreneurship education is/should be embedded in the development of entrepreneurial university. In 2016, a special edition of the journal "Industry and Higher Education" included five articles dedicated to entrepreneurship and the role of the university. In the introductory article, Davey et al. (2016) discussed how entrepreneurship is understood in the context of the university and its role in entrepreneurship, while in 2017, Kirby and Ibrahim (2017) reviewed these twin concepts of entrepreneurship education and the entrepreneurial university in a factor-driven economy, Egypt.

4.2.1 Entrepreneurship Education

Entrepreneurship education initially started in the late 1940s in the United States, and it was only in the 1980s that courses began to be taught in the United Kingdom and Europe (Kirby & Ibrahim, 2017, p. 40). Today, it is considered one of the growing fields of education worldwide. Entrepreneurship education influences the way of thinking and acting among academics and students in the university context (Davey et al., 2016), and the key competencies of the ability to recognise opportunity and turn ideas into action help academics and students to be more creative, innovative, and self-confident in daily, as well as professional, life. For students, enhanced entrepreneurial competencies and behaviours may lead to new venture creation or contribute towards intrapreneurship as employees. Universities are the ones to create this favourable environment for educating interested students and potential entrepreneurs to change societies (Hannibal et al., 2016).

In 2015, Fayolle and Gailly researched the impact of entrepreneurship education on entrepreneurial attitudes and intention among 275 French students toward entrepreneurship and the identified factors influencing the effects of entrepreneurship education programmes. They proposed a model to measure the initial state and persistence of the impact. The result confirmed that the intention model (the theory of planned behaviour) relates to previous entrepreneurial exposure, which is relevant for increasing entrepreneurial intention. Similarly, Potishuk and Kratzer (2017) also applied the theory of planned behaviour on students' entrepreneurial attitudes and intention, and the results showed that the influence of attitudes on the intention has high explanatory power (Ajzen, 1991; Souitaris et al., 2007; Müller, 2008; Demir & Demiryürek, 2018).

Besides, educators and researchers of the entrepreneurship content and pedagogy have widely discussed these issues. For instance, Sirelkhatim and Gangi (2015) conducted a systematic literature review on this topic and provided a better understanding of its curricula content and teaching methods by analysing 129 articles.

The field of entrepreneurship re-emerged as an essential agenda item of economic policymakers across Europe in the late twentieth century (Wennekers et al., 2002). The European Union introduced some Framework Programmes such as a coherent framework for entrepreneurship education in 2013 and the European entrepreneurship competence framework (EntreComp) in 2016. The intention was to support actions to improve the entrepreneurial capacity of European citizens and organisations as part of the New Skills Agenda for Europe. Several funding opportunities became available through COSME, Horizon 2020, EU Startup Nation Standard, Innovation Radar, and the Digital Innovation and Scale-up Initiative (DISC) to support the development of entrepreneurship competencies. More recently, in 2021, a pilot call on Innovation Capacity Building for Higher Education was announced to promote institutional changes and integration in the innovation ecosystem in Higher Education Institutions (HEIs). These actions introduced at the macro level clearly demonstrate the importance of entrepreneurship and the need for an updated method of teaching to equip graduates to adapt to the changing environment. Besides, *HEInnovate* provides a self-assessment tool for HEIs who intend to explore, identify, and exploit their innovative potential.

Morris and Liguori (2016) proposed that there are three categories for entrepreneurship education: (i) business basics, (ii) entrepreneurship basics, and (iii) entrepreneurial mindset and competencies. The first two categories are mainly based on theories, and these can be taught online with a traditional approach. However, the third category, related to entrepreneurial mindset and competencies, is not easily taught by the traditional online teaching method. It needs a more interactive environment and learning from real-world experiences through techniques such as experiential learning techniques. Ratten and Jones (2020) and Liguori and Winkler (2020) have discussed the changing nature of entrepreneurship education due to the COVID-19 pandemic. They also argued that soft skills and resilience are the essential competencies required to be taught in entrepreneurship education. In order to teach entrepreneurial mindset and competencies online, new approaches are required to adapt to new contextual market conditions to challenge the impact of COVID-19 (Salamzadeh & Dana, 2020).

4.2.2　Entrepreneurial Universities

Many researchers have tried to define the term entrepreneurial university (Burton, 1998; Chrisman et al., 1995; Etzkowitz, 2003; Kirby, 2006; Guerrero et al., 2014, 2015), and among them, perhaps the most accepted idea is that "Entrepreneurial University can innovate, recognise and create opportunities, take risks and respond to challenges. It sells its services in the knowledge industry and is a natural incubator that supports its academics, technicians and students to create new ventures" (Kirby, 2020a).

Similarly, Williams (2003) defined it as

> "a natural incubator, providing support structures for teachers and students to initiate new ventures: intellectual, commercial and conjoint". It is about a University that has: "the ability to innovate, recognise and create opportunities, work in teams, take risks and respond to challenges, on its own, seeks to work out a substantial shift in organisational character to arrive at a more promising posture for the future." (Guerrero et al., 2006)

Kirby and Ibrahim (2017) highlighted a set of formal and informal institutional factors affecting the development of the entrepreneurial university, which helps to identify the needs to be considered for the transformation process. Frameworks, models, and tools are widely introduced on and around the entrepreneurial university, and many case studies are conducted by researchers from both developed and developing countries (Guerrero et al., 2006; Kawamorita et al. 2016; Kirby, 2006; Kirby et al., 2011; Kirby & Ibrahim, 2017; Peterka & Salihovic, 2012; Salamzadeh et al., 2015; Salamzadeh et al., 2017; Tajpour et al., 2020).

In 2020, a systematic literature review on entrepreneurial university transformation was conducted by Stolze (2020). From 18 countries, 36 HEIs were analysed and suggested that exogenous (external macro and meso environments) and endogenous (internal micro environments which directly affect an institution's ability to act accordingly) factors constantly influence HEIs to be more entrepreneurial. Similarly, Kawamorita et al. (2020a, b, c, d) illustrate that being entrepreneurial is the key for HEIs to survive in a competitive global market. However, despite the importance of HEIs being proactive in responding to challenges, not all HEIs should aim to transform fully towards entrepreneurial universities as many have no potential/capacity to do so. Therefore, as the first step, it is more feasible to focus on its ecosystem to create synergies at the meso level, spreading the entrepreneurial culture at their institutions (Stolze, 2020).

4.2.3 COVID-19 Pandemics and Higher Education

The outbreak of the COVID-19 pandemic has become a significant disruption for HEIs, leading to financial challenges worldwide. Besides this, the pandemic appears to have accelerated the critical trends in higher education, such as digital transformation, the necessity for embedded entrepreneurial mindset/skills in formal education, and the introduction of a new policy approach. These challenges and opportunities for Higher Education Institutions (HEIs) have already been studied by many authors from different countries, as listed in Table 4.1.

Most of the HEIs have been forced to shift their education programmes to distance learning, not to terminate the education but to continue delivering the programmes online (using asynchronous and/or synchronous methods). As a result, most of the literature has been on the impact of the COVID-19 pandemic on either online teaching and generally learning or entrepreneurship, not on the universities in general, the entrepreneurial university in particular, or entrepreneurship education specifically.

According to the relevant literature reviewed, most of the studies on Higher Education and COVID-19 were on the impact of this pandemic on online education/digital communication/entrepreneurship (Abdulrahim & Mabrouk, 2020; Ali, 2020; Amir et al., 2020; Dubey & Pandey, 2020; Hebebci et al., 2020; Obaid AI-Youbi et al., 2020; Moralista & Oducado, 2020) but not on the universities (Kawamorita et al., 2020a, b, c, d). Many studies on online education are especially presented as it is clear that society needs these flexible and resilient education systems. Ali (2020) conducted a meta-analysis on Online and Remote Learning in HEIs. The findings reveal that universities are going through digital transformation in teaching and learning across the world. Also, he highlighted that there are many essential functions in ICT integrated learning to be concerned apart from resources, such as staff readiness, confidence, student accessibility, and motivation. Similarly, Kawamorita et al. (2020a, b, c, d) identified the importance of capacity to use the technology among teaching staff and learners (students). They presented a case study of one of

Table 4.1 Literature on COVID-19 pandemics and Higher Education published in 2020

Author/s	Country	Study focus	Conclusion
Abdulrahim and Mabrouk (2020)	Saudi Arabia	The effectiveness of the digital transformation, how the fourth industrial revolution can improve productivity, learning outcome, and well-being work environment in these uncertain circumstances	Digital learning is distinct from traditional learning, and the finding shows the improvements in students learning outcome and enhanced the faculty member's capabilities. Successful application of technical systems, which improved staff productivity and work environment
Brammer and Clark (2020)	Asia, Australia, and the United Kingdom	Management education: reflections on challenges, opportunities, and potential futures	Flexible education, future thinking, and resilience building are required for sustainable HEI management. COVID-19 led to the structural change in HE, driven by the competitive dynamics of brand strength, shifting student demands, and the development and diffusion of new learning technologies
Kawamorita et al. (2020b)	The Middle East (Iran, Turkey, Iraq, United Arab Emirates, Oman, Jordan, Kuwait, and Lebanon)	The main challenges faced by entrepreneurial universities and their responses to those challenges	General and mission-related challenges were identified. The research finding can be used as a guideline for entrepreneurial universities to play their role in innovation ecosystems actively
Kawamorita et al. (2020a)	Turkey	Impact of the Covid-19 pandemic in Higher Education (distance learning) and continuous challenges and solutions at Ondokuz Mayis University	Despite these new challenges, the pandemic positively impacted the perception of academic staff who were reluctant towards distance education before at OMU. This shift to online education due to the pandemic created a great opportunity to change their (educator) negative view to positive ones
Kedraka and Kaltsidis (2020)	Greece	Investigation of the online education experience at Democritus University of Thrace	Although students have positive feedback, new teaching methods and strategies for improving distance learning in higher education are necessary

(continued)

Table 4.1 (continued)

Author/s	Country	Study focus	Conclusion
Korkmaz and Toraman (2020)	Turkey	Research on problems educators experienced in online learning practices during the pandemic; the changes they expect to take in the future	Most of the educators experienced some challenges during the online education practices, and therefore improvements are necessary, including the training for teaching staff to adapt to this digital environment
Özer (2020)	Turkey	The current structure and the four major problems of VET in Turkey are discussed; the improvements made in VET after the introduction of Turkey's 2023 Education Vision are reviewed; the contribution of VET to the fight against the COVID-19 pandemic is analysed	The finding shows that the importance of a strengthened VET system is key in the Turkish context. Also, creating the link of VET curricula with academic skills, taking into account the technological transformations at the global scale
Rizun and Strzelecki (2020)	Poland	Investigation of first-year students' expectations about the education shift to distance learning (GETAMEL)	The most important factors identified were the feeling of pleasure in online education and a sense of self-efficacy
Toquero (2020)	The Philippines	Analysis of HE working system in the Philippines and opportunities for HEIS to respond to the educational problems that arise due to the COVID-19 pandemic	HEIs need to seize the opportunity to strengthen their evidence-based practices, provide accessible mental-health-related services, and make the curriculum responsive to the needs of the changing times
Yılmaz İnce et al. (2020)	Turkey	Research on knowledge and views of students about distance education	The opportunities of the participants as having computers and the internet affect their views on distance education
Liguori and Winkler (2020)	Global	Discussed how the pandemic is impacting entrepreneurship education globally and call for additional scholarship and the development of additional resources for online entrepreneurship education (editorial)	Fewer studies are conducted in this area at the moment. SAGE Publishing provided open access to all of the Entrepreneurship Education and Pedagogy (EE&P's) teaching cases for 30 days to help the educators. Also encouraged more research on learning innovations

(continued)

Table 4.1 (continued)

Author/s	Country	Study focus	Conclusion
Wang et al. (2020)	China	Risk management of COVID-19 by universities in China	Chinese universities have made significant contributions to emergency risk management (alumni resource collection, medical rescue and emergency management, mental health maintenance, control of staff mobility, and innovation in online education models)

Source: Authors' own work

the universities in Turkey (i.e. OMU) and how it is facing ICT adoption by offering appropriate training and guidance for the users. ICT has become a must for the digital transformation process of HEIs worldwide.

However, since the implementation of such online/distance learning programmes, lack of training on how to utilise the technology in response to COVID-19 is discussed by many HEIs (Abdulrahim & Mabrouk, 2020; Brammer & Clark, 2020; Kedraka & Kaltsidis, 2020; Toquero, 2020; Yılmaz İnce et al., 2020; Kawamorita et al., 2020a), and also, the European Commission has announced a call for proposals to tackle the issues in this area. Some studies have focused on studies such as Wang et al. (2020), who proposed solutions to respond to risks and problems faced at Chinese Universities, including medical security, emergency research, professional assistance, positive communication, and hierarchical information-based teaching. Brammer and Clark (2020) explored Management Education in Business Schools where more international students and staff are involved by sharing a perspective on the impacts of COVID-19 in Asia, Australia, and the United Kingdom. They concluded that COVID-19 affects the structural changes in HEIs, by a number of factors creating shifting demands such as the development and diffusion of new learning technologies, a decrease in international student recruitment, and the entry of large technology companies into the market (Brammer & Clark, 2020). As a result, they highlighted that the COVID-19 pandemic might result in the closing, merging, and restructuring of universities due to the lack of funding.

HEIs face more problems in developing countries due to the limited infrastructure available to respond to the pandemic. Kawamorita et al. (2020a, b, c, d) conducted qualitative research and presented the main challenges and answers to those challenges by entrepreneurial universities in the Middle East. Their findings showed two types of challenges and solutions applicable by entrepreneurial universities (general and mission related) and provided a guideline for HEIs to help the innovation ecosystems deal with the ongoing crises.

Therefore, the authors intend to fill the gap in the literature by investigating the relationship between entrepreneurship education and entrepreneurial activity in the COVID-19 era. It is the main contribution of this research. The specific objective is to determine whether, as a result of the pandemic, universities expect to become more or less entrepreneurial and to:

(a) Identify the challenges that HEIs face due to the pandemic and how they respond to them.
(b) Understand the digital transformation and technological empowerment of teaching, learning, researching, and university management.

To accomplish these objectives, this chapter focuses on Turkey as an efficiency-driven economy (GEM, 2020) and applies the case study method to better understand the entrepreneurial university framework in this context.

4.3 Aims and Methodology

This chapter attempts to understand the impact of the COVID-19 pandemic on Turkish universities, particularly concerning their entrepreneurial orientation. This chapter focused on the third mission of entrepreneurial universities (teaching, research, and entrepreneurship) (a) before and (b) after the pandemic.

This research aims to (i) examine how entrepreneurial universities are perceived among Turkish universities (considering the formal and informal institutional factors towards the entrepreneurial university development) and their institutional goals, (ii) identify what and how entrepreneurship education is offered at their universities and how current challenges and opportunities are linked with the education provided, and (iii) provide recommendations to overcome these challenges during the COVID-19 pandemic and to deal with the transformation process in Turkey quickly and efficiently.

4.3.1 The Data-Gathering Phase

The questionnaire survey was sent to all the 206 HEIs in Turkey via the official correspondence university system to achieve the objectives mentioned earlier. Only 22 universities responded, which is about 10% of the total number of HEIs in Turkey. The sampling frame for this study was the Vice-Chancellor or his/her delegated representative from the management who could complete the survey.

Data were collected online via Google Form in August 2020. The participants were instructed that, upon proceeding with the online survey, they would be granted consent to participate in the research voluntarily; also, they were given the option to respond anonymously. An online survey was chosen as the most optimal method for collecting data during this dynamically changing pandemic condition and situation. The online survey is also faster and requires no contact between people, thus being more convenient than traditional methods. Nulty (2008) and Cook et al. (2000) confirmed in their research that the response rates for online surveys are much lower than those obtained when using on-paper surveys; however, it can reach a larger number of a population. The questionnaire was developed based on the related literatures such as those of Kirby and Ibrahim (2017) and Guerrero et al. (2014), as

Table 4.2 Questionnaire survey structure

Section	Information asked	Question number	Type of research question
1	Perception of the term "the entrepreneurial university"	1–4	Mixed
2	Details of the institution towards its approach to entrepreneurship	5–8	Closed
3	University contribution towards the pandemic	9–12	Mixed
	Expected number of students and responses	13–15	
	Online education	16–17	Closed
	R&D	18–22	
	The difficulties/challenges the institution has experienced and/or expects to experience due to the COVID-19 pandemics	23–25	Open ended
4	Details of the respondents	26–28	Open ended (optional)

Source: Authors' own work

well as from the online resources (Kirby, 2020a, b). It was divided into four sections, including open and closed questions as in Table 4.2.

4.3.2 The Data Analysis Technique and Tool

The case study approach was chosen as a suitable method for this study to explore complex issues in real-life settings (Crowe et al., 2011). Descriptive statistics were employed to understand the features of a specific data set by providing summaries about the sample and measures of the collected data.

4.4 Research Findings

In this section, both primary and secondary research findings are presented, aiming to identify the formal and informal institutional factors affecting the entrepreneurial university's development in the Turkish context by addressing the challenges and barriers they are facing.

4.4.1 The Turkish Context

Turkey is an emerging economy growing faster than in other countries in the world (Sivabalan & Ismail, 2020). According to the GEM Classification model (GEM, 2020), the efficiency-driven economy faces rapid economic growth with fast social changes. The number of people involved in early-stage entrepreneurial activity in Turkey is much less compared to other developing countries. The education level of those early-stage entrepreneurs is lower, whereas the number of established business entrepreneurs is relatively higher (Karadeniz & Ozdemir, 2009). The government has been trying to foster an entrepreneurial culture through tax reforms (i.e. reduction or exemption) and new regulations. Also, many support programmes have been announced to provide funds, incentives, training, and education for entrepreneurs. However, it was only after 1995 that entrepreneurship education has been offered at universities in Turkey. Moreover, it has been treated as one of the elective courses limited to business administration programmes in some universities. Along with a better understanding of the subject, many universities now recognise the importance of entrepreneurship education, which is necessary for students majoring in business and students in different disciplines. As a result, it is now a compulsory subject in some universities, and entrepreneurship is taught through interdisciplinary approaches (Gürol & Atsan, 2006). Various actors and institutions have been working together to enhance the capacity for entrepreneurship in Turkey, especially within the last 10 years. For instance, in 2013, The Scientific and Technological Research Council of Turkey (TUBITAK) took the lead and introduced an annual index of the top 50 entrepreneurial and innovative universities. The main aim of introducing this index was to foster the development of entrepreneurship ecosystems within and around higher education institutions (Gür et al., 2017). The twin concepts of entrepreneurship education and the entrepreneurial university are relatively new in Turkey; therefore, there has been little published research on the topic.

There are currently 206 universities in Turkey, including 129 public universities and 77 private or foundation ones (Council of Higher Education, Turkey, 2020). The council of higher education manages all HEIs in Turkey (YÖK in Turkish Language), responsible for strategic planning as well as establishing and maintaining quality assurance mechanisms for higher education. The number of international students has been increasing every year, and in 2020, it exceeded 200,000. This clearly shows that the country has considerable potential to be one of the leading countries in higher education in a global market. Even during the pandemic, the number of international students is growing in 2021 (hurriyetdailynews.com, 2021).

The first COVID-19 case in Turkey was identified in March 2020. Since then, strict regulations have been introduced by the government to deal with the situation. One of the regulations that affected the HE sector was the temporary termination of education. As a result, all universities and private schools were forced to switch to distance learning without having sufficient training and preparation (Kawamorita et al., 2020a). However, the Ministry of Education introduced distance learning via three TV channels, as televised education has been available since the mid-1970s, and it is still a popular medium for education, especially in rural Turkey, due to its accessibility (Kawamorita et al., 2020c). The challenges and opportunities in HE after the outbreak of COVID-19 have already been studied (Korkmaz & Toraman, 2020; Kawamorita et al., 2020a; Yılmaz İnce et al., 2020) but have focused on the impact of the pandemic on distance learning education specifically, not on the university and the way it operates.

Despite the unfavourable environment during the pandemic, the GEM Report for Turkey (GEM, 2020) identified several successful collaboration projects in the entrepreneurial ecosystem. For example, an initiative called "Coronathon Türkiye" (Erhan & Gümüş, 2020) was launched by multiple actors, including universities, NGOs, governmental institutions, and private companies, to tackle the challenges caused by the COVID-19 outbreak. As a result, over 1500 participants contributed to 36 h of virtual work, with more than 120 online mentors and 12 new start-ups. This suggests that Turkish entrepreneurs have adapted quickly to remote working, which was not common before the outbreak (GEM reports for Turkey, 2020). This also confirms Karadeniz and Ozdemir's (2009) findings that the country offers favourable entrepreneurial environmental conditions such as the people's positive attitudes towards entrepreneurship and the market openness in a rapidly changing environment. In their study, the main barriers to innovation for entrepreneurs were identified as inadequacies in the government R&D policy, insufficient intellectual property rights, lack of information on technology, lack of financial sources, and inadequate tax incentives. Despite the improvements in the higher education system and sufficient infrastructure, Turkey is still behind compared to some emerging economies, and much needs to be done to create a better entrepreneurial climate.

4.4.2   Survey Findings

The questionnaire was sent to all 206 HEIs in Turkey, in which 22 responses were received. The collected evidence provides the current and future of the impact of the pandemic on universities, including the perception and declaration of "the entrepreneurial university", institutional approach towards the Entrepreneurship University, contribution towards the pandemic, expected student recruitment, online education, R&D, and difficulties or challenges HEIs experienced/expected.

(a) Perception of the "Entrepreneurial University"

According to the results, all of the HEIs agree with the definition of an entrepreneurial university (Table 4.3: Q1) as "…has the ability to innovate, recognise and create opportunities, take risks and respond to challenges. It sells it services in the knowledge industry and is a natural incubator that supports its academics, technicians and students to create new ventures".

Awareness of the international accreditation council for entrepreneurial and engaged universities scored between 40% and 60%, but with a score of 59.1%, it is better known than *HEInnovate* with 40.9% (Table 4.3: Q4), a free self-assessment tool for HEIs that was initiated by the European Commission, DG Education and Culture, and the OECD LEED Forum.

As shown in Table 4.3: Q5, 72.7% of the respondents answered that entrepreneurship is embedded within the mission and vision of their universities, while 77.3% (Table 4.3: Q6) consider both teaching and research as a part of the embedded institutional perspective. However, as shown in Table 4.3: Q7, 36.4% of the

HEIs do not teach entrepreneurship to students, and 50% of them teach entrepreneurship within the field of business and some other degree programmes. Only 13.6% of the HEIs are teaching entrepreneurship education in all degree programmes.

And 63.6% consider themselves as an entrepreneurial university. The criteria for identifying entrepreneurial universities were as follows: (1) entrepreneurship is embedded within the mission and vision of the university, and (2) universities are characterised by high levels of efforts of transformation towards developing institutional entrepreneurial initiatives. The collected information includes the general information as a result of the COVID-19 pandemic, awareness towards the concept of the entrepreneurial university, and self-assessment towards entrepreneurial university and university names.

(b) University Outcomes

According to Table 4.3: Q9, half of the Turkish HEIs think that the pandemic does not affect (remains the same) the transformation towards an entrepreneurial university. However, 31.8% believe that their universities will be more

Table 4.3 Questionnaire survey structure

Sections	Questions	Choice	Percentages
1. Perception of entrepreneurial university	1. Do you agree with the following definition of an entrepreneurial university? An entrepreneurial university "…has the ability to innovate, recognise and create opportunities, take risks and respond to challenges. It sells its services in the knowledge industry and is a natural incubator that supports its academics, technicians and students to create new ventures"	Yes	100
		No	0
	2. If no, what would be your definition?		
	3. Are you aware of the Accreditation Council for Entrepreneurial and Engaged Universities?	Yes	59.1
		No	40.9
	4. Are you aware of the OECD instrument HEInnovate?	Yes	40.9
		No	59.1
2. University outcomes	5. Is entrepreneurship embedded within the mission and vision of your university?	Yes	72.7
		No	27.3
	6. Is it on a par with	Teaching	9.1
		Research	13.6
		Both	77.3
	7. Do you teach entrepreneurship to your students?	All	13.6
		Business	50
		No	36.4
	8. Would you regard your university as an entrepreneurial university?	Yes	63.6
		No	36.4

(continued)

Table 4.3 (continued)

Sections	Questions	Choice	Percentages
3. The impact of the COVID-19 pandemic on student recruitment, digital transformation, and universities	9. Do you think that as a result of the pandemic your university will become	Less entrepreneurial	18.2
		More entrepreneurial	31.8
		Remain the same	50
	10. Has your university been involved in helping fight the pandemic?	Yes	72.7
		No	27.3
	11. If yes to question 10, how?	Researching for a vaccine	18.8
		Making facemasks etc	18.8
		Home office	6.3
		Providing support to	56.3
	13. Do you expect that, as a result of the pandemic, student numbers will	Increase	4.5
		Reduce	31.8
		Remain the same	63.6
	14. Do you expect that, as a result of the pandemic, international student numbers will	Increase	9.1
		Reduce	77.3
		Remain the same	13.6
	15. If you expect a reduction in student numbers, how do you intend to respond?	Find alternative sources	4.8
		Increase international recruitment	19
		Reduce expenditure	14.3
		Increase our distance learning	61.9
	16. How much of your university's teaching has been moved online as a result of the pandemic?	100%	59.1
		70–99%	18.2
		50–69%	9.1
		1–29%	13.6
	17. How much of your university's teaching will be moved to online as a result of the pandemic?	100%	22.7
		70–99%	31.8
		50–69%	13.6
		30–49%	18.2
		1–29%	13.6
	18. Will the number of university research	Increase	45.5
		Reduce	31.8
		Remain the same	22.7
	19. Will the research	Remain the same	57.1
		Become more applied	42.9
	20. Will the income from research	Increase	18.2
		Reduce	45.5
		Remain the same	36.4
	21. Will more income for research come from collaboration with employers?	Yes	40.9
		No	59.1
	22. Will more emphasis be placed on commercialising the intellectual property generated by the university's research?	Yes	42.9
		No	57.1

Source: Authors' own work

entrepreneurial due to the pandemic, and the remaining 18.2% have the opposite view: they will be less entrepreneurial. Although half of the HEIs think entrepreneurial orientation remains the same, 72.7% said that their universities had been involved in helping fight the pandemic (Table 4.3: Q10). Table 4.3: Q11 demonstrates the actions taken on identified challenges include providing support to the health services (more than half, 56.3%) followed by researching for a vaccine (18.8%) and making face masks and/or protective clothing while others include a more flexible working style, such as working from home (18.8%).

(c) The Impact of the COVID-19 Pandemic on Student Recruitment and Digital Transformation

Regarding student recruitment, 63.6% (Table 4.3: Q13) say that the number will remain the same; however, 77.3% expect that the number of international students will be decreased (Table 4.3: Q14), which is a large part of the income for many universities. Table 4.3: Q15 shows that an increase in distance learning provision seems to be the priority solution (69.1%) to respond to the consequences which will be caused by the decrease in the student numbers. Some 19% suggested that increased international recruitment activity would be another way, followed by the reduced expenditure (14.3%). Only 4.8% think that finding alternative sources of income is necessary to overcome the financial challenges. Digital transformation of teaching activity rapidly increased in Turkey. As a result, shown in Table 4.3: Q16, 59.1% answered that 100% of the university's teaching had been moved online as a result of the pandemic. On the other hand, 13.6% answered that less than 29% is conducted online. Over 50% of HEIs expected that more education will be moved to online (Table 4.3: Q17).

(d) The Impact of COVID-19 Pandemic on Universities

As a result of the pandemic, 45.5% said that the university would get involved in more research (Table 4.3: Q18). Despite this, only 18.2% think the income from research will be increased (Table 4.3: Q20), while 42.9% believed there would be a shift to more applied research (Table 4.3: Q19). More than half of the HEIs expect that less emphasis will be placed on commercialising the intellectual property generated by the university's research (Table 4.3: Q22), though fewer HEIs expect their positive performance through collaboration with employers (Table 4.3: Q21).

The last three questions were designed to identify the difficulties/challenges the institution has experienced and/or expects to experience due to the COVID-19 pandemic difficulties/challenges. These questions were open ended, and the main challenges which Turkish HEIs identified would appear to be (i) adaptation to distance learning, (ii) lack of funding, and (iii) decreased number of students. It was highlighted that distance learning should be given more importance, and the use of technological devices should be introduced to academic staff. Other challenges include lack of health services and vaccine studies, lack of cooperation with industry, lack of incentives, and less productivity in projects and publication. Also, a concern was raised by one of the universities that, in a medical school, "students need to have contact with patients for their education while fighting with the pandemic".

4.4.2.1 Social and Economic Impacts at the Local, National, and International Level

The expected challenges once the pandemic is over was asked as the final question in the questionnaire. The most mentioned expected challenge highlighted was "the changes" in terms of a redefinition of the working condition. Then, educational settings as universities are expected to change their vision after the pandemic. Also, the adaptation to face-to-face training, the relationship styles, and the way of doing business to get used to old normal were among the other issues.

4.5 Conclusion

This chapter has focused on exploring the impact of COVID-19 on Turkish universities and the development of entrepreneurial universities in the country in accordance with government policy. While the pandemic could create conditions whereby universities might become more closely involved with their communities and recognise more clearly their third mission responsibilities, the restrictions brought about by the pandemic might hinder this development. Hence this chapter explores this specific issue. It does so by surveying all 206 of Turkey's universities. Interestingly, though, only 10% of them responded, which might suggest that either they were too busy dealing with the consequences of the pandemic or the topic was of no importance to them. Whatever, this has two implications. First, it suggests that there is a need for further research to identify why most universities did not respond, and second, it means that the findings of the study do not necessarily represent the total population of universities in the country.

Based on the responses received from what was effectively a 10% sample, however, it would appear that Higher Education Institutions in Turkey:

(i) Have a good understanding of what entrepreneurial universities are and are in the transformation process.
(ii) Are involved in entrepreneurial activities to deal with the COVID-19 crises.
(iii) Have or expect to have financial challenges as a result of the pandemic and believe that entrepreneurship is one of the keys for survival.

Clear evidence was found demonstrating how Turkish HEIs are becoming more entrepreneurial by responding to the challenges such as (i) adaptation toward distance learning, (ii) reduced income and funding, and (iii) a decrease in the number of students, especially from other countries.

Although Turkish HEIs appear to be fully supporting online education as a result of the COVID-19 crisis, much more needs to be done. In particular, there is a need to evaluate the impacts of distance education and improve the current performance due to the lack of the required skills in the use of technological devices and tools on the part of the academic staff. This is consistent with similar findings of the impact of COVID-19 on Higher Education (Kawamorita et al., 2020a, b, c, d). Furthermore, these crises affect all aspects of university operations, and therefore, HEIs should be flexible, focusing on priorities, and act entrepreneurially to deal with the changing environment.

While this study has provided some insights on the expectations and concerns of a sample of Turkey's universities, the small sample size may affect the reliability of the results, but it would seem that the pandemic could be creating the conditions in which the transformation of Higher Education is encouraged and facilitated. Hence the study addresses a critical gap in the body of understanding on the impact of the pandemic. More research is needed, though, to monitor both developments in Turkey and other educational systems. As the pandemic has demonstrated, if the grand challenges that the world is facing are to be addressed successfully, universities have an important part to play, especially given the nature of the global knowledge economy. Certainly, they need to respond to challenges, innovate, and incubate new solutions to problems.

References

Abdulrahim, H., & Mabrouk, F. (2020). COVID-19 and the digital transformation of Saudi higher education. *Asian Journal of Distance Education, 15*(1), 291–306. Retrieved from https://eric.ed.gov/?id=EJ1289975.

Ajzen, I. (1991). The theory of planned behavior. *Organisational Behavior and Human Decision Processes.* https://doi.org/10.1016/0749-5978(91)90020-T

Ali, W. (2020). Online and remote learning in higher education institutes: A necessity in light of COVID-19 pandemic. *Higher Education Studies.* https://doi.org/10.5539/hes.v10n3p16

Amir, L. R., Tanti, I., Maharani, D. A., Wimardhani, Y. S., Julia, V., Sulijaya, B., & Puspitawati, R. (2020). Student perspective of classroom and distance learning during COVID-19 pandemic in the undergraduate dental study program Universitas Indonesia. *BMC Medical Education.* https://doi.org/10.1186/s12909-020-02312-0

Brammer, S., & Clark, T. (2020). COVID-19 and management education: Reflections on challenges, opportunities, and potential futures. *British Journal of Management.* https://doi.org/10.1111/1467-8551.12425

Clark, B. R. (1998). Creating entrepreneurial universities: organizational pathways of transformation. Issues in Higher Education. Elsevier Science Regional Sales, 665 Avenue of the Americas, New York, NY 10010 (paperback: ISBN-0-08-0433545; hardcover: ISBN-0-08-0433421, $27).

Chrisman, J. J., Hynes, T., & Fraser, S. (1995). Faculty entrepreneurship and economic development: The case of the University of Calgary. *Journal of Business Venturing.* https://doi.org/10.1016/0883-9026(95)00015-Z

Cook, C., Heath, F., & Thompson, R. L. (2000). A meta-analysis of response rates in Web- or internet-based surveys. *Educational and Psychological Measurement.* https://doi.org/10.1177/00131640021970934

Council of Higher Education, Turkey. (2020). Retrieved 25 December 2020, from https://www.yok.gov.tr/en/homepage

Crowe, S., Cresswell, K., Robertson, A., Huby, G., Avery, A., & Sheikh, A. (2011). The case study approach. *BMC Medical Research Methodology.* https://doi.org/10.1186/1471-2288-11-100

Davey, T., Hannon, P., & Penaluna, A. (2016). Entrepreneurship education and the role of universities in entrepreneurship: Introduction to the special issue. *Industry and Higher Education.* https://doi.org/10.1177/0950422216656699

Demir, H., & Demiryürek, K. (2018). Determination of entrepreneurship tendencies of university students: The case of OMU faculty of agriculture. *KSU Journal of Agriculture and Nature, 21*(Special Issue), 168–176. https://doi.org/10.18016/ksutarimdoga.vi.472966

Dubey, P., & Pandey, D. (2020). Distance learning in higher education during pandemic: Challenges and opportunities. *The International Journal of Indian Psychology, 8*(2), 43–46. https://doi.org/10.25215/0802.204

Erhan, Ç., & Gümüş, Ş. (2020). Opportunities and risks in higher education in the postpandemic period. In *Reflections on the pandemic*. Turkish Academy of Science.

Etzkowitz, H. (2003). Research groups as "quasi-firms": The invention of the entrepreneurial university. *Research Policy*. https://doi.org/10.1016/S0048-7333(02)00009-4

Global Entrepreneurship Monitor Reports for Turkey. (2020). *Immediate impact January–July 2020*, Retrieved 25 December 2020, from https://www.gemconsortium.org/economy-profiles/turkey-2/policy

Guerrero, M., Kirby, D. A., & Urbano, D. (2006). *A literature review on entrepreneurial universities: An institutional approach*. Autonomous University of Barcelona, Business Economics Department, Working Paper Series, (06/8).

Guerrero, M., Urbano, D., & Salamzadeh, A. (2014). Evolving entrepreneurial universities: Experiences and challenges in the Middle Eastern context. In *Handbook on the Entrepreneurial University*. Edward Elgar.

Guerrero, M., Urbano, D., & Salamzadeh, A. (2015). Entrepreneurial transformation in the Middle East: experiences from Tehran Universities. *Technics Technologies Education Management, 10*(4), 533–537.

Gür, U., Oylumlu, İ. S., & Kunday, Ö. (2017). Critical assessment of entrepreneurial and innovative universities index of Turkey: Future directions. *Technological Forecasting and Social Change, 123*, 161–168. https://doi.org/10.1016/j.techfore.2016.09.008

Gürol, Y., & Atsan, N. (2006). Entrepreneurial characteristics amongst university students. *Education + Training*. https://doi.org/10.1108/00400910610645716

Hannibal, M., Evers, N., & Servais, P. (2016). Opportunity recognition and international new venture creation in university spin-offs-cases from Denmark and Ireland. *Journal of International Entrepreneurship, 14*(3), 345–372.

Hebebci, M. T., Bertiz, Y., & Alan, S. (2020). Investigation of Views of Students and Teachers on Distance Education Practices during the Coronavirus (COVID-19) Pandemic. *International Journal of Technology in Education and Science, 4*(4), 267–282. https://doi.org/10.46328/ijtes.v4i4.113

Hurriyetdailynews.com. (2021, April 3). International institutions revise Turkeys growth forecasts. *Hürriyet Daily News*. https://www.hurriyetdailynews.com/international-institutions-revise-turkeys-growth-forecasts 163644.

Karadeniz, E., & Ozdemir, O. (2009). Entrepreneurship in Turkey and developing countries: A comparison of activities, characteristics, motivation and environment for entrepreneurship. *MIBES Transactions, 3*(1), 30–45.

Kawamorita, H., Altun, E., & Kizilkaya, R. (2020a). Impact of the Covid-19 pandemic in higher education: Case study on distance education at Ondokuz Mayıs University, Turkey. In *Conference: Information systems and communication technologies in the modern educational process. IV International scientific and practical conference*. Perm.

Kawamorita, H., Salamzadeh, A., & Demiryurek, K. (2016, February). Academic entrepreneurship: Some evidence from a Turkish University. *SSRN Electronic Journal*, 1–9. https://doi.org/10.13140/RG.2.1.1194.7285.

Kawamorita, H., Salamzadeh, A., Demiryurek, K., & Ghajarzadeh, M. (2020b). Entrepreneurial universities in times of crisis: Case of Covid-19 pandemic. *Journal of Entrepreneurship, Business and Economics, 8*(1), 78. Retrieved from www.scientificia.com

Kawamorita, H., Takahashi, N., & Demiryurek, K. (2020c). Media literacy and rural women entrepreneurship: Experience from Japan and Turkey. *Nordic Journal of Media Management, 3*(1), 361–383. https://doi.org/10.5278/njmm.2597-0445.5898

Kawamorita, H., Yazici, E., & Kizilkaya, R. (2020d). Internationalisation experience at Ondokuz Mayis University, Faculty of Agriculture as the leading faculty of our University. In *II international forum "Dialogue of young scientists: Science talks"*. Kazakh National Agricultural University.

Kedraka, K., & Kaltsidis, C. (2020). Effects of the COVID-19 pandemic on university pedagogy : Students' experiences and considerations. *European Journal of Education Studies, 7*(8), 17–30. https://doi.org/10.46827/ejes.v7i8.3176

Kirby, A. D. (2020a). *Entrepreneurial university and COVID-19: Opportunities for entrepreneurial transformation?* Retrieved 25 August 2020, from https://www.aceeu.org/news/spotlightarticle/id/7

Kirby, A. D. (2020b). *Coronavirus and the entrepreneurial university*. Retrieved 25 August 2020, from https://www.advance-he.ac.uk/news-and-views/coronavirus-and-entrepreneurial-university

Kirby, D. A. (2006). Creating entrepreneurial universities in the UK: Applying entrepreneurship theory to practice. *Journal of Technology Transfer*. https://doi.org/10.1007/s10961-006-9061-4

Kirby, D. A., Guerrero, M., & Urbano, D. (2011). Making universities more entrepreneurial: Development of a model. *Canadian Journal of Administrative Sciences, 28*(3), 302–316. https://doi.org/10.1002/CJAS.220

Kirby, D. A., & Ibrahim, N. (2017). Entrepreneurial education and the entrepreneurial university: The challenge of creating an institutional entrepreneurship ecosystem in a factor driven economy. *Technology Transfer and Entrepreneurship*. https://doi.org/10.217 4/2213809903666160531105838

Korkmaz, G., & Toraman, Ç. (2020). Are we ready for the post-COVID-19 educational practice? An investigation into what educators think as to online learning. *International Journal of Technology in Education and Science, 4*(4), 293–309. https://doi.org/10.46328/ijtes.v4i4.110

Liguori, E., & Winkler, C. (2020). From offline to online: Challenges and opportunities for entrepreneurship education following the COVID-19 pandemic. *Entrepreneurship Education and Pedagogy*. https://doi.org/10.1177/2515127420916738

Moralista, R. B., & Oducado, R. M. F. (2020). Faculty perception toward online education in a state college in the Philippines during the coronavirus disease 19 (COVID-19) pandemic. *Universal Journal of Educational Research*. https://doi.org/10.13189/ujer.2020.081044

Morris, M. H., & Liguori, E. (2016). Teaching reason and the unreasonable. In M. Morris & E. Liguori (Eds.), *Annals of entrepreneurship education and pedagogy* (Vol. 2, pp. xiv–xxii). Edward Elgar Publishing.

Mowafy, A. (2020). *How 'entrepreneurial universities' are tackling the effects of COVID-19 in Egypt*. The American University in Cairo School of Business – Business Forward. http://businessforwardauc.com/2020/04/08/how-entrepreneurial-universities-are-tackling-the-effects-ofcovid-19-in-egypt/

Müller S. (2008). *Encouraging future entrepreneurs: The effect of entrepreneurship course characteristics on entrepreneurial intention*. University of St. Gallen, Business Dissertations.

Nulty, D. D. (2008). The adequacy of response rates to online and paper surveys: What can be done? *Assessment and Evaluation in Higher Education*. https://doi.org/10.1080/02602930701293231

Obaid AI-Youbi, A., Al-Hayani, A., Bardesi, H. J., Basheri, M., Lytras, M. D., & Aljohani, N. R. (2020). The King Abdulaziz University (KAU) pandemic framework: A methodological approach to leverage social media for the sustainable management of higher education in crisis. *Sustainability (Switzerland)*. https://doi.org/10.3390/su12114367

Özer, M. (2020). The contribution of the strengthened capacity of vocational education and training system in Turkey to the fight against Covid-19. *Yuksekogretim Dergisi, 10*(2), 134–140. https://doi.org/10.2399/yod.20.726951

Peterka, S. O., & Salihovic, V. (2012). *What is entrepreneurial university and why we need it?* 1. Medunarodni Znanstveni Simpozij Gospodarstvo Istocne Hrvatske – Jucer, Danas, Sutra.

Potishuk, V., & Kratzer, J. (2017). Factors affecting entrepreneurial intensions and entrepreneurial attitudes in higher education. *Journal of Entrepreneurship Education*.

Ratten, V., & Jones, P. (2020). Covid-19 and entrepreneurship education: Implications for advancing research and practice. *International Journal of Management Education*. https://doi.org/10.1016/j.ijme.2020.100432

Rizun, M., & Strzelecki, A. (2020). Students' acceptance of the covid-19 impact on shifting higher education to distance learning in Poland. *International Journal of Environmental Research and Public Health, 17*(18), 1–19. https://doi.org/10.3390/ijerph17186468

Salamzadeh, A., & Dana, L. P. (2020). The coronavirus (COVID-19) pandemic: Challenges among Iranian startups. *Journal of Small Business & Entrepreneurship, 1-24*. https://doi.org/10.1080/08276331.2020.1821158

Salamzadeh, A., Farsi, J. Y., Motavaseli, M., Markovic, M. R., & Kawamorita, H. K. (2015). Institutional factors affecting the transformation of entrepreneurial universities. *International Journal of Business and Globalisation, 14*(3), 271–291. https://doi.org/10.1504/IJBG.2015.068620

Salamzadeh, A., Kawamorita, H., & Salamzadeh, Y. (2017). Entrepreneurial universities and branding: a conceptual model proposal. *World Review of Science, Technology and Sustainable Development, 12*(4), 300. https://doi.org/10.1504/wrstsd.2016.082188

Sirelkhatim, F., & Gangi, Y. (2015). Entrepreneurship education: A systematic literature review of curricula contents and teaching methods. *Cogent Business & Management, 2*(1), 1–11. https://doi.org/10.1080/23311975.2015.1052034

Sivabalan, S., & Ismail, N. (2020). Bloomberg.com, Bloomberg, Retrieved 25 August 2020 from www.bloomberg.com/news/articles/2020-08-17/turkey-s-homemade-economic-pain-won-t-cost-traders-any-sleep

Souitaris, V., Zerbinati, S., & Al-Laham, A. (2007). Do entrepreneurship programmes raise entrepreneurial intention of science and engineering students? The effect of learning, inspiration and resources. *Journal of Business Venturing*. https://doi.org/10.1016/j.jbusvent.2006.05.002

Stolze, A. (2020). A meta-ethnography on HEIs' transformation into more entrepreneurial institutions: Towards an action-framework proposition. *Industry and Higher Education*. https://doi.org/10.1177/0950422220922677

Tajpour, M., Kawamorita, H., & Demiryurek, K. (2020). Towards the third generation of universities with an entrepreneurial approach. *International Journal of Technoentrepreneurship, 4*(2), 122–133. https://doi.org/10.1504/IJTE.2020.113927

Toquero, C. M. (2020). Challenges and opportunities for higher education amid the COVID-19 pandemic: The Philippine context. *Pedagogical Research, 5*(4), em0063. https://doi.org/10.29333/pr/7947

Universities UK. (2020). Retrieved 28 December 2020, from https://www.universitiesuk.ac.uk/covid19

Wang, C., Cheng, Z., Yue, X.-G., & McAleer, M. (2020). Risk management of COVID-19 by universities in China. *Journal of Risk and Financial Management*. https://doi.org/10.3390/jrfm13020036

Wennekers, S., Uhlaner, L., & Thurik, R. (2002). Entrepreneurship and its conditions: a macro perspective. *International Journal of Entrepreneurship Education, 1*(1), 25–64.

Williams, G. (2003). *The enterprising university: Reform, excellence and equity*. The Society for Research into Higher Education and Open University Press.

Yılmaz İnce, E., Kabul, A., & Diler, İ. (2020). Distance education in higher education in the COVID-19 pandemic process: A case of Isparta Applied Sciences University. *International Journal of Technology in Education and Science, 4*(4), 343–351. https://doi.org/10.46328/ijtes.v4i4.112

Chapter 5
Opportunities and Threats Facing Early-Stage Digital Startups During the COVID-19 Pandemic

Asef Karimi, Navid Mohammadi ⓘ, and Shaghayegh Sakhteh

5.1 Introduction

The widespread outbreak of the Coronavirus disease 2019 (COVID-19) pandemic has thus far led to lifestyle modifications. The nationwide quarantine and closure caused by this disease started in the city of Wuhan, the capital of Hubei Province, China, and spread quickly across the world (Gössling et al., 2020). Changes arising from this condition have had significant impacts on national and international economies (Kuckertz et al., 2020) and have subsequently influenced most industries and businesses (Kim et al., 2020). Nearly all economists believe that the given pandemic is something astonishing, variable, and very important that has dramatically caused changes in political and economic arenas (Winston, 2020). Industries including hospitality and tourism, e.g., restaurants, hotels, tourist attractions, transportation, etc. (Ateljevic, 2020; Chang et al., 2020; Gössling et al., 2020; Higgins-Desbiolles, 2020; Liew, 2020; Yang et al., 2020), sports, education, exports, and imports, just to name some (Wells et al., 2020), have been accordingly subjected to the strongest effects among other industries. The recommended preventive measures for COVID-19 such as reduction in working hours, social distancing, teleworking, increase in layoffs, and downsizing have severely challenged businesses, giving rise to the failure of various types of small and large ones (Amankwah-Amoah et al., 2020). This crisis has so far had many consequences and effects on businesses,

A. Karimi (✉)
Faculty of Management and Accounting, College of Farabi, University of Tehran, Tehran, Iran
e-mail: asef.karimi@ut.ac.ir

N. Mohammadi · S. Sakhteh
University of Tehran, Tehran, Iran
e-mail: Navid.m@ut.ac.ir; sh_sakhteh@ut.ac.ir

entrepreneurs, small- and medium-sized enterprises (SMEs), as well as startups, both in developed and developing countries (Castro & Zermeño, 2020; Kuckertz et al., 2020; Salamzadeh & Dana, 2020). Small businesses and startups are assumed to be more vulnerable than large entities, since they are placed at lower levels in terms of financial capacity, assets, and productivity. In addition, decline in demands for startup products and services in the short term may be a factor in putting such companies at risk of failure (Indriastuti & Fuad, 2020).

The COVID-19 pandemic would be a turning point in the history of such businesses, creating many opportunities and threats. According to the Organization for Economic Cooperation and Development (OECD), this condition has generally changed consumption patterns and customer behavior and has resulted in paradigm shifts and competitiveness of businesses in the market (Wenzel et al., 2020). One of the most important approaches adopted by businesses and startups to deal with the threats and to seize the opportunities coming from this pandemic is digitalization (Indriastuti & Fuad, 2020). Given the importance of this category of businesses, this research focused on digital startups.

Several definitions have been to date presented for startups, but in general, it is worth noting that startups refer to companies with profitable, scalable, and reproducible models of business (Salamzadeh & Dana, 2020). In this sense, those in their infancy life cycle are called early-stage startups. At this point, startups are required to supply innovative products and services and differentiate between themselves and competitors in the market. Making such distinctions would be very important for their survival (Glaveckaitė, 2020). In addition, they need to decide when and in what market to offer their products or services in order to have the greatest chance of success (Marmer et al., 2011). With the development of the digital age and the movements towards online and digital businesses, startups have also taken big steps in this direction by exploiting novel technologies (Elia et al., 2020).

The startup ecosystem of Iran, as a developing country, has truly switched on its activities since 2010 and hundreds of successful startups such as *Snapp*, *TAPSI*, and *Digikala* have developed. Majority of these startups are digital and online (Beigi et al., 2020). Following the COVID-19 pandemic, the entrepreneurial ecosystem in Iran has experienced significant changes, so that the failure rate of startups has dramatically increased (Salamzadeh & Dana, 2020). As a major crisis, COVID-19 has also created many opportunities and threats for startups in Iran and has altered their business models (Etemad, 2020). These prospects and challenges need to be fully identified and then properly organized for further utilization. Unfortunately, little research has been until now done in this field, and only a few articles have identified the challenges caused by the COVID-19 pandemic on mature businesses (Salamzadeh & Dana, 2020). To fill this gap, this chapter aims to identify the opportunities and threats for digital startups in their infancy life cycle during this condition in Iran. It is not also a long time since the emergence of this disease around the world, so there is a need to conduct different studies to shed light on dark points through identifying the effects of COVID-19 on businesses at various levels. Therefore, any research in this area can generate many valuable outputs. Among the innovations of this study was evaluating digital startups particularly early-stage ones. The results of this chapter would thus elucidate some points within the startup ecosystem in Iran during the pandemic and give directions to startups, accelerators, as well as the components of startup ecosystems in other countries with the same entrepreneurial ecosystems.

In this chapter, the research carried out on businesses and startups during the COVID-19 pandemic is initially examined, and then, the activities of digital startups through this crisis were investigated. Subsequently, the research method and the study population are presented, the research results are analyzed, and finally, this chapter provides findings and suggestions for future research.

5.2 Literature Review

5.2.1 SMEs and Startups During COVID-19

The COVID-19 pandemic has so far had many positive and negative effects on SMEs and startups, leading to their failure and even their growth. Some startups have failed due to their low flexibility and others have made the best use of opportunities, thanks to their high alertness and adaptability. Research conducted in this regard has acknowledged that the pressures imposed on startups during this pandemic have made them continue their life through seeking alternative measures and appropriate solutions tailored to these new conditions. Accordingly, COVID-19 has acted as a catalyst for further innovation, and business managers and founders of startups have been obliged to change their strategies in full (Papadopoulos et al., 2020; Salamzadeh & Dana, 2020).

In Iran, some startups, such as *Eseminar*, have exploited such opportunities and their revenues have increased, but others have abandoned competitions in the face of challenges. During the COVID-19 pandemic, some governments, such as Germany, have been also implementing a wide variety of measures to support businesses and startups via tax subsidies, reduction in working hours, bank credits, as well as special lending facilities. Some banks have also offered special support programs for startups, including growth loans and joint venture programs (Kuckertz et al., 2020). However, early-stage startups in Germany have been deprived of such support, as one of the main conditions for lending to startups is having profitable businesses. In this respect, early-stage startups have so far failed to pass the valley of death, and sometimes not even the breakeven point (Kuckertz et al., 2020). Therefore, COVID-19 has produced much more challenges for such startups. Another threat facing these entities has been sales volume decrease and fixed costs, putting their survival at risk. Moreover, many stakeholders and investors have had no interest in making investments in startups, since they have been only seeking short-term solutions to overcome this crisis (Kuckertz et al., 2020).

Over the last year since the COVID-19 outbreak, many studies have been conducted on various businesses during this pandemic, each one reflecting on the effects of the disease on startups. For example, Salamzadeh and Dana (2020),

examining mature startups, identified several challenges facing such small businesses during the COVID-19 pandemic and revealed that startups in Iran were
generally drawn against five categories of threats, including financing, human
resource management, support measures and mechanisms, market and marketing,
crisis management, and others (Salamzadeh & Dana, 2020). As well, Rowan and
Galanakis (2020) focused on threats for agri-food startups (European Startups)
and even explored mature startups and destructive innovation projects in this area.
Accordingly, the effect of COVID-19 on the success of each project was recognized and the main challenges, including teleworking and remote monitoring, use
of artificial intelligence, machine learning, and the like, were identified (Rowan &
Galanakis, 2020). In a review of 16 mature startups and businesses, Kuckertz
et al. (2020) also investigated the impact of this pandemic and identified some in
40 countries such as Namibia or Nepal, including destructed infrastructure of
businesses, inadequate financial resources, as well as changes in business models,
policies, internal processes, and other such cases, as extracted from some interviews (Kuckertz et al., 2020). Moreover, Bacq et al. (2020) discussed the rapid
response of startups to social conditions during the COVID-19 pandemic (Bacq
et al., 2020). As suggested by Almeida et al. (2020), startups (Portuguese tech
startups) needed to review customer needs and their experiences with purchases
for survival during this condition and even make use of digital media to provide
their services (Almeida et al., 2020). Hasanat et al. (2020) additionally noted that
among the challenges facing Malaysian e-commerce companies importing their
products from other nations, including China, were limits for transport caused by
the disease around the world, inventory depletion, no access to raw materials, and
many more (Hasanat et al., 2020).

5.2.2   Digital Startups During COVID-19 Pandemic

One of the effects of COVID-19 on businesses and startups is pushing them towards
digitalization and creating opportunities for digital startups. This solution can be
right for transition from the pandemic era (Indriastuti & Fuad, 2020). The emergence of this crisis has also made people and businesses more eager to move towards
novel technologies. Businesses and startups have been also trying to offer their
products and services on digital platforms and provide better solutions to new needs
arising in the market (Almeida et al., 2020). Among the benefits of the digitalization
of businesses, sustained competitive advantage, increased efficiency in business
processes, higher levels of customer satisfaction, facilitated decision-making, and
accelerations in strategic changes can be thus noted (Indriastuti & Fuad, 2020). The
COVID-19 pandemic has correspondingly had a positive effect on sustainable consumption among customers online (Tran, 2020). In this regard, startups engaged in
e-commerce during this crisis have benefited a lot (Indriastuti & Fuad, 2020).
Digikala, the most important online sales platform in Iran and the Middle East, has

also well managed the situation to its advantage. In addition, *Eseminar*, holding online meetings and conferences in Iran, has seized the opportunity and has multiplied its revenues by ten times.

But shifts towards digitalization can be sometimes considered as challenges to business managers, because changes can bring businesses and startups to predicament and a state of uncertainty. In general, the success of a business in the process of transformation to digitalization depends on the acceptance of employees, suppliers, key partners, and consumers (Almeida et al., 2020). Unquestionably, startups are much more agile, and such changes have been easier forthem, especially startups that have made use of the lean startup method to fulfill their objectives (Ximenes et al., 2015).

5.3 Research Methodology

5.3.1 Research Design and Procedure

This chapter examines the opportunities and threats for early-stage digital startups in Iran during the COVID-19 pandemic. For this purpose, the qualitative method along with in-depth interviews with the founders of 13 Iranian early-stage digital startups was employed. The unstructured interviews, lasting 45–120 min, were thus conducted with at least two members of the startup team. The analysis of the data derived from the interviews as well as coding opportunities and threats for these startups were further completed via thematic analysis (Braun & Clarke, 2006). In order to assess the validity of this research, a PhD student of entrepreneurship was invited to code the interviews individually and to compare the codes extracted.

5.3.2 Sources of Data

Snowball sampling was applied to the following target population: (a) startups in their infancy life cycle or the so-called early-stage startups, (b) digital startups, (c) early-stage startups with less than two years of life cycle, and (d) startups whose target market was Iran.

Iranian digital startups were selected for this research, since Iran is a developing country and hence a developing startup ecosystem. To identify the opportunities and challenges, in-depth interviews, lasting 45–120 min, with cofounders of 13 startups were conducted. There were also attempts to interview at least two members of each startup, which constituted 31 people in total. The total time of the interviews was also more than 30 h. The details about the startups examined in this chapter are presented in the table below (Table 5.1).

Table 5.1 Selected startups

Case	Scope	Year of establishment	Number of cofounders	Number of interviewed cofounders	Total time of interviews	Job titles of interviewees
1	E-commerce	2019	4	2	2.5	CEO, CTO
2	Logistic	2019	5	3	3	CEO, CTO, marketing manager
3	Agri-tech	2020	4	2	1.5	CEO, product manager
4	Food	2018	3	2	2	CEO, marketing manager
5	E-commerce	2020	4	2	3	CEO, marketing manager
6	E-commerce	2019	4	3	2.5	CEO, CTO, marketing manager
7	Tourism	2019	5	3	3.15	CEO, CTO, marketing manager
8	Blockchain	2019	4	2	2.15	CEO, CTO
9	Game	2020	5	3	2.5	CEO, marketing manager, product manager
10	Game	2018	3	2	2.45	CEO, CTO
11	Fin-tech	2019	3	2	1.45	CEO, marketing manager
12	IOT	2019	4	3	3.15	CEO, CTO, marketing manager
13	IOT	2019	3	2	2.15	CEO, marketing manager
Sum				**31**	**31.5**	

Source: Authors' own table

5.4   Data Analysis

Thematic analysis was employed to evaluate the transcribed interviews in this chapter. For this purpose, second-order codes were extracted from the interviews and then converted into first-order ones. As a final point, these codes were aggregated to form the ultimate construct. The given process was accomplished in parallel for both opportunities and threats and eventually tabulated. To reach the aggregates, the opinions of five experts in entrepreneurship and startup activities elicited through semi-structured interviews. This step was completed to ensure the accuracy of the categorization and coding. This interview was held in the form of an online focus group, and then expert opinions on each code and category were collected, and accordingly the required revisions were made. In the end, the results of interviews conducted in 13 early-stage digital startups were aggregated and finalized by taking advantage of the views of the members in the focus group session. Table 5.2 illustrates the opportunities and threats identified in the interviews (Table 5.3).

A total number of 13 opportunities and 19 threats were accordingly identified within four categories, i.e., market and marketing, startup team, operational and management issues, and financial and economic activities, as described below.

5.4.1 Opportunities and Threats Related to Market and Marketing

Following the COVID-19 pandemic, governments decided to impose restrictions such as reduced working hours, travel restrictions, nationwide quarantine, and closure of all guilds and businesses except emergency services (Iwuoha & Aniche, 2020; Lai et al., 2020). Accelerators, growth and innovation centers, and shared workspaces were no exception. These centers are the principal place of deployment, operation, and service startups (especially early-stage ones) (Sperindé & Nguyen-Duc, 2020). The closure of accelerators also impeded the growth process of startups, and it took a long time for these centers to adapt to the current situation. One of the strategies recruited by accelerators during this pandemic has been moving towards accelerated online and virtual processes. Unfortunately, this change has not still formed well in the entrepreneurship ecosystem of Iran, so the growth and development speed of startups has greatly reduced. As pointed out by one of the interviewees, "The closure of workshops and some activities of mentors as well as the quarantine of the team have caused our activities to stop for a few months" (Case 5). Given that shared workspaces in Iran are sometimes private, restrictions and closure laws had not been operated uniformly in all. Some centers have been closed and others have reduced their working hours, but in general, startup routine activities have changed. Many of the startups using shared workspaces as a workplace have shut them down and have been forced to relocate to other areas with a lower cost or work in their home. The decline in face-to-face interactions has also led to a wave of digital and online businesses, and the existing ones have been focused on developing digitalization and innovation (Soto-Acosta, 2020). The increasing number of competitors and their movement towards digitalization has given rise to competitive environments for businesses, especially startups, and has created a red ocean for early-stage startups. On the other hand, startups in need of importing raw materials or products to advance their businesses have faced many challenges. Some of these problems include lack of imported resources and raw materials due to restrictions

Table 5.2 Opportunities facing early-stage digital startups during COVID-19 in Iran

Aggregate dimensions	Second-order codes	First-order codes
Market and marketing	Expanding marketing and service activities via analyzing customer behavior online	Consumer behavior can be fully observed and monitored online, so there is an opportunity to analyze it at a much lower cost
	Showing tendency in society towards in-person and digital transactions	COVID-19 has provided a great opportunity to create a much deeper and larger market for offline and online businesses as well as e-commerce.
	Discovering new needs by users within the digital space	People turning to the digital space have encountered services they have not seen before, resulting in the discovery of new needs in the digital context.
	Building a digital culture among customers and startups	Pre-pandemic customers have become individuals interested in the digital space and online transactions.
	Detecting a rising trend in consumer demands for some products and services	COVID-19 has created a huge market for customers to buy health items virtually. As well, educational platforms and startups have been in great demand owing to people's extra leisure time.
Startup team	Boosting creativity and ideation among team members due to having much more time	Given the increase in people's free time and saving travel time, team members have more time to sleep on the issues and come up with new ideas and creativity.
	Empowering team members	With regard to the increase in team members' overtime, these individuals can give a boost to their capabilities.
Operational and management issues	Augmenting productivity	If a process is well managed, the productivity of startup operations will increase dramatically. Also, the speed of work amplifies and there is no need to spend a lot of time every day to get to work.
	Building a teleworking culture	COVID-19 has led to the implementation of teleworking culture in organizations and startups.
	Developing new business models	Innovation becomes obvious in business models by startups since they take advantage of the paradigm shift created by COVID-19.
Financial and economic activities	Adding to likelihood of raising capital for digital startups	Considering movements towards digitalization, investors are more inclined to invest in digital startups.
	Reducing workspace costs	Teleworking, with all its problems, has reduced many of costs associated with shared and private workspaces.
	Benefiting government support during COVID-19	Some financial and spiritual facilities have been allocated to startups during the pandemic, which have been really helpful.

Source: Authors' own table

Table 5.3 Threats facing early-stage digital startups during COVID-19 in Iran

Aggregate dimensions	Second-order codes	First-order codes
Market and marketing	No access to imported products and raw materials attributable to travel restrictions	Some items being imported from abroad and sold on e-commerce platform have been completely eliminated due to travel restrictions between countries.
	Rising prices of imported materials	Lack of access to imported products and raw materials has greatly increased their prices
	Increasing competitions in digital businesses	Losing customers and increasing competitions in digital and online businesses are other major challenges, and only startups with more speed and flexibility can win.
	Closure of accelerators	Closure of accelerators has caused many early-stage startups have no possible forms of development and regular training, which is a great challenge to new entrepreneurs.
	Lack of access to shared workspace	Startups previously based in a shared workspace tend to work in the same space again, but COVID-19 has closed many of these common spaces and has made them more costly.
Startup team	Reduced number of workforce	COVID-19 has led to the withdrawal of talented workforce from startup teams.
	Startup collapse because of separation of team members	The closure of university dormitories and the quarantine of cities have caused team members to move away and startup team to collapse completely.
	Decreased motivation among team members	Restrictions on team travel and increased quarantine have caused fatigue and lower team motivation.
	Lower team member interactions	Teleworking has dramatically reduced interactions between team members as a big challenge.
	Need for new members	Due to the paradigm shift in businesses, there has been a need to change the capabilities of team members in some startups.
	Reduced commitment in team members	Being away from the startup challenge space has reduced the commitment of team members and generally led to their closure.

(continued)

Table 5.3 (continued)

Aggregate dimensions	Second-order codes	First-order codes
Operational and management issues	Lower productivity and speed of work	In many cases, teleworking has not had enough productivity and has completely challenged startup performance.
	Cessation of activities in production department, technical supervision, testing, etc., requiring physical presence of workforce	There is difficulty in operational oversight of parts of work process that require physical presence.
	Difficulty in shipping and logistics	There are increased requests to sell products and to reduce logistics caused by traffic restrictions for online stores.
	Decelerated administrative and government-related processes caused by teleworking	Administrative processes related to company registration and the like have become prolonged due to teleworking of administrative staff of government organizations.
Financial and economic activities	No access to investor network	Attracting capital has become extremely difficult owing to the closure and remote operation of accelerators, venture capital funds, and the like.
	Decreased revenues	Decreased revenues in startups due to changes in consumer behavior.
	Increased costs	Costs of research and development have soared and business models of startups have altered following changes in consumer behavior.
	Problems in repaying bank loans	Due to declining startup revenues, it has become extremely difficult for teams to pay back loan banks.

Source: Authors' own table

on transfers between countries as well as a significant growth in prices due to the bans and high exchange rate for the US dollar in Iran. In this sense, one of the startup founders stated that "Many of the raw materials used for our products were being imported from China, and the COVID-19 pandemic caused us to face a market shortage for a while, and at last we procured them at twice the price" (Case 1). In the wake of restrictions on transport and reduced social activities, many customers and users who had already no incentives to shop online have become persuaded to meet their needs through online platforms. Such modifications in consumer lifestyle have helped owners of startups and enterprises to monitor consumer behavior in the online context and consequently develop their products and services according to their needs. This change has also dramatically reduced research and development costs in startups. In addition to purchases, online meetings and training classes as well as many other activities have been among the new needs raised by users following the COVID-19 pandemic, indicating modifications in people's traditional lifestyle into a digital one. As an example, one of the interviewees said that "COVID-19 was very helpful for us and demands for our services compounded. With the advent of this pandemic, we even witnessed the reconciliation of traditional people with the Internet" (Case 6). Upon the digitalization of people's lifestyle, the type of needs has also changed, leading to the discovery of new needs and the creation of demands for startups whose services were not popular. "COVID-19 and obligations to use the digital space have made people familiar with new technologies in online and digital media and they have recognized their needs for some products" (Case 2). Online consumer behavior as well as its analysis and monitoring have also given startup marketing teams the opportunity to save resources and energy. As one of the interviewees reiterated, "Analyzing customer behavior through online tools and social networks makes us able to monitor and analyze their travels and provide services tailored to their needs at the right time" (Case 11). The occurrence of this pandemic around the world has even changed consumption patterns regardless of geographical location and has consequently created a wave of growing demands for some services and products. Hospitals and healthcare centers have also faced huge demands, reducing their capacity to provide services. On the other hand, some products, including cleaning products and disinfectants, have faced multiplied demands. In response to such demands, businesses have increased their production capacity and human resources, and many investors have shown their tendency towards making investments in this area. In addition, extra leisure time and time savings due to teleworking have augmented demands for some services such as education, games, and entertainment. While many products and services have encountered a decrease in demands in this era, many of the startups providing services and products in the fields of health, education, and entertainment have gained substantial profits. As declared by one of the interviewees, "During the pandemic, we had a wave of user inputs on our gaming platform, reflecting the increasing attractiveness of digital entertainment for people" (Case 10).

5.4.2   Opportunities and Threats Related to Startup Teams

In many startup teams, members were from different cities, which could make it difficult to bring team members together because of quarantines and restrictions in cities. One of the main reasons why team members might be from different cities is that the general idea of a startup normally comes up within university dormitories, training classes, schools, and academic contexts, and in many cases, students from different cities come together in these places (Muñoz-Bullon et al., 2015). Because of quarantines, many team members were unable to attend, which had led to the separation of team members and, in some cases, the collapse of the teams. As one interviewee put it, "The quarantine of the cities prevented one of the technical forces from being present, and we had to continue with a smaller capacity, which was really challenging" (Case 12). On the other hand, the collapse of the team has made startups to attract new teammates, wherein finding them in line with the objectives of the team and the spirit of the startup was also challenging (Forbes et al., 2006). In this regard, one of the interviewed respondents said that "The separation of our marketing personnel due to living in another city was one of the heaviest expenses we paid. It was hard to replace someone who could quickly adapt to the team spirit and align with other members, so we had to pay salaries, regardless of recruiting a teammate, which was not possible for us" (Case 13). In response to this constraint, startups have organized group meetings and activities in the form of online platforms, but this change has led to reductions in commitment among some team members and subsequently caused problems in the startup process. "The teleworking hindered the work process, and the members lost their commitment to work due to their distance from the work environment and lack of a teleworking culture, which was a real challenge by itself" (Case 4). Teleworking has further diminished interactions between team members, in turn giving rise to many interpersonal challenges along with team performance decline. As one of the interviewees reiterated, "Our communications moderated during teleworking, and all team members were not aware of each other's challenges, our motivation and performance also demoted" (Case 8). As stated in another interview, "I lost motivation to continue my job at the beginning of the pandemic and it took some time to adapt myself to the existing conditions in the market" (Case 7).

By imposing travel bans during COVID-19, much time was saved, giving team members the opportunity to spend time investing in their skills and developing their capabilities. For example, one of the founders said that "During this pandemic, due to the decrease in our in-person activities and the increase in free time, we held weekly training sessions with members, which helped broaden the team's skills and knowledge, and we could make the most of the time saved from teleworking" (Case 3). As well, the extra leisure time for the teams led to the growth of creativity and emergence of new ideas in order to generate innovative business models. In the words of one of the interviewees, "We had much free time during the pandemic, and this gave us the opportunity to spend time researching and developing to improve or establish business models suitable for the current situation" (Case 9).

5.4.3   Opportunities and Threats Related to Operational and Management Issues

Teleworking can cause problems for operations and activities of many startups. Some problems might be unavoidable and others might even originate from poor management (Salamzadeh & Dana, 2020). Compared with developed countries, teleworking is a new concept in Iran and the culture of teleworking has not still matured (Valmohammadi, 2012). Following the changes in the practice of teleworking, individuals' commitment to reduce and advance tasks has become unbalanced. In addition, founders or team leaders have faced challenges caused by agile team management. One of the main consequences of this issue is lower productivity of team members and generally startups. As maintained by one of the interviewees, "All through the COVID-19 pandemic, tasks became much more difficult to monitor, and we failed to reach the key performance indicators on time due to haphazardness of most activities" (Case 1). In addition, part of the startup activities dependent on government departments and agencies became disrupted and even decelerated as a result of reduced working hours and human resource capacity. This was mentioned in many of the interviews. For example, one of the interviewees said that "We spent much more time than normal to get the permission. We referred to many organizations, but they were not responsive, so we felt really tired" (Case 5).

Given the type of services, teleworking was not respected as a solution in many startups and caused the complete cessation of work process and sometimes the dissolution of such startups. One of the members our work process in the quote, "We needed the technical supervision of one of the members our work process, but this stage of work was stopped and we could not do anything because he was living in another city" (Case 12).

In contrast, many startup teams were able to adapt well to the conditions and to do away with the significant increase in their productivity. As one of the founders maintained, "Teleworking reduced wasted time and we could improve productivity much more, and consequently our work speed multiplied" (Case 13). Gradually, with the requirements of teleworking, startups adapted to the current situation, and over time, the complexity of this situation dwindled, and teleworking culture in the startup community enhanced. For example, one of the interviewees reiterated that "On the early days of COVID-19, the situation was very unfamiliar and knotty to me, and I could hardly focus on teleworking, but over time, I could adapt to this situation and realize that there were many benefits to this practice. I did not know about it. Now it has become difficult for me to work in person and there is no necessity to do it" (Case 6). The COVID-19 challenges and constraints arising from it have also posed threats to startups and have consequently diminished demands for their products and services. Following these threats, many startups have adjusted their business models to meet the new conditions and the needs in society, and some have even developed new business models. In this regard, one interviewee added that "With the advent of COVID-19 and subsequent changes in customer behavior and lifestyle, we decided to work on a new business model to meet the concerns and needs of all people in the pandemic era, so we introduced a new model for our business with the features to suit the current needs" (Case 4).

5.4.4 Opportunities and Threats Related to Financial and Economic Activities

The COVID-19 pandemic has led to numerous financial and economic problems for startups. In other words, the principal concerns in startups, i.e., financial challenges, have become much more highlighted (Kuckertz et al., 2020; Rowan & Galanakis,

2020). One of the most important challenges was no access to investor network. Attracting capital also became extremely difficult due to the closure of accelerators, venture capital funds, and the like. In this respect, one of the founders stated that "We were negotiating with an investor, unfortunately infected with COVID-19, and our consultations were canceled" (Case 8). In addition, changes in the needs and consumption patterns as well as customer demands have given rise to lower demands and thus a drop in startup revenues. At the same time, their fixed costs, such as those for workspace, human resources, etc., have remained stable. This reduction in startup revenues made it impossible for those who had borrowed from banks to repay their loans. "During this period, we faced a decrease in sales and revenues; unfortunately we also had problems paying off our loans" (Case 1). In general, the costs of doing research and development and those of changing business models of startups, increasing prices of transportation and raw materials, and many other such things have caused significant financial challenges to startups. "During COVID-19, goods and materials were not available in the market for a long time, and after they were at hand, they had a significant price increase due to higher customs costs" (Case 6).

On the other hand, the pandemic raised benefits and opportunities for startups, leading to their economic recovery. Among these opportunities was investors' willingness to invest in startups in the digital domain. "We could attract good capital during this period. I think the reason was the observation by investors in terms of increasing demands and people's cravings for the Internet and digital businesses" (Case 5). During COVID-19, government support institutions also granted facilities and exemptions to various startups, covering the costs and potential losses and providing an opportunity to empower and engage them in research and development for further innovation in business models. Accordingly, one of the startup founders said that "We could get credit facility from the Innovation and Prosperity Fund that saved us, so we could spend the budget on adding new features to our work" (Case 12). The COVID-19 pandemic also led to savings for fixed costs, including the costs of workspace in many startups. This was contributing for early-stage startups with limited financial resources. As declared by one of the interviewees, "The closure of the shared workspace and the teleworking of the team was repulsive for us at first, but after a while, as the personnel got used to this practice, we realized how much it could save us money" (Case 10).

5.5   Conclusion and Suggestions for Future Research

The COVID-19 pandemic is regarded as one of the biggest crises occurring in the past decades, facing human societies. It has had numerous positive and negative effects on different communities and has even dramatically led to lifestyle modifications in general. Economy and businesses have not spared the crisis and have undergone many positive and negative changes. Following adaptations in lifestyles, consumer needs and behavior have been completely modified and a paradigm shift has arisen in the market. Ventures, at different levels, have been struggling with different challenges, but the most sensitive ones have been early-stage startups. Given that such companies are in their infancy with no financial power, they may collapse due to a small crisis or they can make the most of the crisis as pivots shrink. For this purpose, many opportunities and threats have emerged for these startups, leading to their rise or fall. Given the changing consumer behavior from offline to online, digital startups have strongly grown during COVID-19 and they have also seized many opportunities. Accordingly, this study is an attempt to examine 13 different cases from early-stage digital startups through in-depth interviews with startup team members, to extract their experiences during the one-year pandemic, and to recognize prospects and challenges drawn against this category of businesses. To this end, thematic analysis was used and 31 startup team members received in-depth interviews, lasting 45–120 min. At least two members of each startup team were interviewed, so that the opportunities and threats for startups could be detected in different aspects. The target population recruited in this study included startups that had met the following four conditions, namely, (a) startups in their infancy life cycle or the so-called early-stage startups, (b) digital startups, (c) early-stage startups with less than two years of life cycle, and (d) startups whose target market was Iran.

After analyzing the interviews, 13 opportunities and 19 threats within four categories, i.e., market and marketing, startup team, operational and management issues, and financial and economic activities, were identified, as fully described in the previous section. Among the most important opportunities for startups in this period, highly mentioned in the interviews, were the reduced costs of workspace, accelerated work process, discovery of new users' needs in the digital space, and use of government support in the course of COVID-19. In addition, the most significant challenges facing startups were collapses due to separation of team members, reduction in team members' commitment, and lower speed of administrative and government-dependent processes, due to teleworking and decline in startup revenues.

This chapter focused on startups in their infancy life cycle, or in other words, early-stage startups as well as the ones working with digital and new customers based on their lifestyles. In addition to the opportunities and threats, this study was an attempt to give a comprehensive view on the strengths and weaknesses of the startup ecosystem in Iran as a developing country, as a good guide for other similar countries to make use of the results.

Given that a number of opportunities and threats identified here referred to startup ecosystem components such as accelerators, innovation centers, shared workspaces, and government institutions, there is a need to do further research on startup ecosystem conditions during COVID-19. In addition, the priorities and the importance of each opportunity and threat can be determined using different approaches, including Multi-Attribute Decision-Making (MSDM) and to plan on how to deal with them. Moreover, proactive risk management approaches such as Failure Mode and Effects Analysis (FMEA) can be utilized to identify risks in startups and to plan to manage them.

There are too many implications for startups at meso level and policymakers in macro levels. Policymakers need to provide support to overcome the Corona crisis, including lending, facilitating business startup rules, providing free business advice to startups, and helping startups enter the market. In addition, as a hedge fund, they can coinvest with accelerators invest in startups that have a high potential for success to successfully overcome the Corona crisis. Startups can also use the experiences expressed in this research in the language of other startups, and before starting their business, consider these issues and plan for them.

References

Almeida, F., Santos, J. D., & Monteiro, J. A. (2020). The challenges and opportunities in the digitalization of companies in a post-COVID-19 world. *IEEE Engineering Management Review, 48*(3), 97–103.

Amankwah-Amoah, J., Khan, Z., & Wood, G. (2020). COVID-19 and business failures: The paradoxes of experience, scale, and scope for theory and practice. *European Management Journal, 39*, 179–184.

Ateljevic, I. (2020). Transforming the (tourism) world for good and (re) generating the potential 'new normal'. *Tourism Geographies, 22*, 1–9.

Bacq, S., Geoghegan, W., Josefy, M., Stevenson, R., & Williams, T. A. (2020). The COVID-19 Virtual Idea Blitz: Marshaling social entrepreneurship to rapidly respond to urgent grand challenges. *Business Horizons, 63*(6), 705–723.

Beigi, M., Nayyeri, S., & Shirmohammadi, M. (2020). Driving a career in Tehran: Experiences of female internet taxi drivers. *Journal of Vocational Behavior, 116*, 103347.

Braun, V., & Clarke, V. (2006). Using thematic analysis in psychology. *Qualitative research in psychology, 3*(2), 77–101.

Castro, M. P., & Zermeño, M. G. G. (2020). Being an entrepreneur post-COVID-19–resilience in times of crisis: A systematic literature review. *Journal of Entrepreneurship in Emerging Economies, 13*, 721–746.

Chang, C. L., McAleer, M., & Ramos, V. (2020). The future of tourism in the COVID-19 era. *Advances in Decision Sciences, 24*(3), 218–230.

Elia, G., Margherita, A., & Passiante, G. (2020). Digital entrepreneurship ecosystem: How digital technologies and collective intelligence are reshaping the entrepreneurial process. *Technological Forecasting and Social Change, 150*, 119791.

Etemad, H. (2020). Managing uncertain consequences of a global crisis: SMEs encountering adversities, losses, and new opportunities. *Journal of international Entrepreneurship, 18*(2), 125–144.

Forbes, D. P., Borchert, P. S., Zellmer–Bruhn, M. E., & Sapienza, H. J. (2006). Entrepreneurial team formation: An exploration of new member addition. *Entrepreneurship Theory and Practice, 30*(2), 225–248.

Glaveckaitė, Ž. (2020). The development process of the right team in early stage start-ups. *Entrepreneurship and Sustainability Issues, 8*, 1041–1063.

Gössling, S., Scott, D., & Hall, C. M. (2020). Pandemics, tourism and global change: A rapid assessment of COVID-19. *Journal of Sustainable Tourism, 29*, 1–20.

Hasanat, M. W., Hoque, A., Shikha, F. A., Anwar, M., Hamid, A. B. A., & Tat, H. H. (2020). The impact of coronavirus (Covid-19) on E-business in Malaysia. *Asian Journal of Multidisciplinary Studies, 3*(1), 85–90.

Higgins-Desbiolles, F. (2020). The "war over tourism": Challenges to sustainable tourism in the tourism academy after COVID-19. *Journal of Sustainable Tourism, 29*, 1–19.

Indriastuti, M., & Fuad, K. (2020). *Impact of Covid-19 on digital transformation and sustainability in small and medium enterprises (SMEs): A conceptual framework.* Paper presented at the conference on complex, intelligent, and software intensive systems.

Iwuoha, V. C., & Aniche, E. T. (2020). Covid-19 lockdown and physical distancing policies are elitist: Towards an indigenous (Afro-centred) approach to containing the pandemic in suburban slums in Nigeria. *Local Environment, 25*(8), 631–640.

Kim, J., Kim, J., & Wang, Y. (2020). Uncertainty risks and strategic reaction of restaurant firms amid COVID-19: Evidence from China. *International Journal of Hospitality Management, 92*, 102752.

Kuckertz, A., Brändle, L., Gaudig, A., Hinderer, S., Reyes, C. A. M., Prochotta, A., et al. (2020). Startups in times of crisis–A rapid response to the COVID-19 pandemic. *Journal of Business Venturing Insights, 14*, e00169.

Lai, K. Y., Webster, C., Kumari, S., & Sarkar, C. (2020). The nature of cities and the Covid-19 pandemic. *Current Opinion in Environmental Sustainability, 46*, 27–31.

Liew, V. K.-S. (2020). The effect of novel coronavirus pandemic on tourism share prices. *Journal of Tourism Futures.* https://doi.org/10.1108/JTF-03-2020-0045

Marmer, M., Herrmann, B. L., Dogrultan, E., Berman, R., Eesley, C., & Blank, S. (2011). Startup genome report extra: Premature scaling. *Startup Genome, 10*, 1–56.

Muñoz-Bullon, F., Sanchez-Bueno, M. J., & Vos-Saz, A. (2015). Startup team contributions and new firm creation: The role of founding team experience. *Entrepreneurship & Regional Development, 27*(1–2), 80–105.

Papadopoulos, T., Baltas, K. N., & Balta, M. E. (2020). The use of digital technologies by small and medium enterprises during COVID-19: Implications for theory and practice. *International Journal of Information Management, 55*, 102192.

Rowan, N. J., & Galanakis, C. M. (2020). Unlocking challenges and opportunities presented by COVID-19 pandemic for cross-cutting disruption in agri-food and green deal innovations: Quo Vadis? *Science of the Total Environment, 748*, 141362.

Salamzadeh, A., & Dana, L. P. (2020). The coronavirus (COVID-19) pandemic: Challenges among Iranian startups. *Journal of Small Business & Entrepreneurship, 33*, 1–24.

Soto-Acosta, P. (2020). COVID-19 pandemic: Shifting digital transformation to a high-speed gear. *Information Systems Management, 37*(4), 260–266.

Sperindé, S., & Nguyen-Duc, A. (2020). Fostering open innovation in coworking spaces: A study of Norwegian startups. In *Fundamentals of software startups* (pp. 161–178). Springer.

Tran, L. T. T. (2020). Managing the effectiveness of e-commerce platforms in a pandemic. *Journal of Retailing and Consumer Services, 58*, 102287.

Valmohammadi, C. (2012). Investigating the perceptions of Iranian employees on teleworking. *Industrial and commercial Training.*

Wells, P., Abouarghoub, W., Pettit, S., & Beresford, A. (2020). A socio-technical transitions perspective for assessing future sustainability following the COVID-19 pandemic. *Sustainability: Science, Practice and Policy, 16*(1), 29–36.

Wenzel, M., Stanske, S., & Lieberman, M. B. (2020). Strategic responses to crisis. *Strategic Management Journal, 41*(7/18).

Winston, A. (2020). Is the COVID-19 outbreak a black swan or the new normal. *MIT Sloan Management Review, 16*, 154–173.

Ximenes, B. H., Alves, I. N., & Araújo, C. C. (2015). Software project management combining agile, lean startup and design thinking. In *Design, user experience, and usability: Design discourse* (pp. 356–367). Springer.

Yang, Y., Liu, H., & Chen, X. (2020). COVID-19 and restaurant demand: Early effects of the pandemic and stay-at-home orders. *International Journal of Contemporary Hospitality Management, 13*, 3809–3834.

Chapter 6
Developments and Changes in Organization and Management Research in the Post-COVID-19 Era: A Foundationalist Approach

Adel Azar and Mahdi Azizi

6.1 Introduction

Management science, which today, like all other aspects of human life, is facing the coronavirus disease 2019 (COVID-19) crisis, has experienced great changes and challenges during its lifetime. If we consider the emergence of management knowledge from the Industrial Revolution and Adam Smith's theory of division of labor (Jang et al., 2011), or more than a century later, consider Frederick Taylor's School of Scientific Management as the starting point of management knowledge (Taylor, 1911), we can see several crises and challenges that caused foundational changes in management knowledge. For example, paying more attention to human capital as a human being, following the human problems in the factories of the Industrial Revolution era, is one of the first and most famous of these challenges, which caused a paradigm shift in management knowledge (Franke & Kaul, 1978). Confrontation of management knowledge with this crisis caused the growth and development of one of the important areas of management: Human Capital Management. Similarly, other crises can be considered that have led to the growth and expansion of management knowledge.

This chapter aims to investigate the effects of the COVID-19 crisis on management knowledge and identify the necessary changes for surviving in the post-COVID-19 period. As official researches and reports from relevant international organizations acknowledge, the extent and depth of the COVID-19 crisis is such that it has affected various areas of human life at all levels (Greig, 2020). Accordingly, in this chapter, based on a foundational view to the structure of management

A. Azar (✉) · M. Azizi
Faculty of Management and Economics, Tarbiat Modares University, Tehran, Iran
e-mail: Azara@modares.ac.ir; Mahdi.azizi@modares.ac.ir

© The Author(s), under exclusive license to Springer Nature Switzerland AG 2022
N. Faghih, A. Forouharfar (eds.), *Socioeconomic Dynamics of the COVID-19 Crisis*, Contributions to Economics, https://doi.org/10.1007/978-3-030-89996-7_6

knowledge,[1] we have tried to consider the effects of the COVID-19 crisis on different aspects of management knowledge and managerial actions and practices.

To this end, we continue the discussion in three sections. In the first section, we examine the effects of the COVID-19 pandemic on the foundational and philosophical theories of management. In the second part, by focusing on various management disciplines, we examine the effects of the pandemic on a more practical level. In the third part of the discussion, this chapter attempts to focus on the prescriptive theories of management that deals with the crisis and running organizations during the COVID-19 period. In addition to reviewing some prescriptive theories, we try to identify different currents in this area.

In the following section, the discussion is continued by focusing on the theoretical foundations of management and the changes resulting from the crisis on this basis.

6.2 Methodology

In this chapter, the epistemological foundationalism approach is used to systematically investigate the effects of the COVID-19 pandemic on management. A brief overview of this approach illustrates the benefits and results it brings to this chapter.

It is clear that, in order to explain epistemological foundationalism, we first need to look at epistemology. However, foundationalism is an approach at the heart of epistemology. The term "epistemology" comes from the Greek words "episteme" and "logos." "Episteme" can be translated as "knowledge" or "understanding" or "acquaintance," while "logos" can be translated as "account" or "argument" or "reason" (Steup & Ram, 2020). Epistemology is as old as the history of philosophy and covers a variety of subjects, but in all its forms, it seeks to understand one or another kind of cognitive success. Therefore, justification is an essential element of epistemology (Engel, 1992). Epistemological foundationalism is in fact a theory about the structure of justification (Dirilen-Gumus, 2011).

Epistemological foundationalism is based on the important principle that knowledge is layered and has a core and a shell. In other words, according to foundationalism, our justified beliefs are structured like a building: they are divided into a foundation and a superstructure, the latter resting upon the former. Beliefs belonging to the foundation are *basic*. Beliefs belonging to the superstructure are *non-basic* and receive justification from the justified beliefs in the foundation (Steup & Ram, 2020).

Foundationalism has been present in various sciences. For the first time, Euclid of Alexandria, whose unparalleled geometry is still visible, applied this idea and founded Euclidean geometry (Rescher, 1975). The importance of Euclidean

---

[1] Foundationalism is an appropriate research strategy when examining the profound and far-reaching effects of a phenomenon on the dimensions of a knowledge (Azizi et al., 2017) – more details in research methodology.

geometry is that, in an attractive and beautiful way, all its problems and teachings go back to a few limited principles, which has made this geometry uniquely rich and strong. Foundationalism has been applied to other sciences – from medicine to philosophy and politics (Little et al., 2012). This approach also has a special place in the organization and management studies (Thomas & Hatchuel, 2009).

The systematic view that foundationalism provides of management knowledge is particularly useful to the purpose of the present study. When we see management knowledge as a building (or a tree), we can better understand the direct and indirect effects of the COVID-19 crisis on it.

Although different steps have been proposed for foundationalism (Haller, 1988), in this study, the main doctrine of foundationalism, namely, the separation of superstructure from infrastructure and attention to the effects of infrastructure on superstructure, has been the research strategy.

6.3 Theoretical Foundations of Organization and Management that Have Changed Due to COVID-19 Crisis

Although the foundation level as the root of any theory and practice had been less subjected to change, major crises such as the COVID-91 crisis can penetrate to this level as well. However, the changes made at this level will often be minor, even so, it should be noted that due to the infrastructural nature of this level, the smallest changes in it would be the source of great changes and developments in the upper levels of theories and techniques. In this regard, we discuss three schools of thought in management knowledge: utilitarianism, social responsibility, and pragmatism.

6.3.1 Utilitarianism as a Basis for Management

Utilitarianism is recognized and accepted as the main foundation of management theories (Martin, 2006). This theory is one of the most important schools in the philosophy of ethics and political philosophy. Although there are many philosophical debates about what utilitarianism is, the simplest definition of the concept of utilitarianism in management is maximizing the utility (benefits) for the majority of people. Although utilitarianism has different characteristics, it is the *consequentialist* nature of this school that has made it popular in the management science. Accordingly, utilitarianism is considered as the main basis of management theories (Martin, 2006). For example, cost-benefit analysis as the practical aspect of utilitarianism is the soul of many management tools and techniques in various fields (Sagden & Williams, 1978).

In this regard, the COVID-19 crisis has posed a fundamental challenge to utilitarianism by disrupting the *consequentialism* feature of utilitarian techniques. In explanation, utilitarianism in management, using its various tools, establishes a relationship between each management action and its direct and indirect effects on its usability, profitability, and beneficially (i.e., it's utility). After the emergence of the COVID-19, the pandemic has caused many problems and difficulties in establishing such a relationship. More precisely, the pandemic has given rise to the causes and factors that were often overlooked in cost-benefit analysis to make these analyses more effective, simple, and practical. This means that managers can no longer set boundaries for their cost-benefit causal loops. As a result, cost-benefit analyses became ineffective in practice (Azizi et al., 2020).

On the other hand, it is clear that the principle of utilitarianism will be weakened without tools for the cost-benefit analysis. Hence, utilitarianism in the post-COVID-19 era needs to find deeper and more multifaceted analytical tools.

It seems that, in the post-COVID-19 era, some factors that traditionally have been overlooked in utilitarian analysis will find their place in this analytical system. Some of these areas are in a way that will be in conflict with the basic principles of utilitarianism, including the nature of this school, which is directly based on the originality of profit maximization approach. Paying attention to emotions and feelings, spirituality, and ethics can be considered as the most important of these areas.

It is clear that this will pose a new and important challenge for researchers in management philosophy. It is not easy to present theories that incorporate both the principles of utilitarianism and these immaterial realms. However, we are optimistic; the most important innovations always arise from facing the most difficult predicaments.

6.3.2 Social Responsibility as the Basis of Management

Social responsibility is considered as another theoretical basis of management (Ghaffari, 2010). In addition, in the field of action and implementation, many organizations consider social responsibility as the reason and basis for many of their actions.

Social responsibility as the basis of management has its own complexities. On the one hand, this is a very general topic and various scientific disciplines are involved, and, on the other hand, its tremendous importance is broader than the organizational level. As a result, focusing on social responsibility at the organizational level and from the perspective of managers is difficult and complex for most managers, especially managers of large economic and industrial enterprises.

Social responsibility is the ideological notion that organizations should not behave unethically or function amorally and should aim (instead) to deliberately contribute to the welfare of society or societies – comprised of various communities and stakeholders – that they operate in and interact with (Planken, 2013). In other words, social responsibility is a set of duties and responsibilities that an organization should perform in order to care, maintain, and help the community. However, the tasks performed in practice based on social responsibility are limited. The social responsibility approach generally includes tasks such as not polluting, not discriminating in employment, and informing the consumer about the quality of products (Fleming, 2002).

Nevertheless, as we could see in practice in the pre-COVID-19 world, social responsibility is marginalized in most organizations towards utilitarianism and cannot lead the organization in critical dilemmas. Further analysis shows that, in fact, social responsibility is exercised only to the extent that it satisfies the environmental communities of each organization (Fleming, 2012). This situation gradually increases the tendency to show and pretend social responsibility actions, instead of the actual actions. In this regard, in many cases, with the sensitization and vitality of the conditions of organizations, the practice of social responsibility is lost or limited (Taket & White, 2000).

However, amid COVID-19 crisis, the practice of social responsibility has fundamentally changed. With the outbreak of the coronavirus, the importance of social responsibility was given much attention, and demands were made from people, governments, and organizations in this regard (Business Human Rights Report, 2020). In the meantime, what was expected of many organizations under the heading of social responsibility was beyond the capabilities of many of them.

The demands made on organizations under the banner of social responsibility are significant; in an intensive period, many organizations were asked: allocate paid leave for all staff, provide health protection and prevention items to employees, keep their necessary production and services, and even produce new and different goods (Business Human Rights Report, 2020).

As expected, most organizations failed to live up to these expectations and even some of their legal duties in this regard (Susser & Tyson, 2020). This result was completely natural. None of these organizations was created to pay special attention to social responsibility. Social responsibility had only a ceremonial aspect for these organizations. As a result, the credibility and social capital of many organizations faced a serious crisis.

In this regard, it seems that the position of this theoretical basis will change in the post-COVID-19 era. In the future, social responsibility must be presented as a genuine and permanent basis of management decisions and actions and be effective in all decisions of each firm. This change is impossible in the current situation, because such a position for social responsibility is in conflict with the basis of utilitarianism. Fortunately, suggestions for correcting the basis of utilitarianism, including attention to spirituality and emotions, can play an effective role in reducing this conflict.

6.3.3   Pragmatism as the Basis of Management

Many management thinkers consider pragmatism as an inseparable part of *Managerialism* school (Hendry, 2013).[2] Although pragmatism, as one of the most important schools in the philosophy of ethics and politics, embraces complex philosophical issues, in management, a simple reading of pragmatism is accepted: giving originality to action and the result of work as a sign of truth and correctness.

However, pragmatism has also been directly and indirectly affected by the COVID-19 crisis. On the one hand, due to changes in other elements, including the two basic theories of management, namely, *utilitarianism* and *social responsibility*, the third basic principle, *pragmatism*, will inevitably change. For example, paying more attention to social responsibility, or opening the door to spirituality, emotions, and feelings to cost-benefit analysis, will transform the position of pragmatism.

The changes imposed by the COVID-19 crisis on the pragmatism base of organization and management are also noteworthy. In general, with the disruption of temporal and spatial boundaries of causality due to the COVID-19 crisis, the possibility of assessing the correctness of an action based on its results has been seriously challenged, and this means the core of pragmatic thinking in management has faced difficulties.

Nevertheless, the effects of the COVID-19 crisis on pragmatism as a theoretical base of management can also be examined in more detail. For example, one of the most important and practical examples of the introduction of pragmatism into management theories is the literature of *satisficing* decision-making (Bradley, 2015). In fact, Herbert Simon, the inventor of the theory of *satisficing* decision-making, has tried to formulate this theory based on pragmatism (Velupillai, 2016). As we know, the theory of satisficing decision-making states that, by accepting bounded rationality, since it is not possible to examine all the factors and elements involved in each issue, we can consider only partially and satisfactorily and then make our decision. However, managers who remember the experience of the COVID-19 crisis and the many effects that issues have had on their businesses maybe never be satisfied again.

6.4   Organizational Areas Affected by the COVID-19 Crisis

In the previous section, we discussed the developments and changes caused by the COVID-19 crisis on the management philosophical foundations. Using this achievement, in this section, we can examine the developments of the COVID-19 crisis on different dimensions of the organizational theories as well as the functional managerial areas. In each part, we will try to take into account the developments that have

---

[2] "The philosophy or practice of conducting the affairs of an organized group (as a nation) by planning and direction by professional managers" (Merriam-Webster's Dictionary). The most prominent feature of this school is its greater emphasis on means than ends (Hendry, 2013).

taken place directly due to the COVID-19 crisis, as well as the changes that have resulted from the change in the philosophical foundations (which we discussed in the previous section).

6.4.1 Changes in the Organizational Culture

The organizational culture is one of the most complex areas of the organization, which is full of covert and indirect effects on other dimensions and activities of the organization. The effects of the COVID-19 crisis on the organizational culture have taken shape at several different levels. The simplest and clearest level is simple interactive actions in the workplace such as shaking hands or hugging, distance when talking, etc. (Friedman & Westring, 2020).

It is clear that these formalities have completely changed because of the COVID-19 crisis. Nevertheless, in order to analyze the changes in the organizational culture caused by the COVID-19 crisis from the managerial view, it is necessary to pay more attention to the deeper dimensions of the problem.

For this purpose, we are going to study the following six dichotomous dimensions of the organizational culture:

- Process oriented vs. results oriented
- Job oriented vs. employee oriented
- Professional vs. parochial
- Open systems vs. closed systems
- Tight vs. loose control
- Pragmatic vs. normative (Hofstede, 1991)

Researchers in this field of management can identify the effects of the COVID-19 crisis on each of these six dimensions through field research. However, regardless of the organizational culture and its quality, the COVID-19 crisis has had a significant impact on the strength of organizational culture.

By changes of communication patterns in the organization – such as the replacement of virtual communication instead of face-to-face communication in many cases, the reduction of informal groups of conversations in the organization, etc. – many sources of nurturing and strengthening organizational culture have diminished. This has made the organizational culture more in need of attention. It seems that focusing on designing formal procedures for training and conveying organizational stories and values can compensate for the weakness in the informal procedures mentioned. However, this issue in the future will attract a large amount of researches.

Cultural values are another potential topic that post-COVID-19 researches will focus on it. After the COVID-19 crisis, many core values in the organizational culture will lose their place. In contrast, many new concepts will emerge as new values in the organizational culture. Researchers in this field should note that the root of these changes is in the philosophical foundations that we examined in the previous section.

6.4.2   Changes in the Organizational Structures

Although organizational structure is a relatively stable area of management and successive changes in this area are by no means desirable, lively, active, and flexible structures can respond to almost every change in the environment. In fact, here we are dealing with one of the proverbs (a nearly paradoxical spectrum) of organization theory and management, in which *Herbert Simon* has well explained his position with (Simon, 1946): Structures must respond to changes in the elements that affect the organizational structure (which includes a wide range of elements from the environment, the organizational culture, the work processes, etc.) while maintaining their stability.

This has caused the COVID-19 crisis to create many challenges in terms of organizational structure. On the one hand, the COVID-19 crisis has changed almost all the elements that affect how the organizational structure works; therefore, an immediate change in the organizational structure of many organizations becomes necessary and inevitable.

On the other hand, the pressures of the COVID-19 crisis had made the conditions of many organizations so difficult that they could not address the issues of organizational restructuring. As the COVID-19 pandemic gets longer, the situation of organizations gets aggravated.

In addition, the COVID-19 crisis has made agility, flexibility, and multitasking more necessary than ever. The main challenge is that the acquisition of each of the features creates huge costs for the organization, and with the limitations and pressures of the COVID-19 crisis, economic efficiency has become more and more necessary for the organizations.

Of course, we know that this challenge is not an unprecedented one. Organizations often require agility and flexibility, in the face of economic constraints. So, what is so special about the current COVID-19 crisis with respect to the organizations?

As an explanation, the COVID-19 crisis, in addition to exacerbating the situation, has also made maladjusted organizational structure epidemic: Many organizations had advanced for years with their stable structures based on bureaucracy and adhocracy, and before the COVID-19 pandemic, they did not feel any need to move towards more multitasking potentiality, agile, and so on. The main challenge has also occurred for these organizations.

It seems that the post-COVID-19 research in this field is going to be focused on the following topics: flexibility of organizational structure, reducing the time and cost of organizational restructuring, and facilitating communication in the organizational structure.

Therefore, organizational structure researchers must strive to find ways for large industries in addition to emerging businesses, because in the post-COVID-19 world, these industries must also be able to utilize the capabilities of agile, flexible, and multitasking structures.

6.4.3 Changes in the Inter-/ Intra-Organizational Communications

Communication within and between organizations has also been severely affected by the COVID-19 crisis. The disruption of previous communication patterns and networks because of this crisis has made it necessary to pay special attention to continuous communication with employees, partners, consultants, shareholders, and all stakeholders. Some experts in this field have suggested that in this situation it is necessary to form a cohesive team to actively communicate with all stakeholders at the center of the organization (Argenti, 2020).

Moreover, it should be noted that communication problems caused by the COVID-19 crisis are not limited to the quarantine period. Social distancing, in turn, has caused numerous problems in intra-organizational communications. Since no communication can replace informal face-to-face communication (Nardi & Whittaker, 2002), social distancing has also disrupted organizational communication in this regard.

On the other hand, these issues and problems also exist in inter-organizational communication. In addition, with increasing stress and ambiguity, which is one of the main complications of the COVID-19 crisis, maintaining inter-organizational communication (including maintaining relationships with customers and suppliers) becomes doubly difficult.

Accordingly, post-COVID-19 researches should focus on communication patterns in the intra-organization and inter-organizational environment. Clearly, these studies will be deeply related to the studies of the organizational culture and organizational structure. Concurrently, research in the abovementioned three areas (culture, structure, and communications) can create a flow of new research in management. However, the COVID-19 crisis will create new currents in management science, which will be addressed in the next section.

6.4.4 Changes in the Business Processes and Technologies

Work processes and technologies are among the most changing areas in the organizational arena, so it is not surprising that this area has been completely transformed by the COVID-19 crisis.

The first major change by the COVID-19 crisis in this area is the weighting of the scales in favor of automation. After the popularity of automation in the past decades, there has been a lot of criticism about it in recent years. However, the COVID-19 crisis once again sidelined all the criticisms of automation based on employment, the environment, and so on.

In this area, management thinkers should note that the need for automation in the COVID-19 period should not cause to ignore the fundamental drawbacks of this approach. Instead, by developing automated processes and considering other criteria such as environment and employment, automation can be developed in a balanced way.

Furthermore, communication technologies were one of the most important tools considered in the COVID-19 period. Online and virtual communications were introduced not only in many work communications in organizations but also in various types of communications in family as well as personal, educational, religious domains, a few examples, as a safe alternative to face-to-face communication during the COVID-19 period.

However, it is clear that a variety of organizational communication systems were previously designed and widely used. But it should be noted that these systems before the COVID-19 pandemic have always been a complement to face-to-face communication, not a substitute.

Along with technologies, business processes have also undergone extensive changes. The COVID-19 crisis has made it impossible to do much with previous processes. In this regard, each business must find a replacement for its traditional work systems.

Meanwhile, the issue of telecommuting, which is considered as the first option to continue the workflow in the COVID-19 period, has caused many problems and challenges at the organizational level. Thus, future researches in this field will address infrastructure challenges in telecommuting, monitoring and controlling processes, motivation, information protection, and education in telecommuting, which have been major telecommuting challenges during the COVID-19 crisis (Neeley & Beard, 2020).

6.4.5 Changes in the Managerial Decision-Making

Decision-making is considered as the most important and most frequent activity of managers, in which a wide range of management researches have tried to shed light on all its dark dimensions, factors, and aspects. Decision-making is also known as the root of many other important and popular areas of management, including strategy formulation (Mintzberg & Waters, 1990), and has a decisive place in the success or failure of any organization.

The COVID-19 crisis has changed this important field at various levels, including decision-making process, decision-making methodologies and its techniques, etc., which are going to be addressed in separate works in the future (Ali-Ahmadi Jeshfaghn, 2020).

Given the various challenges that have been posed to decision-making in the COVID-19 crisis, it seems that researchers in this field, after this experience, are designing and developing more democratic and participatory decision-making methods. Focusing on the emotions and feelings in decision-making, prioritizing human status rather than maximizing profits in decision-making, and the role of spirituality in decision-making will be the most important values for decision-making in the post-COVID-19 era.

6.4.6 Changes in the Organizational Strategies

It is clear that organizational strategies have a long-term impact on the future of any organization. Thus, if the COVID-19 crisis has also changed organizational strategies, it indicates that the crisis is not only a temporary situation for the theories of organization and management, but has marked a new season for organizations.

As mentioned previously when discussing the field of decision-making, theoretically decision-making should be considered as the root of the strategy formulation (Mintzberg & Waters, 1990). Based on this, it can be concluded that the field of strategy is not immune from the COVID-19 crisis.

One of the strategic trends that has been most affected by the COVID-19 crisis was the desire and strategic move of the organizations towards globalization. There is almost no organization that does not pursue this strategy, and globalization was a goal for all successful organizations (before the COVID-19 crisis, of course).

An important point to consider in relation to this strategy is its full alignment with the principle of cost-benefit analysis (Hitt et al., 2020). But, why has the COVID-19 crisis prepared large organizations to say goodbye to globalization strategy?

It is clear that in the post-COVID-19 era, the strategy of globalization is no longer in line with the principles of cost-benefit analysis as in the past (Gray, 2020). The COVID-19 crisis has shown that globalization drastically increases supply and distribution risks and makes it very difficult to have a deep and lasting relationship with customers and suppliers, which is a prerequisite for resilience in the face of major crises.

This challenge is another example of the effects of the three pillars of management in action: *utilitarianism*, *pragmatism,* and *social responsibility*. Therefore, researchers in the field of strategy in the post-COVID-19 world need to redefine new ideal models for successful organizations.

6.4.7 Changes in the Supply Chain Management

Supply chain management has been one of the most important challenges for organizations during the COVID-19 crisis, which has caused many problems for important factories all around the world and became a new and pervasive challenge (Haren & Simchi-Levi, 2020). This has not been limited to quarantines or factories that require large quantities of perishable raw materials and has covered almost all industry groups (Linton & Vakil, 2020).

Significant research has been done in this area. Many organizations were redesigning their supply chains at the height of the COVID-19 crisis. Management consultants' advice to these organizations is clear: redesign with second sources to back up capacity for supply and redesign to locally sources (Rice Jr., 2020).

However, implementing these recommendations has been particularly challenging for many organizations. As we saw in the previous sections, techniques such as the strategy of globalization and cost-benefit analysis have led organizations to have suppliers and customers from all over the world, shift their manufacturing sectors to countries with cheap labor and so on. Clearly, creating a secure and stable supply chain in such a situation is not easy.

The supply chain was one of the biggest challenges for organizations during the COVID-19 crisis. Therefore, it should be expected that a large volume of research with new approaches in this field would emerge, approaches that, instead of prioritizing cost reduction, prioritize supply chain stability.

6.4.8   Changes in the Quality Management

Quality is one of the basic concepts in management that has had a strong presence in all areas of management – both in the production and services. Although no external factor can undermine the importance of quality in management knowledge and practice, as the COVID-19 crisis has affected our quality of life, the quality of workforce efficiency, product production, and service delivery by organizations have been affected by this crisis (Tarki et al., 2020).

On the other hand, a careful and specialized view on quality management makes it clear that this area has also been deeply affected by the COVID-19 crisis. It should be noted that more up-to-date approaches to quality management, instead of focusing on output, should focus on the process of production or services and consider management in general and more specifically quality measurement at this stage (Li et al., 2019). Accordingly, the COVID-19 crisis has also affected quality management by making sweeping changes in work processes.

Another quality-related issue is the quality of goods, elements, and factors of production and service delivery; this area is not also immune to the effects of the COVID-19 crisis. As will be discussed in detail in the next section, in many industries, including the healthcare industry, labors has been widely affected by the COVID-19 crisis (Caligiuri et al., 2020). On the other hand, the raw materials of production are often the product of other factories and as a result are completely affected by this crisis.

Researchers in the field of quality management after experiencing the COVID-19 crisis seem to focus extensively on the new techniques for sustainability of quality.

It is clear that this is directly related to the supply chain (as an assurance for quality of *input*) and human resource management (as an assurance for quality of *process*). We discussed the first issue in the previous section, and in the next section, we will address the issue of human resource management.

6.4.9   Changes in the Human Resource Management

Just as the COVID-19 crisis has changed various aspects of human life, so is the organizational arena; human capital has undergone the most changes caused by the COVID-19 pandemic. The field of human resource management has undergone changes in various dimensions and aspects, which in some cases have been the source of foundational changes in other areas of management (Caligiuri et al., 2020). Here are some of these areas:

- **Changes in the Necessary Conditions and Qualifications for Obtaining Jobs**

    With the change in technology and methods of work, changes of the patterns of communication and organization at such conditions as well as the evaluation criteria of qualification and competencies to get jobs have also changed.

    From one perspective, it can be said that with the increasing use of virtual communication technologies, the importance of ability to use these technologies has become more important. On the other hand, it should be noted that since communication and coordination problems culminated in the COVID-19 crisis, it is better to have a workforce that is skilled in this area.

    For this purpose, it is necessary to consider communication capabilities as a priority criterion in the conditions and competencies of jobs descriptions and to be used in the selection and recruitment of human resources.

- **The Need for the New Processes to Control Human Resources**

    With changing technologies and work processes, including the increasing use of *teleworking*, there is a need for new ways to supervise human resources. During the COVID-19 crisis, most of the organizations' human resources spend all or part of their working hours telecommuting wherever possible. Therefore, the dominant control mechanism in organizations must be redesigned based on these conditions.

    In this area, there is a variety of online tools to supervise human resources working remotely. In the meantime, before choosing one of these online tools, managers should consider that direct and intense control would always increase the stress level of the human resources (Lu et al., 1999), and therefore prescribing it during the COVID-19 crisis period is not true in any way.

- **The Need for the New Processes to Motivate and Support Human Resources**

    It is clear that as business conditions change, motivation and human resource support also need to be changed. In general, as working conditions become more difficult, the need for motivation and support for human resources increases, and the COVID-19 crisis is no exception.

    However, it should be noted that some major crises, in addition to changing the amount and quantity of need for support and motivation, also change the quality and manner of need for support and motivation. The COVID-19 crisis also requires a change in the way and quality of motivation and support of human resources, because it poses a serious threat to the health of human resources.

Prior to the COVID-19 crisis, the role of ethics and spirituality in motivating human resources was underestimated (Guillén et al., 2015). Given the threats to the health and safety of human resources during the COVID-19 crisis, increasing traditional motivation and financial support is by no means sufficient to deal with the crisis. Accordingly, it seems that researchers in this field should look for new ways of motivating and supporting human resources, which in addition to financial support have other types of supports.

On the one hand, organizations must provide adequate support for employee safety and health. Many researchers have proposed significant strategies in this regard by emphasizing the capabilities of cyberspace and automation technologies (de Caro et al., 2020). On the other hand, especially in terms of motivation, organizations should also include spiritual issues in this area.

- **Organizational Justice**

The COVID-19 crisis has once again shown that organizational justice suffers greatly. During the quarantine period, with social distancing and the rise of telecommuting, research has shown that telecommuting will be more difficult for you if you are woman or black or in racial minority (Roberts & McCluney, 2020). This is an example of unfair organizational standards and practices.

These unfair practices are other examples that show that managerial research needs a social transformation (Bapuji et al., 2020a, b).

It should be noted that all of the above are just a few examples of the effects of the COVID-19 crisis on human resource management. However, COVID-19 is a pandemic human disease and naturally affects labor force more than anything else in the organization.

In the next section, we will look at the last, but not the least area, affected by the COVID-19 crisis: leadership.

6.4.10   Leadership in the Post-Coronavirus Age

In the previous sections, we looked at the developments that the COVID-19 crisis has brought to each of the organizational areas. All of this makes the leadership role more vital in this era. In general, organizations feel the real need for leadership when they are in critical days. The COVID-19 crisis is a perfect example of these critical days.

Although specific and predictable activities for leadership cannot normally be considered, the pressure on organizational leaders during the COVID-19 crisis has prompted researchers to make clear executive proposals for the organizational leaders in this era. Suggestions are as follows: paying more attention to the needs of employees and empathizing with them, daily tracking on supply chain, striving to build employee mental preparedness for any change, updating intelligence on a daily basis, using experts and forecasts carefully, constantly reframing your understanding of what's happening (Reeves et al., 2020b), and, finally, paying attention to the online technologies (Lin, 2020).

Clearly, the main issue is the art of leaders in implementing these points. Focusing on these recommendations shows that organizations are in dire need of multidisciplinary leaders. Therefore, training multidisciplinary leaders is an issue that can attract a lot of attention in the post-COVID-19 world.

6.5   Three General Recommendations

In the previous section, we looked at the most important changes that the COVID-19 crisis has brought to various areas of management. In this section, we want to take a look at the most important recommendations made by management thinkers in the face of this crisis.

The following are three main categories that include most the suggestions of management thinkers to deal with the COVID-19 crisis:

6.5.1   *Technology*

The first solution proposed by the experts in the face of the COVID-19 crisis was to use the capabilities of technology. The use of technology to deal with the COVID-19 crisis is divided into three general categories, each of which was intended to address one of the major problems of organizations:

- *Robotic technologies* to reduce production problems and other physical problems.
- *Communication technologies* and cyberspace to reduce problems in communication, monitoring, telecommuting, etc.
- *Soft technologies*, to adapt the mechanisms of the organization to the new conditions.

It is clear that all three of these approaches were widely used before the COVID-19 pandemic. Nevertheless, what emerged as a major prescription in the COVID-19 era was the design of different ways to expand the use of these technologies. For example: How to transfer the meetings that were previously held face to face to the cyberspace? How to automate more production lines and make them independent of labor? How to shift more staffing works to software and automation instead of labors and reducing the need for human resources in this area? How to make changes to the strategy or decision-making process that are more in line with the conditions of social distancing (and the reduction of informal meetings as one of the main sources for this)?

These and other similar questions are the nature of a series of studies that are going to find solutions to the COVID-19 crisis in the use of technology (Corrêa, 2020). As it is clear from the above questions, this type of research is not limited to specific areas of management and can be applied in different areas of management and organization.

It should also be noted that these prescriptions do not usually fit into the in-depth and revolutionary research of management. As we have mentioned, the use of technology in different sectors and for different needs of organizations is not a new issue, and what has been proposed here by management thinkers is only an emphasis on the previous principles.

However, understanding the currents of research resulting from the COVID-19 crisis is an important issue that requires full attention, so we have addressed this important issue in the conclusion section. Before that, we need to consider two other categories of management prescriptions in the face of the COVID-19 crisis.

6.5.2   More Focus on Social Responsibility

As mentioned earlier, social responsibility has been emphasized seriously as one of the main expectations of organizations during the COVID-19 era. Governments, nongovernmental organizations, and the public sector have demanded many actions from organizations under the heading of social responsibility. In contrast, most organizations failed to meet these expectations.

In this regard, management researchers have also participated in this issue in two ways. On the one hand, like most people and the governments, management theorists also point to the social responsibility of organizations to solve various problems amid the COVID-19 crisis. Employees who could not go to work, goods that should not be priced, products that should be produced more than usual capacity, etc. were all left to the social responsibility of organizations (Bapuji et al., 2020a, b).

On the other hand, paying attention to social responsibility to reduce the inability of organizations to act on its requirements is another area of concern for management researchers in this regard. In this area, there are several works in different fields of management that have introduced a way to deal with various organizational and managerial problems in changing the level of social responsibility (de Bakker et al., 2020). In the previous sections, we came across several examples in this regard.

However, social responsibility is one of the main concepts that management thinkers use to address the challenges posed by the COVID-19 crisis. Of course, this concept in many cases approaches the position of morality and spirituality and in some points overlaps with it. Therefore, in the next section, as the third basic prescription of managerial research in the face of the COVID-19 crisis, we will address the role of ethics and spirituality.

6.5.3   Ethics and Spirituality

Terrible crises have always been a reminder of the importance of morality and spirituality in societies. The COVID-19 crisis is no exception. As we have discussed in previous sections, ethics and spirituality have been introduced as an important solution to various problems caused by the COVID-19 crisis in various organizational areas such as motivation and support of human resources (Rutten & Becker, 2020), social responsibility (Chatterji, 2020), etc.

Meanwhile, the foundational theories of management and organization, which we discussed in the first part of this chapter, are most prone to spirituality and ethics. As we have seen, *utilitarianism*, as one of the main foundations of management and organization, has become increasingly spiritual in the face of the COVID-19 crisis: i.e., cost-benefit analyses, utilitarian criteria, and examples of utility all seriously tended to spirituality.

In this regard, considering the impact of theoretical and philosophical foundations in other areas of management, and by following the tendency of these theoretical foundations to spirituality, we can expect the tendency of other areas of management to ethics and spirituality.

6.6 Conclusions

In this work, we tried to provide a relatively comprehensive picture of the changes that have taken place in management knowledge because of the COVID-19 crisis. For this purpose, first we examined the developments caused by the COVID-19 crisis in the theoretical foundations of management knowledge. To do this, we addressed three theoretical foundations: *utilitarianism*, *pragmatism*, and *social responsibility*.

After, we examined the changes that have taken place in various areas of the organization. For this purpose, we examined various issues such as organizational structure, culture and communication, strategy, supply chain management, and finally leadership. In each case, in addition to reviewing the effects that the COVID-19 crisis has had on these areas, we have tried to depict future researches in these areas and the changes that have resulted from the COVID-19 crisis in these studies.

In the next step, by examining the management prescriptions for overcoming the COVID-19 crisis, we tried to provide a classification of this issue. As we have seen, managerial prescriptions for facing COVID-19 pandemic were generally based on three headings: technology (robotics, cyberspace, and soft), more focused on social responsibility, and spirituality.

In this section, first we try to identify the main streams of managerial researches in the face of the COVID-19 crisis by analyzing these findings.

6.6.1 Managerial Research Currents in the Face of the COVID-19 Crisis

Scientific currents are one of the most important and influential parts in any field of knowledge. Few events can streamline or change them. However, the effects of the COVID-19 crisis have been so dramatic, and we expect two scientific currents due to this crisis. Although it is still too early to deal with the scientific currents caused by COVID-19 crisis, according to the signs that can be seen in the changes and developments of research in each field of management, it can be said that the two different scientific currents are being formed in the face of the COVID-19 pandemic effects on management knowledge:

- **Revolutionary Current**

Normally, we always face revolutionary currents after very big scientific crises. From an epistemological point of view, as *Thomas Kuhn* has pointed out, *scientific revolutions* occur after the confrontation of conventional science with major crises and lead to the creation of new scientific paradigms. Of course, it should be noted that the meaning of crisis here is scientific crises: the continuing inability of the fundamental theories of a science to provide satisfactory answers to some new problems (Kuhn, 2012). However, most of these scientific crises, especially in the applied fields of humanities and most of all in management, are caused by social crises such as the COVID-19 crisis.

For example, as various areas of life became more complex and intertwined because of the COVID-19 crisis, the basis of utilitarianism in many areas became problematic:

- As long as people's safety and health are at risk, they are not motivated by utilitarian factors.
- Sacrifice is one of the solutions to all major crises, but by utilitarian standards, no sacrifice can be expected from anyone.
- Cost-benefit analyses have lost their effectiveness in the complex context of the COVID-19 crisis and so on.

Given the place of utilitarianism theory in management, this could become a real crisis for the management knowledge. In the meantime, if the other schools of thought in the management science, including the followers of religious management, postmodern management, and feminists in management, could provide interesting alternatives to this basic theory, they have laid the groundwork for a scientific revolution.

Accordingly, we called revolutionary research to the researches designed for this purpose that seeks to disprove the philosophical foundations of basic theories of existing management knowledge.

However, although the first preliminary works in this field are emerging after the COVID-19 crisis (e.g., Dolan et al., 2020; Naqvi & Russell, 2020), if we want to discuss more operationally, it needs to give more time to this process. Therefore, for now, we focus on developmental current.

- **Developmental Current**

As we discussed, major social crises are causing scientific crises in the applied social sciences. However, we should note that these scientific crises, in rare cases that are very large and terrible, lead to scientific revolutions (the revolutionary approaches described in the previous section can be the prelude to these revolutions). Nevertheless, in most cases, these crises are answered with developmental current. Developmental currents are in fact the result of the efforts of believers in the traditional paradigm of existing management.

In the developmental current while maintaining the basic principles and theories, new techniques and strategies for overcoming the COVID-19 crisis are being developed. Therefore, except for the section one, most of the works that we have introduced in this chapter fit into this category.

Identifying these two approaches is a very important issue for the subject of this chapter. Here, the separation of foundational areas from other areas, which was done in the first part of the chapter, helped us to be able to distinguish between the two currents much more easily. Each of these two currents, in turn, provides ambitious plans with different goals set for research and organizations.

The future shape of the management knowledge depends on the degree of development and dominance of each of these two currents. Although the developmental current is working hard to provide a variety of techniques and strategies for controlling the COVID-19 crisis, a pure idea from the revolutionary current can change the situation. We can now vigilantly monitor the movements of each of these currents. In the following, we try to examine the effects of the COVID-19 crisis at a more practical level.

6.6.2 Deaths and Births of the Businesses Due to the COVID-19 Crisis

In this section, we will look at the effects that the COVID-19 crisis has had on the decline or creation of businesses. This issue can be considered as one of the practical results of our discussion. Businesses that have been more successful in previous titles and have adapted better to the changes taken place in each of the organizational areas discussed in this chapter have survived. In contrast, the lives of many businesses, large and small, have ended in the face of the COVID-19 crisis.

Although successful experiences in the face of the COVID-19 crisis can be seen from various businesses in many countries around the world, including China, Germany, etc. (Reeves et al., 2020a), in any case, the COVID-19 crisis has caused many bankruptcies and closures. On the other hand, new businesses have been created since the COVID-19 crisis. Examining experiences of similar global crises (such as the Hong Kong Flu and the Spanish Flu) shows that these new businesses grow GDP faster and filling the gap of lost businesses (Carlsson-Szlezak et al., 2020).

In the meantime, businesses, large and small, each had their own problems. Small businesses face problems such as access to capital, liquidity, and being ignored in government policymaking. Financing problems, which are a constant issue for small businesses, have intensified during this period, destroying many small businesses during the COVID-19 crisis. Governments, on the other hand, to escape the unemployment wave, focus on large businesses when designing protection policies and often ignore small businesses (Monson, 2020).

However, it should be noted that despite the greater support of governments for large businesses, it is the smaller businesses that have had more flexibility and thus could adapt more easily to the new conditions. Hence, large businesses faced a serious weakness in this regard.

However, all the organizational areas mentioned in this chapter have undergone significant changes because of the COVID-19 crisis. The inability of any organization to adapt to these changes prepares that organization to decline. That is why management research plays a vital role in this period. Now, it is up to the management researchers to find ways for managers to save organizations.

6.7   Conclusion and Suggestions

This work presents a map of the set of areas of theory and practice in management that has changed most, due to the COVID-19 crisis. In each case, we have tried to discuss the developments that this crisis has created in the practical and theoretical levels.

On this basis, it is suggested that each of the specialized areas that were briefly addressed be examined in separate studies.

On the other hand, experts in other scientific fields are suggested to design and conduct research in their scientific fields in order to study revolutionary and developmental currents.

The severity and extent of the COVID-19 crisis ensure that such currents exist in the researches of all active and living scientific disciplines (especially the applied disciplines of the humanities and social sciences). The tremendous role that these scientific currents play in forming the future of any discipline makes it necessary to address them.

Finally, it is suggested that field researches to be conducted to accurately and quantitatively measure the effects of the COVID-19 crisis and the effects of each of the management prescriptions on the rate of productivity and performance in organizations. In addition, examining the experiences and situation of businesses that have overcome or failed in the face of the COVID-19 crisis will provide many practical lessons for businesses.

References

Ali-Ahmadi Jeshfaghni, H. (2020). Philosophy of behavioral decision-making against the Corona virus epidemics prevalence (case study: The difference between macro-management models in combating COVID-19 in Iran and the United States). *Journal of Marine Medicine, 2*(1), 65–77.

Argenti, Paul A. (2020, March 13). Communicating through the coronavirus crisis. *Harvard Business Review*. URL: https://hbr.org/2020/03/communicating-through-the-coronavirus-crisis

Azizi, M., Adel, A., & Nayeri, M. D. (2020). Participatory decision making in the post COVID-19 period. *Modern Research in Decision Making, 5*(2), 165–192.

Azizi, M., Azizi, S. M., & Latifi, M. (2017). Investigating the effect of utilitarian school on decision-making theories and comparing it with the theory of Islamic growth. *Journal of Islamic Management Research, 3.*

Bapuji, H., de Bakker, F. G. A., Brown, J. A., Higgins, C., Rehbein, K., & Spicer, A. (2020a). Business and society research in times of the corona crisis. *Business & Society, 59*(6), 1067–1078. https://doi.org/10.1177/0007650320921172

Bapuji, H., Patel, C., Ertug, G., & Allen, D. G. (2020b). Corona crisis and inequality: Why management research needs a societal turn. *Journal of Management, 46*(7), 1205–1222. https://doi.org/10.1177/0149206320925881

Bradley, R. (2015). *Decision theory with a human face.* Cambridge University Press.

Business Human Rights Report, COVID-19 and Responsible Business Conduct. (2020). IRL: https://www.business-humanrights.org/sites/default/files/documents/OECD_COVID-19%20 and%20Responsible%20Business%20Conduct_Full%20Note.pdf

Caligiuri, P., De Cieri, H., Minbaeva, D., Verbeke, A., & Zimmermann, A. (2020). International HRM insights for navigating the COVID-19 pandemic: Implications for future research and practice. *Journal of International Business Studies, 1,* 74–80.

Carlsson-Szlezak, P., Reeves, M., & Swartz, P. (2020, March 3). What coronavirus could mean for the global economy. *Harvard Business Review.* URL: https://hbr.org/2020/03/what-coronavirus-could-mean-for-the-global-economy

Chatterji, M. (2020). Caring management in the new Economy, socially responsible behaviour through spirituality. *Journal of Management, Spirituality & Religion, 17,* 1–6.

Corrêa, N. K. (2020). The automation of acceleration: AI and the future of society. arXiv preprint arXiv:2007.04477.

De Bakker, F. G. A., Matten, D., Spence, L. J., & Wickert, C. (2020). The elephant in the room: The nascent research agenda on corporations, social responsibility, and capitalism. *Business & Society. Advance online publication.* https://doi.org/10.1177/0007650319898196

de Caro, F., Hirschmann, T. M., & Verdonk, P. (2020). Returning to orthopaedic business as usual after COVID-19: Strategies and options. *Sports Traumatology, Arthroscopy,* (28), 1699–1704. https://link.springer.com/article/10.1007/s00167-020-06031-3

Dirilen-Gumus, O. (2011). Differences in system justification with respect to gender, political conservatism, socio-economic status and religious fundamentalism. *Procedia-Social and Behavioral Sciences, 30,* 2607–2611.

Dolan, S. L., Raich, M., Garti, A., & Landau, A. (2020, April 28). "The COVID-19 crisis" as an opportunity for introspection: A multi-level reflection on values, needs, trust and leadership in the future. *The European Business Review.*

Engel, M. (1992). Personal and doxastic justification in epistemology. *Philosophical Studies, 67,* 133–150. https://doi.org/10.1007/BF00373694

Fleming, M. (2002, November). *What is safety culture? Rail way safety ever green house.* Sage.

Fleming, P. (2012). *The end of corporate social responsibility: Crisis and critique.* Sage.

Franke, R. H., & Kaul, J. D. (1978). The Hawthorne experiments: First statistical interpretation. *American Sociological Review, 4*(5), 623–643.

Friedman, S. D., & Westring, A. F. (2020, March 10). How working parents can prepare for coronavirus closures. *Harvard Business Review.* URL: https://hbr.org/2020/03/how-working-parents-can-prepare-for-coronavirus-closures

Ghaffari, G. (2010). The logic of comparative research. *Iranian Journal of Social Studies, 3*(4), 64–85. Winter 2009.

Gray, J. (2020). Goodbye to globalization. *The Guardian.* https://www.theguardian.com/world/2001/feb/27/globalisation

Greig, F. (2020). Coronavirus symptoms explained: Meaning of a 'persistent' or 'continuous' cough, high temperature and loss of smell and taste. URL: https://inews.co.uk/news/health/coronavirus-symptoms-explained-persistent-continuous-cough-temperature-high-loss-smell-taste-anosmia-409092

Guillén, M., Ferrero, I., & Hoffman, W. M. (2015). The neglected ethical and spiritual motivations in the workplace. *Journal of Business Ethics, 128*(4), 803–816.

Haller, R. (1988). Justification and praxeological foundationalism. *Inquiry, 31*(3), 335–345.

Haren, P., & Simchi-Levi, D. (2020, February 28). How coronavirus could impact the global supply chain by mid-March. *Harvard Business Review*. URL: https://hbr.org/2020/02/how-coronavirus-could-impact-the-global-supply-chain-by-mid-march

Hendry, J. (2013). *Management: A very short introduction*. Oxford University Press. https://global.oup.com/ukhe/product/management-a-very-short-introduction-9780199656981?cc=gb&lang=en& Print ISBN-13: 9780199656981

Hitt, M., Ireland, R. D., & Huskisson, R. E. (2020). *Strategic management: Concepts: Competitiveness and globalization* (12th ed.). Cengage Learning.

Hofstede, G. (1991). *Cultures and organizations: Software of the mind*. McGraw-Hill.

Jang, Y. S., Steven Ott, J., & Shafritz, J. M. (2011). *Classic readings in organization theory*. Wadsworth Cengage Learning.

Kuhn, T. S. (2012). *The structure of scientific revolutions*. The University of Chicago Press.

Li, Y., Zhang, F. P., Yan, Y., Zhou, J. H., & Li, Y. F. (2019). Multi-source uncertainty considered assembly process quality control based on surrogate model and information entropy. *Structural and Multidisciplinary Optimization, 59*(5), 1685–1701.

Lin, C. (2020, March 17). Delivery technology is keeping Chinese cities afloat through coronavirus. *Harvard Business Review*. URL: https://hbr.org/2020/03/delivery-technology-is-keeping-chinese-cities-afloat-through-coronavirus

Linton, T., & Vakil, B. (2020, March 5). Coronavirus is proving we need more resilient supply chains. *Harvard Business Review*. URL: https://hbr.org/2020/03/coronavirus-is-proving-that-we-need-more-resilient-supply-chains

Little, M., Lipworth, W., Gordon, J., Markham, P., & Kerridge, I. (2012). Values-based medicine and modest foundationalism. *Journal of Evaluation in Clinical Practice, 18*(5), 1020–1026.

Lu, L., Wu, H. L., & Cooper, C. L. (1999). Perceived work stress and locus of control: A combined quantitative and qualitative approach. *Research and Practice in Human Resource Management, 7*(1), 1–15.

Martin, L. L. (2006). *Jeremy Bentham on organization theory and decision making, public policy analysis and administration management, handbook of organization theory and management, the philosophical approach*. Taylor and Francis.

Merriam-Webster's Dictionary. https://www.merriamwebster.com/dictionary/managerialism

Mintzberg, H., & Waters, J. A. (1990). Tracking strategy in an entrepreneurial firm. *Family Business Review, 3*(3), 285–315.

Monson, C. (2020, March 27). What small businesses need to survive the coronavirus crisis. *Harvard Business Review*. URL. https://hbr.org/2020/03/what-small-businesses-need-to-survive-the-coronavirus-crisis

Naqvi, Z. B., & Russell, Y. (2020). A Wench's guide to surviving a 'global' pandemic crisis: Feminist publishing in a time of COVID-19. *Feminist Legal Studies*. https://doi.org/10.1007/s10691-020-09435-1

Nardi, B. A., & Whittaker, S. (2002). The place of face-to-face communication in distributed work. In *Distributed work* (pp. 83–112). Boston Review.

Neeley, T., & Beard, A. (2020). Adjusting to remote work during the coronavirus crisis. *Harvard Business Review*. URL: https://hbr.org/podcast/2020/03/adjusting-to-remote-work-during-the-coronavirus-crisis

Planken, B. (2013). Definitions of social responsibility. In S. O. Idowu, N. Capaldi, L. Zu, & A. D. Gupta (Eds.), *Encyclopedia of corporate social responsibility*. Springer. https://doi.org/10.1007/978-3-642-28036-8_476

Reeves, M., Fæste, L., Chen, C., Carlsson-Szlezak, P., & Whitaker, K. (2020a, March 10). How Chinese companies have responded to coronavirus. *Harvard Business Review*. URL: https://hbr.org/2020/03/how-chinese-companies-have-responded-to-coronavirus

Reeves, M., Lang, N., & Carlsson-Szlezak, P. (2020b, February 27). Lead your business through the coronavirus crisis. *Harvard Business Review*. URL: https://hbr.org/2020/02/lead-your-business-through-the-coronavirus-crisis

Rescher, N. (1975). Foundationalism, coherentism, and the idea of cognitive systematization. *The Journal of Philosophy, 71*(19), 695–708.

Rice, J. B., Jr. (2020, February 27). Prepare your supply chain for coronavirus. *Harvard Business Review*. URL: https://hbr.org/2020/02/prepare-your-supply-chain-for-coronavirus

Roberts, M., & McCluney, C. L.. (2020). harvard business review, https://hbr.org/2020/06/working-from-home-while-black

Rutten, F. T., & Becker, J. (2020). *Comprehending millennial motivation during a crisis-the perceived influence of the employee-leader relationship*. Dissertation, Malmö universitet/Kultur och samhälle). Retrieved from http://urn.kb.se/resolve?urn=urn:nbn:se:mau:diva-22701

Sagden, R., & Williams, A. (1978). *Fundamentals of cost-benefit analysis*. Oxford University Press.

Simon, H. (1946, Winter). The proverbs of administration. *Public Administration Review, 6*(1), 53–67.

Steup, M., & Ram, N. (2020). Epistemology. In E. N. Zalta (Ed.), *The Stanford encyclopedia of philosophy* (Fall 2020 edition). https://plato.stanford.edu/archives/fall2020/entries/epistemology

Susser, P., & Tyson, T. (2020, March 4). What are companies' legal obligations around coronavirus? *Harvard Business Review*. URL: https://hbr.org/2020/03/what-are-companies-legal-obligations-around-coronavirus

Taket, A., & White, L. (2000). *Partnership and participation: Decision-making in the multiagency setting*. Wiley.

Tarki, A., Levy, P., & Weiss, J. (2020, March 20). The coronavirus crisis doesn't have to lead to layoffs. *Harvard Business Review*. URL: https://hbr.org/2020/03/the-coronavirus-crisis-doesnt-have-to-lead-to-layoffs

Taylor, F. W. (1911). *The principles of scientific management*. Harper & Brothers.

Thomas, H., & Hatchuel, A. (2009). A foundationalist perspective for management research: A European trend and experience. *Management Decision, 47*, 1458–1475.

Velupillai, V. (2016). A pragmatic holist: Herbert Simon, economics and "the architecture of complexity". In *New approaches to economic challenges*. OECD.

Part II
Shock Economy and Financial Dynamics

Chapter 7
Lessons from COVID-19 and Its Impact on Reallocation of Resources: A Cross-Country Comparison in Search of a Global Perspective

Jamshid Damooei

7.1 Introduction

COVID-19 took the world by surprise despite a widely previously understood and scientifically proven confidence that the ongoing ecological changes have increasingly made the possibility of occurrences of pandemics and zoonotic diseases a certainty (Gibb et al., 2020).[1]

There have been a significant number of large-scale studies into the environmental drivers of disease based on the focus of climate change. By comparison, much less emphasis has been placed on the impact of other related factors such as land use change, the conversion of natural habitats into agricultural production units, and urban or otherwise anthropogenic ecosystem changes (Gottdenker et al., 2014; Keesing et al., 2010). These changes within their global setting are an important mediator of infection risk in humans.

This study uses a historical context to argue about the impact of pandemics on bringing about drastic changes in the economic system in the world, and it uses conventional and macroeconomic arguments to show the impact of the likely changes in various countries. It argues that COVID-19 may not have brought any new changes in the world; however, it unveiled the fragility of the prevailing economic system in a rapid and unavoidable fashion.

---

[1] See Rory Gibb, David W. Redding, Kai Qing Chin, Christl A. Donnelly, Tim M. Blackburn, Tim Newbold, and Kate E. Jones (2020). Zoonotic host diversity increases in human-dominated ecosystems, Nature volume 584, pages 398–402 https://www.nature.com/articles/s41586-020-2562-8

J. Damooei (✉)
Center for Economics of Social Issues (CESI), School of Management, California Lutheran University, Thousand Oaks, CA, USA
e-mail: Damooei@callutheran.edu

© The Author(s), under exclusive license to Springer Nature Switzerland AG 2022
N. Faghih, A. Forouharfar (eds.), *Socioeconomic Dynamics of the COVID-19 Crisis*, Contributions to Economics, https://doi.org/10.1007/978-3-030-89996-7_7

We use a group of countries, ranging from developed to developing, and employ cross-country comparisons to highlight the existing challenges of the economic systems in these countries. The study brings attention to the impact of environmental changes and their contribution towards possible creation of pandemics. It looks into the historical context of pandemics and how they have brought structural changes in living condition, production possibilities, and mobility of work force within nations.

One of the pivotal arguments of this study is the importance of separating demand for goods and services from meeting the needs of people and communities. The study goes further and selects a number of important areas of need of every society and makes a cross-country comparison among them. The objective is to show that investing on meeting the essential needs of communities through provision of public goods and services can go a long way to create resiliency in those communities when they are faced with unprecedented crisis such as pandemics.

Resiliency towards crisis is also a function of the mindset and attitude of people towards public trust and how it is created or broken. The study indicates the public trust is a complicated subject worthy of a much higher level of scrutiny and investigation. However, it supports the idea that creation of public trust is an important social capital and in every country. The study shows that changed over time through major economic transformation resulted in its decline.

The study brings attention to the role of the public sector in the provision of public goods and services and investment in areas leading to the protection of the economy and the livelihood of people in various countries as an essential element of a new emerging system. It proposes that in many instances, the future world should embark on both the production of global public goods (GPG) and creating and strengthening international cooperation if there is any hope for a sustainable and functioning global economy.

The study questions the efficacy of embarking on market responses to the preparation of support economies for unexpected events and risks such as pandemics. Finally, it uses the ensuing arguments to shed light on the principal elements of resource allocation within countries and the emerging global system in the near future.

7.2 Literature Review

7.2.1 Pandemics in Their Historical Context and Their Impact on Changing Economic Conditions and Social Environment

Pandemics and infectious diseases have brought fundamental changes throughout history as they exposed the dysfunctionality of systems and presented an unacceptable face of the existing systems in serving the needs of people for the continuation of order at the time.

The Black Death (Bubonic plague) of the Medieval period changed the flow of history, although it is hard to measure the impacts statistically in any reliable way. The Black Death changed the role of the working class and led to the refurbishment of capital accumulation structures and welfare distribution (Bell & Lewis, 2004).

Clark (2001) argues that the pressure of time and destruction of sources of production and in particular labor in the Medieval period led to the discovery of two new continents: the Americas. Declining labor supplies led to the shift from feudalism to centralization of governments. Pamuk (2007) argues that production structures shifted from labor to capital-based and productive centers shifted from rural to urban during the Medieval period, and plague had significant effects on these challenges.

The important element of all such historical evidence is that these changes and their consequences occurred within centuries and it was not the mere occurrence of a plague in one particular time which led to such important transformations, but the gradual structural changes that happened which brought countries' economies to their tipping points. This makes an accurate assessment of the impact of the recent pandemic hard to predict, but very important to assess.

There are, however, some assessments which can help us to see the experience of the past in a clear light. Within 5 years, from 1347 to 1352, the Black Death killed 20,000,000 people in Europe, a third of the total population of Europe at that time (Tuchman, 1978). The plague started in Asia and spread through Europe through trading ships.[2] The plague had an important impact on the relationship between the peasants and the lords. As workers died, it became harder to find people who could work on land and the remaining workers began to ask for higher wages.

The increase in wages within the political and social structure of the time brought severe reaction from the ruling class. An English law in 1349 tried to force workers to accept the same wages they received in 1346. A similar law was passed with the aim of fixing wages and forcing workers to accept the existing wages against the prevailing conditions that could lead their increase.

There were, however, other developments which brought the ensuing economic consequences regardless of the passage of laws forcing the workers to accept existing wages, and that was the creation of competition among landlords to offer higher wages to workers in order to secure their wage demand and the ability of workers to consider leaving their home in search of better jobs in other places. The labor mobility would not have occurred if the economic conditions did not change due to labor shortage caused by the plague.

It is hard to ignore the economic impact of the plague, which was a human tragedy that caused a population reduction, brought about a shortage of labor, and finally resulted in an increase in wages and the mobility of workers and improvements in their standard of living.

---

[2] See Barbara Tuchman (1978). A Distant Mirror – The Calamitous 14th Century. New York: Ballantine Books, pp. 92–93.

The problem with such a conclusion, although unavoidable, is that the conclusion provides a Malthusian explanation of how changes in population may create unavoidable economic changes and adjustment. There is, however, a different explanation for such a conclusion, and that is the inevitability of avoidance of economic change if living conditions are impacted by drastic changes that pandemics and all unexpected societal shocks may bring about. In ancient times, the change in population could have had a drastic impact on the labor market and brought about a change in wages, whereas in modern times, this may generate a different set of economic consequences in production and trade sectors in certain countries and in the world as a whole.

Within the context of fourteenth-century economic conditions, the plague brought a fundamental change in agriculture, and the shortage of laborers not only impacted the wages but also the type of products based on their labor demand, and caused a move towards various types of husbandry, mobility of workers, and the enhancement of restrictive laws, which, in time, brought the wave of resistance and political change.

As David Routt (2008) explains, the wake of a new climate created by the Black Death brought rapid changes in the prevailing pattern of boom and bust that used to change on a generational basis.[3] The late Medieval popular uprising with major economic consequences is often linked with the demographic, cultural, social, and economic reshuffling caused by the Black Death. It should also be mentioned that the connection between pandemics and revolts is neither exclusive nor linear. Any single uprising is rarely susceptible to a single-cause analysis, and just as rarely was a single socioeconomic interest group the fomenter of disorder. The outbreak of rebellion in the first half of the fourteenth century (e.g., in urban [1302] and maritime [1325–28] Flanders and in English monastic towns [1326–27]) indicates the existence of socioeconomic and political disgruntlement well before the Black Death (Routt, 2008).[4]

The victims of Spanish flu (1918–1920) were mostly ages 15–40, rather than young or old. While there have been efforts to find the cause of the flu and its impact on the number of deaths, very little efforts have been made to find the connection between these pandemic and other major recent pandemics such as bird flu, swine flu, and SARS in recent times.

From a purely economic point of view, Karlsson et al. (2014) argue that the Spanish flu pandemic was a labor supply shock to the economy, which, on the other hand, leaves physical capital intact. They point out that the primary impact was from the side of labor supply. The data on GDP is not available, and therefore it is hard to make a clear estimation of the pandemic's impact. On the distributional side of the economic impact, they argue that it brought about a higher level of poverty in impacted countries. In a number of countries within Europe and the United States,

---

[3] See The Economic Impact of Black Death by David Routt, University of Richmond, Economic History Association. https://eh.net/encyclopedia/the-economic-impact-of-the-black-death/
[4] Ibid.

this incident brought a delay in these countries in their effort to reach a steady state. Karlsson et al. (2012) follows the example of Théophile et al. (2008) and shortly discuss the predictions from a standard neoclassical growth model.[5] In the neoclassical one-sector model, deriving the short- and medium-term impact of a pandemic is relatively straightforward. The immediate impact of a negative human capital shock is that the ratio between physical and human capital is moved above its steady state level.

Building further on this development, this incidence must have brought a considerable level of capital deepening (excess of physical capital over human capital), which may have led a lower return to human capital, in turn resulting in more investment in human capital. This means that earnings per capital increased the effects on capital incomes per capita, which are the product of sinking interest rates and a larger per-capita capital stock. Moreover, due to the smaller population size, the economy will generally grow faster on a per capita basis than before the pandemic. Poverty and inequality are of course strongly related to returns on factors of production. If wages increase more than capital returns, workers most likely experience an increase in incomes while the income of capital holders decreases.

The empirical evidence for health shocks and economic growth is elusive. However, there are very few empirical studies estimating the economic effects of pandemics.[6] The most significant deduction from an elaborated study of impacts from pandemics on economic performance reached by Karlsson et al. (2014) suggests that epidemics in past experiences have been largely a random shock to regions.[7] They could not identify a socioeconomic rise in the incidence of the epidemic. Their study tentatively concludes that differences in excess mortality rates across regions are largely exogenous. Let us not forget that their study was focused on Sweden in the early part of twentieth century and their conclusion is tentative and within a very restrictive region. Their study also indicates a starkly different result with what might be assumed for the economic conditions of today in many parts of the world. They found that with regard to capital incomes, the pandemic had a strong negative impact, and this impact appears to have been a combination of immediate and medium-term responses.

This study finds that the highest quartile (with respect to influenza mortality) experienced a drop of 5% during the pandemic and an additional 6% afterwards. For

---

[5] See Théophile T. Azomahou, Raouf Boucekkine, and Bity Diene (2008), Economics of Epidemics: A Review of the Theory, Mathematical Population Studies 15(1):1–26. https://www.econstor.eu/bitstream/10419/84878/1/688928587.pdf

[6] See Johansson (2007) and Lachaud (2007). They examine the short and medium-term economic implications of HIV/AIDS, but this pandemic is very different compared to the Spanish flu as it is a much slower process.

[7] See Martin Karlsson, Therese Nilsson, and Stefan Pichler (July 2014), The impact of the 1918 Spanish flu epidemic on economic performance in Sweden: An investigation into the consequences of an extraordinary mortality shock, Journal of Health Economics, https://www.sciencedirect.com/science/article/pii/S0167629614000344

earnings, on the other hand, they were unable to detect any effect either during or after the pandemic.

With regard to poorhouse occupancy rates, Karlsson et al. (2014) find a strong and positive effect, which seems to have appeared only once the epidemic had receded in 1920. For this variable, the top quartile suffered an increase in the poorhouse need rate by 11% compared to the bottom quartile. The increased poorhouse occupancy rates seem to be at odds with the increased scarcity of labor.

Their analysis shows that results are not driven by internal migration, but the pandemic appears to have increased regional employment rates in the industrial sector. This suggests that the pandemic led to a significant reduction in average worker quality. This is a labor market adjustment, which we have only been able to study for one sector of the economy.

7.2.2 The Impact of Environmental Changes on the Creation of Pandemics

The impact of environmental changes in the creation of pandemics is not a new debate; it has been around for decades. The subject brought up a number of questions and some efforts have been made to address them. The question of how the spread of infectious diseases can be the result of climate change caught the attention of many nations and scientific circles.

A study by Mordecai et al. (2020) at Stanford University forecasts how climate change will alter where mosquito species are most safeguarded and how quickly they spread disease, shifting the burden of disease around the world. Their research does not indicate any immunity from harm for developed countries compared with developing countries.[8] The research reveals that the conditions on Earth are becoming more receptive to these changes and we should expect a much higher level of spread of diseases because of global warming around the world.

It is important to acknowledge that mosquitoes and other biting insects transmit many of the most important, devastating, and neglected human infectious diseases, including malaria, dengue fever, chikungunya, and West Nile virus. Economic development and cooler temperatures have largely kept mosquito-borne diseases out of wealthier Northern Hemisphere countries, but climate change promises to tip the scales in the other direction.[9] This clearly presents a new challenge which should be looked at primarily through the lens of environmental degradation rather than any other causal effects.

---

[8] For more information, see Rob Jordan, Stanford Woods Institute for the Environment, 2019, https://earth.stanford.edu/news/how-does-climate-change-affect-disease#gs.jovukv, and for the original paper, see Mordecai et al. (2020), A Climate change could shift disease burden from malaria to arboviruses in Africa LANCET PLANETARY HEALTH 2020; 4 (9): E416–E423.

[9] Ibid.

Hales et al. (2002), Wilson (2001), and Martens et al. (2002) show that changes in infectious disease transmission patterns are a likely important consequence of climate change. This makes it imperative that a community of nations needs to learn more about the underlying complex causal relationships and learn from the existing evidence in their mission to create a realistic predictive future model and bring forward an effective means of mitigating the adverse impacts of pandemics.

The T.H. Chan Harvard School of Public Health, in its discussion of COVID-19 and Climate Change, draws attention to an important question, which is while we do not have direct evidence that climate change is influencing the spread of COVID-19, we know that climate change alters how we relate to other species on Earth in the way that our health and our risk for infection is impacted.[10]

More than 32,000 species are threatened with extinction, which is about 27% of all assessed species, because of the loss of biodiversity[11]. This will bring drastic reductions of populations of endangered species due to human exploitation and loss of habitats, which in turn will bring about more zoonotic viruses. The scenario of COVID-19 is likely to repeat itself an infinite number of times, if relevant and appropriate measures are not taken. These measures are multidimensional and multifaceted.

In many ways, COVID-19 put the economic system around the world into an unexpended stress test, which is still continuing and the process brought up the existing fractures in the system. It also put the prevailing healthcare system in many economies to an even greater test. The role of the existing institutions and their responsibility for the prevention of the damages or abating the social and economic costs of them appeared as an urgent debate, which should have been brought up a long time ago and settled for good. It is regrettable that there is no clear indication in many economies if these issues are going to be settled soon.

7.2.3 Pandemics, Economic Condition, and the Role of Governments in Responding to the Needs and Provision of Public Goods and Services

There have been a number of major pandemics since the turn of the century, such as SARS, MERS, and Ebola, each with devastating impacts and potentially dire consequences for a large number of countries worldwide. However, there has never been such a rapid globalization of a pandemic like COVID-19. The global scale of the pandemic has been tremendous and the economic costs have been colossal and are still rising.

---

[10] See T.H. Chan Harvard School of Public Health, Coronavirus and Climate Change, https://www.hsph.harvard.edu/c-change/subtopics/coronavirus-and-climate-change/

[11] For more information, see https://www.iucnredlist.org/

It is important to have a relevant perspective for the sources of the economic cost of pandemics within the prevailing and the emerging economic structure of various economies. Market-based economies are credited with using the system to provide goods and services for which there are demands. It is also argued that under a truly competitive market structure, a market-based economy allocates the existing scarce resources optimally. There is often, however, little or no efforts to either critically examine the prevailing market structure to show that there is a free market nor any endeavor to make a distinction between the demand for goods or services or needs within an economy. Wants or demands imply willingness to purchase and an ability to purchase. All such goods and services are called private goods and services and they are produced by willing suppliers often for maximization of their profits. The goods and services are provided for all those who are willing to have them and have the financial ability to do so. The standard economic theories suggest within a free market structure, a competitive business environment will result in the creation of economic efficiency, and this in turn brings about economic progress and better lives. The economic entities responding to such demands will continue to operate and, in the process, bring about an efficient allocation of resources.

The missing piece of this story, which brings a much higher level of reality into the lives of human beings, is that not all the goods and services, which are essential for the lives of individuals and groups, are private goods and services and are produced based on demands. Some of the most essential elements of a balanced and humanly conceivable life on Earth are not based on demands, but rather on meeting the needs of individuals, groups, and communities. Meeting the existing or emerging needs is essential for the continuation of life, but those in need may not be able to pay for them, and therefore considering them as demand is incorrect.

Continuing with the perception of responding to demand or wants is an ill-founded concept, which in time can create human disasters, the likes of which we have seen and continue to see during this pandemic. This is one of the primary reasons for the US economy is performing miserably in responding to COVID-19, and this can be seen in a number of other countries around the world.

7.3 Methodology

In order to better demonstrate the economic condition of various countries and evaluate their potential in dealing with the onslaught of COVID-19, we selected 15 countries from various parts of the world for the purpose of looking deeper into their prevailing conditions, which can directly be linked to their ability to combat COVID-19. The selection was based on the economic, political, and social state of these countries built on their degree of economic growth and development, the size of their populations (large and small), and their possible differences on the perception and the actual the role of the public sector, as well as cultural and political differences. It should also be mentioned that this chapter does not claim to have captured and included every socioeconomic, cultural, and political environment and condition of these countries that could and continue to be making significant differences in the varying success of these countries in withstanding the negative consequences of COVID-19.

7.4   Results and Discussion

7.4.1   Selected Essential Indicators of Healthcare Preparedness Before COVID-19

The rapid spread of COVID-19 took many countries by surprise, and within weeks, there was a panic about having the necessary healthcare facilities such as hospital beds, personal protective equipment (PPE), respirators, ICU beds, and even masks for protection of ordinary people, and in many instances, even for frontline healthcare workers and caregivers. The following charts present certain aspects of these abilities in a comparative basis.

The disparity among the countries is striking. In Japan, the ratio is about 13 beds per 1000 people, which is about 4.5 times that of the United States. India is the second most populated country in the world and has the lowest ratio among the group of countries selected. Having beds, particularly in the onset of the outbreak, played an important role and one can argue that it resulted in a higher fatality rate in many countries. The days of peak hospitalization in Spain and Italy that resulted in some measure of prioritization of hospital facilities and beds are still vivid in the

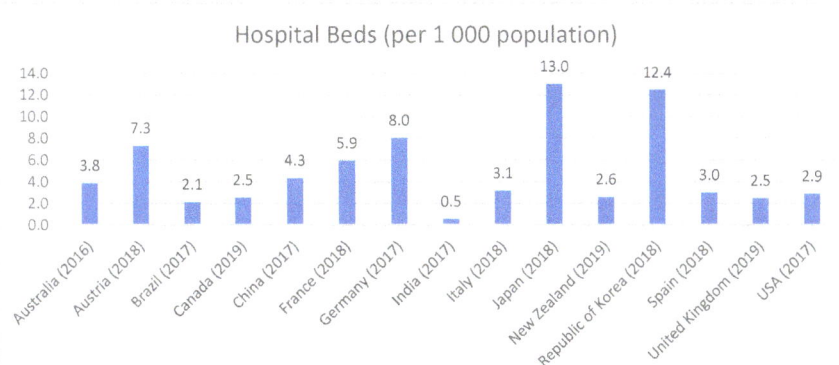

Source: Source: World Health Organization, 2020 (author's own chart)
https://www.who.int/data/gho/data/indicators/indicator-details/GHO/hospital-beds-(per-10-000-population)

Chart 7.1   Hospital beds (per 1000 population)
Source: World Health Organization, 2020 (author's own chart) https://www.who.int/data/gho/data/indicators/indicator-details/GHO/hospital-beds-(per-10-000-population)

memories of people who lived through those hard days. This trend never stopped in many countries and we have heard their occurrences repeatedly during consecutive surges.

Chart 7.1 shows the number of doctors per 1000 people in the selected countries. The rate is varied and there are wide differences among the countries reported in the graph. One of the issues that may bring about a difference with regard to the number of physicians per population group is the method of delivery of healthcare. For example, in some countries, assistant physicians may have a greater role than in other countries, and therefore, this may impact the number of doctors per population group. However, this may not be the case in many of our comparisons, and this could indicate the allocation of resources to healthcare needs for a particular country. The reasons that bring about such differences will be argued in greater depth in the proceeding segments of this study.

Again, the level of preparation for emergencies varies widely among the countries reported. One of the important issues in the provision of healthcare is the demographic needs of the population. It is logical to assume that given the same conditions (controlling for other possible influential variables which may impact the level of medical preparedness), the average age of the population plays an important role. Charts 7.2 and 7.3 provide some relevant and important information.

Chart 7.4 is important since, from the start, it became clear that COVID-19 has a more devastating impact on older people. However, setting COVID-19 aside, having an older population is likely to demand higher attention and budgetary

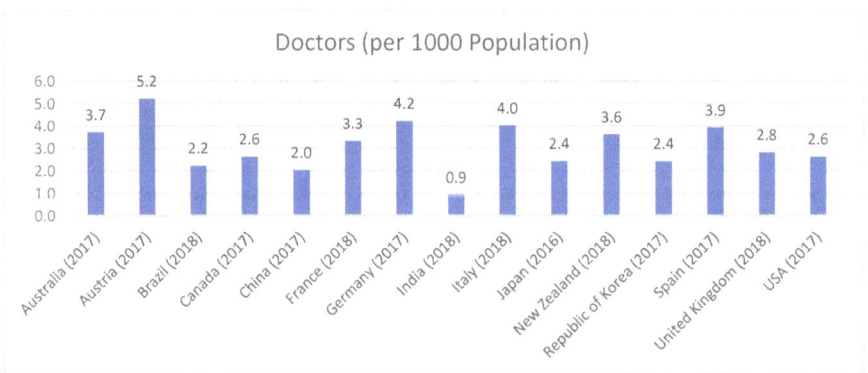

Source: Source: The World Bank, 2020, (author's own chart)
https://databank.worldbank.org/reports.aspx?source=2&series=SH.MED.PHYS.ZS&country=

Chart 7.2 Doctor (per 1000 population)
Source: The World Bank, 2020 (author's own chart) https://databank.worldbank.org/reports.aspx?source=2&series=SH.MED.PHYS.ZS&country=

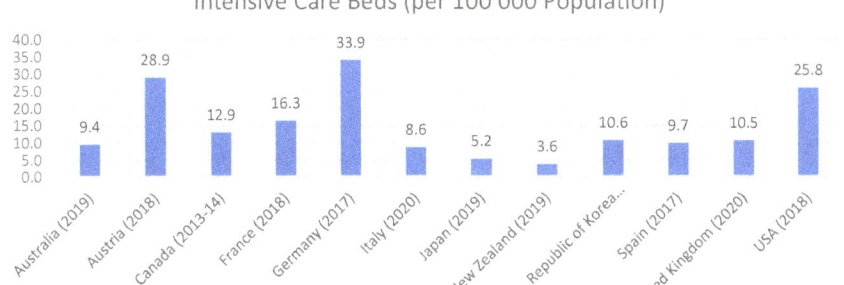

Source: OECD, https://www.oecd.org/coronavirus/en/data-insights/intensive-care-beds-capacity
(author's own chart)
Note: We were not able to find this information for all the countries and only 12 countries are reported

Chart 7.3 Intensive care beds (per 100,000 population)
Source: OECD, https://www.oecd.org/coronavirus/en/data-insights/intensive-care-beds-capacity(author's own chart)
Note: We were not able to find this information for all the countries and only 12 countries are reported

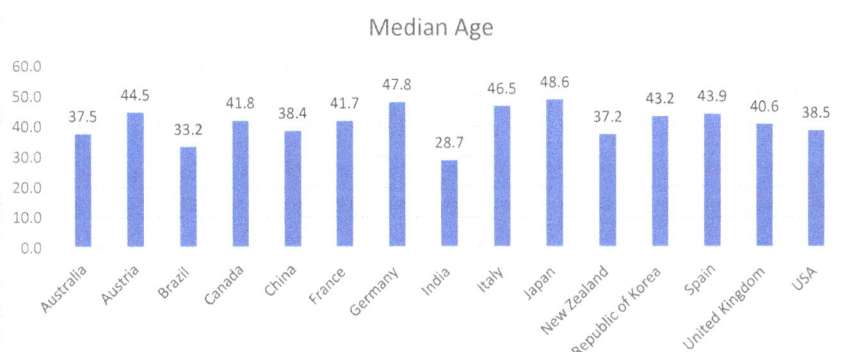

Source: Central Intelligence Agency, 2020, (author's own chart)
https://www.cia.gov/library/publications/the-world-factbook/fields/343rank.html

Chart 7.4 Median age
Source: Central Intelligence Agency, 2020 (author's own chart) https://www.cia.gov/library/publications/the-world-factbook/fields/343rank.html

allocation toward the provision of healthcare services. In other words, meeting the emerging needs of an economy is likely to be strongly and positively correlated to the median age of population of that economy.

7.4.2   Economic Preparedness for Facing Pandemics Through Overall Budgetary Allocation to Meet the Needs and Provision of Healthcare Services

Protecting people in a society is an important topic within the political economy of that society. Understanding the political economy of a nation requires going beyond the explanation of how economic policy decisions are made. It requires a deeper look into the history, the culture, and the social psychology of that nation.

The idea that everyone should protect their own interests and nothing should be expected from others or the government has attraction in a number of countries, and in almost all of them, the question of having equal opportunities for developing such an ability does not come up. The other complication of this philosophy is the message of individualism to the extent that it refutes the collective and social nature of human life. The practical implication of such a belief is the rejection of the role of government. Rejecting the economic role of government brings with it the rejection of paying taxes to cater to the needs of the whole or the role of government in the provision of public goods and services. These are important issues, but paying detailed attention to them falls outside the focus of this study. However, it is not possible to leave them out of this discussion altogether.

The other important issue, which was brought up earlier, is how to think about the role of the private sector in providing what should be considered public goods or services. Despite a general belief that most goods are or should be produced by the private sector as private goods and services is a misconception. It is important to understand the role of markets and their contributions to the production and the availability of many goods and services in every economy, and their impact on resource allocation. However, it is equally important to understand the failure of markets.

Market failure presents itself in multiple ways, such as creation of externality (cost to third party), asymmetry of information (not all parties to a transaction have access to information), and, most importantly, a lack of a market for what should be considered as a need. For example, air quality does not have a market, although the reduction of it can impact a number of markets. Healthcare is one of the most important needs in every society. The argument in defense of this assertion is simple. Every person is entitled to having access to healthcare, regardless of their ability to pay for it. Just like air quality, which impacts the lives of everyone in a community and influences many other related markets, healthcare has also the same kind of impact on many other aspects of life in a society. A clear example of it is the occurrence of pandemics. Viruses do not discriminate between various people, and they

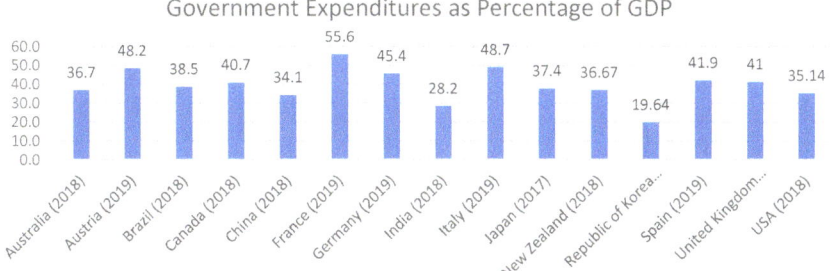

Source: Countryeconomy.com (2020). (author's own chart)
https://countryeconomy.com/countries/compare/uk/usa

Chart 7.5 (Government expenditures as percentage of GDP)
Source: Countryeconomy.com (2020) (author's own chart)
https://countryeconomy.com/countries/compare/uk/usa

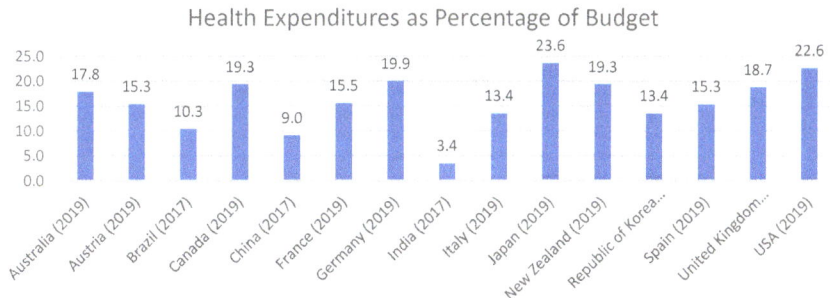

Source: Countryeconomy.com (2020), (author's own chart)
https://countryeconomy.com/government/expenditure/health

Chart 7.6 Healthcare expenditures as percentage of budget
Source: Countryeconomy.com (2020) (author's own chart) https://countryeconomy.com/govern-
ment/expenditure/health

do not care if they have health insurance or not. However, by not treating the diseases, the spread of a virus can go much faster, and its negative impacts may threaten
the lives of all people.

We should also make it very clear that treating healthcare as a need is not because
having access to such service will have a positive impact for all; having access to
healthcare should be treated as the right of every person in a society, regardless of
its justification, based on its impact for the betterment of all people within a society.
The rights of people should be protected regardless any other social side benefits
for all.

Charts 7.5, 7.6, 7.7, 7.8, 7.9, 7.10, 7.11, 7.12, 7.13, and 7.14 and Exhibit 7.1
investigate the following important questions:

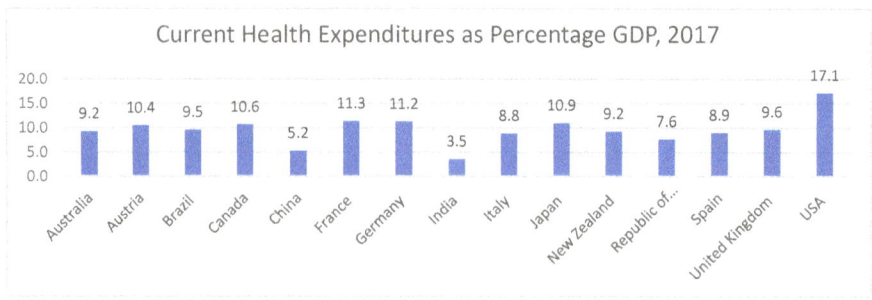

Source: The World Bank, (author's own chart)
https://databank.worldbank.org/reports.aspx?source=2&series=SH.XPD.CHEX.GD.ZS&country

Chart 7.7 Current health expenditures as percentage of GDP in selected countries
Source: The World Bank (author's own chart) https://databank.worldbank.org/reports.
aspx?source=2&series=SH.XPD.CHEX.GD.ZS&country=

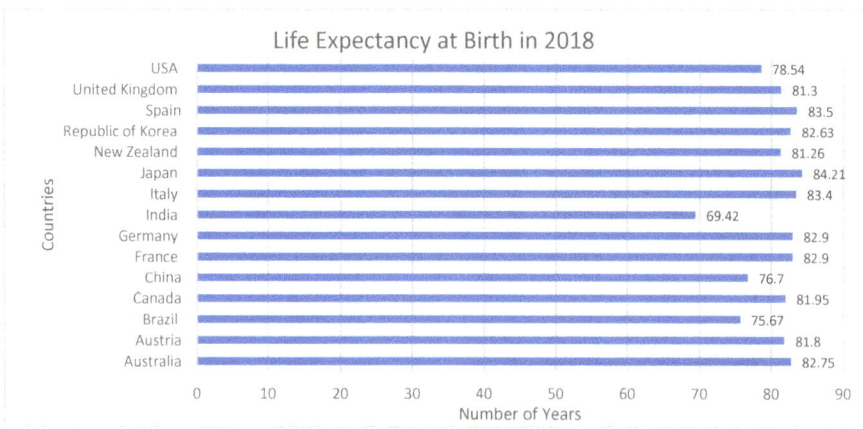

Source: Countryecononomy.com (2020) (author's own chart)
https://countryeconomy.com/demography/life-expectancy

Chart 7.8 Life expectancy at birth in 2018
Source: Countryecononomy.com (2020) (author's own chart)
https://countryeconomy.com/demography/life-expectancy

- How important has the provision of meeting the needs of individuals and groups been in selected countries through their efforts to make it possible by redistribution of national income?
- Is healthcare treated as right of everyone in the countries selected?
- How important has the provision of healthcare services been through the size of budgetary allocation?
- How efficient has the provision of healthcare been in the selected countries?
- Is there an argument for reaching greater efficiency in the provision of public service (or good) if it is assigned to the public sector or private?

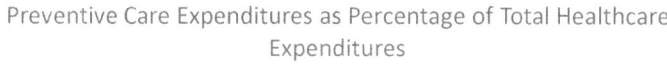

Source: OECD. Stat (2019), (author's own chart)
https://stats.oecd.org/Index.aspx?DataSetCode=SHA
Note: We do not have data for all the countries selected

Chart 7.9 Preventive care as percentage of total healthcare expenditures
Source: OECD. Stat (2020) (author's own chart)
https://stats.oecd.org/Index.aspx?DataSetCode=SHA
Note: We do not have data for all the countries selected

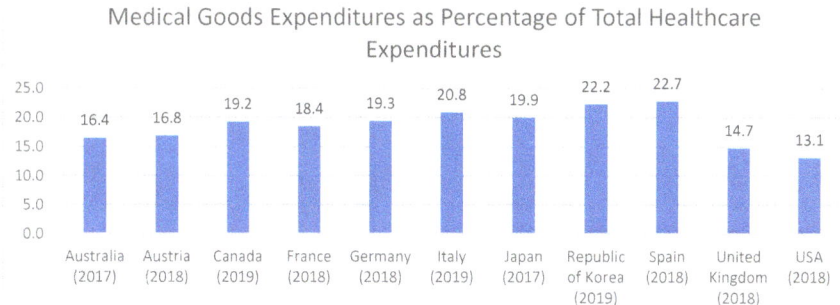

Source: OECD. Stat (2019), (author's own chart)
https://stats.oecd.org/Index.aspx?DataSetCode=SHA
Note: We do not have data for all the countries selected

Chart 7.10 Medical goods expenditures as percentage of total healthcare expenditures
Source: OECD. Stat (2020) (author's own chart)
https://stats.oecd.org/Index.aspx?DataSetCode=SHA
Note: We do not have data for all the countries selected

They provide the information that can be used to open up discussions on all the questions asked above. The most important question for how an economic system considers the role of its public sector in meeting the needs of its population can be seen through the overall expenditure of its government budget as a proportion of its GDP. Chart 7.5 presents this issue most vividly.

Chart 7.5 shows a considerable gap between countries like France, Austria, or Italy and countries like the Republic of Korea or India. The size of the ratio explains the role of government in the redistribution of income. The higher the ratio, the higher the possibility of people in those countries enjoying a higher level of social

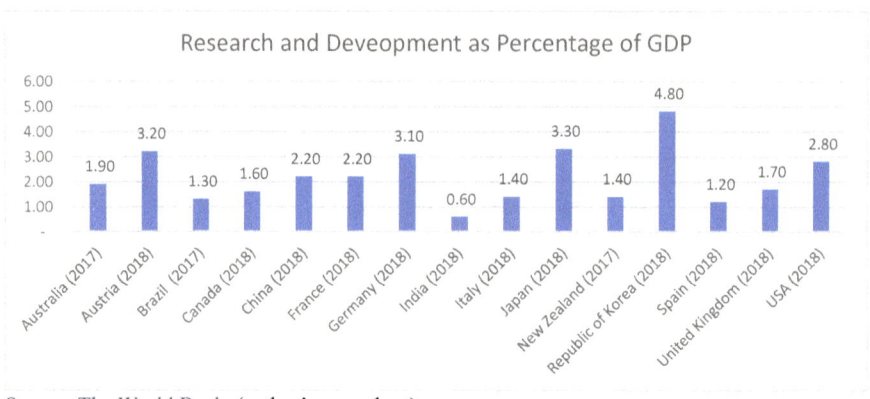

Source: The World Bank, (author's own chart)
https://databank.worldbank.org/reports.aspx?source=2&series=GB.XPD.RSDV.GD.ZS&country

Chart 7.11 Research and development as percentage of GDP
Source: The World Bank (author's own chart) https://databank.worldbank.org/reports.
aspx?source=2&series=GB.XPD.RSDV.GD.ZS&country

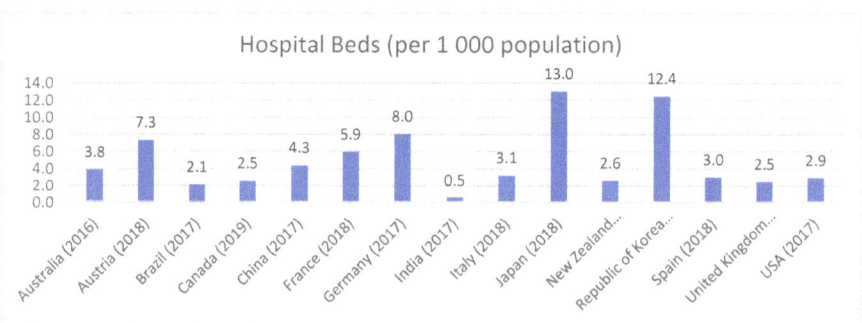

Source: World Health Organization, (author's own chart)
https://www.who.int/data/gho/data/indicators/indicator-details/GHO/hospital-beds-(per-10-000-population)

Chart 7.12 Hospital beds (per 1000 population)
Source: World Health Organization (author's own chart)
https://www.who.int/data/gho/data/indicators/indicator-details/GHO/hospital-beds-(per-10-000-population)

welfare. The argument about where this should be is contentious and by no means settled in the world. There is, however, little doubt about the importance of the impact of government expenditure in providing the basic needs of people and investment in the creation of healthy and well-educated human capital.

Investing in the creation of human capital can be done through direct investment by the provision of basic needs, health, and education through the public and private sectors, or a significant share of it can be placed on the public sector alone. The

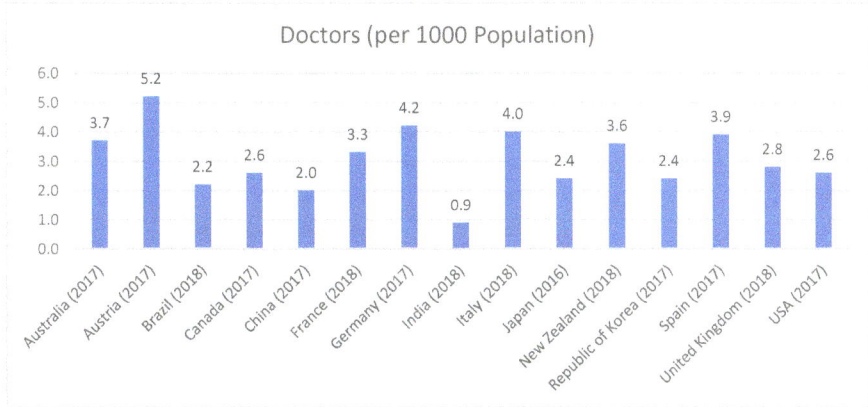

Chart 7.13 Doctor (per 1000 population)
Source: The World Bank (author's own chart) https://databank.worldbank.org/reports.aspx?source=2&series=SH.MED.PHYS.ZS&country=

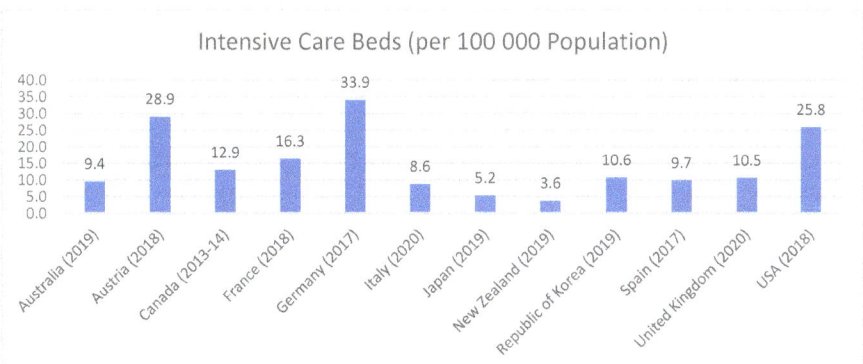

Chart 7.14 Intensive care beds (per 100,000 population)
Source: OECD (author's own chart)
https://www.oecd.org/coronavirus/en/data-insights/intensive-care-beds-capacity
Note: OECD database did not provide information for India, China, and Brazil

efficacy of relying on one or the other is an important topic which falls outside the focus of this study.

One of the most important questions is if, in the selected countries, healthcare is accessible to all through a system entirely financed by the public sector. Furthermore, the question of whether the provision of healthcare is done through a universal system or other means become also very important.

Australia	Universal government funded healthcare system
Austria	Universal public-private insurance system
Brazil	Universal government funded healthcare system
Canada	Universal government funded healthcare system
China	Universal public insurance system
France	Universal public insurance system
Germany	Universal public-private insurance system
India	Non-universal insurance system
Italy	Universal government funded healthcare system
Japan	Universal public insurance system
New Zealand	Universal government funded healthcare system
Republic of Korea	Universal public insurance system
Spain	Universal government funded healthcare system
United Kingdom	Universal government funded healthcare system
United States	Non-universal insurance system

Source: Social Security Programs Throughout the World, 2020 (author's own exhibit)
https://www.ssa.gov/policy/docs/progdesc/ssptw/

Exhibit 7.1 Status of prevailing healthcare systems in selected countries
Source: Social Security Programs Throughout the World (**2020**) (author's own exhibit) https://
www.ssa.gov/policy/docs/progdes**c/ssptw/**

Exhibit 7.1 shows that there are four distinguishable systems through public and private financial arrangements for the provision of healthcare systems in the selected countries. All of the countries, with the exception of the United States and India, have universal healthcare systems. Among the remaining countries, there are three methods of providing universal healthcare systems. The first group, like Australia, Canada, or the United Kingdom, provides a universal government-funded healthcare system. The second group of countries provides a public insurance system. These are countries such as China, France, Japan, and the Republic of Korea. The third group includes Germany and Austria, and they provide a universal public-private insurance system. The important issue is that in 13 countries, providing healthcare is universal, and everyone is entitled to it regardless of their income, employment status, or age.

Having a universal healthcare system is an important step towards the creation of a system that can be resilient towards outside shocks, such as pandemics or other unexpected natural or human-created disasters (other environmental incidences, war, etc.). The economic reason is that such services are considered essential, and their provision does not depend on the decisions of private sector. However, the efficiency of the system in terms of its cost-effectiveness and actual budgetary allocation is also very important. Chart 7.6 brings attention to these very important issues through the performance of the selected countries.

The pattern of budgetary allocation of resources to healthcare is widely different among the selected countries. India represents the lowest of such allocations. The United States, Japan, Germany, Canada, and New Zeeland indicate a higher proportion of budgetary allocation. While Chart 7.6 presents important information about the role of government through its budget in the provision of healthcare, the question of resource allocation to healthcare is not clear if we limit ourselves to the budgetary allocation of a government, since in almost all these countries, the private sector also has a contribution. In a country like the United States, the role of private sector is very crucial, but a lion's share of healthcare expenses is on the shoulder of taxpayers. Furthermore, the cost of healthcare may differ in different countries based on their existing compensation of medical personnel or other cost differentiating market structures. For example, in the United States, drug companies enjoy a different ability to determine their prices than in many European countries. Laws governing patents, which have a determining impact on the cost of drugs, differ widely in different countries. Chart 7.7 provides more information about the cost of healthcare among the selected countries.

Chart 7.7's comparison with Chart 7.6 provides important insight into the structure of healthcare industries within the selected countries. The United States has the highest proportion of cost of healthcare compared with any other country presented in the group. This brings a number of important issues to mind. As a country without a universal healthcare system, the United States spends by far the greatest proportion of its GDP on healthcare, and yet, not all of its residents have access to healthcare. One of the possible implications is the question of cost-effectiveness of the system in the United States. India does not provide universal healthcare system either; however, the allocation of resources through the overall functioning of its economy is low too. One can argue that India, as the second most populated country on Earth, has not brought the needed attention to the health of its residents.

Chart 7.8 provides a better angle to look into the efficacy of the healthcare systems within the selected countries. It is a good indicator of the efficacy of each healthcare system. In other words, life expectancy can be a good indicator of the functionality of a healthcare system.[12]

Chart 7.8 shows that the United States, with the highest percentage of the cost of healthcare as a proportion of its GDP and highest proportion of budgetary allocation, has one of the lowest life expectancies among the group. The comparison between China and the United States is rather alarming. According to the information presented, the United States, as a proportion of its GDP, spends more than three times that of China and its life expectancy is less than 2 years higher than China. This comparison can be done between the United States and almost all other

---

[12] It could be argued that a number of other social factors can impact life expectancy at birth, such as quality of food, culture of exercise, environmental conditions, and other related factors. While we cannot reject the impact of such factors, there is an important and determining impact which comes from prevailing healthcare system within a country. This can also be brought out through the prevalence of preventive care, which is an important part of a universal healthcare under government sector in countries.

countries in the group, and the result tells the same story, which is a prevalence of a highly inefficient healthcare system in the United States. This creates an important discussion: the role of government and its involvement in the provision of healthcare services, as a public service and good, which should be provided to all as an entitlement and not based on the existing demand.

Going further with the discussion of healthcare investment and its provision as an effective policy of being prepared for natural disasters such as COVID-19 and the lessons learned for a better tomorrow and a need for structural changes in the resource allocation, we will look at a number of important areas of investment in the common good of an economy.

Chart 7.9 presents an important picture which requires focused attention. It reveals the importance of preventive care in a healthcare system. Although it is hard to generalize the following conclusion without further research, it can be said that a public sector-financed and sector-run healthcare system may have higher interest in the promotion of a preventive healthcare system since it works more effectively towards the reduction of the overall cost of a healthcare system and a nonprofit-based healthcare system is more likely to be aware and conscious of cost reduction than a profit-based healthcare system. This is not a new argument that for-profit systems focus on profit maximization, whereas a public-financed and public-run system is based on cost-effectiveness and the creation of economies of scale. These are important economic issues with far-reaching consequences on the health of a nation and its level of preparedness to face unexpected healthcare shocks such as COVID-19 in its economic and social life.

Finally, Chart 7.11 looks at the impact of research and development within the selected countries.

Looking into the future and bringing about change through focusing on research and development (R&D) is a vital element of becoming better prepared for the changes ahead. Taking this investigation further, we will look at a number of areas of capacity of the selected countries in provision of needed healthcare services.

The pattern is very uneven. Some countries like Japan, South Korea, Germany, and Austria have a much higher level of preparedness via hospital beds to accommodate possible surges. This level is much lower in countries like India, Brazil, the United States, and the United Kingdom.

A number of important propositions can be suggested in explaining the findings presented in Charts 7.12, 7.13, and 7.14. The first, and probably the most important, suggestion is that countries who treat the provision of healthcare as a demand for all or a large group of its people are likely to pay lesser attention to the provision of such a service as they leave it to the market and demand rather than needs. In such a process, it is quite predictable to end up with an inadequate provision of services and by extension preparation for contingencies. The other proposal is that considering healthcare as a need should be coupled with sufficient allocation of resources to such needs. Finally, it is also important to bear in mind that countries may embark on different methods of providing the needed care. For example, in some countries, a much higher level of care is provided by nurses or assistant physicians than physicians. All such considerations and controlling for their impact may lead us toward better analyses and conclusions. Nonetheless, the issue of treating healthcare as a need has a very important implication within this study.

7.4.2.1   Focusing on the Impact of Pandemic on Low-Income Countries

The plight of low-income countries in dealing with COVID-19 deserves special attention. These countries are often faced with food insecurity and their economic well-being is closely tied to the continuation of their economic ties with developed countries.

Many developing countries have become increasingly integrated into global trade and finance over the past several decades. However, for a significant number of developing countries, the problem is their dependency on developed countries' change in demand in the markets of developed countries for the products exported from low-income countries. This has been observed in recent times, and a good example of it can be found in the international financial crisis of 2008 (Damooei, 2015).[13]

Macroeconomic changes in the world could have triggered a series of their own negative impacts, and there have been serious concerns with regard to developing countries, particularly the low-income group. Past experiences showed that the lowering of interest rates and other economic problems that may lead to devaluation of currencies can lead to increases in the prices of raw materials and other products that are exported by the developing countries. Weak financial positions of countries increase their inability to come up with financial policies to stimulate their economies. The lowering of growth and a rise in poverty become unavoidable in many countries. The inability to provide social protection for people can cause many of these countries to plunge into economic, social, and political instability.[14]

Bisong et al. (2020), in their recent study, indicate that the flow of remittance as an integral part of development finance proved relatively resilient during the 2008 financial crisis and the 2014 Ebola epidemic. However, they are currently under threat by the COVID-19 pandemic. Lockdown measures implemented in host countries have caused many migrants to lose their jobs, consequently reducing remittance flows to developing countries. In 2020, the World Bank estimated a historical decline in global remittances of $110 billion (US dollars), with sub-Saharan Africa (SSA) expected to experience a decline of about 23.1%.[15]

---

[13] See Damooei J. (2015). Economics of the Debt Crisis and Its Impact on the Developing Countries, Ed, The Changing Landscape of Global Financial Governance and the Role of Soft Law, Brill Martines Nijhoff Publishers.

[14] Ibid.

[15] For more information, see Bisong et al. (2020). The impact of COVID-19 on remittances for development in Africa (No. 269). ECDPM Discussion Paper [PDF]. Retrieved from https://elibrary.acbfpact.org/acbf/collect/acbf/index/assoc/HASH0184/a19668a2/637b2693/3273.dir/Impact%20COVID%2019%20remittances%20development%20Africa%20ECDPM.pdf

Developing countries are likely to be the worst affected economically by COVID-19 in the medium and long term. For example, the World Food Program (WFP) predicts that an additional quarter of a billion people will be hungry around the world by the end of 2020 as a result of the pandemic.[16]

Dahab et al. (2020) argue that whenever vaccines, improved therapeutics, or rapid testing for COVID-19 become available, these must be allocated equitably to low-income and crisis-affected populations. They explain that approaches such as containment of importation are likely to have exhausted their potential in the immediate future; not all interventions are of equal value, and the opportunity costs of emphasizing one over the other should be considered. The price of inaction may be high. Suboptimal, inefficient control interventions could, however, be costlier.

The need for paying special attention to low-income countries and finding ways to help them is important for a number of reasons. They range from observing the core value of humanity which is to respond to those in need at a time of crisis, irrespective of where they are within the global community, to recognition of the fact that being together when a pandemic hit the global society is essential if the global society is looking for a lasting solution. Pandemics can only be controlled when we treat the whole community as one.

7.4.3   The Impact of Social Environment on Resilience of Countries to Pandemics

This segment of the research goes beyond the conventional arguments for how and why some countries face adversarial developments with greater resiliency and a number of them do not. This segment requires a much deeper investigation than is offered in this chapter. However, it is important to bring the relevant issues and, to the extent possible, provide relevant observations and evidence which can help us to understand some of the unexpected changes resulting in the escalation of health problems and a loss of lives, what can be termed as unnecessary or avoidable.

It is hard to be accurate about what the final numbers indicate with regard to the rate of infection and mortality. However, we have sufficient information to see that the existing pattern, with some level of confidence, can be predicted in regard to the final outcome and that it will not be very different from what can be observed during the last month of 2020.[17]

While there is clear evidence suggesting that testing, contact tracing, wearing masks, keeping the safety measures regarding gathering and assembling, and occasional lockdowns have been effective, there seems to be a wide variety of

---

[16] For more information, see Carmody, P. (2020). Meta-trends in global value chains and development: interacting impacts with COVID-19 in Africa. Transnational Corporations Journal, 27(2) [PDF]. Retrieved from https://unctad.org/system/files/official-document/diaeia2020d2a8_en.pdf

[17] The paper was finalized and submitted for publication during the end of 2020.

interpretations, which resulted in the rejection of scientific recommendations and a high level of politicization of various simple safety measures. At the same time, a number of countries, and in particular the United States, have not been willing to invest in people and making it economically possible for them to follow the safety measures, in particular with regard to staying away from having to work. The situation makes it impossible to stay away from work, when one cannot make ends meet without work and the paycheck that accompanies it. The battle for surviving COVID-19 and the ability to afford a minimum standard of living does not offer a choice, when those unemployed have no means to meet their basic economic needs.

These issues are complex and deserve their specific studies. However, we will look at some of the most pressing social and political issues which have impacted the overall impact of COVID-19 on the state of the economies of various countries.

7.4.3.1 The Impact of Trust Within an Economy

Public trust and how it is created or broken is a complicated subject worthy of a much higher level of scrutiny and investigation. It is present when one can find loyalty to the constitution of a country or society, its laws, and the existence of a set of ethical principles not defined with a limited boundary of private gain. What is evident when we look at the state of various nations, we observe clear differences between them. For example, in some countries wearing masks by a significant number of people was taken to be a threat to their personal freedom, whereas in most countries it was regarded as an important step to save the lives of others when a pandemic is in place and threatens the lives of many. Why many take a simple and logical act of reducing the spread of a lethal virus as a threat to personal freedom can in part be addressed by a lack of trust in what a government or segments of a government recommends.

Nunn et al. (2018) argue that severe economic downturns are more likely to cause political turnover in countries that have lower levels of generalized trust. The relationship is only found among democracies and for regular leader turnover, which suggests that the underlying mechanism works through leader accountability and the electoral process.[18] A related development, which stems from the inability of the prevailing economic system to instill trust in people, is the hardship and inability of the countries to respond to the desires of its own working people for increased opportunities and receiving a fair share of the prosperity. The latter is most evident in a country like the United States.

The prevailing information and current research show that the overwhelming majority of US workers have not received the benefits of the increased proactivity in labor. The Economic Policy Institute's (EPI) most recent study of 40+ years of US productivity and hourly compensation shines light on the root of the discontent in

---

[18] For more information, see Nathan Nunn et al. (2018), Distrust and Political Turnover, National Bauru of Economic Research (NBER), https://www.nber.org/system/files/working_papers/w24187/w24187.pdf

our society. It shows that the productivity and compensation of average American workers dovetailed from 1948 to 1973. Productivity increased by 96.7% and hourly wages by 91.3%. The average workers were among the recipients of the nation's prosperity. From 1973 to 2014, productivity increased by 72.2% whereas the average hourly wage increased by only 9.2%. If we focus on just 1980 onward, the picture is even clearer. From 1979 to 2013, productivity increased by 62%, while the compensation of 90% of Americans went up by only 15.2%. The average annual compensation increase over this 34-year period was only 0.48%. During the same period of time, the earnings of the top 1% increased by 138%. No wonder the overwhelming majority of Americans feel that they have been left behind.[19]

A similar trend is threatening the well-being of many working people around the world which is the outcome of the emergence of a highly productive economy and service sector-based economy in the post-industrial era, use of automation, and a race to bottom emanating from a rise in the influence of large mega transnational companies in creating the prevailing policies of international trade. The existing evidence shows that wages and salaries of a large proportion of workers have been traded off with increased corporate profits and a depression of worker wages.

Van Biesebroeck (2014), in a survey of literature published by ILO, indicates that wage policies and labor market institutions play a crucial role in building equitable societies and sustainable economies, in which the fruits of progress are shared with all. He indicates that recent trends around the world show that, in many countries, there is a considerable difference and gap between wage growth and the growth of productivity. This trend has led to a decline in the share of national income paid to workers as labor compensation. This in turn brought forward a growing inequality in the personal distribution of income. This change has been structural and comes with incomes increasing much more rapidly at the top than in the middle or at the bottom of the distribution. The author believes that this trend is harmful to social justice and can lead to internal imbalances inducing families to borrow beyond their means and exerting a downward pressure on household consumption and aggregate demand. In some instances, wages have increased more rapidly than labor productivity, eroding external competitiveness and sometimes discouraging investment.[20]

The problem therefore comes down to wage policies today, which should be the center of attention for public policy decisions. Corrective wage policies are crucial in the face of a gradual and certain trend towards a clear path of further disparity of wages in relation to productivity. Appropriate and effective policies need to receive

---

[19] For more information, see Josh Bivens and Lawrence Mishel (2015), Understanding the Historic Divergence Between Productivity and a Typical Worker's Pay, Briefing Paper #406, Economic Policy Institute (EPI). https://www.epi.org/publication/understanding-the-historic-divergence-between-productivity-and-a-typical-workers-pay-why-it-matters-and-why-its-real/

[20] For more information, see Johannes Van Biesebroeck (2015), How tight is the link between wages and productivity? A survey of the literature, International Labor Office, Conditions of Work and Employment Series No. 54. https://www.ilo.org/wcmsp5/groups/public/%2D%2D-ed_protect/%2D%2D-protrav/%2D%2D-travail/documents/publication/wcms_410267.pdf

close attention from governments and social partners who – within their own national context – seek to ensure that minimum wages, collective bargaining, and other labor market institutions contribute to fair, efficient, and inclusive labor markets.

Public trust surely has other dimensions within the culture and history of different countries and nations. The important issue for this particular research is to link this factor to the ability of countries to help themselves to face the negative impacts of COVID-19 and to reduce them. Chart 7.15 presents a comparison between the selected countries for which the information was available.

Chart 7.15 shows trust in government as it refers to the share of people who report having confidence in the national government. Countries like Canada, New Zealand, and Germany score very high. In order to take a historical look at this trend and tie it to the ongoing discussion about the state of the economy and perception of working people, we looked at the change in the United States over the last 75 years. In the graph below, the number shows percentages of people who trust the government (Chart 7.16).

The chart presents a remarkable change over the last 75 years. A significant part of this trend very much captures the same trend in separation of productivity and wages and the gradual disenfranchisement of an overwhelming majority of workers in the United States. This is a destructive trend and may lead to drastic changes in the political environment. Some of the results of this trend can be seen in the rise of populist movements in the United States and in a number of other countries around the world.

We take the issue of trust further and try to see if trust in government is structurally different with trusting other members of the community. This can be presented in Chart 7.17.

Although there are some minor differences, the trust patterns presented among the countries are similar when trust in government or people in general is under

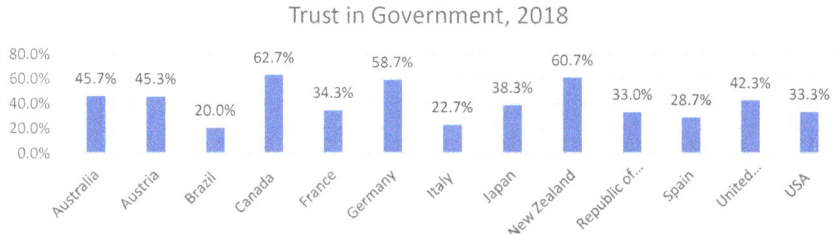

Source: OECD (author's own chart)
https://data.oecd.org/gga/trust-in-government.htm
Note: Data for India and China were not available

Chart 7.15   Trust in government
Source: OECD (author's own chart)
https://data.oecd.org/gga/trust-in-government.htm
Note: Data for India and China were not available

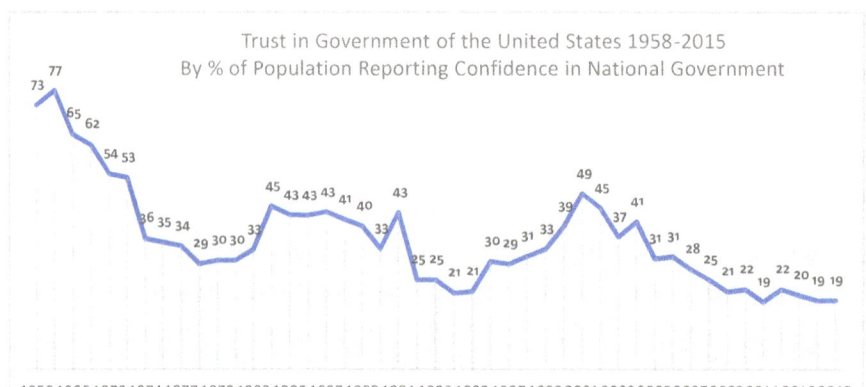

Source: Ourworldindata; (author's own chart)
https://ourworldindata.org/grapher/public-trust-in-government
Note: There is no direct way to compare the results of this survey with other surveys. The important issue is that we are comparing the findings from the same source for all the years reported.

Chart 7.16 Trust in government of United States from 1958 to 2015
Source: Ourworldindata (author's own chart)
https://ourworldindata.org/grapher/public-trust-in-government
Note: There is no direct way to compare the results of this survey with other surveys. The important issue is that we are comparing the findings from the same source for all the years reported

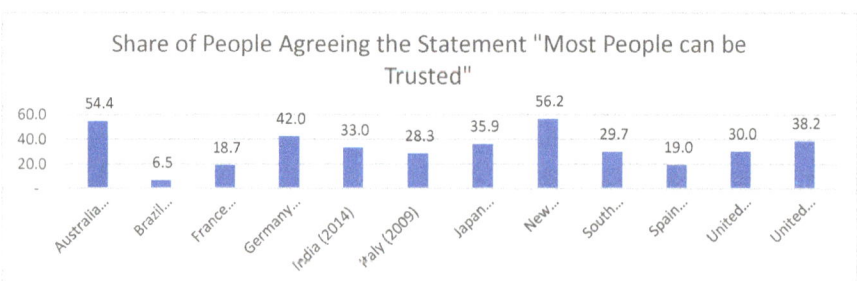

Source: Ourworldindata; (author's own chart)
https://ourworldindata.org/trust
Note: Information for China, Canada and Austria, were not available

Chart 7.17 Share of people agreeing the statement "Most People can be Trusted"
Source: Ourworldindata (author's own chart)
https://ourworldindata.org/trust
Note: Information for China, Canada, and Austria were not available

observation. It shows that an environment of trust appears to be a nationwide environment, and it impacts trust toward their governments and each other in the same manner.

Trust in the government or one another has practical implications in accepting or rejecting decisions which can be examined based on acceptable scientific basis. We have seen the detrimental reactions of societies and their resorting to baseless propaganda and rumors in some countries which pretty much follow a path of distrust when we look closely into such cases. A good example of it is the emergence of claims against wearing masks in the United States and some other countries. To show the fallacy of such claims against the existing scientific evidence in support of using masks and seeing their positive impacts in a number of countries, Table 7.1 offers some relevant and useful information.

7.4.3.2 Having Choice to Withstand Harsh Economic Environment

Many countries over the course of the rise and fall of the COVID-19 virus ordered their residents to observe lockdowns. However, the level of economic assistance to make such lockdowns possible varied among countries.

The practices of various countries have been very different. In a country like China, the lockdown was enforced with a high level of restriction and people were quarantined for a certain number of days with full amenities and healthcare services while the eradication of the virus was in progress. Testing and contact tracing were aggressively followed by countries like South Korea, Singapore, New Zealand, and Australia.

Gibney (2020) from *Nature* writes that efforts to tackle the questions about the success of countries to contain COVID-19 are shown from a database that brings together information on the hundreds of different interventions that have been introduced worldwide. The platform is being prepared for the World Health Organization (WHO) by a team at the London School of Hygiene & Tropical Medicine (LSHTM). The platform gathers data collected by ten groups tracked by interventions, including teams at the University of Oxford, United Kingdom, the Complexity Science Hub Vienna (CSH Vienna), and public health organizations and nonprofit organizations such as ACAPS, which analyzes humanitarian crises.[21]

In Europe, for example, Sweden, the United Kingdom, and the Netherlands are grouped together as countries that acted relatively slowly. In the early stages of their epidemics, all three implemented "herd immunity" strategies, which involved few measures or ones that relied on voluntary compliance, although later, the United Kingdom and the Netherlands switched to more aggressive responses, including countrywide lockdowns. Meanwhile, Germany and Austria stand out as nations that adopted aggressive and early control strategies compared with Italy, France, and Spain, which implemented similar measures, including lockdowns, but later in their epidemics. As a result, Germany and Austria have, per capita, seen a fraction of the deaths from COVID-19 of these other countries in the early and later stages of the pandemic development and spread.[22]

---

[21] For more information, see Elizabeth Gibney (2020), Whose coronavirus strategy worked best? Scientists hunt most effective policies, Nature https://www.nature.com/articles/d41586-020-01248-1

[22] These number changed towards the end of the year. However, the conclusion about their lower death rate remained relatively more favorable due to their policies compared with the other

Table 7.1 Arguments against weaning masks

Arguments against mask requirements during the coronavirus (COVID-19) pandemic, 2020

	Mask requirements are not necessary to stop the spread of coronavirus	Mask requirements give a false sense of security	Mask requirements restrict freedom	Masks present other health risks	Mask requirements have harmful social consequences	Mask requirements are unenforceable
Claim 1	There is insufficient data to support that mask requirements effectively prevent the spread of coronavirus	Mask-wearing mandates encourage people to pursue risky behaviors and activities that could spread COVID-19	Mask requirements are an overreach of government power and are unconstitutional	Wearing masks can cause other health risks	Wearing of masks can generate racist reactions	Local mask laws with unclear enforcement mechanisms are ineffective, counterproductive, and potentially dangerous for employees
Claim 2	The curve has been successfully flattened in areas without mask requirements		Mask requirements are a slippery slope and will lead to more government mandates, bureaucracy, and regulations		Mask wearing inhibits communication and children's social development	Mask mandates for businesses require employees to enforce laws
Claim 3	Mask requirements risk deemphasizing other necessary public health measures				Mask mandates are immoral laws by government-imposed to control human behavior and personal development	Colleges and universities should not ask students to report violations of Covid-19 rules

Source: Ballotpedia (author's own table) https://ballotpedia.org/Arguments_against_mask_requirements_during_the_coronavirus_(COVID-19)_pandemic._2020

Early findings from the Oxford Team also suggest that poorer nations tended to bring in stricter measures than did richer countries, relative to the severity of their outbreaks.[23] For example, the Caribbean nation of Haiti enforced lockdown on confirming its first case, whereas the United States waited until more than 2 weeks after its first death to issue stay-at-home orders.[24]

A large number of countries in the world did not start controlling COVID-19 in a drastic and aggressive manner. Some of them never took the pandemic seriously and as a result brought severe consequences to their countries and people. Among them, Brazil takes a distinct place. The United States and India can be placed in the same group of countries.

Finally, helping people to stay in lockdown can only be successful when people are given the choice by setting in place economic measures which can support people who are out of their jobs with help through relevant fiscal policies and companies through fiscal and monetary policies. We will take a close look at some of these policies in a selected group of countries for which data is available.

Table 7.2 shows a widely different scheme of support for working families and people during the time of the pandemic. Countries like Canada, Germany, Australia, and France have had far greater provisions to support their people and give them a true choice of staying in the state of lockdown than being forced to work and make ends meet. The United Kingdom has some restrictive provisions but has more provisions in support of its people during the pandemic than the United States. The United States has more gaps in its support, and leaving a fair share of it to state provisions makes it more complicated and, in reality, more restrictive. Bearing in mind that states have their own policies and financial abilities, which ultimately depend on assistance from the federal government and the support of a majority of working families, low income remained a problem for millions for much of the duration of the problem up until the completion of this study.

We have to add to this lack of support in the United States the disregard towards the plight of its undocumented immigrants, which in some states are close to 10% of the labor force. This group of workers received the lowest level of support during the pandemic. Bearing in mind that offering the choice of working or following the instruction of governments (federal, state, or regional) and accepting the lockdown orders impacted all workers regardless of their residency, since the virus can spread regardless of one's citizenship. The inability of the government in the United States to help its people has been rather illogical and, in many respects, inhumane.

European countries who followed a more relaxed set of policies and opted for herd immunity at the start of the pandemic.

[23] Oxford Team refers to the Oxford University team of scientists involved in development of COVID-19 vaccine.

[24] Ibid.

Table 7.2 Government support during coronavirus pandemic

	United Kingdom	Australia	Canada	France	Germany	United States
Wage subsidies						
New wage subsidy scheme						Existing but rarely used scheme also allows workers whose hours are cut to claim prorated UI
						No – except for ERC for companies with over 100 employees
Only compensates for hours that employees do not any longer work?	Yes (Apr–Jun must be furloughed completely; Jul–Oct also covers those on reduced hours)	No – receive AU$1500 per fortnight (£410 pw) regardless of hours worked	No – paid 75% of old wage (or, if hours cut, 100% of new wage if that is lower)	Yes – reimbursed for any hours they are unable to work	Yes	>50% turnover fall (ERC); businesses employing <500 people (PPP); businesses can only claim ERC or PPP
Any eligibility requirements	No	30% turnover fall, or 50% for large businesses, 15% for charities	15% turnover fall for first month, 30% for subsequent months	Employees' work must be stopped by coronavirus	Employers must put 10% of workforce on the scheme, must be temporary, unavoidable loss of work	50% (ERC); UI replacement rate varies by state (see below)

	United Kingdom	Australia	Canada	France	Germany	United States
% of wages paid (gross or net)	80% (gross)	Uniform AU$1500 per fortnight (£410 pw) per employee (all of which must go to the employee, regardless of employee's previous earnings or current hours)	Up to 75% previous wage (gross); if hours are cut, scheme pays the lower of 100% of new wage and 75% of previous wage	70% (gross) or €8 (£7) per hour (whichever is higher)	Starts at 60% (gross), increases to 80% over time. Extra 7% for workers with children	$5000 (£3940) in total (ERC); 100% of wages for 8 weeks up to max of $15,385 (£12,100) in total (PPP)
Maximum payment per employee through the scheme	£2500 per month (£580 pw)	AU$1500 per fortnight (£410 pw)	CA$847 (£500) per week	€6927 per month (£1423 pw)	Only available for those paid <€6900 (£6130) pcm	
	United Kingdom	**Australia**	**Canada**	**France**	**Germany**	**United States** Yes (PUA and FPUC)
Unemployment benefits						
New welfare benefit	No – generosity of existing benefit (Universal Credit) increased	Yes (coronavirus supplement to job seeker)	Yes (CERB)	No	No	Varies by state: $600 (£470) per week coronavirus supplement, on top of existing state UI payments (worth 25–50% of previous weekly wage). Total amounts are roughly equal to level for average wage in most states

(continued)

Table 7.2 (continued)

	United Kingdom	Australia	Canada	France	Germany	United States
Level of unemployment benefits available to those who lose their jobs due to Covid-19	£410 per month (£90 pw) for a single, childless adult	AU$1116 per fortnight (£310 pw) for a single, childless adult	CA$1000 per fortnight (£290 pw)	57% of previous daily salary or 40.4% plus €12 (£11) a day, whichever is higher (up to cap of €248 (£220) a day). Minimum €29 (£26) a day	60% (or 67% for parents) of previous net wages below €6900 (£6130) in West Germany and €6450 (£5730) in East	Anyone unemployed through no fault of their own, including casual workers. State-level work history requirements
Eligibility for unemployment benefits	All unemployed and low earners eligible except those with >£16 K savings, or with partner with higher earnings	Anyone with fortnightly earnings under AU$1086 (£290 pw) who is unemployed, a gig/casual worker, sick, or caring for sick people	Anyone earning <CA$1000 per month, who both earned >CA$5000 (£2930) in 2019 and due to Covid-19 is unemployed, sick, or has a career	Anyone who paid contributions for 4 months in past 28 months and did not quit job voluntarily	Anyone who has paid contributions for 12 of past 24 months and be seeking new job	Extra $600 per week for all UI claimants, UI duration extended, extension of UI-equivalent benefits to gig workers and those whose claims had expired (PUA)
Changes made in response to coronavirus	£20 per week extra, made easier for self-employed to qualify	AU$550 per fortnight (£150 pw) extra, partner income test relaxed and asset limits waived	Entirely new benefit	All benefit claimants continue receiving benefits to 31 July, even if entitlement should run out before then	Eligibility period extended for further 3 months	
	United Kingdom	Australia	Canada	France	Germany	United States No – covered by PUA

Compensation for the self-employed

New welfare benefit	Yes	No – covered by jobseeker; sole traders also eligible for job keeper	No – covered by CERB	Yes	No – eligible for business grants, and easier access to basic welfare payment	Must self-certify to have lost some income due to coronavirus and be capable of looking for work
Eligibility criteria	Average annual profits over past 3 years less than £50,000 and have been trading in March 2019	30% turnover fall (job keeper); fall in income to under AU$1086 per fortnight (jobseeker)	Income affected/ stopped by coronavirus or caring commitments, earning less than CA$1000 per month after expenses	Turnover fall of >50%, annual taxable profit of less than €60,000 (£54,000)	60% fall in revenue loss April-May 2020 compared to previous year	Same proportion of 2019 earnings as UI (25–50% of previous weekly wage depending on state), plus $600 per week. Reduces with income earned
Compensation provided	80% of average of past 3 years' profits (regardless of current revenues/profits) for first 3 months; 70% for second phase	Job keeper: AU$1500 per fortnight. Jobseeker: AU$1116 per fortnight for a single, childless adult with income under AU$1086 per fortnight	CA$1000 per fortnight	100% of your income lost compared with same month in 2019	Grants to cover operating costs for 3 months	Varies by state – between US$900 and US$1200 (£710–£950) per week in most states
Maximum amount that can be received through the scheme	£2500 per month (£580 pw) first phase, £2190 (£500 pw) second phase	See above	CA$1000 per fortnight	€1500 per month (£310 pw)	€9000 (£7990)	

Source: Instituteforgovernment (author's own table)
https://www.instituteforgovernment.org.uk/coronavirus-support-workers-comparison

7.5   Need for International Cooperation

Public health measures to prevent, detect, and respond to events are essential to control public health risks, including infectious disease outbreaks. Kandel et al. (2020) used 18 indicators from the International Health Regulations (IHR) for State Party Annual Reporting (SPAR) tool and associated data from national SPAR reports to develop five indices: (1) prevent, (2) detect, (3) respond, (4) enabling function, and (5) operational readiness.[25]

Of 182 countries, 52 or 28% had prevent capacities at levels 1 or 2, and 60 or 33% had response capacities at levels 1 or 2. Of the countries, 81 or 45% had prevent capacities and 78 or 43% had response capacities at levels 4 or 5, indicating that these countries were operationally ready. Of the countries, 138 or 76% scored more highly in the detect index than in the other indices.

However, 44 or 24% of the countries did not have an effective enabling function for public health risks and events, including infectious disease outbreaks: 7 or 4% at level 1 and 37 or 20% at level 2. Of the countries, 102 or 56% had level 4 or 5 enabling function capacities in place. Of the countries, 32 or 18% had low readiness, 2 or 1% at level 1 and 30 or 17% at level 2, and 104 or 57% of countries were operationally ready to prevent, detect, and control an outbreak of a novel infectious disease, while 66 or 36% were at level 4 and 38 or 21% were at level 5.

Lee et al. (2020, July) believe that the Coronavirus crisis may lead to a deeper understanding of international collaborations for developing antivirals and vaccines that are essential to protect us from current and future health security threats.[26] A logical deduction leads to a simple conclusion that working in isolation and constantly reinventing the wheel makes no sense in an international setting when the danger is common to all, and the loss of one is directly related to a loss of all when an international occurrence like pandemic strikes the global community.

Oldekop et al. (2020) argue that COVID-19 brings urgency for a global, rather than an international, development paradigm. This pandemic is a prime example of a development challenge for all countries through the failure of their public healthcare systems as a global public good or service.[27] They argue that this pandemic brought focused attention to the fallacy of any assumption that the global North has all the expertise and solutions to tackle global challenges and has further highlighted the need for multidirectional learning and transformation in all countries

---

[25] See Nirmal Kandel et al. (2020). Health security capacities in the context of COVID-19 outbreak: an analysis of International Health Regulations annual report data from 182 countries Retrieved from https://www.thelancet.com/action/showPdf?pii=S0140-6736%2820%2930553-5

[26] See Doyeon Lee et al. (2020, July). A Strategy for International Cooperation in the COVID-19 Pandemic Era: Focusing on National Scientific Funding Data. MDPI Retrieved from https://www.mdpi.com/2227-9032/8/3/204

[27] For more information, see Johan A. Oldekop et al. (2020, June). COVID-19 and the case for global development. World Development [PDF]. Retrieved from https://reader.elsevier.com/reader/sd/pii/S0305750X20301704?token=BE330080326E997BDA9F7EB322BD0E96A00BA2295EA23FCEC8D8B733996DAED28E2306EF32E42EE948A4E0F5746F54F3

towards a more sustainable and equitable world. Their study presented a strong argument for a global development paradigm through examining the implications of the COVID-19 pandemic across four themes or "vignettes": global value chains, digitalization, debt, and climate change. The core of this argument is that development studies must adapt to a very different context from when the field emerged in the mid-twentieth century.

Barbier and Burgess (2020) argue about the high vulnerability to the COVID-19 pandemic of developing countries. They demonstrate that this problem in part is due to the lack of international support for ensuring progress towards the 17 Sustainable Development Goals (SDGs). Yet the mounting financial burden faced by all countries means that additional support is unlikely to be forthcoming in the near future.[28]

The authors argue that finding innovative policy mechanisms to achieve sustainability and development through cost-effective measures and policies are essential for all countries. This requires identifying affordable policies that can yield immediate progress towards several SDGs together and aligning economic incentives for longer-term sustainable development.[29]

Bhusal (2020) takes a different and rather critical view and, to a great extent, a pessimistic one about the fallout of COVID-19.[30] The author predicts strong tendencies towards greater global challenges for political processes, particularly on the instruments of democracy and the rule of law. He argues that learning from various reports during the pandemic, the post-pandemic world will be characterized by populism, nationalism, intensified citizen surveillance, and curtailed and compromised individual liberties.

The pandemic will also inflict severe damage to globalization, free trade, multilateralism, and development cooperation. A more promising note in this study is that problems witnessed during this crisis, however, are systemic and caused by dysfunctional neoliberal corporate capitalism. In that sense, if there is a political mandate of this crisis – that is to find an alternative to the obsolete and oppressive neoliberal corporate capitalism which has served a few and failed the many.[31]

Brown and Susskind (2020) bring a different perspective in their analyses of COVID-19 and its impact on international cooperation. They argue that many of the tasks involved in public health, and in particular those involved in the control of an

---

[28] For more information, see Edward B. Barbier and Joanne C. Burgess (2020, July). Sustainability and development after COVID-19. World Development https://reader.elsevier.com/reader/sd/pii/S0305750X20302084?token=AD3D70011805A4E15826118046BF7E844F1130CC7B4B381954157A95BC03D37E0B1B378A94F1421201B4C0EC74694D45

[29] Ibid.

[30] See Manoj Kr. Bhusal (2020). The World After COVID-19: An Opportunity for a New Beginning; International Journal of Scientific and Research Publications (IJSRP) [PDF]. Retrieved from http://www.ijsrp.org/research-paper-0520/ijsrp-p10185.pdf

[31] Ibid.

infectious disease like COVID-19, ought to be as treated global public goods (GPG), which can only be delivered through international cooperation.[32]

In the early part of this chapter, we focused our attention on the importance of separating the needs from wants and demands, and the attention that should be given to the production of public goods and service in response to and meeting the essential needs in every economy. The issue of GPG requires its own important emphasis. The most important issue in understanding the significance of treating the response to a global pandemic as a GPG is the inseparability of the lives of one country from the lives within others in such a global crisis. Brown and Susskind argue that the most distinctive and challenging feature of GPG problems is that there is no obvious mechanism for resolving them. With a traditional public good, a national government has the power and authority to intervene to ensure the optimal level of provision is achieved within their particular country.[33]

While national governments are able to change domestic law or build national institutions to ensure the optimal level of a traditional public good is secured within their borders, there are no provisions in international law to impose obligations on other sovereign countries to ensure the optimal overall level of a GPG is secured without their consent. The importance of creating an international mechanism for defending the global community against future pandemics and other global calamities requires new initiatives and practical mechanisms that can be pragmatic and functional. The existing international setting for creating such capacity requires innovative thinking and cooperative spirits within the global society that can perceive all nations as equal partners without the endeavor to subjugate resource-scarce communities as lesser companions. Reaching such a level of understanding within the prevailing power struggle and sense of superiority among a good number of developed countries presents a bleak possibility for success.

7.6 How the Lessons Learned May Impact the Resource Allocations Within the Countries and in the Global Setting

Lessons learned: The following segment provides a list of lessons learned, which will be used to highlight the principles and foundations of resource allocation at the global level. We are out of options, and the road ahead cannot be the same as the past if we are going to have a lasting world and functioning economies within countries for a foreseeable future.

---

[32] See Gordon Brown, Daniel Susskind, International cooperation during the COVID-19 pandemic, Oxford Review of Economic Policy, Volume 36, Issue Supplement_1, 2020, Pages S64–S76, https://doi.org/10.1093/oxrep/graa025

[33] Ibid.

- Pandemics and infectious diseases have brought fundamental changes throughout history as they exposed the dysfunctionality of systems and revealed an unacceptable level of ability of the existing systems in serving the needs of people for a continuation of order at the time.
- It is hard to ignore the economic impact of the Bubonic Plague (Black Death), which was a human tragedy that caused a population reduction, brought about a shortage of labor, and finally resulted in an increase in wages and the mobility of workers and improvements in their standard of living.
- Within the context of fourteenth-century economic conditions, the plague brought a fundamental change in agriculture and a shortage of laborers not only impacted their wages but also the type of products based on their labor demand. It also caused a move towards various types of husbandry, more mobility of workers, and the enhancement of restrictive laws which, in time, brought a wave of resistance and political change.
- The Spanish flu pandemic brought a labor supply shock to the economy, while leaving the physical capital intact. The data on GDP is not available and therefore it is hard to make a clear estimation of its overall impact. On the distributional side of the Spanish flu's economic impact, it is argued that it brought about a higher level of poverty in countries impacted. In a number of countries within Europe and the United States, this incidence brought about a delay in these countries in their effort to reach a steady state (full and optimal utilization of their productive resources).
- On a theoretical ground, the developments during the Spanish flu pandemic brought about a considerable level of capital deepening (an excess of physical capital over human capital) which must have led to a lower return to human capital, in turn resulting in more investment in human capital. This means that earnings per capita increased. The effects on capital incomes per capita, which are the product of sinking interest rates and a larger per-capita capital stock, cannot be very clear.
- Climate change brings attention to an important point: while we do not have direct evidence that climate change is influencing the spread of COVID-19, we know that climate change alters how we relate to other species on Earth in the way that our health and our risk for infection is impacted.
- Wants or demands imply a willingness and an ability to purchase. All such goods and services are called private goods and services, and they are produced by willing suppliers, often for profit. The goods and services are provided for all those who willing to pay for them and have the financial ability to do so.
- Some of the most essential elements of a balanced and humanly conceivable life on Earth are not based on demands, but rather on meeting the needs of the individuals, groups, and communities. Meeting the existing or emerging needs is essential for the continuation of life, but those with needs may not be able to pay for them, and therefore, considering them to be demands is incorrect. Continuing with the perception of responding to demands or wants is an ill-founded concept, which in times can create human disasters, the likes of which we have seen and continue to see during this pandemic. This is one of the primary reasons that the

US economy is performing miserably in responding to COVID-19, and this can be seen in a number of other countries around the world as well.

- In order to better demonstrate the economic conditions of various countries and evaluate their potential in dealing with the onslaught of COVID-19, we selected 15 countries from various parts of the world for the purpose of looking deeper into their prevailing conditions, which can directly be linked to their ability to combat COVID-19.

- This study took a number of essential preparations and investments in countries' healthcare sectors and presented a comparative picture of the selected countries with regard to such revision. The rapid spread of COVID-19 took many countries by surprise, and within weeks, there was a panic about having the necessary healthcare facilities, such as hospital beds, personal protective equipment (PPE), respirators, ICU beds, and even masks for the protection of frontline healthcare workers and, in many instances, for caregivers.

- All of the countries, with the exception of the United States and India, have universal healthcare systems. Among the remaining countries, there are three methods of providing healthcare. One group, which includes Australia, Canada, and the United Kingdom, provides a government-funded universal healthcare system. The second group provides a public insurance system, such as China, France, Japan, and the Republic of Korea. The third group includes Germany and Austria, and they provide a universal public-private insurance system. The important issue is that in 13 countries, providing healthcare is universal, and everyone is entitled to it regardless of their income, employment status, or age.

- The United States in particular had one of the worst levels of preparedness to face COVID-19 and, in total, spent the highest level of cost of healthcare as a proportion of its GDP. Such a high level of expenditure does not come about with any concrete level of performance demonstrated by life expectancy at birth. The study makes it very clear that profit-making as a principal element of the cost of delivery of healthcare in the United States did not create an efficient healthcare system in this country.

- The disparity in the levels of preparedness is not in having a universal healthcare system alone, but it is also a function of the level of expenditure and investment in a country's healthcare system.

- The plight of low-income countries dealing with COVID-19 deserves special attention. These countries are often faced with food insecurity, and their economic well-being is closely tied to the continuation of their economic ties with developed countries. Many developing countries have become increasingly integrated into global trade and finance over the past several decades. However, for a significant number of developing countries, the problem is their dependency on developed countries' changes in demand in their markets for the products exported from low-income countries.

- The need for paying special attention to low-income countries and finding ways to help them are important for a number of reasons. They range from observing the core value of humanity, which is to respond to those in need at times of crisis irrespective of where they are within the global community, to recognizing the fact that working together when a pandemic hit the global society is essential if the global society is looking for a lasting solution. Pandemics can only be controlled when we treat a community as one.

- Severe economic downturns are more likely to cause political turnover in countries that have lower levels of generalized trust. The relationship is only found among democracies and for regular leader turnover, which suggests that the underlying mechanism works through leader accountability and the electoral process.
- In the United States, the overwhelming majority of people did not benefit from the economic growth and increase in productivity over the last 45 years. A similar trend is threatening the well-being of many working people around the world which is the outcome of the emergence of a highly productive economy and a service sector-based economy in the post-industrial era, the use of automation, and a race to bottom emanating from rise in influence of large mega transnational companies in creating the prevailing policies of international trade. The existing evidence shows that wages and salaries of a large proportion of workers have been traded off with increased corporate profits and a depression of worker wages.
- Public trust surely has other dimensions within the culture and history of different countries and nations. The important issue for this particular research is to link this factor of the ability of countries to reach the point at which they can help face the negative impacts of COVID-19 and reduce them.
- Trust in the government or one another has practical implications in accepting or rejecting decisions which can be examined based on acceptable scientific basis. We have seen the detrimental reactions of societies and their resort to baseless propaganda and rumors in some countries which follow a path of distrust when we look closely into such cases.
- A large number of countries in the world did not start controlling COVID-19 in a drastic and aggressive manner. A good number of them either never took this pandemic seriously and as a result brought severe consequences upon their populations. Among them, Brazil takes a distinct place. The United States and India can be placed in the same group.
- Helping people to stay in a lockdown can only be successful when people are given the choice by setting in place economic measures which can support people out of work with help through relevant fiscal policies and by helping companies without workers through fiscal and monetary policies. We will take a close look at some of these policies in a selected group of countries for which data is available.
- Existing records present a widely different scheme of support for working families and all people during the time of pandemics. Countries like Canada, Germany, Australia, and France have far greater provisions to support their people and give them a true choice of staying in a state of lockdown rather than being forced to work and make ends meet. The United Kingdom has a more restrictive provision, but compared with the United States has more provisions in support of its own

people during the pandemic. The United States has more gaps in its support, and leaving a fair share of it to state provisions makes it more complicated and in reality, more restrictive.

- COVID-19 brings about an urgency for a global, rather than an international, development paradigm. This pandemic is a prime example of a development challenge for all countries through the failure of their public healthcare system as a global public good or service.
- Studies indicate a high vulnerability to the COVID-19 pandemic of developing countries. This problem in part is due to the lack of international support for ensuring progress towards the 17 Sustainable Development Goals (SDGs). Yet the mounting financial burden faced by all countries means that additional support is unlikely to be forthcoming in the near future.
- Post COIVD-19, unprecedented economic hardships and social anxieties will become the new normal. However, the pandemic also offers a chance to reflect and revise our course and to come up with an alternative that will be just and fair for the many.
- Some studies present a different and rather critical, and to a great extent, pessimistic view regarding the fallout from COVID-19. They predict strong tendencies towards greater global challenges for political processes, particularly on the instruments of democracy and the rule of law. They suggest that learning from various reports during the pandemic, the post-pandemic world will be characterized by populism, nationalism, intensified citizen surveillance, and curtailed and compromised individual liberties.
- The pandemic will also inflict severe damage to globalization, free trade, multilateralism, and development cooperation. A more promising note in this study is that problems witnessed during this crisis are systemic and caused by dysfunctional neoliberal corporate capitalism. In that sense, if there is a political mandate of this crisis – that is to find an alternative to the obsolete and oppressive neoliberal corporate capitalism which has served a few and failed many.
- The most important issue in understanding the significance of treating the global pandemic as GPG is the inseparability of the lives of one country from others within such a global crisis. The most distinctive and challenging feature of GPG problems is that there is no obvious mechanism for resolving them. With a traditional public good, a national government has the power and authority to intervene to ensure the optimal level of provision is achieved within their particular country.

7.7 The Blueprint for a Better Allocation of Resources Toward Creating a Sustainable World That Can Withstand the Challenges Ahead

While during the time of completing this study the hope of seeing the end of this tragedy is somewhat foreseeable with the introduction and use of a vaccine, there is no definitive estimate of the overall economic costs and how the trend will be tamed and settled. There is also another dimension of this catastrophe, which is its dispro-portionate burden of costs on the fragile shoulders of the poor and the dispossessed within certain countries and across the world. Finally, it is quite clear that due to the impact of COVID-19 on the functioning of economies, the world will not go back to the way it was. The impact may create a larger inequality in the distribution of income and economic opportunities for the poor and the dispossessed if economies do not take measures to correct their existing fundamental economic imbalances. If we look deeper into what has happened, one issue becomes abundantly clear, which is the polarization of people into the two camps of the haves and the have nots. A divided community, nation, or the world as a whole, if not brought back together, will certainly bring about destruction and wars within and among nations. The stark contrast in the end picture is clear: the continuation of life or its destruction. The following elements based on the findings of this study may lead movements toward the correction of our existing economic imbalances:

(I) *Creation of robust fiscal policies for redistribution of income:* We need an economic system that can support and provide the basic needs of its own peo-ple regardless of their prevailing individual or group economic conditions. With higher productivity and the emergence of a robust production sector through innovation and new discoveries, instituting a universal basic income (UBI) in a meaningful development, which is financially possible, will increas-ingly become unavoidable. Having a system that can support all people against all kinds of economic shocks is essential and possible through the emergence of a highly productive economy. The idea of supporting people during a pan-demic is an investment for the protection of the society for a sustainable and resilient economic system. This was clearly demonstrated in the success of communities that can protect themselves by staging successful lockdowns and by solving the basic financial needs of their communities through income sup-port. Having a practical choice means an ability to survive economically dur-ing such measures. It should also be added that the continuation of having income and maintaining consumption has positive macroeconomic impacts on the recovery of the economy.

(II) *Increase in production of public goods nationally and globally:* Within a national economy, the production of public goods is easier to imagine and plan for. Countries such as France and Germany and a number of other European governments' expenditures on the economy through taxation and spending of the proceeds reach 50% or more of their GDPs. In most such countries, healthcare, education, and other areas of basic needs are provided for all their citizens, and these countries have created better economic opportunities for their intergenerational mobility. In the post-COVID world, the idea of continu-ing to have a non-universal healthcare system or having a prominent role for a profit-based healthcare system will be hard to accept. The time we are living in made it very clear to us that looking into our lives as isolated from others is unrealistic, and to some extent, irrational and absurd.

The bigger problem is how to bring about a global system capable of pro-ducing global public goods (GPG). The issue in such an emerging system is to make the case that investment for the good of one nation can benefit when it is extended to all. The pandemic provides this opportunity, and there will be ample information and data to make the case at national and international levels. Preventing and dealing with the fallout of pandemics is not the only area of such needs. The looming fallout of ongoing and accelerating economic and social pressures from global warming and environmental decay on large scales is present and will stay on the horizon. This may, however, still lack an international campaign to gather support for and develop a functional financial system for its implementation.

(III) *Enhancing economic democratization within nations and globally:* Any pre-vailing economic system brings with it its own realities, which, in time, can continue to exist when its functioning system maintains lives and supports a sustainable system for production and distribution of income and supports the lives of its people within its communities. The existing economic system over time has gravitated towards a transnational and very large and powerful corpo-rate system. This has become unsuitable, and the futility of the system can be seen in the accumulation of income and wealth in hands of a few and the deg-radation of the overwhelming majority of people in every corner of the world. This system is destroying itself and in time cannot even benefit those who are its current beneficiaries. The system needs fundamental transformation through a greater role of other players such as labor unions, civil societies, consumers, and non-profit entities, workers' co-ops, and much more. We need reforms and to get ourselves away from an absolute adherence to market-based economic principles toward instead a focus on non-market theories of economic democracy. We need to create a reform agenda supporting practical examples of decentralization and economic liberalization to democratic coop-eratives, public banking, fair trade, and the regionalization of food production and currency. These changes are on the horizon, and already, we see many examples of them growing within the existing system. However, with the greater ability of advanced technology and social and economic entrepreneur-ship, the pace of change will enhance dramatically in the years ahead.

(IV) *International cooperation and development of a shared global vision for change:* This is vital and, at the same time, very complex. History, as indicated in this study, tells us that change is inevitable, and our short historical review of the past showed that times of global pandemics brought about fundamental global changes in their wake. The rise of capitalism, movement of labor, enhancement of technology, and all pivotal changes of the past brought ways and means which, although they came about during dark times, they led humanity toward greater light and offered hope for better lives. History, despite its grim tales of human catastrophe and loss, also tells us how destruc-tive forces allowed humanity to see the road to recovery for better lives in the future. This is not to glamourize the grief of the loss of human lives, which is always tragic and heartbreaking, but it is a call to be vigilant and alert regard-ing the lessons that can be learned. The most important lesson of COVID-19 is to reject the notion that every country and nation must solely focus on their own gains, presuming that the world is based on zero sum gains. Nothing can be further from the truth. The pandemic taught us about the interconnection of our lives better than anything else. Coronavirus passed through all territories and did not ask for our national identities. It hit us hard where we denied ourselves our basic necessities and brought greater losses to those who thought they were an island of only themselves. Our economic policies have to be based on international understanding of our fragility and strengths as a community of nations. There has to be a much stronger international solidarity, joint programing, research and development, international healthcare system, production of GPG, coordination based on economic democratization, and a mobilization of human resources to meet the challenges of a global economy.

This is a difficult process since our historic lessons of the past tell us that at times of economic difficulty and hardship, many communities tend to respond to populist policies and personalities by embracing nationalism and a rejection of seeing our strength in our togetherness as members of a global community. This is in part, and particularly in modern times, a function of a lack of trust in the influence of corporate media and the failure of our educational system. Changes in those areas become important segments of the blueprint for consecutive change.

(V) *Investment in educational systems, changes in power of corporate media, and focusing on social justice in the design of public policies:* First and foremost, education and public media should be considered as public good (service). The corporate bottom-line does not serve the common good. There is a considerable positive externality in both education and the creation of reliable information and appropriate levels of public discourse about public information and news, which often do not find their way to the bottom-line of our international corporations. Investing in both areas are important and have a high return on investment and should be fully utilized. Striving for social justice is not a slogan; it is a recipe for a high return investment in members of our communities beyond the restrictive boundaries of our collective prejudices and misunderstandings of ourselves as interdependent members of the same community. Social justice is not just a moral imperative; it is meeting a necessity for reaching our full potential as a community at the local, national, and international arenas.

(VI) *Adhering to a principle of sustainability within a larger meaning and purview:* Sustainability is to understand and create a path for continuity and prosperity within every community. At times, it may bring upon us a feeling that we do not need it for the good of our own. It simply becomes embodied in our actions, when we transcend our own personal position and present it as being good for the benefit of all. In essence, such feelings are delusional on the part of those who are not the beneficiaries of such perception, and yet support it and the narcissistic and deceptive tendencies of those who benefit from it. The reality is that many may not see the good of all and its relationship to their own good, since they do not feel it in any practical measures in their own lives. This is why the call for a sustainable natural environment over time has fallen on deaf ears. The pandemic brought a version of it to our lives; however, as this study indicates, individuals and groups have not learned the lesson, and in many cases, it has manifested itself in the denial of the real causes and the learning may not support the reason for change. This can only come about through taking up most of the measures we proposed for the future reallocation of resources in the national and global sense. The ideas presented, while a lesson that should be taken as the blueprint for change, can only be enforced through activism and struggling for change, and not just hoping for it. We may find ourselves challenged in the years ahead and see the opposite development. Nonetheless, we should come to agree that without a systemic change, we will threaten our own existence and the pressure for change along these lines will become even more compelling.

7.8   Conclusion

The single most important conclusion of this study is that COVID-19 changed living conditions rapidly and exposed the fragility of the existing social and economic systems of societies around the world. This means that COVID-19 did not cause the destruction of people's lives and the collapse of their economies; rather, it merely brought about the conditions for fractures that have existed for a long time to surface and become more visible and felt in a much more rapid pace. This becomes more evident when we compare and contrast the prevailing conditions and the economic and human consequences of this pandemic in various countries.

Historical changes in the past and their consequences occurred within centuries over time, and the transformations were gradual and structural, which brought countries' economies to their tipping points over a relatively long period of time. Changes in today's world within a universe well connected through the fast movement of information and a much higher level of social consciousness are unlikely to be gradual, and the outcome will show the force of rapid transformation, and in many ways, overtly and even drastically. This can be a promise for a better world rather than living under a threat of destruction if we think about transformation as a change towards the betterment of life on Earth.

The empirical evidence for health shocks and economic growth is elusive. While the impact of COVID-19 on economic growth is likely to remain in the center of prevailing arguments, the reality of it is that the most important consequence of a pandemic is not a temporary interruption of economic growth, but how the existing experiences may shape the future of the production system and how that may impact the distribution of income and wealth within the countries and around the world. Based on the observations, income distribution is more likely to be gravitated towards the highly skilled workforce, and this is likely to worsen the distribution of income and wealth for years past the pandemic.

It is important to have a relevant perspective for the sources of the economic cost of pandemics within the prevailing and the emerging economic structures of various economies. There is often little or no effort to either critically examine the prevailing market structure to show whether we have a "free market" or any endeavor to make a distinction between the demand for goods or services or needs within an economy. The missing piece of this story, which brings about a bitter dose of reality into human beings' lives, is that not all goods and services, which are essential for the lives of individuals and groups, are private goods and services and are produced based on demand. Some of the most essential elements of a balanced and humanly conceivable life on Earth are not based on demands, but rather on meeting the needs of individuals, groups, and communities.

The analyses of the data show that in countries where healthcare services are considered public goods and their governments allocate sufficient finances toward meeting those needs, the fallout from pandemics is less severe. Among them, Japan, South Korea, Germany, Austria, Canada, and New Zealand are great examples. The idea that everyone should protect their own interests and nothing should be expected from others or the government has attraction in a number of countries, and in almost all of them, the question of having equal opportunity for developing such an ability does not come up. The other complication of this philosophy is the message of individualism to the extent that it refutes the collective and social nature of human life. The practical implication of such a belief is the rejection of the role of government.

The plight of low-income countries in dealing with COVID-19 deserves special attention. These countries are often faced with food insecurity and their economic well-being is closely tied to the continuation of their economic ties with developed countries. Developing countries are likely to be the worst affected economically by COVID-19 in the medium and long term. Paying special attention to low-income countries and finding ways to help them is important for a number of reasons: they range from observing the core value of humanity, which is to respond to those in need at time of crisis, irrespective of where they are within the global community, to recognition of the fact that coming together when a pandemic hits the global society is essential if the global society is looking for a lasting solution. Pandemics can only be controlled when we treat the whole community as one.

This study sheds light on the inability of the prevailing economic system to instill trust in people. It argues that the cause of it is the inability of countries to respond to the desires of their own working people for increased opportunities and to receive a fair share of the prosperity. Current trends show that the well-being of many working people around the world is threatened by the emergence of a highly productive and service sector-based economy in the post-industrial era, the use of automation, and a race to the bottom emanating from a rise in the influence of large mega-transnational companies that create the prevailing policies of international trade. The existing evidence shows that wages and salaries of a large proportion of workers have been traded for increased corporate profits and a depression of worker wages. COVID-19 will most certainly worsen this ongoing trend, unless we experience a global rethinking about this issue.

A lockdown of the economy seemed a practical way to control the spread of the infection and countries performed remarkably different with regard to such a clear and obvious measure for effective control. Helping people to stay in a lockdown situation can only be successful when people are given a choice by setting in place economic measures which can support people who are out of their jobs with help through relevant fiscal policies and companies through fiscal and monetary policies.

The study brought up a number of practical policy options which can help to create a sustainable global economic system for recovery from COVID-19 and preparedness for other pandemics which will surely impact the global society repeatedly in the future. These are economic policies aimed at creating a resilient global economic system prepared to withstand the likely pressures in the decades and longer periods of time to come.

We need to produce global public goods (GPG), and this needs to be understood and established through the community of nations. The looming fallout of ongoing and accelerating economic and social pressures from global warming and environmental decay on a large scale are present and will remain on the horizon. This may, however, still lack an international campaign to gather support for and develop a functional financial system for its implementation. With higher productivity and the emergence of a robust production sector through innovation and new discoveries, instituting a universal basic income (UBI), which is financially possible, will increasingly become unavoidable.

We need to create a reform agenda supporting practical examples of decentralization and economic liberalization for democratic cooperatives, public banking, fair trade, and the regionalization of food production and currency. These changes are on the horizon, and already, we see many examples of them growing within existing economic systems. However, with the greater ability of advanced technology and social and economic entrepreneurship, the pace of change will enhance dramatically in the years ahead. The most important lesson of COVID-19 is to reject the notion that every country and nation must solely focus on their own gains, presuming that the world is based on zero-sum gains. Social justice is not just a moral imperative; it is meeting a necessity for reaching our full potential as a community in the local, national, and international arenas. Sustainability is to understand and create a path for continuity and posterity within every community. In a nutshell, we should agree that without a systemic change, we will threaten our own existence and the pressure for change along these lines will become even more compelling.

References

Ballotpedia. (2020). *Arguments against mask requirements during the coronavirus (COVID-19) pandemic, 2020*. Retrieved from Ballotpedia https://ballotpedia.org/Arguments_against_mask_requirements_during_the_coronavirus_(COVID-19)_pandemic,_2020-2021.

Barbara, W. T. (1978). *A distant mirror: A calamitous 14th century* (pp. 92–93). Alfred A. Knopf. Ballantine Books.

Barbier, E. B., & Burgess, J. C. (2020, July). *Sustainability and development after COVID-19*. World Development. Retrieved from https://reader.elsevier.com/reader/sd/pii/S030575 0X20302084?token=AD3D70011805A4E15826118046BF7E844F1130CC7B4B38195415 7A95BC03D37E0B1B378A94F1421201B4C0EC74694D45

Bell, C., & Lewis, M. (2004). Economic implications of epidemics old and new. *World Economics, 5*(4), 137–174.

Bhusal, M. (2020). The world after COVID-19: An opportunity for a new beginning. *International Journal of Scientific and Research Publications (IJSRP)* [PDF]. Retrieved from http://www.ijsrp.org/research-paper-0520/ijsrp-p10185.pdf

Bisong, A., Ahairwe, P., & Njoroge, E. (2020). *The impact of COVID-19 on remittances for development in Africa (No. 269)*. ECDPM discussion paper [PDF]. Retrieved from https://elibrary.acbfpact.org/acbf/collect/acbf/index/assoc/HASH0184/a19668a2/637b2693/3273.dir/Impact%20COVID%2019%20remittances%20development%20Africa%20ECDPM.pdf

Bivens, J., & Mishel, L. (2015). *Understanding the historic divergence between productivity and a typical worker's pay: Why it matters and why it's real*. Economic Policy Institute. Retrieved from https://www.epi.org/publication/understanding-the-historic-divergence-between-productivity-and-a-typical-workers-pay-why-it-matters-and-why-its-real/

Brown, G., & Susskind, D. (2020). International cooperation during the COVID-19 pandemic. *Oxford Review of Economic Policy, 36*(Supplement_1), S64–S76. Retrieved from https://doi.org/10.1093/oxrep/graa025

Carmody, P. (2020). Meta-trends in global value chains and development: Interacting impacts with COVID-19 in Africa. *Transnational Corporations Journal, 27*(2) [PDF]. Retrieved from https://unctad.org/system/files/official-document/diaeia2020d2a8_en.pdf

Central Intelligence Agency. (2020). *The World Facebook*. Retrieved from Country Comparison :: Median age—The World Factbook—Central Intelligence Agency (cia.gov).

Clark, G. (2001). *Microbes and markets: Was the Black Death an economic revolution?* University of California, Davis. Retrieved https://pdfs.semanticscholar.org/d2f7/a23ebb075f7233c993e65a50444e60211a92.pdf

Countryeconomy.com. (2020). *Government health expenditure*. Retrieved from https://countryeconomy.com/government/expenditure/health

Dahab, M., van Zandvoort, K., Flasche, S., et al. (2020). COVID-19 control in low-income settings and displaced populations: What can realistically be done? *Conflict and Health, 14*, 54. Retrieved from https://conflictandhealth.biomedcentral.com/articles/10.1186/s13031-020-00296-8

Damooei, J. (2015). *The debt crisis and its impact on developing countries. In The changing landscape of global financial governance and the role of soft law*. Brill Nijhoff Publishers. Retrieved from https://brill.com/view/book/edcoll/9789004280328/B9789004280328-s016.xml

Gibb, R., Redding, D. W., Chin, K. Q., Donnelly, C. A., Blackburn, T. M., Newbold, T., & Jones, K. E. (2020). Zoonotic host diversity increases in human-dominated ecosystems. *Nature, 584*(7821), 398–402. Retrieved from https://www.nature.com/articles/s41586-020-2562-8

Gibney, E. (2020). Whose coronavirus strategy worked best? Scientists hunt most effective policies. *Nature*. Retrieved from https://www.nature.com/articles/d41586–020–01248-1

Gottdenker, N. L., Streicker, D. G., Faust, C. L., & Carroll, C. R. (2014). Anthropogenic land use change and infectious diseases: A review of the evidence. *EcoHealth, 11*(4), 619–632.

Hales, S., et al. (2002). Potential effect of population and climate changes on global distribution of dengue fever: An empirical model. *Lancet, 360*, 830–834.

Johansson, L. M. (2007). Fiscal implications of AIDS in South Africa. *European Economic Review, 51*(7), 1614–1640. Retrieved from https://www.diva-portal.org/smash/record.jsf?pid=diva2%3A183183&dswid=5481

Jordan, R. (2019). *How does climate change affect disease?* Stanford Woods Institute for The Environment Retrieved from https://earth.stanford.edu/news/how-does-climate-change-affect-disease#gs.jovukv

Karlsson, M., Nilsson, T., & Pichler, S. (2014). The impact of the 1918 Spanish flu epidemic on economic performance in Sweden: An investigation into the consequences of an extraordinary mortality shock. *Journal of Health Economics, 36*, 1–19.

Keesing, F., Belden, L. K., Daszak, P., Dobson, A., Harvell, C. D., Holt, R. D., Hudson, P., Jolles, A., Jones, K. E., Mitchell, C. E., Myers, S. S., Bogich, T., & Ostfeld, R. S. (2010). Impacts of biodiversity on the emergence and transmission of infectious diseases. *Nature, 468*(7324), 647–652.

Lachaud, J.-P. (2007). HIV prevalence and poverty in Africa: micro- and macro-econometric evidences applied to Burkina Faso. *Journal of Health Economics, 26*(3), 483–504.

Lee, D., Heo, Y., & Kim, K. (2020, July). *A strategy for international cooperation in the COVID-19 pandemic era: Focusing on national scientific funding data.* MDPI. Retrieved from https://www.mdpi.com/2227-9032/8/3/204

Martens, W. J. M., Rotmans, J., & Rothman, D. S. (2002). In W. J. M. Martens & A. J. McMichael (Eds.), *Environmental change, climate and health: Issues and research methods* (pp. 197–225). Cambridge University Press.

Mordecai, E. A., Ryan, S. J., Caldwell, J. M., Shah, M. M., & LaBeaud, A. D. (2020). Climate change could shift disease burden from malaria to arboviruses in Africa. *The Lancet Planetary Health, 4*(9), e416–e423. Retrieved from https://earth.stanford.edu/news/how-does-climate-change-affect-disease#gs.jovukv

Nirmal, K. Stella, C., Abbas, O, Jun, X. (2020). *Health security capacities in the context of COVID-19 outbreak: An analysis of International Health Regulations annual report data from 182 countries.* Retrieved from https://www.thelancet.com/action/showPdf?pii=S0140-673 6%2820%2930553-5

Nunn, N., Qian, N, & Wen, J. (2018). *Distrust and political turnover.* National Bauru of Economic Research (NBER). https://www.nber.org/system/files/working_papers/w24187/w24187.pdf

OECD. (2020). *Trust in government (indicator).* Accessed on 15 December 2020. Retrieved from https://data.oecd.org/gga/trust-in-government.htm

OECD. Stat. (2020). *Health expenditure and financing.* Retrieved from https://stats.oecd.org/Index.aspx?DataSetCode=SHA

Oldekop, J. et al. (2020, June). *COVID-19 and the case for global development.* World Development [PDF]. Retrieved from https://reader.elsevier.com/reader/sd/pii/S0305750X20301704?token =BE330080326E997BDA9F7EB322BD0E96A00BA2295EA23FCEC8D8B733996DAED2 8E2306EF32E42EE948A4E0F5746F54F3

Our world in data. *Public trust in government, United States, 1958 to 2015.* Retrieved from https://ourworldindata.org/grapher/public-trust-in-government

Pamuk, Ş. (2007). The Black Death and the origins of the 'Great Divergence' across Europe, 1300–1600. *European Review of Economic History, 11*(3), 289–317.

Routt, D. (2008). *The economic impact of the Black Death* (R. Whaples, Eds.). EH.Net Encyclopedia. Retrieved from http://eh.net/encyclopedia/the-economic-impact-of-the-black-death

Social Security Programs Throughout the World. (2020). Retrieved from https://www.ssa.gov/policy/docs/progdesc/ssptw/

T.H. Chan Harvard School of Public Health, Coronavirus and Climate Change. Retrieved from https://www.hsph.harvard.edu/c-change/subtopics/coronavirus-and-climate-change/V

The World Bank. (2020). *DataBankWorld development indicators..* Retrieved from https://databank.worldbank.org/reports.aspx?source=2&series=SH.MED.PHYS.ZS&country=

The World Bank. *Research and development expenditure (% of GDP).* Retrieved from https://databank.worldbank.org/reports.aspx?source=2&series=GB.XPD.RSDV.GD.ZS&country

Van Biesebroeck, J. (2014). *How tight is the link between wages and productivity?: A survey of the literature.* ILO [PDF]. Retrieved from https://www.ilo.org/wcmsp5/groups/public/%2D%2D-ed_protect/%2D%2D-protrav/%2D%2D-travail/documents/publication/wcms_410267.pdf

Wilson, M. (2001). Ecology and infectious disease. In J. L. Aron & J. A. Patz (Eds.), *Ecosystem change and public health: A global perspective* (pp. 283–324). Johns Hopkins University Press.

World Health Organization. (2020). *Hospital beds (per 10 000 population).* Retrieved from https://www.who.int/data/gho/data/indicators/indicator-details/GHO/hospital-beds-(per-10-000-population)

World Health Organization Global Health Expenditure database. Retrieved from https://databank.worldbank.org/reports.aspx?source=2&series=SH.XPD.CHEX.GD.ZS&country

Chapter 8
Financial Markets and COVID-19

Kunibert Raffer

8.1 Introduction

The present COVID-19 or corona crisis has affected the global economy more gravely than any crisis before, even the financial crisis of 2008. The financial crisis affected real production and most services very little. The corona pandemic has had and continues to have a huge impact beyond the financial sector, on real production, in particular production chains, and the service industry, locking down whole economies. Economies have suffered gravely for many months already and there is no end in sight. Not only countries highly dependent on tourism face much bigger problems than after 2008, when tourism was virtually not affected. Joblessness and income losses of firms and people still or formerly employed are much higher. The need for emergency finance is thus larger.

In both cases, grave government regulatory failures triggered the crisis: flawed regulation of the financial sector mainly in the USA though eagerly followed by others and flawed or highly insufficient veterinary regulations in China, as well as attempts to silence doctors warning of disastrous consequences. While banking regulations have improved after 2008 (most probably not enough, but still), China seems not inclined to tackle the problem. Historical evidence strongly suggest so. SARS coronavirus (SARS-CoV), a virus identified in 2003, also came from China: "SARS-CoV is thought to be an animal virus from an as-yet-uncertain animal reservoir, perhaps bats, that spread to other animals (civet cats) and first infected humans in the Guangdong province of southern China in 2002" (WHO, 2020). Apparently, no action was taken to avoid such catastrophe in the future.

K. Raffer (✉)
Department of Economics (Emeritus), University of Vienna, Vienna, Austria
e-mail: Kunibert.raffer@univie.ac.at

© The Author(s), under exclusive license to Springer Nature Switzerland AG 2022   175
N. Faghih, A. Forouharfar (eds.), *Socioeconomic Dynamics of the COVID-19 Crisis*,
Contributions to Economics, https://doi.org/10.1007/978-3-030-89996-7_8

In contrast to China, the USA was able to divert blame for a comparable epidemy some 100 years ago. The so-called Spanish flu was a contagious disease spread knowingly by the USA all over the globe. The mere fact that the uncensored Spanish press (unlike in all countries at war) published about it labelled a US war crime the Spanish flu. The name stuck, exculpating the USA literally carrying sick soldiers too weak to walk on board of ships to be sent to Europe. Many died before arrival, but quite a few managed to infect US allies first and eventually the whole world. Rightly blaming China nowadays, one must not forget the USA.

Financial markets are affected in several ways. Many debtors will simply become unable to honour their obligations due to lost business caused by the lockdown. The plunge of manufacturing and of service activities logically led to a plunge in export revenues of Southern countries (SCs). Collapsed demand for oil has severely affected oil exporters. As most of them have wisely built up reserves in good years, the drop of export revenues can be mitigated to some extent. Following Kuwait's example, which had established her General Reserve Fund in 1960, this innovative decision was later followed by most oil exporters, especially Norway (cf Raffer, 2006).

Another debt crisis in the South is looming. Understandably, banks have become cautious regarding new credits to sovereign, private or corporate debtors. Huge support programmes for firms and private persons have become necessary and are planned or already decided. There is little demand for private loans such as new mortgages or for consumption. On the other hand, large support measures, such as the EU's €750 billion package, can only be financed via financial markets and largely if not virtually only by countries in the North having creditworthiness.

This contribution is going to discuss corona effects, on the financial sector and on sovereigns. First, SCs are discussed and then the role of international financial institutions (IFIs) that are so much more powerful in the South and the effects on the North. Finally, financial markets and private debtors will be analysed. It seems that COVID-19 is unfortunately likely to be used to reinforce neoliberalism. After a short period of "neglecting" neoliberal targets – such as the economically indefensible Maastricht criteria which at present are temporarily suspended but not abolished – the neoliberal fight against the welfare state and decent social standards will start again and more powerfully. Once (not if) the EU abrogates this suspension, all Euro countries will have to cut down severely to meet again the doubtful Maastricht criteria (cf Raffer, 1998a on their economic "rationale"), whose only aim seems to be to prevent Keynesian policies. Neoliberal cuts will enjoy a heyday. The same goes for SCs. Once the crisis will be considered over, the "need" to follow neoliberal fiscal policies will again be stressed and enforced by IFIs and the European Union (EU). The fact that such policies brought about the greatest catastrophe in history, WWII, seems of no concern.

The financial effects of the crisis will strengthen the global neoliberal fight against the poor and for more inequality as well as those institutions fighting it.

8.2 Financial Effects of Corona

The crisis has produced various negative effects on the financial sector:

- For firms and individuals: Falling incomes render serving existing precarious debts, which tends to increase the percentage of non-performing loans. Getting new loans that might have become necessary will become very difficult if not impossible even for most economically relatively strong borrowers.
- Those governments that can afford to do so offer guarantee schemes for firms with liquidity problems, which are meanwhile most firms in these economies.
- For countries: Losses in export and tax revenues will make serving existing debts precarious. As many countries are already under debt pressure, this will lead to an increase in sovereign defaults. In very many cases, increased health expenditures will also impair countries' financial standing. Downsized and definitely inadequate health systems in SCs, the result of conditionality by the Bretton Woods twins (BWTs), have made things more difficult. In the North, cut-downs have happened as well, though due to neoliberalism and Northern governments' own decisions.
- Foreign direct investment in SCs has been falling. Resources flowing back put another strain on countries' foreign exchange reserves.
- Steeply falling remittances, which are an important source of foreign exchange for quite a few SCs. As remittances have only played a role in recent history, one may well expect it to be one of if not the biggest declines in history.
- Official development assistance (ODA), already – some very few countries excepted – much below promises, is unlikely to increase. On the contrary, one may assume that cash-strapped donors might even reduce the percentage that actually flows to SCs.
- Demand for loans is increasing enormously. Nevertheless, this is a mixed blessing for the financial sector, as the number of good (or perfectly creditworthy) clients is decreasing. Increasing debt loads are not unlikely to render even blue chip debtors less blue and more chipped.

8.3 Effects on the South

The IMF's (2020a) *World Economic Outlook Update, June 2020* simply speaks in its headline of "A Crisis Like No Other", seeing "An Uncertain Recovery". The IMF (2020b) clarifies that it "projects emerging market economies to *shrink* (stress i.o.) by 3.2 % this year – the largest drop for this group on record. By way of comparison, in the global financial crisis, growth for the group took a significant hit but still bottomed out at a positive 2.6 percent in 2009".

The COVID-19 pandemic has widely exposed the debt vulnerability of many SCs, also creating problems for some countries in the North. As no real solutions to sovereign over-indebtedness have been implemented and the human rights oriented and fair solution routinely granted to debtors within countries – insolvency proceedings – has been steadfastly denied to SCs, this is no surprise. Human lives in SCs do apparently not matter. Countries tottering along under unsustainable debt burdens are bound to suffer the next debt crisis even if nothing more than minor disturbances occurred. COVID-19 is far from minor. Not only exports – tourism, especially in cases such as Caribbean island or some European states – but also remittances by people working in the North are bound to fall dramatically. Less economic activity in the North automatically means less money. That economic activity in more advanced SCs has stalled, and direct consequences of corona aggravate the problem. SCs exporting mainly raw materials or simple manufactures to be finished in the North have lost large parts of their markets. This renders honouring one's debts very difficult or impossible, especially so as debt problems had been building up over decades before the corona crisis struck. SC debts have not been reduced to a long-term sustainable burden.

Li (2020), a UN independent expert on foreign debt and human rights, summed up the situation: "Even before the pandemic, 40 percent of low-income countries were struggling to service their debt. Today, to contain the spread of the coronavirus and keep the economy afloat, developing countries would need more than US$2.5 trillion, according to IMF and UN estimates".

Rightly speaking of an "unprecedented economic damage from the COVID-19 crisis", UNCTAD (2020) also estimated liquidity and financing requirements of the South due to the pandemic of at least $2.5 trillion. UNCTAD proposed a four-pronged strategy:

- "a $1 trillion liquidity injection; a kind of helicopter money drop for those being left behind", which is to be financed by reallocating existing special drawing rights at the IMF plus a substantial new allocation.
- "a debt jubilee for distressed economies. An immediate debt standstill on sovereign debt payments … followed by significant debt relief". UNCTAD (2020) refers once again to Germany's London Accord as a "benchmark", estimating that this would amount to "around $1 trillion".
- This cancelation should be implemented in 2020 "overseen by an independently created body". The demand for independent arbitration for SC debts including debtor protection and human rights was first presented in the mid-1980s (*v.* Raffer, 1987 or the *locus classicus* 1990, last updated publication 2016). UNCTAD does not refer to its author, though. Understandably so, as the "Raffer Proposal" strictly demanded equal treatment (=equal losses) for IFIs and creditor governments, a necessary and justified demand that nevertheless made this proposal unwelcome, even though he just recalled the intention of the founders of the BWTs (cf Raffer, 2009). Demanding justice and equity for people in SCs, as well as debtor protection (which means protecting their human right and the Rule of Law, cf. Raffer, 1990), has never been too popular with official creditors. Thus, whenever the so-called insolvency procedures are quoted now, it usually is the IMF's self-serving proposal, the SDRM (Simply Disastrous Rescheduling Mechanism; obviously, the IMF prefers Sovereign Debt Restructuring

Mechanism) protecting the IMF's own money as well as that of other IFIs. It would have increased the IMF's power further.

- A Marshall Plan for health recovery funded by the non-paid though long promised official development assistance (ODA) funds. UNCTAD estimates that an additional $500 billion – a quarter of the last decade's missing ODA – largely in the form of grants for emergency health services and related social relief programmes would be needed. Briefly, those expenditures that BWTs have insisted to be cut down massively when enforcing their "structural adjustment" should again be increased.
- Finally, capital controls are called for as a legitimate means to curtail surges in capital outflows.

Last but by no means least, this UNCTAD document points out that the enormous sum of this "proposed package is similar in size to the amount that would have been delivered to developing countries over the last decade if countries in the Development Assistance Committee of the Organisation for Economic Co-operation and Development had met their 0.7% ODA target".

One may add that the 0.7 target was not imposed on "donors" but has been propagated – though mostly not reached – voluntarily by them. This historic record indicates the chances of UNCTAD's proposal.

The OECD (2020a, p. 5) harbours no illusions regarding ODA: "Coronavirus (COVID-19) risks major setbacks for financing for sustainable development". After reassuringly pointing out "Since many ODA budgets had been finalised before the outbreak of COVID-19, the effect of the global economic recession on ODA levels might not be immediate but lagged" (ibid., p. 9), the OECD (ibid., p. 10) finally turns realistic: "Given DAC members' own budget pressure in 2020, the overall level of ODA could decline in 2020. The OECD calculates that if DAC members were to keep the same ODA to GNI ratios as in 2019, total ODA could decline by USD 11 billion to USD 14 billion, depending on a single-or double-hit recession scenario on member countries' GDP". Thus, ODA is unlikely to be of great help to corona-affected countries. Furthermore, one has to suspect that ODA will again be "all aid short if real help" (Raffer & Singer, 1996, p. 3), especially so as expenditures recorded as ODA are not ODA as officially defined at all, money spent on migrants in donor countries being one better known example. Based on official OECD data, Raffer (1998b; Raffer & Singer, 2001, pp. 83–86) showed that an increasing part of official ODA figures was what the OECD itself "diplomatically" called "broadened", i.e. no real help, though recorded by "donors" themselves as ODA, or simply fake in honest English. In 1994, for example, over 40% of recorded ODA was due to broadening. One should thus not put much faith in ODA. The present wave of migrants (also wrongly called "refugees") means that expenditures for these people within donor countries (called in-donor refugee costs by the OECD) are likely to grow and to be wrongly recorded as ODA.

According to the OECD (2020b) "Private finance for low- and middle-income countries eligible for ODA is projected to plunge by USD 700 billion, a drop 60% larger than in 2008 during the global financial crisis".

Remittances have become an important source of foreign exchange for many countries. The International Bank for Reconstruction and Development (IBRD) predicted the "Sharpest Decline of Remittances in Recent History", expecting remittances to "decline sharply by about 20 percent in 2020 due to the economic crisis induced by the COVID-19 pandemic and shutdown" (World Bank, 2020c).

Sayeh and Chami (2020, p. 16) show that the "economic shock will be magnified by the loss of remittances", which the authors put at "much more than 10 percent of GDP for many countries, led by Tajikistan and Bermuda, at more than 30 percent" (ibid., p. 17). The OECD (2020a, p. 8) expects very strong declines in money sent to SCs. Referring to their Chart 1, Sayeh and Chami (ibid., p. 16) write "As of 2018, remittance flows to these countries reached $350 billion, surpassing foreign direct investment, portfolio investment, and foreign aid as the single most important source of income from abroad". This Chart, however, clearly shows a volume of remittances above $300 billion, but well below $350 billion; judging by looking at the graph, the flows sum up to some $325 or $330 billion. This slight inconsistency does not affect the validity of the argument, though.

The authors (ibid., p. 8) expect global remittance flows to fall by 20% in 2020 as a result of the pandemic. This fall of $65 to maybe $70 billion is nearly half the preliminary ODA total for 2019, which is officially $152.8 billion (OECD, 2020c), but includes expenditures that do not flow to recipient countries at all as mentioned above. Understandably, Sayeh and Chami (2020, p. 18) conclude "Compared with previous economic crises, this pandemic poses an even greater threat to countries that rely heavily on remittance income".

In the IMF Blog, Mühleisen et al. (2020) conclude "Dwindling policy space may force some countries to take recourse to more unorthodox measures". They also notice "A worrisome lack of fiscal space": one-third of developing market economies "have limited or no room for fiscal policy to counter a prolonged crisis". Thus, they have to resort to "unorthodox measures", including "steps to ease credit and financial regulation". As eased financial regulation was the cause of the financial crisis, this seems a dubious strategy. It might produce an additional regional financial crisis.

Policy space is heavily curtailed by credit rating agencies (CRAs), bilateral investment treaties and investor-state dispute settlement. Li (2020, p. 2) points out that CRAs have played a key role in keeping SCs from entering into debt relief discussions. Even "a request … to participate in the DSSI [the G20s' Debt Service Suspension Initiative, KR] could be taken as a signal of distress by credit rating agencies, which would thus affect its [= the country's] borrowing capacity in the future" (ibid.). "Moody's … has already put countries [that] expressed interest in International Financial Institutions' debt moratorium under rating review and downgraded one country participating in the DSSI" (Li, 2020, p. 2).

Economically this is pure idiocy. If a debtor agrees with a group of creditors on a moratorium, this means that creditors not part of this deal are more likely to get paid. Those agreeing to a moratorium do so by their own choice. The logical effect should be an upgrade for the rest if a minimum of economic knowledge existed, which seems apparently not the case.

Eurobond default clauses consider not only non-payment but also a moratorium as default, which would trigger acceleration. Li rightly concludes that such consequences make SCs reluctant "to accept debt relief offers" (ibid.). Thus, one offers what is unlikely to be accepted as those who offer this "relief" know or have to know. It is unlikely that the USA or German Foreign Offices or Ministries of Finance are totally unaware of these legal consequences. They knowingly offered something that could hardly be accepted, parading as "helpers". Some people might call this malicious – but it is totally in line with the so-called development co-operation as it actually operates in real life.

Such facts enforce heavy doubts about the seriousness and honesty of the G20 Initiative. The G20 knew or had to know that "beneficiaries" are unlikely to accept due to norms established by those "generously" proposing this "relief". It is a sad practical joke at best. Assuming that none of those elaborating this initiative knew about financial markets and their constraints are absolutely absurd. The G20 Initiative is a real but badly designed con trick ridiculing SCs, both clumsy and unprofessional.

Aware that their DSSI is unlikely to solve the problem, the G20 already presented a "Common Framework for Debt Treatments beyond the DSSI" (G20, 2020). Their brief paper revisits all failures, errors and injustices of debt management since 1982. Creditors decide as they prefer without any independent checks. Debtors are under strict BWT control as under the heavily indebted poor countries (HIPC) initiatives and the Multilateral Debt Relief Initiative (DRSI). Finally, the document clarifies "In principle, debt treatments will not be conducted in the form of debt write-off or cancellation" (ibid., p. 2). This means the proposed "treatment" falls short of both HIPC and the MDRI, initiatives build on the principle of debt reduction. It basically picks up the failed "Baker Plan", although it does not totally exclude debt reductions. By implementing their idea, the G20 will produce poverty, grave economic damages and decreases in already poor living standards, as official creditors have done over decades. This treatment also opens the door for political pressure on debtors, unlike an insolvency as proposed by Raffer (1990).

8.4 IFIs

As of April 2020, more than 80 countries have called on the IMF for emergency funds to avoid sovereign default (Ellmers 2020). Debt relief agreed on so far is insufficient according to Ellmers, a statement impossible to contradict.

Like virtually all multilateral organisations (for an excellent overview *v.* Financing for Sustainable Development Office, 2020), the BWTs have also and relatively early reacted to corona, offering "relief" of one way or another. Offering mainly loans, the crisis will logically increase their leverage. This again can be used to force neoliberal policies on debtor member countries more powerfully. As their various pandemic-connected activities are presented on their respective homepages, this contribution is not reproducing their various activities and programmes in detail.

– The IBRD Group

The Group of IFIs under the umbrella of the International Bank for Reconstruction and Development (IBRD), which likes to call itself the World Bank, launched its first set of emergency support operations quickly (for details *v*. World Bank, 2020a). This includes support to private business and for health measures. The latter means correcting the effects of cut-downs in public health forced on SCs by the IBRD – and the IMF – before. According to a press released on 19 May 2020, "100 Countries" got "Support in Response to COVID-19 (Coronavirus)" (World Bank, 2020b). The Group pledged $160 billion in grants and financial support over a 15-month period. Of the 100 countries, 39 are in sub-Saharan Africa. All measures by the IBRD can be seen at its homepage.

As "Nearly one-third of the total projects are in fragile and conflict-affected situations" (ibid.), one may wonder how and whether loans will be repaid. In these cases, corona overlaps other developmental problems, which does not make things any easier.

This support is to be given through grants, loans and equity investments. It will be supplemented by the suspension of bilateral debt service, as endorsed by the Bank's governors. IDA eligible countries that request forbearance on their official bilateral debt payments will have more financial resources to respond to the COVID-19 pandemic and fund critical, lifesaving emergency responses. This is a good and proper reaction to the crisis.

Looking at the statutes, one still notices the real intention of the IBRD's founders, which would have been highly useful for the present crisis. Thus, Article IV, Section 4 of the IBRD's statutes speaks of a "relaxation of conditions of payment" in order to "modify the terms of amortization or extend the life of the loan". This is not all. At "its discretion", the Bank may also accept "service payments on the loan in the member's currency for periods not to exceed three years". In this case, repurchasing of the member's currency "on appropriate terms" (an expression giving some leeway) is stipulated. This may be extremely useful if a country has a short-term scarcity of foreign exchange and is likely or foreseeably able to pay in foreign currencies later. Art. IV.4.c.i thus provides a valuable way to defuse short-term (illiquidity) problems that might otherwise trigger default, protracted debt problems and losses suffered by other creditors. It seems like tailor-made for the corona crisis. "Appropriate terms" clearly allow help by adjusting terms to circumstances. Unfortunately, it has not been used during any crisis in the past, and is unlikely to be used adequately now. The IBRD has always insisted on full payment even though its own statutes do not confer this right on the IBRD. Exceptions are the HIPC Initiatives and the MDRI, where the Bank has asked rich members to finance multilateral relief.

Article IV.4.c confers a right onto members suffering "from an acute exchange stringency" (viz. threatening default) to ask for relief. It stipulates:

> If a member suffers from an acute exchange stringency, so that the service of any loan contracted by that member or guaranteed by it or by one of its agencies cannot be provided in the stipulated manner, the member concerned may apply to the Bank for a relaxation of the

conditions of payment. … (ii): The Bank may modify the terms of amortization or extend the life of the loan, or both.

Article IV.4.c specifically demands taking both the Bank and such member's interests into account. One notices that no conditions are stipulated for such relief, except the member's urgent need for help. Of course, this option wisely foreseen by its humane founders has never been used. On the contrary, the Bank has wrongly claimed to be a preferred creditor, thus mala fide causing a lot of misery in their member countries. Respecting Art. IV, which subordinates the IBRD, would have helped Southern members substantially. It still would do so.

The country has the right to ask for relief. The IBRD may – but need not – grant it but has to take the member's interest into account. The Bank does not have to grant relief whenever asked. Nevertheless, Art. IV.4.c certainly constitutes a general obligation to grant relief when and where appropriate, an obligation hardly reconcilable with the purported preferred creditor status and the Bank's behaviour in the past. Other creditors, most clearly the private sector, have no such obligation. They may eventually lose money, and they may grant relief by renegotiation, but they have no obligation to grant relief, let alone take the debtor's interest into account.

This indicates that the Bank's founders wanted to subordinate the IBRD's claims, maybe formulating so clearly because no sovereign insolvency procedure existed. Even overstretching Art. IV.4.c in favour of preference beyond any logic, this biased interpretation could not justify any preference. The often heard "argument" that relief for multilateral debts cannot be granted or would make development finance inoperable was not shared by the IBRD and IDA's founders. HIPC and the MDRI, as well as loan loss reserves they have built up, also prove this wrong.

Steadfastly denying debt relief, claiming mala fide to be a preferred creditor and forcing member countries not to avail themselves of their statutory rights are definitely at severest odds with statutory duties, good governance, the Rule of Law and economic reason.

Art. IV.7 clearly formulates: "In cases of default on loans made, participated in, or guaranteed by the Bank: (a) The Bank shall make such arrangements as may be feasible to adjust the obligations under the loans, including arrangements under or analogous to those provided in Section 4 (c) of this Article". As Section 4.c explicitly allows debt relief, it would be difficult to argue that the obligations to be adjusted exclude the debtor's obligations to the IBRD, unless one is lying. Such absolute clarity has become absent in statutes of IFIs established later (cf Raffer, 2009). Non-multilateral, especially private, creditors may provide similar relief too, but they are not obliged to do so.

Compared with the IBRD, IDA's Articles of Agreement are somewhat vague. Pursuant to Article V.3, titled "Modifications of Terms of Financing", IDA may "agree to a relaxation or other modification of the terms on which any of its financing shall have been provided". Decisions on relief are to be taken "in the light of all relevant circumstances, including the financial and economic situation and prospects of the member concerned".

Summing up, although it is very clear that the IBRD – like other IFIs – is legally not a preferred creditor, the Bank has been able so far illegally to enforce priority at grave human costs. No sovereign victim has ever objected so far. If that should finally and after decades stop during and because of the corona crisis, that could only be welcomed. The Rule of Law would finally be recognised by IFIs. In practice, this is unfortunately still utopian.

The founders of the IBRD and IDA were wiser, more far-sighted, more humane and less racist than the Bank is at present. Even people from the South were supposed to have human rights. To the founders, lives in the Third World obviously still mattered.

– *The International Monetary Fund (IMF)*

Although its claims were initially subordinated to private claims, the IMF has meanwhile no statutory obligation comparable to the IBRD (Raffer, 2006; Martha, 1990). As the BWTs became more neocolonial, the IMF got rid of this subordination existing until the Second Amendment, thus of the intentions of its founders. Martha (1990, p. 825) refers to Schedule B, paragraph 3 on the calculation of monetary reserves on which repurchase obligations were based. It seems logical to argue that the exclusion of holdings "transferred or set aside for repayments of loans during the subsequent year" was done "to give preference in repayment to lenders other than the Fund". This subordination, obviously a parallel to the IBRD's statutory obligations in favour of debtors, is history. Still, no preference exists according to the IMF' statutes.

Naturally, clearly worded stipulations in favour of debtors in need disappeared when regional development banks were established later on (cf Raffer, 2009). Lives in the Third World have come to matter less and less to those preaching human rights more and more loudly to SCs.

The Fund is once again accused of privileging austerity over the lives of vulnerable groups (Bretton Woods Observer, 2020a, b, p. 8), as it has always done, as well as of over-optimistic forecasts. Such over-optimism is a traditional feature of the IMF's, well known and even repeatedly acknowledged by the Fund.

The IMF itself admitted in a joint paper with IDA (2004, p. 13):

> past experience suggesting a systematic tendency toward excessive optimism . . . a common theme behind the historical rise in low-income countries' debt ratios was that borrowing decisions were predicated on growth projections that never materialized . . . analysis of projections made by Fund staff over the period 1990–2001 suggests a bias toward over-optimism of about 1 percentage point a year in forecasts of low-income country real GDP growth. The bias in projecting GDP growth in U.S. dollar terms, however, was considerably larger, at almost 5 percentage points a year.

About 5 percentage points a year is absolutely inacceptable. Not correcting such errors but continuing with over-optimism is damaging members mala fide. The document called for "well-disciplined projections, including by laying bare the assumptions on which they are predicated and by subjecting them to rigorous stress tests that explicitly incorporate the impact of exogenous shocks" (ibid.). These are very basic requirements of projections, which the IMF – according to its own conclusion – had not observed until 2004, and has continued not to observe afterwards. There are many occasions when the IMF itself has admitted this undue bias.

Observing its masters' voice, the IMF downplays the need for help or debt reduction by routinely exaggerating forecasts, thus knowingly prolonging the crisis. It provides an "argument" against meaningful international debt relief (on IFI overoptimism, not only regarding debt cf. Raffer, 2010, pp. 204–211). Briefly, there was no change during the last years.

An IMF Working Paper acknowledged that undue optimism is not restricted to SCs. In the Commonwealth of Independent States: "overoptimism by multilaterals contributed to the high debt levels" (Helbling et al., 2004, p. 1). As prolonged crises mean increased income and importance, economists or lawyers can easily find explanations. As long as Southern members will tolerate this incorrect behaviour, nothing will change. To stop it, victims have to stand up against the Fund and its Northern masters to defend their contractual rights, the Rule of Law and human rights.

The Fund's statutes nevertheless still contain an interesting stipulation. Its Article VIII, 2(b) stipulates:

> Exchange contracts which involve the currency of any member and which are contrary to the exchange control regulations of that member maintained or imposed consistently with this Agreement shall be unenforceable in the territories of any member. In addition, members may, by mutual accord, cooperate in measures for the purpose of making the exchange control regulations of either member more effective, provided that such measures and regulations are consistent with this Agreement.

Munevar and Pustovit (2020) drew attention to this article, arguing that it allows the IMF to impose a debt standstill through the temporary suspension of enforceability of debt contracts in domestic courts of IMF member countries, including the USA and the UK. No doubt, the Fund as well as members could do so, whether they want or do so is in fact a different matter.

Rightly arguing that it "seems inexcusably naïve to expect" that "all private sector creditors will voluntarily suspend debt service payments or join other debt relief initiatives for countries in need", the authors want to use the IMF's statutes as a way of enforcing a standstill quickly and efficiently.

The authors quote IMF sources showing that this avenue had been considered but not taken by the IMF itself. Although members have approached the Fund informally in the past, there exists no record of a formal request: "If such a request were to take place, the IMF Executive Board is bound under Decision no. 446-4 to provide an interpretation" (ibid.).

Looking at the history of the Fund, there is no doubt that Art. VIII was meant as a safety provision. Northern members seem to have pushed this initial intention – like any other SC-friendly stipulations – aside.

To fight COVID, Fisher and Mazarei (2020, p. 1) propose a Pandemic Support Facility (PSF), a new temporary lending instrument, "primarily" for emerging markets. Unfortunately, this would further increase the IMF's arbitrary power over poorer countries.

Unsurprisingly, special drawing rights (SDRs) were brought up again. Since the creation of SDRs in 1969 to supplement the increasingly insufficient supply of dollars and gold in relation to sharply grown world trade and payments, the idea came up to allocate these artificial, supplementary assets to members not in relation to their quotas in the Fund, but to give developing members more SDRs. Early on the idea was to provide more resources to finance development. Now the idea has cropped up again to finance the fallout of COVID-19 in the South. One example is Barry Hermann's (2020) proposal that IMF members agree to a general allocation and that developed countries contribute a part of their allocations to trust funds at the IMF, as well as that similar trust funds be established at the IBRD and regional development banks that are empowered to receive SDRs. Hermann remarks that governments already can and some do contribute SDRs to the trust funds at the IMF for low-income countries. There is precedent. But these contributions are by far not of the dimension needed. Hermann's proposal is more sophisticated than a simple proposal to allot more SDRs to SCs; it is helpful and could be implemented easily – all perfect reasons to prevent it.

The historic record of SDRs is not encouraging. The first proposal to link SDR creation with development finance, allotting more SDRs to "developing countries" than according to their quotas, had been made even before SDRs existed. Of course, proposals followed right after SDRs were established in 1969. The IMF, Research Department (1973) looks down in history: "From the time when academic proposals for issuing an international reserve asset began to appear in the late 1950s, there have been frequent suggestions that the issuance of such an asset should in some manner be made to enhance the flow of resources to less developed countries, and foster economic development".

What discourages optimism regarding Hermann's proposal is that simple Link proposals (more SDRs for SCs) were not the only proposals made. Ideas such as the North giving unused SDRs to IDA to finance development were also made. However, direct link or not all have been blocked. Thus, one has unfortunately to conclude that Hermann's good and helpful proposal will also be blocked by the North.

Gallagher et al. (2020) have proposed an SDR allocation "equivalent of at least $500 billion as part of the global response to the crisis generated by the coronavirus pandemic". They admit, however, that allocations "would be made according to IMF quotas, which means that only a fraction of the allocated SDRs would go to developing and emerging economies" (ibid.) so that "slightly under two-fifths" would be allocated to the South. As this is "certainly too low", the authors advocate a reform of IMF quotas.

This is no doubt needed. The history of quota changes, though, shows that the allocation is still too much determined by the relative importance of members around 1945. Changes have occurred after long and protracted political tug of wars against bitterly defending former "big economies", although China has eventually managed to become the third largest member. Really to support the South via SDRs would need either a substantial change in quotas – absolutely unlikely as voting rights are based on quotas – or another substantial and also unlikely change in the IMF's statutes in order to allow a larger allocation of SDRs for developing countries. After all, more SDRs would reduce the IMF's grip on SCs, as well as on some poor European countries.

Officially, the IMF's position is expressed by Georgieva (2020) "we are looking at other available options. Several low- and middle-income countries have asked the IMF to make an SDR allocation, as we did during the Global Financial Crisis, and we are exploring this option with our membership". Looking at something does not mean doing anything.

The Fund's reactions to the crisis caused accusations that the IMF is effectively bailing out private lenders to some of world's poorest nations. The Jubilee Debt Campaign (2020) found that "$11.3 billion of IMF loans issued to help countries heavily impacted by the coronavirus crisis are effectively being used to bail out private lenders". Loans to 28 highly indebted developing countries are used to pay interest and debts to private creditors according to this source. These are those private creditors that mostly refuse to participate in any activity to help these countries, such as moratoria, as official creditors, including the IMF, officially deplore.

For these countries, this is little help, even though comparatively lower interest rates payable by poor countries to the Fund are some help nevertheless. Quoting the IMF's (2013, e.g., p. 7; pp. 15f) own argument that "debt restructurings have often been too little and too late, thus failing to re-establish debt sustainability and market access in a durable way", Jubilee (2020) sees the IMF as "partly to blame for this as it often breaks its own policy by lending to countries with high debts, thereby delaying necessary debt restructurings". The IMF's record in delaying debt reductions, not least by overoptimistic forecasts (as at present) is not encouraging.

8.5 Financial Effects in the North

Corona (COVID-19) has also caused enormous upheavals in the North that led to huge financial programmes to overcome the crisis. The OECD (2020d, p. 5) states "The pandemic-related surge in government financing needs has resulted in OECD governments raising a record amount of funds from the market. From January to May 2020, governments issued debt securities worth USD 11 trillion – almost 70% higher than average issuance in the same period over the past five years". Compared with pre-COVID estimates, gross borrowing needs have increased by 30%. As could be expected, "While central government borrowing estimates have increased significantly in G7 economies, changes in OECD emerging-market economies have been rather limited". According to the OECD, about 25% of government bonds carried negative interest rates, and 43% of bond issuance was at interest rates between 0% and 1%. While, for example, Germany earns money by borrowing, SCs face increased costs due to COVID-19.

Sums suddenly available due to the pandemic in the North are mind-boggling. The US Coronavirus Aid, Relief, and Economic Security Act ("CARES Act") amounts to an "estimated US$2.3 trillion (around 11% of GDP)" (IMF, 2020c; this source provides a highly commendable survey covering 196 countries). This was not all. The Paycheck Protection Program and Health Care Enhancement Act, for example, amounts to $483 billion (for a list of programmes v. ibid.). In the USA, money is not a limiting factor. Only petty political feuds between the political parties can stop necessary financing due to budget laws way beyond any sane economic reason.

The EU's best-known action is the €750 billion package, called Next Generation EU (NGEU) recovery fund, split into grants (€390 billion) and loans (€360 billion) (cf. European Commission, 2020a; for pointed criticism v. Varoufakis, 2020). Unfortunately, anti-corona measures were again abused to roll back democracy by trying to link all financial transactions to an undefined term, the Rule of Law. Members, such as Hungary, opposed this, claiming that these funds must not be connected to undefined and thus anti-Rule-of-Law exigencies.

The EU's selective use of the Rule of Law seems to fuel suspicions obviously harboured by, for example, Hungary and Poland. Unlike in these two cases, two countries disliked by Brussels, the EU has sometimes been more lenient regarding this principle, of which human rights is part and parcel. The discrimination of the ethnic minority of Russian origin by Baltic states has been treated in a way that made the German weekly *Der Spiegel* (Verseck, 2020) refer to as "Apartheid" when describing the situation. The Czech Republic was allowed to join without abrogating decrees legalising the expropriation and expulsion of people uniquely because of their ethnicity. Their implementation resulted in many people killed with impunity and, finally, a relatively minor remark. Hilpold (2021) noted in the government-owned *Wiener Zeitung* that legal rights of ongoing judges, whose withdrawal in Poland caused Europe-wide outrage, do not even exist in Austria. Unlike Poland and Hungary, these countries are not considered bad boys by Brussels.

This intended attack on the rights of elected national parliaments did not succeed this time, but it will no doubt be repeated. Debt levels high above the Maastricht criteria and the EU's "democracy deficit" and already existing anti-democratic instruments such as the European semester – which still is not a strong instrument so far – will make it easier to overrule democratic institutions.

The European Council (2020, pp. 5f) is quite outspoken: member states have to prepare national recovery and resilience plans to be "assessed by the Commission ... The criteria of consistency with the country-specific recommendations, ... shall need the highest score of the assessment". The "assessment of the recovery and resilience plans shall be approved by the Council, by qualified majority on a Commission proposal". "The positive assessment of payment requests will be subject to the satisfactory fulfilment of the relevant milestones and targets". These – more precisely the Rule of Law – have not necessarily been defined. Thus, Brussels could arbitrarily decide whether a member violated the Rule of Law or any other unspecified "milestones and targets" or not, as was brought up by Hungary. On top of present mechanisms to overrule democratic decisions of democratically elected parliaments by non-elected Commission members and politicians – as, for example, by the European semester – a new arbitrary mechanism is to be established to bring the EU closer to a bureaucratic dictatorship.

Coincidentally, a reform of the European Stability Mechanism (ESM) signed on 27 January 2021 stipulates "a stronger role in future economic adjustment programmes and crisis prevention" (ESM, 2021) for the Mechanism. It will co-operate with the EU Commission in assessing member economies and put pressure on EU members.

What one notes immediately is that parliaments are not even mentioned. Leaders (in German, Führer) decide. Varoufakis (2020) criticises this concept outspokenly, pointing out the foreseeable result that budget restrictions pursuant to Maastricht (in contrast to logic and economic reason) will be even more restrictive once the present COVID-19 situation will be over. And they will again be valid. Thus, Brussels will become more powerful. He rightly foresees a new neoliberal austerity wave destroying welfare in the EU in favour of capital and EU functionaries.

While "democracy" is declared a basic and important value of the EU (cf. European Commission, 2020b), the "European parliament" is not a parliament at all. It has no right to propose bills. The EU and the parliament itself speak of "co-decision" and "participation in the legislative process" (European Parliament, 2020). In no democracy, the parliament co-decides or participates in legislation, but it is the only legislative power. The EU construction is clearly anti-parliamentary, as much so as unelected politicians dare at the moment – the real way to serfdom to paraphrase F.A. Hayek.

To put things in a nutshell, it appears that the COVID-19 crisis has been used by the EU to increase non-democratic decision-making or at least to introduce the basis of such mechanisms further to cut back fundamental rights of national parliaments. COVID-19 was a gift of God to roll back democracy. As Maastricht is only suspended, not abrogated, Brussels clearly seems to wait for the right junction to take these criteria out of the box again in order to foster neoliberalism. Necessary heavy expenditures now to save countries will come in handy when destructing European welfare states further.

8.6 Conclusion

Focusing on economic policymaking and politics in the light of the pandemic, Jordà et al. (2020) conclude in the journal of the BWTs that:

> The COVID-19 pandemic's toll on economic activity in recent months is only the beginning … While the rapid and unprecedented collapse of production, trade, and employment may be reversed as the pandemic eases, historical data suggest that long-term economic consequences could persist for a generation or more.

While one might be inclined to doubt whether studying previous pandemics, such as the Black Death in the 1300s, can really provide guidance – economic policy has somewhat developed since then – the authors are no doubt right. Financial markets will feel the effects at least for many years. The problems created globally by a virus from a Chinese market are likely to haunt us for quite some time. With a bit of bad luck, another virus may break out from an animal market before all the consequences of the present crisis will be overcome.

Unfortunately, China's lack of proper reactions to SARS referred to above lead one to fear that the next spread is possible.

Interest rates are bound to be kept low not to create problems for borrowing governments and the EU – with grave impacts on market financed pension schemes. Poor people in SCs will have to suffer due to debt pressure. While consequences are dire for people, especially the poor, and for democracy, some are on the winning side. IFIs are able to increase their importance, leverage and incomes. The EU is likely to be happy to have another "reason" to destroy democracy further. The financial consequences of COVID-19 thus go very much beyond financial markets only.

References

Bretton Woods Observer. (2020a, Autumn). *Civil Society raises alarm about IMF's continued backing of austerity amidst pandemic*. Unsigned. https://www.brettonwoodsproject.org/2020/10/civil-society-raises-alarm-about-imfs-continued-backing-of-austerity-amidst-pandemic/

Bretton Woods Observer. (2020b, Autumn). *Over optimistic IMF forecasts risk dire consequences for COVID-19 responses*. Unsigned. https://www.brettonwoodsproject.org/2020/10/over-optimistic-imf-forecasts-risk-dire-consequences-for-covid-19-response/

Ellmers, B. (2020). *The Global South needs debt relief*. https://www.ips-journal.eu/regions/global/article/show/the-global-south-needs-debt-relief-4286/

ESM. (2021). *ESM reform*. https://www.esm.europa.eu/about-esm/esm-reform

European Commission. (2020a). *Recovery plan for Europe*. https://ec.europa.eu/info/live-work-travel-eu/health/coronavirus-response/recovery-plan-europe_en#key-instruments-supporting-the-recovery-plan-for-europe

European Commission. (2020b). *The EU values*. https://ec.europa.eu/component-library/eu/about/eu-values/

European Council. (2020). Special meeting of the European Council (17, 18, 19, 20and 21July 2020), Brussels, 21July 2020, EUCO 10/20 CO EUR 8 CONCL 4. https://www.consilium.europa.eu/en/press/press-releases/2020/07/21/european-council-conclusions-17-21-july-2020/

European Parliament. (2020). *The European Parliament: Powers*. https://www.europarl.europa.eu/factsheets/en/sheet/19/parlamentul-european-competente

Financing for Sustainable Development Office. (2020). *Funding mechanisms for COVID-19 responses*. https://www.un.org/development/desa/financing/sites/www.un.org.development.desa.financing/files/2020-05/Mapping%20of%20COVID-19%20Response.pdf

Fisher, M., & Mazarei, A. (2020, July). *A possible IMF pandemic support facility for emerging-market countries*. Peterson Institute for International Economics, Policy Brief.

G20 11 (2020, November 13) *Extraordinary G20 Finance Ministers and Central Bank Governors' Meeting Final Statement* (mimeo), https://www.bundesfinanzministerium.de/Content/EN/Standardartikel/Topics/world/G7-G20/G20-Documents/2020-11-13-extraordinary-g20fmcbg-statement-of-november-13.pdf?__blob=publicationFile&v=7

Gallagher, K. P., Ocampo, J. A., & Volz, U. (2020). *IMF Special Drawing Rights: A key tool for attacking a COVID-19 financial fallout in developing countries*. https://www.brookings.edu/blog/future-development/2020/03/26/imf-special-drawing-rights-a-key-tool-for-attacking-a-covid-19-financial-fallout-in-developing-countries/

Georgieva, K. (2020). *The great lockdown: Worst economic downturn since the great depression*. https://www.imf.org/en/News/Articles/2020/03/23/pr2098-imf-managing-director-statement-following-a-g20-ministerial-call-on-the-coronavirus-emergency

Helbling, T., Mody, A., & Sahay, R. (2004). *Debt accumulation in the CIS-7 countries: Bad luck, bad policies, or bad advice?* IMF Working Paper (WP/04/93).

Hermann, B. (2020). *Financing the pandemic response in developing countries: Voluntary debt relief is no answer; SDR allocation is.* https://www.researchgate.net/publication/343892508_Financing_the_pandemic_response_in_developing_countries_voluntary_debt_relief_is_no_answer_SDR_allocation_is

Hilpold, P. (2021, 14 January). *Unabhängigkeit der Gerichte vor Gericht.* Wiener Zeitung. https://www.wienerzeitung.at/themen/recht/recht/2088585-Unabhaengigkeit-der-Gerichte-vor-Gericht.html

IMF, Research Department. (1973). *Allocation of SDRs and financing of economic development.* published in IMF eLibrary 1996, https://www.elibrary.imf.org/view/IMF071/15394-9781451940220/15394-9781451940220/ch04.xml?language=en

IMF. (2013, April 26). *Sovereign debt restructuring—Recent developments and implications for the fund's legal and policy framework.* IMF.

IMF. (2020a, June). *World economic outlook update.* https://www.imf.org/en/Publications/WEO/Issues/2020/06/24/WEOUpdateJune2020

IMF. (2020b). *COVID-19 response in emerging market economies: Conventional policies and beyond.* IMF Blog. https://blogs.imf.org/2020/08/06/covid-19-response-in-emerging-market-economies-conventional-policies-and-beyond/

IMF. (2020c). *Policy responses to COVID-19, policy tracker.* https://www.imf.org/en/Topics/imf-and-covid19/Policy-Responses-to-COVID-19

IMF & IDA. (2004, September, 20). *Debt sustainability in low-income countries-proposal for an operational framework and policy implications.* http://www.imf.org/external/np/pdr/sustain/2004/020304.pdf

Jordà, O., Singh, S. R., & Taylor, A. M. (2020). The long economic hangover of pandemics. *Finance & Development, 57*(2), 12–15.

Jubilee Debt Campaign. (2020). *$11 billion of IMF loans are bailing out private lenders.* https://jubileedebt.org.uk/press-release/11-billion-of-imf-loans-are-bailing-out-private-lenders

Li, Y. (2020, May 14). *Debt standstill for distressed countries must go beyond 2020, Geneva.* https://www.ohchr.org/EN/NewsEvents/Pages/DisplayNews.aspx?NewsID=25888&LangID=E

Mühleisen, M., Gudmundsson, T., & Ward, H. P. (2020, August). *COVID-19 response in emerging market economies: Conventional policies and beyond.* IMF Blog.

OECD. (2020a). *The impact of the coronavirus (COVID-19) crisis on development finance.* http://www.oecd.org/coronavirus/policy-responses/the-impact-of-the-coronavirus-covid-19-crisis-on-development-finance-9de00b3b/

OECD. (2020b). *COVID-19 impact on external private finance in developing countries.* http://www.oecd.org/coronavirus/en/#data

OECD. (2020c). *Official development assistance – ODA 2019 preliminary data.* https://www.oecd.org/dac/financing-sustainable-development/development-finance-standards/official-development-assistance.htm

OECD. (2020d). *Sovereign borrowing outlook for OECD countries 2020,* Special COVID-19 Edition.

Martha, R. S. J. (1990). Preferred creditor status under international law: The case of the International Monetary Fund. *International and Comparative Law Quarterly, 39*(4), 801–826.

Munevar, D., & Pustovit, G. (2020). *Back to the future: A sovereign debt standstill mechanism – IMF Article VIII, Section 2(b),* Eurodad. https://eurodad.org/Entries/view/1547199/2020/05/19/Back-to-the-Future-A-sovereign-debt-standstill-mechanism-IMF-Article-VIII-Section-2-b

Raffer, K. (1990). Applying chapter 9 insolvency to international debts: An economically efficient solution with a human face. *World Development, 18*(2), 301–313.

Raffer, K. (1998a). Is a revival of Keynes's ideas likely? (some comments on chapters by Gerald M. Meier and Sir Hans W. Singer). In S. Sharma (Ed.), *John Maynard Keynes – Keynesianism into the twenty-first century* (pp. 116–127). Edward Elgar.

Raffer, K. (1998b). Looking a gift horse in the mouth: Analysing Donors' aid statistics. *Zagreb International Review of Economics & Business, 1*(2), 1–21.

Raffer, K. (2006). *Macro-economic evolutions of Arab economies: A foundation for structural reforms.* Paper presented at the high-level roundtable partnership for Arab development: A window of opportunity at the OPEC Fund for International Development on 5 May 2006; OFID Pamphlet Series no. 36, 2007.

Raffer, K. (2009). *Preferred or not preferred: Thoughts on priority structures of creditors.* Paper presented at the 2nd meeting of the ILA sovereign insolvency study group, 16 October, Washington, DC. https://homepage.univie.ac.at/kunibert.raffer/net.html

Raffer, K. (2010). *Debt management for development, protection of the poor and the millennium development goals.* Edward Elgar. [Paperback edition 2011].

Raffer, K. (2016). Debts, human rights, and the rule of law: Advocating a fair and efficient sovereign insolvency model. In M. Guzman, J. A. Ocampo, & J. E. Stiglitz (Eds.), *Too little, too late, the quest to resolve sovereign debt crises* (pp. 253–269). Columbia University Press.

Raffer, K., & Singer, H. W. (1996). *The foreign aid business: economic assistance and development co-operation.* Edward Elgar. [Paperback edition 1997].

Raffer, K., & Singer, H. W. (2001). *The economic north-south divide: Six decades of unequal development.* Edward Elgar. [Paperback editions 2002, 2004].

Sayeh, A., & Chami, R. (2020, June). Lifelines in Danger. *Finance & Development, 57*(2), 16–19.

UNCTAD. (2020). *UN calls for $2.5 trillion coronavirus crisis package for developing countries.* https://unctad.org/en/pages/newsdetails.aspx?OriginalVersionID=2315

Varoufakis, Y. (2020). *While EU leaders squabble, the Elephant in the room remains unnoticed.* https://www.yanisvaroufakis.eu/2020/07/18/while-eu-leaders-squabble-the-elephant-in-the-room-remains-unnoticed/

Verseck, K. (2020). *Angst vor der russischen Minderheit.* https://www.spiegel.de/politik/ausland/estland-und-lettland-das-problem-mit-der-russischen-minderheit-a-1169422.html

WHO. (2020). *SARS (severe acute respiratory syndrome).* https://www.who.int/ith/diseases/sars/en/

World Bank. (2020a). *How the World Bank Group is helping countries with COVID-19 (coronavirus).* https://www.worldbank.org/en/news/factsheet/2020/02/11/how-the-world-bank-group-is-helping-countries-with-covid-19-coronavirus

World Bank. (2020b). *World Bank Group: 100 countries get support in response to COVID-19 (coronavirus).* https://www.worldbank.org/en/news/press-release/2020/05/19/world-bank-group-100-countries-get-support-in-response-to-covid-19-coronavirus

World Bank. (2020c). *World Bank predicts sharpest decline of remittances in recent history.* https://www.worldbank.org/en/news/press-release/2020/04/22/world-bank-predicts-sharpest-decline-of-remittances-in-recent-history

Chapter 9
Forecasting Monetary Policy Rates in the COVID-19 Era for South Africa

Thobeka Ncanywa and Ombeswa Ralarala

9.1 Introduction

Despite some commendable progress in the South African monetary policy in the democratic era, the country has been grappling with negative effects of credit downgrades, high unemployment rate and slow economic growth among others. As if that was not enough, in December 2019, there was an announcement of the global deadly disease COVID-19 virus in China, which spread to all countries including South Africa. One of the ways adopted by the South African government was to immediately apply a stay-at-home lockdown to reduce the spread of the virus. The lockdown system implies that the economy comes to a standstill. In this period, we have been observing the South African Reserve Bank reducing interest rates, intending to stabilise the economy as there are many channels that this can influence the economy (SARB, 2020).

On that note, it is important to forecast how the change in monetary policy rates can affect the economy. Forecasting in monetary policy involves the monetary policy committee making financial decisions on what resources to utilise in the long term and gains from the resources informed by the future behaviour of those resources (Brooks, 2008). In this context, changes such as reducing or increasing interest rates will reveal forecasts on how the country will perform, and accurate forecasts will yield more satisfying gains from acting on them. The World Health Organization (2020) reported that the pandemic resulted in interest rates historically at their lowest not only in South Africa but worldwide. Gupta et al. (2020) also noted that the global growth of gross domestic product will be expected to decrease. It was also notable that the virus impacted the world stock market negatively

T. Ncanywa (✉) · O. Ralarala
Department of Economics, University of Limpopo, Mankweng, South Africa
e-mail: Thobeka.ncanywa@ul.ac.za; ombeswa.ralarala@ul.ac.za

© The Author(s), under exclusive license to Springer Nature Switzerland AG 2022
N. Faghih, A. Forouharfar (eds.), *Socioeconomic Dynamics of the COVID-19 Crisis*,
Contributions to Economics, https://doi.org/10.1007/978-3-030-89996-7_9

including those of developed markets. Due to the outbreak of coronavirus, there was an increase in the American stock market volatility (Baker et al., 2020).

The pandemic caused massive economic uncertainty including the aspects of market lockdown that spiked inflation, exchange and interest rate uncertainties. Variability in inflation and exchange rate can be bad for planning purposes as there is great uncertainty in the behaviour of these variables. Nyoni (2018) claims that due to the impact the changes in these variables have on the economy, they, thus, are one of the most watched and analysed monetary policy rates. One of the most important elements when undertaking managerial decisions is forecasting (Majhi et al., 2009). In developing theoretical models and approaches, policymakers have taken into consideration the importance of forecasting as a way to a more proper decision-making process (Pejović & Karadžić, 2020). Thus, to forecast the impact of the concerned monetary policy rated during COVID-19, the study used a univariate model called the autoregressive integrated moving average (ARIMA) modelling, exponential smoothing and generalised autoregressive conditional heteroscedasticity (GARCH) multivariate modelling, vector autoregression (VAR), impulse response functions and variance decomposition. It was imperative to find out how the South African monetary policy rates will behave through and after the COVID-19 era. The chapter will focus on monetary policy rates such as inflation rate, bank rate and foreign exchange rate.

9.2   Literature Review

As much as it has been stated in Gujarati (1995) that forecasting models are theoretic, the monetary policy follows goals, targets and instruments to have a sound economy. The main goal of monetary policy is price stability (Mishkin, 2007; Bernanke & Woodford, 1997; SARB, 2020). To achieve this goal, countries adopt a target using instruments in their exposal. For instance, in South Africa, price stability has been attempted to be achieved by adopting an inflation-targeting framework. The South African inflation rate framework was adopted in the year 2000 and is maintained between 3% and 6% (SARB, 2020). The SARB acknowledge that controlling inflation is advantageous due to its flexibility and transparency (SARB, 2020). Mishkin (2007) discussed five main elements of the inflation-targeting framework such as the public announcement of the target; institutions commit to price stability, a strategy to set policy instruments, transparency and accountability.

For SARB to maintain the 3–6% band of inflation, interest rate such as repurchase rate or bank rate is used as instruments. The Reserve Bank employs a process called monetary policy transmission mechanism (Fig. 9.1). Figure 9.1 illustrates channels of monetary policy which show how monetary policy decisions affect the economy and how to bring price stability. In addition to the monetary policy transmission mechanism, SARB employs a process called open market operations (OMOs) in domestic and foreign exchange markets to achieve price stability. Domestically, the SARB is responsible to manage liquidity in commercial banks.

The SARB uses OMOs as one of the instruments to influence liquidity in the money market. OMOs involve the buying and selling of domestic securities at the Reserve Bank's initiative. This instrument has been used by the SARB since the early 1980s when South Africa shifted from direct to market-related measures to influence monetary conditions. Any change in the demand for money will result in the central bank reaction to control interest rates in the short term. This will be done by raising the money base supply, meaning the central bank will purchase a financial asset through OMOs. Conversely, to reduce the money base, the central bank can sell the financial assets through OMOs (SARB, 2020).

Foreign exchange is one of the channels in the transmission mechanism shown in Fig. 9.1. This channel is viable because the country is integrated into the global economy. South Africa follows a flexible policy and has adopted a flexible exchange rate (SARB, 2020). The channel follows the change in repurchase rate that affects the foreign exchange rate, which in turn touches net exports and ultimately aggregate demand in the economy. For instance, when there is an announcement of the decrease in the repo rate, called an expansionary monetary policy, local deposits become attractive compared to those in other currencies. There is a decrease in the exchange rate as domestic goods are affordable compared to foreign goods; this increase in net exports will lead to a rise in output. There are three ways that the exchange rate channel can influence the economy: the direct effect, the operation via current account surplus and the expected producer price inflation (Aron et al., 2014).

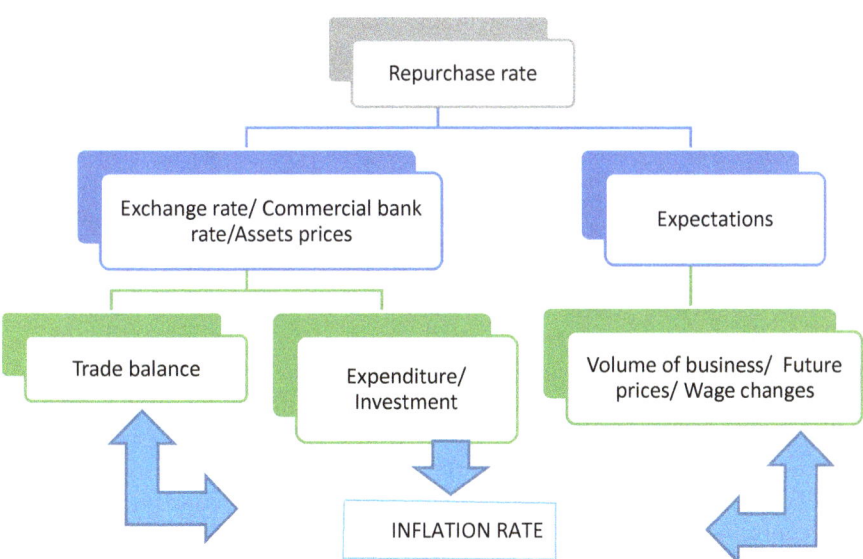

Fig. 9.1 South African monetary policy transmission mechanism. (Source: Authors own figure from SARB)

Evidence of studies that dealt with forecasting of inflation and the exchange rate has been documented globally. For instance, Dzupire (2020) documented a relationship between inflation and exchange rates, where it was argued that due to high volatility and heteroscedasticity of these variables the generalised autoregressive conditional heteroscedasticity (GARCH) methodology was used in the study. The assessment noted that both these variables influence consumer prices mostly through exports and imports. Humala and Rodríguez (2010) supported this argument by using univariate and multivariate models to examine pressures in a currency that aimed at reducing the volatility of the exchange rate in Peru. The study suggested that monetary authorities must be consistent with reduced volatility goal. Bokhari and Feridun (2006) also stated that when it comes to inflation forecast and modelling, autoregressive integrated moving average (ARIMA) models outperform the vector autoregressive (VAR) methodology in Pakistan. However, Najand and Bond (2000) used univariate and random walk models to compare forecasting accuracy techniques in four countries. The study discovered that for all four countries, structural models performed better than both ARIMA and random walk models.

Wickremasinghe (2019) reasoned that multivariate volatility models are the most preferred econometrics approaches when it comes to variables that have high volatility and clustering. Diebold and Nerlove (1989) assessed temporal volatility patterns in several dollar spot exchange rates. The study started by formulating and estimating univariate models and then followed by the use of multivariate models. All seven nominal spot exchange rates showed the existence of ARCH. It was claimed that the models adopted capture volatility and clustering factors better. Bautista (2003) adopted a multivariate GARCH approach in the interaction between exchange and interest rate. The study was conducted using weekly data from 1988 to 2000 in the Philippines. It was concluded that the exchange rate and interest rate had a correlation that was far from constant. This was reported to be as a result of decisions taken by policymakers in response to exogenous events. Fengler et al. (2017) used GARCH models in comparing the exchange rates of two currencies. Thus, it can be argued that when forecasting of variables such as interest rate, exchange rate and inflation, univariate and multivariate forecasting come in handy as these variables show to be highly volatile.

Monetary policy variables have a critical role in trade, socio-economy and the economy as a whole. Thus, accurate forecasting of these variables is of utmost importance. Erdem et al. (2005) analysed the Istanbul Stock Exchange indexes focusing on the exchange rate, interest rate and inflation price volatility spillovers for the 1991–2004 period. To test for univariate volatility spillover of these variables, EGARCH was used. The test proved that strong unidirectional spillover volatility existed from inflation and interest rate to exchange rate. Nyoni (2018) modelled and forecasted the Nigerian Naira for the period 1960–2017. To achieve the goal of the study, forecast evaluation statistics (ME, RMS, MAE, MPE and MAPE) were used. The forecast evaluation statistics showed that the Nigerian Naira needs to be devalued to prevent it from a continual depreciation. The policy implication was also argued to restore the stability of the exchange rate in Nigeria.

Shaibu and Osamwonyi (2020) also used multivariate and ARIMA univariate approaches to forecast Nigerian inflation for the period 1988 to 2017. According to the authors, ARIMA modelling was one of the most appropriate approaches when forecasting inflation. The studies also noted that interest rate, exchange rate and money supply impacted inflation greatly in Nigeria for the period 1988 to 2017. The above literature proves that regulating monetary policy rates can ensure their stability. Catik and Karaçuka (2012) analysed inflation forecasting power of artificial neural networks for Turkey using with univariate models for the period 1982–2009. It was concluded that a model such as ARIMA performs better when it comes to one-step ahead forecasting, whereas unobserved components model excel with dynamic forecasts.

9.3   Methodology

South Africa is in the recovery process to boost the economy after a shutdown of the whole economy due to the COVID-19 pandemic. This chapter aims to find the best monetary policy forecasts that can be utilised to influence the economy in the recovery process. The econometric methodology of the time series models is used to achieve the set aim.

9.3.1   Data

Forecasts of monetary policy rates, namely, inflation rate, bank rate and foreign exchange rate, are determined using monthly secondary time series data. Data for these variables are obtained from the South African Reserve Bank scanning from 1994 to 2020.

9.3.2   Model Estimation

Forecasting of the monetary policy rates such as inflation, bank and foreign exchange rates is analysed in a univariate and multivariate set-up as alluded in Chatfield (2001). Univariate forecasting use forecasts that are determined by the present and previous values of a variable forecasted (Gujarati, 1995). Examples of univariate forecasts are ARIMA models and exponential smoothing methods. Multivariate forecasts include values of one or more explanatory variable(s). Examples of multivariate forecasts are simultaneous equation regression and vector autoregression models.

9.3.2.1 Univariate Modelling

In an attempt to achieve the set objective, univariate modelling of the monetary policy rates is employed. For this analysis, a univariate model called the autoregressive integrated moving average (ARIMA) modelling and exponential smoothing is employed. A univariate model is a dispersal of a variable at time t (can be inflation, bank rate or foreign exchange rate) to determine forecast using past and present information of the variable and the error term. Therefore, within the ARIMA (p, I, q) univariate forecasting, there is a p-order of an autoregression, an I-order of integration and q-order of moving average process. ARIMA models were first introduced by Box and Jenkin in 1970 (Brooks, 2008; Chatfield, 2001; Gujarati, 1995).

In ARIMA models, the Box-Jenkin methodology which consists of identification, estimation and diagnostic checking steps is adopted (Brooks, 2008, Gujarati, 1995). The identification step finds out if the data follows a pure AR, a pure MA and a combination ARMA or ARIMA process. In the identification step, a correlogram can be used to assist. Correlograms are used in conjunction with theoretical tools such as partial autocorrelation function (PACF) and autocorrelation (ACF). Then, the resulting PACF and ACF coefficients are checked using the rule of thumb for the autocorrelation coefficient. According to Brooks (2008), it is difficult to find the order of the model using ACF and PACF. To determine the appropriate model order, the Akaike and Schwarz information criteria can be used. The rule of thumb is to pick the model order that gives the minimum information criteria value.

There are two types of forecast mentioned in Brooks (2008), namely, dynamic and static forecasts. Dynamic forecasts are a multiple-step forecast starting at the beginning of the sample period which can quickly converge upon long-term mean values. The static forecast follows sequential steps from one period to the next. So, forecasts are constructed, and construction is followed by testing if they are accurate, meaning testing for forecast accuracy. To test for forecast accuracy, we can employ several measures such as mean absolute error (MAE), root mean squared error (RMSE), Theil's U-statistic and mean absolute per cent error (MAPE). The RMSE assumes that unbiased errors and that terms are normally distributed (Willmott & Matsuura (2005). The smaller the RMSE, the better, meaning that the lower values of RMSE imply that there are minor forecast errors (Brooks, 2008).

Furthermore, the exponential smoothing methodology is employed to test for forecast accuracy including single, double and Holt-Winters. The reliable MAE value should be below 100 to account for out-of-sample variability (Chatfield et al., 2001). Decomposition of forecast errors into bias proportion, variance proportion and covariance proportion. Significant bias proportion implies that forecasts are not biased (Brooks, 2008).

9.3.2.2 Multivariate Modelling

Monetary policy rates are operating in a relay of the monetary policy transmission mechanism. It is for that reason that in this chapter multivariate models are constructed to measure the relationship between the monetary policy rates. A multivariate modelling analysis measures the relationship between two or more explanatory variables. Multivariate modelling is useful to foresee the behaviour of future value(s) of the dependent variable based on future value(s) of explanatory variables through forecasting. We need out-of-sample forecasting as it determines forecasts of future values of the dependent variable, given the values of the explanatory variables (Gujarati, 1995).

To forecast the effects of how these rates can affect each other and for how long, generalised autoregressive conditional heteroscedasticity (GARCH), vector autoregressive (VAR), impulse response functions and variance decomposition are employed. It is noted in Brooks (2008) that impulse response functions suggest the effects of shocks between the dependent variable and its explanatory variables. Another VAR forecasting method is the variance decomposition, which is slightly different from the impulse response function. VAR variance decomposition entails movement in the shocks of the dependent variable and also of other variables in the system (Brooks, 2008). Variance decomposition and impulse response function yield similar outcomes and are usually employed together. To remedy the challenge that forecast errors can be correlated, orthogonalised impulse responses are used (Brooks, 2008).

Multivariate models such as VAR do not always yield improved forecasts but may result in short-horizon forecasts (Chatfield, 2001). So forecasting through the GARCH family is crucial particularly for variables characterised by volatility clustering, which refers to wide movements of these variables (Gujarati, 1995; Ding & Granger, 1996). These variables can have high volatility in one 1 followed by low volatility in the next month. There are numbers of these models especially to forecast volatile variables such as inflation and foreign exchange rates, namely, generalised ARCH, exponential-GARCH (E-GARCH) and the Glosten, Jagannathan and Runkle GARCH (GJR). An ARCH model refers to error term variance that is explained by the previous time' error terms. Then when the error terms and the conditional variance are squared in the previous period, the ARCH is generalised to GARCH. The multivariate analysis of the inflation rate regressed against bank rate, and the foreign exchange rate is adopted.

9.4 Results and Discussions

The monetary policy variables under study need to be tested for the presence of unit roots, as this is the common feature in time series data. Variables that contain a unit root result in inappropriate forecasts (Brooks, 2008; Gujarati, 1995). Table 9.1 tabulate results of unit roots using the augmented Dickey-Fuller tests.

Table 9.1 Unit root results of the augmented Dickey-Fuller

Variables		T-statistic	Critical values			Probability	Decision
			1%	5%	10%		
	A constant and linear trend						
Inflation	At level	−2.165	−3.987	−3.424	−3.135	0.506	Non-stationary
	At 1st diff.	−12.77	−3.987	−3.424	−3.135	0.000	Stationary
Bank rates	At level	−2.694	−3.987	−3.424	−3.135	0.239	Non-stationary
	At 1st diff.	−13.01	−3.987	−3.424	−3.135	0.000	Stationary
Forex	At level	−1.748	−3.987	−3.424	−3.135	0.727	Non-stationary
	At 1st Diff.	−13.39	−3.987	−3.424	−3.135	0.000	Stationary

Source: Authors own table from SARB data
Notes: *Diff.* differenced, *FOREX* foreign exchange rate

It is shown in Table 9.1 that inflation, bank rate and foreign exchange rate have a unit root and therefore are non-stationary at levels. They turn out to be stationary after first differencing, which implies that there is first-order integration [I (1)].

Correlograms also confirm that the monetary policy variables (inflation, bank rate and foreign exchange rate) are first-order integrated, as they become stationary after first differencing (Fig. 9.2a–c). This implies that when forecasts are determined, differenced variables should be used to remove the existing unit root. This is crucial especially for the ARIMA models to determine the I-order of variables because forecast with a unit root is inaccurate and inappropriate (Pejović and Karadžić (2020)).

9.4.1 Forecasts of Inflation

ARIMA (p, I, q) modelling is used to find the best forecasts of inflation. Using the Box-Jenkins methodology to find the best forecasts, the first step involves finding the best model with values of p, I and q. Table 9.2 indicates nine trials of different models for values of p, I and q as (1, 1, 1), (1, 1, 2), (1, 1, 3), (1, 1, 4), (1, 1, 5), (1, 1, 6), (1, 2, 1), (4, 2, 1) and (9, 1, 1).

In Table 9.2, different statisticsare used to decide which model can give the best forecasts with minimum forecast error. According to Pejović and Karadžić (2020), lowest and significant coefficients of autoregressive (ar) and moving average (ma), lowest Akaike's Information Criteria (AIC) and Bayesian Information Criteria (BIC) and highest log-likelihood value can indicate the best model to be chosen for forecasts. Looking at the results in Table 9.2, model (1, 1, 4) is chosen as the best as it has both significant ar and ma though ar is not the lowest and the highest log likelihood. AIC and BIC are not used to choose the best model here, because where AIC (2910) is lowest, log likelihood is not the highest and ar is insignificant and high. So the choice is based on the model that satisfies many statistics than the others.

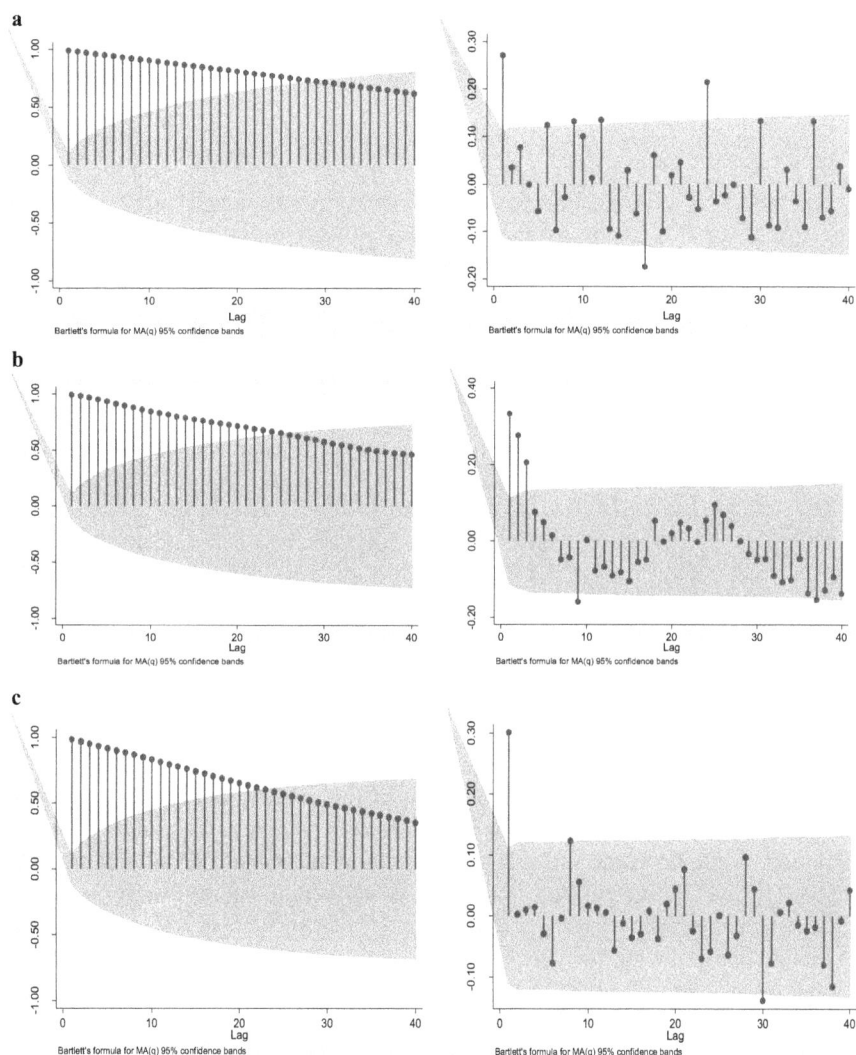

Source: Authors own figure from SARB data

Notes: LFOREX- logged foreign exchange rate; LCPI- Inflation; MA- Moving Average

Fig. 9.2 (**a**) Correlograms of inflation and differenced inflation. (**b**) Correlograms of bank rate and differenced bank rate. (**c**) Correlograms of foreign exchange rate and differenced foreign exchange rate
Source: Authors own figure from SARB data
Notes: *LFOREX* logged foreign exchange rate, *LCPI* inflation, *MA* moving average

Table 9.2 ARIMA models of inflation

	(1,1,1)	(1,1,2)	(1,1,3)	(1,1,4)	(1,1,5)	(1,1,6)	(1,2,1)	(4,2,1)	(9,1,1)
L1 ar	.003	.993***	.310	.993***	.993***	.269	.260***	.281***	.697
L2 ar								.075	.195
L3 ar								.090	.092
L4 ar								.053	.025
L5 ar									.105
L6 ar									.253**
L7 ar									.293**
L8 ar									.127
L9 ar									.080
L1 ma	.284	1.38***	.025	1.35***	1.35***	.599***	−1	1.00	
L2 ma		.402***	.062	.340***	.340***	.118			
L3 ma			.048	.080	.080	.061			
L4 ma				.111**	.114	.029			
L5 ma					.002	.076			
L6 ma						.123			
AIC	2925	2941	2923	2943	2941	2933	2912	2910	2939
BIC	2910	2922	2900	2917	2911	2899	2897	2883	2894
Log-L	1466	1475	1467	1478	1478	1475	1460	1462	1481

Source: Authors own table from SARB data

Notes: *ar* autoregressive, *ma* moving average, AIC-Akaike's information criteria, BIC-Bayesian information criteria, *Log-L* log likelihood

After choosing the 'best' model from trials in Table 9.2, static and dynamic forecasts are determined. Figure 9.3 shows the forecasts and the actual values of inflation based on the first-order ar, first differenced inflation and fourth-order moving average (1, 1, 4). It can be seen in Fig. 9.3 that the fitted values overlap with the actual values indicating that forecast error is very close to zero. This implies that inflation forecasts are the best, meaning South Africa should continue trusting inflation targets as they portray best forecasts. This is in agreement with the studies found in Bokhari and Feridun (2006).

Further analysis of forecasting using exponential smoothing for inflation is done. Figure 9.4 illustrates that the forecasts closely follow the actual data, and therefore the model fits the data well. This confirms what Fig. 9.3 realised that inflation forecasts are the best for South Africa. Accuracy measures of inflation forecast also yield the best forecasts (Chatfield et al., 2001). For instance, the optimal exponential coefficient is 0.0109, the sum of squared residuals is 0.001631973, and the root mean squared error is 0.0022870686. Brooks (2008) alluded that measures of forecast accuracy should be close to zero to declare the best forecasts. On that note, looking at these inflation forecasts, it can be seen that inflation forecasts are the best (Catik and Karaçuka, 2012; Lütkepohl, 2005; Monteforte and Moretti, 2013; Naraidoo and Paya, 2012).

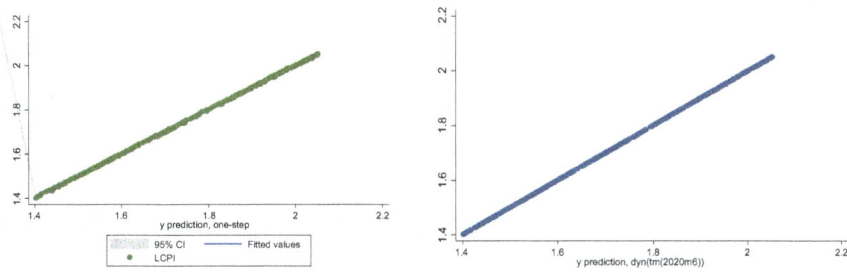

Fig. 9.3 Static and dynamic forecasts of inflation
Source: Authors own figure from SARB data
Notes: *LCPI* inflation, *y* fitted values of inflation, *dyn (tm (2020m6))* Stata software code for dynamic prediction 6 months ahead

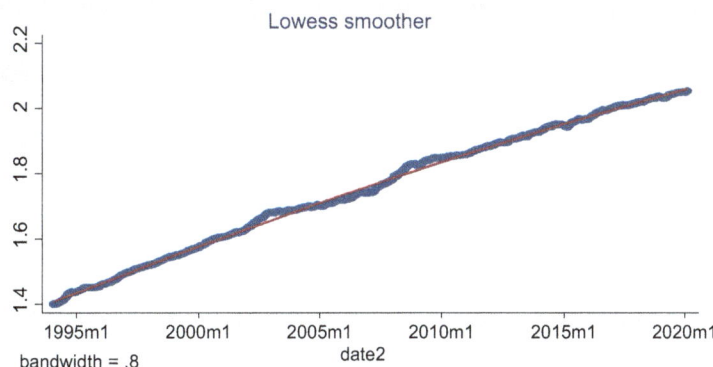

Fig. 9.4 Exponential soothing of inflation
Source: Authors own figure from SARB data
Notes: *m1* month 1, *LCPI* inflation

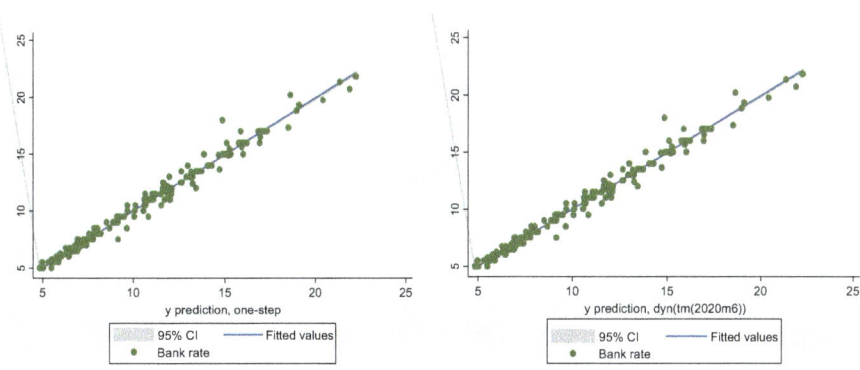

Fig. 9.4 Static and dynamic forecasts of bank rate
Source: Authors own figure from SARB data

9.4.2   Forecasts of Bank Rate

Bank rate as the rate charged by the South African Reserve Bank is important for forecasting, especially in the COVID-19 period. This is because it is the instrument used by monetary authorities to control the economy for contractionary and expansionary monetary policy. Same procedures that were undertaken in inflation forecasts are also followed in this section. After identifying the order of stationarity that bank rate has a unit root and becomes stationary after first differencing, then the best ARIMA model was chosen. In Table 9.3, based on the low AIC, lower and significant ma and significant ar, models with first-order ar, first-order integration and sixth-order ma are chosen (1, 1, 6).

After choosing the model (1, 1, 6) from trials in Table 9.3, static and dynamic forecasts are determined as shown in Fig. 9.4. In Fig. 9.4, it can be realised that as much as many fitted values overlap with the actual values, starting at the tenth period, many fitted points are far from the actual values. This indicates that bank rate forecasts are best in the short horizon and therefore can be used in the short run. This can be beneficial in disaster periods like the COVID-19 era, where economic contractions need an immediate recovery to put the economy back to

Table 9.3 ARIMA models of bank rate

	(1,1,1)	(1,1,2)	(1,1,3)	(1,1,4)	(1,1,5)	(1,1,6)	(1,2,1)	(4,2,1)	(9,1,1)
L1 ar	.706***	.617***	.473***	.578	.479	.909***	.336***	.263***	.373**
L2 ar								.175***	.327***
L3 ar								.096**	.205***
L4 ar								.054	.013
L5 ar									.037
L6 ar									.018
L7 ar									.022
L8 ar									.011
L9 ar									156***
L1 ma	.421	.364***	.213	.318	.222	1.19***	1.00	1.00	.652***
L2 ma		.101*	.116**	.090	.119	.469***			
L3 ma			.077	.057	.083	.418***			
L4 ma				.038	.021	.258***			
L5 ma					.031	.104*			
L6 ma						.107**			
AIC	320	320	321	323	325	319	335	327	320
BIC	335	339	343	349	354	353	350	353	365
Log-L	156	155	155	155	154	151	163	157	148

Source: Authors own table from SARB data

Notes: *ar* autoregressive, *ma* moving average, *AIC* Akaike information criteria, *BIC* Bayesian information criteria, *Log-L* log linear equilibrium. However, policymakers need to have a plan to boost the economy in the long run.

Exponential smoothing procedure further confirms that bank rate forecasts are not the best as the fitted values move far from the actual values as shown in Fig. 9.5. These results are further confirmed by the forecast accuracy measures that the optimal exponential coefficient is 0.3186, the sum of squared residuals is 54.901533 and root mean squared error is 0.41948355. It should be noted that these values are not close to zero and therefore there is a large forecast error. Therefore, for South African data, bank rate does not yield best forecasts with the ARIMA and exponential smoothing models. On that note, a more fractionally differenced ARIMA model called ARFIMA is employed to find the best estimates. Figure 9.6a shows the spectral density of bank rate, which illustrate that the ARFIMA modelling can recognise both long- and short-run effects that are confounded by the ARMA model.

Notes: *y* fitted values of bank rate, *dyn (tm (2020m6))* Stata software code for dynamic prediction 6 months ahead

Figure 9.6b predicts good forecasts of bank rate. This is demonstrated by predicted values that fit the original series well and the similar flow of the fractionally differenced series to the original. This led to plotting dynamic forecasts of bank rate 3 months ahead. As can be seen in Fig. 9.7, the bank rate shows good forecast 3 months after the sampled time in a 90% confidence interval.

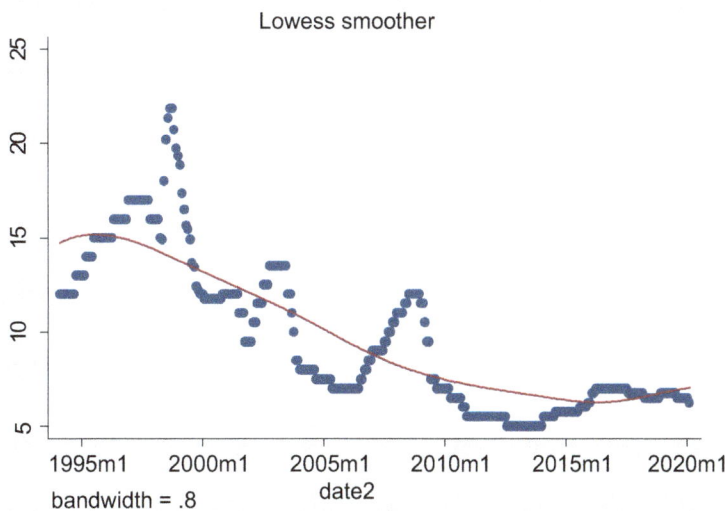

Fig. 9.5 Exponential smoothing of bank rate
Source: Authors own figure from SARB data
Note: *m1* month 1

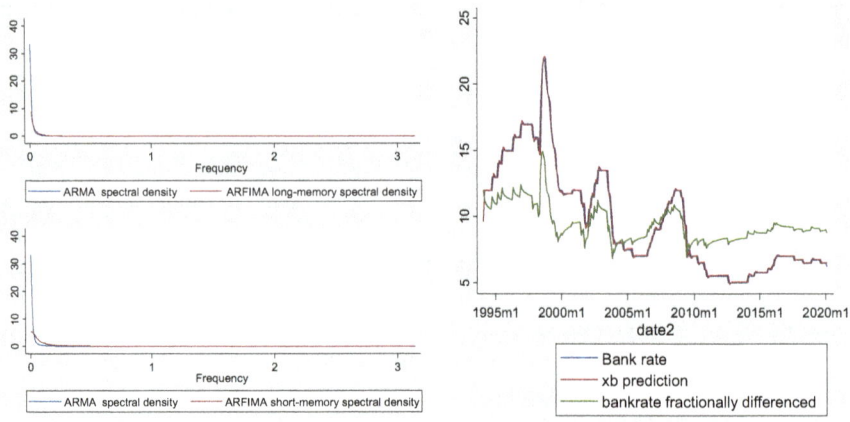

Fig. 9.6 (**a**) ARFIMA spectral density of bank rat. (**b**) Bank rate forecasts with ARFIMA
Source: Authors own figures from SARB data
Notes: *ARMA* autoregressive moving average, *ARFIMA* autoregressive fractionally integrated moving average

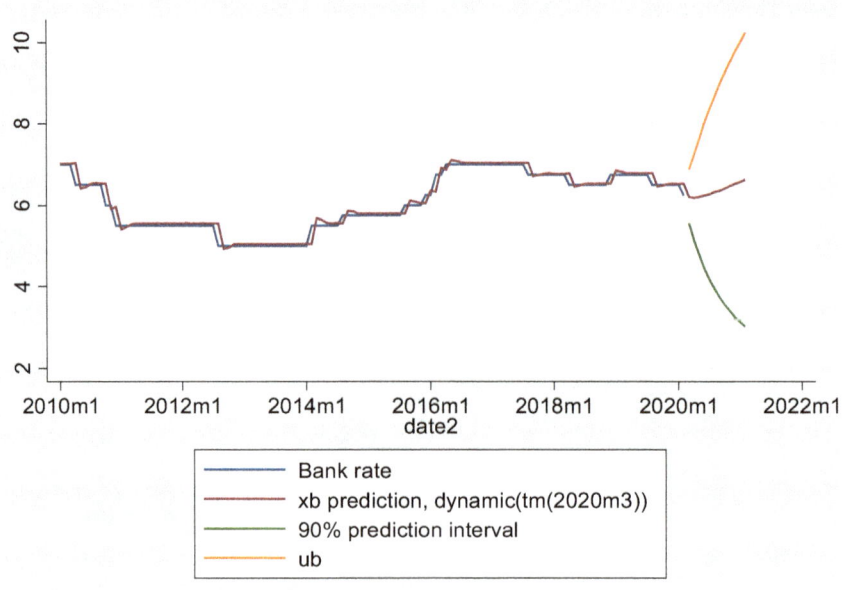

Fig. 9.7 Dynamic forecast of bank rate 3-month post-2020
Source: Authors own figures from SARB data
Notes: *xb* calculates linear prediction from fitted values, *m1* month 1

9.4.3   Forecasts of Foreign Exchange Rate

The foreign exchange rate is crucial for export and import activities, and a country should export more than importing. After trials of ARIMA models of foreign exchange rate have been run, the model that best explains foreign exchange is (4, 2, 1). This model has a lower and significant ar, lowest AIC and BIC and higher log likelihood. It turns out that foreign exchange rate works best after second differencing (I=2), as can be seen in Table 9.4 that second-order integration yield lower and significant ar estimates.

Table 9.4   ARIMA models of foreign exchange rate

	(1,1,1)	(1,1,2)	(1,1,3)	(1,1,4)	(1,1,5)	(1,1,6)	(1,2,1)	(4,2,1)	(9,1,1)
L1 ar	.003	.411	.334	.840**	.836**	.269	.303***	.335***	.659***
L2 ar								.108	.225***
L3 ar								.044	.053
L4 ar								.001	.042
L5 ar									.015
L6 ar									.076
L7 ar									.060
L8 ar									.113*
L9 ar									.128**
L1 ma	.329**	.077	.001	1.17***	1.17***	.058	.999	.999	.999
L2 ma		.134	.109	.279*	.276	.074			
L3 ma			.002	.012	.006	.013			
L4 ma				.030	.016	.015			
L5 ma					.011	.019			
L6 ma						.058			
AIC	1748	1746	1744	1743	1741	1739	1733	1731	1741
BIC	1733	1727	1722	1716	1711	1705	1718	1704	1696
Log-L	878.25	878.25	878.26	878.50	878.52	878.83	870.820	872.52	882.90

Source: Authors own table from SARB data
Notes: *ar* autoregressive, *ma* moving average, *AIC* Akaike information criteria, *BIC* Bayesian information criteria, *Log-L* log linear

Table 9.5   GARCH model estimates of inflation

Variable				
Independent variable: inflation	Coefficients	Std. error	Z-stat	Probability
Bank rate	-0.207	0.001	-18.94	0.000
Foreign exchange rate	0.668	0.025	26.30	0.000
Log likelihood = 433.38				

Source: Authors own table from SARB data

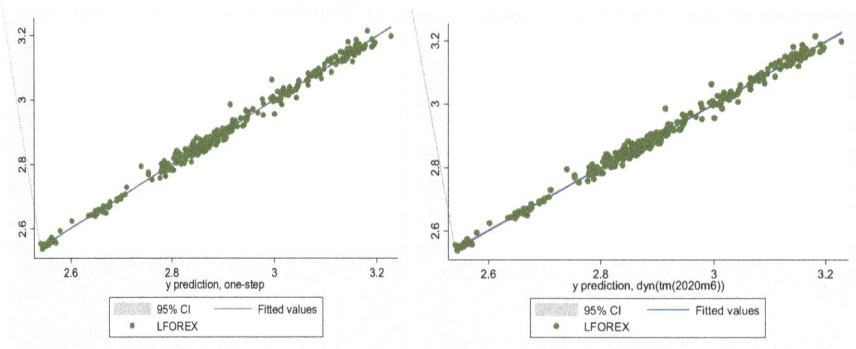

Fig. 9.8 Static and dynamic forecasts of foreign exchange rate
Source: Authors own figure from SARB data
Notes: *y* fitted values of foreign exchange rate, *LFOREX* logged foreign exchange rate

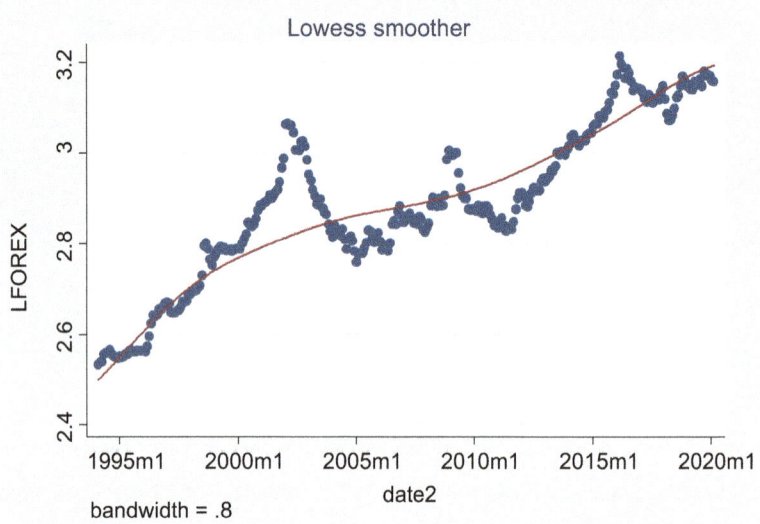

Fig. 9.9 Exponential smoothing of foreign exchange rate
Source: Authors own figure from SARB data
Notes: *m1* month 1, *LFOREX* logged foreign exchange market

The chosen model (4, 2, 1) assist in finding the static and dynamic foreign exchange forecasts (Fig. 9.8). In Fig. 9.8, a few points are not fitted with the actual values in both the static and dynamic forecasts of the foreign exchange rate. These results indicate that the exchange rate has a better forecast than the bank rate.

When further analysis of exponential smoothing and measures of accuracy are employed, it turns out that foreign exchange has better forecasts. Figure 9.9 indicates three phases where foreign exchange rate's fitted values were far apart from

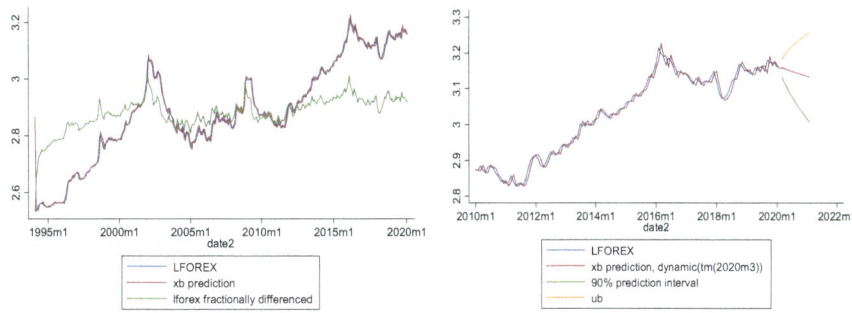

Fig. 9.10 Static and dynamic forecasts of the foreign exchange rate with the ARFIMA model
Source: Authors own figure from SARB data
Notes: *LFOREX* logged foreign exchange rate, *xb dynamic(2020m3)* Stata code for predictions

the actual values in the years 2003, 2010 and 2016. The measures of forecast accuracy confirm that foreign exchange has better forecast as indicated by the optimal exponential coefficient of 0.0001, the sum of squared residuals of 0.072865052 and root mean squared error of 0.015282076. Maintaining a stable exchange rate for countries is in line with the studies of Humala and Rodríguez (2010), Diebold and Nerlove (1989) and Dzupire (2020).

Looking at the three monetary policy variables in this study, it can be seen that inflation gives better forecasts followed by the foreign exchange rate. Additionally, static and dynamic forecasts of the foreign exchange rate in Fig. 9.10 portray good predicted values in the ARFIMA model. Therefore, we can allude that South Africa needs to pay careful attention to fluctuations of the foreign exchange rate as it was central to trading issues.

9.4.4 Multivariate Forecasts

In the multivariate analysis forecasts of inflation (lcpi), bank rate and foreign exchange rate (lforex) are created. The vector autoregressive (VAR) and autoregressive conditional heteroscedasticity (ARCH) methodologies are employed to create these forecasts. The VAR model use differenced data of the three variables as dlcpi, dbankrate and dlforex to control for stationarity. The results of the VAR model yield a significant root mean square error for all variables with inflation = 0.002, bank rate = 0.399 and foreign exchange rate = 0.14. Also, in the VAR, the log likelihood of 2181 is obtained indicating good monetary policy forecasts. After running the basic VAR, the response functions of the model follow. Impulse response functions (IRF) give results of own shocks and comparison to other variables.

Figure 9.11 reports orthogonalised impulse response functions and forecasts of the three variables. It can be seen that a positive shock on bank rate causes an increase on itself until the fourth period which fades away thereafter as indicated in

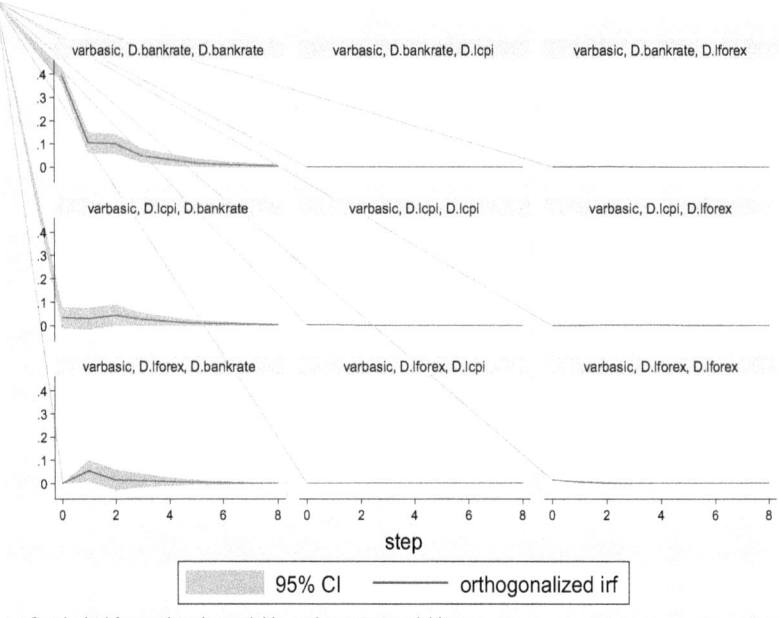

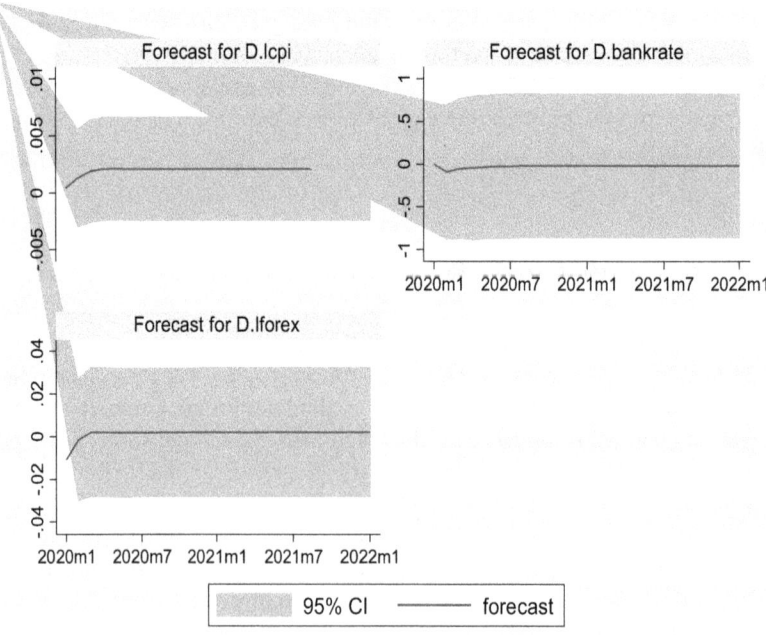

Fig. 9.11 Impulse response functions and forecasts of inflation, bank rate and foreign exchange rate
Source: Authors own figure from SARB data
Notes: *D* differenced, *LFOREX* logged foreign exchange rate, *LCPI* inflation, *IRF* impulse response function

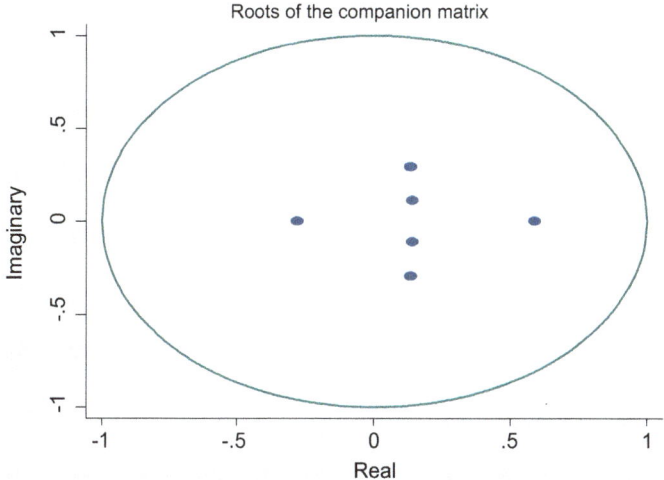

Fig. 9.12 Stability test results
Source: Authors own figure from SARB data

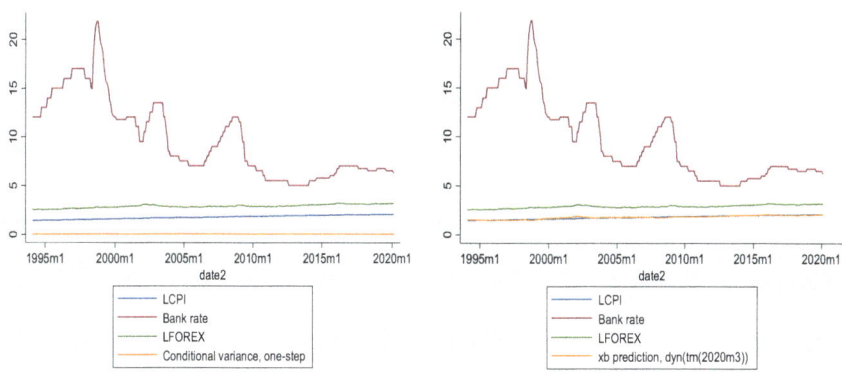

Fig. 9.13 Forecasts of inflation (lcpi), bank rate and foreign exchange rate (lforex) with ARCH model
Source: Authors own figure from SARB data
Notes: *LFOREX* logged foreign exchange rate, *LCPI* inflation

the first row. As for inflation (lcpi) in the second row of Fig. 9.11, there is a slightly constant response of inflation to bank rate overtime. A positive shock of foreign exchange rate causes a decrease in bank rate, followed by an increase in the second period, and fades away in the fourth period. The second picture in Fig. 9.11 illustrates that in the three variables, we have good forecasts as the widths of the confidence intervals grow with the forecast horizon for the next 2 years. The stability of this method is tested with the eigenvalues in the model. It can be shown in Fig. 9.12

that all the eigenvalues are placed inside the circle indicating the stability of the model.

Further analysis of the multivariate modelling with the ARCH methodology follows. After testing for ARCH effects on the series, it has been found that these variables have non-constant variance. Hence, ARCH methodology is used. Experiences of the GARCH are tested and in line with Fengler et al. (2017).

Figure 9.13 confirms what has been realised in the univariate forecasting models that inflation, bank rate and foreign exchange rate yield the best forecast. This implies that the South African monetary policy variables chosen in the study can be used to forecast and shape the economy for the future especially in the COVID-19 era.

9.5   Conclusion and Recommendations

The chapter aimed to determine the best monetary policy rate forecasts for South African during the global COVID-19 pandemic. The best forecast can assist in recovering the economy after a lockdown period due to the pandemic. The monetary policy rates adopted are inflation rate, bank rate and foreign exchange rate. Based on the volatile nature of these rates univariate forecasting models such as autoregressive integrated moving average and multivariate models such as vector autoregressive and autoregressive conditional heteroscedasticity were employed

Findings in both the univariate and multivariate forecasting models link the use of monetary variables in the monetary policy transmission mechanism discussed in the theoretical literature review with ways that the economy can be saved. For instance, the South African monetary policy authorities can stick to the adopted inflation target of 3–6% band. The best inflation forecasts are an indicator that targeting inflation in South Africa is a good choice. The instruments of changing the bank rate called repurchase rate in South Africa are good instruments as forecasts to indicate the movement of the future economy in the post-COVID-19 era. As South Africa has an open economy trading globally, the foreign exchange rate shows that paying attention to it can give good forecasts for the future performance of the economy. It is thus recommended that South African policymakers closely monitor these monetary policy rates as their changes determine some major economic consequences during the pandemic.

References

Aron, J., Farrell, G., Muellbauer, J., & Sinclair, P. (2014). Exchange rate pass-through to import prices, and monetary policy in South Africa. *Journal of Development Studies, 50*(1), 144–164.

Baker, S. R., Bloom, N., Davis, S. J., & Terry, S. J. (2020). *COVID-induced economic uncertainty* (No. w26983). National Bureau of Economic Research.

Bautista, C. C. (2003). Interest rate-exchange rate dynamics in the Philippines: a DCC analysis. *Applied Economics Letters, 10*(2), 107–111.

Bernanke, B. S., & Woodford, M. (1997). *Inflation forecasts and monetary policy* (No. w6157). National Bureau of Economic Research.

Bokhari, S. M., & Feridun, M. (2006). Forecasting inflation through econometric models: An empirical study on Pakistani data. Doğuş Üniversitesi Dergisi, v1 n7 39-47

Brooks, C. (2008). *Introductory econometrics for finance*. Cambridge University Press, 2a Upplagan. ISBN-13, 978-0.

Catik, A. N., & Karaçuka, M. (2012). A comparative analysis of alternative univariate time series models in forecasting Turkish inflation. *Journal of Business Economics and Management, 13*(2), 275–293.

Chatfield, C. (2001). Prediction intervals. In J. S. Armstrong (Ed.), *Principles of forecasting: A handbook for researchers and practitioners*. Kluwer.

Chatfield, C., Koehler, A. B., Ord, J. K., & Snyder, R. D. (2001). A new look at models for exponential smoothing. *Journal of the Royal Statistical Society: Series D (The Statistician), 50*(2), 147–159.

Diebold, F. X., & Nerlove, M. (1989). The dynamics of exchange rate volatility: a multivariate latent factor ARCH model. *Journal of Applied Econometrics, 4*(1), 1–21.

Ding, Z., & Granger, C. W. (1996). Modelling volatility persistence of speculative returns: a new approach. *Journal of Econometrics, 73*(1), 185–215.

Dzupire, N. C. (2020). *Modelling the co-movement of Inflation and exchange rate*, preprints (www.preprints.org).

Erdem, C., Arslan, C. K., & Sema Erdem, M. (2005). Effects of macroeconomic variables on Istanbul stock exchange indexes. *Applied Financial Economics, 15*(14), 987–994.

Fengler, M. R., Herwartz, H., & Raters, F. H. C. (2017). Multivariate volatility models. In *Applied quantitative finance* (pp. 25–37). Springer.

Gujarati, D. (1995). *Basic econometrics*, (International Edition). Prentice-Hall International, Inc.

Gupta, M., Abdelmaksoud, A., Jafferany, M., Lotti, T., Sadoughifar, R., & Goldust, M. (2020). COVID-19 and economy. *Dermatologic Therapy, 33*(4), e13329–e13329.

Humala, A., & Rodríguez, G. (2010). Foreign exchange intervention and exchange rate volatility in Peru. *Applied Economics Letters, 17*(15), 1485–1491.

Lütkepohl, H. (2005). *New introduction to multiple time series analysis*. Springer.

Majhi, R., Panda, G., & Sahoo, G. (2009). Development and performance evaluation of FLANN based model for forecasting of stock markets. *Expert Systems with Applications, 36*(3), 6800–6808.

Mishkin, F. S. (2007). *The economics of money, Banking, and financial markets*. Pearson Education.

Monteforte, L., & Moretti, G. (2013). Real-time forecasts of inflation: The role of financial variables. *Journal of Forecasting, 32*(1), 51–61.

Najand, M., & Bond, C. (2000). Structural models of exchange rate determination. *Journal of multinational financial management, 10*(1), 15–27.

Naraidoo, R., & Paya, I. (2012). Forecasting monetary policy rules in South Africa. *International Journal of forecasting, 28*(2), 446–455.

Nyoni, T. (2018). *Modelling and forecasting Naira/USD exchange rate In Nigeria: A Box-Jenkins ARIMA approach*. MPRA (Munich Personal REPEC Archive), University library LMU, Munich.

Pejović, B., & Karadžić, V. (2020). Econometric Modelling and Forecasting of Interest Rates in Montenegro. *Economic Analysis, 53*(1), 72–83.

Shaibu, I., & Osamwonyi, I. O. (2020). A Comparative Analysis of Inflation Dynamics Models in Nigeria. *International Journal of Academic Research in Business and Social Sciences, 10*(2).

South African Reserve Bank (SARB). (2020). www.resbank.co.za. Accessed online 03 Apr 2020.

Wickremasinghe, G. B. (2019). *Is the PNG foreign exchange market efficient?* Australian National University, Canberra

Willmott, C. J., & Matsuura, K. (2005). Advantages of the mean absolute error (MAE) over the root mean square error (RMSE) in assessing average model performance. *Climate Research, 30*(1), 79–82.

World Health Organization. (2020). www.who.int Accessed online 01 Apr 2020.

Chapter 10
The Effectiveness of the COVID-19 Economic and Social Relief Package as a Poverty Alleviation Strategy in South Africa

Adrino Mazenda, Tyanai Masiya, and David Mandiyanike

10.1 Introduction

The COVID-19 outbreak is not only a health crisis; it is a socio-economic crisis which has impacted all the countries' economic sectors. In the South African context, the pandemic has left all the sectors constrained. Consequently, it has worsened poverty and inequality. In April 2020, the government introduced a R500 billion economic and social relief package (ESRP) which in part sought to cushion the population from poverty and improve food security and, furthermore, to sustain the population for the next 6 months and anticipate the economy re-opening and/or possible development of a vaccine.

Section 27 (1) of the Constitution of the Republic of South Africa, 1996, stipulates that 'Everyone has the right to have access to— (a) health care services, including reproductive health care; (b) sufficient food and water; and (c) social security, including, if they are unable to support themselves and their dependants, appropriate social assistance'.

Section 27 (2) further stipulates that it remains the responsibility of the state to ensure that measures that would lead to the realisation of this right are put in place. Consequently, the National Food and Nutrition Strategy (NFNS) (2013:6) adopted in 2013 states that 'The strategic goal of the National Food and Nutrition Security

A. Mazenda (✉) · T. Masiya
School of Public Management and Administration, University of Pretoria, Hatfield, Pretoria, South Africa
e-mail: adrino.mazenda@up.ac.za; masiya.masiya@up.ac.za

D. Mandiyanike
Department of Political and Administrative Studies, University of Botswana, Gaborone, Botswana
e-mail: mandiyanike@ub.ac.bw

Policy is to ensure the availability, accessibility and affordability of safe and nutritious food at national and household levels'. This strategy also helps to direct the three spheres of government to promote food security, which is accomplished through the following strategies: increased and more targeted public spending on social programmes that has an effect on food security, increased access to food processing and distribution and strategic utilisation of food and trade policies to increase food production and support community-based food production cooperatives through selective government procurement (DAFF, 2013:5–6).

Key in the ESRP is the social grant and the Economic Relief Structural Grant (ERSG), and a reprieve for food insecurity is the temporary increase in both social support grants and business. Government provided relief to meet household's poverty and improve the overall food security position, which fell below the extreme poverty line of R585 (US$33.89) per month (Dean, 2020).

Citing the essence of the ERSG intervention, the possible contentions, coupled with the continued deterioration in the South African economy, due to the closure of business and the incapacitated informal economy, this chapter seeks to investigate the extent to which the ERSP strategy was effective to address the poverty and food security challenges faced by the citizenry. This chapter explores the challenges government faces in the implementation of the ERSG amidst the COVID-19 pandemic and provides recommendations to ensure effectiveness in the implementation of the programme including probable plan for the continued closure of business and the informal economy despite easing certain restrictions/lockdown measures.

The chapter is structured as follows: introduction, adopted research methodology, an extensive literature review relating to poverty and its alleviation, findings on the various themes related to the ESRP as a strategy to alleviate poverty in South Africa and recommendations and conclusions.

10.2   Methodology

This chapter adopted the qualitative research approach. According to de Vos et al. (2014:91), 'qualitative approach aims to answer research questions that provide a more comprehensive understanding of a social problem' (de Vos et al., 2014:91). Babbie and Mouton (2011:270) assert that 'the primary goal of studies using qualitative approach is to describe and understand rather than explain human behaviour'. More importantly, in this article which was based on an extensive review of literature, postulates that a qualitative research approach tends to focus on how people or groups view social reality differently. This approach was the most appropriate for this chapter because it assisted to examine the effectiveness of the COVID-19 economic and social relief package as a poverty alleviation strategy in South Africa.

This chapter utilised secondary data, primarily academic literature; official South African government documents; credible internet sources, primarily daily newspapers; and relevant information from research institutions. Table 10.1 illustrates the primary sources which were consulted.

Table 10.1 Main data sources

Academic sources	Government sources	Research institutions	International institutions
ISI accredited journals	African Peer Review Mechanism (2020)	Institute for Economic Justice (2020)	United Nations (2011, 2020a, b)
Scopus accredited journals	Department of Health (South Africa) (2020)	International Food Policy Research Institute (2020)	World Health Organization (2020)
DHET journals	Department for Communications (South Africa) (2020)	Trade Law Centre, South Africa (2020)	United Nations Children Fund (2020)
	The Presidency (South Africa) (2020)		United Nations Development Programme (2014)
			World Bank (2001, 2018, 2020)
			Debt Rescue (2020)

Source: Authors own table

Generally, the credibility of internet data was considered as information from an authoritative writer or institution. The neutrality of the source of information was also utilised as a criterion to identify truthful and credible data. Thus, secondary sources proved significant in the provision of a broader spectrum and sense of the government's COVID-19 intervention strategies. The rationale was to provide an in-depth analysis and to place this research within the context of existing literature.

A thematic analysis approach was utilised to analyse the data. Wagner et al. (2012:231) define thematic analysis as 'a general approach to analysing qualitative data that involves identifying themes and patterns in the data', while Braun and Clarke (2006) posit that 'thematic analysis minimally organises and describes your data set in detail and also often goes further than this, and interprets various aspects of the research topic' (Braun & Clarke, 2006: 6). Once data was gathered from secondary sources, it was categorised, synthesised and coded to identify themes. The data was presented based on the identified themes.

10.3   Literature Review

Despite poverty being multidimensional, its levels are often measured using income and consumption. This dimension differs from Sen's capability deprivation approach which perceives poverty as the inability to acquire certain capabilities, which differs from social settings and individual beliefs (Sen, 2000; Singh & Chudasama, 2020). The United Nations Development Programme (UNDP) (2014) concurred with Sen's capability approach, with Goal 1 of the Sustainable Development Goals being alleviating hunger and extreme poverty. As such development projects and poverty alleviation programmes in developing countries are aimed to alleviate poverty amongst the poor and vulnerable communities. Keys to these programmes are community participatory demand-driven approaches. These are community members' projects predominantly towards food security and income generation motives. The success of these project-based approaches is occasionally facilitated:

1. Firstly by non-governmental organisations (NGOs), in partnership with developing country regimes. These approaches are at times limited in scope and do not include all the communities (Yalegama et al., 2016).
2. Secondly, economic growth via productive employment, in the form of state-sponsored public work programmes (Ambarkhane, 2013). Economic growth enables governments to spend on the basic necessities of the poor including healthcare, education and housing (Bhagwati & Panagariya, 2012).
3. Thirdly, access to micro-credit to support income-generating projects, which target women and youth (Banerjee & Jackson, 2017). This is important to ensure food security and nutrition and, amongst other, essential basic needs (Banerjee & Jackson, 2017). However, for positive outcomes through the micro-credit programme, services such as skills development, capacity building, technical assistance and initiatives related to enhanced education, health and nutrition as well as sustainable livelihoods should be encouraged (Nawaz, 2010; International Food Policy Research Institute (IFPRS, 2020).

While vital for sustainable livelihoods, economic growth and microcredit frequently exclude the poor and the vulnerable (Sen, 2000). They also neglected to focus on the social, psychological and cultural aspects of poverty. Sen (2000) concedes that social isolation and deprivation of ability are grounds for poverty. His capability framework is centred to promote people's well-being and freedom of choice/social structures. It illustrates the contrast between means and ends, as well as the disparity between substantive freedoms and outcomes. An example is the difference between fasting and starvation (Robeyns, 2005; Singh & Chudasama, 2020).

Improving the capability of the disadvantaged is key to enhance their living conditions (Ambarkhane, 2013). It creates an opportunity for engagement to generate income-related activities (Nguyen & Rieger, 2017). Social inclusion of disadvantaged communities through the eradication of social barriers is as critical as financial inclusion in the reduction of poverty-related interventions (Elkins, 2014). Moreover, social protection is often a series of public actions intended to reduce levels of uncertainty, risk and deprivation. It is an effective method to resolve the issues of injustice and vulnerability (Elkins, 2014). It also promotes gender equity due to equal independence enjoyed by both men and women in economic, social and political engagement (Vyas-Doorgapersad, 2014; Singh & Chudasama, 2020).

The World Bank (2018) reported on a poverty alleviation strategy which incorporates the provision of vital social services to growth for the poor while building financial and social safety nets. Singh and Chudasama (2020) concur with the World Bank. As such, numerous social security and public expenditure programmes continue to serve as instruments to alleviate poverty in many underdeveloped nations globally, as well as in South Africa (Ahmed et al., 2014; IFPRS, 2020; Maphanga & Mazenda, 2019). These social security systems and protection mechanisms have a positive impact on poverty reduction and food security and address social inequality during the COVID-19 pandemic. However, of major concern is the long-term viability of these mechanisms (IFPRS, 2020). According to the International Labour Organization (ILO, 2020), policymakers in developing countries should strive to the best of ability to establish emergency crisis responses with a longer-term outlook to improve social security structures and provide decent jobs, as well as promote changes from the informal to the formal economy. Of significance and in response to COVID-19, they should guarantee the security of income and jobs and encourage decent work, utilise unemployment protection systems and other structures to assist businesses in employee retentions and adjust the public works programme structures in response to the pandemic. Moreover, they should also augment income security through transfer payments by increasing the amount of benefits and expand coverage through current or new programmes and change eligibility requirements, commitments and distribution mechanisms. When available, humanitarian welfare benefits can supplement and further improve national social protection systems (ILO, 2020). Through the ESRP, South Africa has responded to most of the social security requirements specified in the ILO (2020). The social security assistance is enacted through the National Development Plan (NDP) (2030) and forms the basis on which the ESRP is administered. The initiatives involve government assistance to vulnerable households with access to 13 basic services, such as housing, public transport, sanitation and basic education among others. Consequently, the provision of extensive cash transfer benefits in the form of social security grants would benefit over 17 million households (Soudien et al., 2018).

In most developing countries, agriculture is prominent as a poverty alleviation strategy. Its viability is enhanced by the development of comprehensive value chains and market systems (Loison, 2015). The sustainability of the value chain systems depends on available government support and other private role players (Norell et al., 2017; Singh & Chudasama, 2020). Jiang et al. (2020); Zhang et al. (2020); and Zhu and Tian (2020) revealed that COVID-19 has had an adverse effect on the growth of grain production, animal husbandry, recreational agriculture, agricultural food value addition as well as marketing in developing countries. This has subjected the population into abject poverty. Key to overcoming these challenges is the creation of agriculture community-based cooperatives and support organisations, online agricultural marketing networks and government financial assistance (Jiang et al., 2020). Despite South Africa being food secure at the national level, the representation of the disadvantaged poor including women in food production and distribution system is minimal (Von Loeper et al. (2016). The structures for land redistribution are not fully functional (Rudzani, 2012). Since 2013, private entities and urban municipalities such as the City of Johannesburg and the City of Cape Town introduced urban farming support (urban rooftop farming as well as agriculture markets) to reduce poverty amongst the vulnerable. The outcomes are positive, however, inadequate to cover the rest of the vulnerable population in the cities (Naude, 2015).

Finally, good governance is important to implement poverty alleviation programmes. Participatory, responsive and inclusive governance must be encouraged

(Kwon & Kim, 2014). Weak political and administrative governance has a negative effect on the distribution of social services (Davis, 2017). This is concurred by Kwon and Kim (2014); as well as Zouhaier (2019). A good governance approach to alleviate poverty has become a requirement for emerging countries to acquire financial assistance from international donor agencies (Singh & Chudasama, 2020). Most African States have managed to comply with the donor organisation requirements for democracy and good governance. These funds were released by China, the European Union (EU) and the World Bank to help inhibit the socio-economic impact of COVID-19. Of prominence is the EU €10 million pledge to support the implementation of the Africa Joint Continental Strategy for COVID-19 Outbreak (Africa Peer Review Mechanism (APRM), 2020).

10.4 Results and Discussion

This section presents the findings on the effectiveness of the COVID-19 ESRP as a poverty alleviation strategy in South Africa. The findings are presented using the thematic analysis. The key themes included the government's response to the COVID-19 pandemic and how it relates to the alleviation of poverty. The key ESRP poverty alleviation strategies are also expounded upon. Firstly, social grant, social relief of distress grants, food parcel scheme, unemployment benefits and paid holidays are discussed.

10.4.1 Government Responses to the COVID-19 Pandemic, ESRP and Poverty Alleviation

Yustini (2018) contends that to measure the effectiveness of poverty alleviation programmes undertaken by the government, qualitative and quantitative descriptive analysis is conducted. Qualitative analysis is conducted by describing poverty alleviation programmes which will continue and be executed by the government together with other stakeholders. Furthermore, analyse the problems or obstacles encountered during the implementation phase, as well as formulate and develop a model of community empowerment which is considered effective to alleviate poverty. The effectiveness analysis is calculated by comparing the planned targets with the achieved results.

Singh and Chudasama (2020) highlight that globally development projects and poverty alleviation programmes are predominantly aimed at reducing poverty of the poor and vulnerable communities through various participatory and community demand-driven approaches. Economic growth is one of the principal instruments to alleviate poverty and assist the poor through productive employment.

On 23 March 2020, during the COVID-19 'State of the Nation' address, the South African President introduced an initial 21-day national lock-up which, inter alia, included a comprehensive plan to reduce the transmission of the virus and mitigate its economic and social impact. This was the first response to three proposed phases. Keys in this phase were measures, which included tax relief, wage support through the Unemployment Insurance Fund (UIF) and small-scale business rescue funding (Trade Law Centre (TRALAC), 2020).

The second phase introduced on 21 April was aimed to stabilise the economy, address the extreme decline in supply and demand and protect jobs. This phase was a shadow of the R500 billion (US$ 28 767 000 000) ESRP (TRALAC, 2020).

The third phase was an economic strategy aimed to drive the recovery of the economy as the country emerged from this pandemic. Central to this phase was the ESRP introduced by the President on 23 July. This phase built on 21 April ESRP core economic and social strategies to stimulate demand and supply through interventions such as a substantial infrastructure build programme, speedy implementation of economic reforms and other steps to stimulate inclusive economic growth (TRALAC, 2020).

Through both the special COVID-19 grants and the top-up of existing ones, well over R30 billion in additional support has already been provided directly to more than 16 million persons from poor households.

The ESRP which forms the focus of this chapter was bankrolled through reprioritisation of funds within the budget and mobilisation of loans from the International Monetary Fund (IMF) and other funding organisation funders to cushion businesses, workers and households against the menacing social and economic implications of COVID-19 (TRALAC, 2020; Mpeta, 2020). Ramaphosa (2020) acknowledged that more than four million workers had received R42 billion in wage support to protect jobs even while companies were not able to operate.

The three areas of interest include (a) redirecting money to finance COVID-19 health response, (b) delivering targeted assistance to households and individuals for the relief of poverty and social distress and (c) aiding businesses in need and helping to secure jobs by raising employee wages. As of July 2020, over R1.5 billion (US$ 26 071 875 000) of assistance had been allocated to businesses (TRALAC, 2020; Ramaphosa, 2020).

As previously indicated, the provisions (b) on ESRP are the focus of this chapter. The provision is necessary to cushion households against income induced food insecurity, which is necessary through subsidising income. This is executed through the social grant, food parcel benefits and unemployment benefits and payment holidays.

10.4.2   Social Grant

Since the onset of the COVID-19 pandemic, the food security of 8.2 million people who already live below the food poverty line before the pandemic was likely to be highly compromised. Furthermore, food insecurity was likely to be dire for the 0.9 million households who had experienced inadequate access to food prior to the lockdown. Moreover, the nutrition status of 9 million children is compromised without access to school feeding schemes (UN, 2020b). However, South Africa has an elaborate social welfare system with a large proportion of social spending going towards social grants. The social welfare system conforms with the provisions of Sections 24–29 of the Constitution's Bill of Rights, which recognises the socio-economic rights of citizens, including the right to social security. Thus, social grants are in place to improve standards of living and redistribute wealth to create a more equitable society. Approximately 18.3 million people are social support grant beneficiaries. At most, 14 million persons benefit indirectly from the social grant, especially those who live in a household where at least one member is a recipient of a grant.

The social grant scheme is the best means to deliver financial assistance directly to vulnerable and low-income families. At least 40% of the population are recipients of the social grant support (Institute for Economic Justice (IEJ), 2020:2–5).

Furthermore, the child support grant (CSG) supports the largest number of grant recipients (12 991 000), who are mostly women, and receives relatively low monthly payments of R445 (US$26). 40% of households' recipients of the child support grant are dependent on income from informal sector activities, while approximately 60% are unemployed (IEJ) 2020:11). The old age pension supports approximately 3 800 000 recipients, 30% equivalents of the child support grant, with increased monthly payments of R1860 (US$103). Seventy-five per cent of these recipients are women, and the income is shared amongst household members. This group is demographically at risk of COVID-19. Consequently, other population groups at risk include the 1 051 000 recipients of the disability grant, 326 000 foster care grant and 158 000 care dependency grant. These recipients earn between R1860 (US$103) and R1040 (US$60) (IEJ, 2020:12).

However, taking into consideration an average household size of six, for the poor households, with at least one household recipient of the social grant, is inadequate to cushion the impact of poverty and food insecurity. The ESR package requires that recipients of the child support grant were to receive an additional R300 (US$17) from May 2020 and consequently R500 (US$ 29) from June to October 2020. Furthermore, R250 (US$14) was aligned to other categories of the social grant recipients (Mpeta, 2020).

However, it should be noted that the increase of R500 between June and October is only per caregiver from June. Zembe-Mkabile et al. (2020) argue that this arrangement has a major impact on household food security. In their study, the authors noted that primary caregivers welcomed the R500 top-up as a positive move; however, they believed that the increase was inadequate. Outcomes which highlight this inadequacy included:

- Increased food needs as a result of children being housebound
- Loss of non-grant income in some households
- Households with only one or two CSGs as the primary source of income
- Primary caregivers of children receiving the CSG being ineligible for the social relief of distress (SROD) grant

- Loss of school meals for children who received this service when schools were open
- People being unable to rely on their usual reciprocity networks for borrowing money and food
- Food price increases

10.4.3   Social Relief of Distress Grant

Approximately 64% of South Africa's economically active population do not have access to the household grant income. Moreover, approximately 25% of the households earn below R6000 (US$345), who are not recipients of any social grants. The most disadvantaged would be those persons who do not collect grants, have not been registered with the UIF and are unemployed. The number equates to approximately 15 million of economically active men, which is an equivalent of about 9 million households. This group has been targeted by the ESR package, with disbursements of R350 (US$20) social relief of distress (SRD) grant a month for 6 months, starting from May to October 2020 (IEJ, 2020:11). The SRD is a special grant allocated to persons who are unemployed and who do not receive any other social grant from the government, Unemployment Insurance Fund, South African Revenue Service and National Student Financial Aid Scheme and whose refusal of the SRD grant would result in undue hardship. It is received in the form of a food parcel, voucher or cash amount – all equivalent to R350 (US$20). The SRD is administered by the Department of Social Development and is paid to only South African citizens, permanent residents or refugees, who meet any of the following criteria:

- The claimant must have been a recipient of a temporary disability grant that lapsed in March 2020 and could not be renewed due to the lockdown.
- The claimant must be able to prove that they cannot work for medical reasons for a period of 6 months.
- The claimant must have suffered the loss of a breadwinner in the family, and the application should be lodged at least within a 12 months' period from the death.
- The claimant shall not seek maintenance from a parent, child or partner lawfully obligated to pay for maintenance and shall provide evidence that the attempts made to receive maintenance have been ineffective.
- The claimant was confronted with a disaster in their community. A disaster is described as a natural or human incident that involves (or threatens to cause) death, injury or illness, destruction of property or destabilisation of community life, or serious material damage or loss or distress has occurred or is likely to happen.
- The claimant forms part of a child-headed household.

The processing of the application is on a 24-hour turnover period, with applicants accessed for credibility and genuine need of the service (Dhever & Hinckermann, 2020).

The application process is in itself unfavourable to the poor food insecure citizens on two major issues: firstly, lack of identification documentation (ID) amongst the poorest households in the country and. secondly, poorly rolled out campaign initiatives to educate the poor citizens on how to complete the application processes due to COVID-19 including travel and contact restrictions. With this said, the recipients are less than the targeted number which leaves much of the population in the poverty trap (Mpeta, 2020).

Despite of these challenges, the SRD does little to offset the food security challenges citizens face. Congruent to the social grants' disbursements, the SRD falls short of the 13 August 2020 Statistics South Africa extreme poverty line of R585 (US$ 33.89) per month (Dean, 2020). The upper-bound poverty line was set at R1 268 (US$72.91) per person. These statistics revealed that the majority of the South Africa population is subjected to extreme poverty. Firstly, the temporary ESR provision of the child support grant and the unemployed provision of R350 (US$20) does little to offset the extreme poverty line. Consequently, the R250 (US$14) aligned to cushion the disability grant, foster care dependency and old age pension is inadequate. The allowance does little to increase the food security position of poor households, which comprises of at least four to six household members, who are generally dependent on one source of income, that is, the social grant (already below the upper-bound poverty line per person) (IEJ, 2020:12; Dean, 2020).

At macro level, South Africa is food secure, because the country is able to produce sufficient food for its people at a reasonable and affordable price (Dean, 2020). Due to COVID-19, this position has been comprised. There is a high likelihood of food insecurity, especially both the utilisation and access dimensions. Loss of income from informal employment coupled with an almost insignificant increase from the SER grant allocations implies less expenditure on food as the income would be spread amongst other household' basic needs. Loss of income entails high incidences of food and nutrition implications and a food utilisation dimension. Malnutrition levels will rise due to inadequate nutrient intake, particularly the over-consumption of cereal staple meals.

10.4.4   Food Parcel Scheme

The food parcel scheme included the direct distribution of food parcels for 3–4 weeks to ensure that starving households were able to avoid food shortages during the COVID-19 lockdown period. The aid was a temporary and inadequate measure to serve as a substitute for income transfer or wage support. The scheme covered the delivery of food packages, split up by 1,000 non-governmental organisations and private sector organisations. These entities are mostly large retailers and food manufacturers. This undermines small-scale and informal food economies, where most food insecurity households are involved in raising an income and alleviating COVID-19-induced poverty. Furthermore, the distribution exercise faced operational irregularities, because the parcels were packaged for a family of four. This resulted in allocation challenges because certain households comprised of more than four members. Although short-lived, the provision was an important measure to inhibit chronic hunger and starvation.

Additional irregularities were identified in the costing. Food parcels in the private sector averaged around R400 (US$23). The Department of Social Development (DSD) normal parcels cost R700 (US$ 40), while the SRD parcel was overpriced at R1300 (US$74). Another irregularity was on the hidden distrubutution costs, for disbursement of parcels to about 2 million households. The overall cost was inflated by at least 0.5 times, to an estimated R1.5 billion (US$862526,49) (including the distribution costs) (IEJ, 2020:14).

10.4.5   Unemployment Benefits

The UN (2020b) contends that over 740 000 informal workers are at risk of falling below the upper poverty line during the extended lockdown due to COVID-19. Income from the labour market is the leading source of household income in South Africa (>70% total income) and is the primary driver of inequality. Income loss is estimated at between R41 and R53 million for 9.5 million affected employees in the formal sector, while 2.5 million SMME informal workers and owners were affected (93% of the total informal sector) and experienced a loss of between R15 and R17 million (US$ 1 165 027) (UN 2020b). However, there are unemployment benefits.

Key to ESR is the UIF unemployment benefits, which were extended to employees who had been retrenched due to the lockdown. This was primarily in the hospitality industry and persons employed for the short term. The benefits draw from the employees' monthly contribution can serve as a poverty alleviation strategy as well as to increase food access during the COVID-19 crisis. The UIF is not redeemable if an employee has resigned, suspended or absconded from work. However, it is considered redeemable if the Commission for Conciliation, Mediation and Arbitration (CCMA) considers the resignation as a constructive dismissal.

Since April 2020, the UIF disbursed approximately R30 million (US$ 1 724 167) per day (IEJ, 2020). The largest number of claims was made in the personal services sector, including the business and finance, agriculture and finally construction (IEJ, 2020:14). However, during the height of the lockdown, although the UIF was an important social safety net, some authorities argued that its administration had been cumbersome leading to potential recipients failing to access the funds. Vorster (2020) argued that the electronic mechanism utilised for the process is not ideal for many of the claimants in particular those in rural areas who often do not have access to computers, internet facilities, smartphones, scanning facilities and data to surf the internet. The online registration process was generally slow and laborious. These shortcomings created major issues for the claimants. On the other hand, Magubane

(2020) argued that in general employers encountered difficulties in accessing the employee relief funds, while others were accused of not disbursing the funds to the employees or tried to defraud the UIF. All these challenges have a bearing on food security.

10.4.6   Paid Holidays

Households in South Africa accrue a sizeable number of operating costs, including essential services such as municipal bills and private transactions, for example, settle outstanding debt. Consequently, the majority of these households have reduced income, which has consequent implications for poverty and food insecurity. Moreover, it must be accentuated that South African households are already in deep debt. The last quarter of 2019, according to the South African Reserve Bank, saw a household debt-disposable income ratio of 73% (IEJ, 2020:16).

The income tax holidays, municipal rates and rent deferments, including water and electricity vouchers to the households in need, interest rate cuts by the South African Reserve Bank (SARB) as well as paid holidays by the South African banks, were shifted the burden from the consumer who waits for the economy to recover.

In conformance with the paid holidays, the government through the ESRP aided companies in distress and sought to protect jobs by supporting workers' wages. By 3 July 2020, approximately R1.5 billion in funding had been granted to all these firms (TRALAC, 2020).

However, with regard to individual consumers, a study by Debt Rescue (2020) established that only 26% of the respondents reported that they had successfully applied for a paid holiday, while 51% asserted that they did not have savings to fall back on. Furthermore, the study also established that only 11% of those polled believed they could settle their bills as previously after their paid holiday had ended. This revealed that despite the government's temporary measures, an impending threat remains with regard to financial security and, inadvertently, food security of the people.

Ramaphosa (2020) acknowledged that in addition to those businesses which had received direct support, many companies had benefited from tax relief measures worth in the region of R70 billion. This spilled over to millions of South Africans benefiting from the historic reduction in interest rates. Adjustments had been made to the Loan Guarantee Scheme to make it easier for companies of any size to access credit at low interest rates and repayments delayed for up to 12 months (Ramaphosa, 2020).

All these efforts point to the government's acclaimed three-phase strategy to meet the ongoing challenges of COVID-19 – preserve, recover and pivot (UN, 2020b:14). The first priority is to preserve life and health by responding to the health crisis with access to testing and access to medical facilities for all. Access to healthcare service for the most vulnerable needs to be prioritised and ensured that no one remains hungry (UN, 2020a, b).

As for recovery, this would be undertaken by compensating income loss through unemployment grants and insurance. The UN (2020b) added that recovery would also require scaling up and starting massive public works programmes to ensure that as many unemployed and under-employed will be able to find employment, at least on a temporary basis during the next challenging months. In the process, this would reduce dependence on grants. Assistance to small businesses including low interest loans coupled with subsidies and tax reliefs would help the business to restart operations and recover (UN, 2020b).

In the third phase (pivot), the UN (2020b) acknowledged that the intention was not merely to recover, but to pivot the country towards a newly invigorated trajectory of sustainable economic growth and fair participation of people with equal access to services. To achieve this pivot, the government must focus on 'enabling interventions' that would not only respond to the crisis induced by COVID-19 but also help the country achieve its planned goals already elaborated in various policy documents (UN, 2020b).

10.5   Recommendations

Although COVID-19 cannot be blamed as the only reason, it has exacerbated the food security crisis which South Africa faces today. The problem of affordability remains apparent. Therefore, the country must continue to use all three channels of social protection as effectively and efficiently as possible. Furthermore, in order to support effective disbursement of grants, government must consider a multisectoral response that ensures an increase in cash and non-cash resources to poor households and children. Beyond the COVID-19 short-term measures, there is need for a long-term collaborative, national pro-poor strategy that can advance equitable access to food because the funding of the short-term measures will be depleted. For example, the UIF is limited, and the long-term issue the state must deal with is employment and its security. A multi-stakeholder engagement platform should also be established which can constitute a communication and information sharing initiative to enhance food security measures.

10.6   Conclusion

Food security is an urgent issue in many countries, including South Africa. The COVID-19 pandemic exacerbated food insecurity. Following the outbreak of the pandemic, South Africa implemented numerous social safety nets to 'cushion' the poor. Through social grants and unemployment insurance, South Africa deployed income to provide support to the poor during the lockdown. The South African government released a R500 billion (US$ 2 879 935 450) economic and social relief package to help fight the negative effects of COVID-19 on the economy and cushion the vulnerable society from extreme poverty for 6 months (May to October 2020). Of interest in this chapter was the delivery of targeted assistance to households and individuals to relieve poverty and social distress. The sudden and severe shocks imposed by COVID-19 brought to the fore the need to seriously consider the value of implementing channels to transfer income to vulnerable households. Despite the social safety nets introduced by the government, it is apparent that the fiscal space to execute it is limited and government revenue was under severe pressure. Moreover, government support is already revealing signs of it being inadequate. Extant research established that all grant categories complain that the amount is low and inadequate. Even caregivers who ordinarily spent grant money on food for their families, and low levels of misuse thereof, argued that the amounts were inadequate to ensure a nourished child and often supported more people beyond just the children. As such there is a need to reinvent food security that speaks beyond the post-COVID-19 period. There is a need to develop a multi-response strategy and a multisectoral response mechanism to focus on a developmental trajectory that is inclusive and accentuates food security for vulnerable communities.

References

Africa Peer Review Mechanism (APRM). (2020). *Africa's governance response to COVID-19: Preliminary report 2020.* Johannesburg. Retrieved from https://www.aprm-au.org/publication-governance-report/s/africa

Ahmed, I., Jahan, N., & Fatema, T. Z. (2014). Social safety net programme as a mean to alleviate poverty in Bangladesh. *Developing Country Studies, 4*(17), 46–54.

Ambarkhane, D. (2013). Poverty reduction as complimentary processes an approach to inclusive growth. *Journal of Commerce & Management Thought, 4*(4), 904–921.

Babbie, E., & Mouton, J. (2011). *The practice of social research.* Southern Africa.

Banerjee, S. B., & Jackson, L. (2017). Micro-finance and the business of poverty reduction: Critical perspectives from rural Bangladesh. *Human Relations, 70*(1), 63–91.

Bhagwati, J., & Panagariya, A. (2012). *Reforms and economic transformation in India. Series: Studies in Indian Economic Policies.* Oxford University Press.

Braun, V., & Clarke, V. (2006). Using thematic analysis in psychology. *Qualitative Research in Psychology, 3*, 77–101. https://doi.org/10.1191/1478088706qp063oa

DAFF (Department of Agriculture and Fisheries). (2013). Strategic Plan 2003-2004-2017-2018. https://www.gov.za/documents/department-agriculture-forestry-and-fisheries-strategic-plan-20132014-20172018

Davis, T. J. (2017). Good governance as a foundation for sustainable human development in sub-Saharan Africa. *Third World Quarterly, 38*(3), 636–654.

De Vos, A. S., Strydom, H., & Fouche`, C.B., & Delport, C.S.L. (2014). *Research at Grass Roots. For the social sciences and human service professions* (4th ed.). Van Schaik Publishers.

Dean, S. (2020). *Stats SA adjusts 'foods poverty line' to R585 per month.* Retrieved from https://www.farmersweekly.co.za/agri-news/south-africa/stats-sa-adjusts-foods-poverty-line-to-r585-per-month/?utm_medium=FW&utm_source=push&utm_campaign=articles

Debt Rescue. (2020). *85% of South Africans need help financially – Survey.* Retrieved from https://www.iol.co.za/personal-finance/debt/85-of-south-africans-need-help-financially-survey-ec3 8801e-464f-415e-90a9-04a8a1a4d9c2. (28 July 2020).

Dhever, S., & Hinckermann, A. (2020). *COVID-19 Relief for the most vulnerable: Increase in Social Grants and the provision of Social Relief of Distress Grants Fasken.* Retrieved from https://www.lexology.com/library/detail.aspx?g=25186006-2018-458c-b36b-22c58158c46

Elkins, M. (2014). Embedding the vulnerable into the millennium development goals: social protection in poverty reduction strategy papers. *Journal of International Development, 26,* 853–874.

Institute for Economic Justice (IEJ). (2020). *An emergency rescue package for South Africa in response to COVID-19.* 17 April 2020. Retrieved from https://iej.org.za/wp-content/uploads/2020/04/COVID-19-An-emergency-rescue-package-IEJ-17-04-2020-1.pdf

International Food Policy Research Institute (IFPRS). (2020). Linking safety nets, social protection, and poverty reduction – Directions for Africa. *Africa Conference Brief, 2.* Retrieved from https://www.wiego.org/sites/default/files/migrated/publications/files/Adato_Ahmed_Lund_Linking_safetynets_SP_poverty_reduction.pdf

Jiang, H. Y., Yang, C., & Guo, C. (2020). Impact of novel coronavirus pneumonia on agricultural development in China and its countermeasures. *Reform, 2020*(3), 5–13.

Kwon, H., & Kim, E. (2014). Poverty reduction and good governance: Examining the rationale of the millennium development goals. *Development and Change, 45*(2), 353–375.

Loison, S. A. (2015). Rural livelihood diversification in sub-Saharan Africa: A literature review. *The Journal of Development Studies, 51*(9), 1125–1138.

Magubane, K. (2020). *UIF's great struggle: Billions in provision, but SA still needs more.* Retrieved from https://www.news24.com/fin24/economy/labour/uifs-great-struggle-billions-in-provision-but-sa-still-needs-more-20200627 (30 July 2020).

Maphanga, M., & Mazenda, A. (2019). The effectiveness of the expanded public works programme as a poverty alleviation strategy. *Administratio Publica, 27*(3), 1–22.

Mpeta, B. (2020). *South Africa faces mass hunger if efforts to offset impact of COVID-19 are eased.* Retrieved from https://theconversation.com/south-africa-faces-mass-hunger-if-efforts-to-offset-impact-of-covid-19-are-eased-143143

Naude, M. (2015). Urban farmers and urban agriculture in Johannesburg: Responding to the food resilience strategy. *Agrekon, 54*(2), 51–75.

Nawaz, S. (2010). Micro-finance and poverty reduction: Evidence from a village study in Bangladesh. *Journal of Asian and African Studies, 45*(6), 670–683.

Nguyen, T. C., & Rieger, M. (2017). Community-driven development and social capital: Evidence from Morocco. *World Development, 91,* 28–52.

Norell, D., Janoch, E., Kaganzi, E., Tolat, M., Lynn, M. L., & Riley, E. C. (2017). Value chain development with the extremely poor: evidence and lessons from CARE, Save the Children, and World Vision. *Enterprise Development and Micro-finance, 28*(1–2), 44–62.

Ramaphosa, R. (2020). Statement on progress in the national effort to contain the covid-19 pandemic, union buildings, Tshwane, 16 September 2020. Retrieved from https://sona.org.za/assets/200916-c19-president-message.pdf

Robeyns, I. (2005). The capability approach: A theoretical survey. *Journal of Human Development, 6*(1), 93–114.

Rudzani, M. (2012). South Africa's land reform debate: progress and challenges. *SSRN Electronic Journal,* https://doi.org/10.2139/ssrn.2181379.

Sen, A. K. (2000). *Social exclusion: concept, application, and scrutiny* (Social Development Papers No. 1. 2000). Office of Environment and Social Development, Asian Development Bank.

Singh, P. K., & Chudasama, H. (2020). Evaluating poverty alleviation strategies in a developing country. *PLoS ONE, 15*(1), e0227176. https://doi.org/10.1371/journal.pone.0227176

Soudien, C., Reddy, V., & Woolard, I. (2018). *South Africa 2018: The state of the discussion on poverty and inequality: Diagnosis, prognosis, responses.* HSRC Press.

Trade Law Centre (TRALAC). (2020). *South Africa's policy response to the COVID-19 pandemic.* Retrieved from https://www.tralac.org/news/article/14617-south-africa-s-policy-response-to-the-covid-19-pandemic.html

United Nations. (2011). Transforming our world: the 2030 Agenda for Sustainable Development. The UN General Assembly, A/RES/70/1 Retrieved from https://www.refworld.org/docid/57b6e3e44.html

United Nations (UN). (2020a, July 7). *UN report: COVID-19 is reversing decades of progress on poverty, healthcare and education.* New York. Retrieved from https://www.un.org/development/desa/en/news/sustainable/sustainable-development-goals-report-2020.html

United Nations (UN). (2020b). *Covid-19 rapid needs assessment – South Africa.* Retrieved from https://www.dsd.gov.za/index.php/component/jdownloads/?task=download.send&id=221:covid-19-rapid-needs-assessment-report-south-africa-2020-07-08&catid=18&m=0&Itemid=101

United Nations Development Programme (UNDP). (2014). *Eradicate extreme poverty and hunger: where do we stand?* United Nations Development Programme.

Von Loeper, W., Musango, J., Brent, A., & Drimie, S. (2016). Analysing challenges facing smallholder farmers and conservation agriculture in South Africa: A system dynamics approach. *South African Journal of Economic and Management Sciences, 19*, 747. https://doi.org/10.4102/sajems.v19i5.1588

Vyas-Doorgapersad, S. (2014). Gender equality in poverty reduction strategies for sustainable development: The case of South African local government. *Journal of Social Development in Africa, 29*(2), 105–134.

Wagner, C., Kawulich, B., & Garner, M. (2012). *Doing social research. A global context.* McGraw-Hill Education.

World Bank. (2001). *World development report 2000/2001: Attacking poverty* (World development report). Oxford University Press.

World Bank. (2018). *The state of social safety nets 2018.* Retrieved from https://www.worldbank.org/en/topic/socialprotectionandjobs/publication/the-state-of-social-safety-nets-2018

World Bank. (2020, June 8) Projected poverty impacts of COVID-19 (coronavirus). *Brief* . Retrieved from https://www.worldbank.org/en/topic/poverty/brief/projected-poverty-impacts-of-COVID-19

Yalegama, S., Chileshe, N., & Ma, T. (2016). Critical success factors for community-driven development projects: A Sri Lankan community perspective. *International Journal of Project Management, 34*, 643–659.

Yustini, T. (2018). Effectiveness of poverty reduction program with value added creation in agribusiness sector and formulation of strategic plan and policies. *International Journal of Economics and Finance, 10*(4), ISSN 1916-971X E-ISSN 1916-9728.

Zembe-Mkabile, W., Ramokolo, V., & Doherty, T. (2020). *COVID-19 and social grants: Relief measures welcome, but not enough.* Retrieved from https://www.samrc.ac.za/news/covid-19-and-social-grants-relief-measures-welcome not enough

Zhang, H., Hu, L. X., Hu, Z. (2020). Attach great importance to the impact of the new crown disease on the agricultural rural economy – Proper response, precise measures, insurance, supply and increase income. *Farmers Daily*, 2020-02-17.

Zhu, X. K., & Tian, X. H. (2020). New crown pneumonia epidemic will not have a big impact on annual grain production. *Farmers Daily*, 2020-03-05.

Zouhaier, A. (2019). The impact of governance on poverty reduction: Are there regional differences in Sub-Saharan Africa? *Munich Personal RePec Archive.* Retrieved from https://mpra.ub.uni-muenchen.de/94716/1/MPRA_paper_94716.pdf

Chapter 11
Oil Price, Foreign Reserves, and Exchange Rate Nexus During COVID-19

Philip Ifeakachukwu Nwosa and Oluwadamilola Tosin Fasina

11.1   Introduction

The outburst of the coronavirus (COVID-19) stunned the world during the last quarter of 2019. The virus originated from Wuhan City in China before spreading to other parts of the world causing a disaster in terms of loss of lives and degradation of the health sector of many countries. Also, the COVID-19 pandemic created economic crisis globally as countries battled with the containment of the novel virus. Farayibi and Asongu (2020) noted that the economic crisis created by the pandemic is reflected in the demand and supply shocks and an oil price shock which is premised on the effect of the global lockdown measure enforced in different countries in the first and second quarters of the year 2020. In addition, the economic effect of the current health pandemic was greater and has a more adverse effects than previous viral diseases experienced globally, and it has rendered several developed nations handicapped (Okenna 2020).

The global economic damage caused by the spread of COVID-19 indicates that the current health pandemic is one of the largest economic shocks experienced in the world in decades. This is evident in the recession currently experienced by some countries in the world. For instance, the United Kingdom crashed into a recession which saw the economy shrinks by 20.4% in the second quarter of 2020 (CNN 2020). Nigeria which happens to be the largest economy in sub-Saharan Africa is projected to slide into the worst economic recession since the 1980s due to COVID-19 pandemic, with a projection between 3.2 and 7.4% in 2020 (Olurounbi 2020). Recent reports from the National Bureau of Statistics (2020) showed that the

P. I. Nwosa (✉) · O. T. Fasina
Faculty of Social Sciences, Department of Economics, Federal University Oye-Ekiti, Oye-Ekiti, Ekiti State, Nigeria
e-mail: philip.nwosa@fuoye.edu.ng; oluwadamilola.fasina@fuoye.edu.ng

© The Author(s), under exclusive license to Springer Nature Switzerland AG 2022   231
N. Faghih, A. Forouharfar (eds.), *Socioeconomic Dynamics of the COVID-19 Crisis*, Contributions to Economics, https://doi.org/10.1007/978-3-030-89996-7_11

Nigerian economy contracted from 1.87% growth in the first quarter of 2020 to −6.10% in the second quarter of 2020. In addition, it is expected that the economy of advanced countries would contract by 7%, with extension to emerging and developing economies (World Bank 2020).

More so, the global economy experienced a slowdown as a result of the lockdown measures enforced in countries all over the world. One of the effects of the lockdown measures was the decline in global demand for crude oil. Chukwuma et al. (2020) noted that the fall in the price of oil during the pandemic could be traced to demand and supply chain which was put on hold due to the lockdown measures adopted by various countries in a bid to flatten the curve of the virus. The global decline in the demand for oil is projected to be more than the loss of the 2008 global economic recession which was estimated at nearly 1 million barrels per day (Lateef and Samuel 2020). The World Bank (2020) noted that the occurrence of COVID-19 has led to an unprecedented collapse in the demand for crude oil and a crash in the price of crude oil globally. The reduction in the price of oil by 55% between the last quarter of 2019 and the first quarter of 2020 was a serious economic shock to the Nigerian economy (UNDP 2020). This is because the Nigerian economy relied primarily on proceeds from the sale of crude oil to finance a large part of government expenditure. Before the COVID-19 pandemic, the Nigerian economy was on a path of economic recovery from the 2016 economic recession, with growth rate estimated at 2–3% in 2019. However, the 2020 gross domestic product growth rate was revised by the international monetary fund from 2.5 to 2%. This revision was premised on relatively low oil price (reduced demand for oil) as a result of the COVID-19 pandemic.

The sharp decline in oil price increased the vulnerability of the Nigerian economy leading to a reduction in the foreign exchange reserve. Olubusoye and Ogbonna (2020) noted that crude oil accounts for a significant proportion of Nigeria's revenue (in terms of foreign exchange earnings) and to a large extent served as the major contributor to the foreign reserve of Nigeria. The Central Bank of Nigeria stated that the country's foreign reserve declined from $36.57 billion as at June 2020 to $36.12 billion as at July 2020. However, as at February 2020, the foreign reserve was valued at $36.6 billion, while as at January 2020, it was valued at $36.73 billion. The above figures clearly show that during the first and second quarters of 2020, the Nigerian economy experienced a decline in its foreign reserve.

The huge decline in foreign exchange reserves led to a depreciation of Nigeria's exchange rate in relation to other stronger currencies especially the US dollar ($) and British pound (£). Available statistics from the Central Bank of Nigeria showed that between March and August 2020, the naira depreciated by 24.3%. The Central Bank devalued the official rate from ₦306/US$1 to ₦360/US$1 and further to ₦380/US$1 as at August 2020 in a major move aimed at unifying the multiple exchange rate windows.

The vulnerability of the Nigerian economy to the effect of the COVID-19 pandemic in line with the sharp decline in the global price of crude oil and the resultant effect on exchange rate and foreign reserve therefore calls for a country-specific investigation. In addition, given the novel nature of the pandemic, it is imperative to examine its effect on key macroeconomic variables in Nigeria. Consequently, the objectives of this chapter are to:

(a) Appraise oil price, foreign reserves, and exchange rate movements during the COVID-19 pandemic.
(b) Analyze the nexus among oil price, foreign reserves, and exchange rate during COVID-19 pandemic.
(c) Examine the response of foreign reserves and exchange rate to a sudden decline in oil price during COVID-19 pandemic.

For a comprehensive understanding of the impact of COVID-19 on oil price, foreign reserves, and exchange rate, the period of this study covers pre-COVID-19 (September 1, 2019, to December 31, 2019) and periods during COVID-19 (January 1, 2020, to April 30, 2020). A juxtaposition of these periods will reveal the magnitude of the impact of COVID-19 on the variables. This study focused on the COVID-19 period from January 1, 2020 to April 30, 2020, because the consequence of COVID-19 was worst felt during this period in Nigeria and during which various restrictions were placed across the global economy. Also, oil price experienced its worst decline in April 2020, during COVID-19.

In addition, the study focused on oil price, foreign reserves, and exchange rate due to the significance of these variables on the Nigerian economy and given their influence on other macroeconomic variables such as gross domestic product, trade flows, balance of payment and inflation among others. Also, data on oil price, foreign reserves, and exchange rate are available on a daily basis which ensures rigorous econometric analysis on the relationship among the variables. However, data on other macroeconomic variables such as GDP, unemployment, trade and balance of payment are unavailable on daily basis, and as such are not included in the study. Furthermore, the findings from this chapter would serve as a guide to policymakers in a bid to recommend country-specific solutions to salvage the economic havoc caused on the Nigerian economy by current COVID-19 pandemic. The remainder of this paper is structured as follows: Section 2 provides a review of literature, while Sect. 3 presents the methodology. The results and discussions are presented in Sects. 4, and 5 presents the conclusion and recommendations.

11.2 Literature Review

The literature regarding the effect of COVID-19 pandemic on oil price, exchange rate, and foreign reserve in Nigeria is relatively scarce. Otache (2020) examined the effects of COVID-19 pandemic on Nigeria's economy. Findings from the study showed that the effects of the pandemic on the economy include job losses, food insecurity, a steep decline in oil revenues, and economic uncertainties. The study recommended some measures to be adopted by the Nigerian government in order to cope with the devastating effects of the pandemic and similar pandemics in the future. Okenna (2020) investigated the short- and long-term consequences of the

COVID-19 pandemic on the economies of most developing African countries using Nigeria as a case study. The study considered Nigeria as a case study because of her importance, influence, and dominance in the league of developing countries in Africa. They noted that strict macroeconomic monetary and fiscal policies must be implemented to reduce the effect of the pandemic on both small- and large-scale businesses including households in the country.

Gondwe (2020) assessed the impact of COVID-19 on Africa's economic development using a generalized method of moment estimator. The study observed that COVID-19 dragged African economies into a decline of about 1.4% in gross domestic product with smaller economies faced with a contraction of about 7.8%. More so, the study observed that there is a drop in world demand and the resultant commodity price drops affected production and export performance of African countries more than their own COVID-19 control measures. Also, the study identified that Nigeria suffered revenue loss estimated at about −11.4%. The study recommended that African countries must re-examine their respective fiscal and economic policy priorities to enhance health and social support system. Chukwuma et al. (2020) examined the economic progress in sub-Saharan Africa in the period of COVID-19 and fluctuations in oil price in Nigeria, South Africa, and Ghana. The study observed that countries within the sub-Saharan Africa region have been adversely affected by the pandemic which has led to a slow pace in the economic progress of the region. The study recommended that a comprehensive measure is needed to reduce economic losses and measures aimed at alleviating liquidity constraints on vulnerable firms and households which were impacted negatively by the COVID-19 pandemic.

Ayodele et al. (2020) investigated the effect of coronavirus outbreak on the performance and effectiveness of the Nigerian money market, capital market, and foreign exchange market using an exploratory and multiple regression analysis. The study observed that COVID-19 cases are directly related to the foreign exchange rate. The study also observed that COVID-19 pandemic significantly affected the Nigerian financial market. Thus, the study recommended that the federal government of Nigeria should take preventive steps against financial challenges resulting from health risk. Farayibi and Asongu (2020) presented an early review of the macroeconomic impact of the COVID-19 pandemic in Nigeria using a dynamic ordinary least square method of estimation. The study observed that COVID-19 pandemic has insignificant negative impacts on basic macroeconomic variables such as exchange rate, inflation, and gross domestic product growth. The study recommended a deliberate policy action that would stabilize the fluctuations in the economy and enhance the performance of basic macroeconomic variables.

11.2.1   Research Gap in Reviewed Literature

A review of literature indicates that there is a paucity of knowledge on the effect of the pandemic on oil price, exchange rate, and foreign reserves in Nigeria. None of the above studies examined the nexus among oil price, foreign reserves, and exchange rate during the COVID-19 pandemic. More so, previous studies did not examine the response of foreign reserves and exchange rate to sudden oil price shocks during the current health pandemic. Sequel to the above gaps in the literature, this study examined the link among oil price, foreign reserve, and exchange rate during COVID-19, which serves as the original contribution to knowledge by this study.

11.3 Research Methods

To analyze the relationship among oil price, foreign reserve, and exchange rate during COVID-19 pandemic, the study employed both descriptive and inferential estimation techniques. The descriptive statistics involved the use of table and graphs in observing the development in both global and local COVID-19 pandemic, oil price, exchange rate, and foreign reserves during the study period. The inference statistic involved the use of vector auto-regression (VAR) technique for causality estimates, as well as the structural vector auto-regression (SVAR) for the response of exchange rate and foreign reserves to the sudden oil price slump at the international market. The outcome of the inferential statistics is to verify if empirical analysis substantiated the simultaneous decline in the variables during the COVID-19 health pandemic.

11.3.1 Causality Model Specification

To determine the causal nexus among oil price, exchange rate, and foreign reserves, this study adopts a vector auto-regression (VAR) model of the form:

$$X_t = \begin{bmatrix} \text{OP} & \text{EXH} & \text{FRS} \end{bmatrix}^I \tag{11.1}$$

Equation (1) can be expressed as:

$$\text{OP}_t = \sum_{i=1}^{m} \delta_{11} \text{OP}_t + \sum_{i=1}^{n} \delta_{12} \text{EXH}_t + \sum_{i=1}^{r} \delta_{13} \text{FRS}_t + \mu_{1t} \tag{11.2}$$

$$\text{EXH}_t = \sum_{i=1}^{m} \delta_{21} \text{EXH}_t + \sum_{i=1}^{n} \delta_{22} \text{OP}_t + \sum_{i=1}^{r} \delta_{23} \text{FRS}_t + \mu_{2t} \tag{11.3}$$

$$\text{FRS}_t = \sum_{i=1}^{m} \delta_{311} \text{FRS}_t + \sum_{i=1}^{n} \delta_{32} \text{OP}_t + \sum_{i=1}^{r} \delta_{33} \text{EXH}_t + \mu_{3t} \tag{11.4}$$

The VAR models in Eqs. (11.1, 11.2, 11.3, and 11.4) can be expressed in a general form as:

$$y_t = B_0 + B_1 y_{t-1} + B_2 y_{t-2} + B_3 y_{t-3} + \varepsilon_t \qquad (11.5)$$

where y_t is $(n \times 1)$ vector containing each of the n variables in the VAR model, B_0 is an $(n \times 1)$ vector of intercept terms, B_i are $(n \times n)$ matrices of coefficient, and ε_t is an $(n \times 1)$ vector of error terms. In this study $n = 3$, which are oil price (OP), exchange rate (EXH), and foreign reserves (FRS).

To analyze the response of exchange rate and foreign reserves to sudden oil price decline during the COVID-19 pandemic, this study employed the structural vector auto-regression estimation technique. The SVAR model addresses possible endogeneity problem among the variables in a system. In addition, structural VAR models allow us to recover the underlying shocks in the variables during the COVID-19 pandemic and to analyze the dynamic interactions among the variables, as well as the feedback effects on each of the variables through impulse response functions (Davtyan 2015).

11.3.2   Structural VAR Identification

The underlying structural model is obtained by pre-multiplying both sides of the unrestricted VAR by an $(n \times n)$ A matrix:

$$Ay_t = \Gamma_0 + \Gamma_1 y_{t-1} + \Gamma_2 y_{t-2} + \Gamma_3 y_{t-3} + e_t \qquad (11.6)$$

where $\Gamma_0 = AB_i$ for $i = 0, 1, 2,$ and 3 and $e_t = A\varepsilon_t$, which describes the relationship between the structural disturbance e_t and the reduced form disturbances ε_t. It is assumed that the structural disturbances e_t are white noise and uncorrelated with each other, i.e., their variance-covariance matrix is diagonal. The matrix A describes the contemporaneous relation among the variables contained in the vector y_t. Without restrictions on the parameters of the structural model, it is not identified. There are a number of alternative identification procedures proposed in the literature. This study applies the widely used recursive approach proposed by Sims (1980) that restricts A (and correspondingly A^{-1}) to a lower triangular matrix. That is, this identification scheme, also known as Cholesky decomposition, imposes a recursive causal structure from the top variables to the bottom variables. While this recursive approach enables to uniquely identify the structural VAR model, it has $n!$ possible orderings in total (Davtyan 2015).

For the ordering of the variables in the structural model, it is natural to assume that for a small open economy like Nigeria, contemporaneously exchange rate (EXH) does not impact foreign reserve and international oil price, but exchange rate is influenced by foreign reserve and global oil price. Also, contemporaneously foreign reserve (FRS) does not impact global crude oil price (OP); however, foreign reserve is influenced by global oil price (OP). Thus, in the arrangement of the variables in the SVAR model, it is expected that global oil price will come first, followed by foreign reserve and then by exchange rate. Thus, the ordering of the variables for the VAR model is OP, FRS, and EXH.

11.3.3   Impulse Response Functions

Impulse response functions (IRFs) are intuitive tools to analyze interactions among variables in the VAR models. To see this and keep things simple, the study considered VAR(1) for any case without loss of generality, since any VAR(p) can be rewritten as a VAR(1). Firstly, we need to express it in its vector moving average (VMA) representation by using recursive substitution:

$$y_t = B_0 + \sum_{i=0}^{\infty} B_1^i \varepsilon_{t-i} \tag{11.7}$$

To trace the economic impact of an impulse of one of the variables on itself and on other variables in the system, it requires the VMA representation based on the orthogonal structural shocks instead of the reduced form disturbances, which are correlated with each other. Therefore, by using the expression for the reduced form disturbances ε_t, Eq. (11.7) becomes:

$$y_t = B_0 + \sum_{i=0}^{\infty} A^{-1} B_1^i e_{t-i} \tag{11.8}$$

Expressing Eq. (11.8) in a compact form:

$$y_t = A_0 + \sum_{i=0}^{\infty} \Phi_i e_{t-i} \tag{11.9}$$

From Eq. (11.9), the response of y_{t+i} to one unit impulse at time t is obtained. If each element of Φ_i is graph against i periods, the response of each variable in the system from the impulse to the different structural shocks is obtained (Davtyan 2015).

11.3.4   Variable Measurement and Sources

In this study, oil price (OP) is measured by Bonny light crude oil price, exchange rate (EXH) is measured by the official naira to US dollar (₦/US$) exchange rate, and foreign reserve is measured by the gross foreign reserve outstanding. Daily data on oil price, exchange rate, and foreign reserve were obtained from the Central Bank of Nigeria database https://www.cbn.gov.ng. Data on global COVID-19 confirmed cases and deaths were obtained from the World Health Organization (WHO) http://covid19.who.int and the Global Change Data Lab (GCDL) https://

ourworldindata.org, while data on COVID-19 confirmed cases and deaths on
Nigeria were obtained from www.nairametrics.com and the Nigeria Centre for
Disease Control https://covid19.ncdc.gov.ng.

11.4 Data Analysis and Interpretation

11.4.1 Appraisal of COVID-19, Oil Price, Foreign Reserve, and Exchange Rate

The coronavirus (COVID-19) was first discovered in the Chinese town of Wuhan,
on December 1, 2019. The virus rapidly spread to other countries of the world,
recording a whooping number of 9824 confirmed cases and 213 deaths by January
31, 2020. By the end of February 2020, the number of confirmed cases and death
toll has risen to 85,228 and 2921, respectively, making the World Health Organization
declare the virus a global pandemic on March 11, 2020, having affected over 100
countries. As observed in Fig. 11.1, the total confirmed cases and deaths have risen
exponentially over successive months, culminating to 32,613,844 confirmed cases
and 989,728 deaths as at September 26, 2020 (WHO 2020).

With respect to continental distribution, Figs. 11.2 and 11.3 showed that America
had the largest share of both the confirmed cases and death rates. The continent
accounted for about 50% (i.e., 16,285,399) and 55% (547,872) of the global confirmed cases and death rates. The countries most affected in the America continent
include the United States with 7,033,430 confirmed cases and 203,774 deaths and
Brazil with 4,689,613 confirmed cases and 140,537 deaths. Asia accounted for
about 31% (i.e., 10,004,525) and 19% (184,829) of the global confirmed cases and
death rates. The countries most affected in Asia are India with 5,903,932 confirmed
cases and 93,379 deaths and Iran with 439,882 confirmed cases and 25,222 deaths.

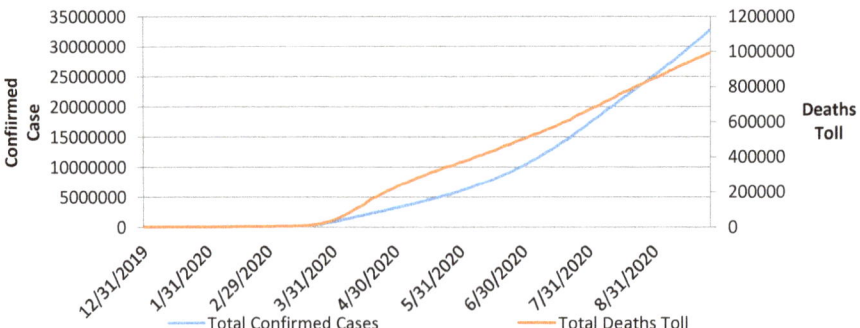

Fig. 11.1 Global COVID-19 confirmed cases and deaths
Source: World Health Organization http://covid19.who.int
Global Change Data Lab (GCDL) https://ourworldindata.org/covid-cases

Fig. 11.2 Continental share of total confirmed cases. Source: European Centre for Disease Prevention and Control (ECDC). https://www.ecdc.europe.eu/en/geographical-distribution-2019-ncov-cases

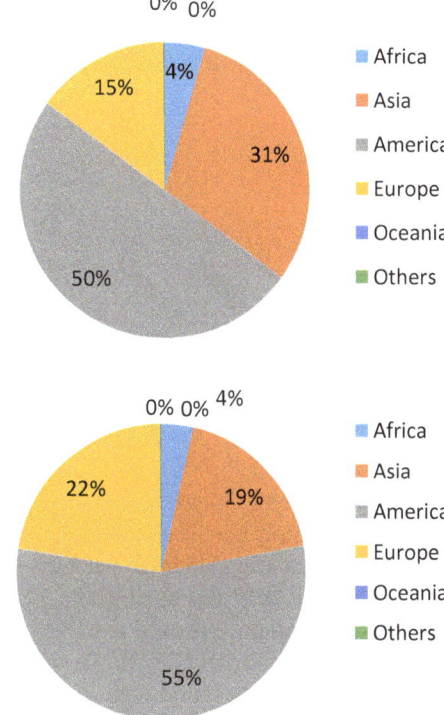

Fig. 11.3 Continental share of total deaths. Source: European Centre for Disease Prevention and Control (ECDC). https://www.ecdc.europe.eu/en/geographical-distribution-2019-ncov-cases

Europe accounted for 15% (i.e., 4,844,339) and 22% (i.e., 221,213) of the global confirmed cases and death rates. The countries most affected in Europe are Russia with 1,136,048 confirmed cases and 20,056 deaths and Spain with 716,481 cases and 31,232 deaths. Africa accounted for 4.4% (i.e., 1.446.132) and 3.5% (i.e., 34,855) confirmed cases and deaths. Countries most affected in Africa are South Africa with 668, 529 confirmed cases and 16, 312 deaths followed by Morocco with 112,522 confirmed cases and 1,998 deaths. Oceania accounted for 0.1% (i.e., 32,753) and 0.096% (i.e., 852) confirmed cases and deaths. Leading countries are Australia with 27,000 confirmed cases and 869 deaths, followed by Guam with 2286 confirmed cases and 42 deaths. Others (which included reports from an international conveyance in Japan) reported less than 1% of both the confirmed cases and death rates, representing 969 cases and 7 deaths.

Nigeria reported its firsts COVID-19 case on February 27, 2020, and the first death was reported on March 24, 2020. Afterward, both confirmed and death cases increased tremendously reaching 58,062 and 1103 confirmed and death cases, respectively, as at September 26, 2020. Nigeria is the fifth African country with the highest reported cases, accounting for 3.6% of the confirmed cases and 3.2% of deaths. Lagos State (with 19,174 confirmed cases and 205 deaths) and the Federal Capital Territory (with 5451 confirmed cases and 74 deaths) reported the highest number of confirmed and death cases in Nigeria (NCDC 2020) (Fig. 11.4).

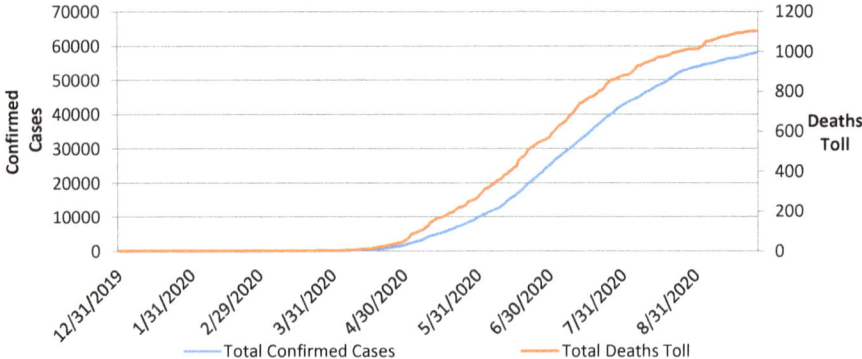

Fig. 11.4 COVID-19 Confirmed Cases and Deaths in Nigeria
Source: Nigerian Centre for Disease Control (NCDC). https://covid19.ncdc.gov.ng

International oil prices are characterized by fluctuations due to changes in demand and supply conditions. Prior to the emergence of the COVID-19 pandemic, the oil price rose from US$60.4 per barrel in early September 2019 to US$71.02 in mid-September 2019 but declined to US$58.56 per barrel in mid-October 2019. Afterward, the oil price peaked at US$72.18 per barrel on January 7, 2020. With the news and rapid spread of COVID-19, which invoked different economic restrictions across countries of the world with consequential impact of oil usage, the demand for oil declined, and coupled with the refusal of Russian and Saudi Arabia to cut down oil production, the oil price slumped to its lowest price of US$7.15 per barrel in April 21, 2020. With gradual reopening of economic activities, there has been resurgence on oil usage, causing a gradual increase in oil price toward its pre-COVID price. As at the second quarter of 2020, the oil price has risen to U$42.49 per barrel with expectation of future increase (Fig. 11.5).

The foreign reserve position before the COVID-19 pandemic stood at US$43.3 billion as at September 2, 2009, declining by 10.85% (US$4.7 billion) to US$38.6 billion by December 31, 2019. In the wake of the COVID-19 pandemic and decline in international crude oil price which contributes largely to Nigerians' foreign earnings, the foreign reserve declined further by 13.47% to US$33.4 billion by April 29, 2020. With the reversal of declining of price due to the gradual reopening of economic activities, the foreign reserves have witnessed upward increase reaching US$36.2 billion as at June 30, 2020. The foreign reserve is expected to increase more due to positive expectation of oil price increases in the future (Fig. 11.6).

With respect to the exchange rate movement, prior to the COVID-19, the exchange rate stood at ₦306/US$1. The decline in international oil price, foreign reserve, and foreign capital inflows pressured the Central Bank of Nigeria (CBN) in devaluating the exchange rate by 17.65% to ₦360/US$1. In a major move to unify

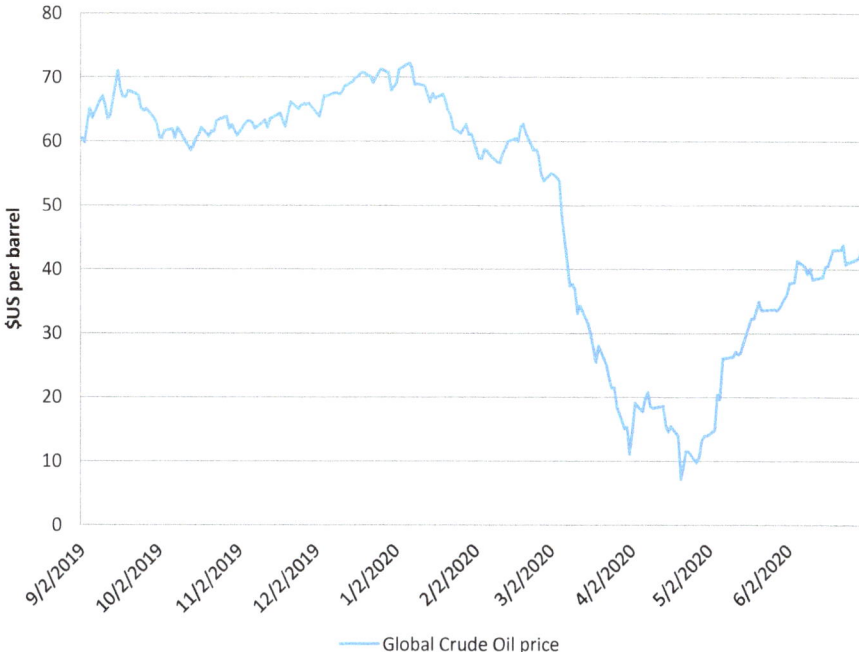

Fig. 11.5 Global oil price September 1, 2019, to June 30, 2020
Source: Central bank of Nigeria. www.cenbank.org

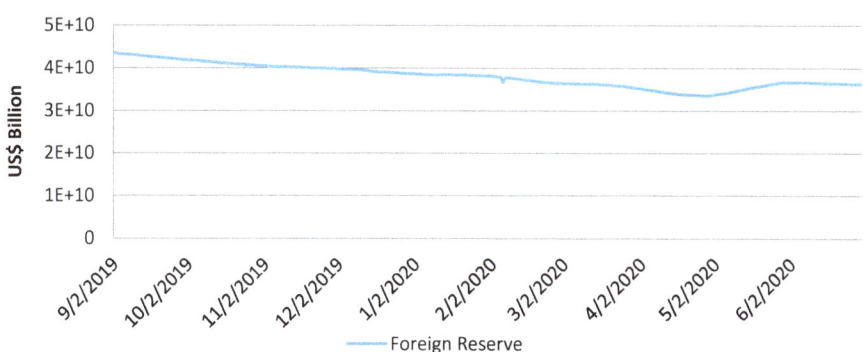

Fig. 11.6 Foreign reserve position in Nigeria September 1, 2019, to June 30, 2020
Source: Central bank of Nigeria. www.cenbank.org

the multiple exchange rate windows, the CBN further devalued the domestic currency by 5.56% on August 20, 2020, thereby making the exchange rate to stand at ₦380/US$1. With rising trends in oil price and foreign reserves, there are expectations that the domestic currency will strengthen against the foreign currencies of the world (Fig. 11.7).

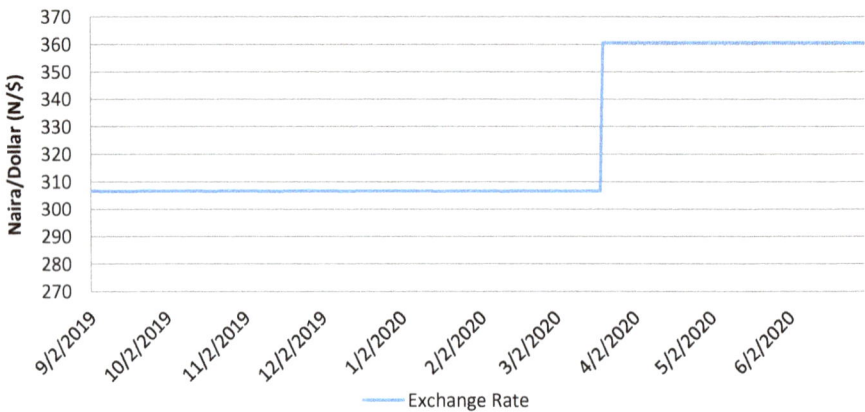

Fig. 11.7 Exchange rate in Nigeria September 1, 2019, to June 30, 2020
Source: Central bank of Nigeria. www.cenbank.org

11.4.2   Data Analysis and Interpretation

11.4.2.1   Descriptive Statistics, Unit Root, Co-integration Estimates, and Lag Selection Criteria

The descriptive statistics below showed that in the pre-COVID-19 era, the mean value of oil price was US$64.54 per barrel, while it declined to US$42.78 per barrel during the COVID-19 era. More so, the standard deviation showed that oil price was more volatile during the COVID-19 era (21.95) than the pre-COVID-19 era (3.11). The mean value of foreign reserve in the pre-COVID-19 era was US$4.08 billion but declined to US$3.63 billion during the COVID-19 era. The standard deviation showed that foreign reserve was more volatile during the COVID-19 era (US$1.62 billion) than in the pre-COVID-19 era (US$1.31 billion). During the pre-COVID-19, the mean value of the exchange rate was ₦306.4/US$1 but depreciated to average value of ₦325.3/US$1 during the COVID-19 era. The standard deviation showed that the exchange rate was more volatile during the COVID-19 era (25.91) than the pre-COVID-19 era (0.04).

The skewness showed that oil price and foreign reserve were positively skewed, while exchange rate was negatively skewed in the pre-COVID-19 era. However, during the COVID-19 pandemic, oil price and foreign reserve were negatively skewed, while exchange rate was positively skewed. The kurtosis showed that all the variables (oil price, foreign reserve, and exchange rate) in both eras were platykurtic, suggesting that the distributions of the variables are flat relative to normal distribution. Finally, in the pre-COVID-19 era, the Jarque-Bera estimate rejected the null hypothesis of normal distribution for all the variables. However, during the COVID-19 pandemic, the Jarque-Bera statistics only rejected the null hypothesis for foreign reserve, while oil price and exchange rate were not rejected. The import from the descriptive statistics showed that the COVID-19 pandemic has

Table 11.1 Descriptive statistics

Statistics/variables	OP	FRS	EXH
	Pre-COVID-19		
Mean	64.535	4.08E+10	306.445
Std. dev.	3.106	1.31E+09	0.0408
Skewness	0.3988	0.3403	−0.2182
Kurtosis	2.3190	2.0768	2.3177
Jarque-Bera (prob.)	3.9871 (0.1362)	4.7690 (0.0921)	2.3774 (0.3046)
	During COVID-19		
Mean	42.784	3.63E+10	325.31
Std. dev.	21.954	1.62E+09	25.905
Skewness	−0.2511	−0.2873	0.6343
Kurtosis	1.3852	1.9063	1.4024
Jarque-Bera (prob.)	10.2476 (0.0060)	5.4695 (0.0649)	14.9134 (0.0006)

Source: Authors' computation 2021

Table 11.2 Phillips-Perron (PP) unit root test

Variables	Level	First difference	Status
	Pre-COVID-19		
OP	−2.1540	−9.8999[a]	I(1)
FRS	−1.8854	−8.6471[a]	I(1)
EXH	−2.6772	−9.1167[a]	I(1)
	During COVID-19		
OP	−0.3405	−8.0273[a]	I(1)
FRS	0.6625	−14.8729[a]	I(1)
EXH	−0.7161	−9.1652[a]	I(1)

Source: Authors' computation 2021
Note: [a] denotes 1% critical values, respectively

significant adverse influence on oil price, foreign reserve, and exchange rate in Nigeria. These findings would be substantiated by further empirical estimates (Table 11.1).

The unit root test showed that the variables were nonstationary at level but became stationary after first differencing. These showed that the variables are integrated at order one, implying that the variables are I(1) series both in pre-COVID era and during COVID-19. Sequel to the unit root results, the co-integration estimate was conducted using Johansen test. The co-integration results showed the absence of a long-run relationship among the variables both in the pre-COVID era and during the COVID-19 period (Tables 11.2 and 11.3).

To ensure appropriate VAR and SVAR estimation, the lag selection criterion was conducted. From Table 11.4, in the pre-COVID-19 era, three lag selection criteria choose lag one (1) as the appropriate lag length, while FPE choose lag zero (0) as appropriate lag length. Furthermore, during the COVID-19 era, four lag selection criteria choose lag one as the most appropriate lag length, while HQ choose lag zero

Table 11.3 Co-integration estimate

Trace test			Maximum eigenvalue test		
Hypothesized no. of CE(s)	Statistics	0.05 Critical values	Hypothesized no. of CE(s)	Statistics	0.05 Critical values
Pre-COVID-19					
None	26.13	29.80	None	16.06	21.13
At most 1	10.07	15.49	At most 1	8.41	14.26
At most 2	1.66	3.84	At most 2	1.66	3.84
During COVID-19					
None	20.79	29.80	None	13.87	21.13
At most 1	6.92	15.49	At most 1	6.76	14.26
At most 2	0.16	3.84	At most 2	0.16	3.84

Source: Authors' computation 2021

Table 11.4 VAR lag order selection criteria

Lag	LR	FPE	AIC	SC	HQ
Pre-COVID-19					
0	NA	9.17e-10[a]	−12.29661	−12.2092	−12.26149
1	7.3369	1.04e-09	−12.17262[a]	−11.82291[a]	−12.03212[a]
2	8.5990	1.15e-09	−12.0689	−11.45690	−11.82303
3	9.4349	1.26e-09	−11.9813	−11.10700	−11.63004
During COVID-19					
0	NA	0.004801	3.174611	3.262662	3.209962[a]
1	23.26858[a]	0.004438[a]	3.095808[a]	3.448011[a]	3.237212
2	6.115706	0.005100	3.233778	3.850133	3.481235
3	5.019383	0.005938	3.383576	4.264083	3.737086

Source: Authors' computation 2021. [a] indicates lag order selected by the criterion
Note: *LR* Sequential modified LR test statistics, *FPE* Final prediction criterion, *AIC* Akaike information Criterion *SC* Schwarz information criterion, *HQ* Hannan-Quinn information criterion

as the most appropriate lag length for estimation. Consequently, this study chooses lag one as the most appropriate lag for estimation.

11.4.3 Causality Estimate

In the pre-COVID-19 period, the causality estimate showed the absence of causation among the variables, implying that these variables did not influence each other in the last quarter of 2019. This is true because, despite the increase in international oil price in the last quarter of 2019 from US$60.4 per barrel in early September 2019 to US$72.18 per barrel in early January 2020, the foreign reserve reported a decrease, while the exchange rate neither appreciated nor depreciated but steadied at ₦306.4/US$.

However, the causality estimate during the COVID-19 showed that international oil price D(OP(-1)) had significant influence on foreign reserves D(LFRS) and exchange rate D(EXH). This showed that changes in international oil price cause change in domestic foreign reserves and exchange rate. These findings are in line with Kumar (2019) and Fratzscher et al. (2014) that changes in international oil price significantly influence exchange rate movement. More so, the causality estimate during COVID-19 showed that foreign reserves D(LFRS(-1)) had significant influence on domestic exchange rate. This is evident as the decline in foreign reserve during the COVID-19 was accompanied by the depreciation of the Naira from ₦306.4/US$1 to ₦360/US$1 and further to ₦380/US$1. The implication of the causality estimate during the COVID-19 period is a unidirectional causal influence from oil price to foreign reserves and exchange rate and a unidirectional causation from foreign reserves to exchange rate during the COVID-19. The outcome of the causality estimate during the COVID-19 pandemic further stressed the adverse impact of the COVID-19 on oil price, foreign reserve, and exchange rate in Nigeria (Table 11.5).

The robustness of the causality estimate is assessed through the VAR residual serial correlation LM estimate. The results of the serial correlation LM test showed that probability values at lags one and two were insignificant at 0.05 critical levels, suggesting that the residuals from the estimate were normally distributed. Thus, the results of the diagnostic test further strengthen the appropriateness of the causality estimates (Table 11.6).

Table 11.5 VAR causality estimate

Variables	D(OP)	D(LFRS)	D(EXH)
Pre-COVID-19			
D(OP(−1))	−0.0645	−0.00003	−0.0031
	(−0.5717)	(−0.4101)	(−1.7869)
D(LFRS(−1))	150.928	0.0416	−1.3492
	(0.9124)	(0.3732)	(−0.5253)
D(EXH(−1))	8.3638	−0.0045	−0.0117
	(1.1895)	(−0.9602)	(−0.1067)
During COVID-19			
D(OP(−1))	0.1443	0.5674	−0.2149
	(1.3058)	(4.7691)[a]	(−1.9179)[b]
D(LFRS(−1))	−6.9440	−0.4647	−0.0031
	(−0.1473)	(−4.7103)[a]	(−3.7122)[a]
D(EXH(−1))	−0.0507	−0.00002	−0.0001
	(−1.2199)	(−0.2950)	(−0.0010)

Source: Author's computation 2021 using e-views 9. [a] implies 1% significance level. t-statistics in () [b] implies 5% significance level

Table 11.6 VAR residual serial correlation LM test

Lags	LM-stat	Prob.
Pre-COVID-19		
1	8.3233	0.5019
2	7.5343	0.5817
During COVID-19		
1	6.1432	0.7255
2	5.9845	0.7415

Source: Author's computation 2021 using e-views 9

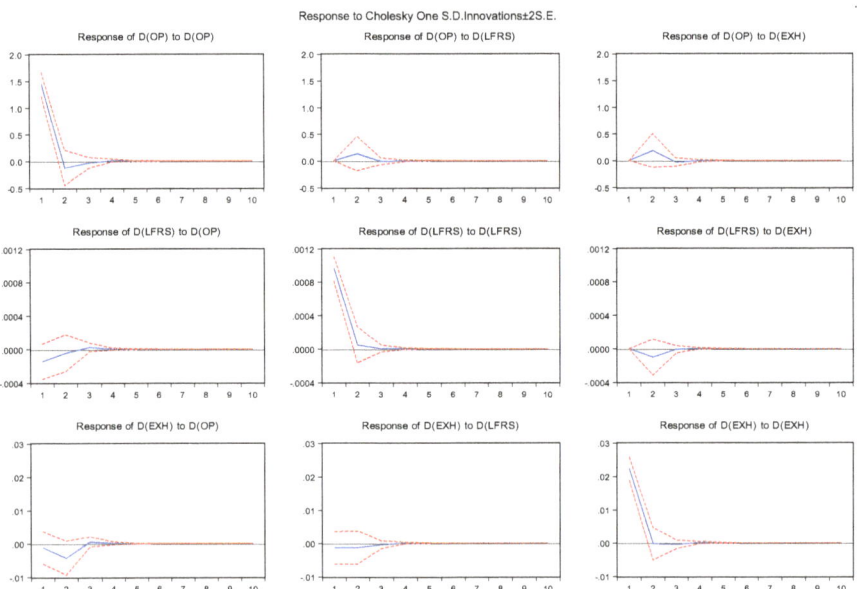

Fig. 11.8 Impulse response function in pre-COVID-19
Source: Author's computation 2021 using e-views 9

11.4.4   Impulse Response Functions

With respect to the objective of this chapter, the impulse response function in the pre-COVID-19 era showed that a sudden decline in oil price resulted in a negative response in domestic foreign reserves over two consecutive periods, while a sudden decline in oil price resulted in a negative response of the exchange rate over two periods, declining from −0.0012 in the first period to −0.0043 in the second period (Fig. 11.8).

With respect to the impulse response function during the COVID-19, Figure 11.8 showed that a sudden decline in oil price also resulted in a negative response of

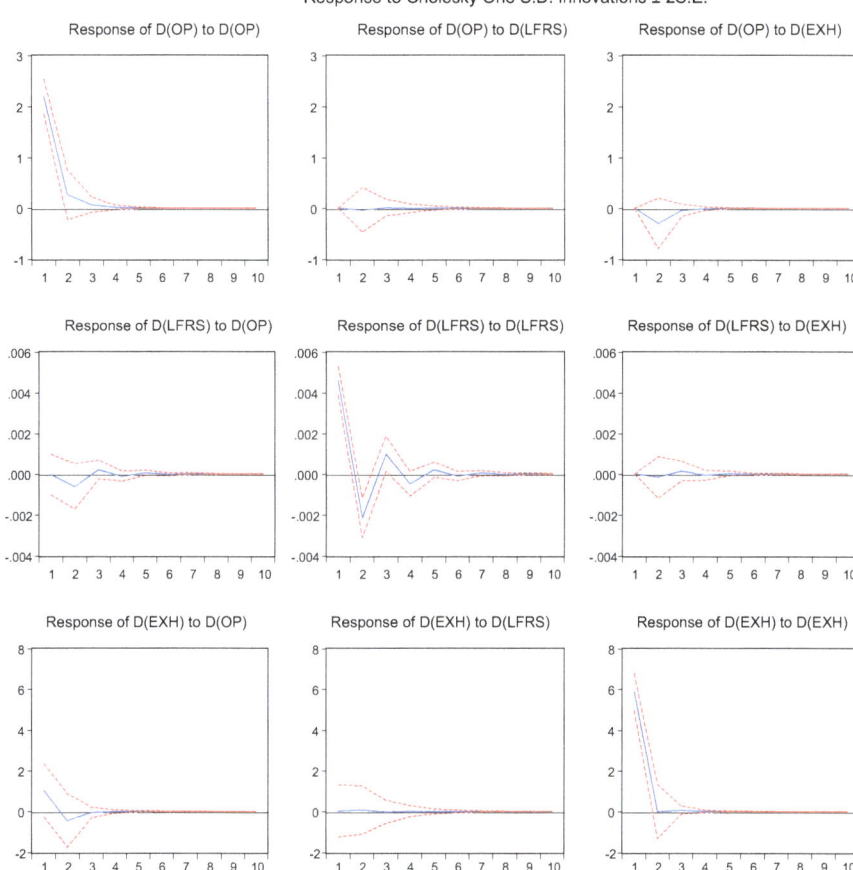

Fig. 11.9 Impulse response function during COVID-19
Source: Author's computation 2021 using e-views 9

domestic foreign reserves over two consecutive periods from −0.00002 in the first period to −0.0006 in the second period, while a sudden decline in oil price resulted in a negative response of the exchange rate over five consecutive periods, declining from 1.0505 in the first period to −0.0039 in the fifth period (Fig. 11.9).

The import from the impulse response functions in Figs. 11.8 and 11.9 showed that the response of foreign reserves and exchange rate during the COVID-19 era to sudden shocks to oil price was more pronounced compared to the response of these variable in the pre-COVID period. This suggests that the COVID-19 pandemic actually had detrimental impacts on foreign reserves and exchange rate in Nigeria.

11.5   Conclusion and Policy Recommendations

This study analyzed the nexus among oil price, foreign reserve, and exchange rate in the pre-COVID-19 era (September 2, 2019, to December 31, 2019) and during the COVID-19 pandemic (January 1, 2020, to April 30, 2020). The study employed both descriptive, VAR, and SVAR estimation techniques. The findings of the study showed that oil price, foreign reserves, and exchange rate had undergone major changes during the COVID-19 period compared to the pre-COVID-19 period. Specifically, the study observed that oil price and foreign reserve experienced decrease during COVID-19, while exchange rate experienced depreciation compared to the pre-COVID era. The descriptive statistics showed that oil price, foreign reserve, and exchange rate were more volatile during the COVID-19 era compared to the pre-COVID-19 era.

The VAR causality estimate showed the absence of causality among the variables in the pre-COVID-19 era, while during the COVID-19 period, the study observed unidirectional causality from oil price to foreign reserves and exchange rate and a one-way causal influence from foreign reserves to exchange rate. The impulse response function from the SVAR model showed that sudden decline in oil price affected foreign reserves and exchange rate more in the COVID-19 period than in the pre-COVID-19 period. The study concluded that the COVID-19 pandemic had significant adverse impact on macroeconomic variables (oil price, foreign reserves, and exchange rate) in Nigeria.

The implications of these results on the Nigerian economy are numerous which include (i) decline in foreign revenue due to oil price decline, (ii) further pressure on the foreign reserves and exchange rate, (iii) cutdown in budgetary oil benchmark from US$57 per barrel to US$25 per barrel, (iv) lack of feasible achievement of 2020 budget, (v) decrease in revenue allocation to the states and tiers of government, (vi) decrease in capital project executions, (vii) expected increase in both domestic and foreign debts, (viii) decrease in the importation of critical manufacturing inputs due to rising challenges in sourcing for foreign currency, (ix) decrease in manufacturing outputs and supply chain crisis, (x) expected increase in inflation rate, (xi) uncertainty in investment and production planning due to uncertainties in exchange rate and inflation rate, (xii) expected increase in unemployment rate, and (xiii) expected increase in hunger and poverty rate in Nigeria during the COVID-19 period.

Drawing from the findings and implications above, this chapter recommends that given the Nigerian economy as a small open economy, with little or no influence on international crude oil price, there is the need for prudent management of the current unstable oil earnings due to the prevailing health pandemic for optimal results. This will reduce pressure on the foreign reserve and exchange rate. Relatedly, there is the need for the government to strengthen the exchange rate through appropriate foreign reserve management by the Central Bank of Nigeria. Also, the various palliative measures of the CBN ₦50 billion COVID-19 intervention programs should be judiciously executed to lessen the consequence of COVID-19 on both the households and business firms.

References

Ayodele, T., Akinyede, O.M., & Iyabode, M. (2020). Corona virus (COVID-19) pandemic and Nigerian financial market. https://doi.org/10.2139/ssrn.3656284/

Chukwuma, O. J., John, O. W., Kolawole, R. T., Chukwudi, I. A., Uchechi, O. R., & Owole, I. R. (2020). Revisiting economic progress in selected countries in Sub-Saharan Africa: Covid-19 and oil price drop. *Journal of Business and Economic Management, 8*(8), 244–250.

CNN (2020). United Kingdom crashes into deepest recession of any major economy. https://www.google.com/amp/s/amp.cnn.com/cnn/2020/08/12/economy/uk-economy-gdp/index.html

Davtyan, K. (2015). Interrelation among Economic Growth, Income Inequality, and Fiscal Performance: Evidence from Anglo-Saxon Countries.

Farayibi, A.O., & Asongu, S.A. (2020). The economic consequences of the COVID-19 pandemic in Nigeria. Working papers of the African governance and development institute, 20/042, African governance and development institute.

Fratzscher, M., Schneider, D. & Robays, I. (2014). Oil Price, exchange rate and asset prices. ECB Working Paper, No. 1689. https://papers.ssrn/so13/paper.cfm?

Gondwe, G. (2020). Assessing the impact of COVID-19 on Africa's economic development, United Nations Conference on Trade and Development (UNCTAD). https://unctad.org/en/publicationslibrary/aldcmisc2020d3_en.pdf&ved/

Kumar, S. (2019). Asymmetric impact of oil prices on exchange rate and stock prices. *The Quarterly Review of Economics and Finance, 72*, 41–51. https://doi.org/10.1016/j.qref.2018.12.009

Lateef, O.A., & Samuel, C.G. (2020). The global health hazards and economic impacts of Covid-19 on the Nigerian economy, Centre for the study of the economies of Africa. http://cseaafrica.org/the-implication-of-covid19-on-the-nigerian-economy/

Nigeria Centre for Disease Control (NCDC) (2020). Cases tracking dashboard for Nigeria, NCDC corona virus COVID-19 micro site. https://covid19.ncdc.gov.ng

Okenna, N. P. (2020). Overview of the impact of COVID-19 pandemic on the Nigerian economy. *International Journal of Engineering Applied Sciences and Technology, 5*(3), 116–119.

Olubusoye, O.E., & Ogbonna, A.E. (2020). COVID-19 and the Nigerian economy analyses of impacts and growth projections. Centre for petroleum, energy economics and law COVID-19 discussion papers series, University of Ibadan.

Olurounbi, R. (2020). Nigeria: Pandemic to poverty in post COVID-19 Future. https://www.theafricareport.com/33300/pandemic-to-poverty-nigeria-in-the-post-covid-future/

Otache, I. (2020). The effects of the COVID-19 pandemic on the Nigeria's economy and possible coping strategies. *Asian Journal of Social Sciences and Management Studies, 7*(3), 173–179.

United Nations Development Programme (UNDP) (2020). The impact of COVID-19 pandemic in Nigeria: A socio-economic analysis. https://www.ng.undp.org/content/nigeria/en/home/library/the-impact-of-the-covid-19-pandemic-in-nigeria-a-socio-economic-html.

World Bank (2020). Global economic outlook during the COVID-19 pandemic: A changed world. https://www.worldbank.org/en/news/feature/2020/06/08/the-global-economic-outlook-during-the-covid-19-pandemic-a-chnaged-world.

World Health Organization (2020). World Health Organization disease (COVID-19) dashboard. https://covid19.who.int

Part III
Politics and Sociology of the COVID-19 Crisis

Chapter 12
COVID-19 and China's Quest for Global Hegemony

Angela Ajodo-Adebanjoko

12.1 Introduction

The year 2020 will go down in history as the year that the world witnessed one of the worst pandemics: an outbreak that paralysed social, economic, political and religious activities globally. The outbreak of the novel coronavirus disease (COVID-19), which was declared a pandemic on March 11, 2020, witnessed the collapse of national and international interactions following the closure of borders and suspension of air travels as well as lockdown of entire economies in about 94% of the countries of the world. COVID-19 which was first reported in Wuhan, a city in China, on December 31, 2019, was declared a pandemic more than 2 months later by the World Health Organization, and between that time and August 28, 2020, there were 24, 466, 482 confirmed cases globally, while about 831,827 had died and 16,000,137 had recovered (John Hopkins University, 2020). Economies have also virtually come to a standstill leading to loss of jobs, while health facilities have been overwhelmed and individuals have been isolated. The virus continues to grow exponentially with its economic impact being more severe than that of the severe acute respiratory syndrome coronavirus (SARS-CoV) in 2002 and Middle East respiratory syndrome coronavirus (MERS-CoV) in 2012, while the political consequences are harder to predict as analysts argue that it could be significant and long-lasting.

The country at the centre of the pandemic, China, has come under scrutiny by various governments around the world. Its conduct in the midst of the ongoing pandemic has raised questions and generated suspicion of an attempt by the country to destabilise other economies through the deployment of the virus regarded as a bioweapon of warfare. Although the country has equally suffered from the effect of the virus, the number of deaths recorded by the country has raised eyebrows. China

A. Ajodo-Adebanjoko (✉)
Department of Political Science, Federal University Lafia, Lafia, Nasarawa State, Nigeria

© The Author(s), under exclusive license to Springer Nature Switzerland AG 2022   253
N. Faghih, A. Forouharfar (eds.), *Socioeconomic Dynamics of the COVID-19 Crisis*,
Contributions to Economics, https://doi.org/10.1007/978-3-030-89996-7_12

initially reported 3869 deaths which is revised to 4632 after much criticisms. Besides, the country's claim that the virus originated from bats or wet market in Wuhan has been refuted with allegations that there is enormous evidence that the virus originated in the Wuhan Institute of Virology of Chinese Academy of Sciences (CNN, 2020). The scope, spread, mode of transmission and overwhelming impact of the disease have raised the questions as to where and when the virus originated, what China knows about the mode of transmission and when, how transparent China has been in alerting the world to the danger of the virus and if the coronavirus is a natural or man-made virus (bioweapon) deployed by China against the rest of the world. These questions are understood against the backdrop that from earliest times to the modern era man has used lethal substances (man-made viruses) for assassination purposes, not only against individual enemies but also occasionally against armies to further their imperial ambition, as a result of which thousands of people have died (Friedrich, 2003). The German and Japanese armies have both used man-made viruses as biological weapons of warfare and such weapons as in the case of Japan's are seen as formidable tools to further imperialistic plans (Friedrich, 2003). At its height, Japan's biological weapons' program employed more than 5000 people and killed as many as 600 prisoners a year in human experiments in one of its 26 centres, while tests were conducted on prisoners and unsuspecting civilians with at least 25 different disease-causing agents (Friedrich, 2003).

Like in Japan, the Wuhan Institute of Virology of Chinese Academy of Sciences in Wuhan has a P4 laboratory which handles dangerous viruses and where dangerous experiments are alleged to be carried out, and it is for this reason that China is accused of having a history of infecting the world and viewed with suspicion in the ongoing health crisis (CNN, 2020). China's handling of the spread of the virus is another case in point. There are allegations by the United States that China hid vital information about the severity of the virus in addition to stockpiling supplies, while France stated that 'things happened that the world did not know' (Morrison, 2020). Ian Jones, professor of biomedical sciences at Reading University, believed that there was an early cover-up in Wuhan, perhaps a few days to a week, before the threat was accepted and that 'we will never know if faster action in those first days could have averted the outbreak' (Éanna, 2020). This view of a cover-up is also shared by Fareed Zakaria who believed that Wuhan tried to cover up the outbreak and thus China's early errors likely made a deadly outbreak worse (Grewal, 2020). The allegations are compounded by the fact that Taiwan claims that the virus had been detected in Wuhan as early as November 17, 2019, while the declaration of the disease as a pandemic on March 11 by the WHO who is accused of being China-centric, at a time when there were already more than 120,000 confirmed cases throughout 114 countries and nearly 4400 deaths, is viewed as belated (Aljazeera, 2020a; New Zealand Herald, 2020; Chung, 2020). Besides this, it has been alleged that China has prevented any investigations by individuals and even the WHO and researchers into the origin of the virus while detaining doctors who raised early alarm bells that could have stopped the spread of the disease, and as Western countries battled with their own domestic epidemic, a newly stabilised China seized a chance to portray itself as the emerging superpower by engaging in what might be called PPE (personal protective equipment) diplomacy, in 1 month sending abroad four million face masks (several of them defective), aid and debt relief to African nations and dispatching a trainload of supplies on to virus-stricken Madrid, while the United States was overwhelmed by crisis and was unable to give assistance to other countries (Foreign Policy, 2020; Pendlebury, 2020). Most of China's actions in the midst of the crisis are alleged to be an attempt to boost its economy which was at its lowest ebb owing to the trade dispute with the United States prior to the pandemic and dominate the world considering that its economy is second only in size to the United States' (Broom, 2019). Referring to China's quest for global leadership, Ward believes that China's vision of global pre-eminence goes back to decades with President Xi Jinping merely 'taking the mask off' in recent years. If all these allegations are true and anything to go by, then there are indeed lots of hard questions for China to answer when full investigations are conducted into the origin, nature and spread of the virus (Gupta, 2020; Aljazeera, 2020a).

12.2 Literature Review

12.2.1 COVID-19: Origin, Transmission and Impact

Generally, coronaviruses (CoV) are a large family of hundreds of viruses that cause illness ranging from the common cold, pneumonia and fever to more severe diseases such as breathing difficulty and lung infection, while the novel coronavirus disease (COVID-19) is an infectious disease caused by a newly discovered coronavirus and is transmitted by respiratory droplets of saliva or discharge from the nose when an infected person coughs, sneezes, speaks or breaths (WHO, 2020; Sasmita & Sha, 2020; Scripps Research Institute, 2020). Coronavirus is a virus primarily of animal origin (bats and rodents) and represents a major group of RNA viruses that cause diseases in mammals and birds with the first coronavirus discovered in chickens (Akinwumi, 2020; Gumel, 2020). According to Gumel (2020):

> The name "coronavirus" is derived from the Latin word "Corona" for crown or wreath. It signifies "the characteristic appearance of the virions (the infective form of the virus), which have a fringe of large, bulbous surface projections creating an image reminiscent of the solar corona or halo". In other words, "coronaviruses" are the crown-jewel of all viruses …Zoonotic scientists estimate that there are millions of viruses in the wild, and humans are always vulnerable to mutations in these zoonotic viruses that could trigger pandemics.

Coronaviruses can be found all over the world and are responsible for about 10–15% of common colds, mostly during the winter, and the virus was detected for the first time in the Netherlands in 2004 in a baby that was suffering from bronchiolitis. The coronaviruses that cause mild to moderate disease in humans are called 229 E, OC43 (the first discovered to be able to infect humans), NL63 and HKU1. There have been various coronaviruses in history such as the severe acute respiratory syndrome coronavirus (SARS-CoV) which originated in Guangdong Province in China in 2002 and spread to 29 countries, resulting in 8000 cases and 744 fatalities globally, and Middle East respiratory syndrome coronavirus (MERS-CoV) which originated in Saudi Arabia in 2012 and spread to 27 countries resulting in 2519 cases and 866 deaths (Gumel, 2020).

The novel coronavirus, code-named COVID-19 by the WHO, is a shortened version of coronavirus disease 2019, and it means that the specific virus that causes this disease is the COVID-19 virus although the formal name for the virus given by the International Committee on Taxonomy of Viruses is the 'severe acute respiratory syndrome coronavirus 2' (SARS-CoV-2), because it is related to the virus that caused the SARS outbreak in 2003 (New Scientist, 2020). An acute respiratory disease, COVID-19 was first discovered in Wuhan, China, in December 2019. Yan-Rong et al. identified COVID-19 as the third introduction of a highly pathogenic and large-scale epidemic coronavirus into the human population in the twenty-first century. They further stated that SARS-CoV-2 belongs to β-coronavirus, with highly identical genome to bat coronavirus, pointing to bat as the natural host. Declared a pandemic – an uncontrolled disease with a worldwide spread – by the WHO, COVID-19 assumes this label after the 2009 swine flu outbreak, which killed hundreds of thousands of people (New Zealand Herald, 2020).

COVID-19 affects all humans although the elderly and those with underlying illnesses such as hypertension, diabetes and heart conditions are the major victims. The mode of transmission of the virus is from animals to humans and vice-versa and from human to human. It is this latter mode of transmission that has become a public health emergency of international concern. More than 212 countries and 818 territories around the world have been affected by the coronavirus pandemic (Worldometer, 2020; John Hopkins University, 2020) which has negatively impacted the world of sports, tourism, education and a host of other businesses and in the absence of a vaccine or treatment has ushered in a 'new normal' which includes regular hand washing and sanitising, social distancing and lockdown of entire economies.

As of May 2020, the United States, the United Kingdom, Italy, France, Spain and Brazil are six of the countries with the highest number of deaths with 104,001; 38,161; 33,229; 28,714; 27,121; and 26, 901, respectively (Epidemic Statistics, 2020). The COVID-19 pandemic has also led to 94% of the world's economy being locked down and an unpredictable market shock, both on demand and supply, amid the progressive shutdown of national economic activities necessary to stem the epidemic. Analysts predict that the economic blow resulting from the current health disaster will bring even more dire consequences while predicting a global recession (Olugbile, 2020; Pendlebury, 2020). In addition, the pandemic has led to unprecedented job losses in different parts of the world. For instance, about 36 million Americans have filed for unemployment, while big economies like those of the United States, France, the United Kingdom and China among others have shrunk (CNN, 2020; BBC, 2020a). The world's largest economy, the United States, shrank by 4.8%, the worst since 2008, while the United Kingdom's economy shrank by 5.8% and is heading for its worst crash in 300 years with the possibility of contracting by 14% from 15% as was in the case in 1709 according to the Bank of England (CNN, 2020). The German economy, the biggest in Europe, has also been pushed into recession by the pandemic contracting by 2%, while the African Development Bank (AFD) estimates that the pandemic could cost the world economy $8.8tn (BBC, 2020a, b). Other economies have such as those of France and China have also shrunk as a result of the pandemic. The COVID-19 health crisis is regarded as Italy's most severe crisis since World War II, with the economy likely to suffer the deepest recession in the country's history.

From a small Chinese city in Wuhan in Hubei Province to countries around the world, the emergence and spread of COVID-19 as a global health emergency have generated controversies across the globe as countries accuse China of not being transparent in disclosing the impact of the virus as seen from the high number of deaths outside China. The argument is that China did not publish the accurate number of deaths, while the Chinese cities such as Beijing, Shanghai and Guangzhou were not affected by the virus despite the fact that the virus was first detected in the country. As a result, it has been alleged that COVID-19 could have been a biological weapon deployed by China to weaken other economies particularly that of the United States (Bryner, 2020). This has led to a blame game between the United States and China; US President Donald Trump while criticising China's handling of the virus has referred to the virus as 'Chinese virus', 'Wuhan virus' or 'foreign virus', while China in defiance denies that the virus originated with it claiming that it was imported by the US military cyclist and fabricated to curb its (China's) rise as a global economic power (Morrison, 2020; Kossaify, 2020; Yuan, 2020; Molter & Webster, 2020; Diresta, 2020).

Controversies on the origin of the virus continue among researchers. While some argue that the virus is not man-made and could not have originated from a laboratory, others believe that it could have originated from the lab, while others are not sure as to its origin (Arab News, 2020; Kossaify, 2020). Bakhos Tannous, an expert in cancer and viral infections, stated that 'There's always a question mark (over) whether the virus could have been made in a lab, simply because it's technically possible to change the structure of the virus'; he, however, concluded that looking at the historical natural evolution of coronaviruses, he doubted that the novel coronavirus is a lab product (Arab News, 2020). In his view, Prof. Stephen Turner believes that the virus most likely originated in bats (Graham, 2020), while Garry et al. (2020) in their analysis of public genome sequence data from SARS-CoV-2 and related viruses found no evidence that the virus was made in a laboratory or otherwise engineered and therefore concluded that the virus originated through natural processes. Hussanin however, states that genomic comparisons suggest that the SARS-Cov-2 virus is the result of a recombination between two different viruses, meaning the exact origin of the virus is still unclear. Thus, the debate on the origin of the novel coronavirus continues.

12.2.2 COVID-19, Biological Weapons and Biological Warfare

In the absence of a cure or vaccine and amidst the continued spread and devastating impact of the novel coronavirus across the globe, one persistent myth is that the virus was made by scientists and escaped from a lab in Wuhan, China, where the outbreak began (Bryner, 2020). In other words, the theory is that COVID-19 is not a natural virus but a man-made virus – a biological weapon fabricated by China in its attempt to destabilise the world economy. The use of biological weapons has long been a part of the history of humanity (Grey & Spaeth, 2006). Biological weapons which can be transmitted through the air and used in explosives (artillery, missiles, detonated bombs) include any microorganism (such as bacteria, viruses or fungi) or toxins (poisonous compounds produced by microorganisms) found in nature that can be used to kill or injure people (Grey & Spaeth, 2006). Some biological weapons include Ebola virus disease (EVD); *Yersinia pestis* bacterium, a CDC Category A organism, spread from person to person, causing pneumonic plague and symptoms such as fever and weakness leading to respiratory failure, shock and death at an advanced stage; Marburg virus which causes Marburg haemorrhagic fever (Marburg HF); bunyavirus which causes human infections such as hantavirus pulmonary syndrome (HPS), Rift Valley fever and Crimean-Congo haemorrhagic fever; and aflatoxin which leads to cell or organ death and cirrhosis liver disease resulting in liver failure and cancer (Grey & Spaeth, 2006).

The use of bioweapons in warfare has been on for centuries and is thought to predate recorded history, though the crude use of biological weapons was first documented in written and visual form as early as 600 BC, the year an Athenian General Solon contaminated the water supply of the besieged Greek city of Cirrha with black hellebore root (Grey & Spaeth, 2006). Some of the earliest form of bioweapons included decomposing bodies of animals and humans, poison, plagues and viruses. In 400 BC, Scythian archers infected their arrows with decomposing bodies or blood mixed with manure, and in 300 BC dead animals were used to contaminate wells and other sources of water, while in the Battle of Eurymedon in 190 BC, Hannibal defeated King Eumenes II of Pergamon by firing earthen vessels full of venomous snakes into the enemy ships, and in the twelfth century AD, Barbarossa used the bodies of dead and decomposing soldiers to poison wells during the battle of Tortona. During the siege of Kaffa in the fourteenth century AD, the attacking Tatar forces hurled plague-infected corpses into the city in an attempt to cause an epidemic within enemy forces. The Black Death pandemic of 1340 which broke out in Italy and led to the death of 25 million people in Europe for a period of 4 years was said to have been imported to Italy from the Black Sea port of Kaffa, where Mongol forces had used plague-infested bodies as bioweapons. In 1710, a Russian army fighting Swedish forces hurled plague-infested corpses over the city's walls, while in 1763 British troops passed blankets infected with smallpox virus to the Indians, causing a devastating epidemic among their ranks.

Bioweapons of warfare were also used in the 1900s. During World War I (1914–1918), the German armies developed anthrax, glanders, cholera and a wheat fungus specifically for use as biological weapons and were alleged to have spread plague in St. Petersburg, Russia, infected mules with glanders in Mesopotamia and attempted to do the same with the horses of the French Cavalry (Grey & Spaeth, 2006). During the period, anthrax was used extensively to disrupt economic and political life, and as a result of the brutal consequences of chemical and biological warfare during the war, the international community agreed to the first multilateral agreement in 1925 (the Geneva Protocol) to ban the use of biological and chemical weapons in war (Grey & Spaeth, 2006). During World War II, the Japanese army poisoned more than 1000 water wells in Chinese villages to study cholera and typhus outbreaks, while Japanese planes dropped plague-infested fleas over Chinese cities or distributed them by means of saboteurs in rice fields and along roads, and some of the effect of these bioweapons persisted for years and killed more than 30,000 people in 1947, long after the Japanese had surrendered (Britannica, 2020; Friedrich, 2003). Bioweapons were also developed in the Cold War era by the Soviet Union and the United States, as well as their respective allies, but these were never used but during the Vietnam War, Viet Cong guerrillas used needle-sharp punji sticks dipped in faeces to cause severe infections after an enemy soldier had been stabbed (Friedrich, 2003).

12.3   Discussions

China's indictment in the ongoing pandemic is based on the fact that many believe that it could have prevented the spread of the virus. Thus, it is believed that like in the past, the coronavirus could have been deployed by the country as a bioweapon of warfare. Kossaify (2020), however, argues that while it has become increasingly difficult to disentangle these theories from serious news reports, the virus may have originated in a Chinese lab not as a bioweapon, but as part of Chinese experiments intended to show the world that China is better equipped than the United States in its ability to identify and combat viruses and pandemics. China on its part has not only continuously denied that it had covered up the extent of its coronavirus out-break but suggested that the idea that the virus originated in its lab was a conspiracy theory propagated by conservative supporters of US President Donald Trump (Hale, 2020; VOA News, 2020a, b). Pandey and Pathak (2020), however, question how the world would expect China to be trusted to tell the truth about a global pandemic, perhaps because the country has always denied wrongful acts such as human rights abuses committed against its own citizens and religious groups. In 2018, there were allegations of persecution of Uyghurs Muslims, with more than a million arbitrarily imprisoned in reeducation camps, in Xinjiang, according to the Council on Foreign Relations (Maizland, 2019), and in 2019, there were also cases of Christians being jailed and churches being closed (Kuo, 2019).

12.3.1 The International System and the Struggle for Power and Influence

China's indictment in the ongoing pandemic will be better understood from the standpoint that international relations and the international system are characterised by competition and the survival of the fittest. The battle for supremacy has always been a feature of international politics. As Morgenthau (1967) postulated, international politics is the struggle for power which is reflected in all interactions at the international level, social, economic, political and diplomatic, and is made worse by the fact that there is no central or supergovernment (i.e., a governing body that has power over other governments). While the UN plays this role, its powers are limited by the veto power possessed by its permanent members and particularly by the rivalry between the United States and China who have used their veto power to forestall progress at different times. The struggle at the international level is often conflictual lending credence to Marx and Engel's (1948) postulation that the 'history of all existing societies is the history of class struggle', although at the international level the struggle is that of influence. All through history, nations have sought to dominate one another. Before the contemporary international system which is said to have existed for less than 500 years, states did not possess sovereignty, and as such, equality was out of the question. In addition, the conduct of international relations in the various state systems was narrow in scope and conducted in the name of ruler or leader. In the Holy Roman Empire, for instance, international relations were conducted in the name of the Pope who was regarded both as the temporal and spiritual leader of the empire. Thus, there was an absence of a 'distinctively modern idea of state as a forum of public power separate from both the ruler and the ruled and consisting of the supreme political authority within a certain defined territory'. With the signing of the Treaty of Westphalia in 1648, the role of the Pope as both the spiritual and temporal leader of the Holy Roman Empire was brought to an end, and independence was granted to all the dependent units within the Holy Roman Empire. As a result, states were now viewed as equal and free to conduct their international relations their own way, independent of any superior power. This ushered in a new international system characterised by sovereign statehood, international law and diplomatic relations.

According to Goldstein and Pevehouse (2013), the basic structures and principles of international system are deeply rooted in historical developments. As such, three stages in the development of the international system have been identified, namely, the multipolar world, the bipolar world and the unipolar world. The multipolar world falls within the period of the two world wars (1900–1950). Before the beginning of this period, the world was dominated by great powers such as Britain, Russia and Prussia, Spain and the Netherlands with Britain playing the role of balancer. The rise of Napoleon after the French Revolution which began in 1789 upset the European order as France moved eastward its border invading other counties and establishing a French empire. The subsequent defeat of Napoleon led to the formation of the Congress of Vienna (1814–1815) which created a collective hegemonic or multipolar system comprising Great Britain, Russia, France, Prussia and Austria. These powers attempted to devise the rules of engagement at the international level that will ensure international order and promote stability in Europe. The major powers embarked on collective action for the following reasons; in spite of Great Britain's global economic and political commitments and ambition to expand its sphere of influence abroad, it required peace in Europe, while Russia also desired a quiet Europe to be able to expand south into the Ottoman empire. Both countries therefore realised that to further their expansionist ambition, there is the need for a stable Europe which will require that Austria regained its independence from France and for a long-term stability France would have to be brought back into the European system. It was this that eventually led to the formation of the Concert of Europe comprising the five powers. China was not one of the major powers during the multipolar world order and views the Concert of Europe as 'an instrument of the Great Game played by the Imperial powers' due to the humiliations she suffered during the period which included the scramble for China, the Second Opium War, colonisation and spheres of influence, loss of sovereignty and joint invasion by Great Powers (Weizhun, 2014).

By the beginning of the twentieth century, three new rising powers of the United States, Japan and Italy emerged. The world during World War II effected major changes in the nature and operation of the world and changes in the nature and operation of the world political system. On the political front, a series of shifts have occurred after 1945 that involved the actors and the polar structure of the system. World War II destroyed the long-lasting decaying, mostly European-based multipolar structure. In this stead emerged a bipolar structure dominated by the Soviet Union and the United States. In this structure, the United States was the military and economic superpower and the leader of the pole. The Soviet Union, though incredibly damaged, was the leader of the other pole. The USSR never matched the United States economically but had a huge conventional armed forces, a seemingly threatening ideology and, by 1949, with atomic weapons, held an unusual position during the Cold War, oscillating between both camps, refusing to align with either, and was at odds with many of the non-aligned countries (Latham, 2010; Yu, 2013). After a period of enmity with both superpowers, the United States and the USSR, Beijing achieved a working relationship with the countries of the Western camp, and her orientation during the period had global weight in that at each stage she was, and was seen as, powerful enough to tip the balance between the two superpowers and profoundly influence the global stage, even if she could never independently shape the world to the same extent as the United States and USSR (Chen, 2001). This bipolar or 'Cold War' era came to an end with the dissolution of the hegemonic section (Eastern Europe) of the Soviet Russian Empire in 1989 and the further dissolution of the imperial core (Soviet Union) in 1991, and this ushered in a unipolar world order with the United States as the sole superpower and hegemon. Under this arrangement, the United States intervenes in other countries' local wars, decides how UN General Assembly reacts to issues, confers legitimacy and recognition on friendly states and describes their enemies as 'axis of evil' and as a hegemon and exports her language, ideology, religion and ethics, customs, democratic values and institutions to other nations whether it is good or detrimental to them. Despite this arrangement, other emerging centres of power like China and India have been showing significant economic potentials, while the State of Israel is considered to be a military superpower, and other regional powers such as Brazil in Latin America, Republic of South Africa in sub-Saharan Africa, Russia in Central Asia and Germany and France in Europe are other critical powers to reckon with. This arrangement has made the onset of rivalry and conflict inevitable. China in particular has been showing more potentials of a superpower with its economic prowess and nursing the ambition of becoming a global hegemon. Her unprecedented economic growth is anticipated to translate into increased diplomatic influence and power, and this has led some scholars to conclude that it will replace the United States as the future global hegemon (Mehmood Zaeen Hassan, 2019).

12.3.2 China's Quest for Global Hegemony

Experts in international politics agree that every state nurses the ambition of becoming a force to reckon with in the international arena. Even small states within a region may seek to take advantage of its natural endowments to lead others. For instance, in the days of Libya under Muammar Gaddafi, the latter sought a United States of Africa under his leadership. While some analysts may consider this a personal ambition, there is no doubt that Gaddafi thought that he/Libya had the potentials to lead Africa because of the country's oil wealth. China like other nations of the world nurses this ambition of becoming a superpower – a country that has global influence over others in cultural, technological, military and political spheres – and though an economic power and emerging as a strong contender for the position, a regional great power as it is in Asia isn't the same as being a global superpower which must have the capacity to project dominating power and influence anywhere in the world, and sometimes in more than one region of the globe at a time, and so may plausibly attain the status of global hegemon (Goldring, 2020, Curtis, 2019). A defining aspect of US superpower, which emerged from the Cold War division of the globe, is the extensive network of alliances it enjoys which range from the 30 nations of North Atlantic Treaty Organization (NATO) to the 1951 Anzus Pact with Australia and New Zealand, plus a number of bilateral military agreements with countries like Japan and South Korea, and the Five Eyes intelligence-sharing alliance between the United States, the United Kingdom, Australia, Canada and New Zealand, while China ranks low in regional alliances with few formal allies, even within Asia (Curtis, 2019). Goldring (2020) argues further that:

> Part of America's rise to power was due to the post-WWII Bretton Woods Conference of 1944, in which delegates from around the world agreed that exchange rates would be rooted in gold, with the US dollar being the reserve currency. This rendered the dollar the most important currency in the world, and as a result, the US became the world's foundation for economic stability. China, however, doesn't have the trust that the world showed the US after WWII; the country's persistent adherence away from Western ideals will keep the

world at large from getting too close…China's current population of over one billion people puts a large strain on its natural resources… Until China's demographics are adjusted to reflect a more balanced society across age, genders and socioeconomic status, their rise to superpower status is likely to be nonexistent.

China or the People's Republic of China is a communist state which has been ruled by the Chinese Communist Party since 1949 (Pendlebury, 2020). The most populous nation on Earth with 1,397,715,000 billion people, China remains a one-party state. Since 1949, the country has had six leaders, namely, Mao Zedong (1949–1954), Liu Shaoqi (1959–1968), Deng Xiaoping (1983–1990), Jiang Zemin (1990–2005), Hu Jintao (2005–2012) and Xi Jinping (2012–present), and since the late 1970s and the accession to the presidency of Deng Xiaoping, the Chinese Communist Party has been on an extraordinary mission to transform the country's economy until a slowdown in the third quarter of 2019, owing to the trade war with the United States, which saw a 27-year low, economic growth, has been phenomenal (China Sage, 2020). Of all China's leaders, Xi seems to be close to actualising the country's imperial ambitions which Ward refers to as the big picture: the objective of dominating in global affairs on a longer-term time frame with the idea of restoring their position – they claim that they used to be the world's supreme power and are now going to return to that. In a speech in 2019, Xi Jinping used the word 'struggle' no less than 60 times and pledged that by 2049 (the centenary of the Chinese Communist Party's seizing power), China will have achieved 'the great rejuvenation of the Chinese nation', and on January 23, 2020, the day of the Wuhan lockdown and with corpses lying in the streets, he spoke at a reception in Beijing, where he ignored the looming disaster and told of the need to 'race against time and keep abreast with history to realise the first centenary goal of the dream of national rejuvenation' (Pendelbury, 2020). Under Xi's leadership, China has sought to exert its economic influence in not only Asia but also Europe and Africa. In 1999, China was the United Kingdom's 26th largest export market, and by 2018, it was the fourth largest source of imports to the United Kingdom. Annual Chinese imports in the country have grown for 19 years running, and in Italy, figures showed it at an annual £22.1 billion. In 2019, long before coronavirus, it was predicted that this relentless surge would see the Chinese outstrips the US economy sometime in 2020 (Pendlebury, 2020). In 2019, Italy joined China's New Silk Road project also known as the Belt and Road Initiative (BRI) involving a wave of Chinese funding for major infrastructure projects around the world, in a bid to speed Chinese goods to markets further afield. Italy became the first member of the G7 group of developed economies to sign up to China's global investment programme and the largest economy among the 15 European Union countries that are BRI members, a move that has raised concerns among Italy's Western allies with critics seeing it as representing a bold bid for geopolitical and strategic influence (BBC News, 2019). Being the third largest economy in Europe with 15% of the Eurozone GDP, including Italy in the BRI, was important and largely symbolic for Chinese ambitions in Europe, suggesting the growing role of China in the world. The ambitious BRI MoU signed between Rome and Beijing included 50 agreements, covering economic, cultural and infrastructural areas (Zeneli & Capriati, 2020). It is estimated that about 200 Italian businesses are now controlled by Chinese owners (not including the ones owned by Chinese living in Italy), while China's central bank holds stakes in several Italian blue chips like Fiat, Telecom Italia, Generali and Eni, among others (Bell, 2020). In Africa, China has signed series of trade agreements with countries within the regions. During the Forum on China-Africa Cooperation (FOCAC) held in Beijing in 2018, China promised to provide $60 billion in financial support to Africa (Africanews, 2018). In recent years, African countries and markets have been flooded with substandard goods from China, while the Chinese continues to make effort to usurp Western influence on the continent.

Before the COVID-19 pandemic, China was battling with an economy that was hard hit by the US trade war. As a result, it entered a 'crisis' due to the lack of trade of companies from Europe and the United States that are based in China, while Chinese shares fell by 40% of their value, and the currency was devalued. It would therefore be understood why some scholars argued that China would seek every means including using a biological weapon to overthrow US hegemony. Although critics may discredit this, arguing that such an attempt by China despite signing agreements to end biological warfare will be immoral, politics is not a profession that encourages moral reflection or insight as 'The ends justify the means' (Eskew, 2020). Besides, apart from the cases that occurred in the past which may be regarded as the era of 'incivility', biological weapons are viewed as formidable tools to further imperialistic plans (Friedrich, 2003).

The possibility of a country using biological weapons in an era of international law is deemed impossible. However, the weakness of international law is often exploited by States as Russia did in the Crimea case, and China may want to do likewise. According to Pandey and Pathak (2020) in international law, in order to hold a State responsible for an internationally wrongful act, first, it must be a breach of international obligations and, second, that breach must be attributable to the State as per Article 2 of the Draft Articles on Responsibility of States for Internationally Wrongful Acts. Thus, the primary question will be whether China violated international law by its omission to share critical information with the World Health Organization (WHO). Article 6 of the International Health Regulations by the WHO mandates countries to provide timely and sufficiently detailed information about the potential public health emergencies, while Article 10 seeks verification from States of unofficial reports of pathogenic microorganisms by which States are bound to provide transparent information within 24 h. In the first instance, it could be argued that Beijing breached this by intentionally withholding critical information both in China and abroad, censored private entities to disseminate COVID-19 information, rejected the WHO's offers of epidemic investigative assistance and withheld early reports of medical staff infections, misleading the WHO to believe that human-to-human transmission was not possible (Pandey & Pathak, 2020). China's actions could be interpreted as an instance of transboundary harm, which is an offence under international law, and based on this, a State or States have the right to bring the country before the International Court of Justice for harms to its citizens and its economy and breach of Article 22 of the WHO, which provides for enforcement of international health regulations. The challenge with this, however, is that the WHO has not indicted China for any wrongdoing but rather has commended the country on the handling of the pandemic. Nevertheless, the US state of Missouri says it is suing the Chinese government over its handling of the coronavirus which it says has led to severe economic losses and for not stopping the spread of the virus which has led Missouri residents to have suffered economic damage worth tens of billions of dollars, although it is doubtful how far this can go since based on the principle of sovereign equality US courts have no jurisdiction over the Chinese government (Harper, 2019).

12.4   Conclusion

The struggle for power and supremacy has been one of the defining features of the international system. From the Concert of Europe or Congress of Vienna (1814–1815) to the multipolar world, the bipolar world and the current unipolar world, nations have sought to dominate one another in their interactions. As the realists put it, international politics is a struggle for power between self-interested states, and whatever the ultimate aim of international politics, power is always the ultimate aim. Morgenthau (1967) argued that statesmen and people may ultimately seek freedom, security, prosperity or power itself; they may define their goals in terms of a religious, philosophic, economic or social ideal; they may also try to further its realisation through non-political means, such as technical cooperation with other nations or international organisations; but when they strive to realise their goal by means of international politics, they do so by striving for power. Multiple economic indicators show that China continues to rise and may transition into one out of three possible hegemonic paths: first, into a free trade-encouraging and free trade-sustaining hegemon; second, into an aggressive, coercive and dominating hegemon; and third, into a Dutch-style hegemonic path. However, the impact of COVID-19 on economies of nations particularly the United States could pave way for China as an economic hegemon.

China is reckoned as one of the countries with the worst human rights abuses in the twenty-first century. The lack of religious liberty and forceful castration of families in order to achieve its one child policy are areas where the issue of morality is lacking in the country. The argument therefore is that a country which engages in such immoral acts could employ any means in the competitive global system to launch itself to the position of a hegemon. In an analysis of what China knew about the virus and when, Zakaria (2020) and Grewal (2020) argued that Wuhan tried to cover up outbreak and thus China's early errors likely made a deadly outbreak worse. As the novel coronavirus (COVID-19) continues to ravage the world with treatment and vaccine still elusive, the world economy coming to a virtual standstill and people forced to live in isolation, largely because one of the most powerful countries in the world either chose to be in denial or actively muzzled information in the initial stages, people and governments are demanding for greater transparency and honesty on the part of China as crucial in helping to better understand the origin of the virus (Gupta, 2020; Kossaify, 2020).

While China's role in the spread of the virus is still under scrutiny, there has been a talk of 'reckoning' from UK Foreign Secretary Dominic Raab who said that the country's relations with China will no longer be business as usual once the crisis is over (Pendlebury, 2020; Ani, 2020). There is therefore the need for a thorough investigation into China's role in the origin and spread of the COVID-19 virus, and if found guilty, appropriate sanctions should be meted on the country. Under international law, the global community has legal recourses such as removal of China from leadership positions and memberships, as China now chairs 4 of 15 UN organisations, reversing China's entry into the World Trade Organisation (WTO), suspension of air travel to China for a certain period and broadcast of Western media in China, undermining of China's infamous internet stateful firewall and requiring that China make full reparations for the injury caused by their internationally wrongful act (Pandey & Pathak, 2020).

References

Africanews. (2018). *China promises $60 bn aid to Africa as 2018 FOCAC summit opens*. https://www.africanews.com/2018/09/03/china-promises-60-bn-aid-to-africa-as-2018-focac-summit-opens/

Akinwumi, A. (2020). *Covid-19 Coronavirus infection*, Covid-19 health education by Deeper Christian Life Ministry, Lagos Nigeria.

Aljazeera. (2020a, April 17). *China's Wuhan revises coronavirus death toll up by 50 percent City says 1,290 more people died of COVID-19 than previously thought after cases were missed in early days of outbreak*. https://www.aljazeera.com/news/2020/04/china-wuhan-revises-coronavirus-death-toll-50-percent-200417042241868.html

Ani. (2020). *British leaders press Chinese on origin and handling of virus*. https://www.asiapacificnews.net/news/264725038/uk-raises-hard-questions-on-origin-of-covid-19

Arab NEW. (2020, April 16). *Serious questions over coronavirus origin fuel conspiracy theories*. https://www.arabnews.com/node/1660591/world

BBC. (2020a) Coronavirus pushes German economy into recession., *BBC News*.

BBC. (2020b). Coronavirus 'could cost global economy $8.8tn) ADB. *BBC News*.

BBC News. (2019). *Italy joins China's New Silk Road project*. https://www.bbc.com/news/world-europe-47679760. 23 Mar 2019.

Bell, K. (2020) *China is buying up Italy, one company at a time*. https://qz.com/280247/china-is-buying-up-italy-one-company-at-a-time/

Broom, D. (2019). *China by numbers: 10 facts to help you understand the superpower today*. https://www.weforum.org/agenda/2019/06/china-by-numbers-10-facts-to-help-you-understand-the-superpower-today/

Bryner, J. (2020). *The coronavirus was not engineered in a lab. Here's how we know*. https://www.livescience.com/coronavirus-not-human-made-in-lab.html

Chen, J. (2001). *Mao's China and the Cold War*. University of North Carolina Press.

China Sage. (2020). *How the Chinese government operates*. https://www.chinasage.info/government.htm

Chung, F. (2020). *Covid 19 coronavirus: World Health Organisation accused of 'parroting Chinese propaganda'*. https://www.nzherald.co.nz/opinion/news/article.cfm?c_id=466&objectid=12322113

CNN. (2020). Pompeo: "Enormous Evidence" Virus originated in Chinese Lab, CNN. Encyclopædia Britannica (2020). Biological Weapons Proliferation, Encyclopædia Britannica.

Curtis, S. (2019). *China kick-starts development of 6G technology less than a week after rolling out its superfast 5G network.* https://www.dailymail.co.uk/sciencetech/article-7656417/China-kick-starts-development-6G-technology-week-rolling-5G-network.html

Diresta, R. (2020). *For China, the 'USA Virus' is a Geopolitical Ploy in a new era of tinfoil-hat diplomacy, official sources are legitimizing conspiracy theories from the internet.* https://www.theatlantic.com/ideas/archive/2020/04/chinas-covid-19-conspiracy-theories/609772/

Éanna, K. (2020). *China was slammed for initial COVID-19 secrecy, but its scientists led the way in tackling the virus.* https://sciencebusiness.net/international-news/china-was-slammed-initial-covid-19-secrecy-its-scientists-led-way-tackling-virus

Epidemic Statistics. (2020). *COVID-19 stats-Realtime coronavirus statistics with chart.* https://epidemic-stats.com/coronavirus

Eskew, C. (2020). *A question of morality in politics.* https://www.washingtonpost.com/blogs/post-partisan/wp/2014/05/13/a-question-of-morality-in-politics/

Foreign Policy. (2020). *China Casts Itself as Global Savior While U.S. and EU Focus on Virus at Home.* https://foreignpolicy.com/2020/03/19/china-us-eu-coronavirus-great-power-competition/

Friedrich, F. (2003). *The history of biological warfare.* https://www.ncbi.nlm.nih.gov/pmc/articles/PMC1326439/

Garry, R. F., Holmes, A. R., & Andersen K. (2020) The proximal origin of SARS-CoV-2 in COVID-19 coronavirus epidemic has a natural origin. *Sciencedaily.* https://www.sciencedaily.com/releases/2020/03/200317175442.htm

Goldring, K. (2020). *Is China the next superpower?* https://www.theperspective.com/debates/china-next-superpower/

Goldstein, J., & Pevehouse, C. J. (2013). *International relations.* Pearson/Oxford University Press.

Graham, R. (2020). *Coronavirus outbreak: How did coronavirus start and where did it come from? Was it really Wuhan's animal market? It's likely Covid-19 originated in bats, scientists say. But did it then spread to pangolins and humans?* https://www.theguardian.com/world/2020/apr/15/how-did-the-coronavirus-start-where-did-it-come-from-how-did-it-spread-humans-was-it-really-bats-pangolins-wuhan-animal-market

Grewal, K. (2020). *China delayed Covid warning by 6 days, there was a 'cover-up' going on: Fareed Zakaria report.* https://theprint.in/world/china-delayed-covid-warning-by-6-days-trump-didnt-act-for-6-weeks-fareed-zakaria-report/428807/

Grey, M. R., & Spaeth, K. R. (Eds.). (2006). *The bioterrorism sourcebook.* McGraw-Hill.

Gumel, A. B. (2020). Using Mathematics to understand and control the 2019 novel coronavirus pandemic. *Akada Lafia Telegram*, 3 May 2020.

Gupta, S. (2020). *Beijing must answer some hard questions on Covid-19*, https://www.msn.com/en-in/news/newsindia/beijing-must-answer-some-hard-questions-on-covid-19/ar-BB11epcx

Hale, E. (2020). *Politics of coronavirus: Taiwan, China and WHO Deadly outbreak lays bare challenges of political situation faced by democratic island that China claims as its own.* https://www.aljazeera.com/news/2020/02/politics-coronavirus-taiwan-china-200205080601495.html?utm_source=website&utm_medium=article_page&utm_campaign=read_more_links

Harper, J. (2019). *Coronavirus: Missouri sues Chinese government over virus handling* https://www.bbc.com/news/business-52364797

John Hopkins University. (2020). *COVID-19 dashboard by the Centre for Systems Science and Engineering (CSSE) at John Hopkins University.*

Kossaify, E. (2020) *Serious questions over coronavirus origin fuel conspiracy theories.* https://www.arabnews.com/node/1660591/world

Kuo, L. (2019). *In Chengdu, In China, they're closing churches, jailing pastors – And even rewriting scripture.* https://www.theguardian.com/world/2019/jan/13/china-christians-religious-persecution-translation-bible

Latham, M. E. (2010). The Cold War in the Third World, 1963-1975. In *The Cambridge History of the cold war: Volume II crises and Détente* (pp. 258–280). Cambridge University Press.

Maizland, L. (2019). *China's Repression of Uighurs in Xinjiang*. https://www.cfr.org/backgrounder/chinas-repression-uighurs-xinjiang

Marx, K., & Engels, F. (1948). *The communist manifesto*. International Publishers.

Mehmood Zaeem Hassan. (2019). *Reassessing realities of a multi-polar world order*. https://moderndiplomacy.eu/2019/09/03/reassessing-realities-of-a-multi-polar-world-order/

Molter, V. & Webster, G. (2020). *Coronavirus conspiracy claims: What's behind a Chinese diplomat's COVID-19 misdirection*. https://fsi.stanford.edu/news/china-covid19-origin-narrative

Morgenthau, H. J. (1967). *Politics among nations: The struggle for power and peace*. Alfred Knopp.

Morrison, S. (2020). *Emmanuel Macron questions China's handling of Covid-19: things happened we don't know about*. https://www.standard.co.uk/news/world/emmanuel-macron-questions-chinas-handling-of-coronavirus-outbreak-a4416581.html

New Scientist. (2020). *Covid-19*. https://www.newscientist.com/term/covid-19/

New Zealand Herald. (2020, March 12). *Coronavirus: World Health Organisation officially declares a pandemic*. https://www.nzherald.co.nz/world/news/article.cfm?c_id=2&objectid=12315921&ref=art_readmore

Olugbile, F. (2020). *Covid-19 and the conspiracy theories*. https://businessday.ng/columnist/article/covid-19-and-the-conspiracy-theories/

Pandey, R., & Pathak, O. (2020). *COVID19 | Will China be held accountable at the ICJ?* https://www.moneycontrol.com/news/trends/legal-trends/covid19-will-china-be-held-accountable-at-the-icj-5175711.html

Pendlebury, R. (2020). *China's post-pandemic power grab: Beijing is desperate to overtake America as the world's economic superpower – And with the West brought to its knees by the virus, who can stop it, asks RICHARD PENDLEBURY*. 20 Apr 2020. https://www.dailymail.co.uk

Sasmita, P. A., & Sha, M (2020). Epidemiology, causes, clinical manifestation and diagnosis, prevention and control of coronavirus disease (COVID-19) during the early outbreak period: A scoping review. *Infectious Diseases of Poverty*, *9*, 29, https://idpjournal.biomedcentral.com/articles/10.1186/s40249-020-00646-x

Scripps Research Institute. (2020). *COVID-19 coronavirus epidemic has a natural origin*. https://www.sciencedaily.com/releases/2020/03/200317175442.htm

VOA News. (2020a, April 19). *COVID-19 Pandemic: China dismisses claims Coronavirus originated in lab*. https://www.voanews.com/covid-19-pandemic/china-dismisses-claims-coronavirus-originated-lab

VOA News. (2020b, April 19). *China dismisses claims Coronavirus originated in lab*. https://www.voanews.com/covid-19-pandemic/china-dismisses-claims-coronavirus-originated-lab

Weizhun, M. (2014). Muddle or march: China and the 21st century concert of powers. *Revista Brasileira de Política Internacional*, *57* no.spe Brasflia. https://www.scielo.br/scielo.php?script=sci_arttext&pid=S0034-73292014000300243

WHO. (2020). *What is a Coronavirus?* https://www.un.org/en/coronavirus

Worldometer. (2020). *Countries where COVID-19 has spread*. https://www.worldometers.info/coronavirus/countries-where-coronavirus-has-spread

Yu, M. (2013). From two camps to three worlds: The party worldview in PRC textbooks (1949–1966). *The China Quarterly*, *215*, 682–702. https://doi.org/10.1017/S0305741013001021

Yuan, S. (2020) *China in coronavirus propaganda push as US ties worsen State media lauds China as global leader in fight against disease in bid to defuse criticism it allowed virus to spread*. https://www.aljazeera.com/news/2020/04/coronavirus-spreads-leads-theories-origin-200407073509327.html?utm_source=website&utm_medium=article_page&utm_campaign=read_more_links

Zakaria, F. (2020) *Fareed Zakaria investigates what China knew, and when, as COVID-19 raced around the world*. https://cnnpressroom.blogs.cnn.com/2020/05/22/fareed-zakaria-investigates-what-china-knew-and-when-as-covid-19-raced-around-the-world/

Zeneli, V., & Capriati, M. (2020). *Is Italy's economic crisis an opportunity for China?* https://thediplomat.com/2020/04/is-italys-economic-crisis-an-opportunity-for-china

Chapter 13
COVID-19 and the Cultural Challenges of the Rights of Contemporary African Ancestors

Benson Ohihon Igboin

13.1 Introduction

COVID-19, "a result of natural contingency as its purest" (Zizek, 2020, p. 14), has presented surreal challenges to global community with different degrees of intensity. According to Slavoj Zizek (2020), the developed countries seem not to bother too much about those who have died or those who will eventually die as a result of coronavirus, but they are paying serious attention to sliding economic fortunes and political uncertainties occasioned by the pandemic. Focusing on how to redound the markets that are in panic does not countenance the whole length of the implications of the pandemic. There is therefore the need to begin a process of reorganising the world in ways that will be more meaningful than it is at present as different blocs need to jettison divisive political correctness and work towards saving humanity (Zizek, 2020, p. 44). While Zizek's penetrative arguments and panaceas are genuine, they however do not also emphasise the fate of those who have died, particularly from African religious and cultural perspectives.

The novel coronavirus otherwise known as 2019-nCov or COVID-19 originated from Wuhan, China, in late 2019. The coronavirus is "a highly transmittable and pathogenic viral infection caused by severe acute respiratory syndrome virus 2 (SARS-CoV-2)" (Shereen et al., 2020, p. 91). Wuhan, a business province in China, experienced the first outbreak, which claimed almost 2000 lives and infected over 70,000 people in the first 50 days. Health experts posit that COVID-19 probably

B. O. Igboin (✉)
Department of Religion and African Culture, Adekunle Ajasin University,
Akungba-Akoko, Ondo State, Nigeria
e-mail: benson.igboin@aaua.edu.ng

Academic Associate of the Research Institute of Theology and Religion, University of South Africa, Pretoria, South Africa

© The Author(s), under exclusive license to Springer Nature Switzerland AG 2022   269
N. Faghih, A. Forouharfar (eds.), *Socioeconomic Dynamics of the COVID-19 Crisis*,
Contributions to Economics, https://doi.org/10.1007/978-3-030-89996-7_13

originated in bats or pangolins. While Chinese researchers describe it as the Wuhan virus or 2019 novel coronavirus, the International Committee on Taxonomy of Viruses (ICTV) calls the virus SARS-CoV-2 and the disease COVID-19. The idea behind SARS-CoV-2 is that coronaviruses are viruses that are capable of causing diseases in both humans and animals such as severe acute respiratory syndrome (SARS), which spread widely in 2002–2003.

On 31 December 2019, China formally reported the incidents of pneumonia of unknown cause to the World Health Organisation (WHO). By January 2020, the WHO (2020a) directed that all protocols concerning public health and surveillance of influenza and severe acute respiratory infections be observed. By 5 January, the WHO had announced a risk assessment report of the Wuhan situation, thus putting the world in red alert. By 11 March 2020, the WHO declared COVID-19 a pandemic.

The first case of infection outside China was Thailand in January 2020, while in Africa, it was Egypt followed by Algeria and Nigeria in February 2020 (WHO, 2020b). Gradually, the novel coronavirus spread to different parts of the world, which led to shutting down of countries and cities depending on the gravity of infection. While the WHO coordinates, monitors, prescribes, regulates and reports activities at the global level, regional and national governments and institutions have taken primary lead in the management and fight against the spread of COVID-19 in their respective territories. The closing of various ports and setting up or activating disease control centres are determined by individual countries. Till date, there has been no agreed recipe for the coronavirus, though attempts are being made to develop vaccines. Countries like Italy, the United States, the United Kingdom and so on have experienced high numbers of fatalities putting a lot of stress on their medical facilities. In fact, apart from conspiracy theories that have shrouded its emergence, its cure has been largely politicised, thus resulting in more fatalities (Abaido & Takshe, 2020, Odubanjo, 2020). Apart from the conspiracy theories that involve the development of vaccines, predictions that Africa will be most hit with devastating casualties have also raised critical concern among Africans (John, 2020). For example, Adam Vaughan (2020) expresses shock that the number of cases reported in Africa was lower than predicted regardless of the appalling state of medical facilities, corruption in governance, weak economy and institutions. He further hinges his astonishment on the experience of previous handling of such epidemics as Ebola and Lassa fever, which, he argues, forms the basis for the prediction of Africa's vulnerability to COVID-19. However, some believe that the nature of African weather, the nature of her population (being young), the nature of the virus itself and prayers, among others, account for the low cases recorded thus far in the continent (Africa Centre for Strategic Studies, 2020).

However, the COVID-19 pandemic is seriously affecting the globe in ways that are yet to be fully estimated. By now, there are glimpses of its effects, especially how it has challenged global health infrastructures and calls for more nuanced humane projects and programmes that should be geared towards safer humanity. From Wuhan where the pandemic started and spread to over 200 countries, it will be premature to give an accurate number of people who have either been infested or died from it. This is simply because the pandemic has not yet been curtailed as the demographics keep rising daily. However, as Zizek (2020) observes, leaders of different countries do not care about the dead; their focus is how to revamp the economy in panic. This forms his major basis for reopening economic and social spaces even though they are actually not yet safe.

Historically, COVID-19 is not the first global pandemic Africa would experience. There was the Spanish influenza of 1918–1920, which claimed almost "two percent of Africa's population within six months", making Africa, specifically sub-Saharan Africa, the hardest hit "of all six continents" (Phillips, 2014). Howard Phillips (2014) explains the origin, the nature of the spread and the consequences of influenza without giving attention to how Africans disposed their dead. Shadreck Chirikure (2020) concentrates on how Africans were able to reduce the fatalities arising from the influenza by observing social distancing, which he also argues can be observed in the present COVID-19 pandemic to curtail its spread. He does not consider the burial of the dead and its implications on African societies. In fact, many other scholars (e.g. Ohadike (1981, 1991), Heaton and Falola (2014), Oluwasegun (2015)) who have studied the influenza devoted their researches towards its origin, impacts on family and economic, political and discursive issues, particularly deconstructing its historiography. Also, studies in Ebola and Lassa fever, two epidemics that have also claimed many lives, particularly in West Africa recently, do not concern themselves with the cultural rights of African ancestors. However, the WHO (2017, p. 1) prescribes what it calls "safe and dignified burials" rather than befitting or proper burial, as will be explained later. In safe and dignified burial protocols, it is the medical or health officials that conduct the burial of the dead, while the family members and "priests" and "imams" are actively allowed to perform religious rites for the deceased. The protocols place more emphasis on Muslim and Christian burial rites than indigenous rites. Although the WHO believes that the families of the deceased should observe the burial, the family members do not actually perform the burial in accordance with laid down cultural and ritual procedures. Honestly, if various governments across Africa had even paid attention to the WHO's (2017) burial protocols with further modifications, the serious agitation for proper burial would have been minimised.

Generally, government does not always put religious and traditional beliefs and measures into consideration when formulating policies on health, especially during outbreak of epidemics or pandemics. Studies have shown that such neglect has not helped in curtailing diseases in many communities in Africa as the people believe more in their cosmological and traditional responses to outbreak and management of diseases than the Western protocols. Angellar Manguvo and Benford Mafuvadze (2015) elaborate:

> In West African context, diseases and death are generally perceived as a culmination of natural and metaphysical causes. Metaphysical causes entail the spiritual realm such as witchcraft and punishment from God or ancestral spirits for breaking taboos and various forms of transgressions.... The way people conceptualize the etiology of a disease generally dictates their response to it. Given that in some affected communities in West Africa, Ebola is linked to the metaphysical realm, it is not surprising that diviners and spiritual healers are often consulted for treatment.

In addition, government has also not paid critical attention to how the traditional religious adherents observe their burials. Although government is concerned about the health status of the population, the adherents are interested in both life and death. Accordingly, great importance is accorded burial of the dead because of the consequences that might result from improper burial of the dead. Manguvo and Mafuvadze (2015) again elucidate:

> It is widely believed that the transition should be facilitated by the surviving relatives through funeral and burial rituals. In the event that the deceased fails to attain the more elevated rank of ancestral spirit, it is believed that their spirit may return and punish the living relatives…. Most West African communities… place significant value on the rituals and resist adoption of alternative methods that minimize the spread of the virus such as cremation.

Africans are very interested in what happens to the dead as well as those who are alive. African cultural beliefs and practices, particularly in relation to burial of the deceased and the ancestors' rights, are important aspects of African traditional religion and culture. Physical burial of the dead is a criterion for assuming the status of an ancestor. But bad death caused by unknown or incurable disease (like coronavirus, as some have assumed at least for now) causes the deceased to lose the right of being buried properly. COVID-19 has raised critical questions in this regard because it is perceived to be a source of bad death, and some of its victims are cremated, not buried. Since previous scholarship has not paid in-depth attention to the rights of the ancestors especially in times of epidemics or pandemics, this chapter intends to fill this gap.

Manguvo and Mafuvadze (2015) have called government attention to the need to creatively balance its policy on outbreak of epidemics or pandemics and traditional communities' belief systems in order to win their confidence. Their argument invariably stretches towards the rights of the ancestors which is the thrust of this chapter. Although rights discourse has been a lively one among people of different cultural backgrounds, it is usually framed around the living individual who is thought of as having rights that must be enjoyed and protected. This conceptualisation naturally ousts the dead, as not capable of enjoying rights. The chapter interrogates this conception and reveals that in traditional Africa the ancestors are a part of the human community and, therefore, enjoy some form of "human" rights so long as they dispense their responsibilities creditably while alive. But enjoying such rights also depends on dying well and being buried, not cremated. Is COVID-19 a source of bad death that deprives the deceased from proper burial? Wouldn't e-burial suffice for the repose of the souls of the ancestors? In the meantime, it is pertinent to clarify the assumptions of rights of the ancestors in Africa.

13.2   Constructing the Rights of the African Ancestors

We begin by asking the following questions: Should we talk about rights for the dead when those who are living hardly enjoy their so-called inalienable human rights? How exactly do we conceive the rights of the dead in Africa? These questions are relevant to the world in different ways and for different reasons. For the African, the world is not just the physical manifestation that we all live in; it has a complex cosmic dimension that instantiates a bond, which the material conception of rights alone cannot countenance. This can better be understood from the perspective that in Africa, "the human community is made up of both the living and the dead as well as the yet to be born" (Salazar & Nicholls, 2019, p. 130). For instance, the arguments for and against abortion may not have been settled fully in Africa, given the fundamental connection between the living, the dead and the unborn, at least from the traditional perspective. Thus, abortion does not only raise ethical issues but also metaphysical concern as it relates to cosmic harmony. In this regard, it seems also imperative to think, particularly within African cultural and religious worldview, that the debate, whether or not the dead have rights, should be provoked. In stirring the hornet's nest, one is not unmindful of the inherent conclusions that some might have reached, though within certain cultural lens or landscape, that the dead do not have or should not have rights, like the unborn. Such conclusion, if reached, is contra to the two-dimensional, composite worldview of Africa (Igboin, 2011).

In addition to the questions raised above, we ask whether or not the term "human" fits into the discourse of the dead when discussing "their rights". The immediate meaning of "human" will appertain to the living, a person or people, and since it is a qualifier of "rights", it may ordinarily convey no other meaning than to relate it literally to the living and not the dead. It is also conceived as a distinguishing mark from the animal; hence, in rights discourse, we hear about "animal rights". Taken generally together, therefore, "human" relates to a physical living being, hence human being, human nature, human weakness, human relations, human interest, human resources, human race and, now, human rights. "Human" can also be understood better when we differentiate it from God. In this case, when we speak of human, we think of the mundane, the existential, the terrestrial rather than the metaphysical (Igboin, 2013).

The Western conception of human being and human life and time is lineal; in this case, an individual is a living being; and that quality of being human ceases at physical death. At death, the individual dissolves and loses personality. Nevertheless, our first locale of rights for the dead, namely, in the here and now, may apply; the second does not seem to appeal to the West, at least, theoretically. The first is only possible in a different sense, from the African cultural matrix. In this case, the rights for the dead revolve around their property which the living may fight over or for legally when encroached. The legal tussle or struggle to retrieve what "belongs" to the dead is not in any way meant to satisfy the dead in the literal sense of it; it is on the contrary meant to enrich the living. Cast in this mode, the human person that is dead may not be said to have rights to enjoy the privilege of his/her property being restored to the family. This is because rights are purely conceived for the living individual. It is also as a consequence of this that the unborn is thought to be without rights (Igboin, 2013).

Alfred Schutz's (1967) philosophy of culture aptly depicts the above position. Schutz argues that there is no relationship between the living and the dead in Western culture in the sense that the African conceives such relationship. What can be known about the ancestors is through documents and monuments left behind. It is these that can be studied to gain faint knowledge of the ancestors. Sylvanus Nnoruka (2009, p. 75) explains this when he thinks that the sphere of the ancestors is "a world of Others of whom I may have knowledge and whose actions may influence my own life, but upon whom I cannot act in any manner". Schutz (1967, p. 214) further posits that the domain of the ancestors is "completely indeterminate and indeterminable". The same applies to the unborn whom he argues cannot be known as individuals. They are "anonymous" and, therefore, can "scarcely be qualified" (Schutz, 1967, p. 135). In a rationalistic culture like this, it is impossible to construct human rights for the dead and the unborn because the former have lost their personal individuality at death, while the latter do not yet acquire or possess any personal individuality that should qualify them for human rights. This leaves Schutz (1967, p. 136) with the world of the "contemporaries" with whom we may not have been physically related but that we coexist in time. He adds that he can also gain experience of the contemporaries by derivation from previous immediate experiences of contemporaries in face-to-face situation or through those who one is presently related but who as fellows must have had experience with other people not directly known to one. Schutz concludes that the only real world or true existence is the present empirical world where social relations are possible. Accordingly, "a social relation between contemporaries consists in the subjective chance that the reciprocally ascribed typifying scheme (and corresponding expectations) will be used congruently by the partners" (Nnoruka, 2009, p. 74). Humanity therefore lies within the contemporaries only, which is the locale of human rights.

Gerrie ter Haar (2011) does not fully agree with Schutz's position, particularly as it relates to human rights and African religion and culture. Haar argues that there is a need to study particular cultures under which human rights are discussed and practised. This is because culture and religion carry different weight of meaning for different people. "Religion is for many people a vital mode of thinking about the world and the place of human beings in it. For this reason, it behoves us to think more deeply about the relationship between religion and human rights than is usual" (Haar, 2011, p. 295). In other words, human rights should not usually be based on legal and formal institutions as the West largely constructs it. Haar (2011, p. 299) notes that "there are many people, particularly in developing countries, who do not base their concept of human rights in any human authority or resource in the first instance, but rather on a divine or spiritual power". She further argues that for some religions that are not book-based such as traditional African religion, there are usually clear references to the supernatural in their advocacy and adjudication of human rights. Just as religion generally poses itself as an alternative source of power to political power, the traditional religions reorder human life by making much more available sources of power to deal with evil and animate life. According to her, "spiritual power provides an alternative to political power, an opportunity that is of particular importance for the relatively powerless" (Haar, 2011, p. 302). She argues that there is a nexus between religion and human rights because of the moral dimension and characterisation of the good and evil. As such, "religion may become a dominant factor in establishing human rights, due to a belief that the rights held by human beings have their ultimate origin in the spirit world" (Haar, 2011, p. 303). She further avers that:

> fundamental to the relationship between religion and human rights, therefore, is the question of what people believe constitutes a human being. What qualities do people suppose make a person truly human? What precisely entitles a human being to make a claim to full humanity? The answer to such questions can be found only by considering popular conceptions of humanity, which can be very different in different cultures. In Bantu-speaking parts of Africa, for example, the concept of 'human being' include various categories of spirit beings and the human dead as well as living humans. (Haar, 2011, p. 304)

As a result of this complex relationship, "restoring broken relations in the widest sense, not only between victim and perpetrator, but also with the wider community as represented in both the visible and invisible worlds, including ancestors and other spirits, becomes the ultimate objective, which often clashes with more secular expressions of justice and peace" (Haar, 2011, p. 304). The experience of interconnectedness of the visible and invisible worlds of Africa cannot but be brought to human rights discourse if we must understand the concept more holistically.

In any case, as much as we would like to agree with Haar, the vacuum she leaves opens borders on the rights of the ancestors in Africa, especially in times of epidemics or pandemics like the COVID-19. In addition to the conception of being "human" described above, the African conceives human in a broader, cyclical spectrum. The unborn are human, and the dead are also human in different, but related, ways. The foetus is not referred to as an "it" in Africa, because as soon as conception is established, the "who" the woman is carrying and nurturing in her womb is a living human person, a "he" or a "she" and never an "it". Since the foetus is not a dispensable lot or a neuter gender, he or she is accorded rights: right to life and right to live. (It is for this purpose that sacrifices are offered on behalf of the unborn. During such sacrifices, the foetus is prayed for, spoken to and assured of family readiness to admit him/her as a member. Thus, the initiation into familyhood starts from conception, and does not even end at death.) In fact, in many African communities like Iuleha, even when a natural abortion (miscarriage) or a stillbirth occurs, the child is not just disposed; some rituals are accorded mainly to ward off a recurrence. People mourn grievously because a life is lost even though they are also happy that the mother survives. But when a pregnant woman is treated or handled in a way that results in abortion, the culprit is "customarily" tried for "murder" of the unborn and has to propitiate the ancestors and pay compensation to the woman. In any case, the stigma of being a "murderer" hardly erases as it is retold to generations of the lineage or community. Even an inadvertent action that results in abortion of a foetus also carries some form of penalty. Thus, in many African communities, the joy of being pregnant is usually expressed in ceremonies and rituals.

Laurenti Magesa (1997) agrees that the unborn are full members of the family and community and therefore have the right of relationship, though in a limited form. In fact, it is not infrequent to observe expectant parents symbolically and "actually" conversing with the unborn. The special care for the pregnant woman is not only because of her, but also for the unborn. He also argues that the unborn have some fundamental rights even though they may not be directly involved in the pursuit of morality and rights. Still, they are members of a given community, albeit in *potency*, and care must be taken that they are not wronged by the living in any way. The most serious wrong against the latter would be for the living to deprive them of the chance to be born and to participate in the life of the family and clan in this world. Such an action would deprive them of the most fundamental right (Magesa, 1997, p. 67; Idowu, 1973).

Magesa (1997, p. 83) further argues that the unborn already possess humanity or personality to a large extent. He avers: "to the new *person* coming into the visible world, all of the ancestors are almost like 'gods' requiring *his* or *her* allegiance". This is why John Mbiti (1969, p. 120) is highly criticised for referring to the unborn baby as an "it" when he argued that the unborn "child is constantly flooded with religious activities and attitudes starting long before it is born". Mbiti (1969, p. 107) further says that it is the responsibility of the family to ensure that the foetus' "existence is not terminated. The family provides for its continuation, and prepares for the coming of those not-yet-born". Mbiti's self-contradiction is made plain when he posits that in African marriage, the living, the dead and the unborn converge in a mystical union that defines the compositeness of the African world. In his words, "it is the point where all the *members* of a given community meet: the departed, the living and those yet to be born" (Mbiti, 1969, p. 133). By this latter admission, we can establish that the unborn are human members of the African community. And once they are now physically born, their umbilical cords are usually buried in the earth in anticipation that the remainder would join sometime in the future for full unification – at the point of physical death. This is why burying the dead in the earth is critically important to the African.

Mbiti's (1969, p. 69) phrase "the living dead" in reference to the ancestors unambiguously confers some essence of being human on the dead. Mbiti argues that the living dead are those, though dead physically, yet live in a different dimension, which is still felt as though physically present in the community. They are called the living dead because they are yet to complete the process of dying. Thus, "they are still part of their human family". Geoffrey Parrinder (1954, p. 8) had earlier described the African ancestors as those who have "survived death and to be living in spiritual world, still taking a lively interest in the affairs of their families". In this context, the ancestors exist in the African two-dimensional world. It is for this reason that Mbiti (1969, p. 83) argues that "the living-dead are bilingual: they speak the language of men, with whom they lived until 'recently', and they speak the language of spirits and God, to whom they are drawing nearer ontologically". And they live as an invisible form in their families and communities. As such, "the living-dead are still 'people', and have not yet become 'things', 'spirits' or 'its'. They return to their human families from time to time, and share meals with them, however symbolically. They know and have interest in what is going on in the family" (Mbiti, 1969, p. 83).

The other controversial term is "rights". Benezet Bujo (1997) makes a critique of two notions of human rights that he considers too narrow and Eurocentric, while Hans Kung (1991) argues that a global ethic is possible on the platform of Western normative concepts. In other words, the world's survival is only now possible "if there is no longer any room in it for spheres of differing, contradictory and even antagonistic ethic. This one world needs one basic ethic. This one world society certainly does not need a unitary religion and a unitary ideology, but it does need some norms, values, ideals and goals to bring it together and to be binding on it". In addition, "The importance of the idea of human rights for today's situation of human history lies in the fact that it brings a common normative basis for the living together of all people in peace and justice regardless of a (possible) religious or ideological foundation" (Kung, 1991, p. 43). While Bujo agrees in principle with these assertions with regard to human rights discourse, he nevertheless objects to them because they are obviously a product of Western philosophy and can be meaningfully engaged only within Western cultural precinct. He contends that such notions of human rights as depicted by these scholars are a fallout of the Enlightenment that confers rights on the individual and defines the human being in exclusion of the society. Such a background that is outright Western does not admit those cultural and religious experiences as real and meaningful that do not fall within Western ambit.

Thus, as Haar (2011) contends, there is the need to engage the concept of rights from not only rational but also religious perspective, particularly African religious and cultural lenses, which in our argument here encapsulate both the unborn and the dead. We, therefore, argue that the dead have some form of rights which they must enjoy in order for the living to enjoy their own rights and to live a harmonious and peaceful life.

13.3   Methodological and Theoretical Frameworks

The phenomenological method of inquiry is adopted for this chapter because of its suitability in investigating African cultural and religious *weltanschauung* – world-view. This approach to religious phenomena involves both emic-insider and etic-outsider observations and thus ensures that the present writer's assumptions are bracketed out and a more accurate and nuanced descriptions of the object of experience are presented (Schilbrack, 2016, p. 36; Gardiner, 2016, p. 60; Danfulani, 2019, p. 13). Its descriptive model provides account of causal link between ritual observance for the dead and consequences of failure to do so. Ritual behaviour is important to understanding religious phenomena because it helps to engage in what is embodied and embedded in its social and cultural realms.

I have earlier discussed that African worldview is not only cyclical but also composite and as such embodies the living, dead and yet to born. This trio composite-ness of the African *weltanschauung* is grounded in cosmotheandric theory. According to Raimon Panikkar (1993) who propounded the theory, cosmotheandrism, which is a derivative from Greek words *cosmos* (earth), *theos* (God) and *anthropos* (human), defines an ontological link that ensures respect for God, humanity and cosmos. This trio is not just a unity; it is an identity that is derived from the union. It thus means that the identity is not possible without the union. Explaining this unity and identity, Panikkar (1982, p. 127) says:

> In the final analysis, *simplicity and complexity are not dialectically opposed*, because the ultimate structure of the universe does not need to be conceived as dialectical. Their relation is dialogical. They have meaning not in opposing and contradicting each other so as to generate some "higher" synthetic amalgam, but as a mutually constitutive relation, so that the one does not make sense without the other and each mutually supports the other.

Benson Igboin (2011) argues that the issues of human rights in Africa ought to reflect the tenets of cosmotheandrism rather than the Western rationalistic ways they are treated. In many rural communities, advocacy and implementation of human rights have recourse to supernatural forces (including God, divinities, spirits, ancestors), human (community) authorities (including kings, priests, elders and wise men and women) and cosmic phenomena (including earth, rivers, fire and other natural phenomena). The cosmotheandric consciousness in Africa derives from the synergy that defines the three layers of authority in the community. In his "Spirituality, Covid19 and Ancestor: The Failure of the Perception of Reality in Three Dimensions", Abdi-Basid Adan (2020, p. 2) carefully examines the cosmotheandric theory as it affects these layers in a COVID-19 context thus:

> From this first dimension of reality, the world of microorganism is also another vision of reality. These living species, having the character in terms of spirituality as us, illustrate almost all of our principles in a very different dimension. The famous Covid19 and other pathogenic and deadly elements achieve the same achievements as that of a neutron disrupting a uranium nucleus, when it comes to penetrating a healthy body which unites an intangible being and a body.

In the sections that follow, cosmotheandric theory will be deployed in interrogating and explaining the nexus between the nature of death resulting from COVID-19, proper burial and attainment of the status and rights of an ancestor. This is important because proper burial is the basis for the connection between the human community and the ancestral world on the one hand, and one can only become an ancestor if the deceased is adjudged to have died a good death that warrants the performance of burial rituals. Since burial is critical, the issue of cremation, which is believed to be capable of "extinguishing" the essence or soul of the deceased, remains a contentious one.

13.4   Qualifications, Responsibilities and Rights of the African Ancestors

We begin this section by stating that it is not every dead person in traditional Africancommunities that automatically becomes an ancestor. In fact, becoming an ancestor is "a social elevation. What was human becomes superhuman" (Lugira, 2009, p. 50). Since we talk about the rights of ancestors, it is fundamental to briefly espouse what qualifies a person to assume ancestorhood. This is important because in human rights language, we easily notice that there are prima facie qualifications for enjoying human rights. Generally, to qualify for ancestorhood, a person must have lived a long life; married and given birth to children who will keep the departed in remembrance in the family and community; led virtuous or good life; died peacefully, not violently; and accorded a befitting and proper burial (Igboin, 2014; Asamoah-Gyadu, 2013). Igboin and Igili (2015) argue that the cause of death is critical to becoming an ancestor. They point out that among the Igbo of Nigeria, for example, a person who dies of an unknown or incurable disease is usually denied proper burial. Any sickness that results in isolating an elder until he dies is believed to be a bad one. When an elder is sick, the children and close relatives are duty-bound to be around to keep him in the warmth of the family until he passes on. Igboin (2019) also argues that among the Owan of Edo State, Nigeria, the kind of sickness responsible for the death of a person is important to determine whether or not the deceased will be given a proper burial. Death caused by fire, flood, felled trees and so on is regarded as bad and does not qualify for proper burial in many African communities. However, Bujo (1997) observes that in many African communities, violent death can be waved when the departed is adjudged to have led a virtuous life. As Salazar and Nicholls (2019, p. 129) clearly note among the Akan of Ghana, "Not all the dead are revered as ancestors. A person's manner of life and death while on earth determines whether he or she is considered an ancestor".

A good death is not also enough; the deceased must also be given a "befitting" and "proper" burial. Befitting burial is more often than not conceived in terms of social aspects of funeral ceremonies. These are the external social ceremonies that everyone can easily access and attend. It consists of singing, dancing, eating, drinking, wearing uniform dresses and so on. Befitting burial, in relative terms, costs so much money depending on the financial wherewithal of the families. Poor families concentrate more on proper burial with less emphasis on befitting burial ceremonies. While the wealthy families can hold socials for several days, poor ones manage to hold theirs for a day, and briefly too. Proper burial has to do with careful observance of unabridged and shared rites and rituals associated with burial. In many communities, it is not everyone that partakes in proper burial. Those who are involved are the immediate family members, especially the first son in case of a man and first daughter in case of a woman, and certain age groups that procedurally perform the rites or rituals associated with burial (Igboin, 2014). "Death calls for a ritual disposal of the body of the deceased. Burial rites are performed by the community…. People are very attentive to giving the departed a proper burial. It is important that the spirit of the departed be content in the world beyond and not come back as a dissatisfied ghost to plague those left behind" (Lugira, 2009, p. 76).

In addition, proper burial involves strictly carrying out the last instructions of the deceased concerning their burial; these instructions may concern how to prepare their bodies for burial, sites of grave and sacrifices that should be performed (Turner, 2017; Matthews, 1998). In fact, in some African communities, only those who died an honourable death have a grave as their entitlement and as of right whose instructions about where to bury them can be honoured. According to Shipton (2009, p. 94), "an honourable death is marked by burial inside the homestead". The children of the deceased are expected to ensure both aspects of the burial are carried out meticulously. Responsible children owe their deceased parents this responsibility, which if denied has consequences (Igboin, 2014). But those who die prematurely, like children, are not accorded "burial". In other words, they are not accorded burial rites because they did not fulfil the expectations of life when alive (Bond, 1992).

In any human rights transaction, individual and collective reciprocal responsibilities cannot be overlooked. If the African ancestors must claim and enjoy rights, it necessarily follows that they must also dispense their responsibilities creditably. Ferdinand Ezekwonna (2005, p. 49) posits that among the Igbo of Nigeria, the ground for any ancestor to enjoy any right is that such an ancestor fulfils his or her responsibility to the family or community. In fact, "when a particular ancestor is not fulfilling this purpose, individuals can abandon him. So, it is a sort of give and take". Magesa (1997) emphasises the belief that the responsibilities of the ancestors to their families and communities are mutual; the responses each party receives are dependent on how they carry out their responsibilities. What is implicated in this mutuality is that ancestors cannot be abandoned for non-performance without severe consequences if their families have reneged on their duties to them, especially proper burial. This is so because the ancestors are believed to be more powerful than their human families; they possess a stronger "vital force" that helps them superintend over the affairs of their community. On the basis of their moral uprightness, they can demand obedience in order to continue to ensure and maintain peace and harmony in their families and between their families and themselves. Peace and harmony are "empirical" evidence that the family members have fulfilled their obligations to the ancestors.

Mbiti (1969) enunciates the responsibilities of the family to the ancestors: the observance or breach of which could either lead to blessing or suffering, as the case may be. According to him, it is imperative that proper burial is given to a deceased elder. It is equally important that their instructions are carried out to the letter without corruption. It is incumbent on the family to maintain a high level of social friendliness with the ancestors through symbolic or ritual acts such as offering regular sacrifices, pouring of libation and observing ethical rules that have been handed over to them as contained in traditions and customs. Viewing all of these critically, Magesa (1997) thinks that the ancestors enjoy more rights and dispense more responsibility than their human families because of the limited nature of the latter. He submits that "perhaps the ancestors have even slightly more rights and responsibilities on account of the vital power they possess. As elder members of the community, and because of their proximity to the Divine, it is morally imperative that the ancestors be honoured" (Magesa, 1997, p. 70). He adds that "keeping the ancestors in good humour is an essential task of the living" (Magesa, 1997, p. 70).

Bujo (1997) combines metaphysical, symbolic and physical claims of human rights for the African ancestors. He argues that it is plausible to claim human rights for the ancestors at both ends because in reality the ancestors have rights. "The dead rightly claim honour, reparation, libation of food as well as other things" (Bujo, 1997, p. 153). In addition, the ancestors are rightful owners of some property such as land, water places and parts of forests; they are used with care and respect for the ancestors by their progenies. The grave of an ancestor not only does connect him/her with their family symbolically but also invokes a metaphysical presence as well as a physical evidence of ownership of such a piece of land. It is partly for this reason that cash trees are more often than not planted by the graveside when an elder is buried outside the house. "This tree is proof of the presence and right of ownership of the deceased. At the same time, it is the protection and guarantee of the children's heritage, who always and irrefutably can use it as a form of reference against usurpers" (Bujo, 1997, p. 154). Bujo (1997, p. 154) further posits that not only the ancestors are appeased with symbolic sacrifices, but also physical, material reparation is also demanded:

> This description clearly shows the importance of the dead as far as the problem of human rights is concerned. Since they belong to the community, *in sensu proprio*, they are the subjects of these rights. Hence, one must never expropriate the deceased in Africa. Whoever robs them of their rights can be prosecuted in court and forced to pay compensation. In the process of compensation, mere rituals are not deemed sufficient since reconciliation with the dead demands also that the descendants of the offended relatives are given benefits.

It is only when both forms of appeasement are done that reconciliation can ensue and then peace is realised among the people and the community as a whole. It is no wonder therefore that the Iuleha people of Nigeria would say: "whoever robs the dead of their property will pay back more than what he has stolen" (Igboin, 2003, p. 68). In what follows, I examine how COVID-19 may affect the status of African ancestors.

13.5   Implications of COVID-19 on the Rights of Contemporary Ancestors

The ultimate goal of an elder in Africa is to become an ancestor at death. Although there are some differences in how the dead become ancestors in African communities, it is established that most Africans believe that proper burial is mandatory for transition into the communion of ancestorhood. Among different communities Richard Gehman (2013, pp. 41, 47) researched in, it is unanimously agreed that proper burial is a sine qua non for attaining the status of ancestorhood. Accordingly, "proper burial, following the traditions of the ancestors, is necessary in order to avoid trouble in this life…. Proper burial was very important since bad luck could come if the ancestral spirits were unhappy with the burial". But proper burial is a result of "good death" since "bad death" does not qualify for "burial" at all (Kunhiyop, 2012, pp. 212–214; Balogun, 2018). Since proper burial is a responsibility of the deceased's children, a right of the deceased and a condition of the deceased to be admitted into the realm of the ancestors, the deceased while alive must ensure that they live worthy life and die peacefully.

There are controversies surrounding the classification of the elders that have died as a consequence of COVID-19, Ebola or Lassa fever. Are they to be regarded as dying a good and peaceful death? In traditional African communities, those who died as a result of laziness, incurable disease and accident, died during pregnancy and so on are believed to have died a bad death, and therefore cannot be honoured with burial or venerated as ancestors (Ayantayo, 2013, p. 68). Does death resulting from COVID-19 therefore a bad one?

Among the Iuleha,[1] there are debates as to how best to classify death resulting from COVID-19. One of the arguments is that since more medical knowledge has been gained over the years, certain sicknesses once regarded as unknown and incurable have become treatable and curable. Although there are conspiracy theories shrouding COVID-19 as a mysterious pandemic, the fact that there are attempts at finding vaccine to treat it does not make it an incurable disease. But since it is contagious, traditional ways of observing the rites of proper burial for the victims should be evolved. This group further states that COVID-19 is just like Ebola and Lassa fever, which though are also contagious their victims are not regarded to have died a bad death. Thus, the importance of proper burial, which can involve a minimal number of people, is seriously canvassed by this group. They argue that in the course of time, when COVID-19 would have been effectively addressed, befitting burial, in the form of second burial, can then be done.

The other group of people are of the view that death as a result of COVID-19 should be considered a bad death because those who are infested are corrupt politicians who have allegedly used their positions in government to impoverish the country. Since thus far the names of those who have been announced to have died from COVID-19 are top government officials both present and past, COVID-19 is a disease that has come to place judgement on the corrupt. To this group, COVID-19 is selective in infesting its victims. Such victims, the group argues, if they die, should not be buried but cremated or thrown into the evil forest so that they cannot reincarnate or be venerated as ancestors. This last position is less scientific because the reality is that both the rich and poor have died from the disease.

The initial position of the Federal Government of Nigeria was that those who died of COVID-19 should be considered to have died a bad death, and therefore do not deserve proper burial. According to Information Minister Lai Mohammed, "Nigerians should not forget that these are not the types of corpses that can be claimed for burial because it must be handled by the ministry of health" (Folorunsho-Francis, 2020). The implication of this position is that some people believed to have contracted the disease refused to go to public health facilities to be tested or treated preferring to die at home; when they are eventually accorded a proper burial, they could become ancestors. This unintended result seems to have been the reason why

---

[1] Iuleha is a clan in Owan West Local Government Area of Edo State; it lies on the north-western side of the state and forms part of the Edo North Senatorial District. It has three sub-clans which are Eruere, Aoma and Okpuje in order of seniority. The communities of Eruere include Oshofo, Osi and Oralla; Aoma, Avbiosi, Uzebba, Ivbiughuru, Ukhuse Oke, Ukhuse Osi and Ohia; and Okpuje, Oah, Ivbiodohen, Iloje, Avbioghola, Okeigho, Oromen and Ikpeyan. For detailed description, history and language of Iuleha, see, for instance, Igboin (2003), Agbuku (2019) and Obomeighe (2019).

the government has to alter its earlier position by setting burial protocols to be observed by the families of the deceased (News Agency of Nigeria, 2020). In a more nuanced reasoning, it will be plausible to argue that the government position changed after the burial of the Chief of Staff (CoS) to the Nigerian President when top government officials flagrantly disobeyed all COVID-19 protocols in a bid to accord him a proper burial (Adebowale, 2020; Anagor, 2020). By this very act, it shows that death resulting from COVID-19 could not be regarded as bad death anymore. It is on this basis that families of deceased have been attempting to find ways to at least accord their dead some sort of proper burial.

I pointed out earlier that the WHO's (2017) burial protocols recognise the value of safe and dignified burial. By these protocols, death resulting from COVID-19 cannot be regarded as bad death. It only requires a more careful handling of the corpses in order to ensure that participants in the burial do not contract the disease. Thus, if governments across Africa had paid attention to this existing protocol, the argument that dead resulting from COVID-19 is bad would have been forestalled.

As a result of respect for the dead and proper burial, many families have been identified to have broken the social distancing rules across the African continent. These families argue that even though it is painful to lose their loved ones, it would be a "double tragedy" to deny them a place in the hereafter in the communion of the ancestors by denying them proper burial. They further posit that denying the dead proper burial would expose them to the angst of the dead. Medically, this defiance to social distancing rules has exposed more people to the pandemic. In South Africa, for instance, high rate of COVID-19 spread has been traced to gathering resulting from attending burial ceremonies of the dead. Understanding the high risks such gathering engenders is critical to how effective the measures to contain the pandemic will eventually be for the society (Jaja et al., 2020). In Nigeria, the burial ceremonies of Abba Kyari, former Chief of Staff to the Nigerian President, and Abiola Ajimobi, former Governor of Oyo State, among others, witnessed large crowds that defied COVID-19 burial protocols (Dede, 2020, Sahara Reporters, 2020). In fact, in Ghana, many families have refused to succumb to government directives for "private burial". The people argue that proper burial must be given to their deceased in order to ensure peace in their families (Kaledzi, 2020).

Abidemi Omonisi (2020) observes that globally, most people that have died as a result of COVID-19 are not buried in conventional ways. Due to the restrictions placed by the governments, families have been unable to organise "a very 'befitting' burial for their deceased members". With specific regard to Africa, Omonisi argues that organising a befitting burial for the dead is a religious, social and cultural duty of the deceased's families in order to ensure that "the deceased migrate to join the ancestors in the invisible world. If this is not done, it is generally believed that the dead person may become a wandering ghost and will continue to torment those still living especially family members of the deceased who ought to give the deceased a 'befitting' funeral". Although burial ceremonies cost humongous amount of money, which has been an issue of intense debate, the implications of not according the deceased a befitting and proper burial cannot be underestimated. For the sake of joining the communion of ancestors, Africans, most of the times, do not bury their elders outside their communities. A great cost is incurred to bring corpses home to be buried: "burial, to be considered proper, honourable, meaningful and acceptable... has to be done in the deceased's ancestral land". Omonisi further posits that COVID-19 has seriously affected the elaborate social and cultural ceremonies associated with burial across Africa. He notes that some Africans who died of COVID-19 have been buried outside their countries, while some have been cremated, which is against African cultural and religious belief and practice for the dead, thus losing the dignity of death and burial. What are the implications of these exigent changes for the African religious and cultural practice?

The idea of cremation has been controversial in relation to assuming the status of an ancestor. Emmanuel Onwubiko (2013) argues that cremation law (though voluntary for those who wish to be cremated) of Lagos State, Nigeria, is not sensitive to the cultural and religious values attached to the dead in Africa. According to him, cremation violates the rights of the dead to be buried and denies them the opportunity to become ancestors. Since death by fire is believed to be a bad death and generally attributed to Sango by the Yoruba, cremation also means that proper burial is denied the deceased, and their spirits might haunt their families who accede to cremate them (Laguda, 2013; Igboin, 2016). In Southern Africa also, cremation is a violation of the rights of dead. As earlier hinted, the umbilical cord that was buried, not cremated at birth, looks forward to a mystical reunion with the rest of the body. This reunion is made possible by burying the dead. What this further implicates is that an ancestor is fully whole and integrated as he or she rejoins with the umbilical cord and thus has the powers to superintend over the affairs of the family. Accordingly, "Burial rites are closely related to the ancestors throughout Southern Africa. Africans here don't perform cremations, and all their dead are buried in graves" (Anderson, 2018, p. 87). In this case, death is "a gift of life; the union of a body and that something-else, that flame that goes out with passing. A good death would accord itself to two inscriptions: the world of ancestors and that of generations to come" (Mudimbe & Kilonzo, 2012, p. 56).

13.6   Conclusion

I have argued that COVID-19 has continued to have serious implications for both the living and the dead. While attention is being paid actively towards reviving the economies around the world, little attention is being paid to the victims of the pandemic, especially the dead in African cultural and religious praxis. The concentration on the dead in the African parlance is so because the conception of reality in Africa is different from the West. This is hinged on the reality that Africa is majorly cyclical, recognising the rights of the living, the dead and the unborn. On the basis of this cosmotheandric understanding of reality, I argued that the dead have some form of right they enjoy and should therefore be accorded them if they qualify to enjoy them. Although this may not seem to be agreeable to Western philosophical position, nevertheless giving the ancestors their due rights in Africa is a precondition for a peaceful social harmony and earning the co-operation of the people in fighting the spread of pandemics or epidemics.

Consequently, government should pay attention to the people's cultural belief as a way of winning their confidence in the process of curtailing the spread of diseases. Resort to legislations that are not sensitive to cultural and traditional beliefs of the people does not help in the fight against the spread of diseases. The people resist such legislation or find creative ways to circumvent it, thus increasing the rate of contraction and spread of diseases (Nwaiwu, 2020; Ujumadu, 2020). Sensitisation mechanism and efforts should involve the local people for making them more acceptable and effective. Through this, government would be able to win the confidence of the people, and the people would also view the efforts of government as good measures to protect them against contracting and spreading diseases.

The challenge COVID-19 has raised borders on whether those who have died from it should be regarded as dying a bad death, thus forfeiting the rights of ancestorhood. I argued that there are creative ways of handling issues of this nature: circumstances have dictated that death by COVID-19 should not be viewed as bad death and the victims could be accorded a proper burial in order to assume the status of an ancestor. However, African religious and cultural beliefs are indeed not static, but dynamic, responding to the need of the time. Family members should relate with COVID-19 patients in isolation centres via social media, particularly through video calls. This medium can also be adopted during burial at this time, that is, e-burial should be embraced because it will not only satisfy and ensure proper burial with the presence of the important family members but also safeguard the living from further contracting and spreading the COVID-19 disease.

References

Abaido, G. M., & Takshe, A. A. (2020). COIVD-19: Virus or viral conspiracy theories? *American Journal of Biomedical Science & Research, 8*(2), 122–124.

Adan, A.-B. (2020). Spirituality, Covid19 and ancestor: The failure of the perception of reality in three dimensions. https://www.researchgate.net/publication/340182986

Adebowale, N. (2020). Abba Kyari's burial: SGF Mustapha admits violations of COVID-19 protocols. *Premium Times*, April 20. https://www.premiumtimes.com/news/headlines/388924-abba-kyaris-burial-sgf-mustapha-admits-violations-of-covid-19-protocols.html. Accessed 29 June 2020.

Africa Centre for Strategic Studies. (2020). Five myths about coronavirus in Africa. *Spotlight*, March 27.

Agbuku, F. O. (2019). *An ethnographic survey of Okpuje in Iuleha history and culture*. Sky-Light.

Anagor, A. (2020). Confusion as Nigeria applies dichotomous protocols for burial of Covid-19 victims. *Business Day*, July 5.

Anderson, A. H. (2018). *Spirit-filled world: Religious dis/continuity in African Pentecostalism*. Palgrave Macmillan.

Asamoah-Gyadu, K. J. (2013). *Contemporary Pentecostal Christianity: Interpretations from an African context*. Regnum Books International.

Ayantayo, J. K. (2013). The implications of ancestral veneration manifesting in national symbols for national integration and moral transformation in Nigeria. In A. Adogame, E. Chitando, &

B. Bateye (Eds.), *African traditions in the study of religion, diaspora and gendered societies: Essays in Honour of Jacob Kehinde Olupona* (pp. 61–70). Ashgate.

Balogun, O. A. (2018). *African philosophy: Reflections in Yoruba metaphysics and jurisprudence.* Xeel Publishers.

Bond, G. C. (1992). Living with spirits: Death and afterlife in African religions. In H. Obayashi (Ed.), *Death and afterlife: Perspectives of world religions* (pp. 3–18). Praeger.

Bujo, B. (1997). *The ethical dimension of community: The African model and the dialogue between North and South.* Paulines Publications Africa.

Chirikure, S. (2020). How ancient African societies used social distancing to manage pandemics. *Quartz Africa.* https://www.google.com/amp/sqz.com/africa/1858278/how-ancient-african-societies-managed-pandemics-like-spanish-flu/amp/. Accessed 4 Aug 2020.

Danfulani, U. H. B. (2019). Religion as commodity in a congested Nigerian market: Where does the holy spirit fit within the economy of religion? In J. K. Ayantayo, B. A. Adedibu, & B. O. Igboin (Eds.), *African Pentecostalism: Probity and accountability* (pp. 1–28). Adekunle Ajasin University Press.

Dede, S. (2020). NCDC guidelines and Abba Kyari's burial. https://www.google.com/amp/s/www.pulse.ng/news/local/ncdc-guidelines-and-abba-kyaris-burial-explainer/gy2wzfh.amp. Accessed 5 Aug 2020.

Ezekwonna, F. C. (2005). *African communitarian ethic: The basis for the moral conscience and autonomy of the individual – Igbo culture as a case study.* Peter Lang.

Folorunsho-Francis, A. (2020). Bodies of covid-19 can't be claimed for burial – Lai Mohammed. *The Punch,* April 3. https://healthwise.punchng.com/bodies-of-covid-19-victims-cant-be-claimed-for-burial-lai-mohammed/. Accessed 26 June 2020.

Gardiner, M. Q. (2016). Reforming philosophy of religion: Some methodological cautions. *Method & Theory in the Study of Religion, 28*(1), 54–67.

Gehman, R. (2013). *African traditional religion in the light of the Bible.* Africa Christian Textbooks.

Heaton, M., & Falola, T. (2014). Global explanations versus local interpretations: The historiography of the influenza pandemic of 1918-19 in Africa. https://doi.org/10.1353/hia.2006.0014

Idowu, E. B. (1973). *African traditional religion: A definition.* SCM Press Ltd.

Igboin, B. O. (2003). *An examination of mythology among the Iuleha of Edo State.* Unpublished M. A. Dissertation, University of Ibadan.

Igboin, B. O. (2011). Human rights in the perspective of traditional Africa: A cosmotheandric approach. *SOPHIA: International Journal of Philosophy of Religion, Metaphysical Theology and Ethics, 50*(1), 159–173.

Igboin, B. O. (2013). How dialectical spirituality influences the perception and pursuit of human rights in Africa. In D. Plevak (Ed.), *Human rights: Theory, developments and ethical issues* (pp. 75–96). Nova Publishers.

Igboin, B. O. (2014). Revisiting the basis of the metaphysics of ancestorship in contemporary Africa. In D. Oguntola-Laguda (Ed.), *Death and life after death in African philosophy and religions: A multidisciplinary engagement* (pp. 79–97). Africa Institute for Culture, Dialogue, Peace and Tolerance Studies.

Igboin, B. O. (2016). The Cremation Law of Lagos: Mediating between law and African religious traditions in contemporary Nigeria. Presented at the first Global African Indigenous Religions Conference organised by Pan African Strategic and Policy Research Group (PANASTRAG) in collaboration with Obafemi Awolowo University, held at the Obafemi Awolowo University, Ile—Ife, 8–13 August.

Igboin, B. O. (2019). When I die: The politics of the metaphysics of death. In C. K. Ikwuemesi, C. Ugwu, & C. Agbo (Eds.), *Dying, death and the politics of after-death in Africa: Studies of some Nigerian communities* (pp. 241–151). Galda Verlag.

Igboin, B. O., & Igili, O. J. (2015). Like father, unlike son: A reconstruction of the meta-life of Unoka in Chinua Achebe's things fall apart. *Southern Semiotic Review, 5*(1), 143–163.

Jaja, I. F., Anyanwu, M. U., & Jaja, C.-J. I. (2020). Social distancing: How religion, culture and burial ceremony undermine the effort to curb Covid-9 in South Africa. *Emerging Microbes*

& Infections, 9(1), 1077–1079. https://www.tandfonline.com/doi/full/10.1080/22221751.202 0.1769501 . Accessed 26 June 2020.

John, T. (2020). We are still confused as to why coronavirus does not kill Africans – Scientists. https://topniajaplu.com/we-are-still-confused-as-to-why-coronavirus-does-not-kill-africans-scientists/? Accessed 6 Aug 2020.

Kaledzi, I. (2020). Ghana's morgues congested as families shun private burials. https://www.google.com/amp/s/amp.dw.com/en/ghanas-morgues-congested-as-families-shun-private-burials/a-53107337. Accessed 5 Aug 2020.

Kung, H. (1991). *Global responsibility: In search of a New World ethic.* SCM Press.

Kunhiyop, S. W. (2012). *African Christian theology.* ACTS.

Laguda, D. O. (2013). Religion and government policy formulations: A study of the responses of Muslims to the coroner law system in Lagos, Nigeria. *Politics and Religion, 2*(VII), 399–412.

Lugira, A. M. (2009). *World religions: African traditional religion* (3rd ed.). Chelsea House Publishers.

Magesa, L. (1997). *African religion: The moral traditions of abundant life.* Paulines.

Manguvo, A., & Mafuvadze, B. (2015). The impact of traditional and religious practices on the spread of Ebola in West Africa: Time for a strategic shift. *The Pan African Medical Journal, 22*(1). https://doi.org/10.11694/pamj.supp.2015.22.1.6190

Matthews, D. H. (1998). *Honoring the ancestors: An African cultural interpretation of Black religion and literature.* Oxford University Press.

Mbiti, J. S. (1969). *African religions and philosophy.* Heinemann.

Mudimbe, V. Y., & Kilonzo, S. M. (2012). Philosophy of religion on African way of believing. In E. K. Bongmba (Ed.), *The Wiley-Blackwell companion to African religions* (pp. 411–451). Blackwell Publishing Ltd.

News Agency of Nigeria. (2020). Social distancing compulsory at burial of Covid-19 death – LASG. *The Guardian* Nigeria, April 19. https://guardian.ng/news/social-distancing-compulsory-at-burial-of-covid-19-death-lasg/. Accessed 26 June 2020.

Nnoruka, S. I. (2009). *Solidarity: A principle of sociality – A phenomenological-hermeneutical approach in the context of the philosophy of Alfred Schutz and an African culture.* Living Flames Resources.

Nwaiwu, C. (2020). Printing Association faults Anambra Burial Law, says it's suffocating. *Vanguard* (Nigeria), August 5.

Obomeighe, A. A. (2019). *Iuleha history and language studies.* Headmark Publishers.

Odubanjo, D. (2020). The biggest threats to Nigeria managing COVID-19: Panic, politics and indecision. *The Conversation.* https://www.google.com/amp/s/thecoversation.com/amp/the-biggest-threats-to-nigeria-managing-covid-19-panic-politics-and-indecision. Accessed 5 Aug 2020.

Ohadike, D. C. (1981). The influenza pandemic of 1918-19 and the spread of cassava cultivation on the lower Niger: A study in historical linkages. *The Journal of African History, 22*(3), 379–391.

Ohadike, D. C. (1991). Diffusion and physiological responses to the influenza pandemic of 1918-19 in Nigeria. *Social Science & Medicine, 32*(12), 1393–1399.

Oluwasegun, J. M. (2015). Managing epidemic: The British approach to 1918–1919 influenza in Lagos. *Journal of Asian and African Studies* (2015). https://doi.org/10.1177/0021909615587367

Omonisi, A. E. (2020). How Covid-19 pandemic is changing the Africa's elaborate burial rites, mourning and grieving. *The Pan African Medical Journal, 35*(2) https://www.panafrican-medjournal.com/content/series/35/2/81/full/. Accessed 26 June 2020.

Onwubiko, E. (2013). The UnAfricanness of Lagos Cremation Law. *The Nigerian Voice*, July 3. https://www.thenigerianvoice.com/news/117994/the-unafricanness-of-lagos-cremation-law.html. Accessed 26 June 2020.

Panikkar, R. (1982). *Blessed simplicity: The monk as universal archetype.* Seabury.

Panikkar, R. (1993). *The Cosmotheandric experience: Emerging religious consciousness.* Orbis Books.

Parrinder, G. E. (1954). *African traditional religion.* Hutchinson's University Library.

Phillips, H. (2014). Influenza pandemic (Africa). In U. Daniel et al. (Eds.), *1914–1918-online International Encyclopedia of the First World War*. Freie Universitat. https://doi.org/10.15463/ie1418.10431

Sahara Reporters. (2020). Ex-Oyo Governor, Ajimobi, Buried at private residence in Ibadan. saharareporters.com/2020/06/28/ex-oyo-state-governor-ajimobi-buried-private-residence-ibadan. Accessed 5 Aug 2020.

Salazar, H., & Nicholls, R. (2019). *The philosophy of spirituality: Analytical, continental and multicultural approach to a new field of philosophy*. Brill.

Schilbrack, K. (2016). Theorizing religion and the role of philosophy. *Method & Theory in the Study of Religion, 28*(1), 35–38.

Schutz, A. (1967). *The phenomenology of the social world* (G. Walsh & F. Lehnert, Trans.). Northwestern University Press.

Shereen, M. A., Khan, S., Kazmi, A., Bashir, N., & Siddique, R. (2020). COVID-19 infection: Origin, transmission, and characteristics of human coronaviruses. *Journal of Advanced Research, 24*, 91–98.

Shipton, P. (2009). *Mortgaging the ancestors: Ideologies of attachment in Africa*. Yale University Press.

Ter Haar, G. (2011). Religion and human rights: Searching for common ground. In G. Haar (Ed.), *Religion and development: Ways of transforming the world* (pp. 298–314). Hurst & Company.

Turner, G. (2017). *Honoring ancestors in sacred space: The archaeology of an eighteenth-century African-Bahamian cemetery*. UF Press.

Ujumadu, V. (2020). Expensive burials over in Anambra as Obiano accents to new law. *Vanguard* (Nigeria), June 2.

Vaughan, A. (2020). We don't know why so few Covid-19 cases have been reported in Africa. *New Scientist*, March 10.

WHO. (2017). How to conduct safe and dignified burial of a patient who has died from Ebola or Marburg virus disease. WHO_EVD_GUIDANCE_Burials_14.2_eng.pdf.

WHO. (2020a). Pneumonia of unknown cause – China. https://www.who.int/csr/don/05-january-2020-pneumonia-of-unknown-cause%2D%2Dchina/en/. Accessed 6 Aug 2020.

WHO. (2020b). A second COVID-19 case is confirmed in Africa. https://www.afro.who.int/news/second-covid-19-case-confirmed-africa. Accessed 5 Aug 2020.

Zizek, S. (2020). *Pandemic: Covid-19 shakes the world*. Or Books.

Part IV
Psychology of the COVID-19 Crisis

Chapter 14
Psychological Perspectives on COVID-19

Sara Hosseini-Nezhad, Saba Safdar, Pegah Hosseini-Nezhad,
and Lan Anh Nguyen Luu

14.1 Introduction

A substantial body of research confirms the finding that SARS-CoV-2 (the novel coronavirus) and COVID-19 (the disease) have had a significant effect on individuals' psychological wellbeing and response (Browning et al., 2021). It is reported that social distancing, quarantine, self-confinement, and discordance between economic and social status, as well as social media misinformation related to COVID-19, are among the main determinants of atypical feelings of sadness, fear, anger, helplessness, loneliness, and stress and, at worst, may prompt suicidal ideations and attempts (Khan et al., 2020). Similarly, it has been reported that in the long term, both the virus and the national lockdown/quarantine orders may result in panic, anxiety, depression, obsessions, paranoia, hoarding behaviours, as well as post-traumatic stress disorder (PTSD) (Dubey et al., 2020a).

This chapter reviews some of the recent literature on the evolutionary perspective of pathogen avoidance and the terror management theory as frameworks in understanding the psychological consequences of COVID-19. Additionally, the

S. Hosseini-Nezhad (✉)
Doctoral School of Psychology, Faculty of Education and Psychology, Eötvös Loránd University (ELTE), Budapest, Hungary

S. Safdar
University of Guelph, Guelph, ON, Canada
e-mail: ssafdar@uoguelph.ca

P. Hosseini-Nezhad
Semmelweis Medical University (SOTE), Budapest, Hungary

L. A. N. Luu
Faculty of Education and Psychology, Eötvös Loránd University (ELTE), Budapest, Hungary
e-mail: lananh@ppk.elte.hu

© The Author(s), under exclusive license to Springer Nature Switzerland AG 2022
N. Faghih, A. Forouharfar (eds.), *Socioeconomic Dynamics of the COVID-19 Crisis*,
Contributions to Economics, https://doi.org/10.1007/978-3-030-89996-7_14

COVID-19 pandemic's negative mental health consequences (e.g., anxiety disorders, depressive disorders, PTSD, loneliness, addictive behaviours, stigmatization, and domestic violence) will be addressed.

Furthermore, we draw attention to the impact of the COVID-19 pandemic on vulnerable groups (i.e., children, parents, elderly individuals, marginalized groups, COVID-19 patients, etc.) as well as on interpersonal relationships. Finally, we will discuss the COVID-19-related psychological interventions (e.g., cognitive behaviour therapy (CBT))[1] and the immunization (or vaccination) strategies used globally to combat the negative impact of COVID-19 pandemic.

14.2   Methodology

An electronic search – using mainly Google Scholar, ResearchGate, ScienceDirect, the National Center for Biotechnology Information (NCBI), and a basic Google search – was performed to collect the relevant literature. The following string of search terms related to our topic was used and combined using the Boolean operator "AND": "mental health" AND "COVID-19," "mental health" AND "pandemic," "psychological health" AND "COVID-19," "depression" AND "COVID-19," "anxiety" AND "COVID-19," "suicide" AND "COVID-19," and so forth.

Overall, 782 articles were identified using the search terms; however, only 184 studies (e.g., both empirical and theoretical) were included. The remaining articles (598) were rejected due to a wide range of reasons, including those deemed irrelevant to the research topic, unrelated to the health and psychological field, and dated.

14.3   Behavioural Immune System (BIS)

It is believed that the BIS functions as the "first crude line of defence" against the threat of pathogens (Schaller, 2006). Like the physiological adaptive immune system that detects and eliminates pathogenic intruders, the BIS detects the presence of infectious pathogens in the environment, provoking adaptive psychological responses (i.e., emotional and cognitive reactions) to illness and thereby promotes behavioural avoidance of pathogenic agents (Schaller, 2011; Schaller & Park, 2011). Specifically, the BIS entails emotions, cognitions, and behaviours activated by perceiving particular types of stimuli (e.g., a morphologically abnormal look) (Schaller, 2006), which stimulate particular emotions (e.g., disgust) and cognitions (e.g., cues that the abnormal look will induce a disease) and further facilitate behavioural responses (e.g., avoiding/excluding the person with abnormal appearance)

---

[1] CBT is a type of psychotherapy based on the *cognitive model*, which states that individuals' reactions (i.e., emotional, behavioural, and physiological reactions) towards situations are influenced by their thoughts about the situations not the situation per se (Beck, 2011).

(Schaller, 2006). The emotional reaction, disgust, is stated to be the core element of BIS and is aroused not only when individuals perceive things that present real pathogen infectious risks but also when they perceive things that have a superficial resemblance to actual pathogens (Schaller, 2011). BIS has been evolved in order to prevent making false-negative errors (i.e., falsely inferring that a pathogen is not present when in fact they are present), which makes it more vulnerable to the risk of producing tons of false-positive errors (i.e., falsely inferring that a pathogen is present when they are absent) (Schaller & Park, 2011).

Furthermore, activation of BIS carries both costs (e.g., calorie consumption, missing opportunities) and benefits (e.g., detecting and avoiding things/people that bear the possibility of infections) (Schaller, 2006; Schaller & Park, 2011). Since not all contexts bear the same degrees of infection risks, nor all people exhibit similar levels of vulnerability towards infectious diseases, BIS is thus marked by the "functional flexibility" concept (Ackerman et al., 2018; Schaller et al., 2007), which specifies that in situations where people perceive themselves as vulnerable to pathogen infection, they exhibit stronger perceptual sensitivity towards individuals or things that tend to bear a real threat of infection (Schaller, 2011; Schaller & Park, 2011). For example, it is reported that individuals with greater vulnerability perception to infection showed "ethnocentrism"; "xenophobia," favouring in-group contact than out-group contact; "prejudice"; and greater "disgust," with regard to pathogen cues, compared to individuals with lower vulnerability perception to infection (Ackerman et al., 2018; Schaller, 2011; Schaller & Park, 2011). Research has also demonstrated that certain personality traits make individuals more exposed to a pathogen and more vulnerable to infectious diseases such as "extraversion" (i.e., the degree to which individuals are outgoing or not) and "openness to experience" (i.e., curious, take risks, and tend to diverge from cultural norms) (Murray & Schaller, 2016; Schaller & Park, 2011). In line with the rationale of the cost/benefit analysis, individuals who show more emotional distress when the risk of pathogen exposure is high also have lower degrees of extraversion (Murray & Schaller, 2016; Schaller & Park, 2011).

The BIS functional flexibility principle works not only on the individual level but also on a societal level, such that in geographical regions where the prevalence of infectious diseases is higher, human societies are collectively more prone to show psychological behaviours related to disease risk (e.g., higher xenophobia and conformity levels, lower extraversion levels, etc.) or behavioural norms (e.g., using more cooking spices which act as natural antibiotics, less sexually promiscuous behaviour, higher personal hygiene, etc.) (Murray & Schaller, 2016; Schaller & Park, 2011). It is believed that the geographical differences in the prevalence of pathogens are associated with various aspects of cross cultural differences (Murray & Schaller, 2016; Schaller & Park, 2011). For instance, in areas where infectious diseases are more prevalent, cultures are more collectivistic (Fincher et al., 2008; Murray & Schaller, 2016), as it is believed that collectivistic (i.e., high emphasis on tradition and conformity) and individualistic cultures (i.e., tolerant attitudes towards deviance from norms) are likely to arise and persist under ecological conditions marked by higher and lower pathogen prevalence, respectively (Fincher et al., 2008; Schaller & Park, 2011).

Responses to the COVID-19 pandemic can be explained through the BIS, as "pandemics activate a behavioural immune system" (McKay & Asmundson, 2020, p. 110). Study participants (Makhanova & Shepherd, 2020), who perceived themselves as more vulnerable to diseases, manifested stronger reactions towards the threat of COVID-19 (i.e., increased anxiety about COVID-19, a perception that COVID-19 is a greater concern than influenza and that individuals ought to adjust their behaviours to fight against the spread of COVID-19, perceptions that protective behaviours and staying home during illness are important) and higher tendency to engage in preventative behaviours (i.e., more cautious behaviours when shopping, visiting stores less often, and fewer face-to-face encounters). Furthermore, women relative to men showed a higher degree of "germ aversion" (i.e., higher emotional and behavioural reactions to the potential pathogen) and "perceived infectability" traits (i.e., perceiving themselves as more vulnerable to disease); additionally, women reported stronger reactions towards the COVID-19 threat.

Similarly, Shook et al. (2020) assessed whether individual differences regarding the level of perceived vulnerability to disease (i.e., "germ aversion," "perceived infectability," and "pathogen disgust") were correlated with concerns about COVID-19 and engagement in prescribed COVID-19 preventative hygiene behaviours (i.e., social distancing, handwashing, sanitizing, masks wearing, etc.) in a large US sample. The findings indicated that greater levels of germ aversion, perceived infectability, and pathogen disgust were significantly associated with greater concern about COVID-19 and greater preventative hygiene behaviours. Other factors associated with greater concern about COVID-19 were being a woman, older age, and more "liberal," "agreeable," "conscientious," and "open to experience," among other factors. Moreover, being a woman was significantly more related to more frequent handwashing and being a man to higher facemask wearing.

It is stated that cultural context affects how people respond to the threat of COVID-19 (Ryder et al., 2020). For instance, individuals in societies with tight cultures[2] are more inclined to accept and comply with COVID-19 restrictive rules than individuals in loose cultures[3] (Gelfand et al., 2021; Ryder et al., 2020). It has been found that societies with tight cultures (e.g., China, Taiwan, and Vietnam) have been more effective in regulating COVID-19 cases and mortality rates than societies with loose cultures (e.g., Brazil, Spain, and the USA) (Gelfand et al., 2021).

---

[2] Tight cultures "have many strong norms and a low tolerance of deviant behavior" (Gelfand et al., 2011, p. 1100).

[3] Loose cultures "have weak social norms and a high tolerance of deviant behavior" (Gelfand et al., 2011, p.1100).

14.4 The Terror Management Theory (TMT)

The TMT considers all anxieties as essentially originating from the fear of death (Solomon et al., 1991). According to the TMT, self-esteem and cultural viewpoints serve as buffers against anxieties, including death-related anxiety (Greenberg et al., 1986, 1997; Harmon-Jones et al., 1997). The TMT can provide insight into the COVID-19 threat and how people behave in response to it. Pyszczynski et al. (2020) argue that whether or not individuals consciously accept that the coronavirus is significantly threatening or not, the fear of death plays a significant part in directing their attitudes and behaviours associated with the virus (Pyszczynski et al., 2020). The TMT proposes two different terror management defence mechanisms (i.e., "distal" and "proximal" defence) to explain how people cope with death anxiety. The proximal defence entails suppressing conscious thoughts of death via denial or distraction, while the distal defence involves unconscious thoughts of death by reliance on one's "self-esteem" and "cultural worldviews" (Pyszczynski et al., 1999). Some of the proximal defence strategies which people engaged in coping with the pandemic include "diversion-seeking behaviours" (i.e., alcohol use, excessive eating, and TV watching), trivializing threat perception (i.e., underestimating the contagion effect or lethality of the virus as declared by health-care professionals, minimizing the coronavirus by comparing it to other diseases such as influenza, etc.), and more adaptive proximal defence strategies of taking the preventative measures recommended by medical experts to prevent infection (i.e., social distancing, sanitizing, wearing masks, etc.) (Pyszczynski et al., 2020). Examples of distal defences employed by people to cope with the COVID-19 involve individuals' emphasis on increasing self-esteem and affirming their cultural values and political beliefs (i.e., conservatives perceive the virus as less threatening than liberals) (Pyszczynski et al., 2020).

14.5 Psychological/Behavioural Reactions

14.5.1 Anxiety

Anxiety is the typical reaction to stressful circumstances, and the COVID-19 pandemic has created substantial distress globally (Rehman et al., 2021; Roy et al., 2020). A systematic review and meta-analysis (Salari et al., 2020) among the general population, mainly in Asia and Europe (e.g., China, Egypt, Iran, Italy, the UK, etc.), reported that the prevalence of stress was 29.6% and that of anxiety was 31.9% during the COVID-19 outbreak. A more extensive systematic review and meta-analysis (Santabárbara et al., 2020) among 161,556 people, across 21 different countries (e.g., Argentina, Australia, Austria, Bangladesh, China, Egypt, El Salvador, Germany, Greece, India, Iran, Ireland, Israel, Italy, Mexico, Peru, Portugal, Saudi Arabia, Spain, Turkey, and the UK), found that the prevalence of anxiety among the general population during the pandemic was 25%. Another pooled prevalence rate of anxiety and stress during the COVID-19 among 113,285 individuals from a total of 16 studies (e.g., 11 studies from China, 2 from India, and 1 from Italy, Spain, and Iran) was found to be 35% and 53%, respectively (Lakhan et al., 2020). In the following, we present examples of various types of anxieties that people experienced during the pandemic.

14.5.1.1 Generalized Anxiety Disorder (GAD)

GAD is a type of anxiety disorder marked by pervasive worries almost every day for at least 6 months about various aspects of day-to-day life and is accompanied by such symptoms as fatigue, restlessness, poor concentration, irritability, sleeping problems, etc. (American Psychiatric Association [APA], 2013).

Huang and Zhao (2020) found a high prevalence of GAD among the people in China during the pandemic, with a higher prevalence among younger participants and those who spent a lot of time focusing on COVID-19. The prevalence rates of GAD among adults in Ireland during the first stage of COVID-19 quarantine orders indicated that more than a quarter of the participants screened positive for GAD or depression, with the risk factors identified as being younger, female, encountering wage loss due to COVID-19, seeing themselves and/or their loved ones infected with the virus, and higher perceived risk of viral contamination (Hyland et al., 2020).

Meanwhile, the COVID-19 pandemic's impact on a large sample population in Cyprus revealed that over half of the participants experienced anxiety symptoms (41% mild GAD and 23.1% moderate-severe GAD) (Solomou & Constantinidou, 2020). Similar to the aforementioned studies, in this study, women and younger individuals were at higher risk of increased anxiety symptoms. Some of the other risk factors included being a student and unemployed, having a previous psychiatric illness, demonstrating higher compliance with safety measures against COVID-19 (i.e., personal hygiene), and experiencing higher levels of dissatisfaction with the quality of life.

Worries or stress levels concerning COVID-19 (i.e., getting COVID-19, dying from COVID-19, family members getting COVID-19, etc.) were found among Americans and Israelis (i.e., health-care workers, students, teachers, etc.) who reported more worries about their family getting infected by COVID-19 rather than themselves getting infected. Additionally, their worries concerning COVID-19 significantly correlated with reaching sufficient criteria for GAD (Barzilay et al., 2020). Various studies also found generalized anxiety symptoms during COVID-19 among Germans (Bäuerle et al., 2020; Petzold et al., 2020), Chinese (Cao et al., 2020; Gao et al., 2020), Bangladeshis (Islam et al., 2020), and Italians (Gualano et al., 2020).

14.5.1.2 Health Anxiety (HA)

HA can be defined as extreme and unnecessary worries about one's own health (Bailer et al., 2015), and in DSM-5, a high level of HA is among the diagnostic criteria for somatic symptom disorder (SSD),[4] as well as illness anxiety disorder (IAD)[5] (APA, 2013).

Several studies investigated HA among individuals during COVID-19. During a virus outbreak, people with high HA engage in compulsive behaviours such as excessive handwashing, social isolation, and panic buying (Asmundson & Taylor, 2020b). Women and people with current or past mental health disorders and chronic illnesses all had greater levels of trait HA, according to one study on Turkish people (Özdin & Özdin, 2020). Landi et al. (2020) carried out a research in Italy during the COVID-19 lockdown, and the findings revealed that higher HA was significantly correlated with negative mental health outcomes (i.e., depression, anxiety, and "peritraumatic distress"), and this correlation was mediated by global psychological flexibility processes (i.e., "defusion," "committed action," and "acceptance"). In other words, both defusion (i.e., distancing and observing negative thoughts) and committed action (i.e., committing to achieve one's goals) lowered the adverse impacts of trait HA on psychological health, while acceptance (i.e., accepting negative thoughts) increased the negative impacts of trait health anxiety. Furthermore, being younger and female were more significantly associated with heightened HA and adverse psychological health.

In another study (Jungmann & Witthöft, 2020) which was conducted in Germany with a general population, trait HA significantly moderated the relationship between COVID-19-associated cyberchondria (i.e., compulsive checking up on COVID-19 on the internet, distress due to web searches, etc.) and the current level of anxiety about the coronavirus. The influence of COVID-19-related experiences and stress on five psychological health outcomes, including HA among American adults, indicated that higher levels of perceived stress related to COVID-19 strongly predicted higher levels of HA (Gallagher et al., 2020). HA was shown to be a significant predictor of increased fear of the COVID-19 pandemic across individuals representing 28 nations (e.g., Austria, Canada, Chile, India, Norway, Russia, the UK, United Arab Emirates, the USA, etc.) (Mertens et al., 2020).

Among the US residents (White, Black, Hispanic, Asian, and mixed ethnic background), HA, COVID-19 anxiety (i.e., physiological symptoms triggered by COVID-19-associated information and thoughts), and COVID-19 anxiety syndrome (e.g., "avoidance," "worrying," and "threat monitoring") mediated the relationship between the big five personality traits and the depression and generalized anxiety symptoms (Nikčević et al. 2020). Four of the big five personality traits (agreeableness, conscientiousness, extraversion, and openness) and neuroticism

---

[4] A high level of anxiety about one's symptoms and health usually present for more than 6 months.

[5] A high level of anxiety about having or getting a serious illness, without the presence (or mild presence) of somatic symptoms, for at least 6 months.

were correlated with HA, COVID-19 anxiety, and depression and generalized anxiety symptoms negativity and positively, respectively. Additionally, a positive correlation between HA, COVID-19 anxiety, and COVID-19 anxiety syndrome was observed (Nikčević et al. 2020).

14.5.1.3 Coronaphobia

The outbreak of COVID-19 has increased fear globally (Ahorsu et al., 2020). The terms "fear of COVID-19" and "coronaphobia" have been used in the literature to refer to the fear of becoming infected by the novel coronavirus (Arora et al., 2020). During pandemics, many people express several fears, including the fear of getting infected, of interacting with contaminated fomites, of others who may transmit the virus (i.e., xenophobia), and of the social and economic outcomes of the pandemic (i.e., job loss) (Taylor et al., 2020). The research findings on the psychological responses to the past epidemics and pandemics imply different psychological factors to play roles in coronaphobia, such as intolerance of uncertainty, perceived susceptibility to an illness, and anxiety tendencies (Asmundson & Taylor, 2020a). Mertens et al. (2020) have found that the significant predictors of increased fear about the COVID-19 pandemic among the participants from 28 countries included psychological vulnerability variables (e.g., "intolerance of uncertainty," individual proneness to worrying, and HA), voluntary exposure to the media about COVID-19, one's "general health," "perceived control" (i.e., preventing being infected by the virus), and perception of risk for loved ones. Coronaphobia is also reported to have been prevalent among frontline nurses in the Philippines, with females, married, full-time nurses having higher anxiety regarding coronavirus (coronaphobia) (Labrague & De Los Santos, 2020). Furthermore, data from a large representative adult population in the USA indicated that participants scored a high level of fear of coronavirus (7 out of 10), a high level of clinical depression, and a mild moderate anxiety (Fitzpatrick et al. 2020). Compared to their counterparts, females, Asians, Hispanics, non-natives, married individuals, and families with children displayed a higher degree of COVID-19 fear.

Meanwhile, Ahorsu et al. (2020) have developed a psychometric assessment tool (Fear of COVID-19 Scale, FCV-19S), assessing the fear of COVID-19 among the general population in Iran. The tool was shown to have robust psychometric properties and was reliable and valid in measuring the fear of the COVID-19. The scale was reported to be effective in providing important information regarding the fear of COVID-19 and thus assist public health initiatives in reducing people's fear, stigma, and anxiety connected to it (Ahorsu et al., 2020). The Fear of COVID-19 Scale has been validated in Italian (Soraci et al., 2020), Arabic (Alyami et al., 2020), Amharic (Elemo et al., 2020), Bangla (Sakib et al., 2020), French (Mailliez et al., 2020), Hebrew (Bitan et al., 2020), and Spanish (Huarcaya-Victoria et al., 2020) samples, to name a few.

Moreover, one Turkish study (Pak et al., 2021) presented evidence that the association between the intolerance of uncertainty and emotional eating was mediated by fear of COVID-19 and depression, with intolerance of uncertainty having a significant, positive, and direct impact on the fear of COVID-19. In addition, fear of COVID-19 was shown to positively predict depression.

One meta-analysis study (Şimşir et al., 2021) (e.g., studies conducted in Bangladesh, Brazil, China, Greece, Hong Kong, Iran, Israel, Italy, Japan, Malaysia, Pakistan, Peru, Saudi Arabia, Spain, Turkey, the UK, United Arab Emirates, and the USA) systematically examined the relationships between fear of COVID-19 and mental health conditions (e.g., "anxiety," "depression," "stress," "distress," "traumatic stress," and "insomnia") among the general population. The result indicated a significant and positive relationship between COVID-19 fear with all the mental health conditions; COVID-19 fear strongly correlated with anxiety, distress, and traumatic stress, moderately correlated with stress and depression, and modestly (a small correlation) correlated with insomnia.

14.5.2 Post-traumatic Stress Disorder (PTSD)

One of the main PTSD criteria in DSM-5 (APA, 2013) is described as "exposure to actual or threatened death, serious injury or sexual violence" (APA, 2013, p. 271). Other criteria include symptoms, such as flashbacks, intrusive distressing memories, continuous negative emotions (i.e., anger, fear, horror, shame), concentration problems, hypervigilance, sleeping problems, the inability to feel positive feelings (i.e., happiness, satisfaction), etc. (APA, 2013).

PTSD is expected to arise in some people due to the COVID-19 pandemic (Kenneavy, 2020). Several studies have investigated COVID-19-related PTSD among the general population, students, and health-care professionals. Tang et al. (2020) assessed the PTSD and depression prevalence and psychological outcomes among a large sample of home-quarantined Chinese college students shortly after the COVID-19 outbreak in China. Feeling extreme fear was the most significant risk factor for developing PTSD and depressive symptoms among the students, followed by other factors such as residing in severely hit regions, having a short night's sleep, and being in the final university year.

Within the first month of the COVID-19 outbreak, a 12.8% prevalence of PTSD was observed among Chinese citizens between 14 and 35 years old (Liang et al., 2020). Participants' negative coping styles mediated the relationship between psychological distress and PTSD, while gender moderated this relationship. Additionally, the prevalence of PTSD among females and males was significantly intensified with a rise in psychological distress; however, it was even more intensified among males (Liang et al., 2020).

One month after the outbreak of the COVID-19, PTSD symptoms were experienced by 4.6% of the people in China (i.e., among the general public, including some health-care workers, as well as among a few suspected and confirmed COVID-19 patients) (Sun et al. 2020b). Some of the factors related to the severity of the symptoms were being a woman, experiencing poor sleep quality, and being a high-risk individual. The prevalence of COVID-19-related PTSD symptoms among the Italian population was 7.6%, and sleep quality, generalized anxiety, and psychological distress were all significant predictors of the level of PTSD symptoms (Casagrande et al., 2020). Similarly, in another research in Italy (Forte et al., 2020) using a large sample size, the prevalence of PTSD was 29%, and a significant relationship was found between COVID-19 PTSD scores and general distress and sleep disturbance. In a general population in Ireland, a prevalence of 17.7% for PTSD was found, with individuals scoring high on COVID-19-related PTSD demonstrating anxiety/depression (Karatzias et al., 2020). PTSD has also been reported among people in Tunisia during the pandemic, and factors such as being a woman, exposed to confirmed COVID-19 cases, as well excessive media consumption about COVID-19 were all associated with a higher tendency for the development of PTSD (Fekih-Romdhane et al., 2020). PTSD symptoms have been reported among health-care professionals (HCP) in Greece (Blekas et al., 2020), with women meeting significantly higher criteria for displaying symptoms of PTSD (i.e., intrusive memories, avoidance, and hypervigilance) compared to men. Health-care workers in India and Singapore also reported PTSD ($n = 67$, 7.4% of HCW) during the pandemic (Chew et al., 2020). Additionally, physical symptoms (e.g., headache) experienced in the earlier months of the outbreak were revealed to be significantly related to other psychological outcomes, including PTSD (Chew et al., 2020).

14.5.3   Hoarding Behaviours

During a crisis, people can experience a high urge to hoard (VanDyke et al., 2020). Hoarding behaviour refers to the act of excessively accumulating assets for later use beyond what is required for current necessities and is an evolutionary and innate response to the perception of a threat (Kirk & Rifkin, 2020). As the COVID-19 pandemic erupted, significant shortages of items and supplies were followed (Long & Khoi, 2020). People started to hoard certain items such as food, hand sanitizers, toilet papers, and face masks (Laato et al., 2020). According to one research (Garbe et al., 2020), the most significant predictor for toilet paper hoarding was a perceived threat, meaning that people accumulated more toilet papers if they felt more threatened by COVID-19. Personality traits (i.e., "emotionality" and "conscientiousness") were reported to be the other predictors of toilet paper hoarding (Garbe et al., 2020). Additionally, personality aspects of emotionality (i.e., "fearfulness," "anxiety," "dependence," and "sentimentality") were shown to increase the feeling of perceived threats, which subsequently facilitated toilet paper hoarding (Garbe et al., 2020). Furthermore, participants with higher conscientiousness (i.e., "organization," "diligence," "perfectionism," and "prudence") were also shown to hoard more toilet paper (Garbe et al., 2020).

Nowak et al. (2020) found a positive correlation between the "Dark Triad traits" (i.e., "psychopathy," "Machiavellianism," and "narcissism") and "collective narcissism" (i.e., "agentic" and "communal") with increased hoarding behaviours (i.e., stockpiling foods, toilet paper, masks, etc.) during COVID-19. People not only hoarded foods and hygiene products during the pandemic but also hoarded guns and ammunition in certain countries. The number of weapon sales has increased in the USA and Canada, reportedly due to justifications of self-defence among Americans and fear of shortages among Canadians (Schwartz, 2020).

14.5.4   Depression

During the COVID-19 pandemic, the prevalence of depression has increased as a result of stressful situations, including financial instability, job loss, and social distancing (Zarefsky, 2020). It is reported that a large number of people might develop clinical depression due to the COVID-19 pandemic (Kanter & Manbeck, 2020). According to DSM-5 (APA, 2013), people with major depressive disorders or clinical depression should experience five or more symptoms – among which are depressed mood, loss of interest in activities, significant weight gain/loss, insomnia/hypersomnia, fatigue, lack of concentration, etc. – for at least 2 weeks; additionally, one of those symptoms must at least include a "depressed mood" or "loss of interest or pleasure."

The depressive symptoms among a nationally representative group of US adults before and during the COVID-19 pandemic indicated that, generally, the prevalence of symptoms of depression was more than three times higher during COVID-19 than the pre-pandemic (Ettman et al., 2020). A meta-analysis of 12 studies conducted in different places (namely, China, Denmark, India, Italy, the UK, and Vietnam) suggested that the prevalence of depression from the pooled samples during the pandemic was 25% – seven times more than the worldwide prevalence rate of depression in 2017 (3.44%) (Bueno-Notivol et al., 2020). One global study (Shah et al., 2021) among individuals from the USA (28.3%), Pakistan (26.2%), Canada (10.8%), the UK (7.8%), and other countries (26.9%) (e.g., Australia, Costa Rica, Finland, Germany, Greece, Hungary, Ireland, Lebanon, Malaysia, Netherlands, Norway, Oman, Qatar, Romania, Saudi Arabia, Spain, Sri Lanka, Switzerland, Trinidad, Turkey, the UAE) reported that 58.6% of the respondents displayed signs of depression ("mild depression" [16.1%], "moderate depression" [20.1%], "severe depression" [10.8%], and "extremely severe depression" [11.7%]) during the COVID-19 pandemic. Depression level was significantly higher among students, unemployed, and those residing in Canada, the UK, and Pakistan, respectively (Shah et al., 2021).

14.5.4.1   Suicide

It has been reported that with the spread of COVID-19 pandemic, suicide rates will increase (Gunnell et al., 2020). Various cases of pandemic-related suicides in different countries, such as Bangladesh, Germany, India, Italy, the UK, and the

USA, have been reported (Sher, 2020). For instance, a Bangladeshi young man committed suicide by hanging himself after only having cold symptoms and fever. An autopsy later revealed he, in fact, did not have COVID-19. His suicide was in response to others around him and he himself, thinking he was infected, as well as the people's extreme negative reactions directed towards him (Mamun & Griffiths, 2020). The causative factors of COVID-19-related suicide among 69 cases in India were mainly pertained to fear of COVID-19 infection, followed by financial problems, feelings of loneliness, isolation and quarantine measures, COVID-19 job-related anxiety, and being diagnosed with COVID-19 (Dsouza et al., 2020). In contrast, in Pakistan, the majority of the causes of suicide among the 16 cases were reported to be a lockdown-related economic recession, while only a few were due to fear of COVID-19 infection (Mamun & Ullah, 2020). Furthermore, an analysis of pandemic-related suicidal ideations among the US population showed 10.7% of the participants had seriously considered suicide in a month preceding the survey, and suicidal ideations were significantly higher among those 18–24 years of age, minority groups (i.e., Hispanics and Black Americans), "unpaid adult caregivers," and "essential workers" (Czeisler et al., 2020). Worldwide report of suicide cases, mainly from India, among health-care professionals (i.e., doctors, nurses, and paramedics) revealed that infection with the virus was the most frequently reported cause of suicide, followed by job-related anxiety, fear of infection, fear of spreading the virus to others, inability to save patients, and the anxiety of witnessing COVID-19 patients psychological suffering and deaths (Jahan et al., 2021).

14.5.5   Loneliness/Social Isolation

Imposed quarantines or isolation policies to prevent the spread of the novel coronavirus around the world – which incorporate lockdowns, gathering restrictions and travel ban, and event cancellations – have caused psychological problems, especially for vulnerable groups (i.e., children, adolescents, women, elderly people, minorities, groups with lower socio-economic status (SES), and individuals with a previous psychiatric illness) (Usher et al., 2020). Social isolation related to COVID-19 can lead to various psychological health conditions – even in individuals with no pre-existing psychological problems – such as depression, panic, anxiety, insomnia, and loneliness (Usher et al., 2020).

Many studies have investigated the loneliness and social isolation related to the COVID-19 pandemic. During the initial lockdown months, a survey of adults in the USA showed an increase in the level of loneliness, with individuals in shelters scoring the highest (Killgore et al., 2020). Loneliness during the outbreak has also been reported among people in the UK (Groarke et al., 2020). The prevalence of loneliness among nationally representative data of 15,530 people in the UK was 35.9% during COVID-19, with younger individuals, women, and those who currently experience or previously experienced COVID-19-related symptoms displaying higher levels of loneliness; by contrast, those who had a paid job and a partner experienced a lower level of loneliness compared to their counterparts (Li & Wang, 2020). Loneliness as a result of social distancing measures was reported to pose the most significant risk factor for depression and anxiety during the COVID-19 outbreak among people in Israel (Palgi et al., 2020). Similarly, loneliness was significantly associated with the physical and mental health of residents in Hong Kong (Tso & Park, 2020). Loneliness has also been observed during the COVID-19 outbreak among old people, including Dutch citizens (Van Tilburg et al., 2020), Hong Kong citizens (Wong et al., 2020), and Austrians (Heidinger & Richter, 2020).

Contrary to the expectations that social restriction measures would impact loneliness to some extent, Luchetti et al. (2020) did not find a significant change in loneliness in response to the COVID-19 measures among Americans as they perceived increased social and emotional support.

14.5.6 Addictive Behaviours

The COVID-19 pandemic is expected to increase addictive behaviours (i.e., alcohol consumption, smoking, and internet addiction) (Sun et al. 2020a), as such addictive behaviours were shown to have increased among people in China during the pandemic (Sun et al. 2020a). While a literature review (Mallet et al., 2021) reported that there is a significant risk of rising substance use disorder during the lockdown, those with opioid use disorder are particularly vulnerable to withdrawal and relapse. Similarly, another literature review (Dubey et al. 2020b) reported an increase in substance abuse (i.e., alcohol, opioid, and cigarette) and behavioural addiction (e.g., internet addiction) during the COVID-19 pandemic and the lockdown.

Conversely, Auer et al. (2020) found an overall decrease in gambling behaviour among online players (sports bettors) from Sweden, Germany, Finland, and Norway during the COVID-19. The amount of wagering among the sports bettors significantly declined during the pandemic compared to pre-pandemic, reportedly because players had less money to gamble as their income dropped due to the pandemic, or did not choose to gamble in front of their family members, or even chose to invest more time on family and other tasks (i.e., gardening, home decoration) (Auer et al., 2020).

A study on internet-related activities (i.e., smartphone and social media use and gaming) among elementary school children in China (median age = 10 years old) before the COVID-19 pandemic and following COVID-19-school closure indicated that the amount of time children used smartphones and social media significantly increased; however, no significant increase in gaming was observed (Chen et al., 2021). Furthermore, children whose level of internet activities increased by 15 or 30 minutes a day demonstrated an elevated level of psychological distress (Chen et al., 2021).

14.5.7 Potential Consequences of Psychological/
Behavioural Reactions

14.5.7.1 Stigmatization

History has shown that epidemic outbreaks have been associated with increased stigma, discrimination, and xenophobia (Villa et al., 2020), and these are all continuously increasing as a consequence of COVID-19 (The United Nations Department of Global Communications [DGC], 2020). Stigma can give rise to stereotyping, labelling, and discrimination and can occur when individuals associate a disease such as COVID-19 with a specific group of people or nationality (Centers for Disease Control and Prevention [CDC], 2020). Individuals who might face stigma during the pandemic include racial and ethnic minorities, those with COVID-19, health-care workers (CDC, 2020), and marginalized people (such as the homeless and migrant workers) (Bhattacharya et al., 2020).

There has been an increase in discrimination towards Asians during the COVID-19 pandemic (Roberto et al., 2020). There are reports of xenophobia against Asians in Australia, Canada, New Zealand, the USA, and across Europe (including Croatia, Finland, France, Germany, Hungary, Italy, and the UK) (Roberto et al., 2020). COVID-19 has facilitated the propagation of racism, leading to increased insecurity and xenophobia; this might be linked to the growth of hate crimes against Asians during the pandemic (Gover et al., 2020).

Various cases of COVID-related stigmatization of health-care providers, people with COVID-19, and recovered patients have occurred worldwide – with health-care professionals being prevented from using public transit, insulted, physically attacked, and receiving eviction orders from their rental homes (Bagcchi, 2020). Although there have been reports of stigmatization against health-care workers, it is noteworthy to mention that there are also reports that the pandemic has made the work of the health-care workers become prominently more visible to people to the point that they are being regarded as heroes (Hennekam et al., 2020).

14.5.7.2 Domestic Violence

Domestic violence is an abusive behaviour used by one person against another to obtain or exert power and includes violence against an intimate partner (through stalking, sexual, physical, and psychological violence), a child (through neglect, psychological, sexual, and physical abuse), and the elderly (through financial, sexual, physical, and intentional neglect) (Huecker & Smock, 2020).

Approximately 1 out of 3 women (35%) worldwide have experienced intimate partner violence (IPV) (World Health Organization [WHO], 2017), which happens to people of various ethnicities, cultures, genders, SES, sexual orientations, and religions (Evans et al., 2020). All types of violence, especially domestic violence against women and girls, have increased since the COVID-19 pandemic (UN

Women, n.d.). The rate of domestic violence against women after the COVID-19 outbreak escalated in numerous countries such as China (300%), Brazil (50%), Cyprus, France, New Zealand (30%), Spain (20%), and the UK (25%) (Noman et al., 2021).

Since the start of lockdown in Peru (Agüero, 2020), domestic violence-related calls for help have increased by 48%. Meanwhile, IPV-related homicides against women have increased in the UK and Mexico as a result of COVID-19 restrictions; additionally, the lockdown has decreased women's capability to escape their abusive partners (Valera, 2020). In Canada, domestic and IPV still keep increasing during the second wave of the pandemic, reporting 20,334 women's domestic violence calls between October 1, 2020, and December 31, 2020, compared to 12,352 during the same time span the previous year (Thompson, 2021). This is attributed to reduced possibilities for women to escape their homes and seek support and connections with family and friends during the pandemic (Thompson, 2021).

14.5.7.3 Interpersonal Relationship Problems

The COVID-19 pandemic has unusually altered interpersonal relationships, compelling people to live closer to certain individuals and further away from others (Y.-L. Liu, 2020). Quarantine life has required close and persistent connection with families and spouses; however, it has created isolation from friends and communities (Y.-L. Liu, 2020). The quarantine impact on various Chinese citizens' relationship types (i.e., with partners, friends, local community inhabitants, Chinese in China, and Chinese abroad) indicated that participants were most likely to report their partnership enhanced since the pandemic. However, this did not apply to those partners who displayed the highest distress level since increased psychological distress was correlated with a decline in an intimate partnership. Respondents in other relationship types (e.g., friends, local community inhabitants, Chinese in China, and Chinese outside of China) were most likely to report a decline in their relationships. For these relationships – except for intimate partnership – elevated distress and being in quarantine were positively correlated with relationship enhancement (Goodwin et al., 2020).

Satisfactions and changes in intimate relationships before and during the pandemic, relationship causal attribution (i.e., the presumed reason for the negative spouse behaviour), as well as "responsibility attribution" (i.e., perception about spouse's behaviours as deliberate, egocentric, and reprehensible) were investigated among US residents (Williamson, 2020). The results did not reveal any significant changes in relationship satisfaction and causal attributions over time; however, overall, responsibility attribution declined significantly. Participants with more positive coping mechanisms and less conflict had elevated relationship satisfaction, and their causal and responsibility attributions declined.

14.5.8   Vulnerable Populations

14.5.8.1   Children/Adolescents

COVID-19 has globally influenced people's lives; however, the virus has had a more significant influence on children and adolescents' psychosocial development compared to adults (Singh et al., 2020). Lockdown, quarantine, and social distancing measures, uncertainties about the pandemic, long-term school closures, parental stress, and deaths of loved ones have impacted the mental health of children and adolescents (Imran et al., 2020). During the pandemic, children have experienced poor sleep and appetite, high agitation, a lack of attention, clingier and more dependent behaviours, uncertainty, and separation anxiety (Singh et al., 2020). Until now, there has been little research investigating the prevalence of psychological disorders among children and adolescents during the pandemic; however, the existing research has revealed an increase in depression and anxiety among children and adolescents (Racine et al., 2020). Chen et al. (2020) examined depression and anxiety among 1036 quarantined children and teenagers aged 6 to 15 years in China, and the result revealed 11.8% of participants with depression, 18.9% with anxiety, and 6.6% with both depression and anxiety. During the pandemic, the psychological impact of quarantine among 121 children and adolescents between the ages of 9 and 18 in India indicated that children and adolescents in quarantine suffered higher psychological distress than those not quarantined, with "worry" (68.6%), "helplessness" (66.1%), and "fear" (62.0%) being the most predominant feelings encountered in quarantine (Saurabh & Ranjan, 2020).

14.5.8.2   Parents/Families

The COVID-19 pandemic has created anxiety for most parents and pregnant mothers, and those with young children have experienced even greater anxiety and depression (Roos & Tomfohr-Madsen, 2020). An analysis of the prevalence of anxiety and depression among mothers with children aged 0–8 years old (including expecting mothers) during the pandemic indicated clinical anxiety and depression among mothers of children between the ages of 0 and 18 months (anxiety 36.3%, depression 33.2%), 18 months and 4 years (anxiety 32.6%, depression 42.5%), and 5 and 8 years (anxiety 29.6%, depression 43.4%) (Cameron et al., 2020).

A national survey in the USA (Patrick et al., 2020) of parents of children younger than 18 years old indicated that since the start of the pandemic, the families' mental health and children's behavioural health were negatively impacted. Additionally, families experienced medical care delays, loss of routine child care, and more food insecurity (i.e., food affordability) during the pandemic (Patrick et al., 2020).

14.5.8.3 The Elderly

The elderly are highly impacted by the COVID-19 pandemic since old age is directly related to a case fatality rate (Kar, 2020). The idea that the elderly are especially vulnerable to COVID-19 can lead to fear among old people (Dubey et al. 2020a). Additionally, isolation and social distancing aggravate mental illnesses and increase the likelihood of depression and anxiety among old individuals (Fontes et al., 2020). Other reasons behind the negative impact of the COVID-19 pandemic on the elderly's mental health involved the replacement of mental health care by telemedicine during the pandemic since most elderly individuals have restricted access or are unable to work with smartphones and the internet and the infeasibility to reach their outpatient clinics to receive their prescription due to quarantine measures and restrictions on public transport (Tsamakis et al., 2021). Furthermore, the media have depicted COVID-19 as an elderly illness leading to stigma, stereotyping, and discrimination towards them, contributing to their enhanced isolation (Tsamakis et al., 2021).

14.5.8.4 Marginalized Groups (i.e., Refugees, Immigrants, and Homeless Individuals)

Refugees, immigrants, and visible minorities are at higher risk of getting infected with the novel coronavirus as they tend to live in densely populated settings with limited access to efficient health care (Kluge et al., 2020; Ryder et al., 2020). The uncertainties following migration in terms of immigration/refugee status, healthcare benefits, the lack of a job, and unfamiliarity with the guidelines for hospital admission can all influence the psychological health of immigrants or refugees, and these uncertainties are further exacerbated by the pandemic-related uncertainties (Sieffien et al., 2020). It is suggested that the COVID-19 pandemic and its health and social impacts – including social isolation, quarantine, fear of illness and death for family members back home, food and medicine insecurity, and a lack of trust in health services due to unfamiliarity with the host language – may trigger past traumas among refugees, hence worsening their psychological health (Rees & Fisher, 2020).

Another vulnerable group is homeless individuals, who are very susceptible to contracting COVID-19 because they live in crowded areas, lack access to healthcare services, and have poor health status (Lima et al., 2020; Perri et al., 2020; Tsai & Wilson, 2020). Their greater risk of coronavirus exposure may adversely impact their psychological health (Tsai & Wilson, 2020). The prevalence of psychological disorders during the pandemic (i.e., substance use disorders, anxiety disorders, affective disorders, psychotic disorders, and dual disorders) among a group of homeless people in a province in Spain was 63%, with substance use disorders being the most prevalent disorder (Martin et al., 2020).

14.5.8.5 People with Pre-existing Psychiatric Disorders

Individuals with pre-existing mental health illnesses are more vulnerable to aggravated psychological disorders due to COVID-19, regardless of the type of mental illness (Mental Health America [MHA], n.d.). People with previous psychological disorders are particularly "sensitive" to lockdown, physical distancing, food accessibility, and overall disruption of their everyday life (Johnson, 2020). It has been reported that the increase in relapse rates is common for all previous psychological disorders during COVID-19 (Chatterjee et al., 2020). Based on an analysis of a representative sample of adults in the USA and Canada, those people with preexisting psychological disorders (i.e., anxiety or mood-related disorders) were more adversely impacted by higher COVID-related stress, self-isolation distress, contamination fear, xenophobia, traumatic stress, and so on, compared to previously healthy individuals (Asmundson et al., 2020).

14.5.8.6 Health-Care Workers (HCWs)

HCWs, particularly those who directly provide care to an individual with confirmed or suspected COVID-19, are under extreme pressure from COVID-19 as a result of the high risk of becoming infected, insufficient protection, isolation, perceived stigma, and being negatively evaluated by patients. Hence, the likelihood that they suffer from psychological issues (i.e., anxiety, fear, insomnia, or depression) increases (Que et al., 2020). A literature review (Spoorthy et al., 2020) on COVID-19-related psychological problems encountered by HCWs indicates that health-care workers have experienced a significant level of anxiety, depression, and insomnia due to the pandemic; some of the factors that correlated with their increased psychological problems included age, gender, profession, workplace, lack of social support, self-efficacy, etc.

14.5.8.7 COVID-19 Patients/Survivors

As a result of the rapid increase in COVID-19-related death rates, those being diagnosed with COVID-19 have been facing mental issues such as anxiety and depression (Zhang et al. 2020b). Anxiety and depression were also reported among COVID-19 patients in China, in addition to poor quality of sleep (Dai et al., 2020). Patients continue to experience psychological problems after recovery. Psychiatric symptoms among 402 adult COVID-19 survivors indicated high rates of PTSD, depression, anxiety, insomnia, and obsessive-compulsive symptoms (Gennaro Mazza et al., 2020).

Similarly, clinical depression and anxiety and a few suicidal attempts were reported among COVID-19 survivors in China (Mei et al., 2021); additionally, mental health issues were significantly greater among COVID-19 patients than in the general population. Some of the risk factors that raised the likelihood of more serious psychological health problems were being a woman, retested positive for novel coronavirus, living alone, and having comorbid physical disorders and low levels of education and wage (Mei et al., 2021).

14.5.9   Interventions

There are new effective psychological interventions that must be implemented and delivered to those in need (Soklaridis et al., 2020). Several groups of people benefit from such interventions, including frontline health-care professionals, COVID-19 patients, as well as individuals experiencing new-onset psychological distress or the exacerbation of their pre-existing mental health condition as a result of infection, losing loved ones to infection, or the impact of social distancing (Inchausti et al., 2020).

In one new intervention model utilized in West China Hospital during COVID-19, internet technology was used to integrate several health-care professionals, including physicians, psychiatrists, psychologists, and social workers, into a platform to help patients and their families, as well as the medical staff (Zhang et al. 2020a). The psychological crisis management of the West China Hospital model is a pyramidal model, with the government as its core leader; at the top of the pyramid is a team of experts delivering training and education to all levels below. At the base of the pyramid are community volunteers providing psychological support to quarantined people, medical staff, etc. Above the base, there are telephone hotlines, online consultations through *WeChat*, and two integrated apps for online registration (*Huayitong* and *Psyclub* applet) that identify those in need of intervention through questionnaires such as the Mood Index Questionnaire and Patient Health Questionnaire-9. Further up the pyramid, the psychological rescue team provides proper interventions based on the result of the previously administered questionnaires. Later, all the individuals are tracked regardless of their evaluation results (Zhang et al. 2020a).

Similarly, several other artificial intelligence technologies such as Tree Hole Rescue were utilized in China to identify individuals with suicidal tendencies. These emergency interventions were done by monitoring and analysing suspicious posts on *Weibo* (a Chinese microblogging website) and asking volunteers to intervene to prevent suicide (S. Liu et al. 2020b). Additionally, free electronic books, as well as communication programs such as *Weibo*, *WeChat*, and *TikTok*, were made available for the mental health education of the public and health-care workers (S. Liu et al. 2020b). For instance, online psychological support such as CBT for depression, anxiety, and insomnia in China was offered through *WeChat* (S. Liu et al. 2020b).

Meanwhile, in Canada, to help various parts of the population – such as the youth, essential workers, homeless/marginally housed, substance abusers, developmentally disabled, and their families – cope with pandemic-induced stress, anxiety, and uncertainty, the Centre for Addiction and Mental Health (CAMH) provided population-specific information sheets (Centre for Addiction and Mental Health [CAMH], 2020). In addition, further information was provided via the Mental Health Commission of Canada, the Canadian Mental Health Association (CMHA), and the Kids Help Phone (CAMH, 2020). Furthermore, Wellness Together Canada, a partnership between the public and private sector and the federal government, was developed to offer online and virtual resources (e.g., assessment tools, self-guided care, peer support, and counselling) to help Canadians deal with the psychological effects of the pandemic (CAMH, 2020). Similarly, the Canadian Psychological Association (CPA) has released factsheets and information on COVID-19 (e.g., Ryder et al., 2020).

Moreover, in certain Canadian provinces such as Ontario, patients had access to the programs *MindBeacon* for internet-based CBT (iCBT) (CAMH, 2020) and *BounceBack* – a free Ontario online peer-to-peer discussion forum managed by the CMHA and designed to help adults (19+) and youth (15–18 years of age) manage their mild-to-moderate depression, anxiety, and stress (BounceBack Ontario, n.d.). All of these Canadian interventions have resulted in a decrease in anxiety levels, although the already elevated levels of depression and loneliness have seen no change (CAMH, 2020).

The web-based psychological interventions have been proposed in the literature as one of the useful methods to alleviate the mental effects of social distancing; however, this may be inadequate for South Asian countries where the internet usage rate is low (32–68%) (Mia & Griffiths, 2021).

Generally, although professional psychological interventions have been reported to help individuals deal with the pandemic's negative psychological impact, research has also reported that professional mental health services alone can be inadequate to deal with the psychological consequences of the COVID-19 crisis (Mia & Griffiths, 2021). For instance, in countries (e.g., South Asian countries) where they are facing economic crisis and sanctions, other programs aiming at economic-related mental health problems could be helpful (i.e., by providing basic food supplies to poor and disadvantaged groups, which will improve their confidence and help them deal with negative psychological effects) (Mia & Griffiths, 2021).

Additionally, racial and ethnic inequalities in accessing mental health services have been reported during the pandemic (e.g., Blacks and Latinos with significantly lower access to mental health services in the USA) (Substance Abuse and Mental Health Services Administration [SAMHSA], 2020). The rise of the second wave of the Black Lives Matter protests has increased awareness of the impact of institutional discrimination and racism on wellbeing and other areas that are critical in COVID-19 pandemic relief (e.g., jobs, "housing," and "education") (Moreno et al., 2020).

It is stated that the permanent cure for the COVID-19 pandemic, hopefully, would be a safe immunization (vaccination) program that is administered globally, providing wide-ranging clinical, social, and economic advantages (Schaffer DeRoo et al., 2020). However, since COVID-19 vaccines have arrived in recent months (the first mass immunization program launched at the beginning of December 2020, and 175.3 million doses of vaccines have been delivered as of February 15, 2021), it is still too soon to realize the long-term strength and length of the protection the vaccines provide (WHO, 2020). However, vaccination would be an effective method of minimizing the disruptive consequences of the pandemic, protecting certain disadvantaged demographic classes (e.g., elderly people), and reducing the socioeconomic pressure of this pandemic (Gori et al., 2021).

At the same time, it is reported that one of the greatest public health issues is people's negative attitudes towards vaccinations (i.e., lack of trust in the advantages of vaccines, concerns about unpredicted side effects, etc.) which will be significant obstacles to the long-term management of the COVID-19 pandemic (Paul et al., 2020).

14.6 Discussion

This chapter began by discussing BIS and TMT's theoretical backgrounds to better grasp the psychological consequences of COVID-19 on various groups.

In the majority of the studies discussed, we see that the pandemic negatively impacts people across all groups (e.g., ages, genders, socio-economic statuses, nationalities, ethnicities, etc.) to some extent. However, the psychological responses to the threat of the COVID-19 are more salient among the more vulnerable groups such as the elderly individuals, marginalized groups, people infected with the COVID-10 virus, and those with pre-existing psychiatric conditions, among other groups.

We have also observed that some demographic subgroups (e.g., gender) experienced more aggravated mental health during the pandemic; as such, women relative to men have reported having experienced higher anxiety, PTSD, and loneliness, among other mental health issues. Similar results were found in a study conducted 1 month after the emergence of COVID-19 in Wuhan, China, among 258 samples in which women are reported to have significantly higher PTSD symptoms compared to men (N. Liu et al. 2020a). Another study also reported that women had been significantly more impacted psychologically by the COVID-19 than men, regardless of working at home or on the front lines (Thibaut & van Wijngaarden-Cremers, 2020). Females (both women and girls) have been more significantly impacted by the COVID-19 pandemic reportedly due to various factors, mainly rooted in gender inequalities. For instance, it is reported that elevated rates of school drop-outs due to school closures caused by COVID-19 would disproportionately impact adolescent girls worldwide, as a large number of these girls reside in countries with the highest gender inequality in educational opportunities (UNESCO, 2020). This will result in an elevated risk of sexual abuse, early marriage/forced marriage, and early pregnancy (UNESCO, 2020) and subsequently adds to their feelings of depression, sadness, and hopelessness since education for a majority of these girls is the only path out of poverty, which is no longer available to them during the pandemic (Caprino, 2020). Furthermore, women account for a relatively larger percentage of caregiving roles (e.g., childcare and eldercare) in all sectors (e.g., formal and informal) as well as domestic tasks (e.g., cleaning and cooking) (Almeida et al., 2020; Gausman & Langer, 2020; Madgavkar et al., 2020). Moreover, a large number of frontline health-care workers (e.g., nurses) are women (Gausman & Langer, 2020; Madgavkar et al., 2020), and they disproportionately do the vast majority of the total unpaid jobs (75%) worldwide (Madgavkar et al., 2020).

The fact that the COVID-19 has impacted everyone to some extent can be explained through fear of death rooted in TMT. It is suggested that COVID-19-triggered mortality salience (e.g., massive COVID-19 death toll) affects individuals' attitudes and behaviours, even those who underestimate the risk of the virus (Pyszczynski et al., 2020). The COVID-19 crisis had unprecedented personal, social, economic, and political costs, and according to TMT, the root cause of all the concerns regarding these issues is the risk of death from the SARS-CoV-2 (Pyszczynski et al., 2020). TMT posits that the tension between a passion for survival and an awareness of death's inevitability generates paralysing fear (terror) (Pyszczynski, 2004). However, the pandemic has elicited a wide range of responses (e.g., distal and proximal defence) among people to cope with their existential terror. Some people embraced more adaptive and healthier approaches (e.g., follow COVID-19 protective health measures, achieve meaning in existence, pursue close interpersonal interaction, enhance self-esteem, and reinforce beliefs in cultural worldviews), while some adopted unhealthier and destructive ones (e.g., denial and avoidance) (Pyszczynski et al., 2020). Meanwhile, TMT states that fear of death can be experienced at "contextual" (i.e., where the context underlines the inevitability of death) and "dispositional" levels (i.e., individual variations in their response to the life contingencies that reveal inevitability of death) (Greenberg et al., 1994; Silva et al., 2021). The reason why vulnerable individuals respond to the threat of COVID-19 even more negatively might be due to the fact that the risk of death is even more salient to these groups either at the contextual or individual levels, leading to a greater fear in them as they are aware of being more at risk of dying from the COVID-19. This is partially supported by a recent study conducted on 352 Brazilians, which found that individual differences (dispositional level) regarding COVID 19 related fear of death significantly predicted psychological health, meaning that participants who manifested higher fear of death related to COVID-19 experienced worse psychological health, and this was mediated by higher anxiety, related to COVID-19. However, this relationship was not significant on the contextual level, meaning that the salience of death in the context (i.e., checking news about COVID-19-related mortalities) did not significantly predict heightened anxiety and lower mental health (Silva et al., 2021).

People have adopted different coping strategies to manage their COVID-19-related existential terror (anxiety); however, they continue to fight between proximal and distal defences against death, as they struggle between efforts to keep themselves protected from this lethal virus and the wish that economy and pre-pandemic life ("normal life") restart (Pyszczynski et al., 2020). That said, people are unable to manage their existential terror effectively since COVID-19 obstacles (e.g., job and income loss) in addition to the prescribed healthy measures (e.g., lockdown and social distancing) undermine distal defences by hindering or eliminating the "anxiety-buffering" sources (i.e., interpersonal connections, jobs, education) that people usually depend on to find meaning in life and retain "equanimity" (Pyszczynski et al., 2020).

Similarly, COVID-19 can be understood through the lens of BIS. As previously mentioned, BIS is rooted in the principle of functional flexibility, meaning that the BIS activates depending on contextual cues and individual variations in traits (Schaller & Park, 2011; Shook et al., 2020). As such, we observed that vulnerable individuals were more at risk of COVID-19 and experienced high BIS sensitivity across the studies. As noted earlier, individuals with pre-existing mental illness showed higher contamination fears, COVID-related stress, and traumatic stress than healthy individuals. Another example illustrated earlier was that stigmatization was observed more among individuals with a higher vulnerability perception to infectious disease. Stigmatization reportedly functioned as an extra (besides adaptive intense fear responses) and an effective BIS in human populations before the development of public health services, meaning that the feeling of disgust aiming at humans and not only at things could be beneficial if it rationally revealed which individuals are infected and can transmit the virus, so people could avoid them (Brewis et al., 2020).

TMT and BIS each provide a great deal of insights into the responses of the individuals during COVID-19. However, TMT puts more focus on people's responses to death, searching for the essence of life, or "symbolic" immortality, whereas BIS focuses on infectious pathogen from an evolutionary viewpoint, attempting to analyse human responses before contamination happens (Pan, 2020).

14.7 Conclusion

Although the COVID-19 pandemic has had an impact on both physical and psychological health (Fiorillo & Gorwood, 2020), history has demonstrated that the psychological health consequences of disasters linger for longer than that of physical health, indicating that the high demands for mental health care would extend far after the coronavirus pandemic (Panchal et al. 2021).

During a pandemic, both terror management mechanisms and the BIS can be triggered simultaneously, such that to manage the fear of death individuals might become "rigid" in their worldviews and get irritated if others challenge their views and, at the same time, they avoid anything that provokes fear of virus infection (Josephs, 2020).

Individuals with the highest vulnerabilities and across various ethnicities, races, occupations, and social and economic groups have been disproportionately impacted by the COVID-19 pandemic (The Lancet Public Health, 2021). The pandemic has exacerbated and escalated the "sharp inequalities" everywhere (Baroud, 2020); although the COVID-19 pandemic will eventually be resolved, the inequalities are making this process slower (Pizzigati, 2021). As these inequalities have previously damaged the societies, it is expected that they will continue to damage in the post-pandemic (Baroud, 2020). Therefore, in order to protect the future wellbeing of the population, it is critical and urgent for societal changes to take place by implementing a population health approach that is wide-ranging and equity-oriented, which is a critical component of creating a more "resilient society" that is better equipped to respond to later pandemics (The Lancet Public Health, 2021).

References

Ackerman, J. M., Hill, S. E., & Murray, D. R. (2018). The behavioral immune system: Current concerns and future directions. *Social and Personality Psychology Compass, 12*(2), e12371. https://doi.org/10.1111/spc3.12371

Agüero, J. M. (2020). COVID-19 and the rise of intimate partner violence. *World Development, 137*, Article 105217. https://doi.org/10.1016/j.worlddev.2020.105217

Ahorsu, D. K., Lin, C.-Y., Imani, V., Saffari, M., Griffiths, M. D., & Pakpour, A. H. (2020). The fear of COVID-19 scale: Development and initial validation. *International Journal of Mental Health and Addiction*. https://doi.org/10.1007/s11469-020-00270-8

Almeida, M., Shrestha, A. D., Stojanac, D., & Miller, L. J. (2020). The impact of the COVID-19 pandemic on women's mental health. *Archives of Women's Mental Health, 23*, 741–748. https://doi.org/10.1007/s00737-020-01092-2

Alyami, M., Henning, M., Krägeloh, C. U., & Alyami, H. (2020). Psychometric evaluation of the Arabic version of the Fear of COVID-19 Scale. *International Journal of Mental Health and Addiction*. https://doi.org/10.1007/s11469-020-00316-x

American Psychiatric Association. (2013). *Diagnostic and statistical manual of mental disorders: DSM-5* (5th ed.) https://www.psychiatry.org/psychiatrists/practice/dsm

Arora, A., Jha, A. K., Alat, P., & Das, S. S. (2020). Understanding coronaphobia. *Asian Journal of Psychiatry, 54*, Article 102384. https://doi.org/10.1016/j.ajp.2020.102384

Asmundson, G. J. G., & Taylor, S. (2020a). Coronaphobia: Fear and the 2019-nCoV outbreak. *Journal of Anxiety Disorders, 70*, Article 102196. https://doi.org/10.1016/j.janxdis.2020.102196

Asmundson, G. J. G., & Taylor, S. (2020b). How health anxiety influences responses to viral outbreaks like COVID-19: What all decision-makers, health authorities, and health care professionals need to know. *Journal of Anxiety Disorders, 71*, Article 102211. https://doi.org/10.1016/j.janxdis.2020.102211

Asmundson, G. J. G., Paluszek, M. M., Landry, C. A., Rachor, G. S., McKay, D., & Taylor, S. (2020). Do pre-existing anxiety-related and mood disorders differentially impact COVID-19 stress responses and coping? *Journal of Anxiety Disorders, 74*, Article 102271. https://doi.org/10.1016/j.janxdis.2020.102271

Auer, M., Malischnig, D., & Griffiths, M. D. (2020). Gambling before and during the COVID-19 pandemic among European regular sports bettors: An empirical study using behavioral tracking data. *International Journal of Mental Health and Addiction*. https://doi.org/10.1007/s11469-020-00327-8

Bagcchi, S. (2020). Stigma during the COVID-19 pandemic. *The Lancet Infectious Diseases, 20*(7), 782. https://doi.org/10.1016/s1473-3099(20)30498-9

Bailer, J., Kerstner, T., Witthöft, M., Diener, C., Mier, D., & Rist, F. (2015). Health anxiety and hypochondriasis in the light of DSM-5. *Anxiety, Stress, & Coping, 29*(2), 219–239. https://doi.org/10.1080/10615806.2015.1036243

Baroud, R. (2020, December 21). *The great divider: Covid-19 reflects global racism, not equality.* CounterPunch. https://www.counterpunch.org/2020/12/21/the-great-divider-covid-19-reflects-global-racism-not-equality/

Barzilay, R., Moore, T. M., Greenberg, D. M., DiDomenico, G. E., Brown, L. A., White, L. K., Gur, R. C., & Gur, R. E. (2020). Resilience, COVID-19-related stress, anxiety and depression during the pandemic in a large population enriched for healthcare providers. *Translational Psychiatry, 10*(1), Article 291. https://doi.org/10.1038/s41398-020-00982-4

Bäuerle, A., Teufel, M., Musche, V., Weismüller, B., Kohler, H., Hetkamp, M., Dörrie, N., Schweda, A., & Skoda, E. M. (2020). Increased generalized anxiety, depression and distress during the COVID-19 pandemic: A cross-sectional study in Germany. *Journal of Public Health, 42*(4), 672–678. https://doi.org/10.1093/pubmed/fdaa106

Beck, J. S. (2011). *Cognitive behavior therapy: Basics and beyond* (2nd ed.). Guilford Press.

Bhattacharya, P., Banerjee, D., & Rao, T. S. (2020). The "untold" side of COVID-19: Social stigma and its consequences in India. *Indian Journal of Psychological Medicine, 42*(4), 382–386. https://doi.org/10.1177/0253717620935578

Bitan, D. T., Grossman-Giron, A., Bloch, Y., Mayer, Y., Shiffman, N., & Mendlovic, S. (2020). Fear of COVID-19 Scale: Psychometric characteristics, reliability and validity in the Israeli population. *Psychiatry Research, 289*, Article 113100. https://doi.org/10.1016/j.psychres.2020.113100

Blekas, A., Voitsidis, P., Athanasiadou, M., Parlapani, E., Chatzigeorgiou, A. F., Skoupra, M., Syngelakis, M., Holeva, V., & Diakogiannis, I. (2020). COVID-19: PTSD symptoms in Greek health care professionals. *Psychological Trauma: Theory, Research, Practice, and Policy, 12*(7), 812–819. https://doi.org/10.1037/tra0000914

BounceBack Ontario. (n.d.). *Get started*. https://bouncebackontario.ca/

Brewis, A., Wutich, A., & Mahdavi, P. (2020). Stigma, pandemics, and human biology: Looking back, looking forward. *American Journal of Human Biology, 32*(5), e23480. https://doi.org/10.1002/ajhb.23480

Browning, M. H. E. M., Larson, L. R., Sharaievska, I., Rigolon, A., McAnirlin, O., Mullenbach, L., Cloutier, S., Vu, T. M., Thomsen, J., Reigner, N., Metcalf, E. C., D'Antonio, A., Helbich, M., Bratman, G. N., & Alvarez, H. O. (2021). Psychological impacts from COVID-19 among university students: Risk factors across seven states in the United States. *PLoS One, 16*(1), Article e0245327. https://doi.org/10.1371/journal.pone.0245327

Bueno-Notivol, J., Gracia-García, P., Olaya, B., Lasheras, I., López-Antón, R., & Santabárbara, J. (2020). Prevalence of depression during the COVID-19 outbreak: A meta-analysis of community-based studies. *International Journal of Clinical and Health Psychology, 21*(1), Article 100196. https://doi.org/10.1016/j.ijchp.2020.07.007

Cameron, E. E., Joyce, K. M., Delaquis, C. P., Reynolds, K., Protudjer, J. L. P., & Roos, L. E. (2020). Maternal psychological distress & mental health service use during the COVID-19 pandemic. *Journal of Affective Disorders, 276*, 765–774. https://doi.org/10.1016/j.jad.2020.07.081

Caprino, K. (2020, July 13). *How the pandemic is negatively impacting women more than men, and what has to change*. Forbes. https://www.forbes.com/sites/kathycaprino/2020/07/13/how-the-pandemic-is-negatively-impacting-women-more-than-men-and-what-has-to-change/?sh=7e03100554ba&fbclid=IwAR2mjMftRmx1kTCJEucS-vkV0aLN4X6WLWisvQlovH-xc07Zf3rOTzQjDTc

Cao, W., Fang, Z., Hou, G., Han, M., Xu, X., Dong, J., & Zheng, J. (2020). The psychological impact of the COVID-19 epidemic on college students in China. *Psychiatry Research, 287*, Article 112934. https://doi.org/10.1016/j.psychres.2020.112934

Casagrande, M., Favieri, F., Tambelli, R., & Forte, G. (2020). The enemy who sealed the world: Effects quarantine due to the COVID-19 on sleep quality, anxiety, and psychological distress in the Italian population. *Sleep Medicine, 75*, 12–20. https://doi.org/10.1016/j.sleep.2020.05.011

Centers for Disease Control and Prevention. (2020, June 11). *Reducing stigma*. CDC. https://www.cdc.gov/coronavirus/2019-ncov/daily-life-coping/reducing-stigma.html?fbclid=IwAR2bPBTFmboAEQyjnJIGmypF40JJOa53xucfFdF0_gxChY8qKL0CcekcidM

Centre for Addiction and Mental Health. (2020). *Mental health in Canada: Covid-19 and beyond: CAMH policy advice*. CAMH. http://www.camh.ca/-/media/files/pdfs%2D%2D-public-policy-submissions/covid-and-mh-policy-paper-pdf.pdf

Chatterjee, S. S., Malathesh, B. C., & Mukherjee, A. (2020). Impact of COVID-19 pandemic on pre-existing mental health problems. *Asian Journal of Psychiatry, 51*, Article 102071. https://doi.org/10.1016/j.ajp.2020.102071

Chen, F., Zheng, D., Liu, J., Gong, Y., Guan, Z., & Lou, D. (2020). Depression and anxiety among adolescents during COVID-19: A cross-sectional study. *Brain, Behavior, and Immunity*. https://doi.org/10.1016/j.bbi.2020.05.061

Chen, I. H., Chen, C. Y., Pakpour, A. H., Griffiths, M. D., Lin, C. Y., Li, X. D., & Tsang, H. W. H. (2021). Problematic internet-related behaviors mediate the associations between levels of internet engagement and distress among schoolchildren during COVID-19 lockdown: A longitudinal structural equation modeling study. *Journal of Behavioral Addictions*. https://doi.org/10.1556/2006.2021.00006

Chew, N. W. S., Lee, G. K. H., Tan, B. Y. Q., Jing, M., Goh, Y., Ngiam, N. J. H., Yeo, L. L. L., Ahmad, A., Khan, F. A., Shanmugam, G. N., Sharma, A. K., Komalkumar, R. N., Meenakshi, P. V., Shah, K., Patel, B., Chan, B. P. L., Sunny, S., Chandra, B., Ong, J. J. Y., … Sharma, V. K. (2020). A multinational, multicentre study on the psychological outcomes and associated physical symptoms amongst healthcare workers during COVID-19 outbreak. *Brain, Behavior, and Immunity, 88*, 559–565. https://doi.org/10.1016/j.bbi.2020.04.049

Czeisler, M. É., Lane, R. I., Petrosky, E., Wiley, J. F., Christensen, A., Njai, R., Weaver, M. D., Robbins, R., Facer-Childs, E. R., Barger, L. K., Czeisler, C. A., Howard, M. E., & Rajaratnam, S. (2020). Mental health, substance use, and suicidal ideation during the COVID-19 pandemic - United States, June 24-30, 2020. *Morbidity and Mortality Weekly Report, 69*(32), 1049–1057. https://doi.org/10.15585/mmwr.mm6932a1

Dai, L.-L., Wang, X., Jiang, T.-C., Li, P.-F., Wang, Y., Wu, S.-J., Jia, L.-Q., Liu, M., An, L., & Cheng, Z. (2020). Anxiety and depressive symptoms among COVID-19 patients in Jianghan Fangcang Shelter Hospital in Wuhan, China. *PLoS One, 15*(8), Article e0238416. https://doi.org/10.1371/journal.pone.0238416

Dsouza, D. D., Quadros, S., Hyderabadwala, Z. J., & Mamun, M. A. (2020). Aggregated COVID-19 suicide incidences in India: Fear of COVID-19 infection is the prominent causative factor. *Psychiatry Research, 290*, Article 113145. https://doi.org/10.1016/j.psychres.2020.113145

Dubey, S., Biswas, P., Ghosh, R., Chatterjee, S., Dubey, M. J., Chatterjee, S., Lahiri, D., & Lavie, C. J. (2020a). Psychosocial impact of COVID-19. *Diabetes & Metabolic Syndrome: Clinical Research & Reviews, 14*(5), 779–788. https://doi.org/10.1016/j.dsx.2020.05.035

Dubey, M. J., Ghosh, R., Chatterjee, S., Biswas, P., Chatterjee, S., & Dubey, S. (2020b). COVID-19 and addiction. *Diabetes & Metabolic Syndrome: Clinical Research & Reviews, 14*(5), 817–823. https://doi.org/10.1016/j.dsx.2020.06.008

Elemo, A. S., Satici, S. A., & Griffiths, M. D. (2020). The Fear of COVID-19 Scale: Psychometric properties of the Ethiopian Amharic version. *International Journal of Mental Health and Addiction*. https://doi.org/10.1007/s11469-020-00448-0

Ettman, C. K., Abdalla, S. M., Cohen, G. H., Sampson, L., Vivier, P. M., & Galea, S. (2020). Prevalence of depression symptoms in US adults before and during the COVID-19 pandemic. *JAMA Network Open, 3*(9), Article e2019686. https://doi.org/10.1001/jamanetworkopen.2020.19686

Evans, M. L., Lindauer, M., & Farrell, M. E. (2020). A pandemic within a pandemic — Intimate partner violence during Covid-19. *The New England Journal of Medicine, 383*, 2302–2304. https://doi.org/10.1056/NEJMp2024046

Fekih-Romdhane, F., Ghrissi, F., Abbassi, B., Cherif, W., & Cheour, M. (2020). Prevalence and predictors of PTSD during the COVID-19 pandemic: Findings from a Tunisian community sample. *Psychiatry Research, 290*, Article 113131. https://doi.org/10.1016/j.psychres.2020.113131

Fincher, C. L., Thornhill, R., Murray, D. R., & Schaller, M. (2008). Pathogen prevalence predicts human cross-cultural variability in individualism/collectivism. *Proceedings of the Royal Society B: Biological Sciences, 275*(1640), 1279–1285. https://doi.org/10.1098/rspb.2008.0094

Fiorillo, A., & Gorwood, P. (2020). The consequences of the COVID-19 pandemic on mental health and implications for clinical practice. *European Psychiatry, 63*(1), e32. https://doi.org/10.1192/j.eurpsy.2020.35

Fitzpatrick, K. M., Harris, C., & Drawve, G. (2020). Fear of COVID-19 and the mental health consequences in America. *Psychological Trauma: Theory, Research, Practice, and Policy, 12*(S1), S17–S21. https://doi.org/10.1037/tra0000924

Fontes, W., Gonçalves Júnior, J., de Vasconcelos, C. A. C., da Silva, C. G. L., & Gadelha, M. S. V. (2020). Impacts of the SARS-CoV-2 pandemic on the mental health of the elderly. *Frontiers in Psychiatry, 11*, 841. https://doi.org/10.3389/fpsyt.2020.00841

Forte, G., Favieri, F., Tambelli, R., & Casagrande, M. (2020). COVID-19 pandemic in the Italian population: Validation of a post-traumatic stress disorder questionnaire and prevalence of PTSD symptomatology. *International Journal of Environmental Research and Public Health, 17*(11), Article 4151. https://doi.org/10.3390/ijerph17114151

Gallagher, M. W., Zvolensky, M. J., Long, L. J., Rogers, A. H., & Garey, L. (2020). The impact of Covid-19 experiences and associated stress on anxiety, depression, and functional impairment in American adults. *Cognitive Therapy and Research, 44*, 1043–1051. https://doi.org/10.1007/s10608-020-10143-y

Gao, J., Zheng, P., Jia, Y., Chen, H., Mao, Y., Chen, S., Wang, Y., Fu, H., & Dai, J. (2020). Mental health problems and social media exposure during COVID-19 outbreak. *PLoS One, 15*(4), Article e0231924. https://doi.org/10.1371/journal.pone.0231924

Garbe, L., Rau, R., & Toppe, T. (2020). Influence of perceived threat of Covid-19 and HEXACO personality traits on toilet paper stockpiling. *PLoS One, 15*(6), Article e0234232. https://doi.org/10.1371/journal.pone.0234232

Gausman, J., & Langer, A. (2020). Sex and gender disparities in the COVID-19 pandemic. *Journal of Women's Health, 29*(4), 465–466. https://doi.org/10.1089/jwh.2020.8472

Gelfand, M. J., Raver, J. L., Nishii, L., Leslie, L. M., Lun, J., Lim, B. C., … Yamaguchi, S. (2011). Differences between tight and loose cultures: A 33-nation study. *Science, 332*(6033), 1100–1104. https://doi.org/10.1126/science.1197754

Gelfand, M. J., Jackson, J. C., Pan, X., Nau, D., Pieper, D., Denison, E., Dagher, M., Van Lange, P. A. M., Chiu, C. Y., & Wang, M. (2021). The relationship between cultural tightness-looseness and COVID-19 cases and deaths: A global analysis. *Lancet Planet Health*, S2542-5196(20)30301-6. https://doi.org/10.1016/S2542-5196(20)30301-6

Gennaro Mazza, M., De Lorenzo, R., Conte, C., Poletti, S., Vai, B., Bollettini, I., Melloni, E. M. T., Furlan, R., Ciceri, F., Rovere-Querini, P., & Benedetti, F. (2020). Anxiety and depression in COVID-19 survivors: Role of inflammatory and clinical predictors. *Brain, Behavior, and Immunity, 89*, 594–600. https://doi.org/10.1016/j.bbi.2020.07.037

Goodwin, R., Hou, W. K., Sun, S., & Ben-Ezra, M. (2020). Quarantine, distress and interpersonal relationships during COVID-19. *General Psychiatry, 33*(6), Article e100385. https://doi.org/10.1136/gpsych-2020-100385

Gori, D., Reno, C., Remondini, D., Durazzi, F., & Fantini, M. P. (2021). Are we ready for the arrival of the new COVID-19 vaccinations? Great promises and unknown challenges still to come. *Vaccine, 9*(2), 173. https://doi.org/10.3390/vaccines9020173

Gover, A. R., Harper, S. B., & Langton, L. (2020). Anti-Asian hate crime during the COVID-19 pandemic: Exploring the reproduction of inequality. *American Journal of Criminal Justice, 45*, 647–667. https://doi.org/10.1007/s12103-020-09545-1

Greenberg, J., Pyszczynski, T., & Solomon, S. (1986). The causes and consequences of a need for self-esteem: A terror management theory. In R. F. Baumeister (Ed.), *Public self and private self* (pp. 189–212). Springer-Verlag.

Greenberg, J., Pyszczynski, T., Solomon, S., Simon, L., & Breus, M. (1994). Role of consciousness and accessibility of death-related thoughts in mortality salience effects. *Journal of Personality and Social Psychology, 67*(4), 627–637. https://doi.org/10.1037/0022-3514.67.4.627

Greenberg, J., Solomon, S., & Pyszczynski, T. (1997). Terror management theory of self-esteem and cultural worldviews: Empirical assessments and conceptual refinements. *Advances in Experimental Social Psychology, 29*, 61–139. https://doi.org/10.1016/s0065-2601(08)60016-7

Groarke, J. M., Berry, E., Graham-Wisener, L., McKenna-Plumley, P. E., McGlinchey, E., & Armour, C. (2020). Loneliness in the UK during the COVID-19 pandemic: Cross-sectional results from the COVID-19 Psychological Wellbeing Study. *PLoS One, 15*(9), Article e0239698. https://doi.org/10.1371/journal.pone.0239698

Gualano, M. R., Lo Moro, G., Voglino, G., Bert, F., & Siliquini, R. (2020). Effects of Covid-19 lockdown on mental health and sleep disturbances in Italy. *International Journal of Environmental Research and Public Health, 17*(13), Article 4779. https://doi.org/10.3390/ijerph17134779

Gunnell, D., Appleby, L., Arensman, E., Hawton, K., John, A., Kapur, N., Khan, M., O'Connor, R. C., Pirkis, J., & the COVID-19 Suicide Prevention Research Collaboration. (2020). Suicide risk and prevention during the COVID-19 pandemic. *The Lancet Psychiatry, 7*(6), 468–471. https://doi.org/10.1016/s2215-0366(20)30171-1

Harmon-Jones, E., Simon, L., Greenberg, J., Pyszczynski, T., Solomon, S., & McGregor, H. (1997). Terror management theory and self-esteem: Evidence that increased self-esteem reduced mortality salience effects. *Journal of Personality and Social Psychology, 72*(1), 24–36. https://doi.org/10.1037/0022-3514.72.1.24

Heidinger, T., & Richter, L. (2020). The effect of COVID-19 on loneliness in the elderly. An empirical comparison of pre-and peri-pandemic loneliness in community-dwelling elderly. *Frontiers in Psychology, 11*, 2595. https://doi.org/10.3389/fpsyg.2020.585308

Hennekam, S., Ladge, J., & Shymko, Y. (2020). From zero to hero: An exploratory study examining sudden hero status among nonphysician health care workers during the COVID-19 pandemic. *Journal of Applied Psychology, 105*(10), 1088–1100. https://doi.org/10.1037/apl0000832

Huang, Y., & Zhao, N. (2020). Generalized anxiety disorder, depressive symptoms and sleep quality during COVID-19 outbreak in China: A web-based cross-sectional survey. *Psychiatry Research, 288*, Article 112954. https://doi.org/10.1016/j.psychres.2020.112954

Huarcaya-Victoria, J., Villarreal-Zegarra, D., Podestà, A., & Luna-Cuadros, M. A. (2020). Psychometric properties of a Spanish version of the Fear of COVID-19 Scale in general population of Lima, Peru. International Journal of Mental Health and Addiction, 1–14. https://doi.org/https://doi.org/10.1007/s11469-020-00354-5.

Huecker, M. R., & Smock, W. (2020). *Domestic violence.* StatPearls. http://www.ncbi.nlm.nih.gov/books/NBK499891/

Hyland, P., Shevlin, M., McBride, O., Murphy, J., Karatzias, T., Bentall, R. P., Martinez, A., & Vallières, F. (2020). Anxiety and depression in the Republic of Ireland during the COVID-19 pandemic. *Acta Psychiatrica Scandinavica, 142*(3), 249–256. https://doi.org/10.1111/acps.13219

Imran, N., Aamer, I., Sharif, M., Bodla, Z., & Naveed, S. (2020). Psychological burden of quarantine in children and adolescents: A rapid systematic review and proposed solutions. *Pakistan Journal of Medical Sciences, 36*(5) https://doi.org/10.12669/pjms.36.5.3088

Inchausti, F., MacBeth, A., Hasson-Ohayon, I., & Dimaggio, G. (2020). Psychological intervention and COVID 19: What we know so far and what we can do. *Journal of Contemporary Psychotherapy, 50*, 243–250. https://doi.org/10.1007/s10879-020-09460-w

Islam, M. S., Ferdous, M. Z., & Potenza, M. N. (2020). Panic and generalized anxiety during the COVID-19 pandemic among Bangladeshi people: An online pilot survey early in the outbreak. *Journal of Affective Disorders, 276*, 30–37. https://doi.org/10.1016/j.jad.2020.06.049

Jahan, I., Ullah, I., Griffiths, M. D., & Mamun, M. A. (2021). COVID-19 suicide and its causative factors among the healthcare professionals: Case study evidence from press reports. *Perspectives in Psychiatric Care.* https://doi.org/10.1111/ppc.12739

Johnson, H. R. (2020). *Position paper: The impact of COVID-19 on mental health.* Psychiatry Advisor. https://www.psychiatryadvisor.com/home/topics/general-psychiatry/position-paper-the-impact-of-covid-19-on-mental-health/

Josephs, L. (2020, March 19). *Terror management and your marriage.* Psychology Today. https://www.psychologytoday.com/ca/blog/between-the-sheets/202003/terror-management-and-your-marriage

Jungmann, S. M., & Witthöft, M. (2020). Health anxiety, cyberchondria, and coping in the current COVID-19 pandemic: Which factors are related to coronavirus anxiety? *Journal of Anxiety Disorders, 73*, Article 102239. https://doi.org/10.1016/j.janxdis.2020.102239

Kanter, J., & Manbeck, K. (2020, April 1). *COVID-19 could lead to an epidemic of clinical depression, and the health care system isn't ready for that, either.* The Conversation. https://theconversation.com/covid-19-could-lead-to-an-epidemic-of-clinical-depression-and-the-health-care-system-isnt-ready-for-that-either-134528?fbclid=IwAR1MPxidnTc1y5Tw7wKDWRHij8oGJGwIzK2OcUm8z8O03NQWDiaPLQ6fmJA

Kar, N. (2020). COVID-19 and older adults: In the face of a global disaster. *Journal of Geriatric Care and Research, 7*(1), 1–2.

Karatzias, T., Shevlin, M., Murphy, J., McBride, O., Ben-Ezra, M., Bentall, R. P., Vallières, F., & Hyland, P. (2020). Posttraumatic stress symptoms and associated comorbidity during the COVID-19 pandemic in Ireland: A population-based study. *Journal of Traumatic Stress, 33*(4), 365–370. https://doi.org/10.1002/jts.22565

Kenneavy, J. (2020, July 16). *How to guard against pandemic PTSD.* Edward-Elmhurst Health. https://www.eehealth.org/blog/2020/07/pandemic-ptsd/#:~:text=PTSD%20won't%20be%20the,being%20in%20the%20long%2Dterm

Khan, K. S., Mamun, M. A., Griffiths, M. D., & Ullah, I. (2020). The mental health impact of the COVID-19 pandemic across different cohorts. *International Journal of Mental Health and Addiction.* https://doi.org/10.1007/s11469-020-00367-0

Killgore, W. D. S., Cloonan, S. A., Taylor, E. C., Miller, M. A., & Dailey, N. S. (2020). Three months of loneliness during the COVID-19 lockdown. *Psychiatry Research, 293*, Article 113392. https://doi.org/10.1016/j.psychres.2020.113392

Kirk, C. P., & Rifkin, L. S. (2020). I'll trade you diamonds for toilet paper: Consumer reacting, coping and adapting behaviors in the COVID-19 pandemic. *Journal of Business Research, 117*, 124–131. https://doi.org/10.1016/j.jbusres.2020.05.028

Kluge, H. H. P., Jakab, Z., Bartovic, J., D'Anna, V., & Severoni, S. (2020). Refugee and migrant health in the COVID-19 response. *The Lancet, 395*(10232), 1237–1239. https://doi.org/10.1016/s0140-6736(20)30791-1

Laato, S., Islam, A. K. M. N., Farooq, A., & Dhir, A. (2020). Unusual purchasing behavior during the early stages of the COVID-19 pandemic: The stimulus-organism-response approach. *Journal of Retailing and Consumer Services, 57*, Article 102224. https://doi.org/10.1016/j.jretconser.2020.102224

Labrague, L. J., & De Los Santos, J. (2020). Prevalence and predictors of coronaphobia among frontline hospital and public health nurses. *Public health nursing (Boston, Mass.)*, 10.1111/phn.12841. Advance online publication. https://doi.org/10.1111/phn.12841

Lakhan, R., Agrawal, A., & Sharma, M. (2020). Prevalence of depression, anxiety, and stress during COVID-19 pandemic. *Journal of Neurosciences in Rural Practice, 11*(4), 519–525. https://doi.org/10.1055/s-0040-1716442

Landi, G., Pakenham, K. I., Boccolini, G., Grandi, S., & Tossani, E. (2020). Health anxiety and mental health outcome during COVID-19 lockdown in Italy: The mediating and moderating roles of psychological flexibility. *Frontiers in Psychology, 11*, 2195. https://doi.org/10.3389/fpsyg.2020.02195

Li, L. Z., & Wang, S. (2020). Prevalence and predictors of general psychiatric disorders and loneliness during COVID-19 in the United Kingdom. *Psychiatry Research, 291*, Article 113267. https://doi.org/10.1016/j.psychres.2020.113267

Liang, L., Gao, T., Ren, H., Cao, R., Qin, Z., Hu, Y., Li, C., & Mei, S. (2020). Post-traumatic stress disorder and psychological distress in Chinese youths following the COVID-19 emergency. *Journal of Health Psychology, 25*(9), 1164–1175. https://doi.org/10.1177/1359105320937057

Lima, N. N. R., de Souza, R. I., Feitosa, P. W. G., Moreira, J., da Silva, C. G. L., & Neto, M. L. R. (2020). People experiencing homelessness: Their potential exposure to COVID-19. *Psychiatry Research, 288*, Article 112945. https://doi.org/10.1016/j.psychres.2020.112945

Liu, Y.-L. (2020, June 5). *Is Covid-19 changing our relationships?* BBC Future. https://www.bbc.com/future/article/20200601-how-is-covid-19-is-affecting-relationships

Liu, N., Zhang, F., Wei, C., Jia, Y., Shang, Z., Sun, L., … Liu, W. (2020a). Prevalence and predictors of PTSS during COVID-19 outbreak in China hardest-hit areas: Gender differences matter. *Psychiatry Research, 112921*. https://doi.org/10.1016/j.psychres.2020.112921

Liu, S., Yang, L., Zhang, C., Xiang, Y.-T., Liu, Z., Hu, S., & Zhang, B. (2020b). Online mental health services in China during the COVID-19 outbreak. *The Lancet Psychiatry, 7*(4), e17–e18. https://doi.org/10.1016/s2215-0366(20)30077-8

Long, N. N., & Khoi, B. H. (2020). An empirical study about the intention to hoard food during COVID-19 pandemic. *Eurasia Journal of Mathematics, Science and Technology Education, 16*(7), Article em1857. https://doi.org/10.29333/ejmste/8207

Luchetti, M., Lee, J. H., Aschwanden, D., Sesker, A., Strickhouser, J. E., Terracciano, A., & Sutin, A. R. (2020). The trajectory of loneliness in response to COVID-19. *American Psychologist, 75*(7), 897–908. https://doi.org/10.1037/amp0000690

Madgavkar, A., Krishnan, M., White, O., Mahajan, D., & Azcue, X. (2020, July 15). *COVID-19 and gender equality: Countering the regressive effects.* McKinsey & Company. https://www.mckinsey.com/featured-insights/future-of-work/covid-19-and-gender-equality-countering-the-regressive-effects

Mailliez, M., Griffiths, M. D., & Carre, A. (2020). Validation of the French version of the fear of COVID-19 scale and its associations with depression, anxiety and differential emotions. *Research Square.* https://doi.org/10.21203/rs.3.rs-46616/v1

Makhanova, A., & Shepherd, M. A. (2020). Behavioral immune system linked to responses to the threat of COVID-19. *Personality and Individual Differences, 167*, Article 110221. https://doi.org/10.1016/j.paid.2020.110221

Mallet, J., Dubertret, C., & Le Strat, Y. (2021). Addictions in the COVID-19 era: Current evidence, future perspectives a comprehensive review. *Progress in Neuro-Psychopharmacology and Biological Psychiatry, 106*, Article 110070. https://doi.org/10.1016/j.pnpbp.2020.110070

Mamun, M. A., & Griffiths, M. D. (2020). First COVID-19 suicide case in Bangladesh due to fear of COVID-19 and xenophobia: Possible suicide prevention strategies. *Asian Journal of Psychiatry, 51*, Article 102073. https://doi.org/10.1016/j.ajp.2020.102073

Mamun, M. A., & Ullah, I. (2020). COVID-19 suicides in Pakistan, dying off not COVID-19 fear but poverty? - The forthcoming economic challenges for a developing country. *Brain, Behavior, and Immunity, 87*, 163–166. https://doi.org/10.1016/j.bbi.2020.05.028

Martin, C., Andrés, P., Bullón, A., Villegas, J. L., de la Iglesia-Larrad, J. I., Bote, B., Prieto, N., & Roncero, C. (2020). COVID pandemic as an opportunity for improving mental health treatments of the homeless people. *International Journal of Social Psychiatry.* https://doi.org/10.1177/0020764020950770

McKay, D., & Asmundson, G. J. G. (2020). Substance use and abuse associated with the behavioral immune system during COVID-19: The special case of healthcare workers and essential workers. *Addictive Behaviors, 110*, Article 106522. https://doi.org/10.1016/j.addbeh.2020.106522

Mei, Q., Wang, F., Bryant, A., Wei, L., Yuan, X., & Li, J. (2021). Mental health problems among COVID-19 survivors in Wuhan, China. *World Psychiatry, 20*(1), 139–140. https://doi.org/10.1002/wps.20829

Mental Health America. (n.d.). *Living with mental illness during COVID-19 outbreak– preparing for your wellness.* https://mhanational.org/living-mental-illness-during-covid-19-outbreak-preparing-your-wellness

Mertens, G., Gerritsen, L., Duijndam, S., Salemink, E., & Engelhard, I. M. (2020). Fear of the coronavirus (COVID-19): Predictors in an online study conducted in March 2020. *Journal of Anxiety Disorders, 74*, Article 102258. https://doi.org/10.1016/j.janxdis.2020.102258

Mia, M. A., & Griffiths, M. D. (2021). Can South Asian countries cope with the mental health crisis associated with COVID-19? *International Journal of Mental Health and Addiction.* https://doi.org/10.1007/s11469-021-00491-5

Moreno, C., Wykes, T., Galderisi, S., Nordentoft, M., Crossley, N., Jones, N., … Arango, C. (2020). How mental health care should change as a consequence of the COVID-19 pandemic. *The Lancet Psychiatry, 7*(9), 813–824. https://doi.org/10.1016/S2215-0366(20)30307-2

Murray, D. R., & Schaller, M. (2016). The Behavioral immune system: Implications for social cognition, social interaction, and social influence. *Advances in Experimental Social Psychology, 53*, 75–129. https://doi.org/10.1016/bs.aesp.2015.09.002

Nikčević, A. V., Marino, C., Kolubinski, D. C., Leach, D., & Spada, M. M. (2020). Modelling the contribution of the Big Five personality traits, health anxiety, and COVID-19 psychological distress to generalised anxiety and depressive symptoms during the COVID-19 pandemic. *Journal of Affective Disorders, 279*, 578–584. https://doi.org/10.1016/j.jad.2020.10.053

Noman, A. H. M., Griffiths, M. D., Pervin, S., & Ismail, M. N. (2021). The detrimental effects of the COVID-19 pandemic on domestic violence against women. *Journal of Psychiatric Research, 134*, 111–112. https://doi.org/10.1016/j.jpsychires.2020.12.057

Nowak, B., Brzóska, P., Piotrowski, J., Sedikides, C., Żemojtel-Piotrowska, M., & Jonason, P. K. (2020). Adaptive and maladaptive behavior during the COVID-19 pandemic: The roles of Dark Triad traits, collective narcissism, and health beliefs. *Personality and Individual Differences, 167*, Article 110232. https://doi.org/10.1016/j.paid.2020.110232

Özdin, S., & Özdin, Ş. B. (2020). Levels and predictors of anxiety, depression and health anxiety during COVID-19 pandemic in Turkish society: The importance of gender. *International Journal of Social Psychiatry, 66*(5), 504–511. https://doi.org/10.1177/0020764020927051

Pak, H., Süsen, Y., Nazlıgül, M. D., & Griffiths, M. (2021). The mediating effects of Fear of COVID-19 and depression on the association between intolerance of uncertainty and emotional eating during the COVID-19 pandemic in Turkey. *International Journal of Mental Health and Addiction.* https://doi.org/10.1007/s11469-021-00489-z

Palgi, Y., Shrira, A., Ring, L., Bodner, E., Avidor, S., Bergman, Y., Cohen-Fridel, S., Shoshi Keisari, S., & Hoffman, Y. (2020). The loneliness pandemic: Loneliness and other concomitants of depression, anxiety and their comorbidity during the COVID-19 outbreak. *Journal of Affective Disorders, 275*, 109–111. https://doi.org/10.1016/j.jad.2020.06.036

Pan, X. (2020). Exercise under death-anxiety: Investigating individual exercise psychology and behavior from perspective of terror management and behavioral immune system introduction. *Journal of Applied Sports Sciences, 1*, 3–21. https://doi.org/10.37393/JASS.2020.01.1

Panchal, N., Kamal, R., Cox, C., & Garfield, R. (2021, February 10). *The implications of COVID-19 for mental health and substance use.* Kaiser Family Foundation (KFF). https://www.kff.org/coronavirus-covid-19/issue-brief/the-implications-of-covid-19-for-mental-health-and-substance-use/

Patrick, S. W., Henkhaus, L. E., Zickafoose, J. S., Lovell, K., Halvorson, A., Loch, S., Letterie, M., & Davis, M. M. (2020). Well-being of parents and children during the COVID-19 pandemic: A national survey. *Pediatrics, 146*(4), Article e2020016824. https://doi.org/10.1542/peds.2020-016824

Paul, E., Steptoe, A., & Fancourt, D. (2020). Attitudes towards vaccines and intention to vaccinate against COVID-19: Implications for public health communications. *The Lancet Regional Health - Europe, 1*, 100012. https://doi.org/10.1016/j.lanepe.2020.100012

Perri, M., Dosani, N., & Hwang, S. W. (2020). COVID-19 and people experiencing homelessness: Challenges and mitigation strategies. *Canadian Medical Association Journal, 192*(26), E716–E719. https://doi.org/10.1503/cmaj.200834

Petzold, M. B., Bendau, A., Plag, J., Pyrkosch, L., Mascarell Maricic, L., Betzler, F., Rogoll, J., Große, J., & Ströhle, A. (2020). Risk, resilience, psychological distress, and anxiety at the beginning of the COVID-19 pandemic in Germany. *Brain and Behavior, 10*(9), Article e01745. https://doi.org/10.1002/brb3.1745

Pizzigati, S. (2021, January 5). *In 2021, let's ring a global alarm on inequality that everyone can hear.* Counter Punch. https://www.counterpunch.org/2021/01/05/in-2021-lets-ring-a-global-alarm-on-inequality-that-everyone-can-hear/

Pyszczynski, T. (2004). What are we so afraid of? A terror management perspective on the politics of fear. *Social Research, 71*, 827–848.

Pyszczynski, T., Greenberg, J., & Solomon, S. (1999). A dual-process model of defense against conscious and unconscious death-related thoughts: An extension of terror management theory. *Psychological Review, 106*(4), 835–845. https://doi.org/10.1037/0033-295x.106.4.835

Pyszczynski, T., Lockett, M., Greenberg, J., & Solomon, S. (2020). Terror management theory and the COVID-19 pandemic. *Journal of Humanistic Psychology, 61*(2), 173–189. https://doi.org/10.1177/0022167820959488

Que, J., Shi, L., Deng, J., Liu, J., Zhang, L., Wu, S., Gong, Y., Huang, W., Yuan, K., Yan, W., Sun, Y., Ran, M., Bao, Y., & Lu, L. (2020). Psychological impact of the COVID-19 pandemic on healthcare workers: A cross-sectional study in China. *General Psychiatry, 33*(3), Article e100259. https://doi.org/10.1136/gpsych-2020-100259

Racine, N., Cooke, J. E., Eirich, R., Korczak, D. J., McArthur, B., & Madigan, S. (2020). Child and adolescent mental illness during COVID-19: A rapid review. *Psychiatry Research, 292*, Article 113307. https://doi.org/10.1016/j.psychres.2020.113307

Rees, S., & Fisher, J. (2020). COVID-19 and the mental health of people from refugee backgrounds. *International Journal of Health Services, 50*(4), 415–417. https://doi.org/10.1177/0020731420942475

Rehman, U., Shahnawaz, M. G., Khan, N. H., Kharshiing, K. D., Khursheed, M., Gupta, K., Kashyap, D., & Uniyal, R. (2021). Depression, anxiety and stress among Indians in times of Covid-19 lockdown. *Community Mental Health Journal, 57*, 42–48. https://doi.org/10.1007/s10597-020-00664-x

Roberto, K. J., Johnson, A. F., & Rauhaus, B. M. (2020). Stigmatization and prejudice during the COVID-19 pandemic. *Administrative Theory & Praxis, 42*(3), 364–378. https://doi.org/10.1080/10841806.2020.1782128

Roos, L. E., & Tomfohr-Madsen, L. (2020, August 16). *Family mental health crisis: Parental depression, anxiety during COVID-19 will affect kids too*. The Conversation. https://theconversation.com/family-mental-health-crisis-parental-depression-anxiety-during-covid-19-will-affect-kids-too-144050

Roy, D., Tripathy, S., Kar, S. K., Sharma, N., Verma, S. K., & Kaushal, V. (2020). Study of knowledge, attitude, anxiety & perceived mental healthcare need in Indian population during COVID-19 pandemic. *Asian Journal of Psychiatry, 51*, Article 102083. https://doi.org/10.1016/j.ajp.2020.102083

Ryder, A., Berry, J. W., Safdar, S., & Yampolsky, M. (2020, May 27). *"Psychology works" fact sheet: Why does culture matter to COVID-19?* Canadian Psychological Association. https://cpa.ca/docs/File/Publications/FactSheets/FS_CultureAndCOVID-19.pdf

Sakib, N., Bhuiyan, A., Hossain, S., Al Mamun, F., Hosen, I., Abdullah, A. H., Sarker, M. A., Mohiuddin, M. S., Rayhan, I., Hossain, M., Sikder, M. T., Gozal, D., Muhit, M., Islam, S., Griffiths, M. D., Pakpour, A. H., & Mamun, M. A. (2020). Psychometric validation of the Bangla Fear of COVID-19 Scale: Confirmatory factor analysis and Rasch analysis. *International Journal of Mental Health and Addiction*, 1–12. https://doi.org/10.1007/s11469-020-00289-x

Salari, N., Hosseinian-Far, A., Jalali, R., Vaisi-Raygani, A., Rasoulpoor, S., Mohammadi, M., Rasoulpoor, S., & Khaledi-Paveh, B. (2020). Prevalence of stress, anxiety, depression among the general population during the COVID-19 pandemic: A systematic review and meta-analysis. *Globalization and Health, 16*(1), Article 57. https://doi.org/10.1186/s12992-020-00589-w

Santabárbara, J., Lasheras, I., Lipnicki, D. M., Bueno-Notivol, J., Pérez-Moreno, M., López-Antón, R., De la Cámara, C., Lobo, A., & Gracia-García, P. (2020). Prevalence of anxiety in the COVID-19 pandemic: An updated meta-analysis of community-based studies. *Progress in Neuro-Psychopharmacology & Biological Psychiatry, 109*, Article 110207. https://doi.org/10.1016/j.pnpbp.2020.110207

Saurabh, K., & Ranjan, S. (2020). Compliance and psychological impact of quarantine in children and adolescents due to Covid-19 pandemic. *The Indian Journal of Pediatrics*. https://doi.org/10.1007/s12098-020-03347-3

Schaffer DeRoo, S., Pudalov, N. J., & Fu, L. Y. (2020). Planning for a COVID-19 vaccination program. *The Journal of the American Medical Association (JAMA)*. https://doi.org/10.1001/jama.2020.8711

Schaller, M. (2006). Parasites, behavioral defenses, and the social psychological mechanisms through which cultures are evoked. *Psychological Inquiry, 17*(2), 96–101.

Schaller, M. (2011). The behavioural immune system and the psychology of human sociality. *Philosophical Transactions of the Royal Society B, Biological Sciences, 366*(1583), 3418–3426. https://doi.org/10.1098/rstb.2011.0029

Schaller, M., & Park, J. H. (2011). The behavioral immune system (and why it matters). *Current Directions in Psychological Science, 20*(2), 99–103. https://doi.org/10.1177/0963721411402596

Schaller, M., Park, J. H., & Kenrick, D. T. (2007). Human evolution and social cognition. In R. I. M. Dunbar & L. Barrett (Eds.), *Oxford handbook of evolutionary psychology* (pp. 491–504). Oxford University Press.

Schwartz, N. S. (2020, April 8). *Why Canadians and Americans are buying guns during the coronavirus pandemic.* The Conversation. https://theconversation.com/why-canadians-and-americans-are-buying-guns-during-the-coronavirus-pandemic-135409

Shah, S. M. A., Mohammad, D., Qureshi, M. F. H., Abbas, M. Z., & Aleem, S. (2021). Prevalence, psychological responses and associated correlates of depression, anxiety and stress in a global population, during the coronavirus disease (COVID-19) pandemic. *Community Mental Health Journal, 57*, 101–110. https://doi.org/10.1007/s10597-020-00728-y

Sher, L. (2020). The impact of the COVID-19 pandemic on suicide rates. *QJM: An International Journal of Medicine, 113*(10), 707–712. https://doi.org/10.1093/qjmed/hcaa202

Shook, N. J., Sevi, B., Lee, J., Oosterhoff, B., & Fitzgerald, H. N. (2020). Disease avoidance in the time of COVID-19: The behavioral immune system is associated with concern and preventative health behaviors. *PLoS One, 15*(8), Article e0238015. https://doi.org/10.1371/journal.pone.0238015

Sieffien, W., Law, S., & Andermann, L. (2020, June 23). *Immigrant and refugee mental health during the COVID-19 pandemic: Additional key considerations.* The College of Family Physicians of Canada. https://www.cfp.ca/news/2020/06/23/06-23-1

Silva, W. A. D., Brito, T. R. S., & Pereira, C. R. (2021). Anxiety associated with COVID-19 and concerns about death: Impacts on psychological well-being, *176*, Article 110772. https://doi.org/10.1016/j.paid.2021.110772

Şimşir, Z., Koç, H., Seki, T., & Griffiths, M. D. (2021). The relationship between fear of COVID-19 and mental health problems: A meta-analysis. *Death Studies*. https://doi.org/10.1080/07481187.2021.1889097

Singh, S., Roy, D., Sinha, K., Parveen, S., Sharma, G., & Joshi, G. (2020). Impact of COVID-19 and lockdown on mental health of children and adolescents: A narrative review with recommendations. *Psychiatry Research, 293*, Article 113429. https://doi.org/10.1016/j.psychres.2020.113429

Soklaridis, S., Lin, E., Lalani, Y., Rodak, T., & Sockalingam, S. (2020). Mental health interventions and supports during COVID- 19 and other medical pandemics: A rapid systematic review of the evidence. *General Hospital Psychiatry, 66*, 133–146. https://doi.org/10.1016/j.genhosppsych.2020.08.007

Solomon, S., Greenberg, J., & Pyszczynski, T. (1991). A terror management theory of social behavior: The psychological functions of self-esteem and cultural worldviews. *Advances in Experimental Social Psychology, 24*, 93–159. https://doi.org/10.1016/s0065-2601(08)60328-7

Solomou, I., & Constantinidou, F. (2020). Prevalence and predictors of anxiety and depression symptoms during the COVID-19 pandemic and compliance with precautionary measures: Age and sex matter. *International Journal of Environmental Research and Public Health, 17*(14), Article 4924. https://doi.org/10.3390/ijerph17144924

Soraci, P., Ferrari, A., Abbiati, F. A., Del Fante, E., De Pace, R., Urso, A., & Griffiths, M. D. (2020). Validation and psychometric evaluation of the Italian version of the Fear of COVID-19

Scale. *International Journal of Mental Health and Addiction*. https://doi.org/10.1007/s11469-020-00277-1

Spoorthy, M. S., Pratapa, S. K., & Mahant, S. (2020). Mental health problems faced by healthcare workers due to the COVID-19 pandemic–A review. *Asian Journal of Psychiatry, 51*, Article 102119. https://doi.org/10.1016/j.ajp.2020.102119

Substance Abuse and Mental Health Services Administration. (2020). Double jeopardy: COVID-19 and behavioral health disparities for Black and Latino communities in the U.S. https://www.samhsa.gov/sites/default/files/covid19-behavioral-health-disparities-black-latino-communities.pdf

Sun, Y., Li, Y., Bao, Y., Meng, S., Sun, Y., Schumann, G., Kosten, T., Strang, J., Lu, L., & Shi, J. (2020a). Brief report: Increased addictive internet and substance use behavior during the COVID-19 pandemic in China. *The American Journal on Addictions, 29*(4), 268–270. https://doi.org/10.1111/ajad.13066

Sun, L., Sun, Z., Wu, L., Zhu, Z., Zhang, F., Shang, Z., Jia, Y., Gu, J., Zhou, Y., Wang, Y., Liu, N., & Liu, W. (2020b). Prevalence and risk factors of acute posttraumatic stress disorder during the COVID-19 outbreak. *medRxiv*. https://doi.org/10.1101/2020.03.06.20032425

Tang, W., Hu, T., Hu, B., Jin, C., Wang, G., Xie, C., Chen, S., & Xu, J. (2020). Prevalence and correlates of PTSD and depressive symptoms one month after the outbreak of the COVID-19 epidemic in a sample of home-quarantined Chinese university students. *Journal of Affective Disorders, 274*, 1–7. https://doi.org/10.1016/j.jad.2020.05.009

Taylor, S., Landry, C. A., Paluszek, M. M., Fergus, T. A., McKay, D., & Asmundson, G. J. G. (2020). Development and initial validation of the COVID Stress Scales. *Journal of Anxiety Disorders, 72*, Article 102232. https://doi.org/10.1016/j.janxdis.2020.102232

The Lancet Public Health. (2021). COVID-19-break the cycle of inequality. *The Lancet Public Health, 6*(2), E82. https://doi.org/10.1016/S2468-2667(21)00011-6

The United Nations Department of Global Communications. (2020). *COVID-19: UN counters pandemic-related hate and xenophobia*. United Nations. https://www.un.org/en/coronavirus/covid-19-un-counters-pandemic-related-hate-and-xenophobia?fbclid=IwAR1adlSzqRf0yncV8qJo6tVluydbfPYY8DUPII62iex3jodI12jNLEsewLA

Thibaut, F., & van Wijngaarden-Cremers, P. J. M. (2020). Women's mental health in the time of Covid-19 pandemic. *Frontiers in Global Women's Health, 1*. https://doi.org/10.3389/fgwh.2020.588372

Thompson, N. (2021, February 15). *Reports of domestic, intimate partner violence continue to rise during pandemic*. CBC News. https://www.cbc.ca/news/canada/toronto/domestic-intimate-partner-violence-up-in-pandemic-1.5914344

Tsai, J., & Wilson, M. (2020). COVID-19: A potential public health problem for homeless populations. *The Lancet Public Health, 5*(4), E186–E187. https://doi.org/10.1016/s2468-2667(20)30053-0

Tsamakis, K., Tsiptsios, D., Ouranidis, A., Mueller, C., Schizas, D., Terniotis, C., Nikolakakis, N., Tyros, G., Kympouropoulos, S., Lazaris, A., Spandidos, D. A., Smyrnis, N., & Rizos, E. (2021). COVID-19 and its consequences on mental health (Review). *Experimental and Therapeutic Medicine, 21*(3), Article 244. https://doi.org/10.3892/etm.2021.9675

Tso, I. F., & Park, S. (2020). Alarming levels of psychiatric symptoms and the role of loneliness during the COVID-19 epidemic: A case study of Hong Kong. *Psychiatry Research, 293*, Article 113423. https://doi.org/10.1016/j.psychres.2020.113423

UNESCO. (2020, March 31). *Covid-19 school closures around the world will hit girls hardest*. https://en.unesco.org/news/covid-19-school-closures-around-world-will-hit-girls-hardest?fbclid=IwAR0MyjQvHhkyi9DSZkQjNshDIZfjVMcRzftoPws66BRDJSY1wPN9e426AbU

UN Women. (n.d.). *The shadow pandemic: Violence against women during COVID-19*. https://www.unwomen.org/en/news/in-focus/in-focus-gender-equality-in-covid-19-response/violence-against-women-during-covid-19

Usher, K., Bhullar, N., & Jackson, D. (2020). Life in the pandemic: Social isolation and mental health. *Journal of Clinical Nursing, 29*(15–16), 2756–2757. https://doi.org/10.1111/jocn.15290

Valera, E. (2020, July 7). *When lockdown is not actually safer: Intimate partner violence during COVID-19*. Harvard Health Publishing. https://www.health.harvard.edu/blog/when-lockdown-is-not-actually-safer-intimate-partner-violence-during-covid-19-2020070720529

Van Tilburg, T. G., Steinmetz, S., Stolte, E., van der Roest, H., & de Vries, D. H. (2020). Loneliness and mental health during the COVID-19 pandemic: A study among Dutch older adults. *The Journals of Gerontology: Series B*, Article gbaa111. https://doi.org/10.1093/geronb/gbaa111

VanDyke, M., Carusa, S., & Warren, T. (2020, March 30). *Understanding hoarding responses to Covid-19: Where did all the toilet paper go?* Anxiety and Depression Association of America. https://adaa.org/learn-from-us/from-the-experts/blog-posts/consumer/understanding-hoarding-responses-covid-19-where?fbclid=IwAR3TKtR6uDrTYkKFHcKL55QValc5HaHR PvKimoc1AFsz8QGvN-v4mjS5bos

Villa, S., Jaramillo, E., Mangioni, D., Bandera, A., Gori, A., & Raviglione, M. C. (2020). Stigma at the time of the COVID-19 pandemic. *Clinical Microbiology and Infection, 26*(11), 1450–1452. https://doi.org/10.1016/j.cmi.2020.08.001

Williamson, H. C. (2020). Early effects of the COVID-19 pandemic on relationship satisfaction and attributions. *Psychological Science, 31*(12), 1479–1487. https://doi.org/10.1177/0956797620972688

Wong, S. Y. S., Zhang, D., Sit, R. W. S., Yip, B. H. K., Chung, R. Y., Wong, C. K. M., Chan, D. C. C., Sun, W., Kwok, K. O., & Mercer, S. W. (2020). Impact of COVID-19 on loneliness, mental health, and health service utilisation: A prospective cohort study of older adults with multimorbidity in primary care. *British Journal of General Practice, 70*(700), e817–e824. https://doi.org/10.3399/bjgp20X713021

World Health Organizations. (2017, November 29). *Violence against women*. WHO. https://www.who.int/news-room/fact-sheets/detail/violence-against-women

World Health Organizations. (2020, October 28). Coronavirus disease (COVID-19): Vaccines. https://www.who.int/news-room/q-a-detail/coronavirus-disease-(covid-19)-vaccines?ad groupsurvey={adgroupsurvey}&gclid=Cj0KCQiAj9iBBhCJARIsAE9qRtA5swVzCzq xzda_JHlDX_Tct7FOJc9LpwpDRWy6egnsp52jaPmu-aIaAjKrEALw_wcB

Zarefsky, M. (2020, August 18). *Why depression, anxiety are prevalent during COVID-19*. American Medical Association. https://www.ama-assn.org/delivering-care/public-health/why-depression-anxiety-are-prevalent-during-covid-19

Zhang, J., Wu, W., Zhao, X., & Zhang, W. (2020a). Recommended psychological crisis intervention response to the 2019 novel coronavirus pneumonia outbreak in China: A model of West China Hospital. *Precision Clinical Medicine, 3*(1), 3–8. https://doi.org/10.1093/pcmedi/pbaa006

Zhang, J., Yang, Z., Wang, X., Li, J., Dong, L., Wang, F., Li, Y., Wei, R., & Zhang, J. (2020b). The relationship between resilience, anxiety, and depression among patients with mild symptoms of COVID-19 in China: A cross-sectional study. *Journal of Clinical Nursing, 29*(21–22), 4020–4029. https://doi.org/10.1111/jocn.15425

Chapter 15
Incorporating the Outcomes of COVID-19 with Other Recent Pandemic Outbreaks on Healthcare Workers: A Systematic Review and Meta-analysis

Amrita Choudhary, Jay Kumar Ranjan, Payal Sharma, and H. S. Asthana

15.1 Introduction

The world is currently undergoing through a major global health crisis, viz., coronavirus disease (COVID-19). The first case of COVID-19 appeared in Wuhan, China, in the month of December (Wang et al., 2020a). Wuhan is considered the epicenter of this global pandemic, which has now spread its arms across 215 nations. As on the morning of 15 June 2020, *7,805,148 confirmed cases* of COVID-19 have been reported across the world, including *a death toll of 431,192 people* (Organisation WH, 2020). These statistics have made COVID-19 a major global health crisis of the century, with no effective treatment available.

Formerly, different parts of the world had already experienced various epidemics and pandemics, e.g., influenza A subtype H1N1, Ebola virus disease (EVD), Middle East respiratory syndrome (MERS), severe acute respiratory syndrome (SARS), yellow fever, etc., (Organization WH, 2017). However, the current COVID-19 pandemic is different from the ones mentioned because of its highly contagious nature; therefore, it is hardly possible to confine it within a limited region (Raviola et al., 2020).

Healthcare professionals are the frontline warriors amidst COVID-19 crisis and are particularly at high risk, because their continuous exposure to the infected surrounding slowly makes them vulnerable to mental exhaustion (Liu et al., 2020a). Majority of healthcare workers are working on long shifts with heavy workload (China NHCotPsRo, 2020) which has sapped them physically and emotionally (Liu et al., 2020a). In addition to that, healthcare providers wear personal protective equipment (PPE) for long hours leading to physical distress, which dampens their

A. Choudhary · J. K. Ranjan (✉) · P. Sharma · H. S. Asthana
Department of Psychology, Banaras Hindu University, Varanasi, India
e-mail: amrita.chaudhary1@bhu.ac.in

© The Author(s), under exclusive license to Springer Nature Switzerland AG 2022
N. Faghih, A. Forouharfar (eds.), *Socioeconomic Dynamics of the COVID-19 Crisis*,
Contributions to Economics, https://doi.org/10.1007/978-3-030-89996-7_15

immune system (Adams & Walls, 2020). The governments all over the world have taken measures such as quarantine of health workers for at least for 14 days prior to visiting home. Various studies have reported that quarantine and social distancing cause many adverse psychological consequences such as irritability, insomnia, poor concentration and indecisiveness (Wu et al., 2009), acute stress reactions (Bai et al., 2004), anxiety (Chong et al., 2004), emotional distress and depression (Chong et al., 2004; Hawryluck et al., 2004), and post-traumatic stress disorder (Sprang & Silman, 2013).

Various researches have been conducted in the past to study the psychological distress caused by pandemics on healthcare professionals; for instance, 10–78% of healthcare workers experienced anxiety (Bai et al., 2004; Chong et al., 2004; Huang et al., 2020; Rossi et al., 2020; Tan et al., 2020), 8–73% felt depression (Bai et al., 2004; Chong et al., 2004; Rossi et al., 2020; Tan et al., 2020), 8–51% faced insomnia (Bai et al., 2004; Chong et al., 2004; Rossi et al., 2020), and 8–89% experienced stress and post-traumatic stress disorder (Bai et al., 2004; Huang et al., 2020; Rossi et al., 2020; Tan et al., 2020; Chan et al., 2005; Chen et al., 2005; Chua et al., 2004; Koh et al., 2005; Lu et al., 2006; Maunder et al., 2006; McAlonan et al., 2007; Nickell et al., 2004). It is evident from the literature survey that a wide variability has been reported among the findings regarding mental health consequences of frontline healthcare workers of pandemics.

Even though the pandemics are crucial public health problems that lead to physical and psychological consequences on forefront healthcare workers, there is no true estimate available for the same. Additionally, there is lack of systemic review and meta-analytic study about mental health consequences of pandemic outbreaks on frontline healthcare workers; therefore, it has been undertaken for the study. Amidst the crisis, the study presented in this chapter would be of great help to the governments, policymakers, and mental health practitioners all over the world, to recognize the resources required for controlling the aftermath of the pandemic.

15.2 Methods and Procedure

15.2.1 Identification of Studies

Databases such as EBSCOhost, PubMed, and Google Scholar were searched up till May 2020. The keywords and database-specific terms were combined to search the articles.

Terms related to pandemic (SARS, influenza H1N1, MERS, EVD, and COVID-19), terms related to mental health consequences (psychological distress, mental health, anxiety, depression, and post-traumatic stress disorder), and terms related to the population of interest (healthcare professionals, healthcare workers, doctors, and nurses) were searched using Boolean logic "AND", "OR".

As per the Preferred Reporting Items for Systematic Reviews and Meta-Analyses (PRISMA) (Moher et al., 2009) guidelines, two authors independently examined and securitized the articles based on the titles and abstracts of the articles as per predefined inclusion and exclusion criteria. After that, full texts of suitable articles were retrieved for further rigorous inspection and evaluation. Apart from the aforementioned, additional articles were identified through manual search of bibliographies, references, and cross-references of the previously identified suitable studies. Further, both the authors who are performing review search processes independently examined the full texts of articles rigorously as per preset inclusion and exclusion criteria. Lastly, both the authors presented their scrutinized articles, and after several rounds of discussion and deliberations, the discrepancies between the authors regarding the final inclusion of articles for the meta-analysis were resolved.

15.2.2 Quality Assessment

The quality of the included articles was assessed using the Strengthening the Reporting of Observational studies in Epidemiology (STROBE) checklist (Von Elm et al., 2008). The checklist comprises 22 different parameters of quality assessment of published articles such as design of the study, variables assessed, sample size, statistical methods, etc. Strobe checklist is suggested for justification and elaboration of observational studies (Da Costa et al., 2011); however it is also popularly used for methodological quality assessment. A summary of the quality assessment is included in the Table 15.1.

15.2.3 Risk of Bias Assessment

The potential risks of biases in individual studies were assessed using the tools available on the website of Evidence Partners. In order to avoid potential publication bias, only cross-sectional studies were included in the present meta-analysis. Therefore, Risk of Bias Instrument for Cross-sectional Surveys of Attitudes and Practices (University CGaM, n.d.) was used for risk of bias assessment, and its findings are presented in Table 15.1.

15.2.4 Inclusion Criteria

The following criteria were used for the inclusion of manuscripts:

1. Manuscripts in which the psychological well-being of healthcare workers is involved in the pandemic level health emergency.

Table 15.1 Risk of bias assessment of cross-sectional studies and quality assessment (using STROBE)

Name of the study	Population representativeness	Response rate	Missing data	Clinically sensible	Reliability and validity of instruments	STROBE scores
Alsahafi et al. (Alsahafi & Cheng, 2016)	Low	Moderate	Low	Moderate	Moderate	18
Bai et al. (2004)	Moderate	Low	Moderate	Moderate	High	20
Tan et al. (2020)	Moderate	Low	Low	Low	Low	20
Chan et al. (Chan & Huak, 2004)	Moderate	Low	Moderate	Low	Low	21
Chew et al. (2020)	Low	Low	Low	Low	Low	20
Chong et al. (2004)	Low	Low	Low	Low	Low	21
Chua et al. (2004)	Low	Low	Low	Low	Low	19
Goulia et al. (2010)	Moderate	Moderate	Moderate	Moderate	Moderate	21
J. Huang et al. (2020)	Moderate	Low	Low	Low	Low	17
Jung et al. (2020)	Low	High	Low	Low	Low	20
Koh et al. (2005)	Low	Low	Moderate	Low	Low	20
Lancee et al. (2008)	Low	Moderate	Moderate	Low	Low	19
Lai et al. (2020)	Moderate	Low	Moderate	Low	Moderate	22
Lehmann et al. (2015)	Moderate	Low	Low	Low	Low	18
Lehmann et al. (2016)	Moderate	Moderate	Moderate	Low	Low	21
Li et al. (2015)	Moderate	Moderate	Low	Low	Low	19
Liu et al. (2012)	Moderate	Low	Low	Low	Low	19
Loh et al. (2005)	Moderate	Low	Low	Moderate	High	17
Lu et al. (2006)	High	Low	Low	High	Low	20

(continued)

Table 15.1 (continued)

Name of the study	Population representativeness	Response rate	Missing data	Clinically sensible	Reliability and validity of instruments	STROBE scores
Matsuishi et al. (2012)	Moderate	Moderate	Low	Low	Low	22
Maunder et al. (2006)	Low	Low	Moderate	Low	Low	22
Oh et al. (2017)	Moderate	Low	Low	Moderate	Low	21
Nickell et al. (2004)	Low	Moderate	Moderate	Low	Low	19
Park et al. (2018)	High	Moderate	Moderate	Moderate	Low	21
Poon et al. (2004)	Moderate	Moderate	Low	Low	Low	19
Rossi et al. (2020)	High	Low	Low	Low	Low	17
Sim et al. (2004)	Low	Low	Moderate	Low	Low	17
Styra et al. (2008)	Low	Moderate	Moderate	Low	Low	19
Tham et al. (2005)	Moderate	Low	Moderate	Low	Low	20
Verma et al. (2004)	Low	High	Low	Low	Low	19
P. Wu et al. (2008)	Low	Low	Low	Low	Low	19
Wong et al. (2005)	Moderate	Moderate	Moderate	Low	Moderate	21
Xiao et al. (2020)	Low	Low	Low	Low	Low	21
Liu et al. (2020a)	Low	Low	Low	Low	Low	20
Xu et al. (2020)	Moderate	Low	Low	Low	High	18
Lu et al. (2020)	Low	Low	Low	Low	Low	20
Zhu et al. (2020)	Low	Low	Low	Low	Low	21
Y. Huang et al. (Huang & Zhao, 2020)	Low	Low	Low	Low	Low	20
S. X. Zhang et al. (2020a)	Low	Low	Low	Low	Low	18

(continued)

Table 15.1 (continued)

Name of the study	Population representativeness	Response rate	Missing data	Clinically sensible	Reliability and validity of instruments	STROBE scores
Z. Liu et al. (2020b)	Low	Low	Low	Low	Low	20
Guo et al. (2020)	Low	Low	Low	Moderate	High	19
Dai et al. (2020)	Low	Low	Low	Low	Moderate	18
Du et al. (2020)	Moderate	Low	Low	Low	Low	20
Qi et al. (2020)	Low	Low	Low	Low	Low	20
Salman et al. (2020)	Moderate	Low	Low	Low	Low	19
C. Zhang et al. (2020b)	Low	Low	Low	Low	Low	20
G. Wu et al. (2020)	High	Low	Low	Low	Low	18
Kang et al. (2020)	Low	Low	Low	Low	Low	20
Wang et al. (2020b)	Low	Low	Low	Low	Low	19

Authors' own table

2. The inclusion of both genders.
3. Studies should have quantitative data on either frequency or mean values.
4. Studies of cross-sectional nature were included.
5. Written in the English language (or only the Abstract from where data can be derived is in English).

15.2.5   Data Extraction and Selection Procedure

After the finalization of the articles, the manuscripts were thoroughly reviewed. The relevant information was retrieved and recorded in MS Excel spreadsheet. The spreadsheet comprised information related to name of the author, publication year, survey year, location, name of the pandemic, sample size, tools used to measure psychological distress, and the descriptive statistics (i.e., frequency, mean, standard deviation) of persons screened of having psychological distress, etc. Depending upon the nature of results given, both raw data and central tendency values were recorded. A summary of the same is given in Table 15.2.

Table 15.2 Mental health consequences faced by healthcare workers during different pandemics

Author	Survey year	Country	Pandemic	Sample size	Tools	Mental health problem
(Alsahafi & Cheng, 2016)	2015	Saudi Arabia	MERS-CoV	1216	Self-developed questionnaire to measure knowledge, attitude, and behavior	Anxiety
Bai et al. (2004)	2003	Taiwan	SARS	218	Questionnaire for acute stress disorder	Acute stress disorders, anxiety, depression, sleep problem, stigma, and rejection
Tan et al. (2020)	2020	Singapore	COVID-19	296	DASS-21, IES-R	Anxiety, depression, stress, PTSD
(Chan & Huak, 2004)	2003	Singapore	SARS	32	GHQ-28; IES	Anxiety, depressed mood, PTSD
				74	GHQ-28; IES	Anxiety, depressed mood, PTSD
Chew et al. (2020)	2020	Singapore India	COVID-19	906	DASS21, IES-R	Depression, stress, anxiety, PTSD
Chong et al. (2004)	2003	Taiwan	SARS	1257	IES, CHQ, SARS exposure experience	Anxiety, sleep problems, depressed mood, PTSD
Chua et al. (2004)	2003	Hong Kong	SARS	271	PSS-10	Stress
Dai et al. (2020)	2020	China	COVID-19	4357	GHQ	Stress
Du et al. (2020)	2020	China	COVID-19	134	PSS, BDI-II, BAI	Stress, depression, anxiety
Goulia et al. (2010)	2009	Greece	Influenza (H1N1)	469	GHQ-28	Stress
Guo et al. (2020)	2020	China	COVID-19	11,118	WeChat Online Survey Tool	Anxiety, depression
J. Huang et al. (2020)	2020	China	COVID-19	230	Self-assessment scale for anxiety, PTSD-SS	Anxiety, PTSD
(Huang & Zhao, 2020)	2020	China	COVID-19	2250	GAD-7, PSQI, CES-D	Anxiety, depression, sleep problems
Jung et al. (2020)	2015	South Korea	MERS-COV	147	IES, JCQ, Turnover intention, GHQ-12	PTSD

(continued)

Table 15.2 (continued)

Author	Survey year	Country	Pandemic	Sample size	Tools	Mental health problem
Kang et al. (2020)	2020	China	COVID-19	994	PHQ-9, GAD-7, ISI, IES-R	Depression, anxiety, sleep problems, PTSD
Koh et al. (2005)	2004	Singapore	SARS	7636	Fear-related questionnaire, IES	Stress
Lancee et al. (2008)	2004–2005	Canada	SARS	448	KPDS, IES, MBI	Depression, anxiety, PTSD, burnout
Lai et al. (2020)	2020	China	COVID-19	1257	GAD-7, ISI-7,IES-R,	Anxiety, sleep problem, depressed mood, PTSD
Lehmann et al. (2015)	2014	Germany	Ebola	66	SSS-8, GAD-7, PHQ-9	Somatic symptom, anxiety, depression, fatigue
Lehmann et al. (2016)	2014	Germany	Ebola	86	HrQoL (SF-12FACIT, PHQ-9, GAD-7, and SSS-8 SSS-8)	Anxiety, depression
Li et al. (2015)	2015	Liberia	Ebola	52	General psychological status (SCL-90-R)	Somatization, obsessive-compulsive, interpersonal sensitivity, depression, anxiety, anger-hostility, phobic anxiety, paranoid ideation, psychoticism
Liu et al. (2012)	2006	China	SARS	549	CES-D (Chinese version), IES-R (Chinese version)	Depression, post-traumatic stress
Liu et al. (2020a)	2020	China	COVID-19	512	Zung Self-Rating Anxiety Scale	Anxiety
Z. Liu et al. (2020b)	2020	China	COVID-19	4679	Self-Reporting Questionnaire, SAS, SDS	Stress, anxiety, depression
Loh et al. (2005)	2003	Malaysia	SARS	202	Self-developed questionnaire to measure anxiety	Anxiety
Lu et al. (2006)	2003–2004	Taiwan	SARS	24	CHQ-12	Stress
				49	CHQ-12	Stress
Lu et al. (2020)	2020	China	COVID-19	2042	Hamilton Anxiety Scale, Hamilton Depression Scale	Anxiety, depression

(continued)

Table 15.2 (continued)

Author	Survey year	Country	Pandemic	Sample size	Tools	Mental health problem
Matsuishi et al. (2012)	2009	Japan	Influenza (H1N1)	218	IES, 19 stress-related questions	Anxiety, stress, PTSD
				864	IES, 19 stress-related questions	Anxiety, stress, PTSD
Maunder et al. (2006)	2004–2005	Canada	SARS	769	IES, KPDS, MBI (Emotional Exhaustion Scale), Ways of Coping Questionnaire	Stress, PTSD
Oh et al. (2017)	2015	South Korea	MERS-CoV	313	Self-developed questionnaire for measuring stress, professionalism, and nursing intention	Stress
Nickell et al. (2004)	2003	Canada	SARS	326	GHQ-12	Stress
Park et al. (2018)	2015	South Korea	MERS-CoV	187	PSS-10, SF-36, Dispositional resilience scale-15, Stigma	Stress
Poon et al. (2004)	2003	Hong Kong	SARS	1696	STAI, MBI	Anxiety, stigma, and rejection
Qi et al. (2020)	2020	China	COVID-19	801	PSQI	Sleep problems
Rossi et al. (2020)	2020	Italy	COVID-19	1379	GPS, PHQ-9, GAD-, ISI-7, PSS-10	Anxiety, sleep problems, depressed mood, stress, PTSD
Salman et al. (2020)	2020	China	COVID-19	398	GAD-7, PHQ-9	Anxiety, depression
Sim et al. (2004)	2003	Singapore	SARS	277	IES-R, GHQ-28, Coping scale	PTSD, psychiatric morbidity, coping issues
Styra et al. (2008)	2003	Canada	SARS	24	IES-R	PTSD
				120	IES-R	PTSD
				16	IES-R	PTSD
Tham et al. (2005)	2003	Singapore	SARS	96	IES, GHQ-28	PTSD, psychiatric morbidity
Verma et al. (2004)	2003	Singapore	SARS	32	GHQ-28, IES-R, HIV Stigma Scale	Anxiety, depressed mood, stigma and rejection, PTSD
Wang et al. (2020b)	2020	China	COVID-19	1210	IES-R, DASS-21	Depression, anxiety, PTSD

(continued)

Table 15.2 (continued)

Author	Survey year	Country	Pandemic	Sample size	Tools	Mental health problem
Wu et al. (2008)	2006	China	SARS	549	IES-R	PTSD, depression
					CES-D	
Wong et al. (2005)	2003	Hong Kong	SARS	794	18-item distress questionnaire	Stress
Wu et al. (2020)	2020	China	COVID-19	60	SCL-90, SAS, SDS, PTSD Checklist	Anxiety, depression, PTSD, sleep problems
Xiao et al. (2020)	2020	China	COVID-19	180	Self-Rating Anxiety Scale, General Self-Efficacy Scale, SASR, PSQI, SSRS	Anxiety, sleep problems
Xu et al. (2020)	2020	China	COVID-19	120	Anxiety and Depression Rating Scale	Anxiety and depression
S.X. Zhang et al. (2020a)	2020	China	COVID-19	927	ISI, SCL-90-R, PHQ-4	Anxiety, depression, sleep problems
C. Zhang et al. (2020b)	2020	China	COVID-19	1563	ISI, PHQ-9, GAD-7, IES-R	Sleep problems, depression, anxiety, PTSD
Zhu et al. (2020)	2020	China	COVID-19	5062	PHQ-9, GAD-7, IES-R	Depression, anxiety, PTSD

Authors' own table

DASS21 Depression Anxiety Stress Scale-21, *IES-R* Impact of Event Scale-Revised, *IES* Impact of Event Scale, *GHQ-28* General Health Questionnaire-28, *PTSD-SS* Post Traumatic Stress Disorder-Symptom Scale, *CHQ* Chinese Health Questionnaire, *PSS-10* Perceived Stress Scale-10, *GAD-7* Generalized Anxiety Disorder-7, *PHQ-9* Patient Health Questionnaire-9, *SSS-8* Somatic Symptom Severity-8, *MBI* Maslach Burnout Inventory, *ISI-7* Insomnia Severity Index, *CES-D* Center for Epidemiologic Studies Depression Scale, *BDI* Beck Depression Inventory, *STAI* State-Trait Anxiety Inventory, *GPS* Global Psychotrauma Screen, *JCQ* Job Content Questionnaire, *KPDS* Kessler Psychological Distress Scale, *TSIBS* Trauma Stress Institute Belief Scale, *VTS* Vicarious Trauma Scale, *DTS* Davidson Trauma Scale, *PSQI* Pittsburgh Sleep Quality Index, *SASR* Stanford Acute Stress Reaction, *SSRS* Social Support Rating Scale, *SAS* Self-reporting Anxiety Scale, *SDS* Self-reporting Depression Scale, *BAI* Beck Anxiety Inventory

15.2.6 Statistical Analysis

The present meta-analysis was conducted using the computer software R (3.5.3). The level of significance of the analysis was 5% (two-tailed tests). Three packages, i.e., "metafor," "matrix," and "xlsx" were used for conducting meta-analysis. The command library "xlsx" was used to extract and upload the MS Excel sheet in R console. Further, the "escalc()" function was used for the calculation of effect size (Viechtbauer, 2010). The package "metafor" uses "xi" and "ni" as generic input commands for event and sample size, respectively; "mi" and "sdi" for mean and standard deviation, respectively (Viechtbauer, 2010). The metaphor package uses rbind() command to combining rows of the effect sizes derived from raw data and mean values. Subsequently, effect size with random effect method was computed using function rma() (Viechtbauer, 2010). Further, "forest" function was used to generate the forest plot. Finally, funnel plot was plotted to estimate the publication bias. Egger's unweighted regression test was also performed to verify the publication bias, which was obtained by executing the regtest() function.

15.3 Results

15.3.1 Search Results

As indicated in Fig. 15.1, 3096 articles were identified through initial search in various search engines. Out of these, 3023 were excluded as the title/abstract was not relevant as per predefined inclusion criteria. Full texts of the remaining articles were reviewed for further analysis. Thereafter several rounds of discussions and deliberations regarding methodologies and findings of the remaining 73 articles, only 49 articles were retrieved for meta-analysis. The data extracted from these articles is included in Table 15.2.

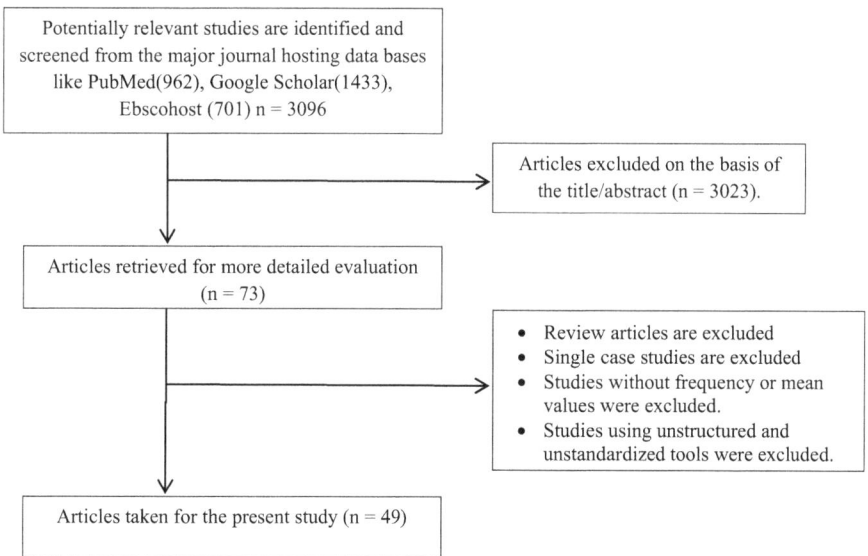

Fig. 15.1 Flow diagram of the study identification process. (Authors' own figure)

15.3.2 Meta-analysis of Different Psychological Problems Faced by Healthcare Workers

The present meta-analysis is based on 49 studies, which reported mental health consequences of 59,552 healthcare workers who were frontline warriors during major global health crisis, viz., SARS, MERS, influenza H1N1, EVD, and COVID-19. Majority of studies have reported anxiety, depressive symptoms, stress, sleep problems, and post-traumatic stress symptoms as major mental health issues among the healthcare professionals. Therefore, these variables were considered for the present meta-analysis.

The results of the meta-analysis (Table 15.3) indicate that anxiety (7%), depression (5%), stress (5%), sleep problems (8%), and post-traumatic stress symptoms (6%) are common mental health problems reported by healthcare workers during the current outbreak of COVID-19. On the other hand, 5% of health workers reported anxiety, and 7% reported depressive symptoms during the spread of Ebola virus disease. Similarly, during the outbreak of influenza (H1N1), doctors and nurses reported stress (12%), anxiety (8%), and post-traumatic stress symptoms (17%). SARS outbreak led to anxiety (11%), depressive symptoms (5%), stress (7%), sleep problems (6%), and post-traumatic stress symptoms (14%) among health workers. Lastly, 13% of healthcare workers reported stress during the era of MERS-COV.

Initially, the present authors had hypothesized that "all studies share a common effect size." Cochran Q that is known as a test of heterogeneity was applied for testing the hypothesis. The computed Q values are greater than df (Q > df), and associated p values are significant ($p < 0.001$). Consequently, it has been inferred that significant amount of heterogeneity was present across the studies (Table 15.3, Figs. 15.2, 15.3, 15.4, 15.5 and 15.6). I^2 indicates the percentage of variation across studies that are due to heterogeneity and not due to chance factor (Higgins et al., 2003). All the I^2 values range from 97.19% to 99.96%, which again indicates that there is high amount of heterogeneity present across the studies related to different mental health issues of frontline health workers during pandemic outbreaks (Table 15.3).

Funnel plots are scatterplots which act as visual aid to detect heterogeneity or publication bias. It is assumed that studies with high precision will be plotted around the average, and those with low precision will spread on either side of the average. Deviation from the funnel shape distribution is an indicator of publication bias. Underreporting of small or nonsignificant outcome is one of the most prominent reasons for the presence of publication bias. In the study presented in this chapter, the visual representation of funnel plots (Figs. 15.7, 15.8, 15.9, 15.10 and 15.11) indicates presence of possible publication bias in the present study. However, Duval and Tweedie's trim and fill analysis suggests that no more additional study were required to avoid the publication bias.

Table 15.3 Mental health consequences across different pandemics

Pandemic	No. of articles	Mental health consequences	Estimate	C.I. (95%)	Q-test	Df	I² (%)
Ebola	3	Anxiety	0.51	0.08–1.11	239.57**	5	97.19
		Depression	0.68	0.01–1.34	285.43**	5	97.73
Influenza (H1N1)	2	Anxiety	1.20	1.16–1.24	0.35	1	0.00
		Stress	0.78	0.48–1.09	206.01**	2	98.84
		PTSD	1.71	1.31–2.12	58.62**	1	98.29
SARS	18	Anxiety	1.11	0.52–1.70	5255.30**	7	99.86
		Depression	0.50	0.01–1.02	1349.68**	6	99.83
		Sleep	0.60	0.19–1.00	127.32**	1	99.21
		Stress	0.71	0.50–0.92	382.89**	6	99.40
		PTSD	1.48	0.73–2.22	15122.96**	10	99.93
MERS-COV	4	Stress	1.26	0.31–2.21	1800.56**	2	99.84
COVID-19	22	Anxiety	0.71	0.42–1.01	7334.39**	19	99.96
		Depression	0.46	0.39–0.52	1824.79**	16	99.16
		Sleep	0.80	0.53–1.07	1769.72**	8	99.85
		Stress	0.49	0.29–0.67	1093.57**	5	99.74
		PTSD	0.56	0.40–0.70	2046.48**	9	99.62

Authors' own table
**significant at 0.0001

15.4   Discussion

The globally hastened spread of various pandemics has created extensive amount of panic and anxiety around the world, not only in the general population but also among healthcare workers. Healthcare workers are always at high risk for contamination during the treatment process of infectious diseases. Therefore, disease outbreaks have laid various physical as well as psychological challenges for the well-being of healthcare workers (Brooks et al., 2020).

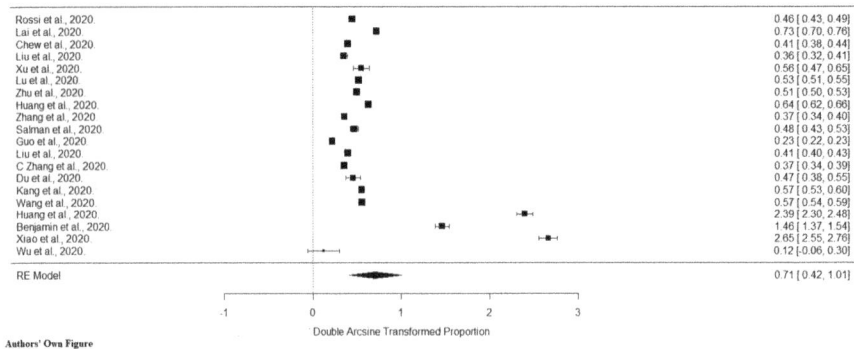

Fig. 15.2 Forest plot for symptoms of anxiety during Covid-19 (Authors own figure)

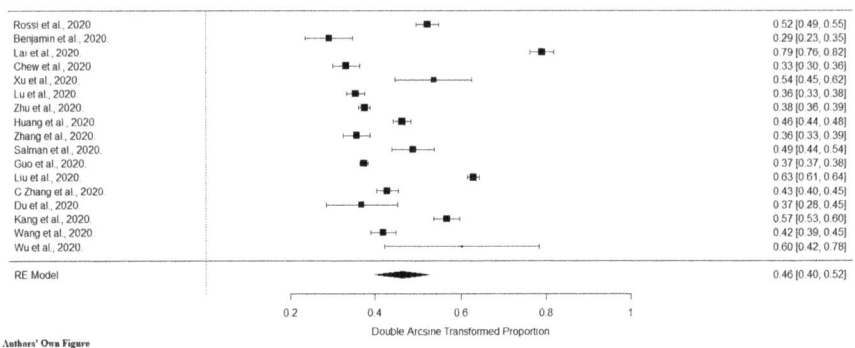

Fig. 15.3 Forest plot for symptoms of depression during Covid-19 (Authors own figure)

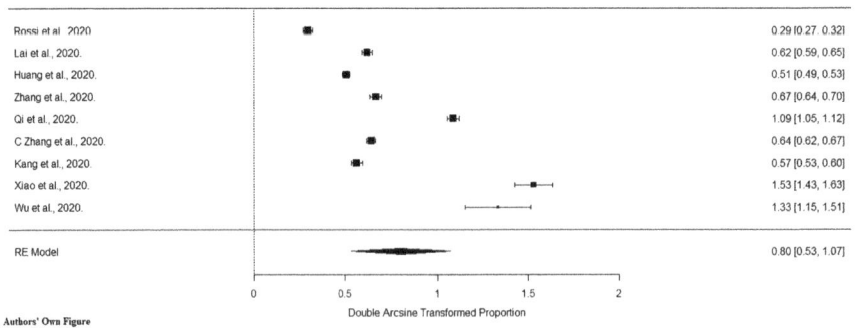

Fig. 15.4 Forest plot for sleep problems during Covid-19 (Authors own figure)

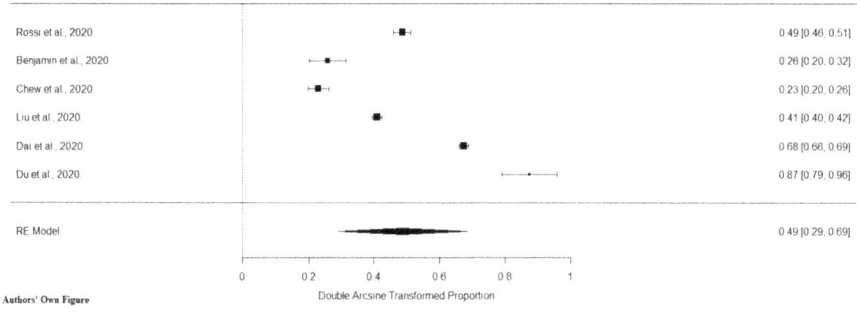

Fig. 15.5 Forest plot for stress during Covid-19 (Authors own figure)

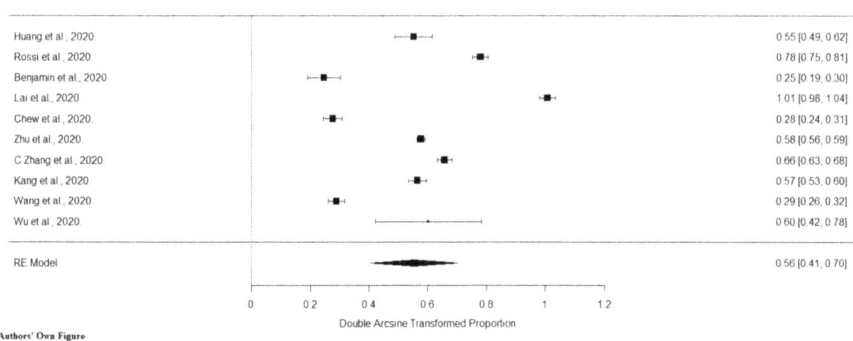

Fig. 15.6 Forest plot for post traumatic stress symptoms during Covid-19 (Authors own figure)

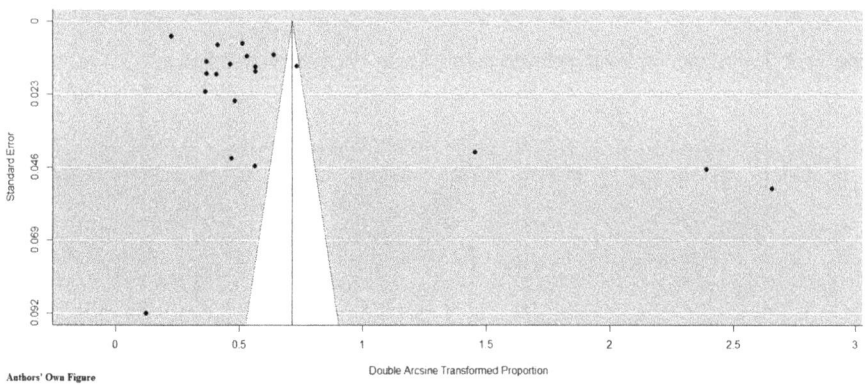

Fig. 15.7 Funnel plot for symptoms of Anxiety during Covid-19 (Authors own figure)

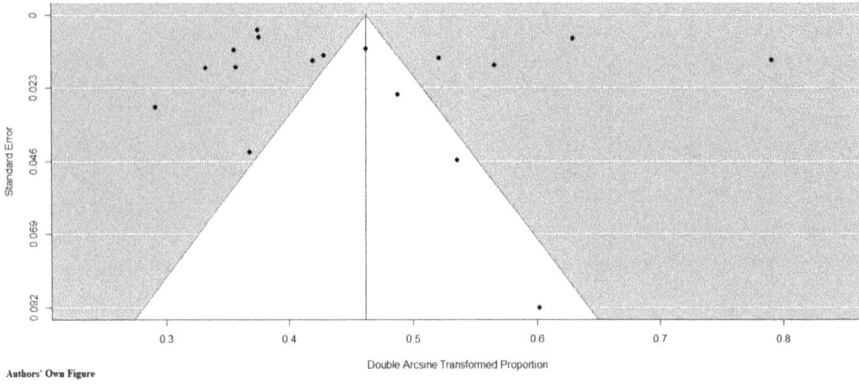

Fig. 15.8 Funnel plot for symptoms of depression during Covid-19 (Authors own figure)

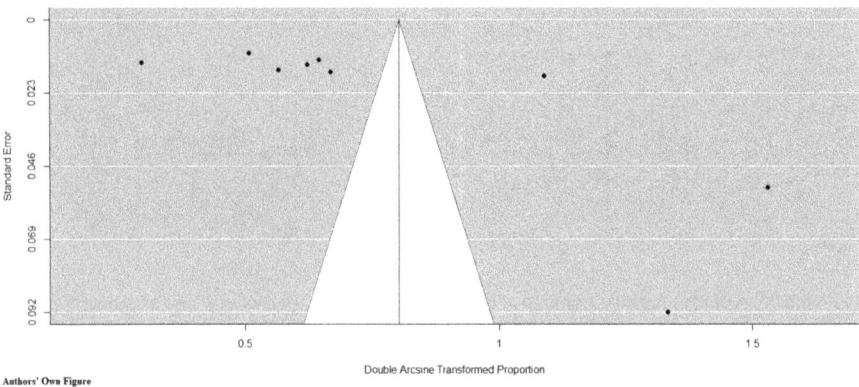

Fig. 15.9 Funnel plot for sleep problems during Covid-19 (Authors own figure)

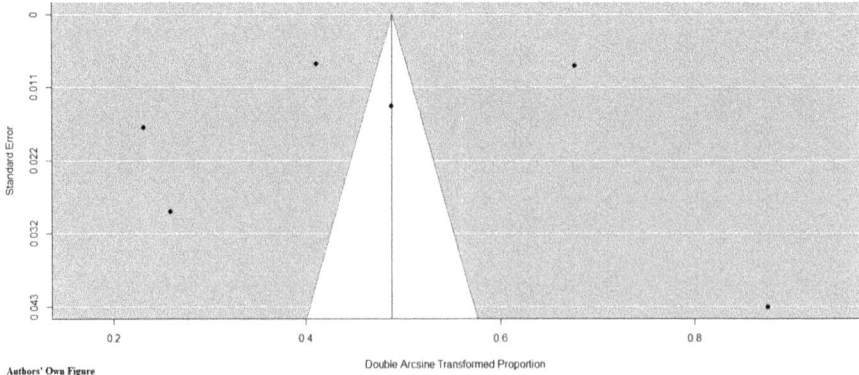

Fig. 15.10 Funnel plot for stress dining Covid-19 (Authors own figure)

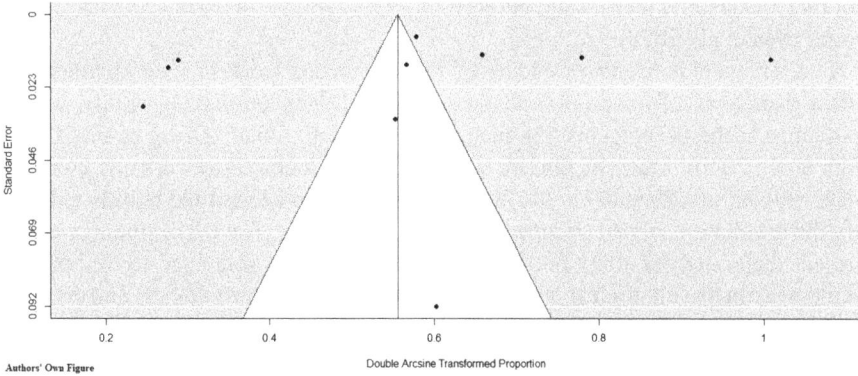

Fig. 15.11 Funnel plot for post traumatic stress symptoms during Covid-19 (Authors own figure)

The finding of the meta-analysis indicates that a significant proportion of health workers are suffering from anxiety (7%), depression (4%), stress-related symptoms (5%), sleep disturbance (8%), and post-traumatic stress symptoms (6%) as a result of COVID-19 outbreak. The present findings may be corroborated with the findings of Lee et al. (2018), as they have reported that health workers who are working in high-risk environment and involved in direct contact with patients either providing routine care or involved in cleaning and disinfection are more prone to the development of many mental health problems.

There are several attributing factors responsible for the genesis and maintenance of mental health problems among frontline healthcare workers. Apart from the biological factors, researchers have identified numerous psychosocial and occupational factors that may lead to mental health issues in the frontline caregivers. Frontline pandemic warriors are the highest risk-prone individuals for the carrier of the virus; therefore, they stay away from their family members and keep themselves in isolation after performing duty (Zhang et al., 2020a). Even after completion of the quarantine period, health workers along with their family members face stigma and discrimination by the neighbors and society, as a result of which, some of them avoid identifying themselves as hospital workers (Koh et al., 2005; Maunder et al., 2003). Some health workers exhibit avoidance behavior even after completion of the quarantine period, and they are reluctant to return to perform duties (Brooks et al., 2020). Apart from the high risk of infection, health workers undergo several occupational challenges such as increased workload, lack of personal protective equipment, inadequate training to deal with any infectious disease outbreak, and uncertainty regarding effective control of disease (Kang et al., 2020; Brooks et al., 2018).

Based on several media reports, some COVID-19 positive patients are neither cooperative nor adhering safety protocols (Today I, 2020). A few patients behave brutally with the ward staff that could be another challenge in the healthcare setting (Times H, 2020). If the psychological and physical needs of healthcare workers are not met adequately, they would be even more susceptible to various mental health issues (Sun et al., 2020).

Further, mental health problems of the healthcare workers may significantly affect their level of attention, understanding, and decision-making ability, which may impede the fight against the pandemic (Lai et al., 2020; Zhang et al., 2020a; Wen et al., 2020). Many healthcare workers show reluctance to work and contemplate resignation (Maunder et al., 2003). Therefore, the need of the hour is to identify the psychological and occupational needs of the caregivers. The findings of the present meta-analysis offer preliminary information and reference to design and implement the psychological intervention, tailored to the psychological and occupational needs of medical workers.

The findings offer an insight into the proactive steps required to protect the well-being of these warriors. The government and hospital management need to maintain the physical and psychological health of health workers during the current COVID-19 struggle.

Although the study addresses the mental health issues faced by healthcare professionals because of any disease outbreak, it has certain shortcomings. Firstly, the studies included in the analysis incorporate different tools and diagnostic criteria, which may have been a source of variability among the findings. Secondly, diagnosing mental health issues in healthcare workers during a pandemic is a difficult task. Amidst the health emergency, burdening the doctors and nurses with long questionnaires is not feasible; therefore, the sample size of certain studies was small. Hence, it is recommended that the government and policymakers should plan frequent screening of mental health in order to identify and address the issues of those healthcare professionals who are serving at high risk. Identification and prevention of mental health issues of these high-risk healthcare workers should be an essential component of global effort in this fight against COVID-19 or any infectious disease.

15.5   Conclusion

Healthcare professionals who are involved in facilitating health care during pandemic outbreaks are at heightened risk of developing mental health problems. Anxiety (7%), depression (5%), sleep disturbances (8%), stress (5%), and post-traumatic stress disorders (6%) are the most common mental health issues experienced by healthcare workers during COVID-19 crisis. As compared to other pandemic outbreaks, sleep disturbances were maximally present among health workers reported during COVID-19 crisis. The strength, intensity, and durability of spread of COVID-19 exceed that of other pandemic outbreaks. Therefore, the need of the hour is to extend psychological help to healthcare professionals who are experiencing mental health-related issues.

References

Adams, J. G., & Walls, R. M. (2020). Supporting the health care workforce during the COVID-19 global epidemic. *Journal of the American Medical Association.*

Alsahafi, A. J., & Cheng, A. C. (2016). Knowledge, attitudes and behaviours of healthcare workers in the Kingdom of Saudi Arabia to MERS coronavirus and other emerging infectious diseases. *International Journal of Environmental Research and Public Health, 13*(12), 1214.

Bai, Y., Lin, C.-C., Lin, C.-Y., Chen, J.-Y., Chue, C.-M., & Chou, P. (2004). Survey of stress reactions among health care workers involved with the SARS outbreak. *Psychiatric Services, 55*(9), 1055–1057.

Brooks, S. K., Dunn, R., Amlôt, R., Rubin, G. J., & Greenberg, N. (2018). A systematic, thematic review of social and occupational factors associated with psychological outcomes in healthcare employees during an infectious disease outbreak. *Journal of Occupational and Environmental Medicine, 60*(3), 248–257.

Brooks, S. K., Webster, R. K., Smith, L. E., et al. (2020). The psychological impact of quarantine and how to reduce it: Rapid review of the evidence. *The Lancet.*

Chan, A. O., & Huak, C. Y. (2004). Psychological impact of the 2003 severe acute respiratory syndrome outbreak on health care workers in a medium size regional general hospital in Singapore. *Occupational Medicine, 54*(3), 190–196.

Chan, S. S., Leung, G. M., Tiwari, A. F., et al. (2005). The impact of work-related risk on nurses during the SARS outbreak in Hong Kong. *Family & Community Health, 28*(3), 274–287.

Chen, C.-S., Wu, H.-Y., Yang, P., & Yen, C.-F. (2005). Psychological distress of nurses in Taiwan who worked during the outbreak of SARS. *Psychiatric Services, 56*(1), 76–79.

Poon, E., Liu, K. S., Cheong, D. L., Lee, C. K., Yam, L.Y.C., & Wang, W. N. (2004). Impact of severe acute respiratory syndrome on anxiety levels of front-line health care workers. *Hong Kong Medical Journal, 10*(5), 325–330.

Chew, N. W., Lee, G. K., Tan, B. Y., et al. (2020). A multinational, multicentre study on the psychological outcomes and associated physical symptoms amongst healthcare workers during COVID-19 outbreak. *Brain, Behavior, and Immunity.*

China NHCotPsRo. (2020). *Press conference of the joint prevention and control mechanism of the State Council.* In China NHCotPsRo (Ed.). National Health Commission of the People's Republic of China.

Chong, M.-Y., Wang, W.-C., Hsieh, W.-C., et al. (2004). Psychological impact of severe acute respiratory syndrome on health workers in a tertiary hospital. *The British Journal of Psychiatry, 185*(2), 127–133.

Chua, S. E., Cheung, V., Cheung, C., et al. (2004). Psychological effects of the SARS outbreak in Hong Kong on high-risk health care workers. *The Canadian Journal of Psychiatry, 49*(6), 391–393.

Da Costa, B. R., Cevallos, M., Altman, D. G., Rutjes, A. W., & Egger, M. (2011). Uses and misuses of the STROBE statement: Bibliographic study. *BMJ Open, 1*(1), e000048.

Dai, Y., Hu, G., Xiong, H., Qiu, H., & Yuan, X. (2020). Psychological impact of the coronavirus disease 2019 (COVID-19) outbreak on healthcare workers in China. *medRxiv.*

Du, J., Dong, L., Wang, T., et al. (2020). Psychological symptoms among frontline healthcare workers during COVID-19 outbreak in Wuhan. *General Hospital Psychiatry.*

Goulia, P., Mantas, C., Dimitroula, D., Mantis, D., & Hyphantis, T. (2010). General hospital staff worries, perceived sufficiency of information and associated psychological distress during the A/H1N1 influenza pandemic. *BMC Infectious Diseases, 10*(1), 322.

Guo, J., Liao, L., Wang, B., et al. (2020). Psychological effects of COVID-19 on hospital staff: A National Cross-Sectional Survey of China Mainland. *Available at SSRN 3550050.*

Hawryluck, L., Gold, W. L., Robinson, S., Pogorski, S., Galea, S., & Styra, R. (2004). SARS control and psychological effects of quarantine, Toronto, Canada. *Emerging Infectious Diseases, 10*(7), 1206.

Higgins, J. P., Thompson, S. G., Deeks, J. J., & Altman, D. G. (2003). Measuring inconsistency in meta-analyses. *BMJ, 327*(7414), 557–560.

Huang, Y., & Zhao, N. (2020). Generalized anxiety disorder, depressive symptoms and sleep quality during COVID-19 outbreak in China: A web-based cross-sectional survey. *Psychiatry Research*, 112954.

Huang, J., Han, M., Luo, T., Ren, A., & Zhou, X. (2020). Mental health survey of 230 medical staff in a tertiary infectious disease hospital for COVID-19. *Zhonghua lao dong wei sheng zhi ye bing za zhi= Zhonghua laodong weisheng zhiyebing zazhi = Chinese Journal of Industrial Hygiene and Occupational Diseases, 38*, E001–E001.

Jung, H., Jung, S. Y., Lee, M. H., & Kim, M. S. (2020). Assessing the presence of post-traumatic stress and turnover intention among nurses post–middle east respiratory syndrome outbreak: The importance of supervisor support. *Workplace Health & Safety*, 2165079919897693.

Kang, L., Li, Y., Hu, S., et al. (2020). The mental health of medical workers in Wuhan, China dealing with the 2019 novel coronavirus. *The Lancet Psychiatry, 7*(3), e14.

Koh, D., Lim, M. K., Chia, S. E., et al. (2005). Risk perception and impact of Severe Acute Respiratory Syndrome (SARS) on work and personal lives of healthcare workers in Singapore what can we learn? *Medical Care*, 676–682.

Lai, J., Ma, S., Wang, Y., et al. (2020). Factors associated with mental health outcomes among health care workers exposed to coronavirus disease 2019. *JAMA Network Open, 3*(3), e203976–e203976.

Lancee, W. J., Maunder, R. G., & Goldbloom, D. S. (2008). Prevalence of psychiatric disorders among Toronto hospital workers one to two years after the SARS outbreak. *Psychiatric Services, 59*(1), 91–95.

Lee, S. M., Kang, W. S., Cho, A.-R., Kim, T., & Park, J. K. (2018). Psychological impact of the 2015 MERS outbreak on hospital workers and quarantined hemodialysis patients. *Comprehensive Psychiatry, 87*, 123–127.

Lehmann, M., Bruenahl, C. A., Löwe, B., et al. (2015). Ebola and psychological stress of health care professionals. *Emerging Infectious Diseases, 21*(5), 913.

Lehmann, M., Bruenahl, C. A., Addo, M. M., et al. (2016). Acute Ebola virus disease patient treatment and health-related quality of life in health care professionals: A controlled study. *Journal of Psychosomatic Research, 83*, 69–74.

Li, L., Wan, C., Ding, R., et al. (2015). Mental distress among Liberian medical staff working at the China Ebola Treatment Unit: A cross sectional study. *Health and Quality of Life Outcomes, 13*(1), 156.

Liu, X., Kakade, M., Fuller, C. J., et al. (2012). Depression after exposure to stressful events: Lessons learned from the severe acute respiratory syndrome epidemic. *Comprehensive Psychiatry, 53*(1), 15–23.

Liu, C.-Y., Yang, Y.-z., Zhang, X.-M., Xu, X., Dou, Q.-L., & Zhang, W-.W. (2020a). The prevalence and influencing factors for anxiety in medical workers fighting COVID-19 in China: A cross-sectional survey. *Available at SSRN 3548781*.

Liu, Z., Han, B., Jiang, R., et al. (2020b). Mental health status of doctors and nurses during COVID-19 epidemic in China. *Available at SSRN 3551329*.

Loh, L.-C., Ali, A. M., Ang, T.-H., & Chelliah, A. (2005). Impact of a spreading epidemic on medical students. *The Malaysian Journal of Medical Sciences: MJMS, 12*(2), 43.

Lu, Y.-C., Shu, B.-C., & Chang, Y.-Y. (2006). The mental health of hospital workers dealing with severe acute respiratory syndrome. *Psychotherapy and Psychosomatics, 75*(6), 370–375.

Lu, W., Wang, H., Lin, Y., & Li, L. (2020). Psychological status of medical workforce during the COVID-19 pandemic: A cross-sectional study. *Psychiatry Research*, 112936.

Matsuishi, K., Kawazoe, A., Imai, H., et al. (2012). Psychological impact of the pandemic (H1N1) 2009 on general hospital workers in Kobe. *Psychiatry and Clinical Neurosciences, 66*(4), 353–360.

Maunder, R., Hunter, J., Vincent, L., et al. (2003). The immediate psychological and occupational impact of the 2003 SARS outbreak in a teaching hospital. *CMAJ, 168*(10), 1245–1251.

Maunder, R. G., Lancee, W. J., Balderson, K. E., et al. (2006). Long-term psychological and occupational effects of providing hospital healthcare during SARS outbreak. *Emerging Infectious Diseases, 12*(12), 1924.

McAlonan, G. M., Lee, A. M., Cheung, V., et al. (2007). Immediate and sustained psychological impact of an emerging infectious disease outbreak on health care workers. *The Canadian Journal of Psychiatry, 52*(4), 241–247.

Moher, D., Liberati, A., Tetzlaff, J., & Altman, D. G. (2009). Preferred reporting items for systematic reviews and meta-analyses: The PRISMA statement. *Annals of Internal Medicine, 151*(4), 264–269.

Nickell, L. A., Crighton, E. J., Tracy, C. S., et al. (2004). Psychosocial effects of SARS on hospital staff: Survey of a large tertiary care institution. *CMAJ, 170*(5), 793–798.

Oh, N., Hong, N., Ryu, D. H., Bae, S. G., Kam, S., & Kim, K.-Y. (2017). Exploring nursing intention, stress, and professionalism in response to infectious disease emergencies: The experience of local public hospital nurses during the 2015 MERS outbreak in South Korea. *Asian Nursing Research, 11*(3), 230–236.

Organization WH. (2017). Emerging diseases.

Organisation WH. (2020). Coronavirus disease (Covid-19). *Pandemic*.

Park, J.-S., Lee, E.-H., Park, N.-R., & Choi, Y. H. (2018). Mental health of nurses working at a government-designated hospital during a MERS-CoV outbreak: A cross-sectional study. *Archives of Psychiatric Nursing, 32*(1), 2–6.

Qi, J., Xu, J., Li, B.-Z., et al. (2020). The evaluation of sleep disturbances for Chinese frontline medical workers under the outbreak of COVID-19. *Sleep Medicine*.

Raviola, G., Rose, A., Fils-Aimé, J., et al. (2020). Development of a comprehensive, sustained community mental health system in post-earthquake Haiti, 2010–2019. *Global Mental Health, 7*.

Rossi, R., Socci, V., Pacitti, F., et al. (2020). Mental health outcomes among front and second line health workers associated with the COVID-19 pandemic in Italy. *medRxiv*.

Salman, M., Raza, M. H., Mustafa, Z. U., et al. (2020). The psychological effects of COVID-19 on frontline healthcare workers and how they are coping: A web-based, cross-sectional study from Pakistan. *medRxiv*.

Sim, K., Chong, P. N., Chan, Y. H., & Soon, W. (2004). Severe acute respiratory syndrome-related psychiatric and posttraumatic morbidities and coping responses in medical staff within a primary health care setting in Singapore. *The Journal of Clinical Psychiatry, 65*(8), 1120–1127.

Sprang, G., & Silman, M. (2013). Posttraumatic stress disorder in parents and youth after health-related disasters. *Disaster Medicine and Public Health Preparedness, 7*(1), 105–110.

Styra, R., Hawryluck, L., Robinson, S., Kasapinovic, S., Fones, C., & Gold, W. L. (2008). Impact on health care workers employed in high-risk areas during the Toronto SARS outbreak. *Journal of Psychosomatic Research, 64*(2), 177–183.

Sun, N., Shi, S., Jiao, D., et al. (2020). A qualitative study on the psychological experience of caregivers of COVID-19 patients. *American Journal of Infection Control*.

Tan, B. Y., Chew, N. W., Lee, G. K., et al. (2020). Psychological impact of the COVID-19 pandemic on health care workers in Singapore. *Annals of Internal Medicine*.

Tham, K., Tan, Y., Loh, O., Tan, W., Ong, M., & Tang, H. (2005). Psychological morbidity among emergency department doctors and nurses after the SARS outbreak. *Hong Kong Journal of Emergency Medicine, 12*(4), 215–223.

Times H. (2020). Health team pelted with stones during Covid-19 screening drive in Indore. *Hindustan Times,* April 2.

Today I. (2020). Tablighi members undergoing Covid-19 treatment not cooperating: Doctors to Delhi government. *India Today,* April 3.

University CGaM. (n.d.). Risk of bias instrument for cross-sectional surveys of attitudes and practices. https://www.evidencepartners.com/wp-content/uploads/2017/09/Risk-of-Bias-Instrument-for-Cross-Sectional-Surveys-of-Attitudes-and-Practices.pdf

Verma, S., Mythily, S., Chan, Y., Deslypere, J., Teo, E., & Chong, S. (2004). Post-SARS psychological morbidity and stigma among general practitioners and traditional Chinese medicine practitioners in Singapore. *Annals of the Academy of Medicine, Singapore, 33*(6), 743–748.

Viechtbauer, W. (2010). Conducting meta-analyses in R with the metafor package. *Journal of Statistical Software, 36*(3).

Von Elm, E., Altman, D. G., Egger, M., et al. (2008). The Strengthening the Reporting of Observational Studies in Epidemiology (STROBE) statement: Guidelines for reporting observational studies. *Journal of Clinical Epidemiology, 61*(4), 344–349.

Wang, C., Horby, P. W., Hayden, F. G., & Gao, G. F. (2020a). A novel coronavirus outbreak of global health concern. *The Lancet, 395*(10223), 470–473.

Wang, C., Pan, R., Wan, X., et al. (2020b). Immediate psychological responses and associated factors during the initial stage of the 2019 coronavirus disease (COVID-19) epidemic among the general population in China. *International Journal of Environmental Research and Public Health, 17*(5), 1729.

Wen, X., Ling, C., & Li, Y. (2020). Several potential risks of novel coronavirus (COVID-19) pneumonia outbreaks in hospitals. *American Journal of Infection Control.*

Wong, T. W., Yau, J. K., Chan, C. L., et al. (2005). The psychological impact of severe acute respiratory syndrome outbreak on healthcare workers in emergency departments and how they cope. *European Journal of Emergency Medicine, 12*(1), 13–18.

Wu, P., Liu, X., Fang, Y., et al. (2008). Alcohol abuse/dependence symptoms among hospital employees exposed to a SARS outbreak. *Alcohol & Alcoholism, 43*(6), 706–712.

Wu, P., Fang, Y., Guan, Z., et al. (2009). The psychological impact of the SARS epidemic on hospital employees in China: Exposure, risk perception, and altruistic acceptance of risk. *The Canadian Journal of Psychiatry, 54*(5), 302–311.

Wu, G., Fang, X., Wu, L., et al. (2020). Analysis on mental health status and needs of health care workers in designated medical institutions of tuberculosis during the epidemic period of COVID-19.

Xiao, H., Zhang, Y., Kong, D., Li, S., & Yang, N. (2020). The effects of social support on sleep quality of medical staff treating patients with coronavirus disease 2019 (COVID-19) in January and February 2020 in China. *Medical Science Monitor: International Medical Journal of Experimental and Clinical Research, 26*, e923549–e923541.

Xu, J., Xu, Q.-h., Wang, C.-m., & Wang, J. (2020). Psychological status of surgical staff during the COVID-19 outbreak. *Psychiatry Research, 112955.*

Zhang, S. X., Liu, J., Jahanshahi, A. A., Nawaser, K., Li, J., & Alimoradi, H. (2020a). When the storm is the strongest: The health conditions and job satisfaction of healthcare staff and their associated predictors during the epidemic peak of COVID-19. *medRxiv.*

Zhang, C., Yang, L., Liu, S., et al. (2020b). Survey of insomnia and related social psychological factors among medical staff involved in the 2019 novel coronavirus disease outbreak. *Frontiers in Psychiatry, 11*, 306.

Zhu, Z., Xu, S., Wang, H., et al. (2020). COVID-19 in Wuhan: Immediate psychological impact on 5062 health workers. *medRxiv*, 2020.2002.2020.20025338.

Part V
The COVID-19 Crisis: Public Health and Biopolitics

Chapter 16
The Spread of the Novel Coronavirus Disease-2019 in Polluted Cities: Environmental and Demographic Factors to Control for the Prevention of Future Pandemic Diseases

Mario Coccia

16.1 Introduction

The main goal of this chapter is to explain the factors determining the transmission dynamics of COVID-19 that is generating a high level of deaths worldwide to suggest policy implications directed to constrain future epidemics in society.

Coronavirus disease 2019 (COVID-19) is a viral infection caused by severe acute respiratory syndrome coronavirus 2 (SARS-CoV-2) that generates clinical symptoms given by fever, dry cough, dyspnea, and pneumonia and may result in progressive respiratory failure and death (Coccia, 2021b; Public Health England, 2020; Zhu et al., 2020). COVID-19 pandemic is still circulating in 2021 with mutations of the SARS-CoV-2 that continue to generate high numbers of COVID-19-related infected individuals and deaths in manifold countries worldwide (Ministero della Salute, 2020; Johns Hopkins Center for System Science and Engineering, 2021). Seligman et al. (2021) show some characteristics of people that are significantly associated with COVID-19 mortality, such as: "mean age of 71.6 years… individuals with nonwhite race/ethnicity (54.8% of deaths; $p < 0.001$); individuals with income below the median (67.5%; $p < 0.001$); individuals with less than a high school level of education (25.6%; $p < 0.001$); and veterans (19.5%; $p < 0.001$)." In this context, the contribution here focuses on a case study of Italy, one of the European countries with the highest fatality rate of COVID-19 in 2020, during the first wave of the global pandemic crisis (Coccia, 2020a, 2021a, b, c, d). Understanding the determinants of transmission dynamics of COVID-19 in Italy, an industrialized

M. Coccia (✉)
CNR – National Research Council of Italy, Moncalieri (TO), Italy
e-mail: mario.coccia@cnr.it

country, is basic for explaining geo-environmental and socioeconomic factors associated with the diffusion of COVID-19 in Western World for generalization of results in other advanced countries to prevent future pandemic disease of similar vital agents (Bontempi & Coccia, 2021; Bontempi et al., 2021; Coccia, 2020a). In particular, statistical analyses here can explain transmission dynamics of COVID-19 over time and space and provide insights to design a strategy of prevention to constrain risk factors for future epidemics that can generate health and socioeconomic issues for nations and globally.

16.2 Study Design

16.2.1 Data and Their Sources

Sources of data are the Ministry of Health in Italy for epidemiological data (Ministero della Salute, 2020), Legambiente (2019) for data of air pollution deriving from the Regional Agencies for Environmental Protection in Italy, il Meteo (2020) for data of climate in Italian province capitals, and finally the Italian National Institute of Statistics for data of the density of population (ISTAT, 2020).

16.2.2 Sample, Period, and Measures

Sample: 55 Italian cities that are provincial capitals, $N = 55$.

Period: from March to April 2020, during the first wave of COVID-19 outbreak in Italy (cf., Fig. 16.1).

Measures

- *Air pollution*. Total days exceeding the limits set for PM_{10} (particulate matter 10 micrometers or less in diameter) or for ozone in the 55 Italian provincial capitals in 2018 (Legambiente, 2019). The annual days of air pollution have stable trend over time and are a main factor that affects the health of people and environment in the long run. The study used 2018 as the baseline year for air pollution data, to set apart the effects of COVID-19.
- *Diffusion of COVID-19*. Number of infected individuals from March 17 to April 28, during the first waves of COVID-19 pandemic in Italy (Ministero della Salute, 2020).
- *Meteorological information*. Average temperature in °Celsius degree (°C) and wind speed in km/h, from February 1 to April 1 2020 (il Meteo, 2020).
- *Interpersonal contact rates*. The population density of cities (individual/km²) in 2019 (ISTAT, 2020).

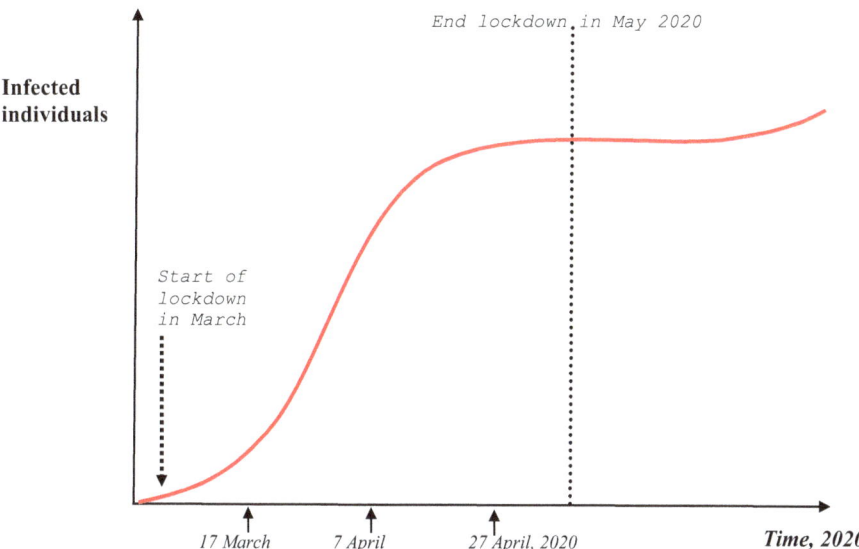

Fig. 16.1 First wave of COVID-19 pandemic in Italy and period under study (from March to April 2020). (Source: Author's own figure)

16.2.3   Data Analysis and Procedure

This study analyzes a database of $N = 55$ Italian provincial capitals, considering variables in the years 2018, 2019, and 2020 to explain the relationships between diffusion of COVID-19 and demographic, meteorological and air pollution data between cities under study (Coccia, 2018a).

Firstly, preliminary analyses of variables are descriptive statistics based on arithmetic mean, std. deviation, coefficients of skewness, and kurtosis to assess the normality of distributions and, if necessary, to fix the distribution of variables with a *log*-transformation.

Statistical analyses are performed categorizing Italian provincial capitals ($N = 55$) in two groups, considering different criteria:

- *Wind speed*

    - Cities with high wind speed, >10 km/h
    - Cities with low wind speed, ≤10 km/h

- *Air pollution*

    - Cities with high air pollution, >100 days per year exceeding the limits set for PM_{10} or for ozone
    - Cities with lower air pollution, ≤100 days per year exceeding the limits set for PM_{10} or for ozone

- *Density of population*

 – Cities with high density of population, >1000 inhabitant/km^2
 – Cities with low density of population, ≤1000 inhabitant/km^2

Secondly, bivariate and partial correlation measures the degree of association between variables using data of infected individuals in different days during the first wave of COVID-19 pandemic in Italy (from March to April 2020).

Thirdly, the regression analysis considers possible relations of dependence of infected individuals from environmental and social factors. In particular, the dependent variable of infected people across Italian provincial capitals is assumed to be a linear function of a single explanatory variable given by total days exceeding the limits set for PM$_{10}$ or ozone (a proxy of air pollution). Variables under study are transformed in logarithmic scale to have normal distributions and apply correctly parametric analyses. As a consequence, the specification of linear relationship for regression analyses is given by a *log-log* model:

$$\log y_t = \alpha + \beta \log x_{t-1} + u \tag{16.1}$$

y = number of infected individuals of COVID-19 in Italian cities
x = total days exceeding the limits set for PM10 or ozone in Italian cities, a measure
   of air pollution
α = constant; β = coefficient of regression; u = error term

This study extends the analysis with a multiple regression model to assess how different factors can affect the diffusion of COVID-19. The specification of the linear relationship is also a *log-log* model as follows:

$$\log y_t = \alpha + \beta_1 \log x_{1,t-1} + \beta_2 \log x_{2,t-1} + u \tag{16.2}$$

y = number of infected individuals of COVID-19 in Italian cities
x_1 = total days exceeding the limits set for PM$_{10}$ or ozone in Italian cities
x_2 = population density in Italian cities, inhabitants per km^2

Equations (16.1–16.2) are analyzed using data of infected individuals at t = March 17, 2020 (starting phase of pandemic wave of the COVID-19 in Italy), at t = April 7, 2020 (growing phase of the pandemic wave of COVID-19 in the presence of quarantine and lockdown in Italy), and at t = April 27, 2020 (maturity phase of the pandemic wave of COVID-19). Ordinary least squares (OLS) method is applied for estimating the unknown parameters of linear models (16.1–16.2). Statistical analyses are performed with the Statistics Software SPSS® version 26.

16.3   Results

Table 16.1 shows that cities with low wind speed (average of 7.3 km/h) have a higher average level of infected individuals than windy cities (average of 12.77 km/h) from March 17 to April 27, 2020. Cities with low wind speed have also a higher average level of air pollution in a meteorological context of lower average temperature.

Table 16.2 confirms previous results considering polluted cities with more than 100 days exceeding limits set for PM_{10} or ozone: a very high level of infected individuals is in polluted cities also having higher average density of population, atmosphere with little wind, and lower average temperature.

Table 16.3 shows that high number of infected individuals is associated with high density of people per km^2 in (polluted) cities because of a higher probability of interpersonal contacts and also an intensive economic activity having higher level of total import and export (cf., Bontempi & Coccia, 2021; Bontempi et al., 2021).

Table 16.4 shows results of the association between variables: a correlation higher than 40% (p-value < .01) is between air pollution and infected individuals from March 17 ($r = .64$, p-value < .01) to April 27, 2020 ($r = .41$, p-value < .01). A lower coefficient of correlation is between density of population and infected individuals over the same period ($r = 31$–48%). The reduction of intensity of the association between variables under study can be due to the effect of quarantine and lockdown applied in Italy from March 9, 2020 onward (Coccia, 2021e). Results also show a negative correlation between number of infected individuals and wind speed among cities from March 17 to April 7, 2020 (on April 27, 2020, the coefficient is not significant).

Table 16.1 Descriptive statistics of Italian province capitals according to wind speed, first wave of COVID-19 in 2020, Italy

	Days exceeding limits set for PM_{10} or ozone	Infected individuals	Infected Individuals	Infected individuals	Density of population inhabitants/ km^2	Temp °C	Wind speed km/h
	2018	March 17, 2020	April 7, 2020	April 27, 2020	2019	Feb to Mar 2020	Feb to Mar 2020
Cities with low wind speed N = 41							
Mean	84.32	536.20	2383.66	3340.26	1517.41	9.05	7.30
Std. deviation	43.31	792.84	2624.029	3666.55	1569.70	2.12	2.77
Cities with high wind speed N = 14							
Mean	53.93	149.57	770.14	1465.64	1265.64	10.36	12.77
Std. deviation	25.87	153.55	633.208	1446.69	2108.31	2.43	3.46

Source: Author's own elaboration

Table 16.2 Descriptive statistics of Italian provincial capitals according to air pollution, first wave of COVID-19 pandemic in 2020, Italy

	Days exceeding limits set for PM$_{10}$ or ozone	Infected individuals	Infected individuals	Infected individuals	Density of population inhabitants/ km^2	Temp °C	Wind speed km/h
	2018	March 17, 2020	April 7, 2020	April 27, 2020	2019	Feb to Mar 2020	Feb to Mar 2020
Cities with high air pollution >100 days exceeding limits set for PM$_{10}$ *N = 20*							
Mean	125.25	881.70	3650.00	4838.05	1981.40	9.19	7.67
Std. deviation	13.40	1010.97	3238.82	4549.41	1988.67	1.46	2.86
Cities with lower air pollution <100 days exceeding limits set for PM$_{10}$ *N = 35*							
Mean	48.77	184.11	1014.63	1637.21	1151.57	9.49	9.28
Std. deviation	21.37	202.76	768.91	1292.26	1466.28	2.62	4.15

Source: Author's own elaboration

Table 16.3 Descriptive statistics of Italian provincial capitals according to density of population in cities, first wave of COVID-19 pandemic in 2020, Italy

	Days exceeding limits set for PM$_{10}$ or ozone	Infected individuals	Infected individuals	Infected individuals	Density of population inhabitants/ km^2	Temp °C	Wind speed km/h
	2018	March 17, 2020	April 7, 2020	April 27, 2020	2019	Feb to Mar 2020	Feb to Mar 2020
Cities with high density >1000 inhabitant/km^2 *N = 25*							
Mean	91.24	665.08	2967.44	4195.42	2584.40	8.63	7.99
Std. deviation	40.24	919.70	3092.46	4333.91	2000.63	2.40	2.79
Cities with lower density ≤1000 inhabitant/km^2 *N = 30*							
Mean	64.37	248.37	1144.20	1727.55	510.77	10.01	9.28
Std. deviation	39.25	386.95	1065.99	1491.47	282.11	1.95	4.41

Source: Author's own elaboration

Table 16.5 confirms a high coefficient partial of correlation between air pollution and infected individuals from March 17, 2020, controlling meteorological factors of cities under study ($r > 58\%$, p-value <. 001). However, a reduction of the coefficient of partial correlation is at April 27, 2020 likely because of full lockdown as measure of containment in society (cf., Coccia, 2021c, h).

Partial correlation in Table 16.6 suggests that the association between number of infected people and air pollution ($r = .54$, in March 17, 2020; $r = .48$, in April 7,

Table 16.4 Correlation, first wave of COVID-19 pandemic in 2020, Italy

	Log Days exceeding limits set for PM_{10} or ozone 2018	*Log* Population density inhabitants/km² 2019	Temp °C Feb to Mar 2020	Wind speed km/h Feb to Mar 2020
Log Infected individuals				
March 17, 2020				
Pearson correlation, *r*	0.643**	0.484**	−0.117	−0.377**
Log Infected individuals				
April 7, 2020				
Pearson correlation, *r*	0.604**	0.533**	−0.259	−0.310*
Log Infected individuals				
April 27, 2020				
Pearson correlation, *r*	0.408**	0.308*	−0.179	−0.164

Source: Author's own elaboration
Note: **Correlation is significant at the 0.01 level
*Correlation is significant at the 0.05 level
$N = 51$ Italian province capitals

Table 16.5 Partial correlation, controlling temperature and wind speed (first wave of COVID-19 in 2020, Italy)

Control variables Temp °C, Feb to Mar 2020 Wind speed km/h, Feb to Mar 2020	*Log* Infected individuals March 17, 2020	*Log* Infected individuals April 7, 2020	*Log* Infected individuals April 27, 2020
Log (air pollution)			
Days exceeding limits set for PM_{10} or ozone			
2018	0.609***	0.585***	0.386**

Source: Author's own elaboration
Note: ***Correlation is significant at the 0.001 level
**Correlation is significant at the 0.01 level
$N = 51$ Italian province capitals

2020, etc.), controlling density of population, is *higher than* correlation between density of population and infected individuals in cities, controlling air pollution ($r = .28$, in March 17, 2020; $r = .36$, in April 7, 2020). These results suggest that air pollution in cities seems to be a critical factor in environment associated with transmission dynamics of COVID-19 in the presence of high density of population, mainly in the starting phase of the pandemic wave of COVID-19 in Italy.

The multiple regression in Table 16.7 reveals how air pollution in cities seems to be one of the driving factors associated with transmission dynamics of COVID-19 having a *stronger* magnitude in the initial phase of pandemic wave of COVID-19

Table 16.6 Partial correlation, controlling air pollution or density of population (first wave of COVID-19 in 2020, Italy)

Control variable	Infected individuals		
	Log Infected	*Log* Infected	*Log* Infected
Density of population	March 17, 2020	April 7, 2020	April 27, 2020
Log (air pollution)			
Days exceeding limits set for PM$_{10}$ or ozone, 2018	0.542***	0.479***	0.316*
Control variable			
Air pollution			
Log (population density)			
Inhabitants/km^2, 2019	0.279*	0.362**	0.15

Source: Author's own elaboration
Note: ***Correlation is significant at the 0.001 level (two-tailed)
**Correlation is significant at the 0.01 level (two-tailed)
*Correlation is significant at the 0.05 level (two-tailed)
$N = 52$ Italian province capitals

(March 17, 2020). In the phase of growth and maturity of the first pandemic wave of COVID-19 (i.e., April 7 and 27, 2020), the determinant of air pollution – associated with high levels of infections – reduces intensity, whereas the factor of human-to-human transmission has a stable level from March 17 to April 7, 2020, *ceteris paribus* (Table 16.7). *This result reveals that transmission dynamics of COVID-19 is due to human-to-human transmission, but in polluted cities, the relation is stronger with a substantial growth of viral infectivity.*

If we decompose the sample in cities with ≤100 and >100 days exceeding limits set for PM$_{10}$ or ozone, then the expected increase of number of infected individuals is higher in polluted cities having more than 100 days exceeding limits set for PM$_{10}$ or ozone (Table 16.8). These results suggest that density of population explains the number of infected individuals, increasing the probability of human-to-human transmission, but the driving role of interpersonal contacts is *stronger* in polluted cities. In particular, on April 7, 2020, in the growing phase of the first pandemic wave of COVID-19 in Italy:

- *In cities with ≤100 days* exceeding limits set for PM$_{10}$ or ozone, an increase of 1% of the density of population, it increases the expected number of infected individuals by about 0.25% (*p*-value = .042).
- *In cities with >100 days* exceeding limits set for PM$_{10}$ or ozone, an increase of 1% of the density of population, it increases the expected number of infected individuals by about 0.85% (*p*-value < .001).

In short, regression analyses on March 17, 2020, in the starting phase of COVID-19 pandemic wave, show that transmission dynamics of COVID-19 has a higher and faster viral infectivity in cities with >100 days of air pollution per year. In particular, *air pollution is definitely an important factor to explain the*

Table 16.7 Parametric estimates of linear models – multiple regression (first pandemic wave of COVID-19 in 2020, Italy)

	Model 1A	Model 1B	Model 1C
	Dependent variable	*Dependent variable*	*Dependent variable*
	Log infected	*Log* infected	*Log* infected
	March 17, 2020	April 7, 2020	April 27, 2020
Constant α	−2.168	1.538	1.407
(St. Err.)	(1.127)	(.854)	(1.701)
(Air pollution)			
Log Days exceeding limits set for PM_{10} in 2018			
Coefficient $\beta 1$	1.266***	0.813***	0.987*
(St. Err.)	(.272)	(.206)	(.411)
(Density of population)			
Log inhabitants/km^2 in 2019			
Coefficient $\beta 2$	0.309*	0.314**	0.244
(St. Err.)	(0.148)	(0.112)	(0.223)
R^2	0.459	0.448	0.185
F-test	22.059***c	21.130***c	5.916**c

Source: Author's own elaboration
Note: ***p-value < 0.01
**p-value < 0.01
*p-value < 0.05
c = predictors: *log* Days exceeding limits set for PM_{10} 2018 year; *log* density inhabitants/km^2 2019

transmission dynamics of COVID-19 in society (cf., Coccia, 2021b; Morawska & Cao, 2020).

Table 16.9 shows the transmission dynamics of COVID-19 considering cities with population density (less than, equal to) ≤ or (greater than) >1000 individuals/km^2. In particular, on April 27, 2020:

- In cities with ≤1000 inhabitants/km^2, an increase of 1% of days exceeding limits set for PM_{10} or ozone, it increases the expected number of infected individuals by about 0.53%.
- In cities with >1000 inhabitants/km^2, an increase of 1% days exceeding limits set for PM_{10} or ozone, it increases the expected number of infected individuals by about 2.00%.

Results confirm that transmission dynamics of COVID-19 accelerates in polluted cities having a high density of population (i.e., >1000 inhabitants per km^2). Moreover, Table 16.9 shows that coefficient of regression in the starting phase of COVID-19 pandemic wave (March 17, 2020) has a small difference between cities with different population density, but in the maturity phase of pandemic wave (on April 27, 2020), the coefficient of regression tends to increase in cities having a higher level of population density (>1000 inhabitants per km^2). These findings here suggest that transmission dynamics of COVID-19 cannot be explained without accounting for complex factors given by the level of air pollution, density of population, commercial activities and other geo-environmental conditions in cities.

Table 16.8 Parametric estimates of the liner relationship of infections on density of population, considering cities with higher or lower level of air pollution (first pandemic wave of COVID-19 in 2020, Italy)

	Cities with ≤100 days exceeding limits set for PM_{10} or ozone, 2018	Cities with >100 days exceeding limits set for PM_{10} or ozone, 2018
Dependent variable: *log* infected March 17, 2020		
Constant α	2.346*	0.242
(St. Err.)	(1.131)	(2.267)
Log Density inhabitants/km² in 2019		
Coefficient $\beta 1$	0.358*	0.816**
(St. Err.)	(0.172)	(0.311)
R^2	0.116	0.276
F-test	4.324*	6.864**
Dependent variable: *log* infected April 7, 2020		
Constant α	4.976	1.670
(St. Err.)	(0.786)	(1.491)
Log Density inhabitants/km² in 2019		
Coefficient $\beta 1$	0.252*	0.849***
(St. Err.)	(0.120)	(0.205)
R^2	0.119	0.488
F-test	17.168***	4.457*
Dependent variable: *log* infected April 27, 2020		
Constant α	5.310**	3.189*
(St. Err.)	(1.848)	(1.566)
Log Density inhabitants/km² in 2019		
Coefficient $\beta 1$	0.203	0.242**
(St. Err.)	(0.281)	(0.215)
R^2	0.016	0.357
F-test	0.521	9.988**

Source: Author's own elaboration
Note: Explanatory variable: *log* density inhabitants/km² in 2019; dependent variable is *log* infected individuals
***p-value < 0.001
**p-value < 0.01
*p-value < 0.05

16.4 Discussion

The intensity of human interaction and commercial activities has accelerated in recent decades because of urban development, population growth, industrialization, and deforestation, with consequential changes in physical, biological, and chemical processes, in economies and society (Coccia, 2005b, 2014, 2017d, 2018b, 2019d, 2021m). In this demographic, economic, and social change, the exposure to air

Table 16.9 Parametric estimates of the relationship of infected people on air pollution, considering cities with population density > or ≤1000 individuals/km^2

	Cities with ≤1000 inhabitants/km^2 2019	Cities with>1000 inhabitants/km^2 2019
Dependent variable: log infected March 17, 2020		
Constant α	−0.121	−1.030
(St. Err.)	(1.562)	(1.366)
Log days exceeding limits set for PM$_{10}$ or ozone, 2018		
Coefficient $\beta 1$	1.199**	1.566***
(St. Err.)	(0.387)	(0.309)
R^2	0.255	0.528
F-test	9.570**	25.756***
Dependent variable: log infected April 7, 2020		
Constant α	3.529**	2.590
(St. Err.)	(1.087)	(1.305)
Log days exceeding limits set for PM$_{10}$ or ozone, 2018		
Coefficient $\beta 1$	0.774**	1.132***
(St. Err.)	(.270)	(.295)
R^2	0.228	0.625
F-test	8.252 **	14.713***
Dependent variable: log infected April 27, 2020		
Constant α	4.720*	−1.206
(St. Err.)	(1.989)	(2.680)
Log days exceeding limits set for PM$_{10}$ or ozone, 2018		
Coefficient $\beta 1$	0.527	2.000**
(St. Err.)	(0.493)	(0.606)
R^2	0.039	0.322
F-test	1.143	10.901**

Source: Author's own elaboration
Note: Explanatory variable: *Log* days exceeding limits set for PM$_{10}$ or ozone, 2018; dependent variable is *log* infected individuals
***p-value < 0.001
**p-value < 0.01
*p-value < 0.05

pollution of particulate matter and ozone has main health effects with increases in mortality and hospital admissions for respiratory and cardiovascular diseases (Bontempi and Coccia, 2021; Bontempi et al., 2021; Coccia, 2020a; Kampa & Castanas, 2008; Hoek et al., 2013). Lewtas (2007) shows that the exposures to air pollution of combustion and fine particulate are associated with genetic damages. The idea that air pollution episodes have a detrimental effect on health and environment is now rarely contested, and acute exposures to high concentrations of air pollutants exacerbate cardiopulmonary disorders in human population (Langrish & Mills, 2014).

In this context of polluted cities, statistical analyses here focus on the association between infected people and air pollution, and meteorological and demographic factors to explain transmission dynamics of COVID-19 over time and space. The main results of the study here, based on a case study of Italy in the first pandemic wave of COVID-19 in 2020, are:

- The acceleration of transmission dynamics of COVID-19 in North Italy has a high association with air pollution and density of people in cities.
- Cities having more than 100 days of air pollution (exceeding the limits set for PM_{10} and other air pollutants, and ozone) have a very high average number of infected individuals, whereas cities having less than 100 days of air pollution have a lower average number of infected people on April 27, 2020.
- Air pollution in cities under study seems to be an important predictor in the initial phase of pandemic wave of COVID-19 (on March 17, 2020, $b_1 = 1.27$, $p < 0.001$) associated with human-to-human transmission ($b_2 = 0.31$, $p < 0.05$). In the phase of maturity of the pandemic wave of COVID-19, the factor of air pollution reduces intensity (on April 27, 2020, $b'_1 = 0.99$, $p < 0.05$) also because of indirect effect of full lockdown in Italy as measure of containment, whereas human-to-human transmission is nonsignificant likely because of quarantine applied in Italy from March to May 2021 (cf., Coccia, 2021b, c, d, e, l).

The study reveals that accelerated transmission dynamics of COVID-19 is in polluted cities and the application of containment measures can reduce human-to-human transmission, but they are necessary but not sufficient policies to stop future pandemic diseases (Chen et al., 2020; Wilder-Smith et al., 2020). This finding suggests that although COVID-19 transmits from human to human, the factor of air pollution supported an accelerated rate of transmission in cities because the novel coronavirus can mix with particulate matter and remain in air having stable atmosphere (little wind) and high humidity, such as North Italy. In particular, results suggested that, among Italian provincial capitals, the number of infected people was higher in cities with >100 days per year exceeding limits set for PM_{10} or ozone, cities located in hinterland zones (i.e., away from the coast), cities having a low average wind speed, and cities with a lower temperature. In hinterland cities (mostly those bordering large urban conurbations, such as Bergamo, Brescia, etc. close to large city of Milan) having a high number of days exceeding PM_{10} and ozone limits, coupled with low wind speed, the average number of infected people on April 7, 2020 more than doubled that of more windy cities that had also exceeded the air pollution limits. In addition, in those cities with over 100 days of air pollution exceeding PM_{10} limits, the average number of infected people on April 7, more than tripled those that had less than 100 days of excessive air pollution. High concentrations of air pollutant induce serious damages to the immune system of people to cope with infectious diseases of (new) viral agents and other diseases (Glencross et al., 2020). In this context, researchers maintain that in an external environment, higher wind speed supports the dilution of air pollution, also decreasing the likely concentration of viral agents within the air and as a consequence reducing the transmission dynamics of viral infectivity among people (Coccia, 2020c, d, 2021a, 2021l).

New findings suggest critical environmental policies, for example, cities in the future should not exceed limits of PM_{10} and $PM_{2.5}$, ozone and other air pollutants for more than 50 days each year, so that the accelerated transmission of viral infectivity and the emergence of other diseases are not triggered in society (Coccia, 2020a). These results provide valuable insight into geo-environmental factors that may accelerate the diffusion of SARS-CoV-2 (the novel coronavirus) and similar viral agents. A socioeconomic strategy to constrain future epidemics similar to the COVID-19 has also to be based on reduction of air pollution for a sustainable development of cities. The reduction of polluting activities and sustainable development impose often huge social costs in the short term on people, households, and families, but they have long-run benefits for human societies. Guo et al. (2019) argue that in recent years, haze pollution is a serious environmental problem affecting cities, proposing policies for urban planning that improve respiratory health. In fact, the improvements in air quality of cities have been accompanied by demonstrable benefits to human health. Moreover, countries should introduce more and more sustainable technologies and organizational, product, and process innovations to cope with viral threats, such as the expansion of testing capabilities to reduce diagnostic delays, artificial intelligence and new ICT technologies for improving diagnostics, development of effective vaccines and antivirals that can counteract future pandemic threats similar to COVID-19, etc. (Ardito et al., 2021; Coccia, 2005, 2015, 2017a, b, c, 2018, 2019a, b, c, 2020b, 2021h; Coccia & Bellitto, 2018; Coccia & Finardi, 2012, 2013; Coccia & Watts, 2020). In brief, the long-term benefits of R&D investments in a sustainable economic development and sustainable technologies are basic aspects for the improvement of environment, atmosphere, air quality, and especially health of people to cope with infectious diseases similar to COVID-19 (cf., the role of labs in the development of science and technology transfer: Coccia, 2005a, 2008, 2019e, f, 2020d, 2021n, 2021o; Coccia and Benati, 2018; Coccia and Cadario, 2014; Coccia and Rolfo, 2000, 2008; Pagliaro and Coccia, 2021).

16.5 Conclusions and Prospects

Italy was the first European country to experience a rapid increase in confirmed cases and deaths of COVID-19 in 2020 (Coccia, 2020h). This study sought to understand how COVID-19 transmitted so rapidly in Italy, analyzing the underlying relationships between infected people and environmental, demographic, and geographical factors that influenced its spread.

The statistical evidence above seems in general to support new results that cities with frequently high levels of air pollution and low wind speed had higher numbers of COVID-19-related infected individuals and deaths. In fact, diffusion of the COVID-19 is higher in cities with low wind speed that prevents the dispersion of air pollutants that can include bacteria and viruses, such as SARS-CoV-2 and its variants, such as Delta and Delta+ (cf., Smets et al., 2016). In short, SARS-CoV-2 spreads through air, particularly in polluted cities with low wind speed, whereas high wind speed can decrease air pollution having viral agents commingled with air pollutants and as a result alleviate the diffusion and lethality of this and other airborne viruses (Coccia, 2020c, d, e, f, 2021a, 2021l). To put it differently, cities mainly located in Northern Italy (highly industrialized regions) with high levels of air pollution, associated with low wind speed because of their morphology and urban location, have a stagnation of air pollution in the atmosphere that can create an appropriate habitat to support the diffusion of SARS-CoV-2 and other viral agents in fall and winter seasons (Fig. 16.2). Climatological factors, such as wind speed and direction, temperature, and humidity, are critical elements for urban ventilation and the atmospheric dispersion of pollutant concentration in cities, also including viral agents (Coccia, 2020c, d, 2021l; Yuan et al., 2019). Considering the benefit of wind as resource that can reduce air pollution and likely viral infectivity with public health benefits, Gu et al. (2020) argue that a strategy to enhance air quality in cities, it is the improvement of urban ventilation: the ability of an urban area to dilute pollutants and heat by improving the exchange of air between areas within and above the urban canopy. Urban ventilation is a critical aspect to ensure acceptable air quality, thermal comfort, and in particular the dispersion of air pollution (Gu et al., 2020; Guo et al., 2017). As a consequence, polluted cities with a low wind-driven natural ventilation have to apply environmental policies to reduce main sources of air pollution (e.g., the application of sustainable and cleaner production) and, at the same time, improve urban ventilation (e.g., reducing heights of new buildings) to foster the dispersion of particulate compound emissions (Peng et al., 2017). Cui et al. (2020) show that reductions in air pollution have avoided premature deaths and related morbidity cases in China. Hence, sustainable policies reduce air pollution and particulate compound emissions and generate significant environmental, public health, social and economic benefits in the long term.

Overall, then, findings here show that the combination of environmental, atmospheric, urban, social, and demographic factors in some regions can sustain, in fall and winter seasons, the stagnation of air pollution also with content of the novel

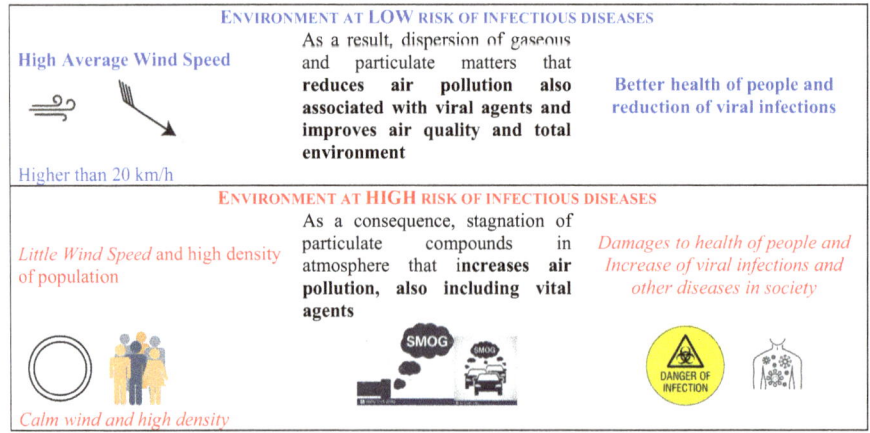

Fig. 16.2 How geo-environmental factors may have accelerated the spread of COVID-19. (Source: Author's own figure)

coronavirus and other viral agents that foster the spread of infectious diseases in cities (Coccia, 2020a, c, d, e, f, h, 2021a). This study suggests that, in order to constrain the impact in society of future epidemics similar to the COVID-19 – *mainly in zones having little wind that prevent pollutant dispersion* – regions and nations have to apply long-run sustainable policies and technologies directed to reduce the sources of air pollution and improve urban ventilation and, as a consequence, air quality in human ecosystem (Coccia, 2019a, 2020g, i, 2021f, g, i; cf. Pronti & Coccia, 2020).

To conclude, this chapter reveals interesting results of transmission dynamics of COVID-19 associated with high air pollution, low wind speed, and high density of population that seem to explain the accelerated diffusion of COVID-19 in Italy and in other similar regions having polluting industrialization. However, these conclusions are of course tentative. There are several challenges to studies on these topics because sources of data may only capture certain aspects of the pandemic diseases and environmental pollution; therefore, and there is need for much more research with new data to explain the relations between viral infectivity, air pollution, meteorological factors, and other social determinants (Coccia, 2021p). Finally, in the presence of high air pollution, low wind speed, and high density of population, this study must conclude that an environmental policy to cope with future epidemics should focus on the reduction of air pollution in hinterland and polluted cities, and improvement of air quality and of healthcare sector (Coccia, 2020e, 2021d, f; Coccia, 2022). In fact, a cautious and intelligent management of the environment is basic to achieve goals of socioeconomic sustainability directed to preserve the health of human society on Earth.

References

Ardito, L., Coccia, M., & Messeni, P. A. (2021). Technological exaptation and crisis management: Evidence from COVID-19 outbreaks. *R&D Management*. https://doi.org/10.1111/radm.12455

Bontempi, E., & Coccia, M. (2021). International trade as critical parameter of COVID-19 spread that outclasses demographic, economic, environmental, and pollution factors. *Environmental Research, 201*, Article number 111514, PII S0013-9351(21)00808-2. https://doi.org/10.1016/j.envres.2021.111514

Bontempi, E., Coccia, M., Vergalli, S., & Zanoletti, A. (2021). Can commercial trade represent the main indicator of the COVID-19 diffusion due to human-to-human interactions? A comparative analysis between Italy, France, and Spain. *Environmental Research*, Article number 111529. https://doi.org/10.1016/j.envres.2021.111529

Chen, S., Yang, J., Yang, W., Wang, C., & Bärnighausen, T. (2020). COVID-19 control in China during mass population movements at New Year. *Lancet (London, England), 395*(10226), 764–766. https://doi.org/10.1016/S0140-6736(20)30421-9

Coccia, M. (2005). A taxonomy of public research bodies: A systemic approach. *Prometheus, 23*(1), 63–82. https://doi.org/10.1080/0810902042000331322

Coccia M. (2005a). Metrics to measure the technology transfer absorption: analysis of the relationship between institutes and adopters in northern Italy. *International Journal of Technology Transfer and Commercialization, 4*(4), 462–486. https://doi.org/10.1504/IJTTC.2005.006699

Coccia M. (2005b). Countrymetrics: valutazione della performance economica e tecnologica dei paesi e posizionamento dell'Italia. *Rivista Internazionale di Scienze Sociali, CXIII*(3), 377–412. Stable URL http://www.jstor.org/stable/41624216

Coccia M. (2008). Measuring scientific performance of public research units for strategic change. *Journal of Informetrics, 2*(3), 183–194. https://doi.org/10.1016/j.joi.2008.04.001

Coccia M. (2014). Steel market and global trends of leading geo-economic players. *International Journal of trade and global markets, 7*(1), 36–52. http://dx.doi.org/10.1504/IJTGM.2014.058714

Coccia, M. (2015). Spatial relation between geo-climate zones and technological outputs to explain the evolution of technology. *International Journal of Transitions and Innovation Systems, 4*(1–2), 5–21. https://doi.org/10.1504/IJTIS.2015.074642

Coccia, M. (2017a). Varieties of capitalism's theory of innovation and a conceptual integration with leadership-oriented executives: The relation between typologies of executive, technological and socioeconomic performances. *International Journal of Public Sector Performance Management, 3*(2), 148–168. https://doi.org/10.1504/IJPSPM.2017.084672

Coccia, M. (2017b). Disruptive firms and industrial change. *Journal of Economic and Social Thought, 4*(4), 437–450. https://doi.org/10.1453/jest.v4i4.1511

Coccia, M. (2017c). Sources of disruptive technologies for industrial change. *L'Industria –Rivista di economia e politica industriale, 38*(1), 97–120. https://doi.org/10.1430/87140

Coccia M. (2017d). New directions in measurement of economic growth, development and under development. *Journal of Economics and Political Economy, 4*(4), 382–395. http://dx.doi.org/10.1453/jepe.v4i4.1533

Coccia, M. (2018). The origins of the economics of Innovation. *Journal of Economic and Social Thought, 5*(1), 9–28. https://doi.org/10.1453/jest.v5i1.1574

Coccia M. (2018a). An introduction to the methods of inquiry in social sciences. *Journal of Social and Administrative Sciences, 5*(2), 116–126. http://dx.doi.org/10.1453/jsas.v5i2.1651

Coccia M. (2018b). An introduction to the theories of institutional change. *Journal of Economics Library, 5*(4), 337–344. http://dx.doi.org/10.1453/jel.v5i4.1788

Coccia, M. (2019a). A theory of classification and evolution of technologies within a generalized Darwinism. *Technology Analysis & Strategic Management, 31*(5), 517–531. https://doi.org/10.1080/09537325.2018.1523385

Coccia, M. (2019b). Why do nations produce science advances and new technology? *Technology in Society, 59*(101124), 1–9. https://doi.org/10.1016/j.techsoc.2019.03.007

Coccia, M. (2019c). The theory of technological parasitism for the measurement of the evolution of technology and technological forecasting. *Technological Forecasting and Social Change, 141*, 289–304. https://doi.org/10.1016/j.techfore.2018.12.012

Coccia M. (2019d). Theories of Development. A. Farazmand (ed.), *Global Encyclopedia of Public Administration, Public Policy, and Governance*, Springer Nature Switzerland AG. https://doi.org/10.1007/978-3-319-31816-5_939-1

Coccia M. (2019e). Metabolism of public organizations: A case study. *Journal of Social and Administrative Sciences, 6*(1), 1–9. http://dx.doi.org/10.1453/jsas.v6i1.1793

Coccia M. (2019f). Theories of Self-determination. A. Farazmand (ed.), Global Encyclopedia of Public Administration, Public Policy, and Governance. Springer Nature Switzerland AG. https://doi.org/10.1007/978-3-319-31816-5_3710-1

Coccia, M. (2020a). Factors determining the diffusion of COVID-19 and suggested strategy to prevent future accelerated viral infectivity similar to COVID. *Science of the Total Environment, 729*(138474) https://doi.org/10.1016/j.scitotenv.2020.138474

Coccia, M. (2020b). Deep learning technology for improving cancer care in society: New directions in cancer imaging driven by artificial intelligence. *Technology in Society, 60*(February), 1–11. https://doi.org/10.1016/j.techsoc.2019.101198

Coccia, M. (2020c). An index to quantify environmental risk of exposure to future epidemics of the COVID-19 and similar viral agents: Theory and practice. *Environmental Research, 191*(December), 110155. https://doi.org/10.1016/j.envres.2020.110155

Coccia M. (2020d). How does science advance? Theories of the evolution of science. *Journal of Economic and Social Thought, 7*(3), 153–180. http://dx.doi.org/10.1453/jest.v7i3.2111

Coccia, M. (2020d). How do low wind speeds and high levels of air pollution support the spread of COVID-19? *Atmospheric Pollution Research*. Advance online publication. https://doi.org/10.1016/j.apr.2020.10.002

Coccia, M. (2020e). How (un)sustainable environments are related to the diffusion of COVID-19: The relation between coronavirus disease 2019, air pollution, wind resource and energy. *Sustainability, 12*, 9709. https://doi.org/10.3390/su12229709

Coccia, M. (2020f). Effects of air pollution on COVID-19 and public health, research article-environmental economics-environmental policy. *ResearchSquare*. https://www.researchsquare.com/article/rs-41354/v1

Coccia, M. (2020g). Critical decision in crisis management: Rational strategies of decision making. *Journal of Economics Library, 7*(2), 81–96. https://doi.org/10.1453/jel.v7i2.2049

Coccia, M. (2020h). How do environmental, demographic, and geographical factors influence the spread of COVID-19. *Journal of Social and Administrative Sciences, 7*(3), 169–209. https://doi.org/10.1453/jsas.v7i3.2018

Coccia, M. (2020i). Fishbone diagram for technological analysis and foresight. *International Journal of Foresight and Innovation Policy, 14*(2/3/4), 225–247. https://doi.org/10.1504/IJFIP.2020.111221

Coccia, M. (2021a). The effects of atmospheric stability with low wind speed and of air pollution on the accelerated transmission dynamics of COVID-19. *International Journal of Environmental Studies, 78*(1), 1–27. https://doi.org/10.1080/00207233.2020.1802937

Coccia, M. (2021b). Effects of the spread of COVID-19 on public health of polluted cities: Results of the first wave for explaining the dejà vu in the second wave of COVID-19 pandemic and epidemics of future vital agents. *Environmental Science and Pollution Research, 28*(15), 19147–19154. https://doi.org/10.1007/s11356-020-11662-7

Coccia, M. (2021c). The impact of first and second wave of the COVID-19 pandemic: Comparative analysis to support control measures to cope with negative effects of future infectious diseases in society. *Environmental Research, 197*, Article number 111099. https://doi.org/10.1016/j.envres.2021.111099

Coccia, M. (2021d). High health expenditures and low exposure of population to air pollution as critical factors that can reduce fatality rate in COVID-19 pandemic crisis: A global analysis. *Environmental Research, 199*, Article number 111339. https://doi.org/10.1016/j.envres.2021.111339

Coccia, M. (2021e). The relation between length of lockdown, numbers of infected people and deaths of Covid-19, and economic growth of countries: Lessons learned to cope with future pandemics similar to Covid-19. *Science of the Total Environment, 775*, Article number 145801, Available online 12 February 2021. https://doi.org/10.1016/j.scitotenv.2021.145801

Coccia, M. (2021f). Pandemic prevention: Lessons from COVID-19. *Encyclopedia 2021, 1*, 433–444. MDPI, Basel, Switzerland, *Encyclopedia of COVID-19, open access journal*. https://www.mdpi.com/journal/encyclopedia. https://doi.org/10.3390/encyclopedia1020036

Coccia, M. (2021g). Comparative critical decisions in management. In A. Farazmand (Ed.), *Global encyclopedia of public administration, public policy, and governance*. Springer. https://doi.org/10.1007/978-3-319-31816-5_3969-1

Coccia, M. (2021h). Evolution of technology in replacement of heart valves: Transcatheter aortic valves, a revolution. *Health Policy and Technology, 10*, Article number 100512, PII S2211-8837(21)00035-6. https://doi.org/10.1016/j.hlpt.2021.100512

Coccia, M. (2021i). Recurrring waves of Covid-19 pandemic with different effects in public health. *Journal of Economics Bibliography, 8*(1), 28–45. https://doi.org/10.1453/jeb.v8i1.2184

Coccia, M. (2021l). How do low wind speeds and high levels of air pollution support the spread of COVID-19? *Atmospheric Pollution Research, 12*(1), 437–445. https://doi.org/10.1016/j.apr.2020.10.002

Coccia M. (2021m). Effects of human progress driven by technological change on physical and mental health. *Studi Di Sociologia, 2*, 113–132. https://doi.org/10.26350/000309_000116

Coccia M. (2021n). Evolution and structure of research fields driven by crises and environmental threats: the COVID-19 research. *Scientometrics*. https://doi.org/10.1007/s11192-021-04172-x

Coccia M. (2021o). Optimal levels of vaccination to reduce COVID-19 infected individuals and deaths: A global analysis. *Environmental Research*, Article n. 112314. https://doi.org/10.1016/j.envres.2021.112314

Coccia M. (2021p). Evolution and structure of research fields driven by crises and environmental threats: the COVID-19 research. *Scientometrics*. https://doi.org/10.1007/s11192-021-04172-x

Coccia M. (2022). Preparedness of countries to face COVID-19 pandemic crisis: Strategic positioning and underlying structural factors to support strategies of prevention of pandemic threats. *Environmental Research, 203*, 111678. https://doi.org/10.1016/j.envres.2021.111678

Coccia, M., & Bellitto, M. (2018). Human progress and its socioeconomic effects in society. *Journal of Economic and Social Thought, 5*(2), 160–178. https://doi.org/10.1453/jest.v5i2.1649

Coccia M., & Benati I. (2018). Rewards in public administration: A proposed classification. *Journal of Social and Administrative Sciences, 5*(2), 68–80. http://dx.doi.org/10.1453/jsas.v5i2.1648

Coccia, M., & Cadario E. (2014). Organisational (un)learning of public research labs in turbulent context. *International Journal of Innovation and Learning, 15*(2), 115–129. https://doi.org/10.1504/IJIL.2014.059756

Coccia, M., & Finardi, U. (2012). Emerging nanotechnological research for future pathway of biomedicine. *International Journal of Biomedical Nanoscience and Nanotechnology, 2*(3–4), 299–317. https://doi.org/10.1504/IJBNN.2012.051223

Coccia, M., & Finardi, U. (2013). New technological trajectories of non-thermal plasma technology in medicine. *Int. J. Biomedical Engineering and Technology, 11*(4), 337–356. https://doi.org/10.1504/IJBET.2013.055665

Coccia M., & Rolfo S. (2000). Ricerca pubblica e trasferimento tecnologico: il caso della regione Piemonte in Rolfo S. (eds) *I nnovazione e piccole imprese in Piemonte*, Franco Angeli Editore, Milano (Italy), ISBN: 9788846418784.

Coccia M., & Rolfo S. (2008). Strategic change of public research units in their scientific activity. *Technovation, 28*(8), 485–494. https://doi.org/10.1016/j.technovation.2008.02.005

Coccia, M., & Watts, J. (2020). A theory of the evolution of technology: Technological parasitism and the implications for innovation management. *Journal of Engineering and Technology Management, 55*(101552) https://doi.org/10.1016/j.jengtecman.2019.11.003

Cui, L., Zhou, J., Peng, X., Ruan, S., & Zhang, Y. (2020). Analyses of air pollution control measures and co-benefits in the heavily air-polluted Jinan city of China, 2013-2017. *Scientific Reports, 10*(1), 5423. https://doi.org/10.1038/s41598-020-62475-0

Glencross, D. A., Tzer-Ren, H., Nuria, C., Hawrylowicz, C. M., & Pfeffer, P. E. (2020). Air pollution and its effects on the immune system. *Free Radical Biology and Medicine, 151*, 56–88. https://doi.org/10.1016/j.freeradbiomed.2020.01.179

Gu, K., Fang, Y., Qian, Z., Sun, Z., & Wang, A. (2020). Spatial planning for urban ventilation corridors by urban climatology. *Ecosystem Health and Sustainability, 6*(1), 1747946. https://doi.org/10.1080/20964129.2020.1747946

Guo, F., Zhu, P. S., Wang, S. Y., Duan, D. W., & Jin, Y. (2017). Improving natural ventilation performance in a high-density urban district: A building morphology method. *Procedia Engineering, 205*, 952–958. https://doi.org/10.1016/j.proeng.2017.10.149

Guo, L., Luo, J., Yuan, M., Huang, Y., Shen, H., & Li, T. (2019). The influence of urban planning factors on PM2.5 pollution exposure and implications: A case study in China based on remote sensing, LBS, and GIS data. *Science of the Total Environment, 659*, 1585–1596. https://doi.org/10.1016/j.scitotenv.2018.12.448

Hoek, G., Krishnan, R. M., Beelen, R., Peters, A., Ostro, B., Brunekreef, B., & Kaufman, J. D. (2013). Long-term air pollution exposure and cardiorespiratory mortality: A review. *Environmental Health, 12*(1), 43. https://doi.org/10.1186/1476-069X-12-43

Il meteo. (2020). *Medie e totali mensili.* https://www.ilmeteo.it/portale/medie-climatiche. Accessed Mar 2020.

ISTAT. (2020). *The Italian National Institute of Statistics-Popolazione residente al 1 gennaio.* http://dati.istat.it/Index.aspx?DataSetCode=DCIS_POPRES1. Accessed June 2020.

Johns Hopkins Center for System Science and Engineering. (2021). *Coronavirus COVID-19 global cases.* https://gisanddata.maps.arcgis.com/apps/opsdashboard/index.html#/bda759474 0fd40299423467b48e9ecf6. Accessed in 4 June 2021.

Kampa, M., & Castanas, E. (2008). Human health effects of air pollution. *Environmental pollution (Barking, Essex: 1987), 151*(2), 362–367. https://doi.org/10.1016/j.envpol.2007.06.012

Langrish, J. P., & Mills, N. L. (2014). Air pollution and mortality in Europe. *Lancet (London, England), 383*(9919), 758–760. https://doi.org/10.1016/S0140-6736(13)62570-2

Legambiente. (2019). *Mal'aria 2019, il rapporto annuale sull'inquinamento atmosferico nelle città italiane.* https://www.legambiente.it/malaria-2019-il-rapporto-annuale-annuale-sullinquinamento-atmosferico-nelle-citta-italiane/. Accessed March 2020.

Lewtas, J. (2007). Air pollution combustion emissions: Characterization of causative agents and mechanisms associated with cancer, reproductive, and cardiovascular effects. *Mutation Research, 636*(1–3), 95–133. https://doi.org/10.1016/j.mrrev.2007.08.003

Ministero della Salute. (2020). *COVID-19 - Situazione in Italia.* http://www.salute.gov.it/portale/nuovocoronavirus/dettaglioContenutiNuovoCoronavirus.jsp?lingua=italiano&id=5351&area=nuovoCoronavirus&menu=vuoto. Accessed May 2020.

Morawska, L., & Cao, J. (2020). Airborne transmission of SARS-CoV-2: The world should face the reality. *Environment International, 139*, 105730. https://doi.org/10.1016/j.envint.2020.105730

Pagliaro M., & Coccia M. (2021). How self-determination of scholars outclasses shrinking public research lab budgets, supporting scientific production: a case study and R&D management implications. *Heliyon, 7*(1), e05998. https://doi.org/10.1016/j.heliyon.2021.e05998

Peng, Y., Ma, X. Y., Zhao, F. Y., Liu, C. W., & Mei, S. J. (2017). Wind driven natural ventilation and pollutant dispersion in the dense street canyons: Wind opening percentage and its effects. *Procedia Engineering, 205*, 415–422. https://doi.org/10.1016/j.proeng.2017.10.392

Pronti, A., & Coccia, M. (2020). Multicriteria analysis of the sustainability performance between agroecological and conventional coffee farms in the East Region of Minas Gerais (Brazil). *Renewable Agriculture and Food Systems, 1-8.* https://doi.org/10.1017/S1742170520000332

Public Health England. (2020). *Novel coronavirus (2019-nCoV) – What you need to know.* https://publichealthmatters.blog.gov.uk/2020/01/23/wuhan-novel-coronavirus-what-you-need-to-know/. Accessed 31 Jan 2020.

Seligman, B., Ferranna, M., & Bloom, D. E. (2021). Social determinants of mortality from COVID-19: A simulation study using NHANES. *PLoS Medicine, 18*(1), e1003490. https://doi.org/10.1371/journal.pmed.1003490

Smets, W., Morett, S., Denys, S., & Lebeer, S. (2016). Airborne bacteria in the atmosphere: Presence, purpose, and potential. *Atmospheric Environment, 139*, 214–221. https://doi.org/10.1016/j.atmosenv.2016.05.038

Wilder-Smith, A., Chiew, C. J., & Lee, V. J. (2020). Can we contain the COVID-19 outbreak with the same measures as for SARS? *The Lancet. Infectious Diseases, 20*(5), e102–e107. https://doi.org/10.1016/s1473-3099(20)30129-8

Yuan, M., Song, Y., Huang, Y., Shen, H., & Li, T. (2019). Exploring the association between the built environment and remotely sensed PM2.5 concentrations in urban areas. *Journal of Cleaner Production, 220*, 1014–1023. https://doi.org/10.1016/j.jclepro.2019.02.236

Zhu, N., Zhang, D., Wang, W., Li, X., Yang, B., Song, J., Zhao, X., Huang, B., Shi, W., Lu, R., Niu, P., Zhan, F., Ma, X., Wang, D., Xu, W., Wu, G., Gao, G. F., Tan, W., & China Novel Coronavirus Investigating and Research Team. (2020). A novel coronavirus from patients with pneumonia in China, 2019. *The New England Journal of Medicine, 382*(8), 727–733. https://doi.org/10.1056/NEJMoa2001017

Chapter 17
High-Performing Machine Learning Algorithms for Predicting the Spread of COVID-19

David O. Oyewola, K. A. Al-Mustapha, Asabe Ibrahim, and Emmanuel Gbenga Dada

17.1 Introduction

Wuhan Jinyintan Hospital was the first to report coronavirus (COVID-19) case on 30 December 2019 from a patient with pneumonia of unknown etiology. Based on the result, the virus had characteristics of the coronavirus family named betacoronavirus 2B (WHO, 2020a). Bat SARS-like coronavirus showed a closed relationship with COVID-19 virus. On 30 January 2020, the World Health Organization (WHO) declared coronavirus as a global public health emergency concern due to an outbreak of respiratory illness. The novel coronavirus was named severe acute respiratory syndrome coronavirus 2 (SARS-COV-2), and the disease has been called coronavirus disease 2019 (COVID-19) by WHO (WHO, 2020b). Common signs of this infection include respiratory symptoms, fever, dry cough, fatigue, sputum production, shortness of breath, sore throat, headache, myalgia or arthralgia, chills, nausea or vomiting, nasal congestion, diarrhea, hemoptysis, and conjunctival congestion. In extreme cases of coronavirus pandemic disease, it may cause kidney failure, death, and severe acute respiratory syndrome (National Center for Immunization and Respiratory Diseases (NCIRD) DoVD, 2020). National health

D. O. Oyewola (✉) · A. Ibrahim
Department of Mathematics & Computer Science, Federal University Kashere, Gombe, Nigeria
e-mail: davidoyewole@fukashere.edu.ng

K. A. Al-Mustapha
Department of Mathematics, Baze University, Abuja, Nigeria

E. G. Dada
Department of Mathematical Sciences, Faculty of Science, University of Maiduguri, Maiduguri, Borno state, Nigeria
e-mail: gbengadada@unimaid.edu.ng

© The Author(s), under exclusive license to Springer Nature Switzerland AG 2022
N. Faghih, A. Forouharfar (eds.), *Socioeconomic Dynamics of the COVID-19 Crisis*, Contributions to Economics, https://doi.org/10.1007/978-3-030-89996-7_17

systems of every nation are currently threatened by the coronavirus (COVID-19) (Center NaI, 2020). To date, Italy has been one of the most affected countries where public health departments, emergency medical systems, and hospitals are struggling to deal with the surge of patients affected by 2019-nCoV (Gardner, 2020). Unfortunately, contagion rates are estimated to rise exponentially in many countries, regardless of their healthcare delivery system. In our healthcare system and hospital, urgent actions are required to provide high-quality medical equipment and high-quality information. The application of translational science in this disaster medicine setting can provide stakeholders and clinicians with acceptable evidence-based medicine concepts (Dong et al., 2020). As of 29 March 2020, this pandemic had spread to 199 countries with 724,759 confirmed cases, 34,020 deaths, and 152,087 recovered cases (https://www.worldometers.info/coronavirus/). Reported symptoms of the disease include dry cough, shortness of breath, fatigue, pneumonia, sore throat, diarrhea, and dyspnea (Li et al., 2020; Zhou et al., 2020). Preventive measures such as masks, hand hygiene practices, avoidance of public contact, case detection, contact tracing, and quarantines have been discussed as ways to reduce transmission (CDC, 2020). Infected people of COVID-19 rely on symptomatic treatment since there is no specific antiviral treatment has proven effective (Huang et al., 2020). The authors (Adhikari et al., 2020) researched on a scoping review proposed by Arksey and O'Malley (2005). To better understand the cause, prevention, diagnosis, and control of coronavirus, 65 articles were analyzed and examined. The research domains, dates of publication, journal language, authors' affiliations, and methodological characteristics were included in the analysis. The results indicated that most of the publication was written using the English language (89.2%). Findings indicated that the published articles related to causes are at the rate of 38.5%, while 67.7% were published by Chinese scholars. However, oftentimes research articles centered on causes, but over time there was an increment of the articles on prevention and control. Studies thus far have shown that the virus origination is in connection with a seafood market in Wuhan, but specific animal associations have not been confirmed. The use of machine learning algorithms is increasing day by day in medical domain for solving problems by analyzing and interpreting large volumes of data (Sarwar & Sharma, 2013). A number of researchers in this field have used machine learning algorithms in order to solve problems in the field of medicine. David Oyewola et al. (2016) compared logistic regression (LR), linear discriminant analysis (LDA), quadratic discriminant analysis (QDA), random forest (RF), and support vector machine (SVM) for diagnosis of breast cancer prediction. The authors classified the patients infected with breast cancer into two categories (malignant and benign). The authors achieved 95.8% accuracy with SVM learning classification in diagnosing breast cancer. So et al. (2017) did the analysis on Diagnosis of Dementia from Clinical Data by machine learning techniques. The authors considered different algorithms such as Naive Bayes, Bayes network, begging, logistic regression, random forest, support vector machine (SVM), and multi-layer perceptron (MLP). The authors classified the patients into normal, mild cognitive impairment, and dementia. The overall accuracy of the diagnosis system was 97% for support vector machine. Dengue disease patients are increasing rapidly in a paper by Iqbal and Islam (2019) compared with K-nearest neighborhood, support vector machine, artificial neural network, Naïve Bayes Classifier, decision tree, logistic regression, and LogitBoost ensemble model. Findings indicated that LogitBoost ensemble model is the topmost classification with accuracy of 92% and sensitivity and specificity of 90% and 94%, respectively. A paper by Beulah Christalin Latha and Carolin (2019) investigates a method termed ensemble classification for prediction of heart disease. In this research, a comparative study was done to decide how ensemble methods can improve weak classifiers in the prediction of heart disease. Findings show that bagging and boosting are effective in improving the accuracy of weak classifiers. In various places including China, England, Germany, and Japan, the author (Diao et al., 2021) examined the distribution and decay duration of the COVID-19 pandemic, where it first spread. The spread and decreasing times were rearranged on the basis of a model with an asymmetric bell shape in the cities of the four investigated nations. To undertake multivariable analyses, they gathered environmental temperature data, absolute moisture, and population density. The finding indicates that the spread and decay durations in the four examined nations have significant relationships ($p < 0.05$) with population density.

The geo-environmental factors of rapid COVID-19 spreads were analyzed by Coccia (2020a) using data on the samples of 55 settlers and data on infected persons in the province and a strategic approach to coping with future COVID-19 epidemic risks. The results indicate the significant level of air pollution associated with COVID-19 in Northern Italy. The results showed that future pandemics such as COVID-19 would have a minimum annual impact; the maximum number of days that can exceed the restrictions for PM10 or ozone, given their climatic circumstances, in Italian provincial or comparable industrialized cities is around 48 days. Bashir et al. (2020) utilized the secondary data obtained from the Centers for Disease Control and Prevention and the Environmental Pollution Agency. They assess the association between the environmental pollution determinants and the COVID-19 outbreaks in California. Spearman and Kendall were used to evaluate the relationship between PM 2.5, PM 10, SO2, NO2, Pb, VOC, and CO in California COVID-19 cases. Findings show a major association between environmentally friendly pollutants such as PM10, PM2.5, SO2, NO2, and CO with pandemic COVID-19. Real-time monitoring of the transmission dynamics is highly crucial to reduce the number of infected persons associated with COVID-19 and fatalities. The author (Coccia, 2020b) suggested the Index c to represent contagious diseases which measures the environmental risk of cities/regions being exposed to future outbreaks of COVID-19 and related vital agents. This Index c summarizes environmental, population, climate, and public health risk factors that determine the exposure to infectious diseases of towns and areas. In general, Index c has a range from 1 to 0 which was applied to Italy. 1 is the environmental and social deficiencies of urban areas, while 0 is the environment reducing the risk of infectious conditions in society. However, Index c is superior indicator for global detection of correlation between potential risk of exposure of cities/regions to infectious diseases and actual risk given by infected individuals and deaths of the COVID-19. Rosario et al. (2020)

examined the connection between meteorological variables such as temperature, humidity, sun radiation, wind speed, and rainfall and COVID-19 infection using the state of Rio de Janeiro, Brazil, as a case study. Solar radiation was shown to have a substantial (0.609, p 0.01) negative association with the occurrence of new corona-viruses (SARS-CoV-2). Wind speed and temperature (maximum and average) had a negative association ($p < 0.01$). The findings show that in a tropical condition, intense sun radiation is the major climatic element that suppresses the proliferation of COVID-19. High temperatures and high wind speeds are other possible causes. Dellicour et al. (2021) offer an analytical approach to examine possible sources of spatiotemporal variability in COVID-19 hospitalization incidence when data are only accessible at the hospital. They applied the approach to Belgium, a nation that was significantly hit by two COVID-19 pandemic waves in 2020, both in terms of death and hospitalization incidence. The findings show a link between the incidence of hospitalization and the local density of nursing home patients, confirming the importance of COVID-19 in Belgium communities. Furthermore, the temporal studies show a strong seasonality in hospitalization incidence, which is related to the seasonality of meteorological factors. Using these connections, they examine the viability of machine learning-based predictive models for predicting future hos-pitalization occurrence. The relationship between atmospheric stability/turbulence including wind speed, air pollution, and the distribution of COVID-19 was studied in order to give insights into environmental risk factors in specific locations (Coccia, 2021a). The findings show that towns with high atmospheric stability, based on low wind speed, and often high levels of air pollution – surpassing acceptable limits of ozone or particle matter – had a greater number of COVID-19-infected people and fatalities. This implies that atmospheric stability, based on low wind speed, decreases the dispersion of gaseous and particulate materials such as air pollution, which can function as a carrier of SARS-CoV-2 in the air, sustaining COVID-19 dissemination in the environment and causing public health issues.

Different researchers have utilized machine learning and deep learning for differ-ent purposes such as malware detection (Mahindru & Sangal, 2020, 2021a, b, c) and sentiment analysis (Basiri et al., 2021). For example, the effectiveness for COVID-19 pneumonia in CR was studied by the deep learning (DL) method (Jang et al., 2020). This is an adult retrospective study in which positive COVID-19 cases were diag-nosed based on reverse transcription polymerase chain reactions between all patients in five emergency departments and in one community center in Korea between 18 February 2020 and 1 May 2020. For comparison CR images without CT scans were classified as positive COVID-19. DL algorithms perform excellently well with 95.6% and 88.7% for sensitivity and specificity, respectively, for the detection of COVID-19 pneumonia on CR, while the area under the curve was 0.921. Coccia (2020c) examined the relationship between wind speed, air pollution, and the dis-semination of COVID-19 to offer insights into how future pandemics and epidemics are restricted and prevented which concentrated on Italy as a case study. Results demonstrate that, in addition to the direct diffusion with human-to-human dynam-ics, high levels of the air pollutants, along with low wind speeds, might contribute to the prolonged continuation of viral particles in the air, thereby promoting the virus infectivity indirectly (SARS-CoV-2). The authors (McCoy et al., 2021) study the health, social, and environmental impacts of COVID-19 per capita transmission (before July 2020) and per capita deaths in US areas. The study used machine learning along with the marginal techniques of prediction to determine the most important parameters for different epidemic measurements of COVID-19. Results reveal that the predictors for both the incidence and death per capita of COVID-19 are strongest for ethnicity and public transportation. Also, Coccia (2021b) studied the link between duration of the lockdown, the number of individuals affected, and fatalities from coronavirus disease 2019 (COVID-19), as well as the degree of GDP growth in nations. The findings suggest that countries with a shorter period of lockdown within 15 days including Austria, Portugal, and Sweden had a higher average confirmed cases divided by population during the first wave of the COVID-19 pandemic than countries with a longer period of lockdown within 60 days such as France, Italy, and Spain. Countries with shorter lockdown time have a lower average death rate of 5.45% than those that have a longer lockdown time with the rate of 12.70%, whereas the average fatality rate varies from March to August 2020 within the first COVID-19 pandemic which indicates that countries with longer lockdown times will be less than countries with a shorter life span (−1.9% vs. -0.72%). In Subudhi et al. (2021), the authors assess the performance of 18 ICU admissions and machine learning algorithms among COVID-19 patients using patient data in the Healthcare Mass General (MGM) database. Results show that ensemble models are superior than other models in both 5-day ICU admission and 28-day COVID-19 admission. Assaf et al. (2020) used three distinct machine learning models to predict patient deterioration depending on patient risk for serious COVID-19 based on status at admission. Among the 6995 patients examined, 162 were hospitalized with non-severe COVID-19, with 25 (15.4%) progressing to critical COVID-19. Machine learning models surpass all other indicators, including the APACHE II score, with 88.0% sensitivity, 92.7% specificity, and 92.0% accuracy in predicting critical COVID-19 (ROC AUC of 0.92 vs. 0.79, respectively). Coccia (2021c) described how air pollution might alter the impact of the COVID-19 pandemic on public health, with a case study of Italy as a focus. The findings showed that the spread of COVID-19 in cities with high levels of air pollution can lead to an increase in the number of COVID-19-infected people and fatalities. The number of sick persons was greater in cities with more than 100 days per year exceeding PM10 or ozone restrictions, cities located in hinterland zones (i.e., distant from the coast), cities with a low average wind speed, and cities with a lower average temperature. A machine learning method is used to discover important clinical parameters to better classify patients to general vs. intensive care unit (ICU) admission and predict death in the COVID-19 pandemic (Hou et al., 2021). Between 7 February 2020 and 27 May 2020, 1874 people were under investigation for COVID-19 at Stony Brook University Hospital in New York. Machine learning was used to predict mortality and ICU admission, with 80% training and 20% testing. In all, 635 patients (aged 6011, 40.2% female) were enrolled in the study. Procalcitonin, C-creative protein, lactate dehydrogenase, D-dimer, and lymphocytes were the top six predictors of death. Procalcitonin, lactate dehydrogenase, C-creative protein, pulse oxygen saturation, temperature, and ferritin rank first through sixth in terms of ICU admission predictions. The top machine learning algorithms predicted death with an accuracy of 89% and ICU admission with an accuracy of 79%. For non-COVID-19 individuals with pneumonia, chest X-ray (CXR) radiography can be utilized as a first-line triage. Khuzani et al. (2020) hypothesized that using a dimensionality reduction method to generate a set of optimal features of CXR images to build an efficient machine learning classifier that can reliably distinguish COVID-19 cases from non-COVID-19 cases with high accuracy and sensitivity, machine learning-based classifiers could reliably distinguish CXR images of COVID-19 patients from other forms of pneumonia. Radiography of chest X-ray (CXR) may be utilized as the first-line triage method for patients with pneumonia not receiving COVID-19. The authors (Coccia, 2021d) hypothesized that the CXR images of COVID-19 patients could be distinguished from other pneumonias using a dimensionally reduction method to create a set of optimum features of CXR images to produce an efficient machine learning classifier capable of differentiating COVID-19 cases from non-COVID-19 with high precision.

In order to determine the impact on human health of effective policies designed to limit the negative effects of COVID-19 pandemic waves and similar infectious diseases in the society, Zhu et al. (2019) studied the comparative analysis of the first and second waves of coronavirus 2019 (COVID-19) and studied the case study on Italy. Statistical analysis of the initial wave of COVID-19 pandemic in Italy suggests that the first wave of data from February 2020 to February 2021 was highly unfavorable for people's health; afterward, negative impacts decreased as of June 2020. The second wave of the COVID-19 pandemic was increasing incidentally confirmed by coronavirus variations between August 2020 and February 2021, compared to the first wave of the COVID-19, but the level of admission to intensive care units and total fatalities was lower. Adebowale et al. (2021) examine and compare patterns of COVID-19 dissemination throughout the first 120 days of the epidemic in Nigeria and seven other countries. Data were collected from the website of the World Bank. A linear, quadratic, cubic, and exponential regression has been used for the fitting of the model. Results reveal that Nigeria's pattern of COVID-19 was comparable to that of Egypt, Ghana, and Cameroon. Nigeria's daily distribution of deaths was comparable to six of the seven countries. In the confirmed COVID-19 cases in Nigeria, there has been a rising tendency. The rate of growth in Nigeria during the lockdown was 5.85 ($R2 = 0.728$, $p < 0.001$). Nevertheless after the lockdown, it was 8.42 ($R2 = 0.625$, $p < 0.001$). The cumulative instances in COVID-19 were the most appropriate for all nations studied using the cubic polynomial model (CPM), and a notable divergence from the exponential growth model was seen. The number of cases projected for Nigeria was 155,467 (95% CI:151,111–159,824, $p < 0,001$) in 3 months (30 September 2020) using CPM. This study aimed to estimate the distribution of COVID in Africa, Asia, Australia/Oceania, Europe, North America, and South America. Analysis of different continents affected by COVID-19 is hardly explored to the best of our knowledge.

17.2   Materials and Methods

17.2.1   Sources, Sample, and Data

The coronavirus (COVID-19) dataset from the Kaggle database has been used for the experiments. The dataset consists of 144 countries and diamond cruise ship of the confirmed, death, and recovered cases of COVID-19 from patients who have contacted coronavirus disease from 22 January 2020 to 14 March 2020.

17.2.2   Modeling and Data Analysis Procedure

- Logistic Regression

  Logistic regression is the appropriate regression method for analysis when the dependent variable is binary. When there are only two possible outcomes for prediction, logistic regression is very effective in predicting the outcomes. Logistic regression can be binomial for predicting binary variable, ordinal for predicting ordinal variable, and multinomial for predicting multinomial variable. The results in the multinomial variable can have more than two possible types (Oyewola et al., 2016).

  The mathematical equation of logistic regression is given as:

$$p = \frac{1}{1 + e^{-b_o + b_1 x_1 + b_2 x_2 + \ldots + b_n x_n}} \tag{17.1}$$

where p is the probability, e is the base of the natural logarithm, and b_o and b_1 are the parameters of the model.

- Support Vector Machine (SVM)

  Support vector machine, which was developed by Vladimir Vapnik, is a machine learning technique for both prediction and classification. SVM is a maximum margin classification algorithm rooted in both machine and statistical learning theory. The technique can be utilized for both nonlinear and linear data. The method involved constructs a set of hyperplane which can be employed for both classification and regression. A maximum distance is achieved by the aid of hyperplane to the closest point of the two classes; such a hyperplane is called an optimal hyperplane. A set of instances that is closest to the optimal hyperplane is called a support vector. Kernel function has a strong mathematical function in SVM for complex learning (Fathima & Manimegalai, 2012).

  The equation is expressed in mathematical form as follows:

$$H = W.X + b = 0 \tag{17.2}$$

where H is the hyperplane, W is the weight, X is the input vector, and b is the bias.

- Recurrent Neural Network (RNN)

Recurrent neural network (RNN) can be defined as a network whose neurons send feedback signals to every layer. Figure 17.1 illustrates the RNN unit which has an internal state that is fed back to the input state and shares the same weights and biases between each of them. The feedback loop of the cell helps the network to communicate with the hidden state h_t to the future time t. X_t denote the input to the cell at time t and Y_t denotes the output to the cell at time t.

Input to the hidden layer equation is given as:

$$h_t = g_n\left(W_{xh}X_t + W_{hh}h_{t-1} + b_h\right) \tag{17.3}$$

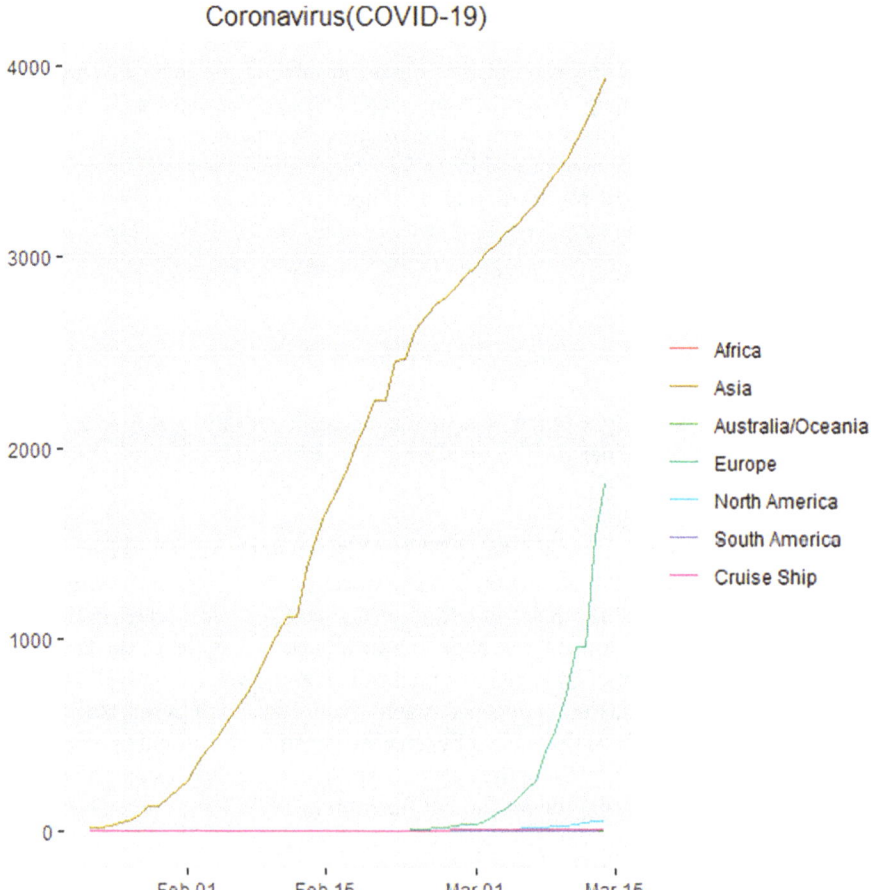

Fig. 17.1 Schematic diagram of recurrent neural network. (Source: Authors' own figure)

where h_t is the hidden layer at t^{th} instant, g_n is the function, W_{xh} is the input to the hidden layer of the weight matrix, X_t is the input at t^{th} instant, h_{t-1} is the hidden layer at $t-1$ instant, and b_h is the bias or threshold value.

Hidden to output layer equation is given as:

$$Z_t = g_n\left(W_{hz}h_t + b_z\right) \tag{17.4}$$

where Z_t is the output vector, W_{hz} is the hidden to output layer weight matrix, and b_z is the bias or threshold.

- Long Short-Term Memory (LSTM)

The LSTM cell is different from the recurrent neural network from two viewpoints (Hochreiter & Schmidhuber, 1997). To start with, LSTM cell is divided into two components, the long-term state c_t and the short-term state h_t. The activation function ρ of the gates denotes the sigmoid function which outputs values in the range [0, 1]. Another reason was that the three control gates along the state path, the forget gate, the input gate, as well as the output gate, are included to control the cell states. The forget gate f_t denotes that nothing should be carried forward from the previous long-term state c_{t-1}. The output gate o_t controls the development of the present short-term state h_t utilizing the data from the present long-term state c_t. For the candidate cell state, the activation function is a hyperbolic tangent function which outputs values in the range [−1, 1]. An important difference of the LSTM cell compared to the simple RNN cell is that its output o_t is equal to the hidden state h_t.

We can describe it mathematically using the following equations:

$$f_t = \rho\left(W_f.[h_{t-1},x_t] + b_f\right) \tag{17.5}$$

$$i_t = \rho\left(W_i.[h_{t-1},x_t] + b_i\right) \tag{17.6}$$

$$c_t = \tan h\left(W_i.[h_{t-1},x_t] + b_c\right) \tag{17.7}$$

$$o_t = \rho\left(W_o.[h_{t-1},x_t] + b_o\right) \tag{17.8}$$

$$h_t = o_t \times \tan h\left(c_t\right) \tag{17.9}$$

where f_t is the forget gate vector, i_t is the input gate vector, c_t is the cell state vector, o_t is the output gate vector, x_t is the input vector, h_t is the output vector, ρ is the sigmoid function, and W, b is the parameter matrix and vector (Fig. 17.2).

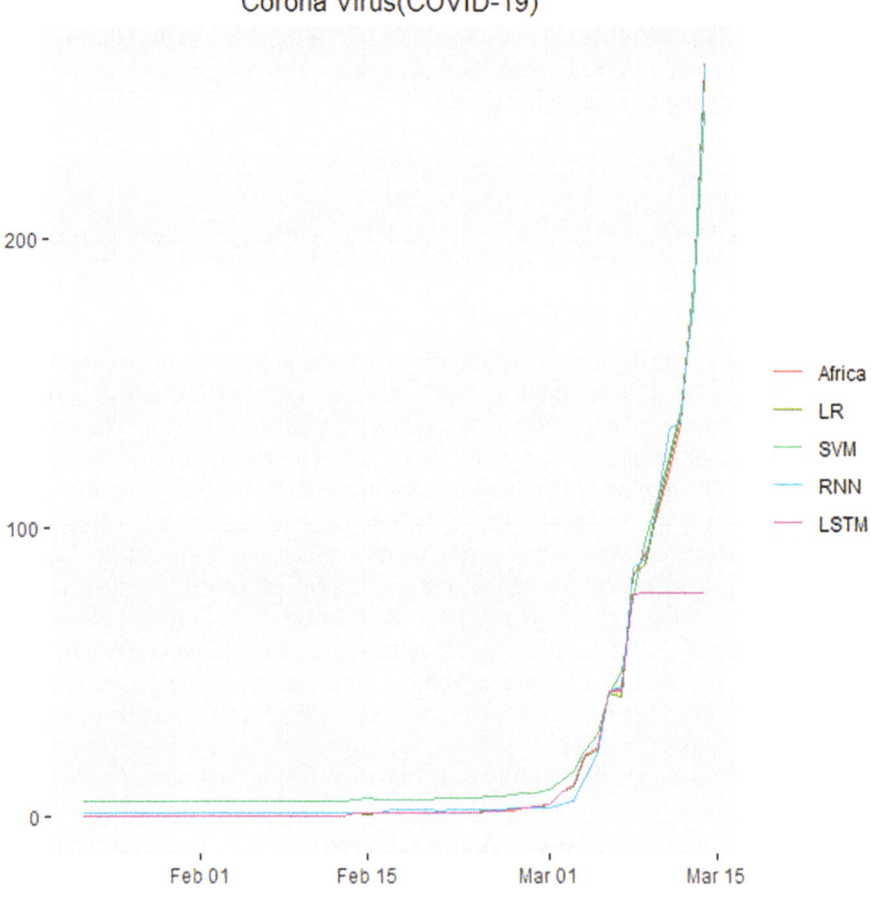

Fig. 17.2 Schematic diagram of long short-term memory (LSTM). (Source: Authors' own figure)

17.2.3 Measure of Variables

Machine learning (ML) is one of the intelligent methodologies that have shown promising results in the domains of classification and prediction. Machine learning usually contains target and input variables. COVID-19 is a virus (more specifically, a coronavirus) identified as the cause of an outbreak of respiratory illness first detected in Wuhan, China.

In the outbreak of these diseases, many patients reported contact with large seafood and animal market, indicating animal to person transmission. Moreover, a large number of infected patients reportedly have no link with the animal markets, suggesting social contact transmission.

The dataset used in this study has daily level information on the number of affected (confirmed), death, and recovery cases from COVID-19. The dataset is a time series data, and so the number of cases on any given day is the cumulative number. The data consists of daily occurrence of confirmed, recovered, and death cases of COVID-19 in each country from 22 January 2020 to 14 March 2020 affected with the disease. Since the disease is pandemic, the daily affected countries were grouped into continents such as Africa, Asia, North America, South America, Europe, and Australia/Oceania and Diamond Princess cruise ship (passengers and crew on board of Japan Diamond Princess cruise ship). In this chapter, we considered only the confirmed cases of those infected with the disease which represents target vectors Y_t at time t, while the input vectors are given in Eqs. (17.12, 17.13, 17.14 and 17.15).

The target variable for each continent is given as:

$$y(t) = \left[y_1(t), y_2(t), \ldots, y_n(t) \right]^T \tag{17.10}$$

We assume the input variable is:

$$b_t = y_t - y_{t-n} \tag{17.11}$$

$$m_t = \left| \sum_{t=0}^{n} b_t \right| - \left(\sum_{t=0}^{2n} \|\|b_t\|\| - \sum_{t=0}^{n} \|\|b_t\|\| \right) \tag{17.12}$$

$$p_t = \frac{1}{t} \sum_{t=0}^{t} y_t \tag{17.13}$$

$$h_t(y) = \alpha y_t + (1-\alpha) h_{t-1} \tag{17.14}$$

$$r_t = h_t(s) - h_t(l) \tag{17.15}$$

where α is the weighting parameter of the confirmed cases in the past having the values from 0 to 1, b_t is the momentum at time t, m_t is trend direction index at time t, p_t is the simple moving average at time t, h_t is the exponential moving average at time t, r_t is the moving average convergence divergence at time t, and s, l are the 12- and 26-day exponential weighted moving average, respectively.

17.2.4   Performance Measures

We assess prediction performance utilizing three measures: mean absolute error (MAE), root mean square error (RMSE), and mean absolute scaled error (MASE).

Mean Absolute Error (MAE)
Consider a set of target or actual returns y_t^n and their predicted values $\hat{y}_t^n$.
MAE is defined as follows:

$$\frac{1}{n} \sum_{n=1}^{n} \left| y_t^n - \hat{y}_t^n \right| \tag{17.16}$$

Root Mean Square Error (RMSE)
RMSE is defined as:

$$\sqrt{\frac{1}{n}\sum_{n=1}^{n}\left(y_t^n - \hat{y}_t^n\right)^2} \tag{17.17}$$

Mean Absolute Scaled Error (MASE)
MASE is defined as follows:

$$\frac{1}{n}\sum_{n=1}^{n}\left(\frac{\left|y_t^n - \hat{y}_t^n\right|}{\frac{1}{n-m}\sum_{n=m+1}^{n}\left|y_t^n - y_{t-m}^n\right|}\right) \tag{17.18}$$

where m is the seasonal period of return r_t^n.

17.3 Results and Discussion

The description of the dataset is shown in Figs. 17.3, 17.4, 17.5, 17.6, 17.7, 17.8, 17.9, 17.10, 17.11, 17.12 and 17.13. The dataset of confirmed, death, and recovered cases of coronavirus was categorized into continents such as Africa, Asia, South America, North America, Europe, and Australia/Oceania and Diamond Princess cruise ship, a cruise ship in Yokohama, Japan. Based on the dataset, Egypt has the highest confirmed cases followed by South Africa, Algeria, Tunisia, Morocco, Senegal, and Reunion, respectively (as shown in Fig. 17.3). Out of the 2600 passengers and 1000 crew members of Diamond Princess cruise ship, 696 tested positive to coronavirus, 325 recovered, and 7 died (Fig. 17.4). Figures 17.5 and 17.6 shows the confirmed, recovered, and death cases in Asia. China has the highest cases of confirmed, recovered, and death cases with 80,977, 65,660, and

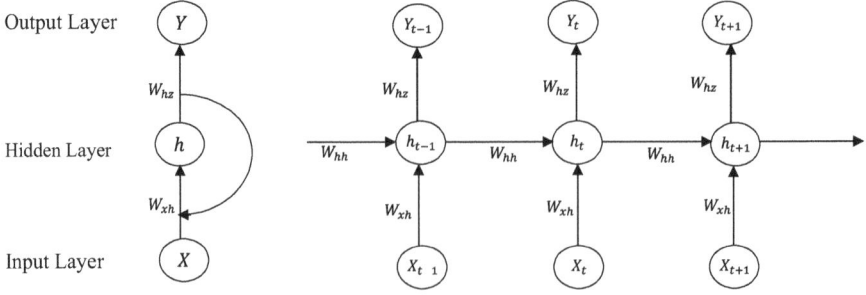

Fig. 17.3 COVID-19 confirmed, recovered, and death cases in Africa. (Source: Authors' own figure)

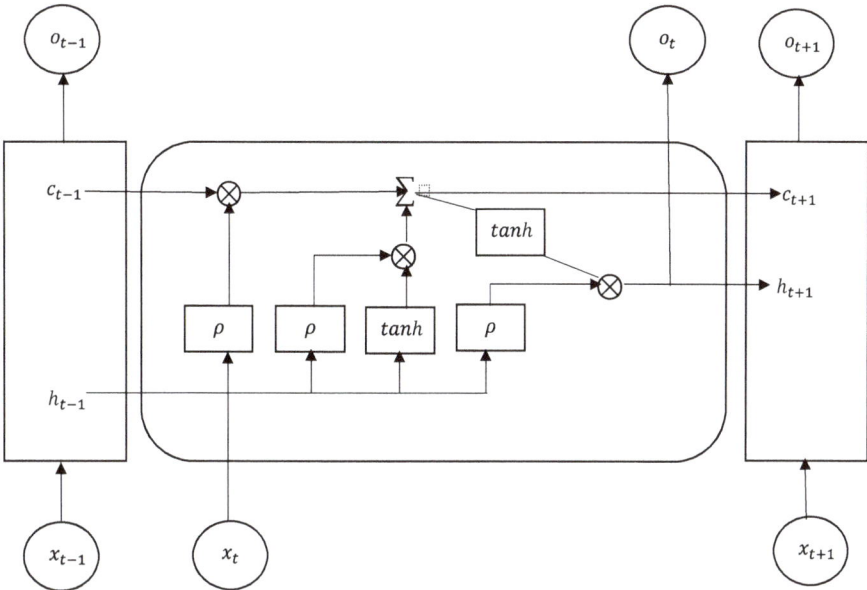

Fig. 17.4 COVID-19 confirmed, recovered, and death cases in Diamond Princess cruise ship. (Source: Authors' own figure)

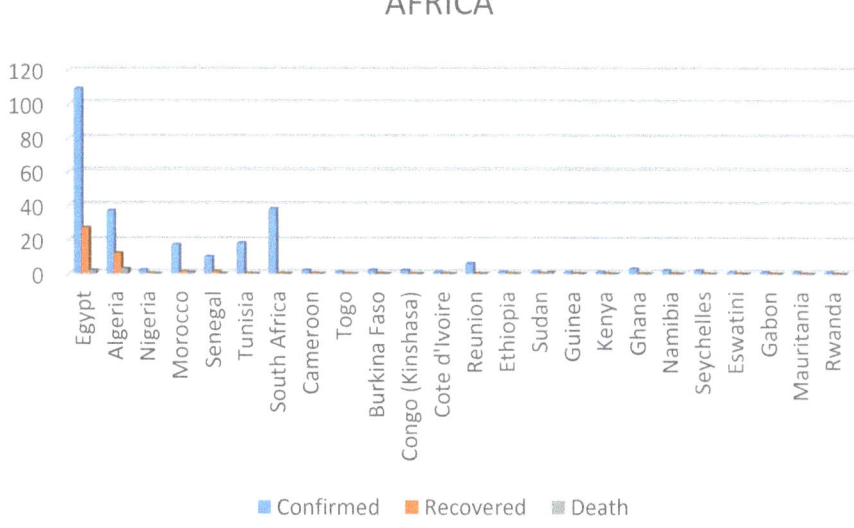

Fig. 17.5 COVID-19 confirmed, recovered, and death cases in Asia. (Source: Authors' own figure)

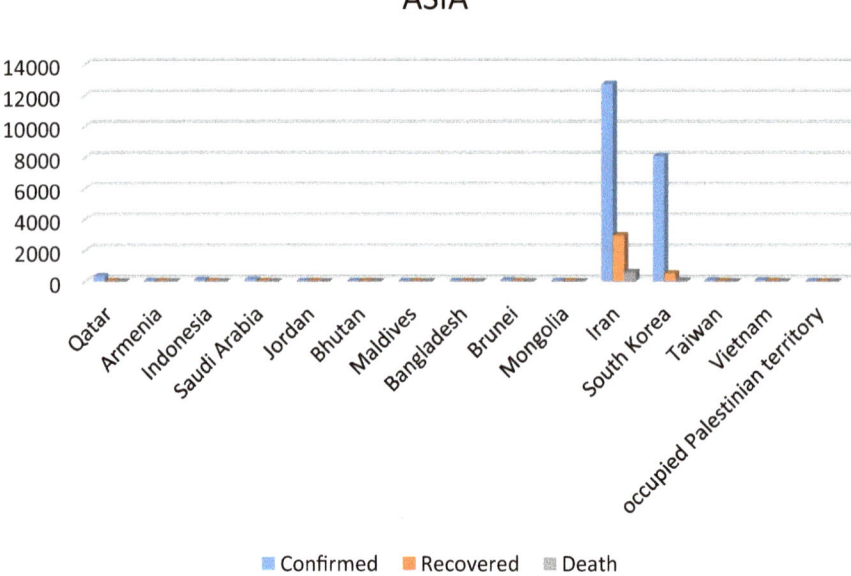

Fig. 17.6 COVID-19 confirmed, recovered, and death cases in Asia. (Source: Authors' own figure)

Fig. 17.7 COVID-19 confirmed, recovered, and death cases in Australia/Oceania. (Source: Authors' own figure)

ASIA

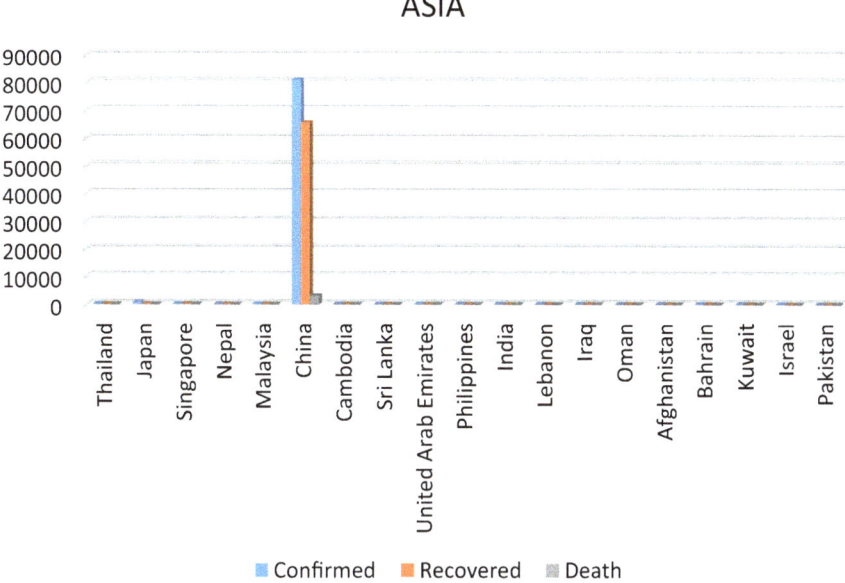

Fig. 17.8 COVID-19 confirmed, recovered, and death cases in Europe. (Source: Authors' own figure)

EUROPE

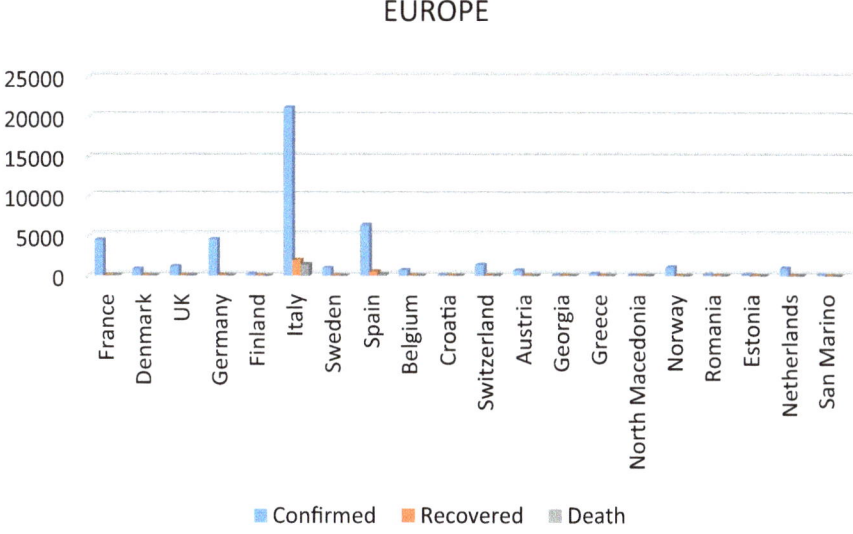

Fig. 17.9 COVID-19 confirmed, recovered, and death cases in Europe. (Source: Authors' own figure)

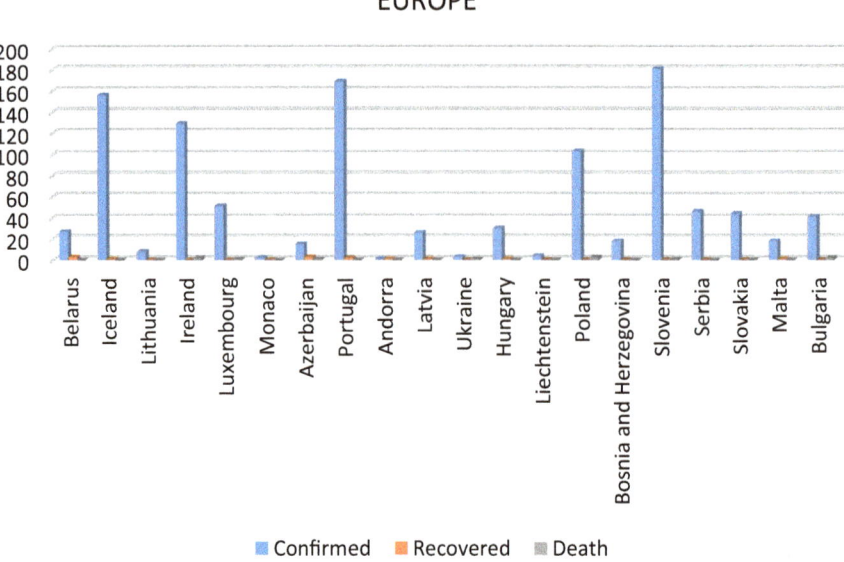

Fig. 17.10 COVID-19 confirmed, recovered, and death cases in Europe. (Source: Authors' own figure)

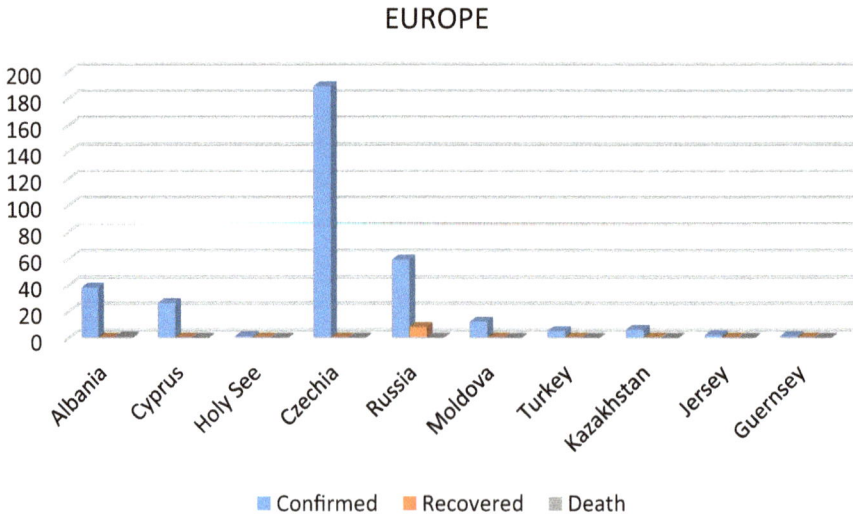

Fig. 17.11 COVID-19 confirmed, recovered, and death cases in Europe. (Source: Authors' own figure)

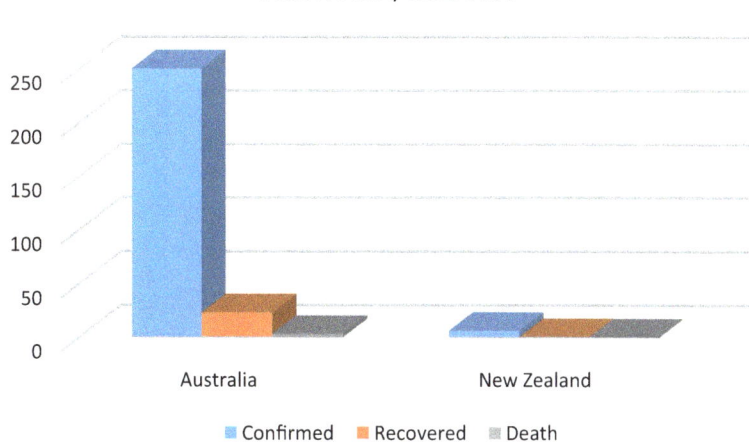

AUSTRALIA/OCEANIA

Fig. 17.12 COVID-19 confirmed, recovered, and death cases in North America. (Source: Authors' own figure)

3193, respectively. Australia/Oceania consists of Australia with 250 confirmed, 23 recovered, and 3 death cases, while New Zealand has 6 confirmed, none recovered, and no deaths (Fig. 17.7). Figures 17.8, 17.9, 17.10 and 17.11 show the confirmed, recovered, and death cases in Europe with Italy having the highest confirmed cases with 21,157, 1966 recovered, and 1441 deaths. In North America, the country with the highest confirmed, recovered, and death cases is the USA with 2727 confirmed, 12 recovered, and 54 deaths as shown in Fig. 17.12. However, in South America, the country with the highest confirmed, recovered, and death cases of COVID-19 is Brazil with 151 confirmed, none recovered, and no deaths (Fig. 17.13).

In this section, we present the result of the transmission of COVID-19, according to results of machine learning techniques such as logistic regression, support vector machine, recurrent neural network, and long short-term memory that were explained above. We then compare them to discern which is more accurate in the predicting spread of the coronavirus. As stated earlier, in Sect. 17.2.1, we used data from the Kaggle database for COVID-19. Data is divided into five segments in order to statistically compare and assess learning algorithms. Figures 17.14, 17.15 and 17.16 are the time series of the confirmed, recovered, and deaths cases of each of the continent utilized in this chapter. The confirmed, recovered, and death cases of COVID-19 pandemic in Asia are at the peak compared to other continents. Most of the continents have stable trends in the months January and February. In mid-February, there are exponential trends of confirmed, recovered, and deaths cases of pandemic diseases which show that the diseases spread faster to other continents. We show the accuracy of these algorithms using mean absolute error, root mean square error, and mean absolute scaled error to predict the

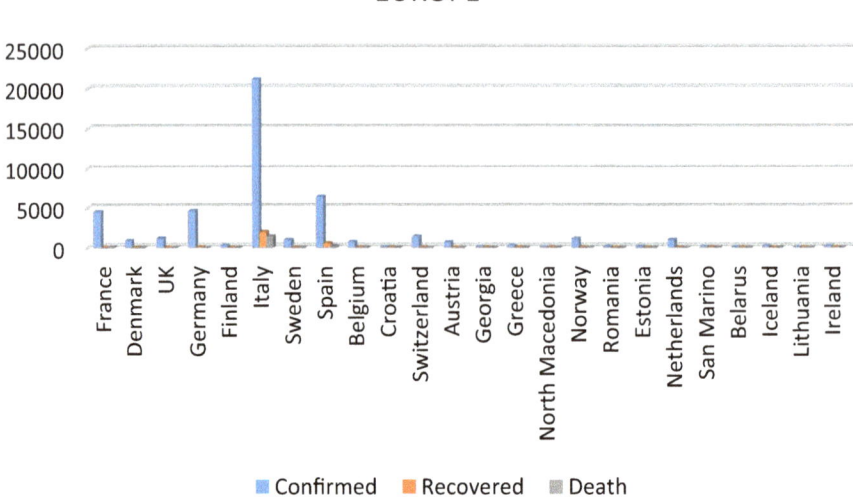

Fig. 17.13 COVID-19 confirmed, recovered, and death cases in South America. (Source: Authors' own figure)

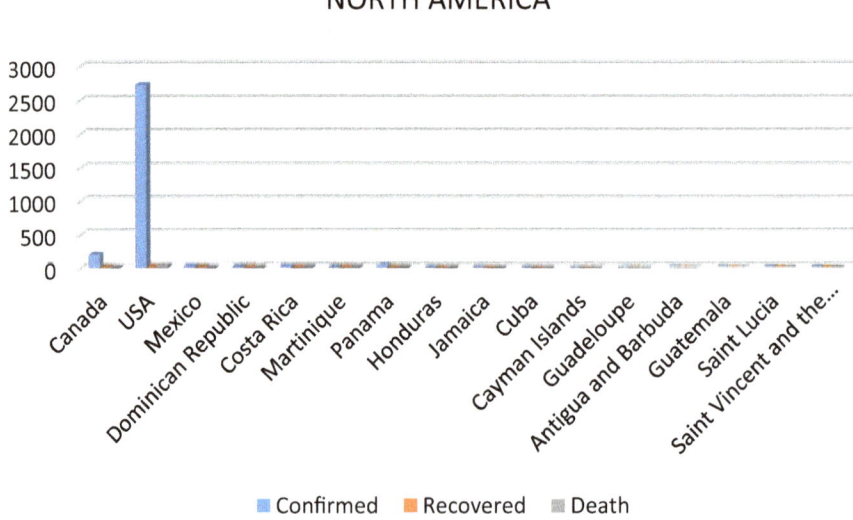

Fig. 17.14 Time series combined cases of the spread of coronavirus. (Source: Authors' own figure)

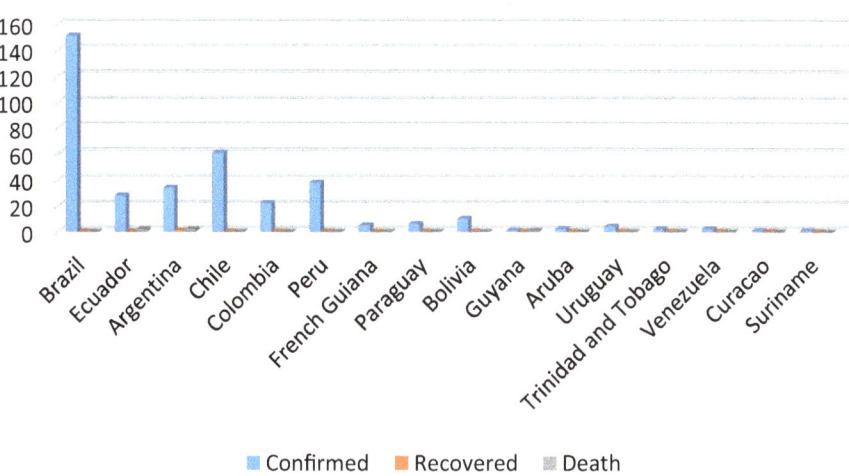

Fig. 17.15 Time series recovered cases of coronavirus. (Source: Authors' own figure)

spread of COVID-19. Each of these accuracies has been obtained from Eqs. (17.16, 17.17 and 17.18).

In this research, we consider four algorithms, i.e., logistic regression (LR), support vector machine (SVM), recurrent neural network (RNN), and long short-term memory (LSTM). The machine learning technique was used to determine the best algorithm among the four which can effectively predict COVID-19 spread in each continent as shown in Figs. 17.17, 17.18, 17.19, 17.20, 17.21, 17.22 and 17.23. The overall performance of each one of the confirmed cases of COVID-19 compared to other algorithms like logistic regression (LR), support vector machine (SVM), recurrent neural network (RNN), and long short-term memory (LSTM). Figures 17.17, 17.18, 17.19, 17.20, 17.21, 17.22 and 17.23 represent the actual continents and predicted value of every one of the algorithms. In this chapter, we also considered the uptrend and downtrend decision taken on the spread of COVID-19 utilizing the predicted value from all the four algorithms. The results demonstrated that logistic regression can predict the spread of pandemic diseases when compared with the actual value of each of the continents and the Diamond Princess cruise ship. Table 17.1 report MAE, RMSE, and MASE of the predicted values. Logistic regression outperforms the remaining three algorithms by achieving smaller errors, implying that the methods are more accurate than any other prediction. The results show that logistic regression can predict the spread of the diseases. The transmission of COVID-19 in Africa, Australia/Oceania, Europe, North America, and South America is very high, while trend of transmission of the disease is stable in Asia and Diamond Princess cruise ship.

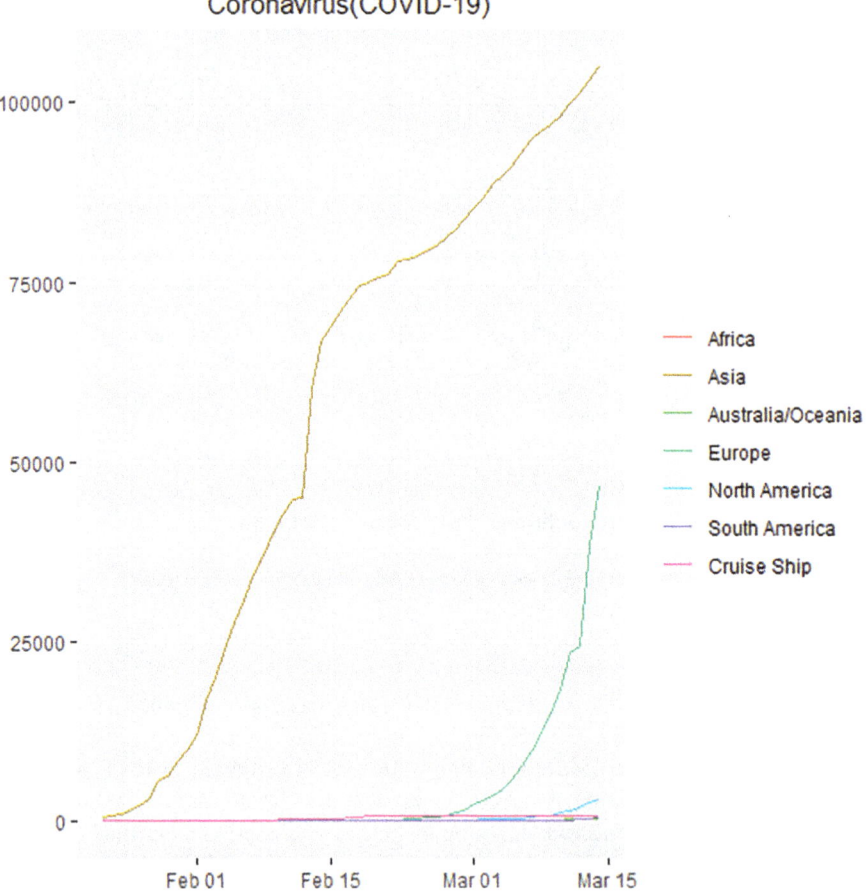

Fig. 17.16 Time series death cases of coronavirus. (Source: Authors' own figure)

Table 17.1 Comparison of COVID-19 models

Continent/ship	Algorithm	MAE	RMSE	MASE
Africa	LR	0.4590791	1.107762	0.03232022
	SVM	5.191755	5.495358	0.3655115
	RNN	1.640905	2.777892	0.1155235
	LSTM	8.249398	30.8881	0.5807766
Asia	LR	57005.25	66846.12	4013.3
	SVM	56883.73	65754.27	4004.745
	RNN	57268.61	67031.95	4031.842
	LSTM	84.76173	88.92752	5.967421
Australia/Oceania	LR	0.6829658	1.031186	0.04603209
	SVM	3.273835	4.137676	0.2206574
	RNN	21.60998	31.52061	1.456519
	LSTM	7.153681	27.78703	0.48216
Europe	LR	44.35829	133.0958	0.01638874
	SVM	344.6199	630.4267	0.1273242
	RNN	2394.434	4249.594	0.8846541
	LSTM	4098.089	10351.17	1.514091
North America	LR	2.276445	4.30547	0.01271177
	SVM	23.71655	28.23568	0.1324343
	RNN	31.08324	76.49514	0.1735703
	LSTM	216.1061	627.1346	1.206746
Diamond princess	LR	4.750852	6.021696	0.08133883
	SVM	24.02565	25.85283	0.4113406
	RNN	6.509865	8.430984	0.1114547
	LSTM	314.8576	422.5014	5.390645
South America	LR	0.5401667	1.176164	0.02800864
	SVM	6.429313	8.979665	0.3333718
	RNN	1.891925	7.903372	0.09809982
	LSTM	12.94701	53.15363	0.6713266

Source: Authors' own table

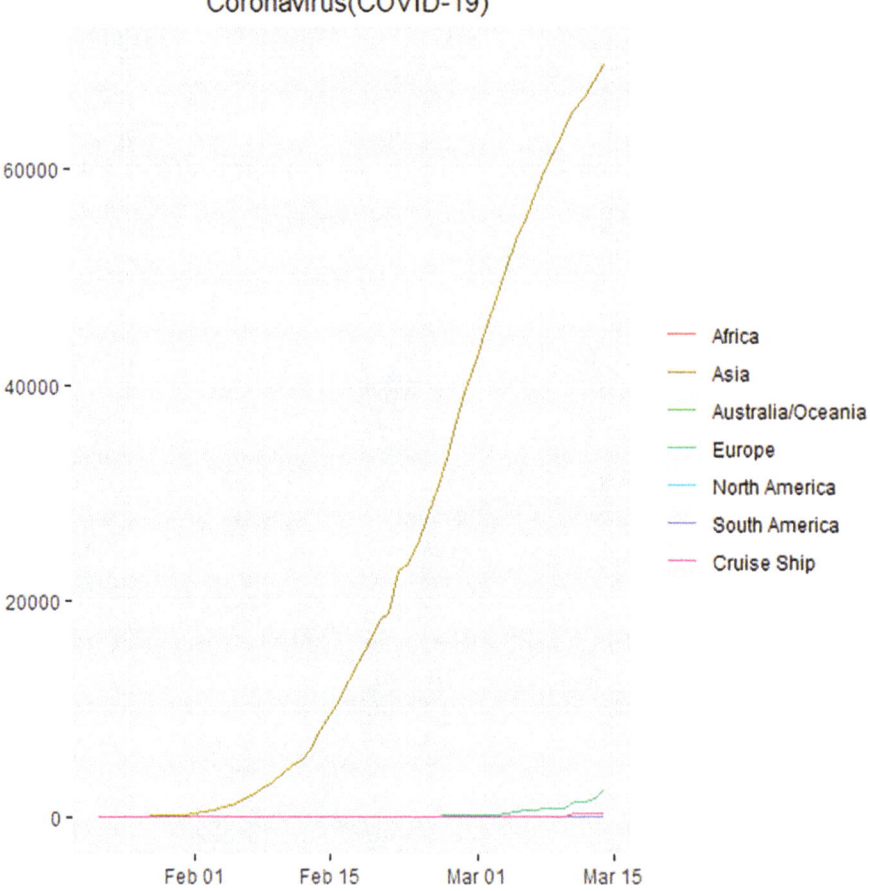

Fig. 17.17 Output prediction obtained from LR, SVM, RNN, and LSTM models. (Source: Authors' own figure)

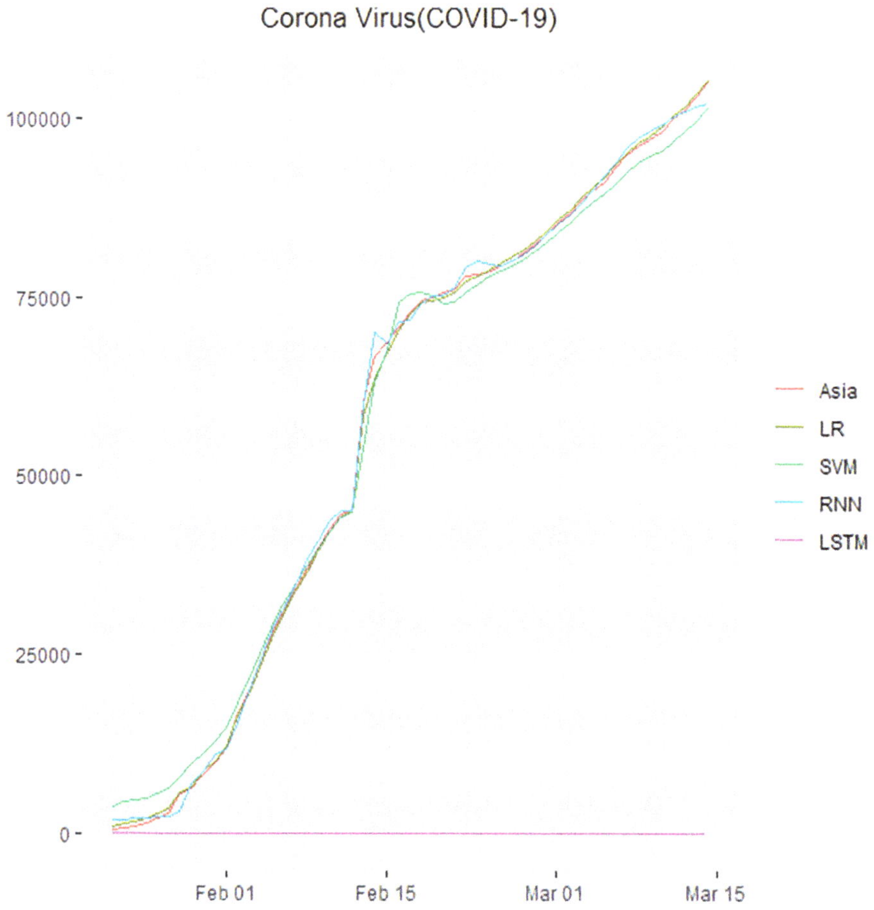

Fig. 17.18 Output prediction obtained from LR, SVM, RNN, and LSTM models. (Source: Authors' own figure)

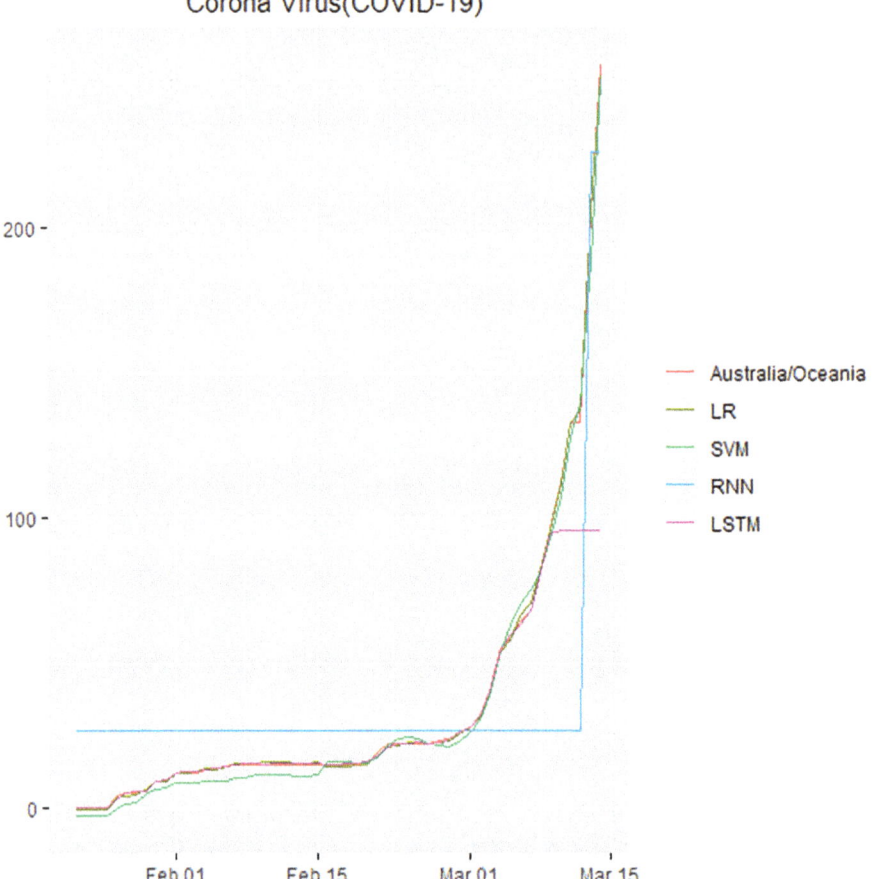

Fig. 17.19 Output prediction obtained from LR, SVM, RNN, and LSTM models. (Source: Authors' own figure)

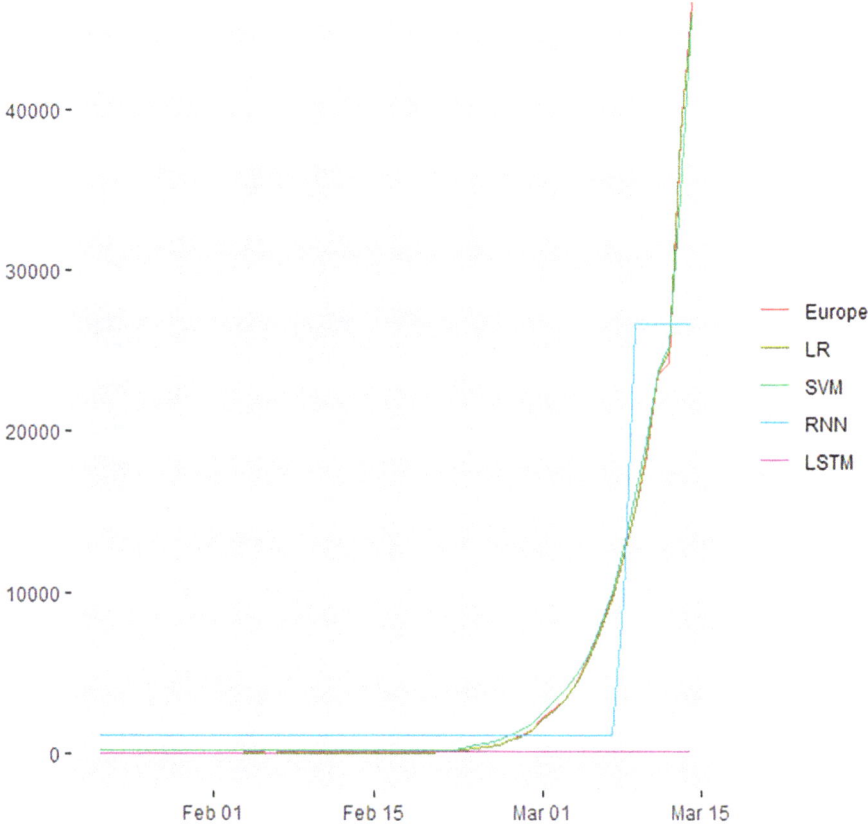

Fig. 17.20 Output prediction obtained from LR, SVM, RNN, and LSTM models. (Source: Authors' own figure)

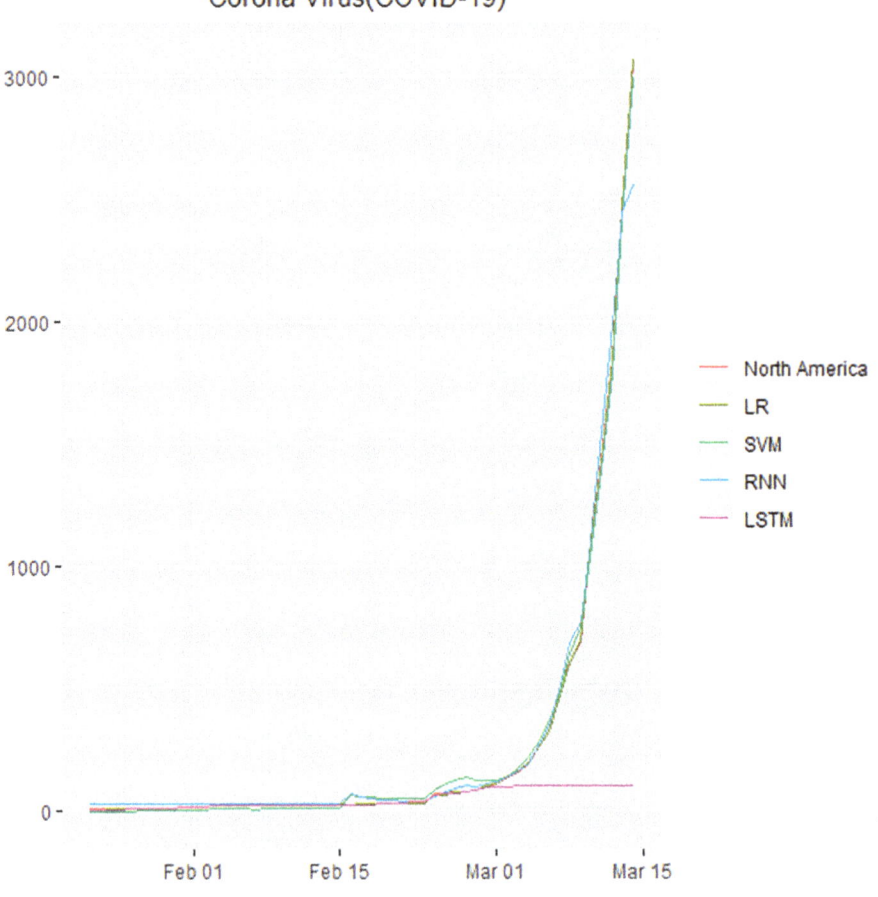

Fig. 17.21 Output prediction obtained from LR, SVM, RNN, and LSTM models. (Source: Authors' own figure)

17.4 Conclusions

In this chapter, we developed a model inspired by the methods used by Kaggle database for the spread of COVID-19 using machine learning techniques. The study reveals that there are exponential trends of COVID-19 in Africa, Europe, Australia/ Oceania, North America, and South America, while trends of transmission of pandemic diseases have been stable in Asia and Diamond Princess cruise ship. As COVID-19 cases continue to rise in Africa, Europe, Australia/Oceania, North America, and South America, there are urgent needs to curtail transmission of the diseases. The main strategies employed in Asia and Diamond Princess cruise ship can also be employed: The first method is preventing the exportation of diseases to other places which blocks transmission and prevents further spread of the disease. The

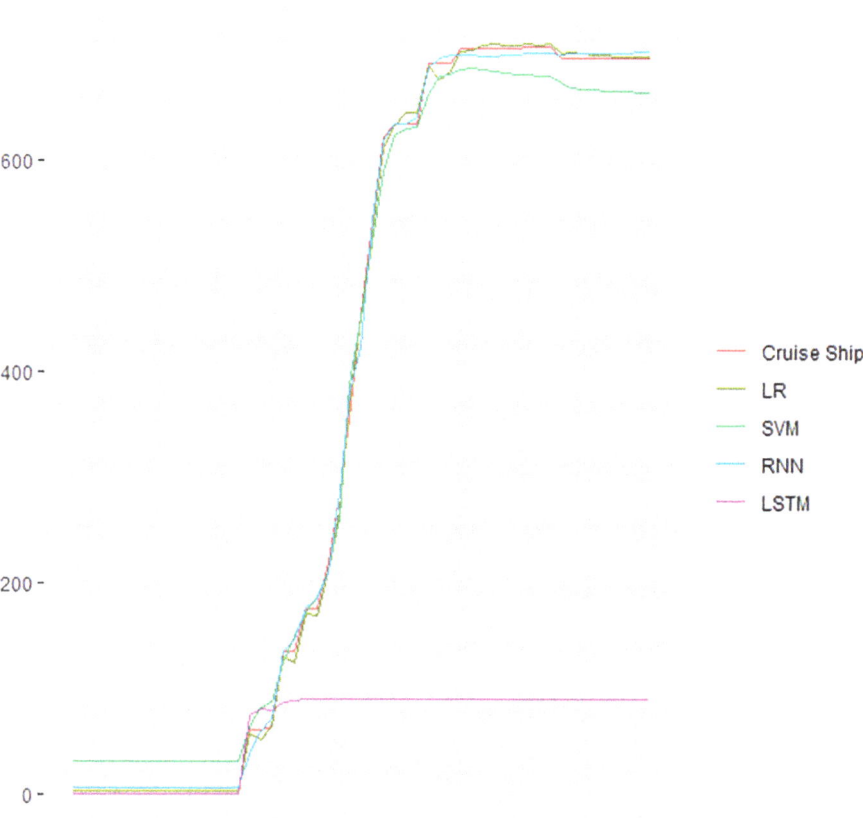

Fig. 17.22 Output prediction obtained from LR, SVM, RNN, and LSTM models. (Source: Authors' own figure)

second method is reducing the intensity of the pandemic which slows down the increase of the affected patients. The third method is reducing clusters of the confirmed cases of the COVID-19 pandemic and self-quarantine. The study here reveals that COVID-19 has been less deadly in Africa than other continents such as Asia, Australia, Europe, and North and South America because of the following reasons:

- Government Policy: Most African governments took drastic measures to try and slow the spread of the COVID-19 virus by public health measures such as avoiding hand shakes, frequent hand washing, social distancing, and wearing of face masks.
- Environmental Factors: A study conducted by Coccia (2021c) reveals greater numbers of infected people and their fatalities associated with COVID-19 in cities with little wind, low average temperature, and often air pollution. The spread

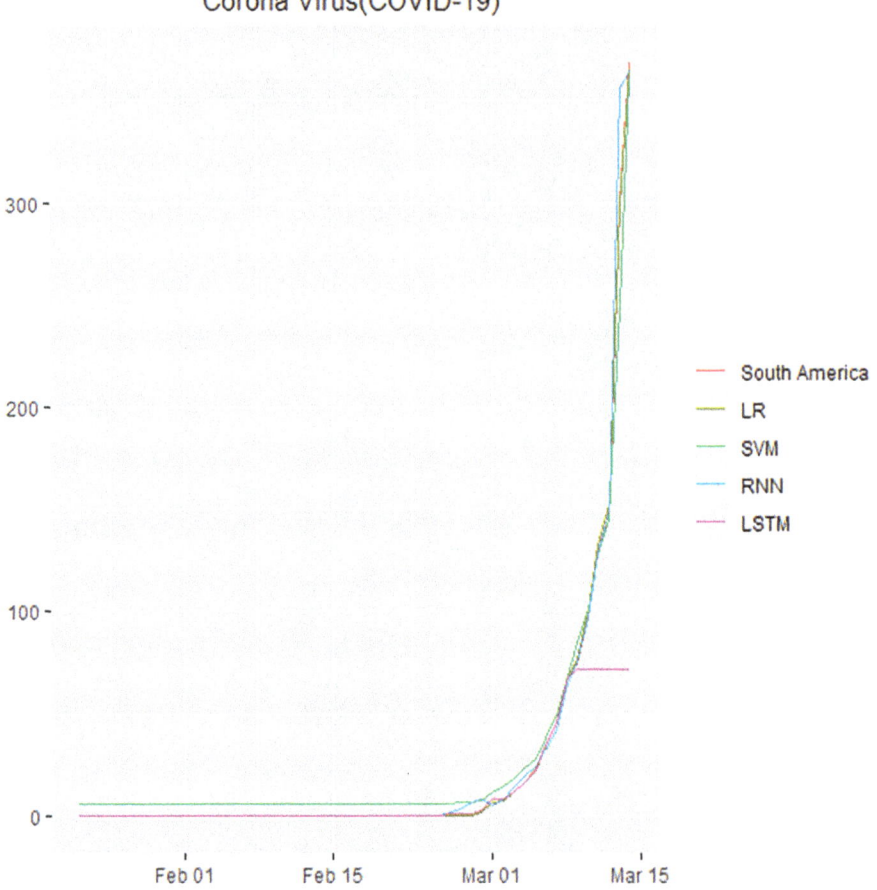

Fig. 17.23 Output prediction obtained from LR, SVM, RNN, and LSTM models. (Source: Authors' own figure)

of the virus accelerated in South Africa than other African countries because the southern hemisphere went into winter. However, when the weather warmed up, the number of reported cases decreased substantially. High temperature experienced in Africa may have resulted in less fatalities than other continents.

There are several challenges to these studies, particularly in real time because the sources of data can only capture certain elements such as confirmed, recovered, and death of patients with COVID-19, but the duration between COVID-19 symptoms and recovered cases was not captured. Also, other underlying ailments were not captured. In future research, we will study a model that can predict COVID-19 more precisely by using disease information of the patient and plan to improve the accuracy.

Appendix

References

Adebowale, A. S., Fagbamigbe, A. F., Akinyemi, J. O., Alarape, S. A., & Obabiyi, S. O. (2021). The spread of COVID-19 outbreak in the first 120 days: A comparison between Nigeria and seven other countries. *BMC Public Health, 21*(1), 129.

Adhikari, S. P., Sha Meng, Y.-J. W., Mao, Y.-P., Ye, R.-X., Wang, Q.-Z., Sun, C., Sylvia, S., Rozelle, S., Raat, H., & Zhou, H. (2020). Epidemiology, causes, clinical manifestation and diagnosis, prevention and control of coronavirus disease (COVID-19) during the early outbreak period: A scoping review. *Infectious Diseases of Poverty*, 1–12.

Arksey, H., & O'Malley, L. (2005). Scoping studies: Towards a methodological framework. *International Journal of Social Research Methodology, 8*, 19–32.

Assaf, D., Gutman, Y., Neuman, Y., Segal, G., Amit, S., Gefen-Halevi, S., Shilo, N., Epstein, A., Mor-Cohen, R., Biber, A., Rahav, G., Levy, I., & Tirosh, A. (2020). Utilization of machine-learning models to accurately predict the risk for critical COVID-19. *Internal and Emergency Medicine, 15*(8), 1435–1443. https://doi.org/10.1007/s11739-020-02475-0. Epub 2020 Aug 18. PMID: 32812204; PMCID: PMC7433773.

Bashir, M. F., Bilal, B. M., & Komal, B. (2020). Correlation between environmental pollution indicators and COVID-19 pandemic: A brief study in Californian context. *Environmental Research, 109652*. https://doi.org/10.1016/j.envres.2020.109652

Basiri, M. E., Nemati, S., Abdar, M., Cambria, E., & Acharya, U. R. (2021). ABCDM: An attention-based bidirectional CNN-RNN deep model for sentiment analysis. *Future Generation Computer Systems, 115*, 279–294.

Beulah Christalin Latha, C., & Carolin Jeeva, S. (2019). Improving the accuracy of prediction of heart disease risk based on ensemble classification techniques. *Informatics in Medicine Unlocked, 16*(2009), 1–9.

CDC. (2020). 2019 Novel coronavirus, Wuhan, China. https://www.cdc.gov/coronavirus/2019-nCoV/summary.html. Accessed 30 Mar 2020.

Center NaI. (2020). Online news: Ministry of Health and Medical Education. Available from: http://dme.behdasht.gov.ir/index.aspx?siteid=1&pageid=3127

Coccia, M. (2020a). Factors determining the diffusion of COVID-19 and suggested strategy to prevent future accelerated viral infectivity similar to COVID. *Science of the Total Environment*, Article Number: 138474. https://doi.org/10.1016/j.scitotenv.2020.1384743

Coccia, M. (2020b). An index to quantify environmental risk of exposure to future epidemics of the COVID-19 and similar viral agents: Theory and practice. *Environmental Research*, Article number: 110155. https://doi.org/10.1016/j.envres.2020.110155.

Coccia, M. (2020c). How do low wind speeds and high levels of air pollution support the spread of COVID-19? *Atmospheric Pollution Research*. PII S1309-1042(20)30293-2. https://doi.org/10.1016/j.apr.2020.10.002

Coccia, M. (2021a). The effects of atmospheric stability with low wind speed and of air pollution on the accelerated transmission dynamics of COVID-19. *International Journal of Environmental Studies, 78*(1), 1–27. Article ID: GENV 1802937. https://doi.org/10.1080/00207233.2020.1802937

Coccia, M. (2021b). The relation between length of lockdown, numbers of infected people and deaths of Covid-19, and economic growth of countries: Lessons learned to cope with future pandemics similar to Covid-19. *Science of the Total Environment*. Available online 12 February 2021, 145801. https://doi.org/10.1016/j.scitotenv.2021.145801

Coccia, M. (2021c). Effects of the spread of COVID-19 on public health of polluted cities: Results of the first wave for explaining the dejà vu in the second wave of COVID-19 pandemic and epidemics of future vital agents. *Environmental Science and Pollution Research*. https://doi.org/10.1007/s11356-020-11662-7

Coccia, M. (2021d). The impact of first and second wave of the COVID-19 pandemic: Comparative analysis to support control measures to cope with negative effects of future infectious diseases in society. *Environmental Research, 197*. Article number 111099, PII S0013-9351(21)00393-5. https://doi.org/10.1016/j.envres.2021.111099.

Dellicour, S., Linard, C., Van Goethem, N., Da Re, D., Artois, J., Bihin, J., Schaus, P., Massonnet, F., Van Oyen, H., Vanwambeke, S. O., Speybroeck, N., & Gilbert, M. (2021). Investigating the drivers of the spatio-temporal heterogeneity in COVID-19 hospital incidence-Belgium as a study case. *International Journal of Health Geographics, 20*(1), 29. https://doi.org/10.1186/s12942-021-00281-1. PMID: 34127000; PMCID: PMC8200785.

Diao, Y., Kodera, S., Anzai, D., Rashed, E. A., & Hirata, A. (2021). Influence of population density, temperature, and absolute humidity on spread and decay durations of COVID-19: A comparative study of scenarios in China, England, Germany, and Japan. *One Health, 12*, 100203.

Dong, E., Du, H., & Gardner, L. (2020). An interactive web-based dashboard to track COVID-19 in real time. *The Lancet Infectious Diseases*.

Fathima, A., & Manimegalai, D. (2012). Predictive analysis for the arbovirus-dengue using svm classification. *International Journal of Engineering and Technology, 2*(3), 521–527.

Gardner, L. (2020). Mapping 2019-nCoV: John's Hopkins University. Available from: https://systems.jhu.edu/research/public-health/ncov/

Hochreiter, S., & Schmidhuber, J. (1997). Long short-term memory. *Neural Computation, 9*(8), 1735–1780.

Hou, W., Zhao, Z., Chen, A., Li, H., & Duong, T. Q. (2021). Machining learning predicts the need for escalated care and mortality in COVID-19 patients from clinical variables. *International Journal of Medical Sciences, 18*(8), 1739–1745. https://doi.org/10.7150/ijms.51235. PMID: 33746590; PMCID: PMC7976594.5.

https://www.worldometers.info/coronavirus/. Accessed on 30 Mar 2020.

Huang, C., Wang, Y., Li, X., Ren, L., Zhao Jianping, H. Y., et al. (2020). Clinical features of patients infected with 2019 novel coronavirus in Wuhan, China. *Lancet, 395*, 497–506. https://doi.org/10.1016/S0140-6736(20)30183-5

Iqbal, N., & Islam, M. (2019). Machine learning for Dengue outbreak prediction: A performance evaluation of different prominent classifiers. *Informatica, 43*(2019), 363–371.

Jang, S. B., Lee, S. H., Lee, D. E., Park, S. Y., Kim, J. K., Cho, J. W., Cho, J., Kim, K. B., Park, B., Park, J., & Lim, J. K. (2020). Deeplearning algorithms for the interpretation of chest radiographs to aid in the triage of COVID-19 patients: A multicenter retrospective study. *PLoS One, 15*(11), e0242759. https://doi.org/10.1371/journal.pone.0242759. PMID: 33232368; PMCID: PMC7685476.

Khuzani, A. Z., Heidari, M., & Shariati, S. A. (2020). COVID-classifier: An automated machine learning model to assist in the diagnosis of COVID-19 infection in chest x-ray images. *medRxiv [Preprint]*, 2020.05.09.20096560. https://doi.org/10.1101/2020.05.09.20096560. PMID: 32511510; PMCID:PMC7273278.

Li, Q., Guan, X., Wu, P., Wang, X., Zhou, L., Tong, Y., et al. (2020). Early transmission dynamics in Wuhan, China, of novel coronavirus-infected pneumonia. *The New England Journal of Medicine*. https://doi.org/10.1056/NEJMoa2001316.

Mahindru, A., & Sangal, A. L. (2020). SOMDROID: Android malware detection by artificial neural network trained using unsupervised learning. *Evolutionary Intelligence*. https://doi.org/10.1007/s12065-020-00518-1

Mahindru, A., & Sangal, A. L. (2021a). MLDroid—Framework for android malware detection using machine learning techniques. *Neural Computing and Applications, 33*, 5183–5240. https://doi.org/10.1007/s00521-020-05309-4

Mahindru, A., & Sangal, A. (2021b). FSDroid:- A feature selection technique to detect malware from android using machine learning techniques. *Multimedia Tools and Applications, 80*, 13271–13323. https://doi.org/10.1007/s11042-020-10367-w

Mahindru, A., & Sangal, A. L. (2021c). HybriDroid: An empirical analysis on effective malware detection model developed using ensemble methods. *The Journal of Supercomputing*. https://doi.org/10.1007/s11227-020-03569-4

McCoy, D., Mgbara, W., Horvitz, N., Getz, W. M., & Hubbard, A. (2021). Ensemble machine learning of factors influencing COVID-19 across US counties. *Scientific Reports, 11*(1), 11777. https://doi.org/10.1038/s41598-021-90827-x. PMID: 34083563; PMCID: PMC8175420.4.

National Center for Immunization and Respiratory Diseases (NCIRD) DoVD. (2020). Coronavirus Disease 2019 (COVID-19) situation summary: Centers for Disease Control and Prevention. Available from: https://www.cdc.gov/coronavirus/2019-nCoV/summary.html

Oyewola, D., Hakimi, D., Adeboye, K., & Shehu, M. D. (2016). Using five machine learning for breast cancer biopsy predictions based on mammographic diagnosis. *International Journal of Engineering Technologies, 2*(4), 142–145.

Rosario Denes, K. A., Mutz Yhan, S., Bernardes Patricia, C., & Conte-Junior Carlos, A. (2020). Relationship between COVID-19 and weather: Case study in a tropical country. *International Journal of Hygiene and Environmental Health, 229*, 113587.

Sarwar, A., & Sharma, V. (2013). *Comparative analysis of machine learning techniques in prognosis of type II diabetes in AI & Society*. Springer Verlag.

So, A., Hooshyar, D., Park, K. W., & Lim, H. S. (2017). Early diagnosis of dementia from clinical data by machine learning techniques. *Applied Sciences, 7*, 1–17.

Subudhi, S., Verma, A., Patel, A. B., Hardin, C. C., Khandekar, M. J., Lee, H., McEvoy, D., Stylianopoulos, T., Munn, L. L., Dutta, S., & Jain, R. K. (2021). Comparing machine learning algorithms for predicting ICU admission and mortality in COVID-19. *NPJ Digital Medicine, 4*(1), 87. https://doi.org/10.1038/s41746-021-00456-x. PMID: 34021235; PMCID: PMC8140139.

WHO. (2020a). Report of the WHO-China Joint Mission on Coronavirus disease 2019 (COVID-19) — February 16–24. https://www.who.int/docs/default-source/coronaviruse/who-china-joint-mission-on-covid-19-final-report.pdf. Accessed 29 Mar 2020.

WHO. (2020b). Novel Coronavirus–China. https://www.who.int/csr/don/12-january-2020-novel-coronavirus-china/en/. Accessed 29 Mar 2020.

Zhou, P., Yang, X. L., Wang, X. G., Hu, B., Zhang, L., Zhang, W., et al. (2020). Discovery of a novel coronavirus associated with the recent pneumonia outbreak in humans and its potential bat origin. *bioRxiv*. https://doi.org/10.1101/2020.01.22.914952

Zhu, N., Zhang, D., Wang, W., Li, X., Yang, B., Song, J., Zhao, X., Huang, B., Shi, W., Lu, R., et al. (2019). A novel coronavirus from patients with pneumonia in China. *The New England Journal of Medicine, 20*, 20.

Chapter 18
Perceptions and Coping Strategies to COVID-19 in a Rural Ghanaian Community

Peter Asare-Nuamah ⓘ, Justina Adwoa Onumah, Christopher Dick-Sagoe, and Kingsley Obeng Kessie

18.1 Introduction

Since its detection in Wuhan in the Hubei Province of China, in December 2019, the novel coronavirus (COVID-19) has gained heightened attention due to its widespread and devastating impact across the globe. By early 2020, COVID-19 had spread to Europe and America, with an escalated number of infected cases and deaths. Studies have linked the rapid spread of COVID-19 to human migration (WHO, 2020b). Nevertheless, Africa observed a slow and delayed spread of the virus compared to other regions of the world (WHO, 2020b). In Africa, the first case of COVID-19 was reported in Egypt on February 14, 2020. However, by April, the African Regional Office of the World Health Organization (WHO) reported more than 10,000 positive cases with over 500 deaths across 52 African countries (WHO, 2020b). In Ghana, in particular, the first case of COVID-19 was reported on March 12, 2020, but had reached about 37,014 confirmed cases on August 3 (Ghana Health Service, 2020).

Coronavirus is not entirely new to the world, due to past incidences of severe acute respiratory syndrome coronavirus (SARS-CoV) and Middle East respiratory syndrome coronavirus (MERS-CoV) (Zhang et al., 2020). However, COVID-19

P. Asare-Nuamah (✉)
University of Environment and Sustainable Development, Somanya, Ghana
e-mail: pasare-nuamah@uesd.edu.gh

J. A. Onumah
CSIR – Science and Technology Policy Research Institute, Accra, Ghana

C. Dick-Sagoe
University of Botswana, Gaborone, Botswana

K. O. Kessie
Kwame Nkrumah University of Science and Technology, Kumasi, Ghana

© The Author(s), under exclusive license to Springer Nature Switzerland AG 2022   403
N. Faghih, A. Forouharfar (eds.), *Socioeconomic Dynamics of the COVID-19 Crisis*,
Contributions to Economics, https://doi.org/10.1007/978-3-030-89996-7_18

causes far more serious and severe respiratory disease (Huang et al., 2020). In a clinical and laboratory study, Huang et al. (2020) noted that dyspnea, fever, sore throat, and dry cough were common symptoms of COVID-19, which spreads mostly through interhuman transmission, with super-spreading events (Perlman, 2020). Consequently, the impact of COVID-19 has been grave and threatening. Studies have highlighted the consequences of COVID-19 on global development, as the pandemic has the potential to thwart efforts toward achieving sustainable development (Agenda 2030). Aside from the loss of lives, COVID-19 affects the human resource capacity of countries and retards economic growth and development. It also strains existing infrastructure (such as hospitals and other healthcare centers) and resources needed for socioeconomic development. Similarly, COVID-19 affects governance and political processes (such as elections) and also puts pressure on governments, who are required to make huge political and financial commitment to address the menace of the pandemic. This is problematic especially in developing economies in Africa, further exposing and questioning the ability of African economies to effectively tackle COVID-19.

Although the initial cases of COVID-19 were mostly confined to urban centers across the globe, the mass movement of people to hinterlands and rural communities, triggered mainly by governments' responses to COVID-19 (Ranscombe, 2020; WHO, 2020b), has escalated exposure and vulnerability of rural communities. Phillipson et al. (2020) argue that the structural features of rural economies, such as home-based working and dispersed population, can cushion their resilience. However, the authors acknowledge that COVID-19 negatively affects rural businesses, agriculture, and household income in rural economies. For Shah (2020), rural communities are likely to be one of the hardest hit areas, due to lack of resources and their demographics. It is also important to highlight that the impact of COVID-19 in rural communities may vary within and between communities, due to the differences in exposure, sensitivity, and adaptive capacity as well as access to socioeconomic resources (Cori et al., 2020; Ranscombe, 2020). According to Horton (2003), research on health needs and diseases have focused excessively on privileged and well-endowed societies with little attention on less endowed and poor communities. Without doubt, COVID-19 cannot be successfully managed without important attention to vulnerable populations, especially in rural communities (Ranscombe, 2020).

Most importantly, understanding how rural communities perceive COVID-19 is crucial, even though there is scarcity of information on rural community perceptions of the pandemic (Ranscombe, 2020; Shah, 2020). Parikh et al. (2020) also call for the extension of public perception to health professionals, to facilitate treatment of COVID-19 patients (Amatya & Khan, 2020). This corroborates the assertion by Zhong and Wong (2004) that managing pandemics demands a better understanding of public perception, which is necessary to drive effective public education and guarantee adherence to available control and treatment measures. WHO (2020a) therefore prioritizes effective communication in its roadmap for COVID-19, to build public trust and enhance informed decision-making. According to Perlman (2020), socioeconomic consequences of COVID-19 are escalated by public fear and panic. Studies have therefore attempted to expand knowledge on public perception during pandemic (Fetzer et al., 2020; Kristiansen et al., 2007; Parikh et al., 2020). For instance, Wiedemann and Schütz (2005) noted that risk perception of a pandemic serves as the basis for precautionary measures. In addition, Renner et al. (2008) argue that precautionary measures are also linked to health beliefs and cognitions.

Globally, precautionary measures to COVID-19 have centered on social distancing, wearing of nose masks, regular washing of hands, applying hand sanitizers, and self-quarantining. Other personal hygiene practices include covering of mouth and nose with elbow when coughing or sneezing and avoiding touching of mouth, nose, and eyes (Fetzer et al., 2020; Parikh et al., 2020). These measures affirm safety responsibilities of individuals during pandemics or disasters. Aside from these personal precautionary measures, governments' responses to COVID-19 range from less intense actions, such as fumigation and disinfection, to harsher and stricter measures, such as lockdowns (Alemanno, 2020; Ranscombe, 2020; Zhang et al., 2020). Zhang et al. (2020) argue that the stricter and swifter response measures are, the lower the rate of spread and infection. Hence, early detection and reporting as well as swift implementation of precautionary and treatment measures are essential to COVID-19 control. Notwithstanding the implementation of both benign and stricter precautionary and control measures, the continuous escalation in the number of infected cases is problematic and creates a troubling situation, especially for developing economies, including Ghana, where poverty and poor access to essential socioeconomic resources are prominent, particularly in rural communities. Hence understanding how vulnerable population perceive and respond to COVID-19 is relevant for policy and planning purposes, including emergency response to control and mitigate the spread of the pandemic (WHO, 2020a). However, there is a dearth of information on how rural communities perceive and respond to COVID-19 in Ghana. This chapter therefore investigates the perceptions and coping strategies to COVID-19 in a rural Ghanaian community.

18.2   Theoretical Framework

This study was guided by the social representations theory propounded by Moscovici (1963, 1984, 1988), which posits that social practices, norms, behavior, and perceptions are inherent in sociocultural setting of society. According to Moscovici (1988: 214), social representations:

> concern the contents of everyday thinking and the stock of ideas that give coherence to our religious beliefs, political ideas and the connections we create as spontaneously as we breathe. They make it possible for us to classify persons and objects, to compare and explain behaviours and to objectify them as part of our social setting. While representations are often to be located in the minds of men and women, they can just as often be found "in the world", and as such examined separately.

The theory therefore argues that a deeper understanding of contemporary psychosocial phenomenon, such as COVID-19, in the case of this study, can be reached if the phenomenon and the associated processes, perceptions, and behaviors are viewed as embedded and inherent in macrosocial, cultural, and historical conditions of society (Moscovici & Duveen, 2000). Farr (1993, 1996) also contends that social representations theory divorces itself from methodological and epistemological individualism as espoused by other social psychological theories. As such, social representations theory assumes that both subject and object are not functionally separable (Moscovici, 1963).

Moscovici (1963) denotes that a collective elaboration of the social object by members of a community, which further influences their behavior and communication, constitutes social representation. Hence, the community's representation of the elaborated social object, in this case COVID-19, becomes their reality. This way, the social reality becomes part of the community's systems and values, which further orients their behaviors, attitudes, perceptions, and communication in their daily activities. According to Wagner et al. (1999), the imagination of social reality or social representations occurs across and not within minds, which illustrates differences in perceptions, attitudes, communication, and behavior of groups regarding a particular reality within the same community. To this end, social representations theory argues that social practices, knowledge, and interactions are characterized by competing versions of reality (Moscovici & Duveen, 2000; Rose et al., 1995) within a specific sociocultural context. The theory has been applied in diverse research fields, such as health (De-Graft Aikins, 2003, 2005), climate change, media, and communication (Höijer, 2010, 2011; Olausson, 2009, 2010), among others.

The application of social representation theory in this study is essential for two reasons: first, it helps to obtain a deeper understanding of how the rural community as a whole perceives and responds to COVID-19, due to the conditioning effect of the environment (social, cultural, historical, and economic, among others); second, the theory helps to observe the differences (contestations) in COVID-19 perceptions and coping strategies of groups (individuals who share same or similar feelings, thought, or actions) within the same community. Thus through social representations theory, this study is able to offer an in-depth understanding of how members of the rural community construct their social reality of COVID-19, as observed in their talks and actions (Wagner et al., 1999).

18.3 Materials and Method

18.3.1 Study Design and Participants

This chapter adopted a qualitative descriptive phenomenology. The adopted approach was employed to generate an in-depth understanding of the subject matter from the sociocultural setting of the participants (Lopez & Willis, 2004). To understand how rural communities perceive and respond to COVID-19 phenomena, their situated context should be studied (Creswell, 2014; Silverman, 2000). This supports the argument that risk perceptions and responses are influenced by socio-cultural setting. The study was also guided by inductive and deductive reasoning. In the case of inductive reasoning, participants' meanings to the subject matter were drawn from the sociocultural setting. Deductively, these meanings were juxtaposed to findings from already existing studies to further generate a general but better understanding from similar but different environmental context.

The study was conducted in Akwansrem (see Fig. 18.1), a rural community in the rural Adansi North District in the Ashanti region of Ghana. Rumors of a COVID-19 case in the community, which generated tension and panic among community members, due to low adaptive capacity and poor access to healthcare, as well as the mass movement of people from urban centers to the community, influenced the need and choice of the community for this study. Akwansrem is located on latitude 6.1863 and longitude −1.4804. According to the Ghana Statistical Service (GSS, 2014), Akwansrem has 527 households and a total population of 2534. Forty (40) participants participated in the study, as the study reached its saturation with the 40th participant. Both purposive and snowball sampling techniques were used to select the participants. To ensure social representations, the study purposively selected participants based on different criteria such as age, gender, religious association, and occupation, among others. However, some of the participants were also suggested by other community members based on their knowledge of the subject matter. Snowballing was particularly important and used for in-depth information on

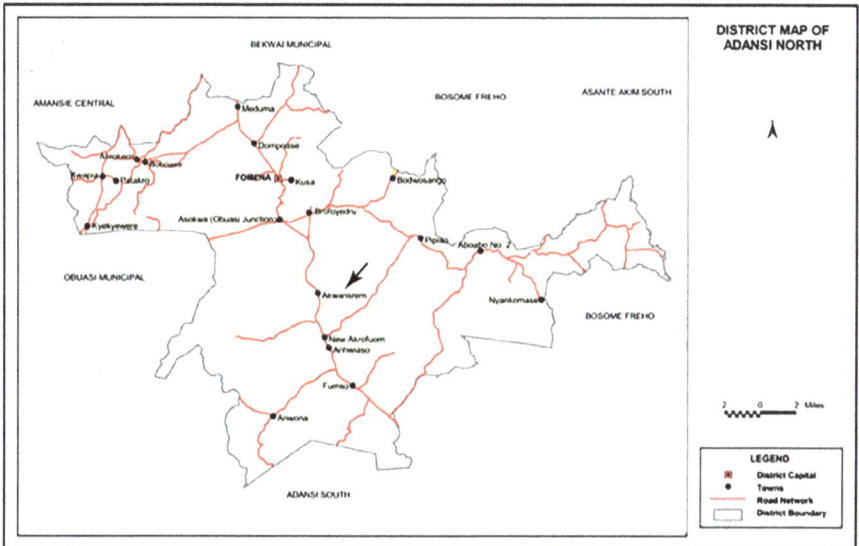

Fig. 18.1 Map of Adansi North District with study setting (Akwansrem) indicated with arrows. (Source: GSS (2014))

nonconventional coping practices. This enabled the study to probe for clarification and detailed information on theme that emerged from previous interviews.

18.3.2 Data Collection Instruments and Procedure

The instruments for the study consisted of semi-structured interview guide and participant observation, which enhanced data triangulation. The use of semi-structured interview guide gave room for the study to ask further questions from emerging themes. Implicitly, all participants were not asked the same questions in the same manner, but rather, emerging themes were further probed in subsequent interviews. Participant observation also allowed the researchers to immerse in the community while adhering to precautionary measures. Data collection and observation, which was undertaken by the first author, started from March to May 2020. This period was crucial to the study, as Ghana's first case of COVID-19 was reported in March, while the imposition and lifting of lockdown and restrictions also took place within this period. Prior to data collection, permission was sought from community gatekeepers. The study also orally sought informed consent from the participants, and only those who consented to participate were involved in the study. In addition, the study adhered to other ethical principles such as voluntary participation, anonymity, confidentiality, and the right to terminate the study.

Interviews were conducted at various places, such as homes, community park, main streets, mills, and market, based on participants' preference. All interviews were conducted in the local language (Twi), and the average time for an interview was 45 minutes. Almost all interviews were recorded upon participants' consent. Transect walks and observation, especially at places of meeting, such as market, mills, pipes, and burial grounds, among others, were employed. The researchers' reflexive position was highlighted during the interviews. Sentences, such as "you know that…" or "we Asantes…" were indicative that the participants were aware of the researchers' knowledge of the community, culture, and belief system. To enhance self-reflexivity and self-representation of the researchers, they maintained neutrality in all cases emerging from facial expressions and participants' views.

Although overt observation helped to understand how the community practiced coping responses in their sociocultural context, perceptions and experiences of individuals vary, and hence the involvement of the participants was necessary for a holistic and deeper understanding of community perceptions and coping responses. The study therefore probed emerging themes in subsequent interviews to generate a deeper understanding, which helped to improve the depth of data. In addition, the participants were informed prior to the interviews that there was no right or wrong answer, which enabled them to express themselves freely in their own language. This reflexive insight helped to gain an in-depth understanding of the participants in their sociocultural setting.

18.3.3 Data Analysis

The study used manual thematic analysis of data. Before the authors analyzed the data, the first author transcribed the interviews from Twi to English, which was shared with the participants to validate the meanings they attached to their real world (Creswell, 2014). The transcripts were perused consistently to identify emerging themes and also draw patterns. The study adopted Braun and Clarke's (2014) stages of thematic analysis: coding and theme identification as well as theme organization and interpretation. The analysis also took cognizance of views that portrayed consensus, conflicts, and absence as well as their frequency. The researchers deliberated on codes and themes to ensure the rigorousness of the data and the study as a whole. In situations where there were divergent views among the researchers regarding a particular code or theme, consensus was reached. The meanings the participants attached to the subject matter are presented in verbatim quotes.

18.4 Results

18.4.1 Participants' Characteristics

Of the 40 participants, there were more males (23) than females (17). The age of the participants ranged between 18 and 68 years. The participants consisted of students (7), teachers (4), farmers (21), and petty traders (8). Except six of the participants who were community members living in cities and towns and had moved back just because of the pandemic, all the participants lived in the community.

18.4.2 Perceptions of COVID-19

The themes that emerged from participants' perceptions of COVID-19 revolved around knowledge of COVID-19 existence, its causes and means of transmission, as well as the symptoms of the disease and general knowledge about the pandemic.

18.4.2.1 Knowledge of COVID-19 Existence

Although all the participants had knowledge of COVID-19, only a section of them (11) knew or perceived it to be a viral infection. Some participants expressed that although they have heard of COVID-19 on radio and television, and even from families and friends, they however, believed COVID-19 did not exist. A participant expressed that "have you not heard a Pastor say the virus does not exist. I strongly agree with the Pastor that COVID-19 is a hoax." Some were also doubtful of

COVID-19 existence specifically in Ghana, even though they believed the disease existed in the world. To this, a participant stated that "if you watch the news, you will see how people are laid in hospital beds in other part of the world. However, in Ghana, we only hear of the number of positive cases without any evidence, such as hospitalization and burial of dead persons, among others."

18.4.2.2 Causes of COVID-19

The participants were ambivalent on the causes of the pandemic. While a few of the participants perceived COVID-19 to be caused by a virus, some of the participants associated the pandemic with Spiritism. For instance, a participant hinted that "the pandemic is a true reflection of an act of God." Another participant also concurred that "if COVID-19 is caused by virus as they claim, we would have had a remedy by now. The pandemic is certainly out of the ability and control of man and only God can do this." This sect of the participants believed that either the pandemic is a sign of the beginning of the end of the world, as stated in the Bible, or it is a reflection of the anger of God on humanity, due to the wickedness and sins of mankind. Still, some of the participants also perceived COVID-19 to be engineered by humans to destroy their fellow human beings. A participant corroborated to this as "everything is possible. We are our own enemies and hence someone somewhere can do this to destroy their fellow human beings."

18.4.2.3 Spread and Symptoms of COVID-19

On how COVID-19 spreads, the perceptions of the majority (38) of the participants converged on droplets and contact. A participant reported that "COVID-19 spreads through droplets from an infected person." Another participant also noted that "when an infected person coughs, sneezes or yawns without covering the mouth or nose, s/he releases droplets that are inhaled by people around, who also get infected." However, it was observed that some community members continued to cough and sneeze without covering their mouth and nose with their elbow or tissue. In the case of contact, most of the participants agreed that body contact and touching infected surfaces and objects could spread the virus. Nevertheless, a participant echoed that "we have heard the pandemic is also spread by animals, such as dogs, cats, bats and pigs, among others."

Almost all the participants were unanimous of their knowledge of the symptoms of the pandemic, largely due to their familiarity with malaria. This was reported by a participant as "we know the symptoms of malaria very well, which are also similar to corona (COVID-19) symptoms." Fever, cold, headache, body pains, and rising temperature were the most common symptoms reported by the participants. In addition, a participant concurred that aside from the similarity of COVID-19 symptoms to malaria, COVID-19 patients also have difficulty in breathing, sore throat, and tightness of chest, which are not found in malaria patients.

18.4.2.4 Misinformation, Public Fear, and Panic Associated with COVID-19 Pandemic

Some participants perceived that although COVID-19 is a global pandemic, it has been excessively hyped and exaggerated, which creates fear and panic in societies. For instance, a participant intimated that "the way people talk about COVID-19 here, as if it is the most dangerous disease on earth and the moment you contract it you must die." Another participant also concurred that "information on COVID-19 creates fear and panic among community members." Some of the participants asserted that misinformation with its associated fear and panic, created by some members of the community, make it difficult for people to go to hospitals when they are sick, especially of malaria, for fear of being told they have COVID-19.

Some participants were also worried that should one person contract COVID-19, it was likely to spread rapidly in the community due to noncompliance to precautionary measures, in addition to the high aged population in the community. However, a section of the participants perceived that mass testing was not relevant as no one in the community had COVID-19. On the contrary, some participants argued that until testing is done, one cannot confidently say someone has or does not have the disease. The participants' perceptions of COVID-19 were largely influenced by their level of education, religious orientation, and access to information from social networks and the media.

18.4.3   COVID-19 and Social Activities and Norms

In terms of the implications of COVID-19 on social activities and norms, social distancing, family support and withdrawal, as well as funeral and burial activities were the major themes expressed by the participants. The participants acknowledged the importance of social distancing during the pandemic; however, in practice, social distancing was scarcely observed in the community. A participant reported that "we have heard that social distancing is essential in a larger community of people but this is a small community and hence we do not strictly observe social distancing." The study observed that at certain places, such as markets, stalls, community water sources (pipes and boreholes), and mills, community members did not adhere to social distancing.

This was more profound among the youth and students as they gathered during the day and at night, on the main streets, to fraternize without observing any social distancing protocol. One participants hinted that "we are used to this and so it is difficult for us to distance ourselves from our friends when we met them." Some youth also forgot that they had to practice social distancing, while others argued that they did not have the disease to warrant social distancing. In addition, although some youth sometimes shook hands, as a common social practice, the study observed that generally, other community members barely engaged in this practice, largely due to the pandemic.

In rural communities, the support for family and community members is a common practice, as reported by the participants. A participant highlighted that "we value community and family support and not even the pandemic will change that." As a result, community members called on their family members in towns and cities, including hotspot areas, to return home. A participant intimated that "some families have called their members in towns and cities to come back to the rural community, until the pandemic recede and things return to normal." This was confirmed by a participant who noted that "many people, especially youths living in Accra and Kumasi, had returned home."

A section of the participants complained that the move could lead to the spread of COVID-19 in the community, as one participant expressed that "we have heard reports of the spread of the disease in other places, due to the movement of people from Accra, Kumasi and other hotspot areas into those communities." However, a participant argued that "they are our family members and therefore we cannot stop them from coming home." The movement of people into the community was particularly observed prior to and during the 3 weeks (March 30 to April 19) lockdown imposed by the Government of Ghana. Those in favor of their family members returning home argued that although the move was necessary to prevent family members in towns and cities from contracting the disease, it was also to reduce the suffering and hardship associated with the lockdown in major towns and cities and hotspot areas.

This chapter observed that during the period of movement of people back to the community, community leaders occasionally announced on the community information centers that those moving in to the community should isolate themselves and also avoid unnecessary gallivanting. It was, however, difficult for migrants to comply with the directive and also challenging for community members and leaders to enforce it. Notwithstanding, people withdrew from community members who traveled to towns and cities and hotspot areas. A participant echoed that "some of us withdraw from people who have traveled to Obuasi, Kumasi, Accra and other places." Another participant hinted that "we have heard that one stall keeper refused to sell to someone who traveled from Accra for fear that the person had COVID-19." Apart from the withdrawal from those who traveled to cities and hotspot areas, some members also withdrew from those who showed symptoms of malaria (feverishness, headache, and general body pains), which are similar to some of the symptoms of COVID-19. According to a participant "…once a person shows malaria or fever symptoms, there is withdrawal of friends from such a person, especially among the youth, as they fear it might be COVID-19 and hence they did not want to be infected."

All the participants concurred that COVID-19 has disrupted social activities, especially funeral and burial rites. A participant expressed that "we cannot have befitting funeral and burial rites due to COVID-19." Although the Government of Ghana's imposition on funerals gave the option for people to bury their family members, however, the participants complained that "it is neither befitting for only few members (maximum of 25 people) to participate in the burial of their family members nor without any befitting funeral rites." A participant quizzed that "you know Asantes love their dead ones and we perform befitting burial and funeral rites. How can we just bury the dead without any funeral? This disease has really disrupted our normal sociocultural practices and norms."

Two burial rites were observed during the data collection period. Both burials and post-burial family gatherings were minimally attended by the public even though there were instances, especially at the cemetery, where community members wanted to find their way into the cemetery to watch and mourn the dead. A participant reported that "those who wished to bury their dead ones due to high cost of keeping them in the morgue had to perform libation and burial rites at the morgue grounds and straightaway bury the dead at the cemetery, without file passing or mourning by families, friends and sympathizers." However, some participants opined that although there would be high morgue cost, they would prefer to suspend the performance of all burial and funeral rites to await complete eradication or an ease in the pandemic and then perform befitting and culturally acceptable burial and funeral rites for their family members.

18.4.4 Coping Strategies to COVID-19

Both conventional and nonconventional preventive and protective coping strategies were employed by the participants and members of the community due to COVID-19.

18.4.4.1 Conventional Coping Strategies

The conventional practices included wearing nose masks, regular hand washing, and applying hand sanitizers. The nonconventional practices involved taking and bathing locally prepared herbal solutions and praying to God. Wearing nose masks within the community was not a common practice among the community members, and only travelers or strangers were seen wearing nose masks. However, the participants reported that they wore nose masks whenever they traveled out of the community. A participant expressed that "if I am not going anywhere, I do not need a nose mask. However, I cannot board a vehicle without a nose mask, so we need to have our nose mask on before we are allowed to board any vehicle." Due to the government's regulations on compulsory wearing of nose mask, especially in public places, transport unions and drivers have implemented a "no nose mask, no boarding" policy. Security agencies within the environs of the community also enforced and ensured that all travelers had their nose masks on. As such, community members were compelled to wear nose masks before boarding any vehicle.

Regular washing of hands was reported by a section of the participants, even though the participants had different views regarding this practice. While some reported that they practiced regular washing of hands with soap, others noted that they rarely practiced regular washing of hands. Some also reported that they only washed their hands when they realized they were dirty. A participant noted that "even though I regularly wash my hands with soap but not under running water. I fetch water and give it to someone to pour it on my hands." The rural condition and poor access to water make regular washing of hands, especially under running water, difficult. Another participant also hinted that "I rubbed soap on my hands and then washed them in a bowl of water." It also emerged that some members of the community only washed their hands when they were about to eat and not necessarily for the purpose of COVID-19 prevention.

Some participants were fed up with regular washing of hands. A participant expressed that "I sell to people and I cannot wash my hands every time I sell to someone or exchange money." Another participant hinted that "even if we wash our hands regularly, we could still get COVID-19. It is only God who can protect us from getting the disease." The study observed that four Veronica buckets were installed in the community in April for the purpose of regular washing of hands. However, by May, only one of them was still in use. The others had been empty for weeks and therefore abandoned, partly due to challenges in accessing water.

Some participants also used hand sanitizers for the purpose of COVID-19 prevention. A participant noted that "had it not been COVID-19, I had never used a hand sanitizer before." Family members in towns and cities supplied sanitizers to their families in the rural community, while others also bought the sanitizers when they traveled. A participant, however, hinted that political aspirants in the constituency within which the community is located also shared hand sanitizers but mainly to their party members. This was confirmed by another participant who expressed that "I got my hand sanitizer from a friend in another community whose husband received them from the aspirant of their party."

18.4.4.2 Nonconventional (Traditional Knowledge) Coping Strategies

Aside from the above conventional coping strategies, some of the respondents also resorted to some unconventional practices. These practices mostly involved using herbal solutions to prevent one from either contracting or spreading COVID-19. For instance, majority of the respondents indicated that they have intensified their intake of ginger, garlic, and lemon. A participant narrated that "I always add garlic and ginger to my food, especially stew and soup." Another also confirmed that "I drink a lot of ginger, garlic and lemon solution these days, due to COVID-19." Some of the participants also intimated they added honey to ginger, garlic, and lemon solutions. The consumption of ginger, garlic, and lemon was all in a bid to boost their immune system against COVID-19.

A section of the participants also prepared concoctions from the bark and leaves of neem tree (*Azadirachta indica*). A participant reported that "whenever I felt feverish, which is a symptom of malaria, I prepared and drank solution from the leaves or bark of neem tree." This, according to the participants, helped in treating malaria and fever, which are also symptoms of COVID-19. This was particularly common among the elderly in the community, even though some youth also took this solution rather than going to the hospital for treatment. An aged woman asserted that "I have always used neem tree to treat malaria and fever." Some of the participants, especially the aged, also bathed with nyanya leaves (*Momordica foetida*) to prevent contracting the virus. A participant explained that "our ancestors and Asante warriors mostly bathed with nyanya leaves before going to war or during an epidemic, to protect themselves. They believed the leaves protected them from bad spirits and diseases. As such, some of the elderly members of the community rubbed nyanya leaves into their bathing water to protect them from contracting COVID-19."

Specifically, among the youth, there was a rise in the consumption of locally made alcohol (*akpeteshie*) due to COVID-19. Some believed the virus cannot withstand alcohol and hence the reason for their intake of *akpeteshie*. For instance, a participant quizzed that "if alcohol in hand sanitizers kills the virus, it means when we drink alcohol, we also kill the virus in our system." In addition, some of the youth also sniffed snuff, a powdered substance made from dried tobacco leaves (*Nicotiana tabacum* L.), to wade off contracting COVID-19. One participant echoed "with my snuff, I know I am covered from contracting COVID-19." The study also observed a rise in the sales and consumption of sobolo (*Hibiscus sabdariffa*) tea, to which the participants affirmed its importance for COVID-19, as it offered several nutritional and health benefits. Some of the participants also resorted to praying to God to protect them from COVID-19. A participant concurred that "whenever I went to the market to sell, I prayed to God to protect me from COVID-19. That is the only thing I can do, because even if you wash your hands, how many times can you do that, especially when selling and exchanging money with people throughout the day?"

18.5   Discussion

The continuous rise in the number of positive cases and death toll, due to COVID-19, coupled with the huge impact of the pandemic, has created the urgent need to find lasting and sustainable solutions to the COVID-19 pandemic (WHO, 2020b). However, fear, panic, and misinformation associated with COVID-19 also create far more negative impact on society. This therefore points to the urgency of effective communication to influence public perception and ensure that governments, in general, and individuals, in particular, make informed decisions, based on accurate, reliable, complete, and trusted information (WHO, 2020a). Understanding public perception, especially in vulnerable communities, is therefore essential to alleviating the impact of the pandemic. This chapter therefore explored public perceptions and response strategies to COVID-19 in a rural Ghanaian community. As postulated by social representations theory, the findings from the study show competing versions of the respondents' reality of COVID-19, based on their perceptions and response strategies. In addition, the cultural and socioeconomic conditioning of the respondents' environment also shaped their perceptions and response strategies to COVID-19.

Indeed, results of this chapter show that participants have knowledge of the COVID-19 pandemic. Most importantly, the participants perceived the existence of COVID-19 to be mostly spread through interhuman contact. The participants also perceived difficulty in breathing, sore throat, headache, body pains, fever, and rising temperature as the major symptoms of COVID-19. These findings confirm the results from existing studies that reported high public perception of the coronavirus pandemic (Fetzer et al., 2020; Kristiansen et al., 2007; Parikh et al., 2020). The participants highlighted misinformation of the pandemic as the major cause of public fear and panic, which affects efforts to seek medical attention, although anxiety, fear, and panic due to COVID-19 contribute to heightened public perception and response (Parikh et al., 2020; Perlman, 2020). Nevertheless, Perlman (2020) argues that public fear escalates socioeconomic consequences of COVID-19 and hence should be alleviated, due to availability of information on the control of the virus. Previous studies have also highlighted the importance of health belief, health cognitions, and risk perception in building public perception during a pandemic (Cori et al., 2020; Renner et al., 2008; Wiedemann & Schütz, 2005).

Nevertheless, the results also reflect misconception among the participants. Some participants perceived COVID-19 to be a hoax or an engineered weapon, while others also associated it with Spiritism. The misconception of the participants may be largely due to religious orientation, even though lack of information and misinformation may also be contributing factors. Religion and therefore religious leaders could play a dominant role in shaping public perception about the existence of COVID-19. This corroborates several studies that emphasized the potential role of religion in influencing attitude, behavior, and perception (Arbuckle & Konisky, 2015; Ysseldyk et al., 2010). The study notes that COVID-19 has disrupted social norms and activities in the community. Specifically, cultural activities such as funerals and burials and the associated rites have been highly affected by the pandemic. Without doubt, funerals and burials are emblems of love for the dead and unity of the living. They create social bond and enhance cultural practices and belief system. The results confirm the argument by Ranscombe (2020) that COVID-19 negatively affects social systems, especially in rural communities. Shah (2020) also reported the disruption in sociocultural practices in rural Appalachia, due to COVID-19.

However members of the rural community have strong affection for their families, evidenced by the support for the return of family members from urban centers where infection rate is high. Parikh et al. (2020) and Ranscombe (2020) remarked mass movement of people from urban centers to rural communities in India. However, the fear of contracting COVID-19 in the studied community led to withdrawal from members who show symptoms of malaria, which are also symptoms of COVID-19. In addition, the results further point to the withdrawal of handshake, especially among the elderly/aged, even though youth and students minimally adhered to social distancing and no handshake. Due to interhuman transmission of COVID-19, social distancing and withdrawal from handshake and affected persons have been reported to lessen the extent of spread of the virus (Zhang et al., 2020). However, the aged are more vulnerable to the pandemic (Huang et al., 2020; Marinis et al., 2020), thereby explaining why they resort more to such withdrawals and other nonconventional practices. According to Power et al. (2018), adapting to health adversity is largely inherent in biopsychosocial conditions of people.

Both conventional and nonconventional practices have been employed by the members of the community as precautionary measures for COVID-19. The study results show that the participants and members of the community wear nose masks, regularly wash their hands, and apply hand sanitizers to protect themselves from contracting COVID-19. Similar findings have been reported in the literature (Fetzer et al., 2020; Parikh et al., 2020). Although MacIntyre et al. (2015) also found nose mask as essential precautionary measures for pandemic such as Ebola, influenza, SARS, and MERS, among others, the study, however, cautioned the use of cloth masks due to high infectious rate compared with medical masks. However, it is important to stress that the extent of practice of these strategies in the rural community differs from that of urban centers. The rural condition and the corresponding poor access to water makes, for instance, regular washing of hands difficult. Low income and poverty in rural communities also affect access to protective equipment including hand sanitizers. Even in the case of nose mask, it was completely of no use to the community members except only when they travel.

Results further show nonconventional practices used by the participants and members of the community, largely due to cultural and traditional knowledge and belief system. The most common practice included drinking ginger, garlic, and lemon concoctions to boost immune systems. Other practices are drinking solution from the bark and leaves of neem tree, bathing with *nyanya* leaves, alcohol consumption, sniffing snuff, drinking sobolo, and praying to God. Studies have pointed out the potency of traditional herbal medicines in treating illness and diseases, particularly in Ghana and Africa, in general (Cocks & Møller, 2002; Konadu, 2008; Tsey, 1997). In Ghana, particularly, in rural communities, neem tree is commonly used to treat malaria. This also explains why traditional herbal practitioners value neem tree as an important medicinal plant (Houghton, 2003). Bathing *nyanya* leaves is influenced by the belief in the spiritual power of the plant, to protect people from evils and diseases, including COVID-19.

Although the study found the consumption of local alcohol as a protective measure among the participants, studies have cautioned the consumption of local alcohol, due to the danger it poses to health (Luginaah & Dakubo, 2003). Addo et al. (2008) also argue that local snuff has higher toxicity than tobacco and hence exposes users to respiratory, cardiovascular, and other health issues. Nevertheless, there is evidence that consumption of *sobolo* significantly improves health conditions (Chang et al., 2014). For instance, studies show that hibiscus teas significantly improves health of diabetic (Mozaffari-Khosravi et al., 2009) and hypertensive (Hopkins et al., 2013; Serban et al., 2015) patients. Interestingly, some participants have resorted to praying to God, as a countermeasure against COVID-19. This is consistent with the study by Hirons et al. (2018), who noted that during hard times, rural dwellers pray to God, as a psychological coping strategy. Such a strategy possibly offers psychological comfort to the participants and community dwellers, as they trust in God to protect them from contracting COVID-19.

18.6 Conclusion

This chapter adopted a qualitative descriptive phenomenology to investigate perceptions and coping strategies to COVID-19 in a rural Ghanaian community. The participants have knowledge of the pandemic even though there are misconceptions among some of them. Results from the study also reflect disruption of sociocultural norms and activities of the participants, due to COVID-19. Both conventional and nonconventional coping and precautionary measures have been adopted by the participants and the community to protect themselves while preventing the spread of the virus in the community. This chapter recommends the urgent need to intensify COVID-19 education, especially in rural communities. Such education should particularly prioritize access to information in rural communities by employing all available media, especially radio, television, and community information centers, as well as opinion leaders, including traditional and religious leaders.

Provision of socioeconomic resources and services should be strengthened and intensified, to enhance adaptive capacity and improve the resilience and livelihood of the rural poor. In addition, local and district administrative authorities should be well-equipped to provide critical services that meet the changing needs of rural communities. Further studies should examine socioeconomic impact of the pandemic on rural livelihood, food security, and agriculture. Identifying health needs of rural communities based on demographics will be relevant for policy and planning purpose. Studies should also examine the efficacies and effects of nonconventional response measures to COVID-19.

References

Addo, M. A., Gbadago, J. K., Affum, H. A., Adom, T., Ahmed, K., & Okley, G. M. (2008). Mineral profile of Ghanaian dried tobacco leaves and local snuff : A comparative study. *Journal of Radioanalytical and Nuclear Chemistry, 277*(3), 517–524. https://doi.org/10.1007/s10967-007-7054-x

Alemanno, A. (2020). The European response to COVID-19: From regulatory emulation to regulatory coordination? *European Journal of Risk Regulation, 11*(2), 307–316. https://doi.org/10.1017/err.2020.44

Amatya, B., & Khan, F. (2020). Rehabilitation response in pandemics. *American Journal of Physical Medicine & Rehabilitation.* Publish Ahead of Print (May). https://doi.org/10.1097/phm.0000000000001477

Arbuckle, M. B., & Konisky, D. (2015). The role of religion in environmental attitudes. *Social Science Quarterly, 96*, 1244–1263.

Braun, V., & Clarke, V. (2014). What can thematic analysis offer health and wellbeing researchers? *International Journal of Qualitative Studies on Health and Well-Being, 9.* https://doi.org/10.3402/qhw.v9.26152

Chang, H., Peng, C., Yeh, D., Kao, E., & Wang, C. (2014). Hibiscus Sabdariffa extract inhibits obesity and fat accumulation, and improves liver steatosis in humans. *Food and Function, 5*(4), 734–739. https://doi.org/10.1039/c3fo60495k

Cocks, M., & Møller, V. (2002). Use of indigenous and indigenised medicines to enhance personal well-being: A South African case study. *Social Science & Medicine, 54*, 387–397.

Cori, L., Bianchi, F., Cadum, E., & Anthonj, C. (2020). Risk perception and COVID-19. *International Journal of Environmental Research and Public Health, 17*(May), 3114. https://doi.org/10.3390/ijerph17093114

Creswell, J. W. (2014). *Research design: Qualitative, quantitative and mixed methods approaches* (4th ed.). Sage Publication.

De-Graft Aikins, A. (2003). Living with diabetes in rural and urban Ghana: A critical social psychological examination of illness action and scope for intervention. *Journal of Health Psychology, 8*, 557–572.

De-Graft Aikins, A. (2005). Healer shopping in Africa: New evidence from rural-urban qualitative study of Ghanaian diabetes experiences. *British Medical Journal, 331*(7519), 737. https://doi.org/10.1136/bmj.331.7519.737

De Marinis, F., Attili, I., Morganti, S., Stati, V., Spitaleri, G., Gianoncelli, L., … Passaro, A. (2020). Results of multilevel containment measures to better protect lung cancer patients from COVID-19: The IEO Model. *Frontiers in Oncology, 10*, 665–673. https://doi.org/10.3389/fonc.2020.00665

Farr, R. (1993). Theory and method in the study of social representations. In D. Canter & G. Breakwell (Eds.), *Empirical approaches to social representations* (pp. 15–38). Clarendon Press.

Farr, R. (1996). *The roots of modern social psychology*. Blackwell.

Fetzer, T., Witte, M., Hensel, L., Jachimowicz, J. M., Haushofer, J., Ivchenko, A., … Yoeli, E. (2020). *Global behaviors and perceptions in the COVID-19 pandemic* (No. 27082). https://doi.org/10.3386/w27082

Ghana Health Service. (2020). COVID-19 daily update - Ghana. Retrieved July 4, 2020, from https://ghanahealthservice.org/covid19/

GSS. (2014). *2010 Population and housing census: District analytical report, Adansi North District*. Accra, Ghana.

Hirons, M., Boyd, E., McDermott, C., Asare, R., Morel, A., Mason, J., … Norris, K. (2018). Understanding climate resilience in Ghanaian cocoa communities – Advancing a biocultural perspective. *Journal of Rural Studies, 63*(August), 120–129. https://doi.org/10.1016/j.jrurstud.2018.08.010

Höijer, B. (2010). Emotional anchoring and objectification in the media reporting on climate change. *Public Understanding of Science, 19*(6), 717–731.

Höijer, B. (2011). Social representations theory: A new theory for media research. *Nordicom Review, 32*(2), 3–16. https://doi.org/10.1515/nor-2017-0109

Hopkins, A. L., Lamm, M. G., Funk, J., & Ritenbaugh, C. (2013). Hibiscus sabdariffa L. in the treatment of hypertension and hyperlipidemia: A comprehensive review of animal and human studies. *Fitoterapia, 85*, 84–94. https://doi.org/10.1016/j.fitote.2013.01.003

Horton, R. (2003). Medical journals: Evidence of bias against the diseases of poverty. *Lancet, 361*, 712–713.

Houghton, P. (2003). Herbal practitioners and pharmacists in Ghana. *The Pharmaceutical Journal, 271*, 93–94.

Huang, C., Wang, Y., Li, X., Ren, L., Zhao, J., Hu, Y., … Gu, X. (2020). Clinical features of patients infected with 2019 novel coronavirus in Wuhan, China. *Lancet, 395*, 497–506. https://doi.org/10.1016/S0140-6736(20)30183-5

Konadu, K. (2008). Medicine and anthropology in twentieth century Africa: Akan medicine and encounters with (medical) anthropology. *African Studies Quarterly, 10*, 2–3.

Kristiansen, I. S., Halvorsen, P. A., & Gyrd-Hansen, D. (2007). Influenza pandemic: Perception of risk and individual precautions in a general population. Cross sectional study. *BMC Public Health, 7*, 48. https://doi.org/10.1186/1471-2458-7-48

Lopez, K., & Willis, D. (2004). Descriptive versus interpretive phenomenology: Their contributions to nursing knowledge. *Qualitative Health Research, 14*, 726–735.

Luginaah, I., & Dakubo, C. (2003). Consumption and impacts of local brewed alcohol (akpeteshie) in the Upper West Region of Ghana : A public health tragedy. *Social Science & Medicine, 57*, 1747–1760. https://doi.org/10.1016/S0277-9536(03)00014-5

MacIntyre, C. R., Seale, H., Dung, T. C., Hien, N. T., Nga, P. T., Chughtai, A. A., … Wang, Q. (2015). A cluster randomised trial of cloth masks compared with medical masks in healthcare workers. *BMJ Open, 5*, e006577. https://doi.org/10.1136/bmjopen-2014-006577

Moscovici, S. (1963). Attitudes and opinions. *Annual Review of Psychology, 14*, 231–260.

Moscovici, S. (1984). The phenomenon of social representations. In M. Farr & S. Moscovici (Eds.), *Social representations*. Cambridge University Press.

Moscovici, S. (1988). Notes towards a description of social representations. *European Journal of Social Psychology, 18*, 211–250.

Moscovici, S., & Duveen, G. (2000). *Social representations: Explorations in social psychology*. New York University Press.

Mozaffari-Khosravi, H., Jalali-Khanabadi, B. A., Afkhami-Ardekani, M., & Fatehi, F. (2009). Effects of sour tea (Hibiscus sabdariffa) on lipid profile and lipoproteins in patients with type II diabetes. *Journal of Alternative and Complementary Medicine, 15*(8), 899–903. https://doi.org/10.1089/acm.2008.0540

Olausson, U. (2009). Global warming – Global responsibility? Media frames of collective action and scientific certainty. *Public Understanding of Science, 18*, 421–436.

Olausson, U. (2010). Towards a European identity? The news media and the case of climate change. *European Journal of Communication, 25*(14), 138–152.

Parikh, P. A., Shah, B. V., Phatak, A. G., & Vadnerkar, A. C. (2020). COVID-19 pandemic: Knowledge and perceptions of the public and healthcare professionals. *Cureus, 12*(5), e8144. https://doi.org/10.7759/cureus.8144

Perlman, S. (2020). Another decade, another coronavirus. *New England Journal of Medicine, 382*, 760–762. https://doi.org/10.1056/NEJMe2001126

Phillipson, J., Gorton, M., Turner, R., Shucksmith, M., Aitken-mcdermott, K., Areal, F., … Panzone, L. (2020). The COVID-19 pandemic and its implications for rural economies. *Sustainability, 12*(10), 3973. https://doi.org/10.3390/su12103973

Power, A., Bell, S. L., Kyle, R. G., & Andrews, G. J. (2018). Hopeful adaptation' in health geographies: Seeking health and wellbeing in times of adversity. *Social Science & Medicine, 231*, 1–5. https://doi.org/10.1016/j.socscimed.2018.09.021

Ranscombe, P. (2020). Rural areas at risk during COVID-19 pandemic. *The Lancet Infectious Diseases, 20*(5), 545. https://doi.org/10.1016/S1473-3099(20)30301-7

Renner, B., Schupp, H., Vollmann, M., Hartung, F.-M., Schmälzle, R., & Panzer, M. (2008). Risk perception, risk communication and health behavior change. *Zeitschrift Für Gesundheitspsychologie, 16*, 150–153. https://doi.org/10.1026/0943-8149.16.3.150

Rose, D., Efraim, D., Gervais, M., Joffe, H., Jovchelovitch, S., & Morant, N. (1995). Questioning consensus in social representations theory. *Papers on Social Representations, 4*(1), 1–155.

Serban, C., Sahebkar, A., Ursoniu, S., Andrica, F., & Banach, M. (2015). Effect of sour tea (Hibiscus sabdariffa L.) on arterial hypertension: A systematic review and meta-analysis of randomized controlled trials. *Journal of Hypertension, 33*(6), 1119–1127. https://doi.org/10.1097/HJH.0000000000000585

Shah, D. T. (2020). The COVID-19 crisis: How rural Appalachia is handling the pandemic? *Marshall Journal of Medicine, 6*(2), 1–3. https://doi.org/10.33470/2379-9536.1287

Silverman, D. (2000). *Doing qualitative research*. Sage.

Tsey, K. (1997). Traditional medicine in contemporary Ghana: A public policy analysis. *Social Science & Medicine, 45*(7), 1065–1074.

Wagner, W., Duveen, G., Farr, R., Jovchelovitch, S., Lorenzi-Cioldi, F., & Markova¨, I., & Rose, D. (1999). Theory and method of social representations. *Asian Journal of Social Psychology, 2*, 95–125.

WHO. (2020a). Communicating risk in public health emergencies. Retrieved June 4, 2020, from http://www.who.int/risk-communication/guidance/download/en/

WHO. (2020b). COVID-19 cases top 10000 in Africa. Retrieved June 4, 2020, from https://www. afro.who.int/news/covig-19

Wiedemann, P. M., & Schütz, H. (2005). The precautionary principle and risk perception: Experimental studies in the EMF area. *Environmental Health Perspectives, 113*(4), 402–405. https://doi.org/10.1289/ehp.7538

Ysseldyk, R., Matheson, K., & Anisman, H. (2010). Religiosity as identity: Toward an understanding of religion from a social identity perspective. *Personality and Social Psychology Review, 14*(1), 60–71.

Zhang, J., Lin, G., Zeng, J., Lin, J., Tian, J., & Li, G. (2020). Challenges of SARS-CoV-2 and lessons learnt from SARS in Guangdong Province, China. *Journal of Clinical Virology, 126*, 104341–104342. https://doi.org/10.1016/j.jcv.2020.104341

Zhong, N., & Wong, G. W. K. (2004). Epidemiology of severe acute respiratory syndrome (SARS): Adults and children. *Paediatric Respiratory Review, 5*, 270–274. https://doi.org/10.1016/j. prrv.2004.07.011

Chapter 19
Government Policy Response to COVID-19 and Stock Market Return: The Case of Iran

Sakine Owjimehr and Ali Hussein Samadi ⓘ

19.1 Introduction

A new virus, later called COVID-19, began to spread in Wuhan, China, in late 2019 and quickly turned into a pandemic. In addition to threatening human health, the virus has had far-reaching negative effects on other aspects of human life, such as education, production, and the financial sector. Due to the widespread impact and the unknown nature of the disease, researchers in health economics and social fields have done numerous studies on COVID-19's mechanism of action.

One of the main sectors of the economy that facilitates the production sector and plays a vital role in any economy is the financial market. With the outbreak of the COVID-19 pandemic, financial markets also experienced many problems. Panic selling due to increasing uncertainty has been the most notable effect of COVID-19 on financial markets. Investors reduced investment and postpone their decisions to wait for any uncertainty to disappear (Wu et al., 2021). Thus, it is important to study how the COVID-19 pandemic affects financial markets. Some researchers have addressed this issue (e.g., Albulescu, 2021; Zaremba et al., 2020; Zhang et al., 2020; Corbet et al., 2020; Akhtaruzzaman et al., 2021; Ashraf, 2020; Sharif et al., 2020; Goodell, 2020).

The rapid spread of COVID-19, as well as its devastating effects on the economy, has led to widespread government intervention in controlling the pandemic. The impact of government intervention policies on financial markets has been studied by several researchers (e.g., Ayadi et al., 2020; Zhang et al., 2020; Narayan et al., 2021; Yang & Deng, 2021; Wu et al., 2021).

S. Owjimehr (✉) · A. H. Samadi
Department of Economics, School of Economics, Management & Social Sciences, Shiraz University, Shiraz, Iran
e-mail: s.ojimehr@shirazu.ac.ir; asamadi@rose.shirazu.ac.ir

© The Author(s), under exclusive license to Springer Nature Switzerland AG 2022   423
N. Faghih, A. Forouharfar (eds.), *Socioeconomic Dynamics of the COVID-19 Crisis*,
Contributions to Economics, https://doi.org/10.1007/978-3-030-89996-7_19

We have also studied the impact of government policy responses on financial markets. But the present study has two contributions. First, we have used Iran as the target community. Iran is the most affected country in the Middle East. Ayadi et al. (2020) observed fluctuations of both the Tehran Stock Market Price Index (TEPIX) and the trading volume of Iran's stock market from 19 Feb 2020 to 22 May 2020. This was when Iran was under severe economic sanctions while foreign aid to Iran was also banned. In other words, the government had to rely only on domestic resources to control the pandemic and reduce its negative impact on the economy. In this context, the role of government action in curbing the pandemic is crucial. Therefore, the question arises as to what has been the impact of Iran's policy responses in curbing COVID-19 on the financial market.

Second, we have used a threshold regression to examine the impact of government intervention on the financial market. Other studies (e.g., Ayadi et al., 2020; Zhang et al., 2020; Narayan et al., 2021; Yang & Deng, 2021; Wu et al., 2021) have used linear regression. In fact, how COVID-19 affects the stock market may depend on the number of confirmed cases, and it is a threshold variable. Government policy responses may be more effective when the rate of infection is very high. An increase in the incidence rate leads to a rise in panic in the community.

So, in this chapter, we use the daily data of Iran's economy from 22 Feb 2020 to 12 June 2021 and apply a threshold regression model.

The remainder of this chapter is organized as follows. Section 19.2 provides some stylized facts about COVID-19 and the stock market in Iran. In Sect. 19.3, the related literature is reviewed. Section 19.4 is devoted to the research methodology. Empirical results and discussions are presented in Sect. 19.5. The last section presents concluding remarks.

19.2   COVID-19 and the Stock Market in Iran

Since early 2020, Iran's economy has been affected by the outbreak of the coronavirus, which has had a profound effect on the economic and social situation. This was at a time when the country had gone through two difficult years, 2018 and 2019, with negative economic growth of 5 and 7%, respectively, because of US sanctions. In fact, COVID-19, severe economic sanctions, and high inflation were the three crises that have put a lot of pressure on Iran's economy since 2020.

From 22 Feb 2020 to 12 June 2021, Iran has experienced four corona waves with more than three million confirmed cases and approximately 85,000 deaths. Figure 19.2 shows the logarithm of confirmed cases of COVID-19 in Iran. As can be seen, the rate of increase in infection in early 2020 is very high but gradually reduces as the number of patients increases.

Like many other countries, the government of Iran intervened to curb the corona and took many steps. Researchers at Oxford University have compiled and reported on government intervention policies for all countries. They have categorized and codified all government actions about COVID-19. Table 19.1 summarizes the report

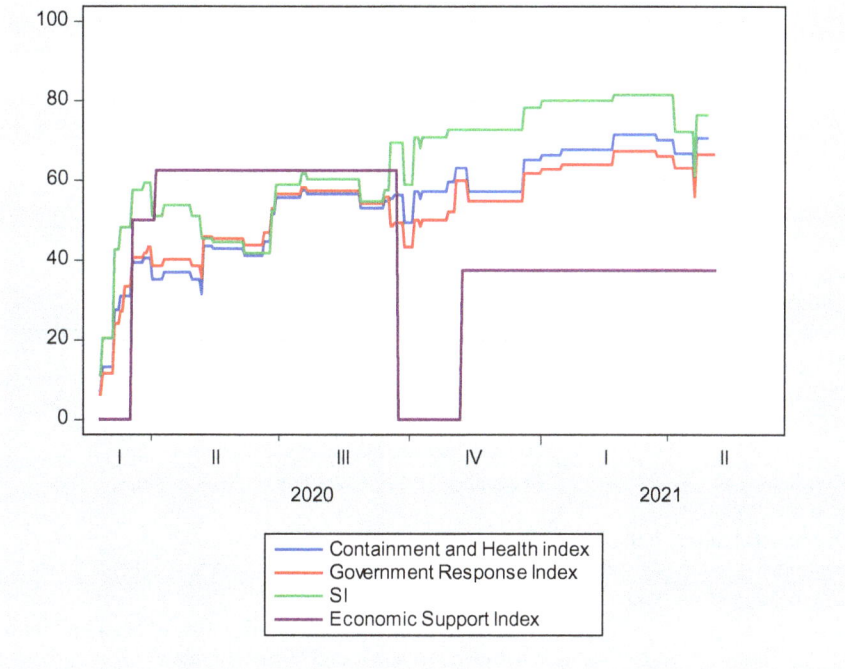

Fig. 19.1 OxCGRT indices of Iran from 22 Feb 2020 to 12 June 2021. (Source: Authors' own figure)

on Iran. It can be seen that Iran has had a mediocre performance in most cases, but it has performed poorly in measures such as economic support and vaccinations. In terms of vaccination, many countries have a score of 5 (universal availability). In the case of Iran, both were due to sanctions and the government's poor financial situation.

In the following, we graph the OxCGRT index in Iran. The OxCGRT includes the stringency index, the government response index, the containment and health index, and the economic support index (Hale et al., 2020). As seen in Fig. 19.1, in the first corona wave (early 2020), government economic support is higher than other indicators. However, with the continuation of COVID-19 (late 2020), the index has fallen due to the financial condition of the sanctioned government and has risen again after a while, but it is at a significant distance from other indicators. In contrast, the other three indices have had a slight upward trend despite some ups and downs.

With the outbreak of the coronavirus, fundamental factors, along with fears of a continuing corona crisis, led to the dominance of supply orders over demand and affected the world stock markets. Several studies have confirmed the negative impact of COVID-19 on financial markets worldwide (e.g., Albulescu, 2021;

Table 19.1 Government policy intervention of Iran

Government policy intervention	Code for Iran	Description
School closing	3 (from 5 March 2020)	Require closing all levels
Workplace closing	3 (from 26 Oct 2020)	Require closing (or work from home) all-but-essential workplaces (e.g., grocery stores, doctors)
Cancel public events	1 or 2	1. Recommend cancelling
		2. Require cancelling
Restrictions on gatherings	Most time 4	Restrictions on gatherings of ten people or less
Close public transport	1	Recommend closing (or significantly reduce volume/route/ means of transport available)
Stay at home requirements	1 or 2	1. Recommend not leaving house
		2. Require not leaving house with exceptions for daily exercise, grocery shopping, and "essential" trips
Restrictions on internal movement	2	Recommend not to travel between regions/cities
International travel controls	3 (from 11 July 2020)	Ban on arrivals from some regions
Income support	0 or 1	0. No income support
		1. Government is replacing less than 50% of lost salary (or if a flat sum, it is less than 50% median salary)
Debt/contract relief for households	First 2, then 1 or 0	0. No
		1. Narrow relief, specific to one kind of contract
		2. Broad debt/contract relief
Public info campaigns	2 (from 12 Jan 2021)	Coordinated public information campaign (e.g., across traditional and social media)
Testing policy	1 or 2	1. Only those who both (a) have symptoms *and* (b) meet specific criteria (e.g., key workers, admitted to hospital, came into contact with a known case, returned from overseas)
		2. Testing of anyone showing COVID 19 symptoms
Contact tracing	0 or 1 or 2	0. No contact tracing
		1. Limited contact tracing – not done for all cases
		2. Comprehensive contact tracing – done for all identified cases
Facial coverings	3 (from Oct 2020)	Required in all shared/public spaces outside the home with other people present or all situations when social distancing is not possible
Vaccination policy	3 (from March 2021)	Availability for all of following: key workers/clinically vulnerable groups/elderly groups

Source: Hale et al. (2020)

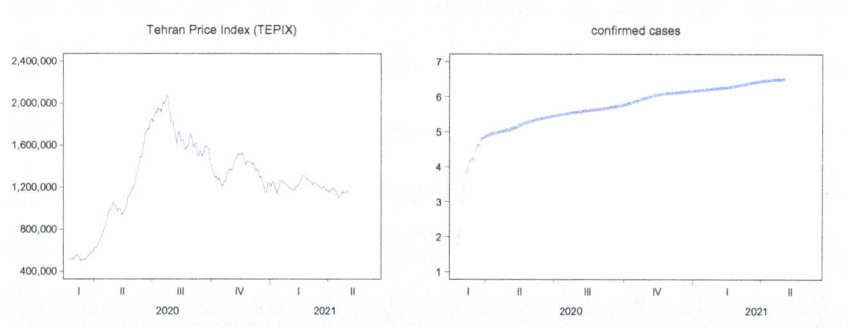

Fig. 19.2 Tehran Stock Market Price Index (TEPIX) and the logarithm of confirmed cases of COVID-19 in Iran from 22 Feb 2020 to 12 June 2021. (Source: Authors' own figure)

Zaremba et al., 2020; Zhang et al., 2020; Corbet et al., 2020; Akhtaruzzaman et al., 2021; Ashraf, 2020; Sharif et al., 2020; Goodell, 2020).

But in Iran, particularly until mid-2020, the stock market situation was completely different. The stock market has experienced unprecedented growth during this period, as Fig. 19.2 shows. Rising liquidity as a driver of market growth combined with the challenge of the recession in business following the outbreak of the corona caused liquidity to move to the stock market. In addition, factors such as expected inflation, rising exchange rates, news related to the capital increase of some companies, and, in particular, government support for the stock market have been factors affecting the growth of the Tehran Stock Market Price Index (TEPIX) in the first wave of the coronavirus.

Gradually, with increasing quarantine, closing borders, and reducing cross-border exchanges, the country's economy and, consequently, the stock market suffered. Industries such as hotels and tourism, restaurants, and transportation were also disrupted. Reduced working hours and successive closures also reduced production and increased firm costs. So, we can see that the TEPIX has decreased from the second half of 2020 onward.

19.3   Literature Review

Until the 1930s, governments had no right to intervene if there was a disequilibrium in the economy, such as rising unemployment or a surplus of demand in the financial markets. Because according to the classical school, the role of governments was limited to establishing order within the country and borders, and the market mechanism (Adam Smith's invisible hand) automatically corrected the disequilibrium.

During the crises of 1929–1933, many economies were hit, and unemployment in Europe and the United States rose to more than 25%, and many factories closed. Under such circumstances, the invisible hand of Adam Smith lost its effectiveness, and Keynes' general theory came to the fore. Thus, permission was granted for government intervention in the economy. In fact, governments today use economic policies such as fiscal, monetary, and income policies to achieve economic goals.

The COVID-19 pandemic is one of the most unexpected crises to hit the world since late 2019. Certainly, no country can overcome such a crisis without the government's intervention.

Here, we first mention the effects of the pandemic on the economy and then investigate the role of the government in controlling the effects of the pandemic on the economy and financial market.

We can classify the economic impact of the COVID-19 pandemic into four stages: (1) business and economic damage, (2) financial contagion, (3) bottom formation, and (4) post-COVID-19 effects (Raza Rabbani et al., 2021). In fact, at first, the pandemic disrupts the demand and supply of goods and services. In this stage, government intervention to control the pandemic through a lockdown and closing the market causes more problems in supply chains.

After the disruption of economic activities, many economies experienced financial contagion. In this stage, panic selling caused sharp downward movement in stock markets. Liquidity starts falling, the market for new funds starts freezing, and central banks are forced to inject liquidity. In this stage, government response policies are only temporary solutions.

The most critical stage is the third stage. Some countries, like Italy, Iran, India, and the United Kingdom, went through this stage in May 2020. In this stage, the financial markets seem to hit rock bottom, small businesses closed due to low liquidity, and unemployment increased.

The fourth stage is characterized by analysis of the severity and seriousness of the economic impact created by the COVID-19, push for deglobalization, less open approach to movement and migration, and search for a long-term solution.

Despite the widespread effects of the pandemic on the economy, we focus here only on its impact on financial markets. One of the important events affecting financial markets is oil price fluctuations (Ibrahim et al., 2020). The spread of the coronavirus in many countries has reduced air and land travel and, consequently, reduced the need for fuel consumption and caused the aviation and tourism industry to depress. Declining oil demand and the imbalance between supply and demand led to lower oil prices. Thus, oil prices fell sharply amid fears of a growing negative impact of the coronavirus outbreak on the corporate business of the world, as well as the economic growth of China and other world economies. As oil prices fell, global stock markets also dropped.

The rapid spread of COVID-19, as well as its devastating effects on the economy, has led to widespread government intervention in controlling the pandemic. Common measures include school closings, travel restrictions, bans on public gatherings, emergency investments in healthcare facilities, new forms of social welfare provision, contact tracing, vaccination campaigns, and other interventions to contain the spread of the virus, augment health systems, and manage the economic consequences of these actions (Hale et al., 2020).

Regarding the impact of government policy responses on financial markets, the types of responses should be considered first. Governments have used various policies and tools to control the pandemic. Each of these policies can have a different or even contradictory effect on financial markets.

Panic selling due to increasing uncertainty has been the most important effect of COVID-19 on financial markets. Investors reduced investment and postpone their decisions to wait for any uncertainty to disappear (Wu et al., 2021).

Yang and Deng (2021) show that government intervention measures such as social isolation, testing, and contact tracing policies have had a positive effect on stock market returns by reducing uncertainty. Meanwhile, government intervention measures and factory closures will reduce supply by cutting off the supply chain and have a negative impact on stock returns.

Economic support policies can increase liquidity in the stock market and reduce investors' fears; thus they can offset the negative impact of COVID-19 on stock market returns (Haroon & Rizvi, 2020; Narayan et al., 2021; Topcu & Gulal, 2020).

Given the extent of the literature, this paper mainly focuses on two points: first, the impact of the epidemic on financial markets and, second, the impact of government policy response measures on the relationship between financial markets and COVID-19. Therefore, in the following, the empirical literature related to these two groups is briefly presented.

19.3.1   The Impact of COVID-19 on Financial Markets

One aspect of the COVID-19 pandemic is that it is not evenly distributed throughout the globe. For example, the number of patients worldwide in April 2021 was more than 150,689,587. South and North America have had the most victims. Among Asian countries, COVID-19 has had the most outbreaks in India. European countries have also been widely afflicted by COVID-19.

Given the heterogeneous distribution of the coronavirus among countries, one cannot expect a homogeneous impact on financial markets around the world. Thus, it has displayed long-term effects in some countries, while its effects have been more transient in some others.

Wang and Enilov (2020) have studied the causality between COVID-19 and stock market returns in the G7 countries. They demonstrated that there is a causal relation between COVID-19 and stock market returns in Canada, France, Germany, Italy, and the United States. But there is no evidence of a causal relationship between COVID-19 and Japan's stock market returns. Overall, the results of the study by Wang and Enilov (2020) indicate the short-term impact of COVID-19 on global financial markets. Ozparlak (2020) used the daily data from China, France, Germany, Italy, the United States, the United Kingdom, Spain, and Turkey from 22 January 2020 to 25 April 2020 and showed that there was a significant long-term relationship between the total number of COVID-19 patients and stock markets and CDS markets in China, France, Germany, the United Kingdom, Spain, and Turkey.

However, such a correlation could not be found in France, Italy, and the United States. Using the time-varying kernel density estimation, Garcin et al. (2020) found the time-varying density of daily price returns of several stock indices, American indices (NASDAQ Composite, S&P 500, S&P 100), European indices (EURO STOXX 50, Euronext 100, DAX, CAC 40), and Asian indices (Nikkei 225, KOSPI, SSE 50), with a particular focus on S&P 500, EURO STOXX 50, and the South Korean KOSPI indices, from 17 April 2015 to 28 May 2020. They described the chronology of the crisis as well as regional disparities. The results of their analysis showed a more limited impact of COVID-19 on the financial markets in China, a strong impact in the United States, and a slow recovery in Europe. But the recovery of the Chinese and South Korean markets was very rapid. Samadi et al. (2021) also used the wavelet coherence and segmented regression methods to investigate the effect of the COVID-19 pandemic on the co-movements of financial markets and concluded that the COVID-19 pandemic did not affect the co-movement of financial markets in Iran.

19.3.2   The Impact of Government Policy Response to COVID-19 on Financial Markets

Government policy responses to the COVID-19 pandemic appear to have had a significant impact on limiting the virus' negative effects on various aspects of the economy, including the financial markets. Ayadi et al. (2020) used a VAR model to analyze the response to the evolution of the COVID-19 pandemic in the financial markets of Australia, Brazil, China, Iran, Russia, Spain, Sweden, South Korea, the United States, Germany, and Tunisia. They found that the response of financial markets to COVID-19 depends on the speed with which each country controlled the virus and prevented it from spreading further. The financial market was less vulnerable to the impact of the pandemic in countries that reacted quickly and limited the virus' proliferation. The effect of the pandemic in these cases was also less persistent to external shocks. Zhang et al. (2020) investigated the impact of the COVID-19 outbreak on financial markets of countries placed on the top 10 list of confirmed COVID-19 cases.[1] Their results show that the pandemic has a negative effect on the financial market. They further stated that government intervention, while helpful, is only effective in the short term in that it can control investors' panic. It does, however, increase uncertainty and may cause long-term problems. Narayan et al. (2021) studied the impact of G7 governments' responses to COVID-19 on their stock market returns. They found that lockdowns, travel bans, and economic stimulus packages all had a positive effect on G7 stock markets. Lockdowns were found to be the most effective in cushioning the effects of COVID-19.

---

[1] According to the data on 27 March 2020.

Rebucci et al. (2020) analyze the quantitative easing (QE) initiative undertaken by 21 developed and emerging economies. They found that QE has not lost effectiveness in developed economies, but the impact of QE on bond yields was much stronger in emerging markets. Wu et al. (2021) used the event study method (ESM) to investigate the relation between COVID-19 and tourism stocks in China. They also studied the impact of government policies on that correlation. Their results indicated that the impact of COVID-19 on tourism stocks has been short term. In this study, the effect of government policies on tourism stocks has been nonlinear. Furthermore, government policies have had a positive effect on stock returns at high quantiles of abnormal returns.

Zaremba et al. (2020) used the stringency index to examine the impact of the stringency of government policy responses on stock market volatility in 67 countries. They used the stringency index based on seven sub-indicators: school closures, workplace closures, cancellation of public events, closure of public transport, public information campaigns, restrictions on internal movement, and international travel controls. Moreover, they used a regression method to observe the effects of the different intervention measures contributing to the stringency index on stock market volatility. They discovered that the stringency index has a positive impact on all measures of stock market volatility. Ibrahim et al. (2020) used OxCGRT to examine the impact of government policy responses on stock market volatility in the following 11 countries: Indonesia, Laos, Malaysia, Myanmar, the Philippines, Singapore, Thailand, Vietnam, China, Japan, and South Korea. Their results showed that in most of these countries, the government measures could reduce stock market volatility.

The results obtained by of Yang and Deng (2021) were much closer to that of Zaremba et al. (2020). They used four comprehensive indicators from the OxCGRT database (stringency index, government response index, containment and health index, and economic support index) for 20 OECD countries from 1 Feb 2020 to 1 Oct 2020. They demonstrated that the number of confirmed cases of COVID-19 decreased stock market returns, and governments' intervention measures, such as social distancing, testing, and contact tracing policies, magnified this negative effect.

Overall, although several studies have been conducted on the impact of government policy responses on financial markets during the coronavirus pandemic, none of these studies have paid attention to different effects of government policy responses depending on the growth rate of confirmed cases of COVID-19. Therefore, the present chapter is different from other studies in this regard.

19.4   Methodology

Following Yang and Deng (2021), the general form of econometric models used to investigate the effect of government intervention on stock market return can be written as Eq. (19.1):

$$\text{Return}_t = \alpha_0 + \alpha_1 \text{Return}_{t-1} + \alpha_3 \text{Covid19}_t + \alpha_4 \text{Intervention}_t + \alpha_5 \text{Ln}(\text{mv})_t + \varepsilon_t$$

$$\tag{19.1}$$

where Return_t is the stock market return and computed as logarithm of (p_t/p_{t-1}), p_t is TEPIX, and Intervention_t is a government intervention variable. For the latter, we used four comprehensive indicators from the OxCGRT database, including SI, government response index, containment and health index, and economic support index. $\text{Ln}(\text{mv})_t$ is the logarithm of market value trade stock, and Covid19_t is the growth rate of confirmed cases of COVID-19.

We consider Covid19_t as the threshold variable and estimate the coefficient of OxCGRT indices for different regimes.

Threshold models have been considered in various studies (e.g., Bai & Perron, 1998, 2003; Hansen, 1999, 2000; Tsay, 1989).

For more explanation, we consider a multiple linear regression model with T observations and m potential thresholds (+1 regimes):

$$\text{Return}_t = X_t \beta + Z_t \delta_j + \varepsilon_t \quad \text{for regime } j = 1, 2, \ldots, m \tag{19.2}$$

The regressors are divided into two groups. The X variables are those whose parameters do not vary across regimes (Return_{t-1}, $\text{Ln}(\text{mv})_t$), while the Z variables have coefficients that are regime-specific (Covid19_t, Intervention_t).

Consider there is an observable threshold variable Covid19_t and strictly increasing threshold values ($\gamma_1 < \gamma_2 < \ldots < \gamma_m$) such that we are in regime j if and only if

$$\gamma_j \leq \text{Covid19}_t < \gamma_{j+1} \tag{19.3}$$

where we set $\gamma_0 = -\infty$ and $\gamma_{m+1} = \infty$. Thus, we are in regime j if the value of the threshold variable is at least as large as the j-th threshold value, but not as large as the $j + 1$-th threshold. For example, in the single-threshold two-regime model, we have:

$$\text{Return}_t = X_t \beta + Z_t \delta_1 + \varepsilon_t \quad \text{if} -\infty \leq \text{Covid19}_t < \gamma_1$$

$$\text{Return}_t = X_t \beta + Z_t \delta_2 + \varepsilon_t \quad \text{if } \gamma_1 \leq \text{Covid19}_t < \infty. \tag{19.4}$$

Parameters are estimated by nonlinear least squares (NLS). To estimate the threshold values γ and determine the number of the regimes, we can use Bai and Perron (2003) test. Bai (1997) and Bai and Perron (1998, 2003) introduced an approach to structural break testing. By considering time as the threshold variable, breakpoint regressions can be seen as threshold regressions. Bai and Perron (2003) extended their approach for threshold regressions. By computing F statistics, they tested $l + 1$ vs. l sequentially determined thresholds.

It should be noted that we use lagged dependent variable (Return_{t-1}) as an explanatory variable. Ordinary least squares (OLS) yield inconsistent estimates in a

Table 19.2 Descriptive statistics of variables

Descriptive statistics	Logarithm of market value	Growth rate of confirmed cases	Containment and health index	Government response index	SI	Economic support index	Return
Mean	9.84	0.437%	54.44	52.94	63.93	41.93	0.0012
Max	10.57	29.3%	71.55	67.29	81.48	62.5	0.025
Min	8.83	0.02%	7.14	6.25	11.11	0.00	−0.021

Source: Authors' own table

dynamic model with correlated errors. This problem is known as serial correlation bias. However, if errors are serially independent, OLS will yield biased but consistent estimates (Stocker, 2007).

Keele and Kelly (2006) showed that "So long as the residuals are not highly autocorrelated, the estimators will exhibit only small amounts of bias." Therefore, after estimating the model, the autocorrelation of residuals will be detected using the Breusch-Godfrey Serial Correlation LM Test. Estimates will be consistent if there is no serial correlation between residual sentences.

19.5   Empirical Results and Discussion

19.5.1   *Data*

We use data of Iran[2] from 22 Feb 2020 to 12 June 2021. First, we test the stationarity property of our data. All variables were stationary except the logarithm of confirmed cases and economic support index. Therefore, we used the growth rate of confirmed cases and the detrended series of the economic support index. Table 19.2 shows the descriptive statistics of our variables, including average, maximum, and minimum of the growth rate of confirmed cases, containment and health index, government response index, stringency index, economic support index, the logarithm of market value trade stock, and return.

According to Table 19.1, the highest growth rate of confirmed coronavirus cases is 29%, and the lowest growth rate is 0.02%. The highest rate of return on the stock market is 0.025, and the lowest rate of return is −0.021. Among the indicators of government intervention, the lowest average belongs to government economic support.

---

[2] Recourse for TEPIX: https://tse.ir/archive.html#/debt

Table 19.3 Result of the threshold regression (stringency index)

Dependent variable: return	Growth rate of confirmed cases less than 0.0638	Growth rate of confirmed cases more than 0.0638
Constant	−0.037 (0.05)	−0.016 (0.34)
SI	0.0001 (0.09)	−0.0001 (0.00)
Growth rate of confirmed cases	−0.04 (0.55)	−0.0007 (0.00)
Non-threshold variables		
Return (−1)	0.35 (0.00)	
Logarithm of market value	0.0026 (0.05)	
Bai-Perron test		
Threshold test	F-Statistic	Critical value
0 VS 1	12.59	11.47
1 VS 2	1.57	12.95
Breusch-Godfrey Serial Correlation LM Test		
	F-Statistic	Critical value
	2.39	0.099

Source: Authors' own table

Table 19.4 Result of threshold regression (government response index)

Dependent variable: return	Growth rate of confirmed cases less than 0.0638	Growth rate of confirmed cases more than 0.0638
Constant	−0.040 (0.06)	−0.24 (0.15)
Government response Index	0.0002 (0.32)	−0.0001 (0.03)
Growth rate of confirmed cases	−0.063 (0.36)	−0.0006 (0.01)
Non-threshold variables		
Return (1)	0.36 (0.00)	
Logarithm of market value	0.0033 (0.05)	
Bai-Perron test		
Threshold test	F- Statistic	Critical value
0 VS 1	12.59	11.47
1 VS 2	1.57	12.95
Breusch-Godfrey Serial Correlation LM Test		
	F-Statistic	Critical value
	1.17	0.31

Source: Authors' own table

Table 19.5 Result of threshold regression (containment and health index)

Dependent variable: return	Growth rate of confirmed cases less than 0.0638	Growth rate of confirmed cases more than 0.0638
Constant	−0.045 (0.03)	−0.23 (0.16)
Containment and health index	0.0002 (0.11)	−0.0001 (0.00)
Growth rate of confirmed cases	−0.046 (0.52)	−0.0006 (0.01)
Non-threshold variables		
Return (−1)	0.36 (0.00)	
Logarithm of market value	0.0033 (0.04)	
Bai-Perron test		
Threshold test	F-Statistic	Critical value
0 VS 1	12.59	11.47
1 VS 2	1.57	12.95
Breusch-Godfrey Serial Correlation LM Test		
	F-Statistic	Critical value
	1.51	0.22

Source: Authors' own table

Table 19.6 Result of threshold regression (economic support index)

Dependent variable: return	Growth rate of confirmed cases less than 0.0638	Growth rate of confirmed cases more than 0.0638
Constant	−0.030 (0.06)	−0.029 (0.06)
Economic support index	−3.93E-05 (0.64)	7.22E-05 (0.00)
Growth rate of confirmed cases	−0.09 (0.17)	−0.0001 (0.05)
Non- Threshold Variables		
Return (−1)	0.36 (0.00)	
Logarithm of market value	0.0033 (0.04)	
Bai-Perron test		
Threshold test	F-Statistic	Critical value
0 VS 1	12.59	11.47
1 VS 2	1.57	12.95
Breusch-Godfrey Serial Correlation LM Test		
	F-Statistic	Critical value
	1.55	0.21

Source: Authors' own table

19.5.2   Result of the Threshold Regression

Model (1) is estimated using the threshold regression method for each of the four government intervention indicators. The results are presented in Tables 19.3, 19.4, 19.5 and 19.6. In all four models, using Bai and Perron test (2003), the number of optimal regimes equals 2.

The threshold variable is the growth rate of confirmed cases of COVID-19. The threshold value is obtained approximately 0.06 based on Bai and Perron's (2003) test. Thus, the first regime is the period when the incidence growth rate is greater than or equal to 0.06, and the second regime is the period when the incidence growth rate is less than 0.06. Based on Fig. 19.2, we can say that the first regime is related to the early outbreak of COVID-19 when the incidence rate has reached 29%.

For all regressions, results of the Breusch-Godfrey Serial Correlation LM Test show that the residuals are not serially correlated, and as a result, the estimates are consistent.

The variables of government intervention index and growth rate of confirmed cases are considered regime-dependent variables. In other words, the coefficients of these two variables plus the intercept are compared in two different regimes. Returns with a lag and market value are also considered non-switching variables. In fact, it is expected that the impact of these variables on stock market returns will not depend on the growth rate of confirmed cases. Tables 19.3, 19.4 and 19.5 show that Iranian stock market returns respond to the three indicators, stringency index, government response index, and containment and health index, very similarly. Thus, in all three cases, in the first regime, where the incidence growth rate is more than 0.06, increasing the incidence growth rate and government intervention indicators has reduced stock market returns. However, in regime two, where the incidence growth rate is less than 0.06, neither of these two variables had an effect on stock returns.

Since the first regime is related to the early outbreak of the coronavirus, according to Fig. 19.1, it can be seen that these days, the stock market index is experiencing very good growth. These days, many people enter the stock market with the encouragement and support of the Iranian government, and, thinking that the corona crisis will not be sustainable, they are active in the stock market. These days, news of the corona and government intervention has reduced stock market returns by a small coefficient.

However, with the rise of confirmed cases and passing the threshold, the destructive effects of the virus on the economy have become apparent. In addition, with the intensification of the recession and rising production costs, the market has become so inactive that none of the news on the increased severity of the government's intervention affects the market return. In other words, the market has adapted to these conditions.

Table 19.6 shows the stock market return response to government economic support. It can be seen that in this case, as for the other three indicators, the government's economic support does not affect the stock market return in the second regime. However, in the first regime, it has had a very small positive effect on return.

It should be noted that due to the poor financial condition of Iran's government, financial support has been very low and sometimes has fallen sharply. It seems that if the value of this index is at an ideal level, it can largely neutralize the negative impact of the other three indicators.

19.6   Conclusion

The start and spread of the COVID-19 pandemic have had various effects on many aspects of human life. One of the most important of which is the economy. The economies of different countries have been affected, depending on the extent of the pandemic. Researchers have conducted numerous studies on the subject. Given the importance of financial markets, one of the focus points has been the impact of COVID-19 on financial markets.

Many studies have investigated the impact of COVID-19 on financial markets. In addition, given the government's involvement in pandemic control, researchers have examined the effectiveness of government interventionist policies. In this regard, some results indicate the positive effect of government policy responses on stock market returns, and some indicate the negative effect of these interventions. Perhaps one of the reasons for the conflicting results is that the nonlinear relationship between government policy responses and stock market returns is not considered. For this reason, in this chapter, a threshold regression has been estimated by considering the confirmed cases as a threshold variable.

The results obtained using Iranian data from 22 Feb 2020 to 12 June 2021 show that government intervention cannot affect the stock market return when the growth rate of confirmed cases of COVID-19 is less than 0.06. However, in a situation with a higher growth rate of the confirmed case of COVID-19, stringency index, government response index, and containment and health index reduce return, but the economic support index increases return. The results of the present chapter are not easily comparable with other studies because threshold regression was used in none of the previous studies. Using linear regression, Ayadi et al. (2020), Zhang et al. (2020), Narayan et al. (2021), and Wu et al. (2021) have concluded that government intervention has a positive effect on the stock market. Using the interaction effects of COVID-19 and government intervention indicators, Yang and Deng (2021) have shown that with the increase of confirmed cases, the impact of indicators on returns becomes negative. The results of their study are consistent with the present chapter.

According to these results, some points can be stated:

1. Investment in the Iranian stock market is heavily influenced by political events and government behavior due to US sanctions. To finance the budget deficit, the government has encouraged people to invest in the stock market and buy government exchange-traded funds (ETFs).

2. Government intervention seems to have been an effective way to control the COVID-19 pandemic, but policymakers have faced a trade-off between citizens' health and stock market return when the growth rate of confirmed cases is high.

References

Akhtaruzzaman, M., Boubaker, S., & Sensoy, A. (2021). Financial contagion during COVID–19 crisis. *Finance Research Letters, 38*, 101604.

Albulescu, C. T. (2021). COVID-19 and the United States financial markets' volatility. *Finance Research Letters, 38*, 101699.

Ashraf, B. N. (2020). Stock markets' reaction to COVID-19: Cases or fatalities? *Research in International Business and Finance, 54*, 101249.

Ayadi, A., Kallel, C., & Rabah Gana, M. (2020). COVID-19 and financial markets: The stories of several countries. *Available at SSRN 3756491.*

Bai, J. (1997). Estimating multiple breaks one at a time. *Econometric Theory, 13*(3), 315–352.

Bai, J., & Perron, P. (1998). Estimating and testing linear models with multiple structural changes. *Econometrica*, 47–78.

Bai, J., & Perron, P. (2003). Computation and analysis of multiple structural change models. *Journal of Applied Econometrics, 18*(1), 1–22.

Corbet, S., Larkin, C., & Lucey, B. (2020). The contagion effects of the COVID-19 pandemic: Evidence from gold and cryptocurrencies. *Finance Research Letters, 35*, 101554.

Garcin, M., Klein, J., & Laaribi, S. (2020). Estimation of time-varying kernel densities and chronology of the impact of COVID-19 on financial markets. *arXiv preprint arXiv:2007.09043.*

Goodell, J. W. (2020). COVID-19 and finance: Agendas for future research. *Finance Research Letters, 35*, 101512.

Hale, T., Webster, S., Petherick, A., Phillips, T., & Kira, B. (2020). *Oxford COVID-19 government response tracker.* Blavatnik School of Government.

Hansen, B. (1999). Testing for linearity. *Journal of Economic Surveys, 13*(5), 551–576.

Hansen, B. E. (2000). Testing for structural change in conditional models. *Journal of Econometrics, 97*(1), 93–115.

Haroon, O., & Rizvi, S. A. R. (2020). Flatten the curve and stock market liquidity–an inquiry into emerging economies. *Emerging Markets Finance and Trade, 56*(10), 2151–2161.

Ibrahim, I., Kamaludin, K., & Sundarasen, S. (2020). COVID-19, government response, and market volatility: Evidence from the Asia-Pacific developed and developing markets. *Economies, 8*(4), 105.

Keele, L., & Kelly, N. J. (2006). Dynamic models for dynamic theories: The ins and outs of lagged dependent variables. *Political Analysis, 14*(2), 186–205.

Narayan, P. K., Phan, D. H. B., & Liu, G. (2021). COVID-19 lockdowns, stimulus packages, travel bans, and stock returns. *Finance Research Letters, 38*, 101732.

Ozparlak, G. (2020). Long run and short run impacts of COVID-19 on financial markets. *Journal of Business Economics and Finance, 9*(2), 155–170.

Raza Rabbani, M., Rahiman, H. U., Atif, M., Zulfikar, Z., & Naseem, Y. (2021). The response of Islamic financial service to the COVID-19 pandemic: The open social innovation of the financial system. *Journal of Open Innovation: Technology, Market, and Complexity, 7*(1), 85.

Rebucci, A., Hartley, J. S., & Jiménez, D. (2020). *An event study of COVID-19 central bank quantitative easing in advanced and emerging economies* (No. w27339). National Bureau of Economic Research.

Samadi, A. H., Owjimehr, S., & Nezhad-Halafi, Z. (2021). The cross-impact between financial markets, Covid-19 pandemic, and economic sanctions: The case of Iran. *Journal of Policy Modeling, 43*(1), 34–55.

Sharif, A., Aloui, C., & Yarovaya, L. (2020). COVID-19 pandemic, oil prices, stock market, geopolitical risk and policy uncertainty nexus in the US economy: Fresh evidence from the wavelet-based approach. *International Review of Financial Analysis, 70*, 101496.

Stocker, T. (2007). On the asymptotic bias of OLS in dynamic regression models with autocorrelated errors. *Statistical Papers, 48*(1), 81–93.

Topcu, M., & Gulal, O. S. (2020). The impact of COVID-19 on emerging stock markets. *Finance Research Letters, 36*, 101691.

Tsay, R. S. (1989). Testing and modeling threshold autoregressive processes. *Journal of the American Statistical Association, 84*(405), 231–240.

Wang, W., & Enilov, M. (2020). The global impact of COVID-19 on financial markets. *Available at SSRN 3588021.*

Wu, W., Lee, C. C., Xing, W., & Ho, S. J. (2021). The impact of the COVID-19 outbreak on Chinese-listed tourism stocks. *Financial Innovation, 7*(1), 1–18.

Yang, H., & Deng, P. (2021). The impact of COVID-19 and government intervention on stock markets of OECD countries. *Asian Economics Letters, 1*(4), 18646.

Zaremba, A., Kizys, R., Aharon, D. Y., & Demir, E. (2020). Infected markets: Novel coronavirus, government interventions, and stock return volatility around the globe. *Finance Research Letters, 35*, 101597.

Zhang, D., Hu, M., & Ji, Q. (2020). Financial markets under the global pandemic of COVID-19. *Finance Research Letters, 36*, 101528.

Chapter 20
Request and Donation Efficiencies in a Crisis: Data Envelopment Analyses of a Philippine Web-Based Emergency Response System

Jackson J. Tan and Richard L. Parcia

20.1 Introduction

At the start of 2020, the highly contagious and potentially fatal novel coronavirus (COVID-19) caused governments throughout the world to halt business activities and nonessential government services within a matter of weeks. Policies enacted by the People's Republic of China to contain the spread of the pathogen within its borders (actions such as social distancing, community quarantines, and mass testing) were also implemented in other countries with varying degrees of success. Implementation of community quarantines induced a cessation of activities in industries from education to manufacturing. Logistics services experienced dramatic reductions in mobility as airports, sea ports, and roads were closed to incoming and outgoing cargo. As all industries were affected by efforts to slow infection rates, supply chains to health-related institutions were greatly debilitated at a time when the number of new infections and deaths related to the virus grew. This shock to healthcare supply chains prompted certain corporations to focus their corporate social responsibility efforts on the amelioration of a potentially catastrophic public health situation (Bunye, 2020; CNN Philippines Staff, 2020; Dumlao-Abadilla, 2020; Gomez, 2020; Manila Bulletin, 2020; The Manila Times, 2020; Tayao-Juego, 2020).

J. J. Tan (✉)
Entrepreneurship Department, College of Commerce and Business Administration, Graduate School, Research Center for Social Sciences and Education, University of Santo Tomas, Manila, Philippines

Ivory Research Interface Data Analysis Services, Pasig City, Philippines
e-mail: jjtan@ust.edu.ph

R. L. Parcia
Graduate School, University of Santo Tomas, Manila, Philippines

© The Author(s), under exclusive license to Springer Nature Switzerland AG 2022   441
N. Faghih, A. Forouharfar (eds.), *Socioeconomic Dynamics of the COVID-19 Crisis*,
Contributions to Economics, https://doi.org/10.1007/978-3-030-89996-7_20

In a response to these events, development and deployment of a virtual donation platform was initiated as part of the corporate social responsibility by a diversified industrial corporation. The earliest confirmed cases of COVID-19 in the Philippines were recorded toward the end of January 2020. In the first 16 days of March, the average daily growth rate of confirmed cases was 33.13%. The national government of the Philippines declared a lockdown of Luzon on 16 March 2020, just as the average death rate from the virus approached 23.77% (Guidotti & Ardia, 2020). On 25 March 2020, the first donations to hospitals were pledged on the corporate platform. Effectively, owners of the diversified industrial corporation filled a crucial role during the crisis in establishing an infrastructure to supply goods necessary for the recovery of infected people (Grube & Storr, 2018). As a form of horizontal coordination, the community-based emergency response platform served as a virtual space whereby donors and hospitals requesting for supplies exchanged information, goods, and services (Rasheed et al., 2019). In states of disaster, conflicts of interest and negotiations were facilitated by information exchanges (Stute et al., 2020).

The purpose of discourse in this chapter is to highlight how data envelopment analysis (DEA) was used in a crisis situation to fortify an already weakened supply chain that supported Philippine hospitals during the initial spread of COVID-19 at the start of 2020. In an effort to determine improvements to the hospital supply chain provided by the emergency response platform, a series of DEA assessments were conducted. The use of an input-oriented, constant returns-to-scale DEA model examined frequencies of donors, individual items requested, total quantity of items requested, and number of requested individual items that received a pledged. The output variable was the total quantities pledged to various hospitals. A second set of analyses examined the levels of efficiency by which cities were served by the platform under an assumption of variable returns-to-scale. In the second set of analyses, inputs that affected the quantity of donated items per thousands in the population were the number of donors, count of individually requested items, requested quantities, and average days a request pended. In exception of the average days a request pended, all other variables were expressed as a proportion of thousands in the population for a city.

At the time requests and donations were made to the platform, growth rates for COVID-19-related deaths and confirmed cases experienced rapid increases. From 12 March 2020 (date of the first doubling of deaths in the country) to 3 April 2020, the average daily growth rate in deaths was 27.52%. The daily average growth rate in confirmed cases during the same period was 20.46%. When set in perspective, at an average daily growth rate of 27.52%, the number of deaths was expected to double in a matter of 4 (3.63) days. In terms of the number of confirmed cases, these were expected to double in 5 (4.89) days. To further emphasize the importance of DEA assessments on cohort hospitals and cities in the platform, from 12 February 2020 to 3 April 2020, national cumulative deaths outnumbered recoveries on an average of 2.12-to-1, respectively. On the date of the first DEA evaluation, 3 April 2020, there were 1036 deaths and 540 recoveries from the virus. On the date of the second assessment, 15 April 2020, there were 3821 cumulative deaths and 2422 aggregate recoveries (Guidotti & Ardia, 2020). It was under these conditions that

DEA appraisals were made to improve the service efficiency for participant hospitals and their respective cities.

Due to the circumstances within which analyses were conducted, a series of limitations were present that constrained the study. Unlike much of the academic discourse related to the DEA technique, data sets used in calculating efficiencies of various decision-making units (DMUs) were not static, or unchanging. With each passing day, data sets changed as new hospitals and donors were added to the database. With dynamic sets of data and limited information from a newly developed system, critical decisions as to the type of data and methodology of analyses used had to be made without the luxury of finding more data from new sources. Confidentiality of the diversified industrial corporation and its subsidiaries involved with the web-based platform was respected in this chapter. Censorship of references to the organizations immersed in the project was observed, in light of requests from the parent company. Data sets used to conduct the DEA assessments are available from the corresponding author upon reasonable request.

In the following sections of this chapter, discussion expounds on the data envelopment analysis technique, along with findings from the assessments of the emergency response platform. The next section will provide precedence as to the use of DEA to analyze healthcare systems, along with an elucidation of members in supply chains to hospitals. The third section will discuss the methodology to perform the analyses in a crisis situation with limited information. Findings from the emergency response portal data receive address in the fourth section. From these findings, the fifth section forwards a series of recommendations. Lastly, a sixth section concludes the chapter.

20.2 Review of Related Literature

20.2.1 Hospital Supply Chains and Crises

Evidence from extant literature discussed how, in a state of crisis, institutions exercised particular strategies that allowed for recovery from such a shock. Strategies for recovery took different forms from multiple sourcing to closer supplier relationships. Technological innovations further fortified relationships with suppliers and expanded supply sources (Ponis & Ntalla, 2016). Benthar et al. (2016) presented the flow of information from hospitals to support services and the project management challenges that this flow faced. Walker (2018) discussed benefits that hospitals experienced from participation in health information exchanges (HIEs). Scavarda et al. (2019) forwarded a cyclical framework of members in a hospital supply chain. Although presented as a specific example, the Scavarda et al. (2019) framework emphasized how members in a hospital supply chain not only were interdependent but also produced externalities that benefited communities that hospitals served.

Ponis and Ntalla (2016) discussed strategies of firms that faced unforeseeable events that disrupted their supply chain network. From a crisis, firms that successfully recovered utilized alternative sources to cover any losses from a failed source. This required that firms held close relationships with suppliers and knowledge of alternative capacities. The paper emphasized that capacity flexibility was the result of close relationships with suppliers and sources. To achieve capacity flexibility entailed that firms engaged in multiple sourcing. Trust within the organization in crisis allowed for firms to quickly recover. To encourage trust within an organization, it was necessary for managers to take a long-term view of operations beyond short-term profits. Practices that resulted in recovery involved collaboration between members of the supply chain. This was further enhanced by technological innovation. Most important in the achievement of recovery from a crisis was the quickness of response to the situation.

Benthar et al. (2016) examined the flow of information between a blood transfusion center and members of the blood supply chain. Information technology was a strategic resource that endowed organizations with competitive advantages. This form of technology reduced information transactions, which improved planning and decision-making in a supply chain.

Walker (2018) examined if participation in a health information exchange network improved hospital efficiency. An HIE served as a platform for the transfer of patient information between organizations in the healthcare system. Timely and accurate information was shared from participation in an HIE. This allowed for coordination between healthcare providers to the benefit of patients. DEA models in the paper were input-oriented as management could control the selection of inputs. The study found that participant hospitals to an HIE network experienced improved technical efficiency and total factor productivity. Hospitals that participated in an HIE network and utilized electronic hospital records were also more likely to have higher total factor productivity.

20.2.2   Data Envelopment Analysis in Hospitals

As a technique of analysis, DEA was utilized in the examination of healthcare systems and sets of hospitals. From Charnes et al. (1978), data envelopment analysis generated estimates of optimal efficiency. Optimal efficiency was a result of an examination of all DMUs in the analysis (Charnes et al., 1978). Conceptually, the method directly compared subjects to their peers (Walker, 2018). According to Büchner et al. (2014), the DEA technique was most often employed in hospital efficiency measurement throughout the extant literature. Afzali et al. (2009) forwarded that in the assessment of hospital case-mix, input variable selection for DEA was crucial. Mazzocato et al. (2010) expounded that medical professionals and hospital support staff must carry a shared understanding of processes involved within the organization, as well as those of organization work flows and the working environment to better effectiveness and efficiency. Lobo et al. (2014) asserted that

Brazilian public and philanthropic hospitals were at the efficient frontier, despite evidence that private hospitals were more efficient on average. Bastian et al. (2016) examined hospitals in the US Department of Defense Military Health System and found that in terms of physician time, and expertise resources necessary to provide services, army hospitals were most efficient. Campos et al. (2016) examined the efficiencies of healthcare systems in autonomous communities within Spain. From the investigations three categories of autonomous communities emerged based on healthcare system efficiency. Shrime et al. (2018) forwarded a method to determine variables for the DEA technique in comparisons of healthcare policies. Kim and Kim (2019) applied hospital cost information to determine efficiencies of members in hospital supply chains. Breitenbach et al. (2021) used country-level data to determine countries that were most efficient in combating the COVID-19 pandemic up to 11 November 2020. Hamzah et al. (2021) examined the Malaysian effort in combating the virus as of April 2020 and forwarded that fewer resources in lower density states impeded the efficiency of these units to improve cumulative recoveries and lower aggregate deaths. Kerstens and Shen (2021) discussed the actions and results of hospitals with government support in Hubei, China, from January to March of 2020. The paper described how hospital efficiencies were affected by government-supported expansions of these facilities within the first 3 months of the pandemic.

Afzali et al. (2009) discussed a framework and criteria for efficiency variable selection in stochastic frontier analysis (SFA) and data envelopment analysis (DEA) constructs with analyses of developing country hospitals. The paper forwarded that the selection of metrics examined productive functions that were internal to the hospital, along with interactive functions, which were programs that allowed the hospital to interact with external stakeholders. Structure metrics examined inputs related to personnel and consumables. Throughput or process metrics captured the level a hospital was in dispose, such as length of stay (conventional metric), or presence of educational health programs (nonconventional metric). Process variables captured the ability of health professionals to make choices which achieved desired outcomes for patients. Output metrics examined hospital activities as number of separations or number of cesarean deliveries (a metric for hospital care quality). The paper forwarded that hospital care quality metrics should be correlated with incidences of larger categories of activities (as surgeries in general) and costs related to care.

Lobo et al. (2014) examined the efficiencies of teaching hospitals in Brazil with data envelopment analyses. Input variables were quantities of beds, number of support services, and labor in terms of full-time equivalent staff. Output variables for the efficiency analyses were frequencies of hospitalizations and highly complex procedures. The study highlighted that an assumption of constant returns-to-scale for a DEA examination was that scale economies did not change with variations in the size of a facility. A variable returns-to-scale DEA assessment assumed that scale economies changed as the size of a facility changed. The paper utilized an output-oriented variable returns-to-scale model. For Brazilian hospitals in the sample, mean efficiency was 0.49. Public and philanthropic hospitals were on average less efficient (0.48) than private hospitals (0.56). Yet, the hospitals at the efficient frontier were public (two hospitals) and philanthropic (three hospitals) in their ownership.

Breitenbach et al. (2021) compared the country-level efficiencies of healthcare systems for 36 countries that dealt with the COVID-19 pandemic. The cross-sectional study utilized data envelopment analysis in an examination of negative outputs from cohort healthcare systems, namely, fatality and infection prevalence rates. Data up to 11 November 2020 were used in the study. Inputs to the DEA models looked at the frequencies in the population of tests for the virus, doctors and nurses, and healthcare expenditure. A series of three models examined the efficiencies of various countries in terms of the outputs recovery, death, and infection rates. Models in the study assumed variable returns-to-scale as various countries had differing resources due to their respective sizes. Countries at the efficient frontier in the paper were Bangladesh, Brazil, Chile, Indonesia, Morocco, and Pakistan. The other 30 cohorts in the study were less efficient than those at the frontier. The paper forwarded that despite greater expenditures on healthcare, developed countries such as Belgium, France, Germany, and the United States were less efficient cohorts. These less efficient countries did not properly utilize their resources to curtail the virus from spreading. The study attributed the inefficiencies to improper policies or slow responses.

Hamzah et al. (2021) discussed the experience of Malaysia as it battled the pandemic through April 2020. The study utilized a network data envelopment analysis (NDEA) method to assess efficiencies of three particular stages in managing the pandemic. Community surveillance, medical care I, and medical care II were the three stages the paper examined. Data for the analyses were at the state-level and categorized between states that had population densities that ranged from low, medium, to high. At the community surveillance phase, the study used cumulative positive cases as an output variable. The frequencies of positive cases in critical care, positive cases in the standard wards, and positive cases using ventilators in critical care were the three output variables for the second phase, medical care I. Output variables for medical care II examined positive and negative outcomes as the cumulative number of recoveries and deaths measured. Another set of input variables received categorization as shared resources. These shared resources were inputs to phases 1, 2, and 3, as well as just between phases 2 and 3. Between the three phases, the frequencies of screening facilities (hospitals and clinics), isolation gowns, N95 masks, and three-ply masks were input assets to the NDEA models. At phases 2 and 3, the number of beds in COVID-19 hospitals and extension centers comprised the shared input. The paper found that efficiency of the entire three-phase pandemic management process depended on the inefficiency of medical care (I and II), more so than community surveillance. High density states were more efficient at the community surveillance and medical care II phases, while low density states showed more efficiency at the medical care I phase. The paper forwarded that fewer resources for low density states impeded the efficiency of these states to produce favorable outcomes (cumulative recoveries and deaths).

Kerstens and Shen (2021) discussed plant capacities of hospitals in Hubei, China, at the start of the COVID-19 pandemic. The 8-week observation window examined the period from 19 January 2020 to 15 March 2020. An exploration of eight plant capacity conditions used data envelopment analysis to determine short-run and long-run efficiencies. Models in the paper reflected the circumstance of government support that allowed hospitals to expand facilities commensurate with the demand of infected patients. In light of substantial resource support from government, models in the paper assumed variable returns-to-scale in calculating for efficiencies. Inputs to the models accounted for personnel (as medical and technical staff), along with the number of beds. The frequency of patients with COVID-19 was the output variable. The paper found that long-run plant capacity affected the number of COVID-19 patients. The assumptions of models in the paper may not reflect conditions of other countries, especially in Southeast Asia, due to differences in government structures and social forces.

20.3   Methodology

Two data envelopment analyses were conducted for this study. The first analysis examined the efficiency of service that participant hospitals received from the web-based emergency response platform. Analyses for the hospital-level data assumed constant returns-to-scale, as information regarding the size of hospital resources could not be ascertained. The second analysis looked at the efficiency by which the platform served cities. This second model assumed variable returns-to-scale as larger cities were expected to have more resources (in the way of hospitals, medical staff, supplies, and the like) than smaller ones. For the DEA models of hospitals served by the platform, the input-oriented model assessed efficiencies as of 3 April 2020. The city-level DEA model was input-oriented and evaluated data as of 15 April 2020.

The community-based emergency response platform was predicated on the idea of creating an information exchange between hospitals and individual donors. At its inception, the platform listed items requested by hospitals and matched these requests to individual donors that pledged some amount to the particular facility. At the time of analysis, 3 April 2020, data from the platform consisted of hospital and donor identifications, number of donors, count of requested items, count of pledged items, number of un-pledged items, total quantities of items requested, total quantities of items pledged, total quantities of un-pledged items, percentage of requests fulfilled, and percentage of requests unfulfilled.

Fulfillment of donations involved delivery arrangements and verification of delivery. Delivery arrangements were agreements made between a donor (pledger) and a hospital. These could take the form of a delivery directly to the hospital by the donor with their own vehicle; the pledger and the hospital arrived at a shared delivery cost agreement; or the hospital could pick up pledged items itself. Only the hospital had the authority to notify the maintainer of the platform that pledged items were delivered by a donor. Such notification by a hospital would signal completion of a request for an item and its quantity. One of the logistics difficulties the web-based platform faced was donors who wanted to pledge items to hospitals in different cities but lacked the logistic resources to complete such a delivery (emergency response platform call center volunteer, personal communication, 18 April 2020).

As the platform was created in a matter of a few weeks before its launch, data that was collected revolved about the supply chain sequence that involved donor procurement and item donations, arrangement for item transport to hospitals, and the confirmation of hospitals upon acceptance of the donated items. Due to the short development and turnaround time of the platform, the industrial corporation that created it did not have the luxury of time to include other hospital specific metrics such as number of infected patients, number of beds, numbers of medical staff, inventories of supplies, and the like. Clearly, the lack of hospital-specific metrics presented a limitation of the study. This limitation in the availability of data stood as a reality in the creation of new web-based platforms, since these applications benefited from incremental improvements overtime.

A collection of data conducted with the data science team of the industrial corporation to determine the number of beds dedicated to COVID-19 patients and numbers of medical staff yielded incomplete information for all cohort hospitals on the platform. Data on medical staff were either not reported or obsolete. Data on the number of infected patients per day at each hospital were inconsistent, as some facilities chose not to report (or stopped reporting) the number of patients and remaining beds due to the risk of extremely burdening already excessively loaded treatment facilities. Hence, due to information asymmetries, the actual sizes of hospitals on the platform (in terms of capacities and resources) could not be determined. It was in light of these limitations that the hospital-level model in this study assumed a constant returns-to-scale as the actual size of each hospital relative to its cohort could not be accurately or consistently determined given the available data. Furthermore, the use of constant returns-to-scale made the assumption that in the short run, hospitals would not be able to expand their facilities quickly, as in the case of Hubei hospitals from January to March of the same year (Kerstens & Shen, 2021).

The fact that hospitals made requests to the private sector through the platform implied a condition of constant returns-to-scale. This condition of constant returns-to-scale existed because hospitals could not expand their facilities in the short term to meet the demands of infected patients in a timely manner. Hospitals did not have the luxury of time to expand resource utilizations. An assumption of Kerstens and Shen (2021) was that (1) hospitals had time and (2) access to government resources to expand facility capacities. Since Kerstens and Shen (2021) examined the long-run inputs and outputs of decision-making units, the discussion of long-run plant capacity utilization explicitly made the assumption that decision-making units had the time to adjust utilizations of inputs (Kerstens & Shen, 2021: 5).

An issue with automated reporting in sudden-onset disasters was a tendency for information to be incomplete or deficient in detail due to the scarcity of time (Stute et al., 2020). Thus, unlike much of the academic literature, where data sets were static for a particular observation horizon, data sets in this study were in a dynamic state. In such a circumstance, not all information was available or known. A usual assumption of many studies that used DEA is that variables captured complete information on decision-making units. In this study, available data from the platform was applied and censured by nearly daily discussions with members of the corporate data science team and platform volunteers about the processes involved in item requisition to donation completion.

Raw data for analyses of hospital requests and donations (pledges) in the emergency response portal came from a subsidiary of the platform maintainer (corporate data science team, personal communication, 18 April 2020). This raw information, in text form, was further curated by the corporate data science team. Information on hospital and donor names, requested items, pledged items, and their corresponding quantities were made available in a master data set for analysis on 3 April 2020. The first analyses were conducted 16 days from the first date donations posted on the platform. Data for the second DEA assessment, 15 April 2020, which examined city-level service efficiencies, required more information than in the initial analysis due to the dearth of aggregate donations. In the subsequent data set, hospital city names and timestamps for requests and donations were included. Again, as time progressed the data set included more information than the previous days.

Curated data sets from the corporate data science team were further wrangled, cleaned, and analyzed by the researcher. Data wrangling, cleaning, and analysis processes were performed in the R statistics environment, version 3.6.3 (R Core Team, 2020). Frequencies for deaths and recoveries in the Philippines were gathered from the package, "COVID-19 Data Hub" (Guidotti & Ardia, 2020). Growth rate calculations for discussions on death and recovery rates in this chapter were facilitated by the package, "dplyr: A Grammar of Data Manipulation," version 0.8.5 (Wickham et al., 2020). Data envelopment analyses were facilitated by the package, "rDEA: Robust Data Envelopment Analysis (DEA) for R," version 1.2–6 (Simm & Besstremyannaya, 2020). Further, data compilation was facilitated by the package, "knitr: A General-Purpose Package for Dynamic Report Generation in R," version 1.28 (Xie, 2020). As much as possible, codes to analyze data from the emergency response platform utilized base R for reproducibility of results. Upon reasonable request, codes to analyze the data in R could be disclosed.

For the second DEA model, population data for each city were drawn from the Philippine Statistics Authority (PSA) based on their Philippine Standard Geographic Code (PSGC). From the PSGC webpage, city- and *barangay*-level populations from the 2015 Census were made available on 31 March 2020 (Philippine Statistics Authority, 2020). Cities and their corresponding populations were matched, as much as possible, according to PSGC number designations. Otherwise, cities were identified by a triangulation of spelling, hospital address location, and discussions with the corporate data science team.

Variables and corresponding values for both hospital- and city-level analyses were similar in composition. A difference between values and variables for both analyses was that the city-level analysis (15 April 2020) measured frequency variables as a proportion of thousands in the population (Verguet et al., 2015; Shrime et al., 2016). Further, the city-level analysis included a variable for the average number of days a request pended before a corresponding donation. For the hospital-level analyses (3 April 2020), input frequency variables were the number of donors (pledgers), count of individually requested items, and total quantity of all items requested. These variables were seen as metrics that captured the interaction of hospitals with individual donors, similar to the methodology of Afzali et al. (2009). The output variable was the total quantity of items donated. Total quantities of items requested were an aggregation of all units for each requested item to grasp the volume of quantity requests. The output variable, total quantities of items donated, was an aggregation of all units for pledged items as a way to determine the volume of donations.

Specification of input variables to the DEA models was based on the understanding of the donation platform supply chain. Part of the responsibilities of the web maintainer was to keep the site up-to-date, with the release of information and reconciliation of donation requests remained in their control. At the request of hospitals, the web maintainer of the site could verify the completion of a donation or withhold donation amounts between parties to the platform. At the conclusion of each day, requests and donation amounts were reconciled and were updated the following day. The information disclosed on the platform still had to undergo a series of verifications as to the validity of each request and donation. Effectively, the web maintainer performed screening activities, monitoring, and censoring request and fulfillment data. For instance, implausible requests and donations (as liquors and spirits) were omitted from the platform. It is from this system of screening that platform volunteers contacted hospitals and donors to intercede for each party. Hence, the selection of input variables to the first DEA model were values that resulted from the screening and verification systems of the web maintainer and its volunteers.

Resultant efficiency scores, θ, for each hospital in the analyses provided information as to DMUs at the efficient frontier, those with a level of efficiency, and those without any efficiency. As information regarding costs involved in the operational sequences from requisition to delivery were not completely disclosed in any of the data sets from the website maintainer, hospital-level DEA assessments were input-oriented and assumed decision-making units experienced constant returns-to-scale. An assumption of constant returns-to-scale was used as base data, and publicly available data did not fully reveal sensible bed capacities, labor-related figures, or expense information usually present in DEA examinations of hospitals and healthcare systems. Constant returns-to-scale was an assumption made based on the data available in the data sets from the platform maintainer. Again, due to the state of crisis that hospital supply chains experienced during the first wave, nonexistent or incomplete data could not be used. Thus, a more conservative estimate of efficiency was determined, based on what could be controlled within the platform.

Peer weights, λ, for each hospital in the DEA assessments served as factors by which to determine reductions of input variable amounts to achieve more efficient service. Use of these weights informed the level by which to adjust allocations of donors, counts of individually requested items, total quantities of requested items, and average request pending times for a particular hospital. As such, modifications to input variables were expected to optimally affect the total quantity of items donated, as the output variable (the total quantity of items from completed donations) was outside of the control of the community-based emergency response platform and was seen as a result of the available figures for input variables.

20.4   Findings

As of the third of April 2020, items requested by hospitals ranged from N95 face masks to a washing machine. The total quantity volume of requests was 311,512 units, yet these were only matched by 8807 units in donations. The ten most requested items accounted for 91.26% of total requests. These items were N95 masks (82,160 units), surgical masks (62,300 units), surgical gowns (26,050 units), vitamin C in an unspecified form (20,500 units), head caps (20,350 units), disposable shoe covers (19,750 units), nitrile gloves (18,500 units), personal protective equipment system kits (14,830 units), disposable goggles (10,795 units), and acrylic face shields (9052 units). Yet, the percentage of these requested amounts that were donated ranged from 0 (vitamin C in an unspecified form and nitrile gloves) to a maximum of 6.63% (acrylic face shield). Figures for the top ten requested items are shown in Table 20.1.

For the first DEA assessment (3 April 2020), descriptive statistics exhibited 75 hospitals with requests to the platform. The number of donors (pledgers) for each hospital ranged from zero to as much as six. Individually requested items per hospital spanned from 1 to as much as 32. Per hospital, the total quantities of items requested ranged from 30 to 52,510. The quantities of donated items for each hospital ranged from 0 to 2045, with a median value of 0. Table 20.2 exhibits the descriptive statistics for each variable of the hospital-level analyses.

The second DEA evaluation (15 April 2020) examined cities served by the platform by virtue of participant hospitals. Cities served by the platform ranged in

Table 20.1 Emergency response platform's ten most requested items

Items	Total requested qty.	Total pledged qty.	Fulfilled %
N95 mask	82,160	1405	1.71
Surgical mask	62,300	3420	5.49
Surgical gowns	26,050	402	1.54
Vitamin C	20,500	0	0.00
Head cap	20,350	1000	4.91
Disposable shoe cover	19,750	425	2.15
Nitrile gloves	18,500	0	0.00
Personal protective equipment kits	14,830	345	2.33
Disposable goggles	10,795	101	0.94
Acrylic face shield	9052	600	6.63

Note: Authors' own table

Table 20.2 Variable summary statistics

Variables	Min.	Median	Mean	Max.
Hospital-level (April 3, 2020)				
Quantities donated (output)	0	0	117.4267	2045
Donors per hospital (input)	0	0	0.7333	6
Count requested items (input)	1	6	6.2267	32
Quantities requested (input)	30	1650	4153.4933	52,510
City-level, (April 15, 2020)				
Quantities donated (output)	0	31.5	498.1905	4642
Donors per city (input)	0	1	1.9524	12
Count requested items (input)	2	6.5	8.2143	47
Quantities requested (input)	130	1979.5	10,823.2619	139,350
Average days pending (input)	2	16	14.3937	21
City populations	51.839	331.5	432.3718	2936.1
Hospitals per city	1	1	1.9762	12

Note: Authors' own table

populations from 51,839 to 2,936,116 people. The median population was 331,451 persons, while the mean population was about 432,372 people (432,371.83 people). There were 42 cities served by the platform. Each city had as many as 12 participant hospitals, or as few as 1. Donors at the city level ranged from 0 to as many as 12. Per city, the count of items requested spanned from two, to as many as 47. Total requested quantities of each item per city ranged from 130 to 139,350 units. The total quantities of matched donations per city ranged from 0 to 4642 units. For the second analysis, in exception of average days pending, all other variables made a proportion of thousands of the city population to capture the scale of people that stood to benefit from platform activities. This same method of scaling variables was also done by Shrime et al. (2018), and Campos et al. (2016) in their assessments of national healthcare policies and healthcare systems, respectively. Table 20.2 shows descriptive statistics for the city-level analyses. Appendix I provides the list of cities serviced by the platform by virtue of participant hospitals in their jurisdictions.

Of the 75 hospitals that participated in the community-based emergency response portal, 29 hospitals were deemed as efficient at some level, θ. From the input-oriented, constant returns-to-scale DEA model, only 8 hospitals of the 75 were deemed as served at the efficient frontier. Less efficiently served hospitals had efficiency scores, θ, which ranged from very close to the efficient frontier at 0.9899 (City of Manila, Hospital 3) to very far from the efficient frontier at 0.1240 (City of Parañaque, Hospital 3). For less efficiently served hospitals, the mean efficiency score was 0.4338, with a median of 0.3897. Efficiency scores for hospitals served by the platform are shown in Table 20.3.

With the city-level analyses, there were 42 cities served by the community-based emergency response platform. From the variable returns-to-scale DEA model, 11 benchmark cities, with efficiency scores at 1, were Bacolod, Cabuyao, General Trias, Iloilo City, Mandaluyong, Mandaue, Manila, Muntinlupa, Pasig, Quezon City, and San Jose Del Monte. Served at near the efficient frontier was San Juan. Of

Table 20.3 Hospital efficiency scores

Hospitals	Efficiency
City of Muntinlupa, Hospital 1	1
City of Bacoor, Hospital 1	1
City of San Pablo, Hospital 1	1
City of General Trias, Hospital 1	1
City of Manila, Hospital 4	1
City of Cabuyao, Hospital 1	1
City of Manila, Hospital 7	1
City of Manila, Hospital 6	1
City of Manila, Hospital 3	0.9899
City of Valenzuela, Hospital 2	0.75
City of Biñan, Hospital 2	0.702
City of Biñan, Hospital 3	0.6543
City of Mandaue, Hospital 1	0.5902
Quezon City, Hospital 2	0.5556
City of Manila, Hospital 1	0.4886
Quezon City, Hospital 11	0.4604
City of Balanga (capital), Hospital 1	0.4545
City of Talisay, Hospital 1	0.438
City of Santa Rosa, Hospital 3	0.3897
City of Manila, Hospital 2	0.3704
City of Pasig, Hospital 3	0.3442
City of Parañaque, Hospital 3	0.3211
Quezon City, Hospital 15	0.2963
City of San Jose Del Monte, Hospital 1	0.2963
City of Pasig, Hospital 2	0.2667
Quezon City, Hospital 7	0.2581
City of Dasmariñas, Hospital 2	0.2162
Quezon City, Hospital 12	0.1429
City of Parañaque, Hospital 3	0.124

Note: Efficiency scores are based on a model that assumes constant returns-to-scale. Author's own table

cities determined as served at some level of efficiency, Roxas City was the least efficiently served. Table 20.4 details efficiency scores for cities at some level of efficiency.

Skewness in peer weights, λ, for both hospital- and city-level analyses reflected the dearth of donations. Weights for each peer hospital ranged from 0 to 1.5. The mean raw peer weighting was 0.2699, with a median weight of 0.149. For peer cities, weights ranged from 0 to 1. The average peer weight for cities was 0.3611, with a median value of 0.3248. The skewness in city peer weights indicated the paucity of donations for requests by hospitals in those cities. For most cities, there were not enough donations to match requests for very necessary and vitally important

Table 20.4 City efficiency scores

City	Efficiency
Bacolod	1
Cabuyao	1
General Trias	1
Iloilo City	1
Mandaluyong	1
Mandaue	1
Manila	1
Muntinlupa	1
Pasig	1
Quezon City	1
San Jose Del Monte	1
San Juan	0.9213
Makati	0.7277
Biñan	0.6749
Talisay	0.6613
Balanga	0.6345
Bacoor	0.6237
San Pablo	0.618
Dasmariñas	0.5646
Parañaque	0.5236
Santa Rosa	0.5145
Valenzuela	0.468
Roxas City	0.3552

Note: Authors' own table

Table 20.5 Summary statistics for efficiency scores, θ, and peer weights, λ

Composite value	Min.	Median	Mean	Max.
Hospital-level (3 April 2020)				
Hospital efficiency score, θ	0.124	0.4886	0.5900	1
Peer weight, λ	0	0.149	0.2699	1.5
City-level (15 April 2020)				
City efficiency score, θ	0.3552	0.9213	0.7951	1
Peer weight, λ	0	0.3248	0.3611	1
Cities less efficient, θ	0.3552	0.6209	0.6073	0.9213

Note: Hospital-level values are from an input oriented, constant returns-to-scale DEA model. City-level values are from an input oriented, variable returns-to-scale DEA model. Author's own table

supplies. This dearth of donations underscored one of the challenges to humanitarian logistics, unavailable supplies suitable to demand and sufficient in quantities (Rasheed et al., 2019). Peer weights for both the hospital- and city-level DEA models were used to determine the amounts by which to reduce inputs so as to bring a particular DMU to optimal service efficiency. Table 20.5 describes the summary statistics for efficiency scores, θ, and peer weights, λ.

20.5   Discussion and Recommendations

The resultant excessive use values for hospital-level DEA appraisals indicated that each input (donors, count of requested items, and quantities requested) was in a state of overutilization. From the DEA assessments, participant hospitals to the platform exhibited an overdependence on individual donors rather than collections of benefactors. The City of Pasig, Hospital 2, was deemed as not excessive in its dependence on donors. Other hospitals in the analysis exhibited a tendency to overly rely on one (an average of 0.9485) to five (maximum value 4.38) donors. Hospitals exhibited the behavior of overly requesting individual items from 1 (minimum value: 0.6891) to 29 (maximum value: 28.39). On average, hospitals requested for six (average value: 5.56) more items than those at the efficient frontier. In consonance with the count of items requested, there were excessive requested quantities for items. Excess requested quantities ranged from nine (minimum value: 8.26) units to as much as 52,032 (maximum value: 52,031.60) units. On average, hospitals requested 6076 (mean value: 6075.25) units more than was optimal. Conceivably, hospitals that made requests to the platform based their request quantities on ensuring access to such supplies rather than actual or projected demand for such articles. Table 20.6 details the levels by which inputs were overutilized by each hospital.

Differences in supply and request volumes evident in the platform were signature of challenges to inventory management in humanitarian logistics. Roark (2005) brought to light that hospital frontline staff might order supplies at a maximum, which allowed for more access to these items by the hospital. Yet, such a quantity was often based on patient lives depending on access to supplies, without basis in foundations of formal business training (Roark, 2005). Dwivedi et al. (2018) highlighted that in disaster-stricken developing countries, demand assessments from sources catalyzed bullwhip effects along the disaster management supply chain due to a tendency for quantity exaggeration. More specifically, the disparity between request and donation quantities was an indication of demand unpredictability at a location and its corresponding quantities (Rasheed et al., 2019). Hence, in crisis situations, extant literature documented that hospital supply chains experienced events where agents placed excessive item and quantity requests to ensure access to supplies for their patients.

A series of recommendations were posited to the corporate data science team on how to improve service efficiencies to hospitals. In exception of the City of Pasig, Hospital 2, a number of donors to particular hospitals were recommended to donate to a different hospital. This recommendation was made in light of the 54 hospitals that did not receive donations by 3 April 2020. The number of donors asked to make pledges to other hospitals was determined by the excessive use figures for inputs, shown in Table 20.6. Hence, the number of overutilized donors to a hospital was rounded up to the nearest whole number. For example, two donors to the City of Valenzuela, Hospital 2, would be asked to pledge to another participant hospital on the platform, since 1.25 donors were overutilized. Further, one donor to the City of

Table 20.6 Hospital-level excess use inputs

Hospitals	Pledgers	Count requested items	Total qty. requests
City of Valenzuela, Hospital 2	1.25	1	1905
City of Balanga, Hospital 1	1.091	2.7275	2594.606
City of Manila, Hospital 2	1.2592	1.8890	1916.36
City of Mandaue, Hospital 1	0.4098	0.8193	4012.142
City of Talisay, Hospital 1	0.562	3.8595	399
Quezon City, Hospital 15	0.7038	3.5189	3695.602
Quezon City, Hospital 2	1.3334	2.6669	2548.406
Quezon City, Hospital 11	1.6189	7.3454	1675.603
City of Biñan, Hospital 2	0.596	6.8510	152
City of San Jose Del Monte, Hospital 1	0.7038	3.5189	52,031.602
City of Manila, Hospital 3	0.0205	0.6891	8.255
City of Manila, Hospital 1	0.5115	4.0917	3295.908
City of Pasig, Hospital 3	0.6558	2.8358	681.994
City of Pasig, Hospital 2	0	11	9400
Quezon City, Hospital 12	1.7142	9.4281	8338.418
City of Parañaque, Hospital 1	4.38	28.3894	18,629.816
City of Dasmariñas, Hospital 2	0.7324	8.5038	7912.456
City of Santa Rosa, Hospital 3	0.6102	5.8472	524.794
City of Parañaque, Hospital 3	0.6788	4.7290	848.512
City of Biñan, Hospital 3	0.3457	1.9137	107.203
Quezon City, Hospital 7	0.742	5.1938	6902.66

Note: Authors' own table

Biñan, Hospital 3, would be asked to make a pledge to a different hospital, as the DEA evaluation determined a donor overutilization level of 0.3457.

With regard to counts of individually requested items, from the hospital-level DEA model, it was recommended that hospitals reduced the number of items requested. In order to provide optimal service, a reduction of 11 requested items would be asked of the City of Pasig, Hospital 2. The City of Parañaque, Hospital 1, would be asked to reduce the number of items it requested by 29 (28.39). Other hospitals with resultant weighted quantities below 1 were recommended to reduce the count of requested items by 1. For instance, the City of Manila, Hospital 3, was determined to over request items by 0.6891, which was 1 (when rounded up to the nearest whole number).

In the same sense that counts of items were inflated, the requested quantities of these items were also determined as overdrawn. Recommendations were made to reduce the requested quantities of items in order to provide optimal levels of service by the community-based platform. As a result, an institution as City of San Jose Del Monte, Hospital 1, was recommended to reduce quantities of requested items by 52,032 (52,031.6) units. The City of Manila, Hospital 3, was recommended to reduce quantities of requested items by 9 (8.26) units.

The resultant excessive use values for city-level DEA assessments indicated that quantities requested and the average days requests pended for filling were suboptimal. In exception of San Juan, where there were no practical amounts by which to reduce either quantities of requested items or average days pending, all other participant cities to the platform were recommended to reduce these input levels. As a mention, San Juan was serviced close to the efficient frontier with an efficiency score, θ, of 0.9213. With the passage of time, more donations to hospitals in the city would bring San Juan into the efficient frontier. Quantities of requested items at inefficiently served cities were inflated an average of 9120 units, with a maximum of 33,992 units (Parañaque) and a median of 7371 units. Further, the average level of request dormancy at inefficiently served cities was 15 (14.39) days, with a maximum of 19 (18.82) days (Roxas City). City-level values for requested quantities and the average days requests pended for inefficiently served cities are shown in Table 20.7. It is of note that the average number of days a request pended for inefficiently served cities is also consistent with the average for all cities on the platform.

From literature on disaster and emergency management, zero lead time was another challenge in humanitarian logistics due to the circumstances of disasters and their magnitudes of impact (Rasheed et al., 2019). Table 20.8 describes the level by which the platform would have to lower quantities of requested items and average days pending to provide more optimal service to a particular city. Data for the city-level analyses were from 15 April 2020. In this data set, more metrics (such as days pending and city population) were included for analyses.

The city-level excess use inputs as shown in Table 20.8 indicate the reduction levels for request quantities and average days pending to efficiently service a particular city. Cities in the table were deemed inefficiently served by the platform. Values of excess use inputs were from a variable returns-to-scale DEA model. In the case of Parañaque, there were four hospitals that made requests to the platform with a total requested quantity of 33,992 units of varying items. The total amount of requested quantities was the maximum for inefficiently served cities. It is of note that the average number of units requested by inefficiently served cities was 9120 (from Table 20.7). Donations made to hospitals in Parañaque amounted to 1185 units. Given the circumstances presented by request quantities and actual donations, it was evident that request amounts were beyond what could be served by the platform for the city. Hence, a recommendation to reduce the quantities of requested items by 21,973 units was made. Further, the number of days a request from Parañaque

Table 20.7 Summary statistics city-level inputs

Input	Min.	Median	Mean	Max.
Quantities requested	700	7371	9120	33,992
Average days pending	10	14.33	14.39	18.82

Note: Summary statistics are for inefficiently served cities. Authors' own table

Table 20.8 City-level excess use inputs

City	Reduction in requested quantity	Reduction in average days pending
Bacoor	9010	4
Balanga	2306	4
Biñan	667	4
Dasmariñas	5273	7
Makati	2331	5
Parañaque	21,973	6
Roxas City	5846	12
San Juan	0	0
San Pablo	10,643	6
Santa Rosa	1062	9
Talisay	228	5
Valenzuela	3723	8

Note: Values are based on a variable returns-to-scale DEA model. San Juan received an efficiency score of 0.9213, which was nearly at the efficient frontier. Hence, there would be no change in lowering the quantities of items requested and the number of days a request pended. Authors' own table

pended was recommended to be reduced by 6 days. The mediation activities of the platform involved communications with individual donors and hospitals in various cities. It was expected that as platform volunteers appealed for reductions in request quantities, and reallocated individual donors to other hospitals, platform service efficiency at the city-level would improve.

20.6   Conclusion

In this chapter, discussion revolved about improvements to service efficiencies for a debilitated national hospital supply chain at the onset of a pandemic. Data envelopment analyses were conducted on information from a community-based emergency response platform. The platform performed as a virtual space where hospitals in need of supplies placed requests for items and their quantities, which were matched by donors. Analyses of data were done at a time when COVID-19 deaths outnumbered recoveries and multitudes of people contracted the pathogen at increased rates each day.

The intent of this chapter was to underscore how DEA was utilized during the crisis to help shore a greatly weakened national hospital supply chain through a community-based platform. This research differed from much of the extant academic literature on DEA as data sets were not static, which complicated wrangling, cleaning, and analysis of data. The research did not have the majesty of time to search for more data or make auxiliary investigations into conceptual nuances in healthcare applications of DEA. Rather, the research was guided and driven by operational understandings from a team of professionals. Hospital-level, input-oriented DEA evaluations assumed constant returns-to-scale as a practice of conservatism due to a lack of complete data on individual hospital capacities, service mix, and costs. For the first DEA assessment on hospitals, input variables were frequencies of donors, individual items requested, and total quantity of items requested. The output variable was the quantity of requested individual items that received a pledged. In the second DEA assessment on cities, efficiency scores were determined by the same inputs as in the hospital-level analyses, along with the average time a request pended until fulfillment. This second DEA model assumed variable returns-to-scale as it was expected that larger cities would have more resources, in the way of hospitals and access to donors, by virtue of their populations. In exception of average pending time, variables for the city-level analyses were scaled by thousands in the population of a city.

From the perspective of the platform in this study, its service as an information exchange with inputs of requests and donations was intended to output a greater volume of items than otherwise would have occurred. From the perspective of hospitals, the emergency donation system allowed them to effectively solicit for inputs (medicines, vitamins, ventilators, and the like) to produce specific outcomes (recovered patients). These hospitals asked for resource donations because they lacked requisite supplies to properly treat patients in a timely manner. In essence, the condition of constant returns-to-scale for an emergency donation system at the hospital level implied that hospitals were not able to expand their resources commensurate to patient demands in time. Hence, as a greater patient load arrived to a hospital with finite resources, strain increased in the system. This strain affected the quality of care each subsequent patient received, as there were less resources for each new case.

From the input-oriented DEA assessments, recommendations to reduce excessively inflated inputs and reallocate donors to other hospitals in need were forwarded. This study found that at the hospital-level, quantity requests for items were magnified. Inputs found in excessive use were recommended to be reduced to improve service to an optimal level. Donors excessively solicited by a hospital were also recommended to make pledges for other hospitals on the platform. Counts of requested items and their corresponding quantities were also suggested to be reduced for optimality.

Acknowledgments The corresponding author would like to acknowledge the professionals at the corporate data science team for their resilience, heroism, sacrifices, and camaraderie throughout the analyses of data from the platform. Further, the authors would like to dedicate this article to the memories of all victims of the COVID-19 pandemic.

Appendix I

The following cities were serviced by the community-based emergency response platform by virtue of hospitals in their respective jurisdictions.

Number	City	Number	City	Number	City
1	Alfonso	15	City of Makati	29	City of Roxas (capital)
2	City of Bacolod (capital)	16	City of Malabon	30	City of San Jose Del Monte
3	City of Bacoor	17	City of Mandaluyong	31	City of San Juan
4	City of Balanga (capital)	18	City of Mandaue	32	San Mateo
5	Batangas City (capital)	19	City of Manila	33	City of San Pablo
6	City of Biñan	20	City of Marikina	34	San Pascual
7	City of Cabuyao	21	Marilao	35	City of San Pedro
8	Daet (capital)	22	City of Masbate (capital)	36	Santa Cruz (capital)
9	City of Dasmariñas	23	Morong	37	City of Santa Rosa
10	City of General Trias	24	City of Muntinlupa	38	City of Santiago
11	City of Iloilo (capital)	25	City of Oroquieta (capital)	39	Talisay
12	City of Imus	26	City of Parañaque	40	City of Tarlac (capital)
13	Kawit	27	City of Pasig	41	City of Valenzuela
14	City of Legazpi (capital)	28	Quezon City	42	City of Zamboanga

References

Afzali, H. H. A., Moss, J. R., & Mahmood, M. A. (2009). A conceptual framework for selecting the most appropriate variables for measuring hospital efficiency with a focus on Iranian public hospitals. *Health Services Management Research, 22*(2), 81–91. https://doi.org/10.1258/hsmr.2008.008020

Bastian, N. D., Kang, H., Swenson, E. R., Fulton, L. V., & Griffin, P. M. (2016). Evaluating the impact of hospital efficiency on wellness in the military health system. *Military Medicine, 181*(8), 827–834. https://doi.org/10.7205/MILMED-D-15-00309

Benthar, O., Benzidia, S., & Fabbri, R. (2016). Traceability project of a blood supply chain. *Supply Chain Forum: An International Journal, 17*(1), 15–25. https://doi.org/10.1080/16258312.2016.1177916

Breitenbach, M. C., Ngobeni, V., & Aye, G. C. (2021). Global healthcare resource efficiency in the management of COVID-19 death and infection prevalence rates. *Frontiers in Public Health, 9*, 638481. https://doi.org/10.3389/fpubh.2021.638481

Büchner, V. A., Hinz, V., & Schreyögg, J. (2014, October 11). Health systems: Changes in hospital efficiency and profitability. *Health Care Management Science, 19.* https://doi.org/10.1007/s10729-014-9303-1

Bunye, I. R. (2020, May 4). Ayala at the front lines. *Manila Bulletin.* https://news.mb.com.ph/2020/05/04/ayala-at-the-front-lines/

Campos, M. S., Fernández-Montes, A., Gavilan, J. M., & Velasco, F. (2016, September). Public resource usage in health systems: A data envelopment analysis of the efficiency of health systems of autonomous communities in Spain. *Public Health, 138,* 33–40. https://doi.org/10.1016/j.puhe.2016.03.003

Charnes, A., Cooper, W. W., & Rhodes, E. (1978). Measuring the efficiency of decision making units. *European Journal of Operational Research, 2*(6), 429–444. https://doi.org/10.1016/0377-2217(78)90138-8

CNN Philippines Staff. (2020, March 17). SMC to produce free rubbing alcohol from Ginebra plant. *CNN Philippines.* https://cnnphilippines.com/business/2020/3/17/San-Miguel-rubbing-alcohol-production.html?fbclid=IwAR3ek2SP6S9njaNVqLUFs88AeQ2PIG9r29oFyJFh_XfVno9m9gDomd1IMbk

Dumlao-Abadilla, D. (2020, March 18). SM Supermalls to waive tenant rentals nationwide. *Inquirer.net.* Retrieved from https://business.inquirer.net/292873/sm-waives-nationwide-mall-rental

Dwivedi, Y. K., Shareef, M. A., Mukerji, B., Rana, N. P., & Kapoor, K. K. (2018). Involvement in emergency supply chain for disaster management: A cognitive dissonance perspective. *International Journal of Production Research, 56*(21), 6758–6773. https://doi.org/10.1080/00207543.2017.1378958

Gomez, J. T. (2020, April 7). 10 websites and applications to help you stay on top of this pandemic. *NOLISOLIPH.* https://nolisoli.ph/77654/10-websites-applications-pandemic-jgomez-04072020/

Grube, L., & Storr, V. H. (2018). Embedded entrepreneurs and post-disaster community recovery. *Entrepreneurship and Regional Development, 30*(7–8), 800–821. https://doi.org/10.1080/08985626.2018.1457084

Guidotti, E., & Ardia, D. (2020) COVID-19 Data Hub. Working paper. https://doi.org/10.13140/RG.2.2.11649.81763.

Hamzah, N. M., Yu, M. M., & See, K. F. (2021). Assessing the efficiency of Malaysia health system in COVID-19 prevention and treatment response. *Health Care Management Science, 24,* 273–285. https://doi.org/10.1007/s10729-020-09539-9

Kerstens, K., & Shen, Z. (2021). Using COVID-19 mortality to select among hospital plant capacity models: An exploratory empirical application to Hubei province. *Technological Forecasting and Social Change, 166,* 120535. https://doi.org/10.1016/j.techfore.2020.120535

Kim, C., & Kim, H. J. (2019). A study on healthcare supply chain management efficiency: Using bootstrap data envelopment analysis. *Health Care Management Science, 22*(3), 534–548. https://doi.org/10.1007/s10729-019-09471-7

Lobo, M. S. C., Ozcan, Y. A., Lins, M. P. E., Silva, A. C. M., & Fiszman, R. (2014). Teaching hospitals in Brazil: Findings on determinants for efficiency. *International Journal of Healthcare Management, 7*(1), 60–68. https://doi.org/10.1179/2047971913Y.0000000055

Manila Bulletin. (2020, April 25). Nestlé PH mounts P500-M 'Kasambuhay' program for 1-M families, frontliners, its people as COVID-19 rages. *Manila Bulletin.* Retrieved from https://news.mb.com.ph/2020/04/25/nestle-ph-mounts-p500-m-kasambuhay-program-for-1-m-families-frontliners-its-people-as-covid-19-rages/

Mazzocato, P., Savage, C., Brommels, M., Aronsson, H., & Thor, J. (2010). Lean thinking in healthcare: A realist review of the literature. *BMJ Quality & Safety, 19*(5), 376–382. https://doi.org/10.1136/qshc.2009.037986

Philippine Statistics Authority. (2020). Philippine Standard Geographic Code (PSGC). Philippine Statistics Authority, Classification Systems, PSGC. https://psa.gov.ph/classification/psgc/downloads/PSGC%20Publication%20March2020.xlsx

Ponis, S. T., & Ntalla, A. (2016). Crisis management practices and approaches: Insights from major supply chain crises. *Procedia Economics and Finance, 39*, 668–673. https://doi.org/10.1016/S2212-5671(16)30287-8

R Core Team. (2020). *R: A language and environment for statistical computing*. R Foundation for Statistical Computing. https://www.R-project.org/

Rasheed, H., Usman, M., Ahmed, W., Bacha, M. H., Zafar, A., & Bukhari, K. S. (2019). A shift from logistic software to service model: A case study of new service-driven-software for management of emergency supplies during disasters and emergency conditions by WHO. *Frontiers in Pharmacology, 10*, 473. https://doi.org/10.3389/fphar.2019.00473

Roark, D. C. (2005). Managing the healthcare supply chain. *Nursing Management, 36*(2), 36–40. https://doi.org/10.1097/00006247-200502000-00012

Scavarda, A., Daú, G. L., Scavarda, L. F., & Korzenowski, A. L. (2019). A proposed healthcare supply chain management framework in the emerging economies with the sustainable lenses: The theory, the practice, and the policy. *Resources, Conservation & Recycling, 141*, 418–430. https://doi.org/10.1016/j.resconrec.2018.10.027

Shrime, M. G., Sekidde, S., Linden, A., Cohen, J. L., Weinstein, M. C., & Salomon, J. A. (2016). Sustainable development in surgery: The health, poverty, and equity impacts of charitable surgery in Uganda. *PLoS One, 11*(12), e0168867. https://doi.org/10.1371/journal.pone.0168867

Shrime, M. G., Mukhopadhyay, S., & Alkire, B. C. (2018). Health-system-adapted data envelopment analysis for decision-making in universal health coverage. *Bulletin of the World Health Organization, 96*(6), 393–401. https://doi.org/10.2471/BLT.17.191817

Simm, J., & Besstremyannaya, G. (2020). rDEA: Robust Data Envelopment Analysis (DEA) for R. *R Package Version, 1*, 2–6. https://cran.r-project.org/web/packages/rDEA/index.html

Stute, M., Maass, M., Schons, T., Kaufhold, M. A., Reuter, C., & Hollick, M. (2020). Empirical insights for designing information and communication technology for international disaster response. *International Journal of Disaster Risk Reduction, 47*, 101598. https://doi.org/10.1016/j.ijdrr.2020.101598

Tayao-Juego, A. (2020, March 29). MSMEs step up. *Inquirer.net*. https://business.inquirer.net/293648/msmes-step-up.

The Manila Times. (2020, April 6). SMC food assistance to poor communities reaches P181 million. *The Manila Times*. https://www.manilatimes.net/2020/04/06/public-square/smc-food-assistance-to-poor-communities-reaches-p181-million/710217/

Verguet, S., Olson, Z. D., Babigumira, J. B., Desalegn, D., Johansson, K. A., Kruk, M. E., Levin, C. E., Nugent, R. A., Pecenka, C., Shrime, M. G., Solomon, T. M., Watkins, D. A., & Jamison, D. T. (2015). Health gains and financial risk protection afforded by public financing of selected interventions in Ethiopia: An extended cost-effectiveness analysis. *The Lancet Global Health, 3*(5), e288 e296. https://doi.org/10.1016/S2214-109X(14)70346-8

Walker, D. M. (2018). Does participation in health information exchange improve hospital efficiency? *Health Care Management Science, 21*(3), 426–438. https://doi.org/10.1007/s10729-017-9396-4

Wickham, H., François, R., Henry, L., & Müller, K. (2020). dplyr: A grammar of data manipulation. *R Package Version, 0*(8), 5. https://CRAN.R-project.org/package=dplyr

Xie, Y. (2020). knitr: A general-purpose package for dynamic report generation in R. *R Package Version, 1*, 28.

Part VI
The COVID-19 Crisis: Food and Agriculture

Chapter 21
How Did COVID-19 Reshape Food Procurement Around the Globe? Effective Operation and Redesign of the Food Retail Industry in China, Portugal, Turkey, and the USA

Yiru Wang, Merve Yanar Gürce, Joao Nuno Lopes, Tite Xu, and Xiang Chen

21.1 Introduction

There have been various pandemic events throughout history (Loske, 2020). During World War I, there was the deadly outbreak of the "Spanish flu," which infected almost one-third of the world's population. The early twenty-first century witnessed the severe acute respiratory syndrome (SARS), immediately followed by the swine flu (H1N1). At the end of 2019, the coronavirus disease 2019 (COVID-19) arose as an unprecedented global public health crisis (Koch et al.,

Y. Wang (✉)
Department of Marketing and Management, School of Business, State University of New York at Oswego, Oswego, NY, USA
e-mail: yiru.wang@oswego.edu

M. Y. Gürce
Department of Business Administration, School of Business, American International University, Al Jahra, Kuwait
e-mail: m.gurce@aiu.edu.kw

J. N. Lopes
Department of Management and Economics, Miguel Torga Institute of Higher Education & University of Beira Interior & NECE – Research Unit in Business Sciences, Covilhã, Portugal
e-mail: joao.nuno.morais.lopes@ubi.pt

T. Xu
Department of Management, Jilin University, Changchun, China
e-mail: txu14@jlu.edu

X. Chen
Department of Geography, University of Connecticut, Storrs, CT, USA
e-mail: xiang.chen@uconn.edu

© The Author(s), under exclusive license to Springer Nature Switzerland AG 2022   465
N. Faghih, A. Forouharfar (eds.), *Socioeconomic Dynamics of the COVID-19 Crisis*,
Contributions to Economics, https://doi.org/10.1007/978-3-030-89996-7_21

2020). With the first case identified in Wuhan, China, COVID-19 rapidly spread to other parts of the world and was declared a "global pandemic" by the World Health Organization (WHO).

Because of the devastating influence of the pandemic, 2020 was a dark year full of many uncertainties. The highly contagious nature of the pandemic makes it extremely transmittable in crowds, and the transmission effects are amplified by its long incubation period, mild symptoms among the infected, and airborne transmission mode. More severely, COVID-19 can exacerbate existing comorbidities within the infected (Pekosz, 2020). The quick spread of the virus caused immediate and growing health consequences in many countries, such as paralyzing their health systems (Baker et al., 2020a, b; O'Donnell et al., 2021). The social impact of COVID-19 is massive and long lasting, including surges in the unemployment rate, stock market crashes, increased poverty rate, and food insecurity. The pandemic also brought about drastic changes to human behaviors and the quality of life. The fear and stress associated with the pandemic induced widespread mental and physical health issues (Bradbury-Jones & Isham, 2020; Naeem, 2020).

Policymakers around the world devised and implemented containment measures to protect people from the COVID-19 infection. Such measures included border closures, national travel bans, regional lockdowns, the closure of schools and nonessential businesses, the use of personal protection equipment (PPE) in public areas, and social distancing. These measures cultivated new habits in education, work, travel, and social life, thus raising new social and economic challenges (Ali Taha et al., 2021; Chen et al., 2021). Food consumption as an essential part of daily life was also largely impacted. For example, it was found that during the pandemic, consumers tended to spend more on essential products with the priority given to food (Ali Taha et al., 2021; Wang et al., 2020). However, the existing studies only explored food consumers' behaviors in a single country. Because of the lack of cross-country studies, we aim to explore how consumers' food procurement behaviors were altered by the pandemic across four different countries in this chapter.

This chapter begins with an introduction to the pandemic, its time frame, and the current status of the pandemic in the countries under study. Then, the chapter presents a literature review of the food retail industry during the pandemic. Following this section, the chapter describes the methodology, the data collection process, and primary findings. Finally, the chapter draws major conclusions from the results and gives practical implications for retail business management. We hope that this study could help policymakers to take steps to protect and reboot the food retail economy in the post-pandemic era.

21.2   COVID-19 Reshaped Food Procurement Globally

21.2.1   COVID-19 in Four Countries

This study focuses on four different countries to understand consumers' perceptions and behavioral changes during the COVID-19 pandemic. These four particular countries were selected due to their unique geographical locations and cultural backgrounds as well as their different coping strategies in response to the pandemic.

China was the first country to report COVID-19 outbreaks. The first case was reported in late December of 2019 (MHC Wuhan, 2020). The pandemic hit China's public health system in an unprecedented manner, with a total of 4854 deaths in the first quarter of 2020 (WHO, 2021). China was also the first country to impose a strict lockdown and then gradually revived its economy from the pandemic (Li et al., 2020; Xu et al., 2021). The Chinese policymakers started to curb the spread of COVID-19 in early 2020 by restricting travel activities and interpersonal contact, such as banning public gatherings and minimizing the use of public transportation, to prevent virus transmission. Unlike other counties that experienced an economic downturn, China's gross domestic product (GDP) grew by 2.3% amid the pandemic (Cheng & Lee, 2021).

In Portugal, the COVID-19 outbreak began in March 2020. At this time, the Portuguese policymakers implemented restrictions on nonessential travel (Vieira et al., 2021) and preventive measures in the public health system. Specifically, people had to stay confined in their homes; they could only go out for essential activities, such as shopping for food and medicine; working remotely was pervasively encouraged; and access to public parks and beaches was also restricted. However, these measures fell short of their desired effects, and the outbreak intensified in the last quarter of 2020 and the first quarter of 2021, with a total of 16,916 deaths (WHO, 2021). The country's GDP dropped 7.6% in 2020 (Goncalves & Khalip, 2021), which was the highest drop since 1936.

The first COVID-19 case in Turkey emerged in March 2020. To prevent further virus spread, the policymakers tried to implement strict preventive measures, such as curfews, travel restrictions, school closures, and limited openings of restaurants (Guney & Sangun, 2021; Satici et al., 2020). COVID-19 prevention campaigns were also carried out to raise public awareness of restricting social activities. Moreover, there were campaigns to promote daily physical exercises as a means to avoid psychological distresses and illnesses (Abiral & Atalan-Helicke, 2020; Grashuis et al., 2020). The outbreak intensified in the second and fourth quarters of 2020 and the first quarter of 2021, with a total of 33,939 deaths (WHO, 2021). The country's GDP had improved by 1.3% over 2020 (Kuxukgomen, 2021).

In the USA, the COVID-19 pandemic posed unprecedented pressure on people, the economy, and society at large. With cases surging rapidly during the holiday season (i.e., the last quarter of 2020), the USA had the most COVID-19 cases and deaths among all countries as of April 2021. The Centers for Disease Control and Prevention (CDC) issued recommendations to battle the pandemic, such as city lockdowns, prohibition of public gatherings, and working remotely for non-essential workers, as well as different hygiene and food safety advices in terms of food procurement, preparation, and consumption on both the consumers' and retailers' ends. In addition, each state implemented its distinct public policies and regulations. The outbreak intensified in the second and fourth quarters of 2020 as well as the first quarter of 2021, with a total of more than 600,000 deaths by June 2021 (WHO, 2021). The country's GDP had fallen 2.3% over 2020 (Cheng & Lee, 2021).

The four countries studied in this chapter shed a unique global perspective on the impacts of the pandemic, as each country imposed different public health policies and had different social-economic changes during the pandemic. It is hoped that this study will provide a comprehensive view of food procurement behaviors in the global context.

21.2.2   The Pandemic Has Reshaped Food Retailing Globally

COVID-19 induced economic downturns around the globe (Petetin, 2020). Countries were forced to implement containment measures to slow down the virus transmission; however, these measures also hindered economic development. As a result, there was a decline in the global GDP during the pandemic, including a 30% decline in the global stock market (Gray, 2020).

Among all the business sectors, the food sector remained operational as it was among one of the few essential sectors during the pandemic (Nakat & Bou-Mitri, 2020). However, this sector underwent a major revamp. There were drastic changes in the food supply change regarding how food was distributed, obtained, prepared, and consumed (Hayes et al., 2021; Naja & Hamadeh, 2020). Due to the many COVID-19 preventive measures, such as lockdowns and the banning of public gatherings, food consumers tended to stockpile groceries in their homes to avoid virus transmission from indoor shopping, dining, and gathering (Cranfield, 2020). Further, many restaurants were forced to close their businesses during the pandemic, with some having to close permanently, as they failed to bear the expense of remaining temporarily closed. The decreased food supply also induced a significant increase in the food price, which eventually increased consumers' overall food expenditure (Pu & Zhong, 2020).

Due to consumers' panic reactions and the multiple lockdowns at the beginning of the pandemic, the demand for some essential products increased exponentially, causing stock shortages at local retailers and, likely, changing the way in which consumers normally undertake food procurement trips (Baker et al., 2020a, b). In the UK, there were only shortages in wheat, flour, and eggs (Trollman et al., 2021), while pork, turkey, and eggs were in short supply in the US market (Hayes et al., 2021). In the long run, the food supply chain was adjusted to meet the increased demand for essential and nonperishable food items such as rice, flour, pasta, and canned products (Ben Hassen et al., 2020; Chedid et al., 2020; Nicola et al., 2020).

Because of the essential nature of food for daily life, during the pandemic, the food sector attracted the most attention from policymakers around the globe (Gray, 2020; Ivanov, 2020). Different public policies were implemented to mitigate food shortage risks, stabilize food prices, and, ultimately, avoid a global food crisis (Ben Hassen et al., 2020). Many of such measures were specifically implemented to meet the food procurement needs of individuals and families during the pandemic. For example, in Wuhan, China, each residential community employed a unique "grid management system," which meant that a group of volunteers was assigned to each community to support the local community members with essential needs, including food and medicine (Chen, 2020). This management system was unique to Chinese society, as almost all of the urban residents live in gated communities. Due to its unique cultural setting, this community model was not found in western countries.

On the other hand, during the pandemic, consumers increased the forms of online food procurement. Research indicated that 46% of consumers made food purchases online for the first time during the pandemic (Wang et al., 2020). US consumers alone spent $5.3 billion on buying food online during April 2020, which was an increase of 37% compared with the previous month (Khandpur et al., 2020). Many US consumers (71%) also indicated that they would continue to procure food online if the pandemic persisted. The increase in online food needs forced food retailers to invest in online platforms and related catering infrastructure, such as roadside pickup lanes or home delivery personnel (Leone et al., 2020; Naeem, 2020).

Following these policy and management changes, studies explored consumers' food procurement behaviors in different countries during the pandemic, with most studies focusing on one specific country (e.g., Chronopoulos et al., 2020, Chang & Meyerhoefer, 2021, Wang et al., 2020). However, there have been very few studies about how such behavioral changes differed across countries. Improving our understanding of the behavioral changes during the pandemic in different countries is essential for policymakers to strategically plan for economic revival. Therefore, this chapter aims to address these timely questions for the post-pandemic recovery: (1) How have consumers' in-store food procurement behaviors changed during the COVID-19 pandemic, relative to their pre-pandemic behaviors, in terms of the shopping time, shopping frequency, transport mode, store type, preventive measures, and shopping experiences? (2) How have in-store risk perceptions impacted consumers' food procurement experiences? Furthermore, this chapter discusses managerial implications for food retailers in preparing for the post-pandemic era.

21.3 Case Study in Four Countries: The Comparison of How Consumers' Food Procurement Behaviors Have Changed During the Pandemic

21.3.1 Data Collection

To better understand how consumers' food procurement behaviors changed during the pandemic, 1600 consumers from four different countries, China (CHN), Portugal (PRT), Turkey (TUK), and the USA, were surveyed regarding their offline food procurement behaviors. The survey asked consumers' food activities, in terms of location, time, frequency, transport mode, and expenditure during their most recent food trip during the pandemic and also asked them to recall their activities 1 year before the pandemic. The four countries were chosen as they are different in geographic location, cultural background, and social-economic development stage. More importantly, the impacts of the pandemic differed in these countries. While China was the first country to report COVID-19 cases, it was also the most successful to curb the widespread of the virus. Portugal and Turkey both suffered from continued increases in new cases but had unified policies and social distancing measures to overcome the hardships. The USA experienced a constant increase in new cases in the early outbreak, but the epidemic curves were shaped differently by state policies.

The web-based survey was launched via different channels in these four countries due to platform availability and popularity, as described in Table 21.1. The survey was conducted in the winter of 2020 when COVID-19 was wide-spreading and consumers were forced to change their regular food procurement patterns.

The survey used in this study was based on the COVID-19 food procurement survey developed by Wang et al. (2020). The survey asked comprehensive questions related to consumer food procurement practices and perceptions during and before COVID-19. Specifically, there were questions about consumers' offline food procurement in terms of location, time, frequency, transport mode, and expenditure

Table 21.1 Details of the data collection in four countries

	CHN	PRT	TUK	USA
Survey platform	Wenjuanxing.com	Google forms	Qualtrics.com	Qualtrics.com
Survey language	Simplified Chinese	Portuguese	Turkish	English
Data collection platform	Social media	Snowball sampling	Social media	Amazon mechanical Turk
Data collection time	Feb 2021	Feb 2021	Feb 2021	Feb 2021
Initial sample size	251	574	275	500
Sample size after screening	239	564	250	500

Authors' own table

during their most recent food shopping trip. The survey also examined consumers' online shopping experiences during the pandemic. Complete answers from 1553 respondents from four countries who passed the attention check questions were recorded and analyzed.

Overall, 44.49% of the survey respondents were female, with 35.63% aged 18–25 years old; 52.00% reported having a college degree or equivalent; 44.14% of the respondents reported being married or in a domestic relationship; and 49.65% reported that they were employed and received wages during the COVID-19 pandemic. Detailed demographic information is listed in Table 21.2.

The findings were condensed into two primary topics, namely, (1) consumers' in-store food procurement behavioral changes during COVID-19 and (2) the factors impacting consumers' in-store food procurement satisfaction. For each topic, we summarized the survey findings, interpreted the findings and the rationale behind changes and their differences across countries, and discussed managerial implications for future business operations.

21.3.2   Changes in Consumers' In-Store Food Procurement

This section examines changes in consumers' food procurement in terms of the shopping time, shopping frequency, transport mode, store type, preventive measures, and shopping experiences during COVID-19 as compared to that before COVID-19.

21.3.2.1   Shopping Time

Survey respondents reported changes in their in-store food procurement time during COVID-19. Before COVID-19, the most common shopping time was in the afternoon (1–5 PM). However, the shopping time window shifted to morning (before 11 AM) and noon (11 AM to 1 PM) during COVID-19, as indicated in Table 21.3.

During COVID-19, with more flexible daily schedules, consumers from all four countries changed the time of their in-store food procurement trips. By coding "Cannot recall" as "N/A," "Morning (before 11 AM)" as 1, and "Evening (after 5

Table 21.2 Demographic information of the sample ($N = 1553$)

	CHN	PRT	TUK	USA
Gender (female %)	71.55%	69.15%	46.40%	36.80%
Age (18–25 %)	63.18%	51.77%	14.00%	15.00%
Education (college degree %)	46.87%	39.01%	63.2%	63.40%
Marital status (married %)	20.08%	25.53%	61.2%	66.00%
Employment (employed %)	35.98%	34.05%	51.60%	75.00%

Authors' own table

Table 21.3 Consumers' in-store food procurement times before and during COVID-19 (N = 1553)

	CHN	PRT	TUK	USA
Before COVID-19				
Morning (before 11 AM)	39.33%	17.37%	6.80%	27.00%
Noon (11 AM to 1 PM)	8.79%	9.22%	20.00%	24.60%
Afternoon (1 PM to 5 PM)	**42.68%**	**63.12%**	**54.00%**	**35.20%**
Evening (after 5 PM)	6.28%	4.43%	9.60%	12.40%
Cannot recall	2.92%	5.86%	9.60%	0.80%
During COVID-19				
Morning (before 11 AM)	**46.44%** (+)	**24.47%** (+)	14.80% (+)	**36.80%** (+)
Noon (11 AM to 1 PM)	12.55% (+)	15.08% (+)	**24.80%** (+)	24.40% (−)
Afternoon (1 PM to 5 PM)	34.32% (−)	51.77% (−)	36.40% (−)	30.40% (−)
Evening (after 5 PM)	6.69% (+)	3.72% (−)	15.20% (−)	7.40% (−)
Cannot recall	0.00%	4.96%	8.80%	1.00%

Authors' own table

PM)" as 4, a paired-sample t-test indicated that consumers from Portugal (M_{Before} = 2.57, M_{During} = 3.37, t = 6.54, p < 0.01), Turkey (M_{Before} = 2.72, M_{During} = 2.54, t = 2.83, p < 0.01), and the USA (M_{Before} = 2.33, M_{During} = 2.08, t = 5.60, p < 0.01) exhibited significant changes in the time they took on in-store food procurement trips, but not consumers from China (M_{Before} = 2.16, M_{During} = 2.01, t = 1.61, p = 0.10).

Next, the analysis of variance (ANOVA) was performed to examine the between-country differences. The results showed no significant differences in the change of shopping time among the different countries (M_{CHN} = 0.17, M_{PRT} = 0.22, M_{TUK} = 0.16, M_{US} = 0.24, F = 0.53, p = 0.66). This result may be due to altered operation time windows in different countries. For example, in the USA, some Walmart stores shortened their regular 24-hour operation time to only 7 AM to 8:30 PM to allow for improved cleaning, restocking, and sustained operations (Walmart, 2020).

21.3.2.2 Shopping Frequency

Survey respondents reported that they had reduced the frequency of food procurement trips since the early outbreak. Before COVID-19, the most common shopping frequency was "2–3 times per week" in all four countries. This frequency decreased to "once per week" during COVID-19 in all countries, as indicated in Table 21.4.

With more flexible daily schedules, consumers from all four countries reduced the frequency of their in-store food procurement trips during COVID-19. By coding "One month or less" as 1 and "More than four times a week" as 5, a paired-sample t-test indicated that consumers from China (M_{Before} = 3.37, M_{During} = 3.00, t = 3.48, p < 0.01), Portugal (M_{Before} = 3.93, M_{During} = 3.10, t = 8.93, p < 0.01), and the USA (M_{Before} = 3.39, M_{During} = 2.99, t = 10.58, p < 0.01) significantly reduced their shopping frequency. The only exception was consumers in Turkey (M_{Before} = 3.55, M_{During} = 3.43, t = 1.58, p = 0.12). The ANOVA was then employed to examine the

Table 21.4 Consumers' in-store food procurement frequencies before and during COVID-19

	CHN	PRT	TUK	USA
Before COVID-19				
Once a month or less	12.97%	3.37%	2.80%	1.60%
2–3 times a month	11.30%	11.17%	7.20%	13.80%
Once a week	21.76%	35.99%	33.60%	36.40%
2–3 times a week	**33.47%**	**41.67%**	**45.20%**	**40.80%**
More than 4 times a week	20.50%	7.80%	11.20%	7.40%
During COVID-19				
Once a month or less	16.74% (+)	4.61% (+)	5.60% (+)	5.20% (+)
2–3 times a month	10.46% (−)	15.96% (+)	7.20% (=)	23.20% (−)
Once a week	**37.25%** (+)	**48.40%** (+)	**38.00%** (+)	**41.80%** (+)
2–3 times a week	27.20% (−)	26.77% (−)	36.80% (−)	27.00% (−)
More than 4 times a week	8.35% (−)	4.26% (−)	12.40% (−)	2.80% (−)

Authors' own table

between-country differences. The results revealed a significant difference in the reduction in change of the shopping frequency among the different countries ($M_{CHN} = 0.37$, $M_{PRT} = 0.40$, $M_{TUK} = 0.12$, $M_{US} = 0.40$, $F = 4.37$, $p < 0.01$).

These results reveal that consumers in the four countries have significantly reduced their in-store food procurement during the pandemic. This result could be due to their safety concerns regarding possible disease transmission in the store. Another explanation could be the altered store operation schedules and the expanded online food procurement industry during the pandemic. For example, in Turkey, online food procurement significantly increased and became the preferred means of food procurement during the pandemic.

21.3.2.3 Transport Mode

Survey respondents reported that they changed their transport modes for food procurement during the pandemic. During the pandemic, public transit was commonly seen as risky (Yıldırım & Güler, 2020). Although governments tried to improve hygiene standards for public transit systems, our survey shows fewer consumers utilized public transit for food procurement.

During COVID-19, consumers from all four countries modified their transport modes for in-store food procurement. Table 21.5 shows that more people chose to use private transportation, such as walking, biking, and driving, while fewer consumers chose to utilize public transit, including buses, subways, and trains. As a result of the lower ridership and the shortage of personnel, public transit systems, such as the Metropolitan Transportation Authority (MTA) in New York City, reduced their operating hours (ITDP, 2020).

In China, slightly more respondents chose to utilize public transportation for in-store food procurement. This result may be due to extremely strict passenger

Table 21.5 Consumers' transport modes for food procurement before and during COVID-19 ($N = 1553$)

	Time	CHN	PRT	TUK	USA
Walk	Before COVID-19	43.93%	14.06%	40.80%	12.20%
	During COVID-19	56.90% (+)	16.19% (+)	44.40% (+)	15.00% (+)
Bike	Before COVID-19	19.67%	0.18%	0.00%	22.80%
	During COVID-19	35.15% (+)	0.36% (+)	7.20% (+)	21.80% (−)
Drive	Before COVID-19	22.18%	79.54%	31.60%	59.40%
	During COVID-19	24.27% (+)	78.83% (−)	42.80% (+)	57.40% (−)
Public transit	Before COVID-19	8.37%	5.16%	1.20%	3.00%
	During COVID-19	9.21% (+)	4.09% (−)	0.40% (−)	1.00% (−)

Authors' own table

monitoring, ventilation, and disinfection measures during the COVID-19 outbreak in China. For example, the ITDP reported that 80% of Chinese cities suspended local public transportation; the metro stations in Beijing were disinfected five times per day, and passengers' body temperatures were screened upon entry into the station (ITDP, 2020). Such procedures may have cultivated a perception of relative safety during the pandemic.

21.3.2.4 Store Type

During COVID-19, changes in consumers' shopping destinations in terms of store types were also noted. The change patterns were mixed. Because of the variation of store types in different countries, we identified the most common store types across different countries for comparison. These stores included national chain supermarkets (e.g., CHN, LianHua, DaRunFa; PRT, Continente, Pingo Doce; TUK, Migros, Carrefour; USA, Walmart, Target), local chain supermarkets (e.g., CHN, not available; PRT, Meu Super, Dia; TUK, Happy Center, Çağrı; USA, Wegmans, Giant Eagle), convenience stores (i.e., CHN, Kede, Quanjia; PRT, gas station, fuel store; TUK, Deli2go, bpShop; USA, 711), and family-owned stores (i.e., CHN, XinFaDi; PRT, Mercado do Bolhao; TUK, Neighborhood Farmers Market, Neighborhood Grocery Store; US, Latham Farmers Market).

As Table 21.6 shows, shoppers from Portugal, Turkey, and the USA utilized national chain supermarkets, local chain supermarkets, and family-owned stores more during COVID-19 compared with that before COVID-19. As the only exception, Chinese shoppers increased the patronization of convenience stores during the pandemic. This result may be due to the fact that convenience stores in China carry a full range of food items, including fresh produce and ready-to-eat items, which fulfilled consumers' essential needs during the pandemic.

Table 21.6 Patronized store types before and during COVID-19

	Time	CHN	PRT	TUK	USA
National chain supermarkets	Before COVID-19	64.44%	87.37%	0.80%	26.10%
	During COVID-19	56.07% (−)	93.42% (+)	4.80% (+)	63.20% (+)
Local chain supermarkets	Before COVID-19	–	32.62%	56.40%	64.60%
	During COVID-19	–	34.93% (+)	59.20% (+)	67.80% (+)
Convenience stores	Before COVID-19	17.99%	6.03%	15.20%	38.80%
	During COVID-19	28.45% (+)	5.32% (−)	13.60% (−)	26.20% (−)
Family-owned stores	Before COVID-19	58.16%	12.77%	47.20%	23.40%
	During COVID-19	35.98% (−)	18.97% (+)	52.80% (+)	24.00% (+)

Authors' own table

Table 21.7 Consumers' in-store preventive measures during COVID-19

	CHN	PRT	TUK	USA
Wearing face masks	94.14%	98.94%	99.60%	89.60%
Wearing face coverings (excluding masks)	5.86%	11.70%	2.00%	14.00%
Wearing gloves	23.01%	1.95%	29.60%	37.80%
Special shopping hours	19.25%	–	47.20%	13.60%
Cart sanitization	17.57%	34.57%	27.20%	38.00%
Social distancing	55.23%	90.78%	92.80%	72.00%
Hand sanitization	42.68%	96.45%	87.20%	60.80%

Authors' own table

21.3.2.5 Preventive Measures

During COVID-19, the most obvious preventive measure that shoppers worldwide adopted was the use of personal protective equipment (PPE), primarily face coverings (e.g., face masks), in public areas. The use of face coverings was enforced by health departments in different countries for in-store patronization. Despite the supply shortage of the PPE at the early stage of the pandemic, PPE supplies were generally available in all countries. Table 21.7 shows the adoption rates of different preventive measures in these four countries during the pandemic.

21.3.2.6 Shopping Experiences

During COVID-19, food consumers had a drastic change in their in-store shopping experiences. These changes manifested in the decreased food supply availability and the increased precautions when shopping in stores. In three out of the four countries surveyed (i.e., CHN, PRT, and the USA), shoppers reported that their in-store food procurement experiences were slightly worse than those before the pandemic. A seven-point Likert scale was used to evaluate consumers' perceptions of food supply, ease of access, payment options, and food price, where 1 was the lowest satisfaction level and 7 was the highest (Table 21.8).

A paired-sample t-test indicated that consumers from China ($M_{Before} = 5.81$, $M_{During} = 5.45$, $t = 5.63$, $p < 0.01$), Portugal ($M_{Before} = 5.94$, $M_{During} = 5.84$, $t = 3.52$, $p < 0.01$), and the USA ($M_{Before} = 5.62$, $M_{During} = 5.41$, $t = 6.37$, $p < 0.01$) reported a significantly worsened in-store shopping experience during the pandemic. The exception was Turkey ($M_{Before} = 5.47$, $M_{During} = 5.90$, $t = -7.56$, $p < 0.01$), where consumers' satisfaction level slightly increased. A possible explanation is that offline food retailers in Turkey frequently announced discount campaigns to attract consumers during the pandemic. Although online food stores significantly expanded their business coverage, offline food stores continued to open new branches during the pandemic.

Then, the ANOVA was adopted to examine the between-country differences in terms of shoppers' in-store food procurement experiences. The results showed that there were significant differences in the in-store shopping satisfaction level between the different countries (from the lowest to the highest: $M_{TUK} = -0.43$, $M_{PRT} = 0.10$, $M_{US} = 0.21$, $M_{CHN} = 0.36$, $F = 50.11$, $p < 0.01$).

At the time of the data collection, COVID-19 had been around for about 1 year, and we hypothesize that the changes in the in-store procurement experiences during COVID-19 were largely due to increased safety concerns. Thus, we hypothesize that in-store shopping safety concerns may contribute to the worsened in-store food procurement experiences.

A seven point Likert scale was used to examine consumers' in-store safety perceptions. A paired-sample *t*-test indicated that consumers from all four surveyed countries perceived that in-store safety worsened during COVID-19. Specifically, China ($M_{Before} = 5.33$, $M_{During} = 4.58$, $t = 5.99$, $p < 0.01$), Portugal ($M_{Before} = 6.57$, $M_{During} = 4.84$, $t = 33.59$, $p < 0.01$), Turkey ($M_{Before} = 6.00$, $M_{During} = 2.66$, $t = 24.72$, $p < 0.01$), and the USA ($M_{Before} = 6.28$, $M_{During} = 4.94$, $t = 18.82$, $p < 0.01$) reported lower ratings during COVID-19 compared with those before COVID-19. A follow-up ANOVA showed that the between-country differences were significant (from the

Table 21.8 Consumers' shopping experiences before and during COVID-19

	CHN	PRT	TUK	USA
Before COVID-19	5.81 (1.12)	5.94 (0.66)	5.47 (0.76)	5.62 (0.75)
During COVID-19	5.46 (1.15)	5.84 (0.72)	5.88 (0.94)	5.41 (0.79)

Authors' own table

lowest to the highest: $M_{CHN} = -0.76$, $M_{US} = 1.33$, $M_{PRT} = 2.09$, $M_{TUK} = 3.34$, $F = 115.10$, $p < 0.01$).

Next, a regression analysis was employed to examine whether safety perceptions impacted the changes in consumers' overall shopping experiences, controlling for their gender, marital status (married or in a relationship = 1, others = 0), and employment status (employed for wages = 1, other = 0), as indicated in Table 21.9, for China, Portugal, and the USA, where there were worse shopping experiences. Worsened safety perception (CHN: $\beta = 0.07$, $t = -2.24$, $p < 0.01$; PRT: $\beta = 0.06$, $t = 3.14$, $p < 0.01$; U.S.: $\beta = 0.11$, $t = 5.44$, $p < 0.01$) was a significant predictor of the change in the shopping experiences. The finding was consistent when the control variables were dropped from the model.

21.4 Study Summary

In this chapter, we have comprehensively analyzed changes in consumers' food procurement behaviors in four distinct countries: China, Portugal, Turkey, and the USA. This chapter strengthens the existing literature by providing a cross-cultural perspective into the social impacts of COVID-19. In-store shopping behavioral changes were analyzed, and the possible causes behind these changes were discussed. To our knowledge, this is among the few empirical studies to provide insights into in-store food procurement using multi-country data during a global health crisis.

From the consumer perspective, results derived from this study indicate that during the pandemic, consumers' in-store food procurement behaviors changed drastically in terms of the shopping time, shopping frequency, transport mode, store type, preventive measures, and shopping experiences across the four countries. From the food retailing perspective, there are many changes to be made, including updating operation systems following national and local public health policies.

Table 21.9 Regression analysis result of the changes in consumers' in-store shopping experiences

	CHN			PRT			TUK			USA		
	Coef.	S.E.	t	Coef.	S.E.	t	Coef.	S.E.	t	Coef.	S.E.	t
Safety perception change	0.07	0.03	2.24	0.06	0.02	3.14	0.03	0.03	1.23	0.11	0.02	5.44
Gender	−0.52	0.14	−3.66	0.06	0.06	0.99	0.1	0.12	0.8	−0.11	0.07	−1.61
Marital status	0.02	0.16	0.14	0.01	0.07	0.18	−0.04	0.12	−0.3	−0.07	0.07	−0.96
Employment status	0.02	0.13	0.18	−0.15	0.07	−2.27	−0.05	0.12	−0.44	−0.11	0.08	−1.48
Intercept	0.44	0.09	4.69	0.003	0.06	0.05	−0.54	0.16	−3.39	0.25	0.09	2.78
R-square	8.69%			2.82%			1.27%			7.50%		

Authors' own table

First, in terms of the *shopping time*, consumers in all countries changed their shopping time during the pandemic. Before COVID-19, afternoon hours were the most common time to shop; however, this preferred shopping time was shifted to morning hours during the pandemic. Consumers, particularly in China, Portugal, and the USA, preferred shopping before 11 AM; on the other hand, more of them chose to shop at noon in Turkey. The different time preferences could be explained by the unique "working from home" practices in Turkey. Since many Turkish people still worked in office buildings during the pandemic, they may have preferred to go shopping during their lunch breaks. In normal times, people in Turkey tend to shop for food after work.

Second, the food *shopping frequency* decreased during the pandemic. This change may have resulted from increased hygiene and safety concerns regarding the rapid spread of the virus in indoor environments. Due to these elevated safety concerns, people preferred to stay home and get their groceries and ready-to-eat foods ordered and delivered from online stores or local stores. Also, local governments encouraged people to support local shops for food deliveries.

Third, during the pandemic, food consumers had different preferences for *transport modes* in all four countries compared to those before the pandemic. In Portugal, Turkey, and the USA, people chose to adopt more private transportation, whereas public transit was the most common transport mode for in-store food procurement in China. This difference could have resulted from the extremely strict health monitoring and disinfection system applied to public transit in China.

Fourth, food consumers had different preferences for *store types* during the pandemic. Our study indicates that when facing different store options, consumers preferred larger supermarkets and family-owned stores, such as farmers' markets, over convenience stores (which normally do not carry fresh produce) during the pandemic. The only exception was China. Chinese consumers increased their patronization of convenience stores during the pandemic. This difference may be due to the unique food retail landscape in China, as many convenience stores and corner stores in China carry a full range of food items, including fresh fruits and vegetables.

Fifth, during the COVID-19 pandemic, people around the world had to adopt new *preventive measures* in their food store visits. They were required to adopt PPE, primarily face masks, and practiced social distancing measures when shopping in stores. The adoption rates of the PPE were considerably high in the four countries (i.e., above or near 90%).

Sixth, food consumers had worsened *shopping experiences* during the pandemic, with the only exception for Turkish consumers. Although Turkish consumers had increased safety concerns, Turkish consumers perceived their in-store food shopping experiences as relatively satisfactory during the pandemic. Surprisingly, they reported even a greater satisfaction level compared with that before the pandemic, albeit not significantly. A critical factor underlying this finding could be the food retailers' marketing strategies in Turkey. Many supermarkets in Turkey announced promotional campaigns during the COVID-19 pandemic (Haberturk, 2021). Although these campaigns were largely criticized by newspapers and social media, Turkish shoppers flocked to stores for deeply discounted items. As a result, many local governments had to temporarily close these stores due to increased health concerns (Haberturk, 2021).

21.5   Managerial Implications

This chapter also sheds insights into the COVID-19 aftermath implications, specifically the food retail industry. There are many changes to be made, including updating operation systems following national and local public health policies. These changes were needed to accommodate the radical changes to people's daily routines, including food procurement. Before COVID-19, consumers patronized various types of stores for food needs. However, during the pandemic, they tended to utilize larger retailers and online retailers for food procurement. As such, retailers need to address consumers' increased hygiene and safety concerns. These consumers' behavioral changes may bring about new competitions as a new food industrial landscape unfolds in the post-pandemic era. We thus propose the following managerial implications for the food retail industry.

Safety and Hygiene Standards After the pandemic, the customers are likely to become more cautious about the in-store safety and hygiene standard than ever before. Therefore, food retailers must prepare for these growing needs. Common areas, including entrances, counters, and shelves, will need to be routinely sanitized to ease shoppers' in-store safety concerns. While retailers must strictly enforce these health and safety guidelines across individual stores, they will also need to improve the communication with the consumers about these guidelines, For example, stores could utilize an "in-store hygiene rating" system, where consumers could rate, comment on, and file complaints about the in-store hygiene and disinfection practices. As a follow-up step, the store managers could respond immediately to consumers' concerns.

Operating Hours During the pandemic, work from home (WFH) was commonly implemented in many countries. Although WFH may be adopted differently post-pandemic, many technology companies, such as Google and Facebook, are likely to allow their employees to WFH permanently. As WFH allows for more flexibility in food procurement, it could shift consumers' shopping time to earlier hours of the day post-pandemic, as the study suggests. Therefore, retailers should consider rearranging their store operating hours (e.g., opening and closing earlier than before) and also adjusting the staff capacity to meet the changing hours.

Online Vending During COVID-19, people had to stay at home to avoid contact with the virus. As such, many consumers switched to online food procurement. However, one study showed that online food prices were comparatively higher than in-store food prices (White, 2016). Thus, it is unclear whether consumers will remain relatively insensitive to food prices and continue online food procurement post-pandemic. Thus, food retailers should consider reaching out to their local communities and identify the online food shopping needs locally to lower the price while maintaining the convenience. Then, they may collaborate with online vendors to regain consumers who choose to continue online shopping.

Supply Chain Management People exhibit panic behaviors, such as hoarding essential items, when facing unexpected situations like COVID-19. Upon the announcement of city lockdowns, shoppers flooded into food stores despite the pandemic threat. Such hoarding behaviors led to food supply shortages in most countries during the early outbreak. In the face of unforeseeable future crises, the food retail industry needs to reconfigure the supply chain, such as improving the monitoring and planning of inventory to ensure affordable food prices. For example, they can engage local producers and suppliers or online vendors in the food supply chain for lower food price and sustaining local food systems. They can also employ new food preparedness innovations (e.g., self-heating food) and emerging distribution channels (e.g., ready-to-cook food by Blue Apron) to achieve higher level of convenience and functionality. These new models were widely preferred during the pandemic.

Indoor Space Reconfiguration The indoor spaces could be reconfigured in three aspects. First, indoor spaces are considered to be breeding grounds for viruses, especially when they are poorly ventilated. Many food retailers operate in an indoor facility, increasing the risk for virus transmission. As the study suggests, consumers tended to shop in large food stores during the pandemic. Therefore, food retailers, especially the national and local chain stores, should prioritize the improvement of the ventilation system by installing air filters that can capture viruses. Also, as the air conditioning system can accelerate the spread of the virus (Chirico et al., 2020), it could be switched to the non-recirculation mode. Second, during the pandemic, large efforts and considerable store spaces were expended on consumer screening (e.g., counting shoppers, checking face covering compliance). In the future, food retailers could relieve these spaces and lower the personnel cost by utilizing modern technologies, such as automatic counting systems, automatic temperature sensors, and face covering detection systems. Third, during the COVID-19 pandemic, consumers widely utilized contactless services for checking store stocking, checking prices, and making payments. In this regard, more self-service facilities (e.g., price checkers, self-checkout counters, voice-controlled kiosks, and e-wallets) can be established to increase shopping flexibility.

Outdoor Space Reconfiguration During the pandemic, public transit was not preferred. As shoppers leaned toward private transport modes, such as walking, bicycling, ride-sharing, and driving, food retailers should consider catering to these changing transportation needs, such as installing more bicycle racks and expanding parking lots. Also, food retailers must consider the increased needs for grocery pick-up, such as installing more roadside pick-up lanes and designating more waiting areas.

Employee Care During the pandemic, food retail employees in all countries were deemed essential workers; and they risked their health for the benefit of others. During and after COVID-19, food retailers should support their employees by all means to increase their overall well-being. Specifically, frontline employees should have their health monitored on a daily basis and should be trained regularly to ensure that they are protected by the highest safety standards. For employees who become infected at work and experience long-lasting health consequences, exclusive and comprehensive health plans should be provided for them. Additionally, retailers should keep a sufficient inventory of PPE items for the employees. Last but not least, the food retailers should encourage their frontline employees for early COVID-19 vaccinations and work collaboratively with local public health departments to prioritize vaccine access for these employees.

21.6 Limitations and Future Research

This study has several limitations. First, this study is focused on the food retail industry and only analyzes consumers' in-store food procurement behaviors in four countries. Future studies could explore other business sectors and more countries to better understand consumers' in-store shopping behaviors. Second, when collecting the data, different countries were at different stages of the pandemic, which may have led to concerns regarding the validity of between-country differences. For example, when collecting data in China, the country had mostly eliminated domestic cases, and many of the pandemic-related measures had been relaxed in low-risk cities. Such time lags may lead to biases in their responses and should be further examined.

21.7 Conclusions

With the ongoing pandemic, the food retail industry is undergoing a major revamp. This chapter aims at exploring the impact of the pandemic on the industry and also proposes adaptation strategies to situations after the pandemic. We have examined food consumers' behavioral changes in four distinct countries: China, Portugal, Turkey, and the USA. These behavioral changes were analyzed, and possible causes behind these changes were discussed. After that, we have proposed the managerial implications for food retailers to better prepare for the post-pandemic situations. To our knowledge, this is one of the first empirical studies to provide insights into in-store food procurement behaviors using multi-country data during a global health crisis.

References

Abiral, B., & Atalan-Helicke, N. (2020). Trusting food supply chains during the pandemic: Reflections from Turkey and the U.S. *Food and Foodways, 28*(3), 226–236. https://doi.org/1 0.1080/07409710.2020.1790147

Ali Taha, V., Pencarelli, T., Škerháková, V., Fedorko, R., & Košíková, M. (2021). The use of social media and its impact on shopping behavior of Slovak and Italian consumers during COVID-19 pandemic. *Sustainability, 13*(4), 1710. https://doi.org/10.3390/su13041710

Baker, S. R., Bloom, N., Davis, S. J., Kost, K., Sammon, M., & Viratyosin, T. (2020a). The unprecedented stock market reaction to COVID-19. *Review of Asset Pricing Studies, 10*(4), 742–758. https://doi.org/10.1093/rapstu/raaa008

Baker, S. R., Farrokhnia, R. A., Meyer, S., Pagel, M., Yannelis, C., & Pontiff, J. (2020b). How does household spending respond to an epidemic? Consumption during the 2020 COVID-19 pandemic. *The Review of Asset Pricing Studies, 10*(4), 834–862. https://doi.org/10.1093/rapstu/raaa009

Ben Hassen, T., El Bilali, H., & Allahyari, M. S. (2020). Impact of COVID-19 on food behavior and consumption in Qatar. *Sustainability, 12*(17), 6973. https://doi.org/10.3390/su12176973

Bradbury-Jones, C., & Isham, L. (2020). The pandemic paradox: The consequences of COVID-19 on domestic violence. *Journal of Clinical Nursing, 29*(13–14), 2047–2049. https://doi.org/10.1111/jocn.15296

Chang, H.-H., & Meyerhoefer, C. D. (2021). COVID-19 and the demand for online food procurement services: Empirical evidence from Taiwan. *American Journal of Agricultural Economics, 103*(2), 448–465. https://doi.org/10.1111/ajae.12170

Chen, J. (2020). Experiencing graduated intimacies during lockdown (Fengcheng): A reflexive and comparative approach to the COVID-19 pandemic in urban China. *Anthropology in Action, 27*(2), 9–19.

Chen, X., Zhang, A., Wang, H., Gallaher, A., & Zhu, X. (2021). Compliance and containment in social distancing: Mathematical modeling of COVID-19 across townships. *International Journal of Geographical Information Science, 35*(3), 446–465.

Chedid, Y., Ubaide, H., Sani, I., & Hamza, Y. (2020). What about BAME? A letter to the editor on 'The socio-economic implications of the coronavirus pandemic (COVID-19): A review'. *International Journal of Surgery, 81*, 105–106. https://doi.org/10.1016/j.ijsu.2020.07.046

Cheng, E., & Lee, Y. N. (2021). New chart shows China could overtake the U.S. as the world's largest economy earlier than expected. *CNBC*. Retrieved from: https://www.cnbc.com/2021/02/01/new-chart-shows-china-gdp-could-overtake-us-sooner-as-covid-took-its-toll.html

Chirico, F., Sacco, A., Bragazzi, N. I., & Magnavita, N. (2020). Can air-conditioning systems contribute to the spread of SARS/MERS/COVID-19 infection? Insights from a rapid review of the literature. *International Journal of Environmental Research and Public Health, 17*(17), 6052.

Chronopoulos, D. K., Lukas, M., & Wilson, J. O. S. (2020). Consumer spending responses to the COVID-19 pandemic: An assessment of Great Britain. *SSRN*. https://doi.org/10.2139/ssrn.3586723

Cranfield, J. A. L. (2020). Framing consumer food demand responses in a viral pandemic. *Canadian Journal of Agricultural Economics, 68*(2), 151–156. https://doi.org/10.1111/cjag.12246

Goncalves, S., & Khalip, A. (2021). UPDATE 2-Portugal's economy fell 7.6% in 2020, biggest drop since 1936. *Reuters*. Retrieved from: https://www.reuters.com/article/portugal-economy-gdp/update-2-portugals-economy-fell-7-6-in-2020-biggest-drop-since-1936-idUSL8N2K82CL

Grashuis, J., Skevas, T., & Segovia, M. S. (2020). Food procurement preferences during the COVID-19 pandemic. *Sustainability, 12*(13), 5369.

Gray, R. S. (2020). Agriculture, transportation, and the COVID-19 crisis. *Canadian Journal of Agricultural Economics, 68*(2), 239–243. https://doi.org/10.1111/cjag.12235

Guney, O. I., & Sangun, L. (2021). How COVID-19 affects individuals' food consumption behaviour: A consumer survey on attitudes and habits in Turkey. *British Food Journal*. https://doi.org/10.1108/Bfj-10-2020-0949

Haberturk. (2021). *Kırmızı Kategorideki Sivas'ta İndirim Covid'i Unutturdu.* Retrieved from: https://www.haberturk.com/sivas-haberleri/86151829-kirmizi-kategorideki-sivasta-market-indirimi-covid-19u-unutturdu-valilik-karari-ile-market

Hayes, D. J., Schulz, L. L., Hart, C. E., & Jacobs, K. L. (2021). A descriptive analysis of the COVID-19 impacts on U.S. pork, Turkey, and egg markets. *Agribusiness, 37*(1), 122–141. https://doi.org/10.1002/agr.21674

Ivanov, D. (2020). Predicting the impacts of epidemic outbreaks on global supply chains: A simulation-based analysis on the coronavirus outbreak (COVID-19/SARS-CoV-2) case. *Transportation Research Part E: Logistics and Transportation Review, 136*, 101922. https://doi.org/10.1016/j.tre.2020.101922

Insititute for Transportation & Development Policy (ITDP). (2020). *How China kept transit running during Covid-19.* Retrieved from: https://www.itdp.org/2020/07/03/how-china-kept-transit-running-during-covid-19/

Khandpur, N., Zatz, L. Y., Bleich, S. N., Taillie, L. S., Orr, J. A., Rimm, E. B., & Moran, A. J. (2020). Supermarkets in cyberspace: A conceptual framework to capture the influence of online food retail environments on consumer behavior. *International Journal of Environmental Research and Public Health, 17*(22), 8639. https://doi.org/10.3390/ijerph17228639

Koch, J., Frommeyer, B., & Schewe, G. (2020). Online shopping motives during the COVID-19 pandemic—Lessons from the crisis. *Sustainability, 12*(24), 10247.

Kuxukgomen, A. (2021). Turkey emerges from COVID-19-hit 202 with 1.8% economic growth. *Reuters.* Retrieved from: https://www.reuters.com/article/us-turkey-economy-gdp/turkey-emerges-from-covid-19-hit-2020-with-1-8-economic-growth-idUSKCN2AT1UE

Leone, L. A., Fleischhacker, S., Anderson-Steeves, B., Harper, K., Winkler, M., Racine, E., Baquero, B., & Gittelsohn, J. (2020). Healthy food retail during the COVID-19 pandemic: Challenges and future directions. *International Journal of Environmental Research and Public Health, 17*(20), 7397. https://doi.org/10.3390/ijerph17207397

Li, J., Hallsworth, A. G., & Coca-Stefaniak, J. A. (2020). Changing food procurement behaviours among Chinese consumers at the outset of the COVID-19 outbreak. *Tijdschrift voor Economische en Sociale Geografie, 111*(3), 574–583. https://doi.org/10.1111/tesg.12420

Loske, D. (2020). The impact of COVID-19 on transport volume and freight capacity dynamics: An empirical analysis in German food retail logistics. *Transportation Research Interdisciplinary Perspectives* 6, 100165.

Naeem, M. (2020). Understanding the customer psychology of impulse buying during COVID-19 pandemic: Implications for retailers. *International Journal of Retail and Distribution Management, 49*(3), 377–393. https://doi.org/10.1108/IJRDM-08-2020-0317

Naja, F., & Hamadeh, R. (2020). Nutrition amid the COVID-19 pandemic: A multi-level framework for action. *European Journal of Clinical Nutrition, 74*(8), 1117–1121. https://doi.org/10.1038/s41430-020-0634-3

Nakat, Z., & Bou-Mitri, C. (2020). COVID-19 and the food industry: Readiness assessment. *Food Control, 121*, 107661.

Nicola, M., Alsafi, Z., Sohrabi, C., Kerwan, A., Al-Jabir, A., Iosifidis, C., & Agha, R. (2020). The socio-economic implications of the coronavirus pandemic (COVID-19): A review. *International Journal of Surgery, 78*, 185–193. https://doi.org/10.1016/j.ijsu.2020.04.018

O'Donnell, N., Shannon, D., & Sheehan, B. (2021). Immune or at-risk? Stock markets and the significance of the COVID-19 pandemic. *Journal of Behavioral and Experimental Finance, 30*. https://doi.org/10.1016/j.jbef.2021.100477

Pekosz, A. (2020). *COVID-19 Scholl of public health expert insights.* Retrieved from: https://www.jhsph.edu/COVID-19/articles/no-COVID-19-is-not-the-flu.html

Petetin, L. (2020). The COVID-19 crisis: An opportunity to integrate food democracy into post-pandemic food systems. *European Journal of Risk Regulation, 11*(2), 326–336. https://doi.org/10.1017/err.2020.40

Pu, M., & Zhong, Y. (2020). Rising concerns over agricultural production as COVID-19 spreads: Lessons from China. *Global Food Security, 26*, 100409.

Satici, B., Gocet-Tekin, E., Deniz, M. E., & Satici, S. A. (2020). Adaptation of the fear of COVID-19 scale: Its association with psychological distress and life satisfaction in Turkey. *International Journal of Mental Health and Addiction*, 1–9. https://doi.org/10.1007/s11469-020-00294-0

Trollman, H., Jagtap, S., Garcia-Garcia, G., Harastani, R., Colwill, J., & Trollman, F. (2021). COVID-19 demand-induced scarcity effects on nutrition and environment: Investigating mitigation strategies for eggs and wheat flour in the United Kingdom. *Sustainable Production and Consumption, 27*, 1255–1272.

Vieira, A., Ricoca, V. P., Aguiar, P., Sousa, P., Nunes, C., & Abrantes, A. (2021). Years of life lost by COVID-19 in Portugal and comparison with other European countries in 2020. *BMC public health, 21*(1), 1–8.

Walmart. (2020). *Temporary changes to our hours to better serve customers*. Walmart.com. Retrieved from: https://corporate.walmart.com/newsroom/2020/03/14/temporary-changes-to-our-hours-to-better-serve-customers

White, M. (2016). *Here's how much extra money you spend buying groceries online*. Money.com. Retrieved from: https://money.com/online-groceries-prices-comparison/

Wang, Y., Xu, R., Schwartz, M., Ghosh, D., & Chen, X. (2020). COVID-19 and retail food management: Insights from a broad-based consumer survey. *IEEE Engineering Management Review, 48*(3), 202–211. https://doi.org/10.1109/EMR.2020.3011054

World Health Organization. (2021). *WHO Coronavirus (COVID-19) dashboard*. Retrieved from: https://covid19.who.int/region/euro/country/pt

Wuhan Municipal Health Commission. (2020). *Expert interpretation of the latest notification of unexplained viral pneumonia*. Retrieved from: http://wjw.wuhan.gov.cn/gsgg/202004/t20200430_1199592.shtml

Xu, J., Gao, M., & Zhang, Y. (2021). The variations in individual consumption change and the substitution effect under the shock of COVID-19: Evidence from payment system data in China. *Growth and Change, n/a*(n/a). https://onlinelibrary.wiley.com/doi/epdf/10.1111/grow.12477

Yıldırım, M., & Güler, A. (2020). COVID-19 severity, self-efficacy, knowledge, preventive behaviors, and mental health in Turkey. *Death Studies*, 1–8. https://doi.org/10.1080/07481187.2020.1793434

Chapter 22
COVID-19 Pandemic and Agriculture: Potential Impact on Legumes and Their Economic Value Chain

Mangena Phetole

22.1 Introduction

Currently, the novel coronavirus disease (COVID-19) that has emerged in Wuhan, China, at the end of December 2019 has rapidly swept across the world infecting millions of people in more than 200 countries. While the virus's exact origin is still under investigations, preliminary research analyses on phylogenetic inferences and genetic sequence analysis suggest that this virus comes from bats, even though the mechanism of dissemination to humans is still unknown (Alanagreh et al., 2020). According to Hu et al. (2015), there are various species of *Rhinolophidae* bats, especially *Rhinolophus sinicus* (horseshoe bats), that harbor genetically diverse strains of coronavirus that cause respiratory diseases in humans. Such diseases include the severe acute respiratory syndrome coronavirus (SARS-Cov) and Middle East respiratory syndrome (MERS), which were also previously reported in China. Within the *Coronaviridae* family, genera such as the *Alphacoronavirus* and *Betacoronavirus* were also reported to mainly infect mammalians, with human coronavirus 229E (HCoV-229E) and human coronavirus NL63 (HCoV-NL63) also transmitted by bats (Hu et al., 2015; Vassilara et al., 2018).

However, there is inadequate literature on the socioeconomic impacts of HCoV-199E and HCoV-NL63, particularly, forecast of the much expected impact of the novel COVID-19 that has already brought world health, travel, and the markets into a standstill. The noticeable changes caused by the new coronavirus already suggest that agricultural services and food supply will be adversely affected, especially in regions like Latin America, Caribbean states, and sub-Saharan Africa where food

M. Phetole (✉)
Faculty of Science and Agriculture, Department of Biodiversity, School of Molecular and Life Sciences, University of Limpopo, Sovenga, Republic of South Africa
e-mail: Phetole.Mangena@ul.ac.za

© The Author(s), under exclusive license to Springer Nature Switzerland AG 2022
N. Faghih, A. Forouharfar (eds.), *Socioeconomic Dynamics of the COVID-19 Crisis*, Contributions to Economics, https://doi.org/10.1007/978-3-030-89996-7_22

security worsened in recent years (FAO, 2020). In contrast, overwhelming literature exists that provide information on how predominant epidemics such as HIV/AIDS or malaria harmfully affect the livelihoods of individuals, communities, and the economy. Additionally, FAO (2020) has already made clear indications that this new crisis may have severe impacts on crop production, particularly harvesting and post-harvest processing of legume crops that are expected to currently enter the market.

Legume crops form part of a large genera of flowering plants along with cereals, all serving as significant sources of feed and balanced nutrition for many people and livestock worldwide. Grain legumes (also known as pulses) are predominant basis for dietary fiber, carbohydrates, vitamins, nitrogen-rich proteins, vegetable oils, and mineral nutrients that are contained within the seeds. These crops provide a greater quality of proteins that are rich in essential amino acids such as lysine and trypto-phan. The crops help to complement cereals that were found to be low in lysine and tryptophan amino acids but comprise significant amount of methionine (Ncube et al., 2016). Furthermore, legumes constitute more than two-thirds of the 80% calo-ries and proteins supplied by plants worldwide (Singh & Singh, 1992). Human beings have utilized legume crops (*Leguminosae*) for decades since the dawn of civilization. Crop species selection and domestication were exclusively based on the plant's growth habit, nutritional value, and health benefits. There are many nutri-tional and functional characteristics already identified in numerous grain legume species across the temperate, subtropical, and tropical regions.

Grain legumes contain about 750 genera and 19,000 plant species that are found within the *Fabaceae* family, which were further divided into three subfamilies: *Caesalpinoideae*, *Mimosoideae*, and *Papilionoideae*. The subdivisions comprise of most of the major cultivated food and feed legume crop species (Table 22.1) (De Ron et al., 2013; Graham & Vance, 2003). Additionally, these crops serve as cover crops that provide soil protection and assist to improve soil characteristics by sup-plying nitrogen as well as serving as green manure. Legumes used as cover crops are normally grown in rotation with the normal cash crops. The legumes used as both forage and grain cover about 180 million hectares, which amounts to an esti-mated 15% of the world's arable agricultural land (Graham & Vance, 2003). According to Graham and Vance (2003), the 15% outlined above accounts for more than 27% of the world's primary agricultural production. This clearly indicates that legumes have a critical role to play in the different sectors of the economy including forestry, fisheries, pharmaceuticals, manufacturing, health, and commercial ser-vices. Legumes are second to *Gramineae* in improving the social and economic structure of countries, particularly for the benefit of the population, gross domestic product (GDP) growth, occupational structure, and education.

Therefore, crop production systems involving legumes serve as a reliable and sustainable solution to alleviate poverty, hunger, and diseases. The increase in grain legumes that enter the domestic and international markets in both processed and raw forms will provide economic stability in many developing countries where people are faced with many socioeconomic and health challenges. Among the health chal-lenges, pandemics such as malaria, HIV/AIDS, cholera, Ebola, and many others have adversely affected the livelihoods of millions of individuals, households, and

Table 22.1 Legumes and examples of cereal crops used for food and feed production. Species of *Leguminosae* and *Gramineae* are also used as cover crops or intercropping, in the tropical, subtropical, and temperate regions

	Common name
Legume crops	
Cajanus cajan	Pigeon pea
Canavalia ensiformis	Jack bean
Cicer arietinum	Chickpea
Dolichos lablab L.	Lablab
Glycine max (L.)	Soybean
Lathyrus sativus	Grass pea
Lens culinaris	Lentils
Mucuna spp.	Mucuna beans
Pisum sativum	Peas
Phaseolus lunatus	Lima beans
Phaseolus vulgaris	Kidney beans
Vigna angularis	Adzuki beans
Vigna faba	Faba beans
Vigna mungo	Black gram
Vigna radiata	Mung beans
Vigna unguiculata	Cowpea
Cereal crops	
Avena sativa	Oats
Digitaria exilis	Fonio
Eragrostis tef	Teff
Fagopyrum esculentum	Buckwheat
Hordeum vulgare	Barley
Oryza sativa	Rice
Pennisetum glaucum	Millet
Phalaris canariensis	Canary grass
Secale cereale	Rye
Saccharum officinarum	Sugarcane
Sorghum bicolor	Sorghum
Triticum spelta	Spelt
Triticum durum	Durum wheat, macaroni wheat
Triticum aestivum	Bread wheat
Zea mays	Maize, corn

Reference sources: Akibobe and Meredia (2012), Fageria et al. (2013) and Amosse et al. (2014)
Author's own table

communities. Gatiso et al. (2018) reported a decrease in household income and crop production in Liberia following the Ebola virus disease (EVD) outbreak. HIV/AIDS was also reported to have negative effects on farm labor availability, crop productivity, consumption/purchase of agricultural products, and health status in rural southeastern Uganda (Parker et al., 2009). These health disasters, including the impact of climate change, have the potential to catalyze the threat to human lives and agricultural production and cause a collapse of the economy in many countries.

This chapter will, therefore, provide a comprehensive review on the trade of major grain legumes, agricultural productivity, and socioeconomic shock expected to be experienced as a consequence spreading of the novel coronavirus disease. The chapter will briefly discuss the predicted impacts of COVID-19 on rural communities subjected to strict curfew regulations. It will report on the unrealized potential of legume agriculture on improving the livelihoods of households in poorer communities and furthermore discusses ways in which modern agricultural technologies may be adopted and used to avert the threat of food insecurity during the lockdown period across the world. Lastly, this chapter will briefly deliberate on how cultivation challenges such as the lack of disease-resistant cultivars, abiotic stress-tolerant varieties, drought, the lack of mechanization, and limited government support on legume research collectively contribute to the lagging transformation in agriculture, whose negative consequences will be much experienced by developing countries during this COVID-19 pandemic outbreak.

22.2 Importance of Legumes in Agriculture, Agro-processing, and the Economy

The extent of legume cultivation, distribution, and use had significantly influenced the population density, growth, and economic prosperity levels, particularly in countries like China, the United States, India, and Nigeria (FAO, 2018). Arable land area cultivated with legumes have been extensively expanded in these countries, amounting to millions of hectares with over hundreds mega tons of yields per annum. Interestingly, legume cultivation allows for the use of varied cropping systems that may involve intercropping, mixed cropping, and rotations of either vegetable or dry grains with cereals (Li et al., 2017). They play an important role in the farming systems and the diets of many people, especially in reducing poverty, improving human nutrition and health, and enhancing ecosystem resilience (Akibobe & Meredia, 2012). Legumes have been under cultivation using traditional and modern agricultural systems for hundreds of years. In China, the cultivation of legumes is widespread, with mung bean and adzuki cultivation dating back to more than 2000 years (Li et al., 2017). This remains a clear indication of the extent to which grain legumes (or vegetable food legumes) have become an integral part of the Chinese cropping systems for generation in both traditional and sustainable modern agriculture.

Legume crops remain key components for providing affordable, high quantity and quality content of dietary proteins and lipids. Table 22.2 illustrates estimates of the protein and lipid content in the seeds of selected legume species. The highest total protein content was detected in the seeds of soybean and velvet bean. The

Table 22.2 Protein and lipid content in the seeds of selected major grain legumes

Crop species	Proteins (g kg^{-1})	Lipids (g kg^{-1})
Black gram	251	18
Broad bean	236	2.55
Chickpea	173	51
Common bean	194	≤9
Cowpea	121.7	58.47
Dry bean	192	24
Faba bean	226	12.5
Lentil	268	1.3
Mung bean	240	12.2
Pea	233	15
Soybean	314	201
Velvet	314.4	67.3
Total average	230	39.36

Sources: Siddhurajan et al. (1996), Yoshida et al. (2009), Fageria et al. (2011), Gasim et al. (2015), Dahiya et al. (2015), Mohatla et al. (2016), Solomon et al. (2017), Grela et al. (2017), and Olivera-Castillo et al. (2017)
Author's own table

Table 22.3 Protein and lipid content in the seeds of major selected cereal crops

Crop species	Proteins (g kg^{-1})	Lipids (g kg^{-1})
Barley	132	35
Corn	102	41
Oat	125	47
Rice	105	22
Sorghum	88	35
Wheat	113	17
Total average	110.8	32.8

Sources: Siddhurajan et al. (1996) and Fageria et al. (2011)
Author's own table

same species were also characterized by a high content of lipids. Among these selected and analyzed legumes, soybean exhibited the highest levels of proteins and lipids even when compared to cereals in Table 22.3. A ban on grain legume export due to COVID-19, particularly an agricultural supply of major commodities such as soybean, will lead to a rapid rise in global soy price and, subsequently, increase in food prices. Food legumes like broad bean (*Vicia faba* L), pea (*Pisum sativum* L), chickpea (*Cicer arietinum*), lentil (*Lens culinaris* Medik), common bean (*Phaseolus vulgaris* L), mung bean (*Vigna radiata* Wilczek), cowpea (*Vigna unguiculata* L. Walp), velvet bean (*Mucuna pruriens*), black gram (*Vigna mungo* (L.) Hepper), pigeon pea (*Cajanus cajan* (L.) Millsp.), and soybean (*Glycine max*

(L.) Merrill) serve various important roles and diversified recipes in ordinary food dishes whose preparation ensures abundant protein contents for the basic nutrition and health of both urban and rural communities across the world (Table 22.2) (Wallace et al., 2016).

Food legumes represent a critical component of agricultural processing for manufacturing of a myriad of products, including foods, nutraceuticals, and pharmaceuticals. The use of legume crops in the manufacturing and tertiary sectors of the economy strengthens the linkages that exist between farmers (small-scale or large-scale business) and the agricultural value chain (Shimeles et al., 2018). According to Verdier-Chouchane and Karagueuzian (2016), these important linkages can be sustainably maintained by improving investments in agricultural technology and innovation that functions mainly to increase crop productivity as well as grain quality in addition to the use of improved agricultural processing technology. In many cases, enhanced crop productivity causes an increase in the growth of agro-processing, which ultimately stimulates agricultural growths by creating the need for expansion and new output markets and increasing farmers' input costs and income (Dube et al., 2018). Studies indicate that improving the use of legume value chain will reveal the nutritional and health benefits required by people faced with challenges such as food insecurity and diseases.

These prospects, including the required improvements in seeds/grain quality, production, stress resistance, post-harvest handling, and marketing, will alleviate the declining legume agri-business in the sector in general or as a result of COVID-19. Furthermore, Chibarabada et al. (2017) stated that improving the sector could also unlock significant economic opportunities for marginalized population groups such as women and children in developing countries. In line with the previous report, Singh and Singh (1992) also reported that approximately 75% of the total world yield of legumes is produced by developing countries, especially rural communities who still rely on conventional agricultural practices for their subsistence. Among this, 12% of this world's total production comes from sub-Saharan Africa where many women and children are still living under extreme poverty and undernourishment. Thus, the production of legumes generally and particularly those that serve as major agricultural commodities needs to be continuously utilized to tackle hunger, malnutrition, and the fight against disease outbreaks. However, many farmers have realized the significant contributions of these crops and their enhanced profitability to the farming business, attributed to the three times higher protein content of the seeds than what is found in cereals (Tables 22.2 and 22.3). Their overall seed composition in the amount of proteins, lipids, carbohydrates, vitamins, fiber, phytochemicals (isoflavonoids, flavonoids, or phenolics), and micronutrients makes the nutritional and economic value of grain legumes to be competitively greater than that of cereals (Dube et al., 2018; Shimeles et al. 2018).

22.3   Current Performance of Grain Legumes in Agriculture

Approximately, more than 90% of the world population depends on agriculture for their food and livelihood. Chibarabada et al. (2017) stated that in South Asia and Sub-Saharan Africa alone, an estimated 70% of the population depend on agriculture, with about 281 and 224 million people, respectively, experiencing some form of undernourishment. However, given the previous and current disease outbreaks (e.g., Ebola and COVID-19), in addition to the uncontrollable population growths, and climate change, these figures are certainly expected to rise drastically in 2021 and beyond. Another factor is the dominant consumption of meat proteins on the daily diets of many populations, especially in developed countries. Roos et al. (2018) reported that a transition toward a less resource-demanding diet is required, to ensure a move from a diet containing animal products to a more plant-based diet, particularly food legumes. Other challenges include the lack of suitable crop varieties for cultivation under unfavorable climatic conditions, water scarcity or drought, the lack of agro-processing facilities used to provide functional legume-based ingredients for food industries, and poor consumer knowledge about the benefits of eating legume-based foods (Roos et al., 2015, 2018).

All of the abovementioned challenges impose negative impacts on the production and trade of legumes, as well as the legume processing industries. From about 30 grain legumes grown for subsistence and farming business, only cowpea, chickpea, dry bean, pigeon pea, and soybean account for more than 90% of the grain legume production reaching the world market (Chibarabada et al., 2017). The remainder of the grain legumes make a combined contribution of less than 10% of food legumes involved in import/export agri-business. These serve as an indication that any upward trends recorded in the increase of grain legume production and trade are always associated with the improved performance of an individual crop species than the whole group of edible legumes, both at farm and business level. As such, continued emergence of sudden pandemics like COVID-19 surge is bound to disrupt progress and continued efforts of increasing the improvement and development of legume-based products. According to the Observatory of Economic Complexity data, legumes were the most traded products with a total of over 1.54 billion US dollars. But between 2017 and 2018, legume exports fell by −0.86% from about 1.55 billion to 1.54 billion USD (OEC, 2020). However, China remained the biggest producer of food legumes due to its wider cultivation of peanuts, followed by India, the United States, Argentina, and Nigeria (Fig. 22.1). Legume production in these countries can be expected to decline like other agricultural commodities due to the business restriction caused by the spread of the COVID-19.

Furthermore, the price of grain legumes has also increased by 5% in real terms from 1990 to 2008 due to output and input production costs, including per capita availability for consumption. It is worth noting that price increases of food legumes are also fueled by the inadequate supply of grains, especially considering the general economic terms. Consumption of grain legumes has also increased at an annual

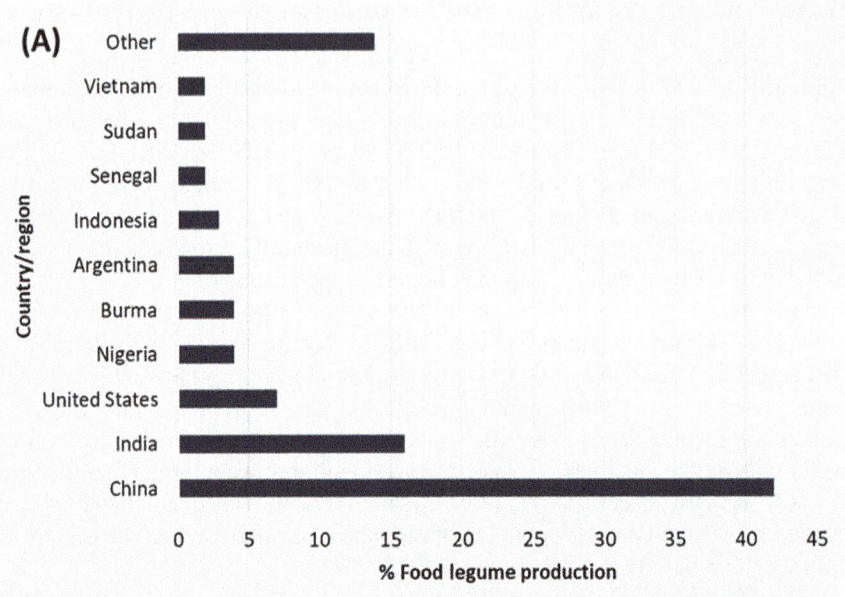

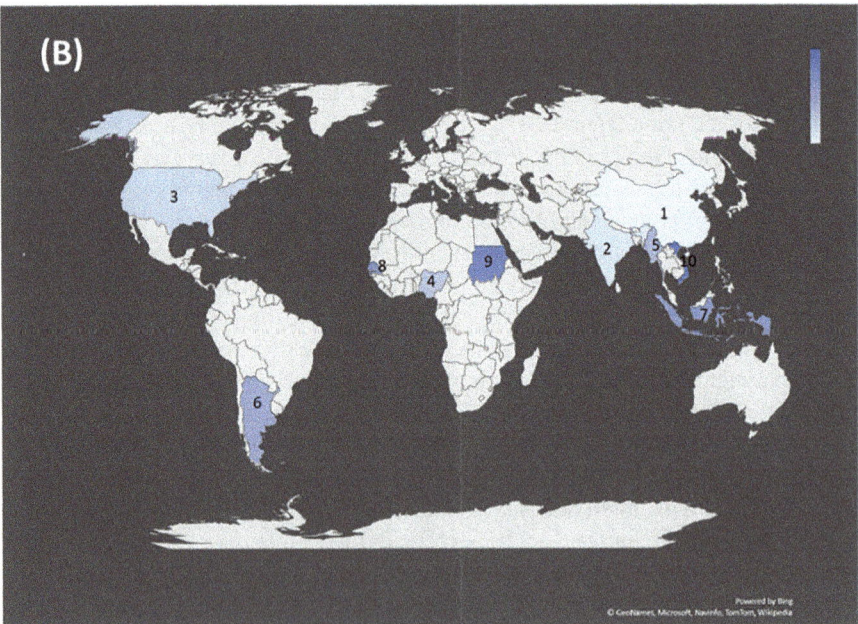

Fig. 22.1 Production and distribution of food legumes in major countries worldwide, which is expected to decline due to COVID-19 surge. The illustrated countries are ranked in ascending order in terms of their average traded quantities in 2019 (Rawal & Navarro, 2019; Merga & Haji, 2019). (Author's own figure)

rate of 1.8% and to more than 35% in developing countries (Anderson et al., 1999, Nedumaran et al., 2015). The demand continues to increase for grain processing in the livestock feed supplement industry, legume foods, and bio-diesel manufacturing, indicating the need for a radical shift in the price structure and utilization patterns of grain legumes. According to their global distribution (Fig. 22.1), these crop species remain the most relevant source of proteins and oil for human food and animal feeds, as well as to prevent diet-related diseases and economic depression (De Ron et al., 2013). A wider global distribution of crop production systems involving legumes is still required in regions that have greater potential and are still not explored for legume cultivation. Although not steady, world legume production has been increasing, reaching a new heights of over hundred million metric tons for selected species such as soybean, peanuts, chickpea, and peas according to recent FAO estimates (FAO, 2018).

22.4   Effect of the COVID-19 Pandemic on Legume Productivity

The grain legumes still lag behind cereals in terms of the area of cultivation and productivity gains. Relative importance of 12 grain legumes that are grown all over the world under different environmental conditions are illustrated in Fig. 22.2. Nedumaran et al. (2015) reported that high cereal productivity, competition from cereal crops, preference and research focus on cereals, and the unstable pulse prices are some of the factors leading to the overall poor performance of grain legumes in the entire agricultural sector. However, these current and future projections could be exacerbated by the COVID-19 outbreak. According to FAO recommendations, planting and harvesting of important legumes such as soybean may proceed but at a speedy pace in regions such as South America (Argentina, Brazil, Bolivia, Paraguay, and Uruguay), Central Africa (Democratic Republic of Congo), and Eastern Africa (Ethiopia, Kenya, and Uganda) (FAO, 2020).

These FAO recommendations were made while many countries were still battling to cope with the COVID-19 surge by introducing new measures to reduce human labor mobility and impose curfews during this pandemic outbreak period. As previously indicated by FAO (2020), the agricultural sector and its production activities are undoubtedly expected to be compromised across the board, turning the health of production, farmers, and farmworkers, as well as the consumers into a system shock. Undoubtedly, legume production will be negatively affected by the pandemic because their agricultural services primarily require adequate number of well-skilled personnel in order to achieve surplus crop production through both small-scale and business farming. Legume production requires improved varieties, inoculants, fertilizer applications, agro-chemicals, machinery, high labor capacity, proper irrigation system, and other extension services carried out by experienced farm works and owners.

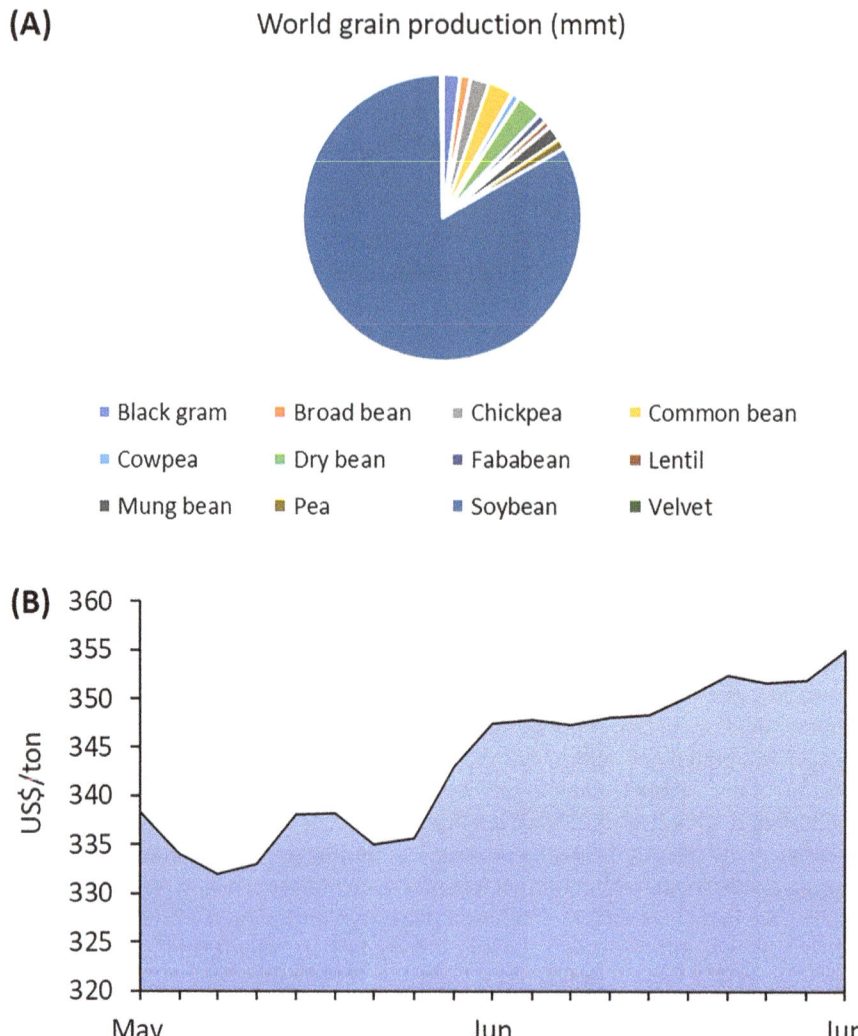

Fig. 22.2 Estimated distribution of the 12 important grain legumes based on market conditions of legumes' major commodities. (**a**) Shows relative value of the legumes as leading food crops. (**b**) IGC grain statistics and oilseed index for legumes in general on month-to-month basis (IGC, 2020; FAO, 2020). (Author's own figure)

However, the work force is simply not readily available due to the rapid spread of COVID-19. Although legumes are still cultivated as marginal crops, largely preferred for rotation and intercropping with cereal crops, their cultivation has to be continued. Additionally, De Ron et al. (2013) reported that crop production systems involving legumes are further favored due to the sustainable role that they play to improve soil properties and their ability to fix atmospheric molecular nitrogen during symbiotic association with *Rhizobia* and to serve as cover crops. Nonetheless, crop production is disturbed by countries implementing and imposing restricting regulations on the different sectors of the economy in both essential and nonessential services. Many did so, based on the impact of the outbreak and rate of COVID-19 infections. Generally, as the virus spreads and cases upsurge worldwide, there are seemingly countless ways in which crop production will soon be hampered by the pandemic. For example, FAO (2020) has highlighted that COVID-19 appears to have already affected seasonal crop cultivation, agro-processing, and logistics of movement of legume grains to different industries for processing.

FAO stated that it is highly likely that the COVID-19 pandemic will result in increased prices of grains and oilseeds, even though the emerging pandemic's overall effects on the agricultural markets are still largely unknown. Most current assessments generally predict a contraction in both supply and demand for agricultural products due to the widely experienced disruption in trade and logistics. Possible reductions in legume production may be attributed to the impact of the current pandemic outbreak to both small-scale producers and agribusiness, eventually trimming world outputs in 2020/2021 to a lower figure. Moreover, the International Grains Council (2020) indicated that the total use of major legume commodities may remain unchanged (on month-to-month basis) at a record of 363 million tons with stocks being lifted on an uprated outlook and the increasing traded volumes influenced by enlarged demand for consumption in Asia (Fig. 22.2).

Furthermore, in comparison to other important crops, the council (IGC, 2020) also predicted a slight increase in world total grain production for maize, wheat, and rice in 2019/2020 (Table 22.4). Major legume commodities such as soybean forecast a much lower global 2019/2020 production, estimated to decrease by 2 million tons (a drop of 7% on a year per year basis) to about 336 million metric tons (Table 22.4). The decreased production together with the scale of processing industries, lack of added value, and differentiation in legume agro-food chain may continue soaring the level of prices much higher than those in the past. International and

Table 22.4 The current standard projections for production and trade of the world's leading grain and oilseed crops

Grain and oilseed	Sub-index	Annual change (%)	2019/2020 production forecast (mt)	2019/2020 trade forecast (mt)
Barley	185	−7	304	157
Maize	172	−15	1118	168
Rice	188	17	497	43
Soybean	181	−1	336	153
Wheat	179	−3	762	178
Total	192	−2	2177	380

Sources: International Grains Council (2020) and COCERAL (2020)
Author's own table
Note: mt million tons

domestic markets will be transversely affected, specifically with negative impacts on the poor in developing countries (Jouan et al., 2019).

The disruption caused in agriculture also implies that cereal prospects for 2020 will still be favorable compared to grain legume crops. Reduction in the labor force mobility will, therefore, have a direct effect on the harvesting of winter irrigated crops. According to the International Crop Research Institute for the Semi-Arid Tropics, the May/June onward period in India is known as the *rabi* season in which legumes like dry bean, gram, and lentil, as well cereals like wheat, cultivated under irrigated tract have reached harvestable stages or are almost at maturity (ICRISAT, 2020). Furthermore, this is also the time when farm harvest in India reach the *mandis* (market) for further processing and trade following approval/purchase by government agencies. The coronavirus outbreak thus leaves agribusiness without harvesting operations and post-harvesting handling of produce in storage and marketing centers. Although international bodies like FAO, the World Health Organization (WHO), and the World Bank Group (WBG) have called for countries to maintain trade flows during the COVID-19 crisis to secure access to essential goods and services, many countries have done less to support domestic production and maintain cross-border or international legume value chain. Thus, projections for grain legume productivity will remain low, especially given that the farming system mainly relies on family's capital and labor force among others, for attaining improved yield productions (Shimeles et al., 2018).

22.5 Effect of Pandemics on the Labor Force and Agriculture

In recent years, the world has already experienced devastating economic losses in agriculture as a result of drought and other major human/animal or plant disease outbreaks. According to de la Fuente et al. (2019), in 2014–2015, devastating human and economic effects were felt by west African countries (Guinea, Sierra Leone, and Liberia), of which Liberia was the hardest hit following the Ebola outbreak. International trade and travel were severely disrupted due to restrictions imposed within Ebola-affected countries. The indirect economic effects resulting from fears of the surge of infections and domestic/international disease containment measures negatively influenced crop production. Generally, under these circumstances, the use of full-time employees or hired workers will be lower, especially in districts containing high number of pandemic incidences. HIV/AIDS was also reported by FAO (2018) to cause a decline of agricultural productions in general and food production in particular. Grain legumes such as beans, groundnuts, and peas, followed by cereals (rice, millet, and maize) were reported to be highly susceptible to HIV/AIDS since they are much more labor-intensive. The many ways in which crop production can be affected include farmer or farmworkers' absenteeism from work due to HIV-related illnesses and the loss of labor from AIDS-related deaths.

All these factors may lead to the reduction of the area of crop cultivation and to the declining yield that may ultimately result in reduced food production and threat to food security. The evidence with respect to the impact of various pandemics like the ones mentioned above on legume agriculture still remain scattered and not well-documented. Much as little is known about the current COVID-19 pandemic. Nonetheless, the already observed effects of COVID-19 demonstrate that farmworkers and farm owners should be supported and provided with the much needed resources to prevent the spread of this disease. Furthermore, this important sector of the economy should be supported to sustain ongoing grain production and trade, radically minimizing potential crushing effects of the pandemic on agricultural production and the entire economy.

22.6 Farmworkers and Farmers' Preparedness for COVID-19 Outbreak

In agriculture, farmworkers and farmers occupy a central place in enhancing food security and economic growth, reducing poverty, and ensuring rural development. These people are at the forefront, leading the most essential sector that can ensure socioeconomic growth by ensuring sustainable development of agriculture in developed and undeveloped countries. Even during this pandemic, most rural poor people still have to depend on agriculture for their livelihoods. Mbagwu et al. (2018) stated that agriculture remains a limestone for many rural communities and their local economy. Therefore, the role of farmworkers and farmers cannot be over-emphasized even during the surging COVID-19 infections across the globe. But farmworkers and farmers' mobility and work during this outbreak period potentially put many lives at risk for exposure to the novel coronavirus. Steege et al. (2009) highlighted that because of limited resources, substandard living conditions, immigration challenges, communication problems, cultural barriers, and discrimination, farmworkers are more vulnerable than the general population. Furthermore, the lack of COVID-19 vaccine, risk reduction training, personal protective equipment, and workplace sanitation and poor general sanitization pose unique exposures and different risks to farmworkers than those faced by farm owners.

Villarejo and Baron (1999) reported that farmworker's lack of health insurance coverage, poverty, inadequate household/individual income, and geographically inaccessible health services put them at high risk than farmers. Without regular access to primary health care, farmworkers are less likely to receive educational materials regarding the novel coronavirus outbreak, personal protective equipment, social distancing, and sanitization. Although unanticipated, COVID-19 pandemic should trigger an emergency alarm for governments to identify priorities for surveillance of farmworkers and farmers. Urgent interventions are necessary by government agencies, health experts, advocates, policy experts, and the private sector to identify issues and urgently generate recommendation regarding farmers and farmworkers' preparedness for COVID-19 response measures. Like other pandemic outbreaks such as malaria, HIV/AIDS, and Ebola, the current disease poses serious risks to legume agriculture and jeopardize international trade.

22.7   Potential Consequences of the Pandemic on Legume Improvement

Although most agricultural commodities' trade and prices have been broadly stable during this pandemic outbreak, some markets began to experience pressure from numerous production, economic, and social factors. The spread of COVID-19 pandemic already exerted pressure on the supply chain, weakened the demand, imposed trade restrictions, and generally caused a decline in the availability of agricultural raw materials. With this worldwide spread of diseases and food insecurity emerging as one of the major policy issues, the structure and operations of key agricultural supply chains need to be optimized (Ge et al., 2015). In order for the agricultural sector to meet demands of the producers and ultimately the consumers they serve, supply chain must improve alignment between crop breeders' efforts and crop production. There is a long-standing relationship between the formal seed system and farming system, with subsequent inclusion of the market, processing industries, and the consumers. Bishaw and Turner (2008) also emphasized that there is a strong link between formal plant breeding system and seed supply. This link serves to collect, conserve, and manage plant genetic resources, improve the germplasm to provide new genetic combinations, and redistribute the newly improved varieties to benefit farmers and consumers (Fig. 22.3).

The reports indicate that effective crop breeding generates new and improved varieties that stimulate organized seed multiplication and marketing by commercial companies. The breeding systems, both conventional and modern, remain the main avenue used to maximize the diffusion and impact of food legumes on gross domestic product (GDP) growth, food security, education, disease alleviation, poverty, and unemployment as illustrated in Fig. 22.3. Owing to the coronavirus outbreak, the demand for improved legume crops and their products will be rapidly increased. The observed restrictions and regulations imposed during this period will result in both domestic and international crop production constraints that unable the sector to meet its demand. The COVID-19 threat on crop improvement and supply chain may be similar to the severe acute respiratory syndrome (SARS) in 2003 and influenza A virus subtype H7N9 (H7N9) in 2013 that severely impacted China's population health and the economy (Qiu et al., 2018). The ability of these diseases to cause reduction of more than 50% of the labor force in various sectors also suggests prohibitions on many plant breeding programs across the globe as some of the nonessential services banned during the lockdown. Galanakis (2020), however, highlighted the importance of sustainability in the seed supply and farming systems in order to reduce the frequency of relevant food and health crisis.

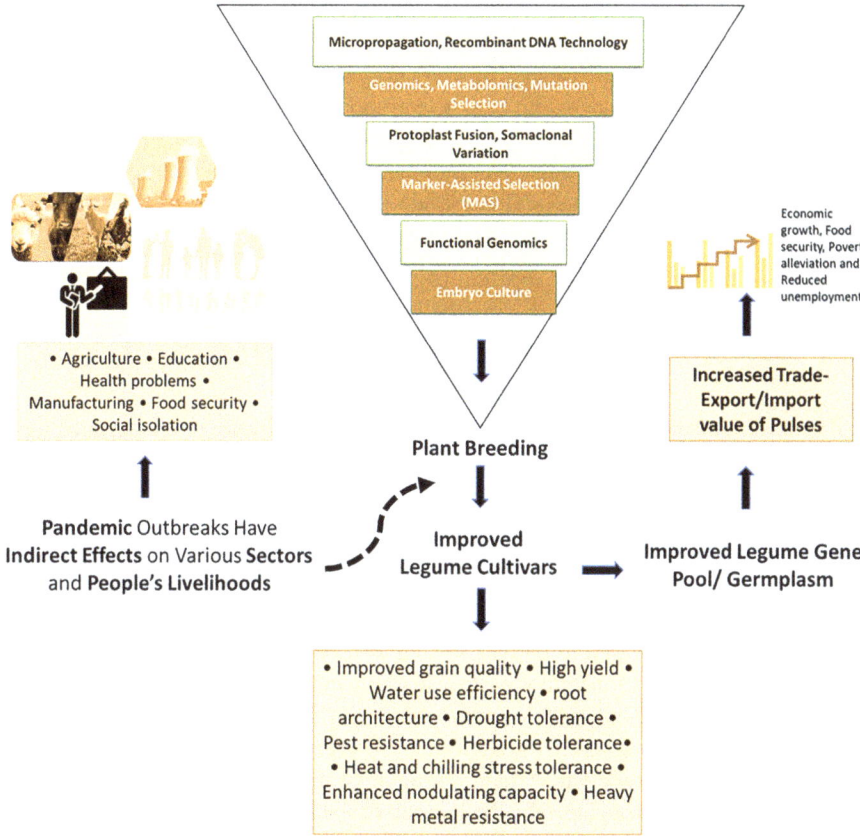

Fig. 22.3 Techniques used for crop improvement of food legumes and their role in the farming systems and agricultural supply chains. These genetic improvement strategies can be potentially explored for use in the development of nutritionally and medicinally enhanced legume varieties utilized in the alleviation of disease outbreaks. (Author's own figure)

Apart from legumes serving as important source of feed and nutrition for humans and animals because of their relatively high seed content of proteins and essential amino acids (Jacob et al., 2016), legume plants provide protein-derived bioactive peptides with many essential roles as health-promoting compounds. The different activities of the peptides include immunomodulatory effects and opioid-like activities (Mejia & Dia, 2010). Immunomodulatory pathways of antimicrobial agents will be very critical in modulating genes involved in immune reactions or neurohormonal systems which regulate immune functions against viruses such as the novel coronavirus (Polak et al., 2015). Breeding of legume crops for improved fiber, proteins, vitamins, and valuable phytochemicals must be continuously sustained in order to develop varieties that may be used to boost the immune systems of consumers infected with such pandemic diseases. Legumes contain remarkable molecular contents, which can be further investigated through advanced genomic and bioinformatic tools to accelerate breeding strategies involved in developing new traits for biofortification (Duc et al., 2015; Cakir et al., 2019). Therefore, legumes can be easily adapted as a strategy to avert global food shortage problem, meanwhile improving the human health response systems against some of the emerging severe respiratory infections. However, as indicated by Cakir et al. (2019), any discussion about legumes that do not take into consideration their genomic properties, susceptibility to biotic and abiotic stress, trade, consumption, value chain, and nutritional and health benefits would be insignificant.

22.8   Mitigation Strategies During COVID-19 Outbreak

To ensure the functionality of crop production and food system, risks, impacts, and vulnerabilities in each of the stages involved on the agricultural value chain must be analyzed (Fig. 22.4). The evaluation and analysis can assist in pinpointing priority areas for developing policies, programs, and investments in agriculture. The developed framework could be used to monitor the use and management of readily available food resources while ensuring continued crop production to support functioning of the food systems and food security. According to FAO, the COVID-19 pandemic framework and all emerged initiatives related to food and agriculture form part of strategic activities of national public interest, requiring special attention and support from all bodies of the individual countries, as well as the support of the general world population. Recognizing the important differences that exist between stages involved in the agricultural value chain, the analysis given in Fig. 22.4 identifies the main risk and impact areas faced by the legume-based food system during the period

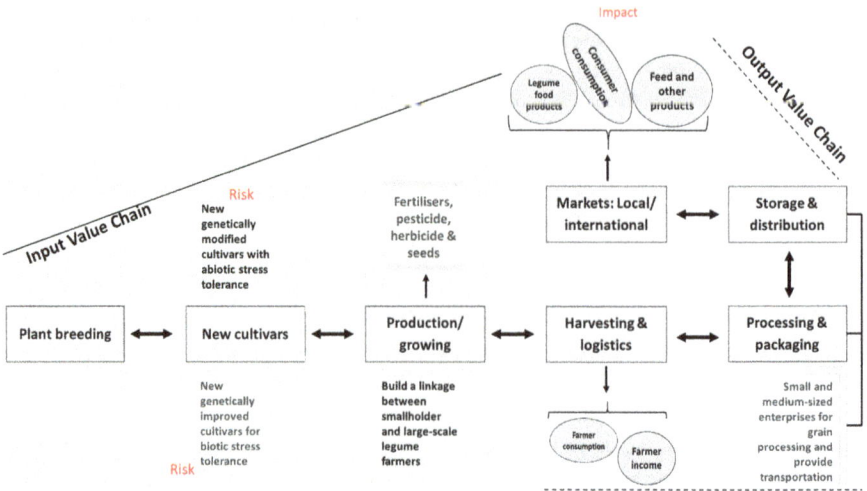

Fig. 22.4 Identifying COVID-19 critical risk and impact area on legume crop production in the agricultural and trade value chain. (Author's own figure)

of the COVID-19 pandemic. The activities can be classified and prioritized according to their different degrees of importance and exposure to COVID-19 risk and impact.

The African region, for example, is among the territories where the COVID-19-associated risks and impacts can be especially serious. According to the United Nations' policy brief, in Africa, hundreds of millions of people were already suffering from hunger and malnutrition before the emergence and spread of the coronavirus (FAO, 2018; Vanlauwe et al., 2019). The report indicated that any further food system disruptions by COVID-19 can result in severe consequences for health and nutrition at a scale unseen for more than half a century. These continued hunger manifestations should be thoroughly monitored at the different stages, from breeding/crop production until the purchase and consumption of agricultural products. As global production trends in grain legumes (pulses, groundnuts, and soybeans) were increasing, even doubling from 148 to over 250 million tons due to an increase in demand for protein meals and oil in the food and feed industry (Gowda et al., 2009), the share of developing countries in the global grain legume production is, however, currently expected to decrease as agricultural operations and trade across borders are restricted. Quarantines and other restrictions will subsequently fuel the severe and long-lasting negative impacts that will be much felt by these developing countries than developed nations.

Food security policies of governments that function to direct agricultural research and extension services are normally responsible for the slow-paced growth of grain legume production in developing countries (Kumar et al., 2014). Many of these countries have increased reliance on grain imports to meet the growing domestic agricultural demands. However, the status quo is to remain as long as these countries continue to obtain low and stagnant yield as a result of drought and lack of transformation in agriculture. Currently, the effects of COVID-19 pandemic on food production in these countries will vary depending on agricultural and food system strategies developed in each country. FAO (2020) indicated that COVID-19 effects will become more profound as the virus continues to spread over time in the absence of additional complementary policies. As such, the impact on food supply, including food legumes, will rely upon crop production rates, developed regulations and trade structures of the countries, levels of curfews, and other market-related issues.

Generally, given these factors, risks and impact analysis in each of the countries' agricultural sector have to be analyzed. Furthermore, risks and vulnerabilities in the food supply have to be determined in order to develop alternative policies and programs in response to COVID-19 (FAO, 2019). Such measure could include joined ventures and cooperation by two or more countries and resource and capacity development to support small-scale farmers who will be the hardest hit and give special attention and support to farm workers and industrial processing workers involved in the agricultural value chain. As indicated by Villarejo and Baron (1999), farm workers are at high risk of contracting the virus than most of the people exposed to the pandemic due to the lack of personal protective equipment and health insurance. However, the main risk remains the ability for countries to guarantee population's access to food and basic services during the outbreak.

22.9   Final Remarks and Conclusions

The main risk caused by the novel coronavirus pandemic will be the loss of income for poor populations complying with health security measures to prevent the spread of the virus. Severe impacts will be felt by countries with the highest levels of poverty, unemployment, and food insecurity since their population's ability to save will decrease. The possible rise in food prices serve also as a threat to food security in low-income families, especially in countries in which the currencies have been devalued. Marginalized populations seeking new sources of employment, food, and health care may be at increased risk of morbidity and mortality from the pandemic owing to several factors including limited economic resources, proper housing, transportation, and hygiene barriers. Steege et al. (2009) previously emphasized that lack of health resources generally make interventions to deal with any severe outbreak of pandemics difficult or impossible to implement, especially among people at lower-income levels.

However, the impact of COVID-19 pandemic on agriculture can be assessed in terms of loss of revenue, unavailability of labor, logistical challenges, and internal/external trade restrictions. The pandemic's impact upon pre-epidemic market share will be inevitably greater and more persistent despite the magnitude of possible trade losses recorded. Furthermore, the effects of the pandemic on crop production and food supply may be classified as "direct," wherein its overall negative impacts on cultivation, harvest, and produce transportation/processing may show ripple effects. COVID-19 has caused immediate and pronounced changes in global food supply systems and consumer food demand (Ker & Cardwell, 2020). While downstream distribution and demand are likely to be hampered by this pandemic, FAO (2019) still projected sharp increases in grain legumes and legume food supply between 2019 and 2020 season attributed to the larger planting in some areas and availability of market stocks. Grain prices are expected to remain stable during this COVID-19 period due to generally well-stocked markets in most countries, resulting from good quantity and quality of harvests in the period 2018–2019, as well as regular internal and cross-border trade flows before emergence of the pandemic.

Some of the additional factors that positively contribute to price stability include availability of off-season products, reduced institutional purchases, reduced regional conflicts (trade and civil wars), and smooth trade-border flows that enable good supply (FAO, 2019). Furthermore, it is worth noting that rainfall deficits in 2019 caused significant production declines across the globe. Southern Africa was severely impacted by frequent droughts, and the reduced first season harvest in East Africa is a result of cyclone damage, leading to constrained production prospects. Expectedly, the combined direct/indirect effects of the pandemic and other crop growth-inhibiting factors (biotic/abiotic stress) on agricultural systems across the globe will be soon witnessed. For example, quarantines and other restrictions are severely affecting labor availability for long breeding programs and large time-critical farming activities (Stephens et al., 2020). This outbreak poses high risks to many other supply chains (Figs. 22.3 and 22.4) distinctively due to long-term disruptions, ripple effects, and highly uncertain future. These COVID-19 impacts are likely to become more widely and deeply felt in the agricultural sector as the crisis continues to escalate (Stephens et al., 2020; Ivanov, 2020).

In conclusion, the most direct economic and social impact of COVID-19 will be the loss of income. But economic sectors like agriculture are likely to suffer from loss of crop productivity, leading to the anticipated shortage of food supply. Already existing reports showed that populations' health depends on high personal hygiene and what people eat. A significant shift from meat-protein-based food to legume plant-based diet is necessary given the multitudes of health benefits associated with the consumption of food legumes. Agriculture remains a multidimensional sector, requiring different forms of interventions to ensure food supply. Its two main critical dimensions (i.e., irrigated and dry land) also demand different levels of sensitivities, plans, and strategies in order to maximize crop yield.

However, the lack of critical resources such as water persuades farmers to invest in breeding programs in order to be assured of decent returns even under periods of any pandemic outbreaks. Direct losses as a result of COVID-19 would be caused by the pandemic itself, while indirect losses are attributed to quarantines or restrictions as a result of the pandemic. Thus, governments are also required to strengthen immediate economic and social relief initiatives. Among these, dry legume seed systems have to be strengthened in order for agriculture to adequately support food and nutrition security.

Acknowledgments This work was supported by the Department of Biodiversity/School of Molecular and Life Sciences and the Department of Research Administration and Development, in the University of Limpopo, Republic of South Africa.

References

Akibobe, C. S., & Meredia, M. K. (2012). *Global and regional trends in production, trade, and consumption of food legume crops*. SPIA report. Department of Agricultural, Food and Resource Economics, Michigan State University, USA, AgEcon Search-Research in Agricultural and Applied Economics, pp. 1–88. https://doi.org/10.22004/ag.econ.136293

Alanagreh, L., Alzoughool, F., & Atoum, M. (2020). The human coronavirus disease COVID-19: Its origin, characteristics and insights into potential drugs and its mechanisms. *Pathogens, 9*(331), 1–11. https://doi.org/10.3390/pathogens9050331

Amosse, C., Jeuffroy, M. H., Mary, B., & David, C. (2014). Contribution of relay intercropping with legume cover crops on nitrogen dynamics in organic grain systems. *Nutrient Cycling in Agroecosystems, 98*, 1–14. https://doi.org/10.1007/s10705-013-9591-8

Anderson, J. W., Smith, B. M., & Washnock, C. S. (1999). Cardiovascular and renal benefits of dry bean and soybean intake. *The American Journal of Clinical Nutrition, 70*(3), 4645–4745. https://doi.org/10.1093/ajcn/70.3.464s

Bishaw, Z., & Turner, M. (2008). Linking participatory plant production to the seed supply system. *Euphytica, 163*, 31–44. https://doi.org/10.1007/s10681-007-9572-6

Cakir, O., Ucarli, C., Tarhan, C., Pekhez, M., & Turgut-Kara, N. (2019). Nutritional and health benefits of legumes and their distinctive genomic properties. *Food Science Technology Campinas, 39*(1), 1–12. https://doi.org/10.1590/fst.42117

Chibarabada, T. P., Mabhaudhi, T., & Modi, A. T. (2017). Expounding the value of grain legumes in the semi– And arid tropics. *Sustainability, 9*, 60. https://doi.org/10.3390/su9010060

COCERAL. (2020). *Grain and oilseeds forecasts*. Bruxelles, Belgium. Available at: http://www.coceral.com/web/june%202020/1011306087/list1187970814/fl.html. Date accessed 30 May 2020.

Dahiya, P. K., Linnemann, A. R., Van Boekel, M. A. J. S., Khetarpaul, N., Crewal, R. B., & Nout, M. J. R. (2015). Mung bean: Technological and nutritional potential. *Critical Reviews in Food Science and Nutrition, 55*, 670–688. https://doi.org/10.1080/10408398.2012.671202

de la Fuente, A., Jacoby, H. G., & Lawin, K. G. (2019). *Impact of the west African Ebola epidemic on agricultural production and rural welfare- evidence from Liberia*. Poverty and equity global practice working paper 207, World Bank Group, pp. 1–36.

De Ron, A. M., Cubero, J. I., Singh, S. P., & Aguilar, O. M. (2013). Cultivated legume species. *International Journal Agronomy, 2013*, Article ID324619. https://doi.org/10.1155/2013/324619

Dube, S. C., das Nair, R., Nkhonjera, M., & Tempia, N. (2018). *Structural transformation in agriculture and agro-processing value chains*. Centre for Competition, Regulation and Economic Development, University of Johannesburg.

Duc, G., Agrama, H., Bao, S., Berger, J., Bourion, V., De Ron, A. M., Gowda, C. L. L., Mikic, A., Millot, D., Singh, K. B., Tullu, A., Vandenberg, A., Palto, M. C. V., Warkentin, T. D., & Zong, X. (2015). Breeding annual grain legumes for sustainable agriculture: New methods to approach complex traits and target new cultivar ideotypes. *Critical Reviews in Plant Sciences, 34*(1–4), 381–411. https://doi.org/10.1080/07352689.2014.898469

Fageria, N. K., Baligar, V. C., & Jones, C. A. (2011). *Growth and mineral nutrition of field crops* (3rd ed., pp. 1–11). CRC Press.

Fageria, N. K., Ferreira, E. P. B., Baligar, V. C., & Knupp, A. M. (2013). Growth of tropical legume cover crops as influenced by nitrogen fertilisation and rhizobia. *Communications in Soil Science and Plant Analysis, 44*, 3103–3119. https://doi.org/10.1080/00103624.2013.832283

Food and Agricultural Organisation of the United Nations. (2018). *Impact of HIV/AIDS on agriculture*. Available at http://www.fao.org/3/ac912e/ac912e06.htm. Date accessed: 8 June 2020.

Food and Agricultural Organisation of the United Nations. (2019). *Crop prospects and food situation*. Vaile delle Terme di Caracalla, Rome, Italy, pp. 1–40. Available at: www.fao.org/giews/. Date accessed: 1 July 2020.

Food and Agricultural Organisation of the United Nations. (2020). *FAO recommendation on planting and harvesting tasks during the COVID-19 outbreak using crop calendars*. Available at http://www.fao.org/2019-ncov/covid-19-crop-calendars/en/. Date accessed: 8 June 2020.

Galanakis, C. M. (2020). The food systems in the era of the coronavirus (COVID-19) pandemic crisis. *Food, 9*(523), 1–10. https://doi.org/10.3390/foods9040523

Gasim, S., Hamad, S. A. A., Abdelmula, A., & Ahmed, A. M. (2015). Yield and quality attributes of faba bean inbred lines grown under marginal environmental conditions of Sudan. *Food Science & Nutrition, 3*(6), 539–547. https://doi.org/10.1002/fsn3.245

Gatiso, T. T., Ordaz-Nemeth, I., Grimes, T., Kuhl, H. S., & Junker, J. (2018). The impact of the Ebola virus disease (EVD) epidemic on agricultural production and livelihoods in Liberia. *PLoS Neglected Tropical Diseases, 12*(8), e0006580. https://doi.org/10.1371/Journal.pntd.0006580

Ge, H., Gray, R., & Nolan, J. (2015). Agricultural supply chain optimisation and complexity: A comparison of analytic vs simulated solutions and policies. *International Journal of Production Economics, 159*, 208–220. https://doi.org/10.1016/j.ijpe.2014.09.023

Gowda, C. L. L., Rao, P., & Bhagavatula, S. (2009). *Global trends in production and trade of major grain legumes*. International conference on grain legumes: Quality improvement, value addition and trade, Indian Society of Pulse Research and Development, Indian Institute of Pulses Research, Kanpur, India. February 14–16. pp. 1–20.

Graham, P. H., & Vance, C. P. (2003). Legumes: Importance and constraints to greater use. *Plant Physiology, 131*, 872–877. https://doi.org/10.1104/pp.017004

Grela, E. R., Kiczorowska, B., Samolinska, W., Matras, J., Kiczorowski, P., Rybinski, W., & Hanczakowska, E. (2017). Chemical composition of leguminous seeds: Part I – Content of basic nutrients, amino acids, phytochemical compounds, and antioxidant activity. *European Food Research and Technology, 243*, 1385–1395. https://doi.org/10.1007/s00217-017-2849-7

Hu, B., Ge, X., Wang, L. F., & Shi, Z. (2015). Bat origin of human coronaviruses. *Virology Journal, 12*, 221. https://doi.org/10.1186/s12985-015-0422-1

International Crops Research Institute for the Semi-Arid Tropics (ICRISAT). (2020). *Containing Covid-19 impacts on Indian agriculture.* ICRISAT Bulletin April 18, 2020. Available at http://www.icrisat.org/containing-covid19-impacts-on-indian-agriculture/. Date accessed: 9 June 2020.

International Grains Council. (2020). *Grain market report.* United Kingdom, London. Available at: https://www.igc.int/en/default.aspx. Date accessed: 21 May 2020.

Ivanov, D. (2020). Predicting the impacts of epidemic outbreaks on global supply chains: A simulation-based analysis on the coronavirus outbreak (COVID-19/SARS-CoV-2) case. *Transportation Research Part E: Logistics and Transportation Review, 136*, 101922. https://doi.org/10.1016/j.tre.2020.101922

Jacob, C., Carrasco, B., & Schwember, A. R. (2016). Advances in breeding and biotechnology of legumes crops. *Plant Cell, Tissue and Organ Culture, 127*, 561–584. https://doi.org/10.1007/s11240-016-1106-2

Jouan, J., Ridier, A., & Carof, M. (2019). Economic drivers of legume production: Approached via opportunity costs and transaction costs. *Sustainability, 11*(705), 1–14. https://doi.org/10.3390/su11030705

Ker, A. P., & Cardwell, R. (2020). Introduction to the special issue on COVID-19 and the Canadian agriculture and food sectors: Thoughts from the pandemic onset. *Canadian Agricultural Economics Society*, 1–40. https://doi.org/10.1111/cjag.12245

Kumar, A., Sharma, P., & Ambrammal, S. K. (2014). Climate effects on food grain productivity in India: A crop-wise analysis. *Journal of Studies in Dynamics and Change, 1*(1), 38–48.

Li, L., Yang, T., Liu, R., Redden, B., Maalouf, F., & Zong, X. (2017). Food legume production in China. *The Crop Journal, 5*(2), 115–126. https://doi.org/10.1016/j.cj.2016.06.001

Mbagwu, F. C., Benson, O. V., & Onuoha, C. O. (2018). *Challenges of meeting information needs of rural farmers through internet-based services: Experience from developing countries in Africa.* The world library and information congress, 84th international federation of library and information conference, Malaysia, July 2018, pp. 1–9.

Mejia, E. G., & Dia, V. P. (2010). The role of nutraceutical proteins and peptides in apoptosis, angiogenesis, and metastasis of cancer cells. *Cancer Metastasis Reviews, 29*(3), 511–528. https://doi.org/10.1007/s10555-010-9241-4

Merga, B., & Haji, J. (2019). Economic importance of chickpea: Production, value and world trade. *Cogent Food & Agriculture, 5*, 1615718. https://doi.org/10.1080/23311932.2019.1615718

Mohatla, K., Mokoboki, K., Sebola, N., & Mashilo, J. (2016). Chemical composition and dry matter yield of cowpea (*Vigna unguiculata* L. Walp) haulms as fodder for ruminants. *Journal of Human Ecology, 56*(12), 77–83. https://doi.org/10.1080/09709274.2016.11907040

Ncube, O., Ndlovu, E., & Maphosa, M. (2016). Physiology of legume grain in formal markets used as seed: Implications for food and nutrition security. *Journal of Food Security, 4*(6), 126–130. https://doi.org/10.12691/jfs-4-6-1

Nedumaran, S., Abinaya, P., Jyosthnaa, P., Shraavya, B., Parthasarathy, R., & Bantilan, C. (2015). *Grain legume production, consumption, and trade trends in developing countries.* Working paper series no. 60, International Crops Research Institute for the Semi-Arid Tropics (ICRISAT), Patancheru, Telangana, India, p. 64.

Observatory of Economic Complexity. (2020). Legume report. Available at http://www.oec.world/en/profile/hs92/207081. Date accessed: 20 May 2020.

Olivera-Castillo, L., Pereira-Pacheo, F., Polanco-Lugo, E., Olivera-Novoa, M., Rivas-Burgos, J., & Grant, G. (2017). Composition and bioactive factor content of cowpea (*Vigna unguiculata* L. Walp) raw meal and protein concentrate. *Journal of the Science of Food and Agriculture, 87*, 112–119. https://doi.org/10.1002/jsfa.2684

Parker, D. C., Jacobsen, K. H., & Komwa, M. K. (2009). A qualitative study of the impact of HIV/AIDS on agricultural households in South-Eastern Uganda. *International Journal of Environmental Research and Public Health, 6*(8), 2113–2138. https://doi.org/10.3390/ijerph6082113

Polak, R., Phillips, E. M., & Campbell, A. (2015). Legumes: Health benefits and culinary approaches to increase intake. *Clinical Diabetes, 33*(4), 193–205. https://doi.org/10.2337/diaclin.33.4.198

Qiu, W., Chu, C., Mao, A., & Wu, J. (2018). The impacts on health, society, and economy of SARS and H7N9 outbreaks in China: A case comparison study. *Journal of Environmental and Public Health, 2018*, Article ID 2710185. https://doi.org/10.1155/2018/2710185

Rawal, V., & Navarro, D. K. (2019). *The global economy of pulses* (pp. 1–190). Food and Agriculture Organisation of the United Nations (FAO). Available at: http://www.fao.org/3/i7108en/i7108en.pdf. Date accessed: 5 June 2020

Roos, E., Karlsson, H., Witthoft, C., & Sundberg, C. (2015). Evaluating the sustainability of diets-combining environmental and nutritional aspects. *Environmental Science & Policy, 47*, 157–166.

Roos, E., Carlsson, G., Ferawati, F., Hefni, M., Stephan, A., Tidaker, P., & Witthoft, C. (2018). Less meat, more legumes: Prospects and challenges in the transition toward sustainable diets in Sweden. *Renewable Agriculture and Food Systems*, 1–14. https://doi.org/10.10147/SI742170518000443

Shimeles, A., Verdier-Chouchane, A., & Boly, A. (2018). Introduction, understanding the challenges of the agricultural sector in sub-Saharan Africa. In A. Shimeles, A. Verdier-Chouchane, & A. Boly (Eds.), *Building a resilient and sustainable agriculture in sub-Saharan Africa* (pp. 9–10). Palgrave Macmillan. https://doi.org/10.1007/978-3-319-76222-7_1

Siddhurajan, P., Vijayakumari, K., & Janardhanan, K. (1996). Chemical composition and protein quality of the little-known legume, velvet bean (*Mucuna pruriens* (L.) DC). *Journal of Agricultural and Food Chemistry, 44*, 2636–2641. https://doi.org/10.1021/jf950776x

Singh, V., & Singh, B. (1992). Tropical grain legumes as important human foods. *Economic Botany, 46*(3), 321–331.

Solomon, S. G., Okomoda, V. T., & Oda, S. O. (2017). Nutritional value of toasted pigeon pea, *Cajanus cajan* seed and its utilisation in the diet of *Clarias gariepinus* (Burchell, 1822) fingerlings. *Aquaculture Reports, 7*, 34–39. https://doi.org/10.1016/j.aqrep.2017.05.005

Steege, A. L., Baron, S., Davis, S., Torre-Kilgore, J., & Sweeney, M. H. (2009). Pandemic influenza and farmworkers: The effects of employment, social and economic factors. *American Journal of Public Health, 99*(Suppl. 2), S308–S315. https://doi.org/10.2105/AJPH.2009.161091

Stephens, E. C., Martin, G., van Wijk, M., Timsina, J., & Snow, V. (2020). Impact of COVID-19 on agricultural and food systems worldwide and on progress to the sustainable development goals. *Agricultural Systems, 183*, 102873. https://doi.org/10.1016/j.agsy.2020.102873

Vanlauwe, B., Hungria, M., Kanampiu, F., & Giller, K. E. (2019). The role of legumes in the sustainable intensification of African smallholder agriculture: Lessons learnt and challenges for the future. *Agriculture, Ecosystems and Environment, 285*, 106583. https://doi.org/10.1016/j.agee.2019106583

Vassilara, F., Spyridaki, A., Pothitos, G., Deliveliotou, A., & Papadopoulos, A. (2018). A rare case of human coronavirus 229E associated with acute respiratory distress syndrome in a healthy adult. *Case Reports in Infectious Diseases, 2018*, Article ID: 6796839. https://doi.org/10.1155/2018/6796839

Verdier-Chouchane, A., & Karagueuzian, C. (2016). Moving towards a green productive agriculture in Africa: The role of ICTs. *African Economic Brief, 7*(7), 1–12.

Villarejo, D., & Baron, S. L. (1999). The occupational health status of hired farm workers. *Occupational Medicine, 14*(3), 613–635.

Wallace, T. C., Murray, R., & Zelman, K. M. (2016). The nutritional value and health benefits of chickpeas and hummus. *Nutrients, 8*(12), 766. https://doi.org/10.3390/nu8120766

Yoshida, H., Saiki, M., Yoshida, N., Tomiyama, Y., & Mizushina, Y. (2009). Fatty acid distribution in triacylglycerols and phospholipids of broad beans (*Vicia faba*). *Food Chemistry, 112*, 924–928. https://doi.org/10.1016/j.foodchem.2008.07.003

Index

Lightning Source UK Ltd.
Milton Keynes UK
UKHW021829240123
415872UK00002B/7